READING CULTURE

CONTEXTS FOR CRITICAL READING AND WRITING

READING CULTURE

CONTEXTS FOR CRITICAL READING AND WRITING

SECOND EDITION

DIANA GEORGE

Michigan Technological University

JOHN TRIMBUR

Worcester Polytechnic Institute

HarperCollins *CollegePublishers*

Senior Acquisitions Editor/Executive Editor: Patricia A. Rossi
Developmental Editor: Marisa L'Heureux
Project Coordination, Text, and Cover Designer: York Production Services
Electronic Production Manager: Christine Pearson
Printer and Binder: R. R. Donnelley & Sons Company
Cover Printer: The Lehigh Press, Inc.

The quote on p. v is from "Culture Is Ordinary," an essay in *Resources of
Hope* by Raymond Williams (London: Verso). Copyright © 1989 by
Raymond Williams.

Reading Culture: Contexts for Critical Reading and Writing

Library of Congress Cataloging-in-Publication Data

Reading culture: contexts for critical reading and writing / [edited by] Diana
George, John Trimbur.—2nd ed.
    p. cm.
  Includes bibliographical references.
  ISBN 0-673-99024-9
  1. College readers. 2. English language—Rhetoric. 3. Critical thinking.
I. George, Diana, 1948–. II. Trimbur, John.
PE1417.R38 1995
808'.0427—dc20   94-26627
                        CIP
ISBN (Teacher Edition) 0-673-99037-0
    95 96 97 9   8   7   6   5

Culture is ordinary; that is
where we must start.

–Raymond Williams

TABLE OF CONTENTS

CHAPTER FIVE: STYLE

CHAPTER SIX: TELEVISION CULTURE

Chapter Seven: Public Space

Chapter Eight: Storytelling

Chapter Nine: Work

Chapter Ten: History

CHAPTER ELEVEN: MULTICULTURAL AMERICA

ALTERNATE CONTENTS

I. JOURNALISM AND POPULAR WRITING

Magazines

II. ACADEMIC AND CRITICAL WRITING

Cross-Cultural Studies

Cultural and Social Criticism

RHETORICAL TABLE OF CONTENTS

COMPARISON AND CONTRAST

PREFACE TO THE SECOND EDITION

Reading Culture is a textbook that asks students to read and write about everyday life in contemporary America. It asks students to look at culture as a way of life that organizes social experience and shapes the identities of individuals and groups. We will be using the term *culture* in this textbook to talk about how people make sense of their worlds and about the values, beliefs, and practices in which they invest their energies and allegiances. One of our central aims is to provide students with reading and writing assignments that will enable them to identify the social patterns and emotional investments in their familiar ways of life and to understand how these ways of life fit into the diverse, mass-mediated, multicultural realities of contemporary America.

Reading Culture assumes that students are already immersed in a wealth of cultural data and that their experiences of everyday life can usefully be brought to attention as material for reflection and deliberation. The reading and writing assignments in *Reading Culture* are designed to promote a critical distancing so that students can begin to observe and evaluate as well as participate in the everyday life of contemporary America. To this end, *Reading Culture* asks students to read in a double sense. First, the range of writing about culture we have assembled here asks students to read carefully and critically, to identify the purposes and assumptions writers bring to the study of culture and the rhetorical patterns they use to enact their aims. Second, *Reading Culture* asks students to read the social world around them, to identify the patterns of meaning in the commonplace, and to put into words the familiar experiences of everyday life that often go without saying.

Reading Culture is organized into eleven chapters. The first chapter, "Reading and Writing About Culture: Music," provides both a general introduction to the study of culture and a case study of rap music. The reading selections in the case study offer background information and differing editorial positions. They serve to illustrate how writing about culture seeks to influence public opinion. The case study also includes a step-by-step sequence of reading and writing activities that introduce students to a number of useful reading strategies—underlining, annotating, and summarizing—and writing strategies—exploratory writing, synthesis, and deliberative judgment.

The ten chapters that form the main part of *Reading Culture* are arranged under a number of broad topics. The two chapters "Generations" and

"Schooling" explore the personal experience of growing up and learning in contemporary America. The next group of chapters, "Images," "Style," "Television Culture," and "Public Space," explore the visual world in which students learn how values and institutions are conveyed in popular media as well as in clothing and hair styles and even the ways in which we organize public spaces. In the chapters that remain, "Storytelling," "Work," "History," and "Multicultural America," students can investigate how the narratives Americans tell about themselves and those that are told about them come to be part of national mythmaking.

We have chosen the reading selections presented here—many of them anthologized for the first time—to provide students with a range of provocative and engaging approaches to the study of culture. The readings include selections from newspaper and magazine journalism, literary essays, memoirs, textbooks, academic books and articles, oral histories, fiction, and songs.

Reading Culture is designed to be used flexibly and creatively. Instructors may wish to ask students to work on the chapters in *Reading Culture* as they are arranged, but this is only one possible order. In the Alternate Contents, we have classified the reading selections in terms of genre and rhetorical modes, and the Instructor's Manual suggests ways to pair or group readings across chapters.

Each reading selection is introduced by a headnote that provides a context for reading and a Suggestion for Reading that directs students to notice particular themes or rhetorical features in the selection. The reading selections are followed by Suggestions for Discussion that raise issues for students to talk about in class or in small collaborative groups. The Suggestions for Writing ask students to consider a range of angles on the issues presented in the reading selection. Typically these writing assignments ask students to interpret a key point or passage in the reading selection, to relate the reading selection to their own experience, and to connect the reading to other readings and to the cultural realities of contemporary America. The Instructor's Manual contains additional resources instructors may wish to draw upon and further suggestions for writing and research activities.

Acknowledgements

There are a number of people we want to thank for their insight and advice. Robert Schwegler deserves credit for helping us conceptualize this project. Joseph Trimmer explained how to make a textbook and offered useful suggestions as a reviewer and as a friend. Constance Rajala made us believe that the project was worth doing. Our editor Marisa L'Heureux has been both supportive and acute in her advice and admonitions. Patricia Rossi brought the book to its final form. We appreciate, as well, the careful readings we received at several stages by the many reviewers of this book: Dana Beckelman, *University of Wisconsin, Milwaukee;* James Berlin, *Purdue University;* Patrick Bizzaro, *East Carolina University;* Jean Carr, *University of Pittsburgh;* John Dick, *University of Texas at El Paso;* Lester Faigley, *University of Texas, Austin;* Donald Gray, *Indiana University;* Sally Harrold, *Southwest Oregon Community College;* David Jolliffe, *University of Illinois at Chicago;* Lisa McClure, *Southern Illinois University;* Christina Murphy, *Texas Christian University;* Thomas Recchio, *University of Connecticut;* Karen Rodis, *Dartmouth College;* Jeff Schiff, *Columbia College;* John Schilb, *University of Maryland;* Charles Schuster, *University of Wisconsin, Milwaukee;* Joe Trimmer, *Ball State University;* and Richard Zbaracki, *Iowa State University;* Reviewers of the second edition were Diane Crotty, *University of Wisconsin, Oshkosh;* Kathy Evertz, *University of Wyoming;* David J. Knauer, *Northern Illinois University;* Lori Ann Miller, *University of California, Irvine;* Michael W. Munley, *Ball State University;* Richard Penticoff, *University of Idaho;* and Rebecca Shapiro, *Purdue University.*

Others have helped as well. Stephen Jukuri, who takes his teaching very seriously, dug through attics to find resources for this second edition and asked his students to help us revise this text. For their kind words and good advice, we do thank them. Bill Williamson took time from his own schedule to make sure that we met our press deadlines. We want to thank Bill Baller for help with the readings on the Vietnam War and Bruce Herzberg and members of the English Department at Bentley College for a helpful discussion of composition readers and multicultural education. Robert Crooks provided us with particularly useful and detailed suggestions.

We also thank our companions Chuck Harris (and Maggie) and Lundy Braun for their patience and faith that we could actually do this a second time. We thank our students at Michigan Technological University and Worcester Polytechnic Institute, and Clare Trimbur, Lucia Trimbur, and Martha Catherine Trimbur for the best confirmation of our intentions we could possibly receive: they recognized themselves and their peers in this project and let us know that the cultural resources we are seeking to tap are vitally important to young people in contemporary America.

Finally, with respect and sadness, we wish to thank Jim Berlin for convincing us that this project was not simply worthwhile but necessary. He taught the earliest versions of *Reading Culture* and helped us see what was useful and what was not. We will miss him, but we will also try to keep his voice of encouragement and healthy skepticism with us as we write and teach.

Diana George
John Trimbur

CHAPTER 1

READING AND WRITING ABOUT CULTURE: MUSIC

culture: education, enrichment, erudition, learning, wisdom, breeding, gentility, civilization, colony, community, crowd, folks, group, settlement, society, staff, tribe, background, development, environment, experience, past, schooling, training, upbringing, customs, habits, mores, traditions

W hat is culture? As the above list of synonyms suggests, this is a difficult question. There are no simple answers or easy ways to define the term, though many have tried. The British cultural historian Raymond Williams says that culture "is one of the two or three most complicated words in the English language." This is so, Williams explains, because the term *culture* has acquired new meanings over time without losing its older senses, and therefore different writers use the term *culture* in quite distinct and sometimes incompatible ways.

For some, culture refers to great works of art, such as Beethoven's symphonies, Shakespeare's plays, Picasso's paintings, or T. S. Eliot's poetry. Taken in this way, culture refers to something that you read; something that you see in a museum, art gallery, or theater; or something that you hear in a concert hall. This culture is often called "high culture" and is closely linked to the idea of *becoming* cultured, of cultivating good taste and discriminating judgment. People who talk about culture in this way often exclude other forms of expression from their idea of what culture means. For example, they might well think that pop stars like Madonna or rap groups like Public Enemy do not properly belong in the domain of culture. And they probably would not include popular entertainment like *The Simpsons,* soap operas, *Monday Night Football,* tabloid journalism, the latest Harlequin romance, or MTV videos, either. In distinguishing high art from low art, this view of culture is largely interested in the classics and in keeping serious art separate from popular culture.

Others, however, take an alternative approach to the study of culture. Instead of separating high art from low, they think of culture in more inclusive terms. For them, culture refers not only to the literary and artistic works critics think of as masterpieces. In this broader view, culture refers to the way of life that characterizes a particular group of people at a particular time. Developed since the turn of the century by anthropologists, though it has now spread into common use, the term *culture* offers a way to think about how individuals and groups organize and make sense of their social experience—at home, in school, at work, and at play. Culture includes all the social institutions, patterns of behavior, systems of belief, and kinds of popular entertainment that create the social world people live in. Taken in this way, culture means not simply masterpieces of art, music, and literature but a people's living experience—what goes on in the everyday lives of individuals and groups.

Reading Culture is a book about interpreting the culture of contemporary America. When we use the term *culture,* we are using a definition that, as you might have guessed, is much closer to the second definition than to the first. We think that the distinction between high and low art is indeed an important one, but not because serious art is necessarily better or more cultured than popular entertainment. What interests us is how the two terms are used in an ongoing debate about the meaning of American culture—about, say, what children should read in school, or about the influence of television and advertising, or about the quality of Americans' popular tastes and their collective self-image as a people. We will ask you to explore these issues in the following chapters to see how arguments about schooling or the media or our national identity tell the story of contemporary American culture. In short, the purpose of this book is not to bring you culture but to invite you to become more aware of the culture you are already living. According to the way we will be using the term, culture is not something you can go out and get. Rather, culture means all the familiar pursuits and pleasures that shape people's identities and that enable and constrain what they do, what they can hope for, and what they might become. Our idea is to treat contemporary America as a vast research project—to understand its ways of life from the inside as you live and observe them.

READING CULTURE

The following chapters offer opportunities to read and write about contemporary American culture. The reading selections group together writers who have explored central facets of American culture. Each chapter raises a series of questions about how American culture organizes social experience and how Americans understand the meaning and purpose of their collective life.

In the following chapters, we will be asking you to think about how the writers we have gathered find patterns in American culture and how they position themselves in relation to contemporary cultural realities. We will be asking you to read not just to understand what the writers are saying but also to identify where they are coming from and what assumptions they are making about cultural issues such as schooling, the media, or American national identity. But we will also be asking you to do another kind of reading, where the text is not the printed word but the experience of everyday life in contemporary America. We will be asking you, that is, to **read culture**—to read the social world around you, at home and in classrooms, at work and at play, in visual images and public places.

Reading a culture means finding patterns in the familiar. In many respects, of course, you are already a skilled reader of culture. Think of all the reading you do in the course of a day. You read not only the textbooks assigned in your courses or the books and magazines you turn to for pleasure. You probably also read a variety of other "texts" without thinking that you are actually reading. You read the clothes people wear, the cars they drive, and the houses they live in to make informed guesses about their social status and how you should relate to them. You read the way social experience is organized on your campus to determine who your friends will be, who the preppies are, the jocks, the hippies, whatever. And you read all kinds of visual images in the media not only for the products they advertise or the entertainments they offer but for the lifestyles they make attractive and desirable. This kind of reading takes place as you move through the daily reality of contemporary America, but it often takes place below the threshold of consciousness. Often, people just take this kind of reading for granted.

To read culture means *not* taking for granted such readings of everyday life. Reading culture means bringing forward for analysis and reflection those commonplace aspects of everyday life people normally think of as simply being *there,* a part of the natural order of things. Reading culture means learning to read those familiar things back into view so that you can begin to understand how people organize and make sense of their lives. To read culture in this way is to see that American culture is not simply passed down from generation to generation in a fixed form but rather is a way of life in which individuals and groups are constantly making their own meanings in the world of contemporary America.

All Americans, of course, are influenced by what cultural critics call the dominant or mainstream culture, whether they feel part of it or not. Everyone, to one extent or another, is shaped by the American way of life and the value it places on hard work, fair play, individual success, romantic love, family ties, and patriotism. After all, to grow up in America means in part learning what the dominant culture values. America is no doubt the most mass-mediated culture in human history, and it is virtually impossible to evade the dominant images of America past and present—whether of the Pilgrims gathered at the first Thanksgiving or of retired pro football players in a Miller Lite commercial.

But for all the power of the American way of life as it is presented by the schools, the mass media, and the culture industry, American culture is hardly monolithic or homogeneous. The culture Americans live in is a diverse one, divided along the lines of race, class, gender, language, ethnicity, age, occupation, region, politics, and religion. America is a multicultural society, and in part because of its very diversity, the culture of contemporary America is constantly changing, constantly in flux. To read culture, therefore, is to see not only how its dominant cultural expressions shape people but also how individuals and groups shape culture, how their responses to and interpretations of contemporary America rewrite its meanings according to their own purposes, interests, and aspirations.

WRITING ABOUT CULTURE

Perhaps the best way to begin thinking about writing about culture is to give you some examples of writing produced in response to a particular phenomenon in recent American cultural history, namely the emergence and widespread popularity of rap music, as well as the many controversies surrounding rap and hip-hop culture. We have chosen a series of writings that deal in various ways with rap music and the social and cultural issues associated with it. The writings that follow present a short case study of rap music and offer some guided steps to do the kind of reading and writing you will be asked to do throughout this book and that teachers in other classes may call on you to do. The steps we present offer a way to read what other writers have written in order to develop your own views, stake out your own position, and write your own version of rap music and the cultural issues it raises.

So, first of all, let's take a look at the written material we have assembled here:

1. Michel Marriott. "Hard-Core Rap Lyrics Stir Black Backlash." *New York Times,* August 15, 1993.

2. Michael Kinsley. "Ice-T: Is the Issue Social Responsibility. . . ." *Time,* July 20, 1992.

3. Barbara Ehrenreich. ". . . Or Is It Creative Freedom?" *Time,* July 20, 1992.

4. Jerry Adler. "The Rap Attitude." *Newsweek,* March 19, 1990.

5. Michele Wallace. "When Black Feminism Faces the Music, and the Music Is Rap." *New York Times,* July 29, 1990.

6. Nelson George. "Niggas With Attitude." *Village Voice,* May 5, 1992.

Notice that these pieces of writing appeared in newspapers and magazines in the 1990s, in the wake of the 2 Live Crew obscenity trial, the controversy over Ice-T's "Cop

Killer," the sexist lyrics in hard-core and "gangsta" rap, and the urban uprising in Los Angeles following the acquittal of police officers in the Rodney King beating case. These are all readily accessible examples of writing from the public press that can be found by consulting such sources as the *Reader's Guide to Periodical Literature.* They are precisely the kinds of writing about culture you might turn up if you were researching rap music on your own. They offer a variety of perspectives on what has become one of the most popular—and troubling—forms of American popular culture.

The selections that follow are not all the same kind of writing. The genres (or types) of writing vary. Not all writing about culture tries to do the same thing or positions the writer in the same way with respect to readers. For this reason, it will be useful to classify the different genres of writing about culture we have assembled in this case study of rap music.

1. The first selection, "Hard-Core Rap Lyrics Stir Black Backlash," by Michel Marriott, is a **feature story** that appeared in the *New York Times* in the summer of 1993. This feature story reports on reactions within the African American community to what Marriott describes as "songs and videos that exalt the immediate gratifications of sexual conquests, remorseless violence, and 'gangsta' values of materialism and self-interest." Marriott interviewed a number of spokespersons for the black community, academics, ministers, and editors, as well as rappers themselves, and the article relies heavily on what Marriott's sources had to say. The style of writing is informative and meant to sound objective. News reporters, of course, are not supposed to allow their biases and opinions to enter into the way they write their stories. But, at the same time, precisely because we expect "just the facts," readers' expectations actually put these writers (and the way they have selected their "facts" and informants and organized their reports) in a powerful position to shape how the public is going to understand and react to the news.

2. The next two pieces are paired **opinion pieces** published next to each other in the July 20, 1992, issue of *Time* magazine, as the controversy surrounding Ice-T's "Cop Killer" was heating up, with figures such as Iran-Contra player Oliver North and actor Charlton Heston on one side calling on Warner Bros. Records to pull the song from the album *Body Count,* and others, such as actor Wesley Snipes, rappers Ice Cube, Public Enemy, and Cypress Hill, and the Recording Industry Association of America, on the other, defending Ice-T and Warner Bros. in the name of freedom of expression. As it turned out, following bomb threats and a call by police officers to boycott Time Warner products, Ice-T agreed to remove the song from the album and ultimately was released from his recording contract with Warner Bros., noting that "you can't be part of the system and make music against the system. . . . Time Warner cannot be in the business of black rage." Each of the opinion pieces— Michael Kinsley's "Ice-T: Is the Issue Social Responsibility. . . " and Barbara Ehrenreich's ". . . Or Is It Creative Freedom?"—takes a stand and makes an argument about the issues underlying the "Cop Killer" controversy. The format here is the familiar one of pro and con, whether "Cop Killer" represents an incitement to violence or a fictionalized response to police brutality. Kinsley's and Ehrenreich's purposes are **argumentative** rather than informative. They want to convince readers that their reading of the controversy, given the situation, is the most reasonable and

persuasive one available. Each piece of writing invites readers to agree with its views and to share its position.

3. The next three pieces are, in many respects, the most interesting examples of writing about culture because they do not limit themselves to simply reporting or positioning themselves in an argument, pro or con. Instead, "The Rap Attitude," by *Newsweek* writer Jerry Adler, "When Black Feminism Faces the Music, and the Music Is Rap," by the black feminist cultural critic Michele Wallace, and "Niggas With Attitude," by *Village Voice* columnist and music critic Nelson George, offer **commentary** on some of the cultural meanings that emerge from rap music. As you will see, while these writers are certainly aware of the controversies surrounding rap music, they have positioned themselves to interpret rather than to argue or to inform. Of course, as you read these commentaries, you will notice ways in which they are both informative and persuasive, but the positions they have taken can best be described as **deliberative** ones that explore some of the wider cultural issues implied by the popularity of rap music—not just whether the lyrics on 2 Live Crew's *As Nasty As They Wanna Be* are obscene or whether Warner Bros. should have released "Cop Killer," but more generally how rap music raises questions about race, class, and gender in contemporary America. Each of these writers, in other words, wants to have a say about the significance of rap music and to influence the climate of public opinion. Taken together, these three examples will give you a sense of the cultural debate activated by rap music.

Before you plunge into the readings, let's take an overview of the reading strategies we recommend that you follow. We know that you already have learned to carry out many of these procedures in the course of your education, but it may be useful, nonetheless, to look at these strategies for a moment, to see what value they might have for you. All of them involve various modes of writing, and all of them can work to help you both to read more carefully and to write your way into the texts you're reading in order to develop your own position.

1. **Underlining:** Most students underline what they are assigned to read—whether it's a textbook, a journal article, or a novel. The purpose of underlining is to catch the key points or memorable passages so that you can return to them easily when you need to study for a test or write a paper.

2. **Annotating:** Sometimes students not only underline what they are reading, they also write comments in the margins of a book or an article. Annotation is a more active kind of reading than underlining because it provides the reader with a written record of his or her experience of the text. It offers readers a technique to write their way into the text. Annotations might include one- or two-word paraphrases of the content, notes on how the writer has structured the piece of writing ("important transition" or "key supporting evidence" or "refutes opposing views"), reactions ("right on" or "nonsense, this is sexist"), or questions about difficult passages to return to. Not everything you read, of course, is worth annotating. You can probably, for example, read the news report below and just underline it. But for many

kinds of writing, annotation can be a valuable way to read and to keep track of your reading.

3. **Summarizing:** Not all students who underline or annotate what they are reading take the next step and summarize what they have read. This is unfortunate because summarizing demands that you take what you have read and put it into your own words. It demands a careful reading that grasps the central idea, selects the main points that support it, and identifies essential details. Writing summaries, that is, can take you a step beyond what you have gained by underlining and annotating. Summarizing builds on these activities by providing you with as accurate an account of what you've been reading as possible. And this can be enormously useful in mastering the material you're reading and making it available to write about.

4. **Exploratory writing:** Exploratory writing offers a way to think out loud about what you have been reading. It's a way to look back at what you have already written into the material you're reading—your underlinings, annotations, and summary—and to bring a reading selection into focus, to draw some inferences from it, and to stake out your own position in relation to it. Exploratory writing often sounds quite personal in tone, but it is not exactly private either. It's a kind of halfway house, really, in between the reactions you might record in your annotations ("this is truly idiotic" or "I couldn't agree more") and the public voice you'd want to assume in a more formal, deliberative essay. One way to think about exploratory writing is that it offers a means to test your personal responses to the public issues you have been reading about, to experiment with ways of explaining and justifying your own reactions so that others will take them seriously, if not necessarily agree with them wholesale. It's not the kind of writing you would turn in to a teacher for a grade, but it's a way of getting there.

5. **Synthesis:** When you do research, as in the case study we have set up for you on rap music, you not only need to explore your responses to what individual writers have said and how they have said it, you will also need to compare how these writers have written on the same topic, how they have positioned themselves in different ways in relation to rap music, and how they have thereby derived a different set of issues to address. Comparing writers' positions and perspectives is what we call synthesis. It's a way of charting the field of discussion so that you can figure out how you want to enter into it—how, that is, you can develop your own position in an informed and knowledgeable way.

6. **Taking a position:** Once you have read through your research materials (underlining, annotating, and summarizing as you go along), written some exploratory writing to clarify your own fix on what individual writers have said, and synthesized the positions a number of writers have taken by bringing them into relation to each other, you are ready to enter the fray—to position yourself in relation to rap music and what others have written about it. Taking a position can be much more than just agreeing or disagreeing with Michael Kinsley's or Barbara Ehrenreich's position on "Cop Killer." Taking

a position doesn't refer simply to making an argument for or against. Rather, taking a position represents a much wider range of writing options than just announcing yourself pro or con in a particular controversy. Often, the most interesting and useful kinds of writing about culture sidestep the pro/con format altogether to stake out a position that casts the issue in question in a new light. This is the power of deliberative writing, as represented by the last three reading selections: they don't seek just to inform or persuade but to lead their readers to rethink their very understanding of the episode and the issues involved.

READING AND WRITING EXERCISES

We offer the following reading and writing exercises as a sequence, but they don't necessarily have to be done in the order we present here. Your teacher may ask you to do all of them or only a few. Our intention is to introduce you to a number of strategies for reading and writing. But we certainly don't assume that all writers doing research will necessarily follow each of the steps in a predetermined order. These are flexible strategies that can be combined in a number of ways. We'll leave it up to you and your teacher to determine what you want to do with them.

Exercise One: Read and underline "Hard-Core Rap Lyrics Stir Black Backlash." Then write a one-page summary of the news report.

Some suggestions for underlining and summarizing: When the work you need to do is a matter of extracting information and getting the facts, details, and issues clear in your mind, you probably turn to underlining (or using a highlighter pen on) what you are reading. This makes a lot of sense. It gives students a way to recall key points when they go back to a textbook to study for a test or a quiz. And it's a good way to get the facts straight.

Students often stop once they have underlined what they have read, figuring they have identified the key points and made them available to return to later on. We recommend, however, that you take a further step and write a summary of what you have read. This, of course, will involve rereading and noticing what you have underlined and perhaps what you missed during the first reading. A good way to do this summary is to use the news reporter's classic questions as a guide: Who? What? When? Where? Why? How?

Michel Marriott

HARD-CORE RAP LYRICS STIR BLACK BACKLASH

◆

I n his latest hit song, the rapper L. L. Cool J rhapsodizes about the erotic promise of the back seat of his jeep to a girl he has lured there to "give it" to her "real raw."

During a recent appearance at the Palladium in Manhattan, MC Lyte rapped about the "ruffneck" attributes she prefers in a man, among them, an "evil grin," a penchant for trouble and a habit of urinating in public.

And the title of a song by the hard-core rapper Dr. Dre has become a popular slogan through the city. The part that can be printed here basically equates women with "hos and trix"—translated, whores and tricks.

APPREHENSION AND FEAR

Perhaps not since rock 'n' roll was born kicking and screaming into the placid 1950's has an expression of youthful rebellion and verve been viewed with so much apprehension and fear by America's adult mainstream as the look, sound and sexual attitudes that characterize much of rap music today.

But unlike earlier controversies—the obscenity case against 2 Live Crew's sexually charged records or the criticism of Ice-T's "Cop Killer"—an emerging backlash to hardcore rap is growing among blacks, many of whom had appeared reluctant to criticize a form of black expression.

"I think a lot of misogynous rap is similar to crack," said bell hooks, a black feminist writer and professor of women's studies at Oberlin College in Ohio. "It gives people a false sense of agency. It gives them a sense that they have power over their lives when they don't."

Given the fast-growing popularity of rap among white youths in the suburbs, Dr. hooks and others worried that some black artists were reinforcing white stereotypes of blacks.

"It's like we have consumed the worst stereotypes white people have put on black people," Dr. hooks said.

Even some rappers said they too were disturbed by the turn the genre has taken in the last several years in glorifying gunplay and drug use and in its negative attitudes toward women.

Some of the complaints were prompted by recent incidents in New York municipal swimming pools in which young girls were taunted or sexually assaulted by young men; in some incidents the youths chanted a popular rap song, "Whoomp! (There It Is)."

But the criticism goes beyond the city's pools.

For more than a month, a group of black men and women called Masses United for Human Rights has been marching along 125th Street in Harlem, demonstrating against the sale of T-shirts with the title of Dr. Dre's song. The group is also trying to block a New York appearance of the Los Angeles–based rapper, which had been scheduled for next month but is now indefinitely postponed, according to one box office that was selling tickets to the show.

Black ministers in New York, Dallas, Los Angeles and Detroit have also begun to challenge lyrics that they say are immoral and self-destructive. The Detroit chapter of the National Association for the Advancement of Colored People is calling for a more critical examination of rap that encourages "stereotypical and inappropriate behavior" while supporting more "positive" rap music, said its leaders.

INFLUENCING BEHAVIOR

"People are outraged, man," said the Rev. Calvin O. Butts III, pastor of the Abyssinian Baptist Church of Harlem who has taken up a crusade against hard-core rap. "You get to the point where you are constantly hearing, over and over, talk about mugging people, killing women, beating women, sexual behavior. When young people see this—14, 15, 16 years of age—they think this is acceptable behavior."

Yet many rap performers casually dismiss the complaints about songs and videos that exalt the immediate gratifications of sexual conquests, remorseless violence and "gangsta" values of materialism and self-interest. "What is said is OK as long as they're paid for it," said Dr. Dre, one of whose videos shows a young man yanking off the bikini top of a young woman playing volleyball at a cookout.

While condemning the sexual attacks at the swimming pools, many rap artists said rap was guilty of no more than accurately reflecting the life of the streets from which the music was spawned some 15 years ago.

"A lot of people are talking about killing," rapper Biz Markie, a 29-year-old native of Harlem, said of best-selling rap lyrics. "That's their way of expressing how it is around their way. A lot of things are happening, and rap is the only way of expressing how people are truly feeling."

Father MC said he was considering naming his upcoming album "Sex Is Law," saying most people were bored with everything but sex and money. Other artists downplayed their influence over their audiences and directed blame at the very parents who are now complaining about the anti-social behavior that they say some rap listeners are exhibiting.

"It is up to the household for parents to control the viewing and listening privileges of their children," said Heavy D, a popular rapper whose music has prospered without the misogynist elements of hard-core rap. "My parents had control.

"Certain things shouldn't be viewed by children," he added.

'MORE SAD THAN MAD'

Even critics of the content of hard-core rap are sympathetic to their origins. Stephanie Stokes Oliver, editor of *Essence,* a black women's magazine, explained that while some lyrics might be painful and offending to women, it is probably pain that produces them.

"I'm more sad than mad about it," she said. "I know a lot of people take out their powerlessness on their family. I think they are taking it out on us, the women."

But Ms. Oliver worries that many young black women don't realize how their portrayal in some songs and videos—as being sexually subservient to men—affects all of them. "They don't see any of this affecting our people," Ms. Oliver said. "They say, 'I know I'm not a bitch, so he's not talking about me, so I'm not offended.'"

HEATED EXCHANGES

An indication of the volatility of the issue could be seen last month when, during the annual meeting of the National Association of Black Journalists, a panel discussion about the message and coverage of rap exploded into heated exchanges between a rapper and some of the journalists.

When asked why some rappers denigrate women in their music, Richard Shaw, better known as Bushwick Bill of the rap group the Geto Boys, defended his lyrics.

"I call women bitches and hos because all the women I've met since I've been out here are bitches and hos," he said. About 100 journalists, most of them women, walked out of the discussion that about 300 people had attended.

Mautana Karenga, professor and chairman of the Department of Black Studies at California State University in Long Beach, said many rappers have a distorted understanding of what black life is. And with the assistance of what he described as powerful white recording companies ever too willing to sell black stereotypes, the rap world is disproportionately magnified.

THE WORST OF STEREOTYPES

Dr. hooks, the Oberlin College professor, added that mainstream white culture also plays a large role in popularizing and enlarging hard-core rap, which is a big seller in suburban record shops. In fact, she asserted that it was the appeal of black people acting out the worst of white stereotypes that has made the music so profitable.

Some rappers said they also believe that some rap is losing its way.

"At first, they were telling the truth," Spunky D, a female member of the rap trio To Be Continued, said of the hard-core or gangster rap that emerged from the West Coast in the late 1980's. "It consisted of everything, the drug dealer, the gang banger, the prostitute; they said everything that was going on in the community.

"But now they're tripping over it," she added. "People are doing what they hear now, and they want to be shooting up people and want to have big money and stuff."

DEATH AND DESTRUCTION

Chuck D, of the New York–based group Public Enemy, has often said that rap music is the Cable News Network of its listeners. If that is so, said Spunky D, who lives in the Oakland, Calif. area, listeners are regularly drummed with news of death and destruction.

Richard Wesley, a successful black playwright and screenwriter, said the popularity of hard-core rap stemmed from the attitudes that attracted young people to rock 'n' roll for decades. "It is anti-establishment, anti-authoritarian and it is rebellious, which are all things to guarantee that it relates to youth," Mr. Wesley said.

"Everybody thought Run D.M.C. was hard when they came out, and then we found out that they were preachers' sons from Hollis, Queens. A lot of these kids are coming from middle-class homes or at least homes with middle-class aspirations."

Yet the celebration of the "ruffneck," as rapper MC Lyte calls it, represents a generations-long paradox of identity in black America, Mr. Wesley said.

ATTITUDES AND MANNERISMS

When a black family is able to give its children the benefits of education, hard work and love, some youth experience a kind of survivor's guilt, Mr. Wesley said. "Middle-class kids want to show that they are still down, so they affect the attitude and mannerisms of kids from much poorer backgrounds." It is, he said, an elemental part of the style and attraction of hard-core rap.

But Juice, half of the rap duo Juice With Soul, said young people must learn to differentiate between fictions on records and the facts of their neighborhoods. "A lot of these kids don't realize that these rappers, they go home to their fancy cars. Nobody is really staying around that hard kind of life no more."

Rapper Biz Markie said critics of rap take it too seriously.

"It's strictly entertainment," he said of his work that often earns him, even on a "bad night," he said, $15,000 a performance. He said he believes much of the debate stems from jealousy on the part of those who do not earn as much money as rappers do.

'THE HOOK AND THE BEAT'

"Rap is making more than politicians, more than the average Joe," he said proudly. Besides, he said, "People don't really go along with the words. They go along with the hook and the beat."

Joseph Simmons, known as Run and one of the few rappers who would permit his actual name to be published, was philosophical about the question of rap music influencing juvenile behavior. Speaking of the sexual assaults in city pools, Mr. Simmons, 28, said, "I don't feel the rappers influence the kids to do what they did in the pool.

"Are we the ones influencing the world?" he asked. "If that was the case, what music was Bill Clinton listening to when he whirlpooled Lani Guinier?" said Mr. Simmons, referring to the President's withdrawal of support for his appointment to be Justice Department's chief of civil rights.

MC Lyte, honey-voiced 22-year-old pioneer among female rappers, said parents, not rappers, have to take more responsibility for how young people behave and think.

"Whatever the youth is doing today, you can't blame it on rap music because they kill in movies, they rape in movies, they do the exact same thing that may or may not go on in a rap song," she said.

SUGGESTIONS FOR DISCUSSION

1. Compare with other members of your class the summaries you have written of "Hard-Core Rap Lyrics Stir Black Backlash." To what extent are they similar? To what extent do they differ? If they differ, how would you account for these differences? Don't assume that one summary is necessarily better or more accurate than another. Instead, try to identify the principles of selection each writer has used.
2. Reread "Hard-Core Rap Lyrics Stir Black Backlash," this time with an eye for the way Michel Marriott has selected details to tell the story. What details, quotes, or incidents do you think are particularly striking? How do you think the reporter's selections would have influenced the way the public responded to rap music in the summer of 1993? Explain.

Exercise Two: Read Michael Kinsley's and Barbara Ehrenreich's opinion pieces from *Time* magazine. Notice how we have underlined and annotated Kinsley's writing. Underline and annotate the piece by Ehrenreich.

Suggestions for annotating: As we mentioned earlier, the purpose of annotating reading selections is to give you a means to write your way into a text. Annotations can be paraphrases (these are really brief one- or two-word summaries), reactions, questions, or observations on how the writer has structured the piece of writing and what assumptions are being made. There's no one right way to annotate readings, and with practice you will develop your own techniques—making annotating a useful and active way to write as you read. Notice that in our annotation of Michael Kinsley's writing, we have paid particular attention to the structure of the argument. We suggest you do the same when you annotate Barbara Ehrenreich's, to see how she makes her case.

Michael Kinsley

ICE-T: IS THE ISSUE SOCIAL RESPONSIBILITY . . .

◆

H ow did the company that publishes this magazine come to produce a record <u>glorifying the murder of police?</u>

poses question making a judgment

> *I got my 12-gauge sawed off*
> *I got my headlights turned off*
> *I'm 'bout to bust some shots off*
> *I'm 'bout to dust some cops off . . .*
> *Die, Die, Die Pig, Die!*

So go the lyrics to *Cop Killer* by the rapper Ice-T on the album *Body Count*. The album is released by Warner Bros. Records, part of the Time Warner media and entertainment conglomerate.

In a *Wall Street Journal* op-ed piece laying out the company's position. Time Warner CO-CEO <u>Gerald Levin makes two defenses.</u> First, Ice-T's <u>*Cop Killer* is misunderstood.</u> "It doesn't incite or glorify violence . . . . It's his <u>fictionalized attempt</u> to get inside a character's head. . . . *Cop Killer* is no more a call for gunning down the police than *Frankie and Johnny* is a summons for jilted lovers to shoot one another." <u>Instead of</u> <u>"finding ways to silence the messenger,"</u> we should be <u>"heeding the anguished cry contained in his message."</u>

presents Time Warner's defense of Cop Killer

This <u>defense is self-contradictory.</u> *Frankie and Johnny* does not pretend to have a political "message" that must be "heeded." <u>If *Cop Killer* has a message, it is that the</u> <u>murder of policemen is a justified response to police brutality.</u> And not in self-defense,

refutes first defense

but in premeditated acts of revenge against random cops. ("I know your family's grievin'—f____ 'em.")

Killing policemen is a good thing—that is the plain meaning of the words, and no "larger understanding" of black culture, the rage of the streets or anything else can explain it away. This is not Ella Fitzgerald telling a story in song. As in much of today's popular music, the line between performer and performance is purposely blurred. These are political sermonettes clearly intended to endorse the sentiments being expressed. Tracy Marrow (Ice-T) himself has said, "I scared the police, and they need to be scared." That seems clear.

refutes sec-
ond defense

The company's second defense of Cop Killer is the classic one of free expression: "We stand for creative freedom. We believe that the worth of what an artist or journalist has to say does not depend on preapproval from a government official or a corporate censor."

Of course Ice-T has the right to say whatever he wants. But that doesn't require any company to provide him an outlet. And it doesn't relieve a company of responsibility for the messages it chooses to promote. Judgment is not "censorship." Many an "anguished cry" goes unrecorded. This one was recorded, and promoted, because a successful artist under contract wanted to record it. Nothing wrong with making money, but a company cannot take the money and run from the responsibility.

states his
own position

magazines
not value-
free

The founder of Time, Henry Luce, would snort at the notion that his company should provide a value-free forum for the exchange of ideas. In Luce's system, editors were supposed to make value judgments and promote the truth as they saw it. Time has moved far from its old Lucean rigidity—far enough to allow for dissenting essays like this one. That evolution is a good thing, as long as it's not a handy excuse for abandoning all standards.

dissent is a
good thing
but suggests
Time Warner
has aban-
doned stan-
dards

No commercial enterprise need agree with every word that appears under its corporate imprimatur. If Time Warner now intends to be "a global force for encouraging the confrontation of ideas," that's swell. But a policy of allowing diverse viewpoints is not a moral free pass. Pro and con on national health care is one thing; pro and con on killing policemen is another.

notes Time
Warner's
dilemma:
censorship
vs. moral ir-
responsibility

A bit of sympathy is in order for Time Warner. It is indeed a "global force" with media tentacles around the world. If it imposes rigorous standards and values from the top, it gets accused of corporate censorship. If it doesn't, it gets accused of moral irresponsibility. A dilemma. But someone should have thought of that before deciding to become a global force.

And another genuine dilemma. Whatever the actual merits of Cop Killer, if Time Warner withdraws the album now the company will be perceived as giving in to outside pressure. That is a disastrous precedent for a global conglomerate.

develops
dilemma fur-
ther

The Time-Warner merger of 1989 was supposed to produce corporate "synergy": the whole was supposed to be more than the sum of the parts. The Cop Killer controversy is an example of negative synergy. People get mad at Cop Killer and start boycotting the movie Batman Returns. A reviewer praises Cop Killer ("Tracy Marrow's poetry takes a switchblade and deftly slices life's jugular," etc.), and TIME is accused of corruption instead of mere foolishness. Senior Time Warner executives find themselves under attack for—and defending—products of their company they neither honestly care for nor really understand, and doubtless weren't even aware of before controversy hit.

Anyway, it's absurd to discuss *Cop Killer* as part of the "confrontation of ideas"— or even as an authentic anguished cry of rage from the ghetto. <u>*Cop Killer* is a cynical commercial concoction, designed to titillate its audience with imagery of violence. It merely exploits the authentic anguish of the inner city for further titillation.</u> Tracy Marrow is in business for a buck, just like Time Warner. *Cop Killer* is an excellent joke on the white establishment, of which the company's anguished apologia ("Why can't we hear what trap is trying to tell us?") is the punch line.

gives his
own view of
Cop Killer

Barbara Ehrenreich

. . . OR IS IT CREATIVE FREEDOM?

Ice-T's song *Cop Killer* is as bad as they come. This is black anger—raw, rude and cruel—and one reason the song's so shocking is that in postliberal America, black anger is virtually taboo. You won't find it on TV, not on the *McLaughlin Group* or *Crossfire,* and certainly not in the placid features of Arsenio Hall or Bernard Shaw. It's been beaten back into the outlaw subcultures of rap and rock, where, precisely because it is taboo, it sells. And the nastier it is, the faster it moves off the shelves. As Ice-T asks in another song on the same album. "Goddamn what a brotha gotta do/To get a message through/To the red, white and blue?"

But there's a gross overreaction going on, building to a veritable paroxysm of white denial. A national boycott has been called, not just of the song or Ice-T, but of all Time Warner products. The President himself has denounced Time Warner as "wrong" and Ice-T as "sick." Ollie North's Freedom Alliance has started a petition drive aimed at bringing Time Warner executives to trial for "sedition and anarchy."

Much of this is posturing and requires no more courage than it takes to stand up in a VFW hall and condemn communism or crack. Yes, *Cop Killer* is irresponsible and vile. But Ice-T is as right about some things as he is righteous about the rest. And ultimately, he's not even dangerous—least of all to the white power structure his songs condemn.

The "danger" implicit in all the uproar is of empty-headed, suggestible black kids, crouching by their boom boxes, waiting for the word. But what Ice-T's fans know and his detractors obviously don't is that *Cop Killer* is just one more entry in pop music's long history of macho hyperbole and violent boast. Flip to the classic-rock station, and you might catch the Rolling Stones announcing "the time is right for violent revolooshun!" from their 1968 hit *Street Fighting Man.* And where were the defenders of our law-enforcement officers when a white British group, the Clash, taunted its fans with the lyrics: "When they kick open your front door/How you gonna come/With your hands on your head/Or on the trigger of your gun?"

"Die, Die, Die Pig" is strong speech, but the Constitution protects strong speech, and it's doing so this year more aggressively than ever. The Supreme Court has just downgraded cross burnings to the level of bonfires and ruled that it's no crime to throw around verbal grenades like "nigger" and "kike." Where are the defenders of decorum and social stability when prime-time demagogues like Howard Stern deride African Americans as "spear chuckers"?

More to the point, young African Americans are not so naive and suggestible that they have to depend on a compact disc for their sociology lessons. To paraphrase another song from another era, you don't need a rap song to tell which way the wind is blowing. Black youths know that the police are likely to see them through a filter of stereotypes as miscreants and potential "cop killers." They are aware that a black youth is seven times as likely to be charged with a felony as a white youth who has committed the same offense, and is much more likely to be imprisoned.

They know, too, that in a shameful number of cases, it is the police themselves who indulge in "anarchy" and violence. The U.S. Justice Department has received 47,000 complaints of police brutality in the past six years, and Amnesty International has just issued a report on police brutality in Los Angeles, documenting 40 cases of "torture or cruel, inhuman or degrading treatment."

Menacing as it sounds, the fantasy in *Cop Killer* is the fantasy of the powerless and beaten down—the black man who's been hassled once too often ("A pig stopped me for nothin'!"), spread-eagled against a police car, pushed around. It's not even a "responsible" fantasy (fantasies seldom are). It's not even a very creative one. In fact, the sad thing about *Cop Killer* is that it falls for the cheapest, most conventional image of rebellion that our culture offers: the lone gunman spraying fire from his AK-47. This is not "sedition"; it's the familiar, all-American, Hollywood-style pornography of violence.

Which is why Ice-T is right to say he's no more dangerous than George Bush's pal Arnold Schwarzenegger, who wasted an army of cops in *Terminator 2*. Images of extraordinary cruelty and violence are marketed every day, many of far less artistic merit than *Cop Killer*. This is our free market of ideas and images, and it shouldn't be any less free for a black man than for other purveyors of "irresponsible" sentiments, from David Duke to Andrew Dice Clay.

Just, please, don't dignify Ice-T's contribution with the word sedition. The past masters of sedition—men like George Washington, Toussaint-Louverture, Fidel Castro or Mao Ze-dong, all of whom led and won armed insurrections—would be unimpressed by *Cop Killer* and probably saddened. They would shake their heads and mutter words like "infantile" and "adventurism." They might point out that the cops are hardly a noble target, being, for the most part, honest working stiffs who've got stuck with the job of patrolling ghettos ravaged by economic decline and official neglect.

There is a difference, the true seditionist would argue, between a revolution and a gesture of macho defiance. Gestures are cheap. They feel good, they blow off some rage. But revolutions, violent or otherwise, are made by people who have learned how to count very slowly to 10.

SUGGESTIONS FOR DISCUSSION

1. Compare the annotations you have written on Barbara Ehrenreich's "... Or Is It Creative Freedom?" with those your classmates have written. If you see differences, don't argue about who's right and who's wrong; instead, identify the advantages

and disadvantages of one style of annotating and another. What do various annotations bring to light or ignore? What do other students' annotations help you understand about the structure of Ehrenreich's argument—about how she establishes
her main point and supports it?

2. A brief summary of Michael Kinsley's "Ice-T: Is the Issue Social Responsibility. . . "
   might look something like this:

   > In "Ice-T: Is the Issue Social Responsibility. . . ," Michael Kinsley rejects Warner Bros.'s
   > defense of "Cop Killer" by arguing that the real issue is neither a matter of Ice-T's fic-
   > tionalized account of black rage against police brutality nor of artistic freedom.
   > According to Kinsley, "Judgment is not 'censorship,'" and if Warner Bros. had exer-
   > cised good sense in the first place, it would never have released "Cop Killer." Kinsley
   > sees "Cop Killer" not as "an authentic anguished cry of rage from the ghetto" but as a
   > "cynical commercial concoction, designed to titillate its audience with imagery of vio-
   > lence."

   Compose a comparable summary of Barbara Ehrenreich's piece. Incorporate some
   brief quotes into your summary. Then compare the summary you have written with
   those others have written, noticing in particular what the summaries quote. Discuss
   the advantages and disadvantages of the quotes you have selected.

3. Compare Kinsley's and Ehrenreich's opinion pieces. What assumptions about their
   readers' beliefs do each of the writers try to tap into? Do you think, given the position each is arguing for, that they have made reasonable assumptions that will allow them to influence public opinion? Is one of the writers, in your view, more effective than the other? If so, what makes the argument effective?

**Exercise Three: Read, underline, and annotate the three final reading selections.
Next write a brief summary of each of the three articles. Then respond to one of
the articles by using exploratory writing.**

Notice we have included a summary and a sample of exploratory writing in response to "The Rap Attitude" by Jerry Adler. But don't let the sample exploratory writing stop you from writing about this article if you want. What you have to say is likely
to be quite different.

Suggestions for exploratory writing: The reading strategies that we've suggested so
far—underlining, annotating, and summarizing—are techniques to gain some control
over what a written text is saying and how it says it. These are ways to get to the heart of
the matter, to see the writer's central idea, and to understand how writers position
themselves in relation to their readers and to their material. Exploratory writing, on the
other hand, has a different set of purposes. It offers a way to position yourself and your
own concerns in relation to what you've read, to engage in a kind of conversation with
a reading selection in which you can ask questions, voice confusion, even talk back to
and contradict the text if you want to. When you do exploratory writing, you should
feel free to take some of the ideas the writer has raised and run with them, even if it
seems that this will take you far afield from the reading itself. Or you may choose to
dwell at length on a particular detail or incident in the reading that strikes you for some
reason or another, even if it isn't the main point you'd identify in a summary. Or you
may find that a particular reading selection reminds you of something you know or
something you've read in a different context. It can be valuable to explore the associations that a particular reading calls up from your experience. In any case, the point to

keep in mind about exploratory writing is that it offers a way to locate yourself in relation to what you've read, to test out your responses and associations to see how they sound and which ones you might tap for more public writing.

Notice that each of the three selections is followed by Questions for Discussion. Your instructor may ask to talk about some or all of these in class. Or you might want to think about them to get ideas about the direction in which you might take your exploratory writing.

Jerry Adler

THE RAP ATTITUDE

L et's talk about "attitude." And I don't mean a good attitude, either. I mean "attitude" by itself, which is always bad, as in, you'd better not be bringing any attitude around here, boy, and, when that bitch gave me some attitude, I cut her good. I mean attitude as a cultural style, marrying the arrogance of Donald Trump to the vulgarity of Roseanne Barr. Comedians have attitude, rock bands have attitude, in America today even *birthday cards* have attitude. In the rap-music group N.W.A, which stands for Niggas With Attitude, you don't have to guess what kind of attitude they mean: jaunty and sullen by turns; showy but somehow furtive, in glasses as opaque as a limousine window and sneakers as white as a banker's shirt. Their music is a rhythmic chant, a rhyme set to a drum solo, a rant from the streets about gunning down cops. Now *that's* attitude.

OK, here it is: the first important cultural development in America in 25 years that the baby-boom generation didn't pioneer: The Culture of Attitude. It is heard in the thundering cacophony of heavy metal and the thumping, clattering, scratching assault of rap—music so postindustrial it's mostly not even *played,* but pieced together out of prerecorded sound bites. It is the culture of American males frozen in various stages of adolescence: their streetwise music, their ugly macho boasting and joking about anyone who hangs out on a different block—cops, other races, women and homosexuals. Its most visible contribution has been the disinterment of the word nigger, a generation after a national effort to banish it and its ugly connotations from the American language. Now it is back, employed with savage irony by black rappers and dumb literal hostility by their white heavy-metal counterparts. *Nigger! Faggot!* What ever happened to the idea that rock and roll would make us free?

Although most Americans may never have heard of them, these are not obscure bands playing in garages and afterhours clubs. In the '70s, urban rappers performed in parks, plugging loudspeakers into lampposts. Now they fill major arenas—although more and more arenas won't have rap concerts any longer, because of fear that the violence can spill over from the stage to the crowd. Public Enemy, a rap group caught up in a protracted anti-Semitic controversy, and N.W.A., have had platinum albums, with more than a million in sales. The heavy-metal group Guns N' Roses sold more than 4 million copies worldwide of the "G N' R Lies" record, whose lyrics insult blacks, homosexuals and "immigrants" inside 10 lines. Major companies are behind them: Public Enemy's releases for the Def Jam label are distributed by CBS/Columbia Records; Guns N' Roses parades its prejudices on Geffen Records, headed by the noted AIDS philanthropist David Geffen.

Attitude! Civilized society abhors attitude, and perpetuates itself by keeping it under control. There are entire organizations devoted to this job, most notably the Parents' Music Resource Center in Arlington, Va. The center has an extensive file of lyrics in rap and heavy-metal music, describing every imaginable perversity from unsafe sex to Devil worship. (The Satanist influence on heavy metal called down a condemnation last week from New York's Cardinal John O'Connor as well.) But executive director Jennifer Norwood is careful to point out that the center takes "no position on any specific type of music." There are rap ballads whose sentiments would not have brought a blush to the cheek of Bing Crosby, and rap acts that promote an anti-drug message. The center does support printing song lyrics on album jackets for the information of parents—although such a step might also make it easier for kids to learn them—and a warning label, which some record companies already apply voluntarily, about "explicit lyrics."

Others who stand against attitude include Florida Gov. Bob Martinez, who asked the statewide prosecutor to investigate the Miami rap group The 2 Live Crew for alleged violations of obscenity laws in the album "As Nasty as They Wanna Be." "If you answer the phone one night and the voice on the other end begins to read the lyrics of one of those songs, you'd say you received an obscene phone call," reasoned Martinez. This proved to be outside the governor's jurisdiction. But a Broward County judge last week cleared the way for prosecutors to charge record-shop owners who *sell* the album; courts would then rule on whether the material was obscene. And the Kentucky-based chain that operates 121 Disc Jockey record stores announced that it would no longer carry records with warning stickers. In part, says company executive Harold Guilfoil, this is a move to preempt mandatory-labeling and sales-restriction laws under consideration in at least 10 states. A Pennsylvania bill that has already passed in one House would require labels for lyrics describing or advocating suicide, incest, sodomy, morbid violence or several other things. "That about takes care of every opera in the world," observes Guilfoil.

Particularly concerned is the Anti-Defamation League, whose civil-rights director, Jeffrey Sinensky, sees evidence in popular music that "hatred is becoming hip." The rap group Public Enemy was the most notorious offender, not even for anything in their music, but for remarks by a nonsinging member of the group, Professor Griff, a hanger-on and backup dancer with the grandiloquent but meaningless title of Minister of Information. Griff, a follower of Louis Farrakhan's Nation of Islam, gave an interview last spring in which he parroted some Farrakhanesque nonsense about Jews being behind "the majority of wickedness that goes on across the globe." After the predictable outcry Griff was fired and the group disbanded; but soon it re-formed, and Griff came back as "Supreme Allied Chief of Community Relations," a position in which he is not allowed to talk to the press. And Public Enemy proceeded to discuss the episode in ominous, if somewhat obscure, terms in "Welcome to the Terrordome," a single prere-leased from its forthcoming album, "Fear of a Black Planet.". . .

"I mean, I made the apology, but people are still trying to give me hell," elaborates Public Enemy's lead rapper, Chuck D. "The media crucified me, comparable to an-other brother who caught hell." If you add up all the Jewish blood that has been spilled over the slander of deicide, it makes Chuck D's sufferings at the hands of his critics seem mild by comparison. The ADL reacted swiftly to what appeared to be a gratuitous incitement to anti-Semitism, and took its protest to where it would do the most good, CBS Records. CBS Records Inc. president Walter Yetnikoff responded with a commit-ment to police future releases for "bigotry and intolerance." While "it goes without say-ing that artists have the right of freedom of expression," Yetnikoff wrote in a memo to the rest of the company, "when the issue is bigotry, there is a fine line of acceptable standards which no piece of music should cross." And once again, Chuck D is saying that Professor Griff will leave the group . . . maybe later this year.

N.W.A.'s attitude even got it into trouble with the FBI. In a letter last summer to N.W.A.'s distributor, FBI Assistant Director Milt Ahlerich observed that the groups' album "Straight Outta Compton" " encourages violence against and disrespect for the law-enforcement officer." But Ahlerich couldn't do much more than make the com-pany "aware of the FBI's position" on lyrics in a song ("F---Tha Police") he couldn't bring himself to name:

> Pullin' out a silly club so you stand
> > With a fake-ass badge and a gun in your hand
> Take off the gun so you can see what's up
> > And we'll go at it, punk, and I'm 'a f--- you up . . .
> I'm a sniper with a hell of a 'scope . . .
> > Takin' out a cop or two . . .

Are even such appalling expressions of attitude protected by the First Amendment? Yes, according to an American Civil Liberties Union official, who told *The Village Voice* that "the song does not constitute advocacy of violence as that has been interpreted by the courts." (Although in plain English, it's hard to imagine what else it might be advo-cating.) Asked whether his music doesn't give the impression that the gang culture in the sorry Los Angeles slum of Compton is fun, Eazy-E, the group's coleader, replied, "It *is* fun," "'F--- tha police' was something people be wanting to say for years but they were too scared to say it," he says. "The next album might be 'F--- tha FBI.'"

Yes, having an attitude means it's always someone else's fault: cops who disrespect (or "dis") you when you walk through a housing project with a gold chain that could lock up a motorcycle, immigrants so dumb they can't speak the language, women who are just asking for it anyway. The outrageous implication is that to *not* sing about this stuff would be to do violence to an artistic vision as pure and compelling as Bach's. The viler the message, the more fervent the assertion of honesty that underlies it. Eazy some-times calls himself a "street historian" to deflect the charge that he is a rabble-rouser. "We're like underground reporters," he says; "We just telling it like it is, we don't hold back." The fact is, rap grows out of a violent culture in which getting shot by a cop is a real fear. But music isn't reportage, and the way to deal with police brutality is not to glorify "taking out a cop or two." By way of self-exculpation, Eazy denies any aspirations toward being a role model. As he puts it, "I don't like anybody want to look at me and stop being theyself."

Even so, Eazy sounds like Edmund Wilson, compared with Axl Rose of Guns N' Roses trying to explain the lyrics to "One in a Million." He says he's mad at immigrants because he had a run-in with a Middle Eastern clerk at a 7-Eleven. He hates homosexuals because one once made advances to him while he was sleeping. This is a textbook definition of bigotry. "I used words like . . . niggers because you're not allowed to use the word nigger," he told his "authorized biographer," Del James, in an interview printed in *Rolling Stone*. "I don't like being told what I can and what I can't say. I used the word *nigger* because it's a word to describe somebody that is basically a pain in your life, a problem. The word nigger doesn't necessarily mean black."

Oh, no? This is an example of what Todd Gitlin, director of the mass-communications program at the University of California, Berkeley, calls the "free-floating rancor" of the youth culture, the "tribal acrimony" that leads to fights over turf, real and psychic. Attitude primarily is a working-class and underclass, phenomenon, a response to the diminishing expectations of the millions of American youths who forgot to go to business school in the 1980s. *If* they had ever listened to anything except the homeboys talking trash, *if* they had ever studied anything but the strings of a guitar, they might have some more interesting justifications to offer. They could quote the sainted Woody Guthrie about "Pretty Boy Floyd," who "laid [a] deputy down" (for disrespecting his wife, as it happened in the song). Apropos of their penchant for exaggerated sexual braggadocio, they could point out that the great jazz pianist Jelly Roll Morton didn't get his nickname because he liked pastry. They could point out that as recently as a generation ago, racial epithets that today would make Morton Downey, Jr., swoon with embarrassment came tripping innocently off the tongues of educated, decent people. *Then* we might have a sensible discussion with them; but they haven't, so we can't.

But of course attitude resists any such attempt at intellectualizing. To call it visceral is to give it the benefit of the doubt. It has its origins in parts of the body even less mentionable, as the pioneering California rapper Ice-T puts it: "Women have some eerie connection with gangsters. They always want the rebel more than the brain. Girls want somebody who can beat everybody up. . . . "

This is the height of gallantry for Ice-T: no one gets killed. More often, when attitude meets woman, woman is by far the worse for it. If she's lucky, she gets made love to with a flashlight ("Shut Up, Be Happy" by Ice-T). Otherwise, she finds herself in the even less healthy company of Eazy-E:

> Now back on the street and
>   my records are clean
> I creeped on my bitch with my
>   Uzi machine
> Went to the house and kicked
>   down the door
> Unloaded like hell, cold
>   smoked the ho'.

It is not just that romance has gone out of music—attitude has done the seemingly impossible and taken sex out of teenage culture, substituting brutal fantasies of penetration and destruction. Girls who want to have fun this way need to have their heads examined.

But that's the point. The end of attitude is nihilism, which by definition leads nowhere. The culture of attitude is repulsive, but it's mostly empty of political content. As Gitlin puts it, "There's always a population of kids looking to be bad. As soon as the establishment tells them what's bad this season, some of them are going to go off and do it." And that's not good, but it's probably not a case for the FBI, either. If we learned one thing from the '60s, it's how *little* power rock and roll has to change the world.

SAMPLE SUMMARY

According to Jerry Adler, "attitude" refers to a kind of arrogant, vulgar, and hostile stance toward the rest of the world taken on by rappers and heavy metal rockers alike. It is, Adler says, a "working-class and underclass phenomenon" that grows out of the "diminishing expectations of the millions of American youths who forgot to go to business school in the 1980s." "Attitude" wants to blame other people, whether the police or Jews or homosexuals or immigrants, and it is particularly brutal toward women, ending up invariably in nihilism.

SAMPLE EXPLORATORY WRITING

Adler has got a point in that a lot of rap and heavy metal rock is filled with what he calls "attitude." I'm bothered too by the sexism, glorification of violence, and anti-Semitism of some rappers. And Axl Rose has got some real problems. I like a lot of rap and some heavy metal too, but too often the music is just an excuse for macho males mouthing off without thinking about what they are saying. On the other hand, I'm not sure Adler is trying hard enough to understand where these people are coming from. I think he's right that "attitude" is a working-class and underclass phenomenon, but he pretty much blows it off at that instead of trying to figure out why so many young people—black and white—are so angry these days. It's an ugly thing, but you've got to get to the roots of why rappers and heavy metal rockers are reflecting the way a lot of people feel.

SUGGESTIONS FOR DISCUSSION

1. What is Jerry Adler's purpose in writing this article? How does he position himself in relation to rap music? How would you describe the voice (or the "attitude") that comes across in his article?
2. Adler says that "attitude" is primarily a "working-class and underclass phenomenon," but he doesn't really explain why. Does this seem an accurate characterization? How would you explain the class origins of "attitude"? Does it make sense, in your view, to group rap music and heavy metal rock together, as Adler does? What does this bring to light? What, if anything, does it ignore?
3. Youth culture has always wanted to shock adults. How different is what Adler calls the "Culture of Attitude" from earlier forms of youth rebellion? What fears of adult society do manifestations of "attitude" bring to the surface?

Michele Wallace

WHEN BLACK FEMINISM FACES THE MUSIC, AND THE MUSIC IS RAP

L ike many black feminists, I look on sexism in rap as a necessary evil. In a society plagued by poverty and illiteracy, where young black men are as likely to be in prison as in college, rap is a welcome articulation of the economic and social frustrations of black youth.

In response to disappointments faced by poor urban blacks negotiating their future, rap offers the release of creative expression and historical continuity: it draws on precedents as diverse as jazz, reggae, calypso, Afro-Cuban, African and heavy-metal, and its lyrics include rudimentary forms of political, economic and social analysis.

But with the failure of our urban public schools, rappers have taken education into their own hands; these are oral lessons (reading and writing being low priorities). And it should come as no surprise that the end result emphasizes innovations in style and rhythm over ethics and morality. Although there are exceptions, like raps advocating world peace (the W.I.S.E. Guyz's "Time for Peace") and opposing drug use (Ice-T's "I'm Your Pusher"), rap lyrics can be brutal, raw and, where women are the subject, glaringly sexist.

Given the genre's current cross-over popularity and success in the marketplace, including television commercials, rap's impact on young people is growing. A large part of the appeal of pop culture is that it can offer symbolic resolutions to life's contradictions. But when it comes to gender, rap has not resolved a thing.

Though styles vary—from that of the X-rated Ice-T to the sybaritic Kwaneé to the hyperpolitics of Public Enemy—what seems universal is how little male rappers respect sexual intimacy and how little regard they have for the humanity of the black woman. Witness the striking contrast within rap videos: for men, standard attire is baggy outsize pants; for women, spike heels and short skirts. Videos often feature the ostentatious and fetishistic display of women's bodies. In Kool Moe Dee's "How Ya Like Me Now," women gyrate in tight leather with large revealing holes. In Digital Underground's video "Doowutchyalike," set poolside at what looks like a fraternity house party, a rapper in a clown costume pretends to bite the backside of a woman in a bikini.

As Trisha Rose, a black feminist studying rap, puts it, "Rap is basically a locker room with a beat."

The recent banning of the sale of 2 Live Crew's album "As Nasty as They Wanna Be" by local governments in Florida and elsewhere has publicized rap's treatment of women as sex objects, but it also made a hit of a record that contains some of the bawdiest lyrics in rap. Though such sexual explicitness in lyrics is rare, the assumptions about women—that they manipulate men with their bodies—are typical.

In an era when the idea that women want to be raped should be obsolete, rap lyrics and videos presuppose that women always desire sex, whether they know it or not. In Bell Biv De-Voe's rap-influenced pop hit single "Poison," for instance, a beautiful girl is considered poison because she does not respond affirmatively and automatically to a sexual proposition.

In "Yearning: Race, Gender, Cultural Politics" (Southend, 1990), bell hooks sees the roots of rap as a youth rebellion against all attempts to control black masculinity, both in the streets and in the home. "That rap would be anti-domesticity and in the process anti-female should come as no surprise," Ms. hooks says.

At present there is only a small platform for black women to address the problems of sexism in rap and in their community. Feminist criticism, like many other forms of social analysis, is widely considered part of a hostile white culture. For a black feminist to chastise misogyny in rap publicly would be viewed as divisive and counterproductive. There is a widespread perception in the black community that public criticism of black men constitutes collaborating with a racist society.

The charge is hardly new. Such a reaction greeted Ntozake Shange's play "For Colored Girls Who Have Considered Suicide When the Rainbow Is Enuf," my own essays, "Black Macho and the Myth of the Superwoman," and Alice Walker's novel "The Color Purple," all of which were perceived as critical of black men. After the release of the film version of "The Color Purple," feminists were lambasted in the press for their supposed lack of support for black men; such critical analysis by black women has all but disappeared. In its place is "A Black Man's Guide to the Black Woman," a vanity-press book by Shahrazad Ali, which has sold more than 80,000 copies by insisting that black women are neurotic, insecure and competitive with black men.

Though misogynist lyrics seem to represent the opposite of Ms. Ali's world view, these are, in fact, just two extremes on the same theme: Ms. Ali's prescription for what ails the black community is that women should not question men about their sexual philandering, and should be firmly slapped across the mouth when they do. Rap lyrics suggest just about the same: women should be silent and prone.

There are those who have wrongly advocated censorship of rap's more sexually explicit lyrics, and those who have excused the misogyny because of its basis in black oral traditions.

Rap is rooted not only in the blaxploitation films of the 60's but also in an equally sexist tradition of black comedy. In the use of four-letter words and explicit sexual references, both Richard Pryor and Eddie Murphy, who themselves drew upon the earlier examples of Redd Foxx, Pigmeat Markham and Moms Mabley, are conscious reference points for the 2 Live Crew. Black comedy, in turn, draws on an oral tradition in which black men trade "toasts," stories in which dangerous bagmen and trickster figures like Stackolee and Dolomite sexually exploit women and promote violence among men. The popular rapper Ice Cube, in the album "Amerikkka's Most Wanted," is Stackolee come to life. In "The Nigga Ya Love to Hate," he projects an image of himself as a criminal as dangerous to women as to the straight white world.

Rap remains almost completely dominated by black males and this mind-set. Although women have been involved in rap since at least the mid-80's, record companies have only recently begun to promote them. And as women rappers like Salt-n-Pepa, Monie Love, M. C. Lyte, L. A. Star and Queen Latifah slowly gain more visibility, rap's sexism may emerge as a subject for scrunity. Indeed, the answer may lie with women, expressing in lyrics and videos the tensions between the sexes in the black community.

Today's women rappers range from a high ground that doesn't challenge male rap on its own level (Queen Latifah) to those who subscribe to the same sexual high jinks as male rappers (Oaktown's 3.5.7). M. C. Hammer launched Oaktown's 3.5.7., made up of his former backup dancers. These female rappers manifest the worst-case scenario: their skimpy, skintight leopard costumes in the video of "Wild and Loose (We Like It)" suggest an exotic animalistic sexuality. Their clothes fall to their ankles. They take bubble baths. Clearly, their bodies are more important than rapping. And in a field in which writing one's own rap is crucial, their lyrics are written by their former boss, M. C. Hammer.

Most women rappers constitute the middle ground: they talk of romance, narcissism and parties. On the other hand, Salt-n-Pepa on "Shake Your Thang" uses the structure of the 1969 Isley Brothers song "It's Your Thing" to insert a protofeminist rap response: "Don't try to tell me how to party. It's my dance and it's my body." M. C. Lyte, in a dialogue with Positive K on "I'm Not Havin' It," comes down hard on the notion that women can't say no and criticizes the shallowness of the male rap.

Queen Latifah introduces her video, "Ladies First," performed with the English rapper Monie Love, with photographs of black political heroines like Winnie Mandela, Sojourner Truth, Harriet Tubman and Angela Davis. With a sound that resembles scat as much as rap, Queen Latifah chants "Stereotypes they got to go" against a backdrop of newsreel footage of the apartheid struggle in South Africa. The politically sophisticated Queen Latifah seems worlds apart from the adolescent, buffoonish sex orientation of most rap. In general, women rappers seem so much more grown up.

Can they inspire a more beneficent attitude toward sex in rap?

What won't subvert rap's sexism is the actions of men; what will is women speaking in their own voice, not just in artificial female ghettos, but with and to men.

SUGGESTIONS FOR DISCUSSION

1. What is Michele Wallace's purpose in writing this article? How does she position herself in relation to the 2 Live Crew legal case? How does she define the terms of discussion in this article?

2. Michele Wallace says that "part of the appeal of pop culture is that it can offer symbolic resolution to life's contradictions." What contradictions does rap try to resolve symbolically? Why does Wallace think that "when it comes to gender, rap has not resolved a thing"?

3. Consider how Wallace deals with the charge that "public criticism of black men constitutes collaborating with a racist society."

Nelson George

NIGGAS WITH ATTITUDE

◆

L
os Angeles—On TNT the night the four cops walked, the Lakers and the Portland Trailblazers were in game three of their play-off series. Forum fans were alerted in the fourth quarter to the state of emergency imposed on the area. The Forum, like the airport and several important thoroughfares, is located in a working-class African American city, a city that was starting to ignite even as A. C. Green boxed out Buck Williams in overtime. You could bet your life that even as the white fans cheered black toughness inside the arena they were fearing it outside.

On CNN, meanwhile, stores were being torched. A gun shop was broken into and its deadly contents carried into homes around South Central. A helicopter captured the bloody beating of a white trucker by angry new jacks—only later did it come to light that four blacks had saved him, two leaving the safety of their homes to do so. At the First A.M.E. church, Mayor Tom Bradley tried to put a pacifier in the mouths of the disgruntled, while the departing Daryl Gates talked of containing the fury that his repressive philosophy had unleashed.

At Kennedy Airport the next morning the 10:30 MGM Grand flight was delayed two hours "because of the riots." One white woman with two blond cherubs and a West Indian nanny got very upset when informed of this delay, but most of the flight's upscale types didn't mention it—at least not loud enough for a black writer and his co-median buddy to overhear. Instead, they used their calling cards and gazed at the "Home" show on ABC.

"There'll be an additional fifteen minutes or so on our flight time today," the pilot announced as the plane passed Philadelphia. "We have to go around the back way into L.A. today—because of all the ruckus going on there all flights were delayed." Midway across America I'm wearing shades and happily listening to Arrested Development when one of the cherubs asks, "Are you high?" Instead of getting up and smacking her mother—my first impulse—I reply, "No, I'm asleep," and think about L.A.

Things got pretty loud this time, but the unstable melting pot has been having quiet riots for years. In the most segregated West Coast metropolis, life has always been cheap for people of color. The habitual nihilism, simmering anger, and casual violence of both the L.A.P.D. and the multiracial gang scene has been escalating ever since my first trip here in 1981. In the African American community, xenophobia toward hispanics and Asians, alienation from a city government run by a prototypical Negro pol, and a genocidal yet fertile youth culture primed black L.A.'s everyday people for the uprising. The naked racism of the acquittal uncorked a big one, but next week, next month, next century, all the small beeps of rioting that make the *Los Angeles Times* Metro section so entertaining will still be there—unless, by some unforeseen miracle, fundamental change occurs between the residents of this brown metropolis and those who presume to control it.

The early '80s choke-hold controversy, the backlash vote against Tom Bradley's run for governor, the Long Beach rap riot, the acceptance of drive-bys in the popular vernacular, *Boyz N the Hood,* the unpunished shooting of a black girl by a Korean grocer—all helped create this boil on the smog-shrouded soil. It's why N.W.A, a/k/a Niggas With Attitude, were to the '80s what the Beach Boys were to the '60s and the Eagles to the '70s—the definitive Southern California band. "Fuck Tha Police" spoke to the fantasies of this city's majority no less than "California Girls" and "Life in the Fast Lane."

As the plane came over the city at about 2:30 L.A. time, smoke billowed up from two, three, four, seven spots out the left side windows. On the right side I saw four others. As the plane passed over the Coliseum, a huge plume of ashy black air floated up under our right wing. We got a beautiful view of the coastline when the plane curved out over the Pacific Ocean—a route determined, I later found out, by South Central residents taking potshots at arriving flights. As we sat on the ground for 25 minutes, an attendant told me the Beverly Center had been closed by looting. I took note for two reasons: This L.A. landmark was in the red-hot center of West Hollywood, an overwhelmingly white liberal (and gay) part of town, and La Cienega Boulevard, which borders this giant mall, was the usual route to my hotel. We were also told that curfews were in effect in Los Angeles, Culver City, and Long Beach—and to hold on to our plane tickets to prove we had pressing business on the street.

An Arab cab driver approached us and asked cautiously, "Where are you going?" When we told him, he wasn't hostile, just concerned. "You sure you have to stay there?" he queried, explaining that on La Cienega south of the Beverly Center motorists were getting pulled from their cars. He wasn't taking that route, and I certainly had no problem with that. I was insistent on my destination only because my hotel, the Mondrian, provided a panoramic view of the city.

From a news station on the cab radio, the voices of authority filled our ears. "We're on full tactical alert," said a Beverly Hills officer. "Fires near MacArthur Park are erupting faster than the Fire Department can respond." "At 98th and Vernon a fireman has been shot." "Avoid all side streets. Use only freeways or main thoroughfares." "All RTD bus service and the Blue Line train service will be canceled." "The Utah-Clippers playoff game is being moved to Saturday afternoon and the Dodgers-Phillies game, scheduled for tonight, will be moved to later in the season." From City Hall the mayor droned on but one line caught my ear: "The police are under orders to take back the streets." And then I looked east and saw a rainbow. Except this rainbow was thick and gray and stretched from midway in the sky down to the ground, with spirals of smoke rising inside like miniature tornadoes.

From the Mondrian's restaurant terrace one can see west from the power towers of Century City across Beverly Hills, the Wilshire District, Mid-City, Koreatown, and the cluster of skyscrapers that defines Downtown. Beyond these areas are places like Inglewood, Ladera Heights, South Central, East L.A., and sundry other hoods. For two hours I sat on that terrace watching fires rage and then smolder. Dowdy white couples, flaxen-haired models, and hip dudes in snakeskin boots stood and pointed at them. As soon as one stream of smoke expired, another puffed up. Fire engines screamed below us. Western Boulevard, a poor man's furniture and appliance strip run by mostly hispanic and Asian merchants that's a major artery into South Central, was lit up. The vibe from the other guests was chilly. Adversity breeds fellowship and I saw people, par-

ticularly white women, making new acquaintances among themselves. No such familiarity came my way.

As the evening fell and the curfew came into effect I started working the phones.
Melissa Maxwell, a young filmmaker living off Wilshire, was very upset. On the way
home she'd witnessed two cars of black youths shooting at each other. A local computer
store had been cleaned out, a window smashed at a nearby bank. Across the street a
business was aflame. Her neighbors in her apartment complex were gathering up their
garden hoses. "There's a Persian carpet outlet on our block," she said nervously, "and
we hear they're going to hit it tonight. If there's a fire in that store it could set off the
whole block."

Cheryl Hill and her man live in West Hollywood two blocks west of Melrose, a
fashionable white area. As thick clouds of smoke filled the air there, residents came outside seeking its source. "We looked around and we were the only blacks on the block,
and we could feel the stares. No one said anything, but white folks were looking at us a
little funny."

Sam Kitt, a white movie executive, was one of the last to leave his Burbank office
building. The studio security guards advised him, "Don't stop for any red lights. If anybody gets in your way, make them a hood ornament." Out in the valley where Sam
lives, the only sign of trouble is a fire "maybe twenty blocks away."

Denise Weeks, a television producer's assistant who lives off Pico in Mid-City,
couldn't talk long. "Everybody on the block's getting their water hoses out," she said
quickly. "There's a fire three blocks away in one direction and another in the other direction four blocks down. Talk to you later."

Dolores Forteno and her video camera had just returned to her home off Western.
"I don't think there's a Korean nail shop left in town. I saw no violence—just fires. Lots
of family-owned businesses burning. The good Chinese food restaurant, the Ethiopian
cleaners, the place we shop for groceries—all gone. It's not a black-Korean thing here
'cause the population is 80 per cent Mexican and Salvadoran, so it's mostly hispanic on
hispanic. They didn't mind me taping. Got them going in and coming out the swap
meet. You got to come over and see it."

Eddie G., an actor from Crenshaw who was staying at the hotel instead of jour-
neying home, took a biblical view. "God's a violent motherfucker," he said. "Forty days
and forty nights of rain is violent. This is his retribution. God's with the niggas on this
one." More profound than his religious interpretation was his news that the Bloods and
Crips had declared a truce and gotten together "to burn this whole motherfucker
down."

This was an observation/rumor that a number of people with gang and rap contacts repeated. The injury of several babies in recent drivebys had apparently led to a
temporary cessation of hostilities. This truce was then extended because of the King
verdict and, according to street talk, channeled into taking black and hispanic fury outside South Central. For hardcore gang-bangers, it was a golden opportunity for the big
payback.

At around nine I walked out into the hotel driveway in a blue jean shirt and pants,
and gazed at Sunset Boulevard. On a normal Thursday the Comedy Store would have
been jumping, cars zooming by, and the hotel's lights on to welcome guests. Tonight
there was nothing to see but stale smoke clouds saturating the air. A hotel employee
told me the Pink Dot down the block had a handwritten sign in the window that read,

"Black Owned," and we both laughed. Three security guards in suits looked me over between their yawns. Then a van rolled by and the brother behind the wheel flashed a gang sign my way. It was time to go inside.

Nine a.m. Friday morning the numbers are coming in: 27 dead, 1,235 injured, 2,000 structural fires, 30 active fires, 3,000 arrested and $200 million in damages—all sure to go much higher. My buddy Chris Rock and I hit the road for Burbank and a celebrities-against-racism event called Wall of Justice. Along Sunset toward Highland, many windows are smashed, Asian store owners are sweeping the sidewalk in front of a diner, and British singer/songwriter Seal drives by in a black convertible. The police have blocked off Hollywood Boulevard going east, now a deteriorating neighborhood that's an L.A. cross between 14th Street and Times Square. There's been massive loot-ing there. Somebody snatched Madonna's old bra from Frederick's of Hollywood.

The Wall of Justice media event draws an eclectic crew—Richard Grieco, Justine Bateman, Debbie Allen, Wesley Snipes, Jimmy Smits, Sean Penn, Anjelica Huston, Joie Lee, Bill Duke, Robert Culp, David Cassidy. A gauze wall has been set up on a Warner soundstage right next to a giant unfinished poster of Mel Gibson and Danny Glover for *Lethal Weapon 3*. The celebs are to sign this wall and then have their names collected on a petition protesting the King verdict. An instant anthem by the unlikely Tom Petty, "Peace in L.A.," is debuted. Wesley Snipes, wearing robes X-Clan would envy, drops a little Afrocentric science on this old-fashioned liberalism when he says from the podium, "The problem is universal racism in this country," but most of the talk is feel-good bromides.

In a corner of the sound stage, Propaganda Films is taping PSAs for the mayor's office, and they've managed to corner N.W.A's Eazy-E and Ren. I'm surprised by their presence but not their attitude. When the nice white-haired woman in the pink dress from the mayor's office asks them to say "Stop the violence" for the camera, Ren just looks through her. Eazy's got on wraparound shades and an adorable smirk. "I can't say that," Ren finally replies. "No," the pink-dress lady asserts, "you must say it." Ren just raises his hands as if to say "Fuck you," and walks away. Eazy, a savvier media manipu-lator, kicks a few lines about "It don't make sense for people to tear up their own neigh-borhood" and steps off.

As actors and directors talk of finding common ground, Ren, one of the FBI-cen-sored voices on "Fuck tha Police," looks around and comments, "Half the mother-fuckers in here are fronting. I wasn't gonna say that stop the violence shit so they could feel good." He takes a call on his mobile phone and then continues: "This Bloods and Crips truce gonna end in just a couple of days. After all the looting's over, it's gonna go back how it was. The good thing about all this is that black people see the police for what he is. Can't trust him. Ain't no justice for a young black man."

On the way back from Burbank we decide to hit Western, not sure we can make it out to South Central and back before curfew. Western Furniture is boarded up. Selected Furniture is being nailed shut. Wilshire TV is burned and gone. These are just a few names of the stores I wrote down—could have been any one of a score of others. Anywhere selling consumer durables, that is—most of the fast-food joints seem untouched.

We cut down a side street onto Virginia Avenue, where two police cars and seven cops guard a mini-mall. As we drive across Mid-City toward the Beverly Center it's clear that the Rodney King uprising was primarily an economic event. Beautiful residential sections just blocks from ransacked mini-malls are untouched and peaceful. Sure blacks robbed blacks. But hispanics robbed hispanics, and blacks robbed hispanics, and everybody robbed Asians, and whites too got their share when the opportunity presented itself.

In 1992 economic outrage isn't bound by geography or race, but by class—no news there except maybe to the mainstream media and government officials. As King himself suggested on Friday, the first two hours of the uprising were probably about the verdict. The night and day that followed around L.A. and the nation were about every bit of hopelessness that's been festering since the '70s. Working and poor Americans have been in a depression since Reagan's first term and all these TV-news–designated "criminals" are going for theirs because they feel so damned deprived.

In 1965 African Americans in urban centers like Watts were seeking their bit of the civil rights miracle that was transforming the South. Their needs were as much economic as social, and those needs were never addressed. Twenty-seven years later a generation has grown up that knows zip about those past hopes and views this world with precious little optimism. Crucially, the folks who wear X hats, view Chuck D and KRS-One as cultural heroes, and know the sound of Tech-9's better than the 10 commandments are not going to respond to racist provocation the way liberals and their African American elders want them to.

Like George Jackson embracing the metaphor of the mythic black stud Stagger Lee, young people—women and men—celebrate the hardest parts of their imaginations and invent themselves as niggas-for-life with no apologies and incredible pride. Shooting AK-47s at cops and attacking Korean grocers whom they've always viewed as economic imperialists is not an aberration. The same bold disdain has been there for years—just aimed mostly at each other, so no one gave a damn. But the nation does now and, like the jury in Simi Valley, it will interpret that attitude to fit its misconceived notions at its own risk.

Friday night on Sunset. No fires can be seen from the terrace, though copters still haunt the sky. Chris and I hit the hotel gym and then stand in our shorts in the driveway, marveling at the quiet of a street we've hung out on so many Fridays after dark. A taxi driver sleeps in his cab. Two parking attendants chill and talk. A black hotel manager in a blue blazer walks out, looks around and says hello. About five minutes later four county sheriffs walk up the driveway and two blue-blazered hotel staffers greet them. The group glances our way and one sheriff, a tall brother with a glistening dome, says, "I know him. That's Chris, the actor." Five minutes later the sheriffs are gone. Celebrity still means something in L.A. But L.A. will never again just mean celebrity.

SUGGESTIONS FOR DISCUSSION

1. Nelson George's article seems to be a report from the frontlines during the uprising that followed the acquittal of four police officers in the Rodney King beating case. But George's piece of writing is not a simple news report meant to inform readers. He situates himself in relation to the events unfolding around him and intersperses his account with commentary. What do you see as the purpose of George's writing? How does he position himself in relation to the uprising? If you were asked to state George's main point in one sentence, how would you do it?

2. George's article is thick with detail—names, places, and incidents. How do these details work together in his article? Do they create a dominant impression of the uprising? How does George use detail to relate rap music to the uprising?

3. The term *attitude* appears in George's title as well as in the title of Jerry Adler's article. Are they using the term in the same way? What differences, if any, do you see?

Exercise Four: Write a one- to two-page synthesis that compares and contrasts the three articles—"The Rap Attitude," by Jerry Adler, "When Black Feminism Faces the Music, and the Music Is Rap," by Michele Wallace, and "Niggas With Attitudes," by Nelson George. Focus your synthesis on how each of the articles provides readers with a different perspective on rap music.

Suggestions for writing a synthesis: It's easy to see that one thing all three articles have in common is that they offer commentary on rap music, its style and cultural context. By this point, you may feel awash in facts, details, commentary, and positions. It can help to sort out what the selections you've read are saying, and one way to do this is to combine two or more of the readings in a synthesis. A synthesis is a way to hold up the readings to each other, to see where they are similar and where they differ. Comparing and contrasting the perspectives these three articles offer readers are useful techniques to chart out the issues and to develop your own position. You might think of writing a synthesis as a preliminary step toward entering the debate about rap music on your own.

Exercise Five: The final writing exercise in this sequence asks you to write a short essay that develops your own position in relation to rap music and what you have read. Think of this essay as deliberative rather than informative or argumentative. That is, though you will need to inform your readers about your topic and take into account some of the controversies surrounding rap music, the purpose of the assignment is not simply to agree or disagree with the writers you've read. The point is to stake out your own position in relation to one of the issues that has emerged for you from the reading and writing you have done.

Suggestions for taking a position: In this assignment, don't limit yourself just to what's reported in the feature story that opens this section or the views represented by Kinsley and Ehrenreich. Taking a position involves deliberating on the significance of rap music and the larger questions it raises about race, class, and gender in contemporary America. It means finding a place on which you can stand to speak publicly about what, in your view, seems to be an especially interesting or significant issue. You might, for example, choose to write about what Jerry Adler calls the "rap attitude," to develop your own views about what causes the kind of macho posturing he finds in both rap and heavy metal. Or you might take off from what Michele Wallace has written about the degrading representations of women in popular culture. Or, you might use Nelson George's impressionistic commentary on the Los Angeles uprising to draw your own conclusions about the connections between rap and life in the inner city.

There are many more issues you could write about. The ones we have just noted are only examples. You have already started to identify important issues in the exploratory writing you've done. Our guess is you will have more than enough to write about. Whatever you decide to write about, don't feel you have to be comprehensive or have the final word. Writers discovering new angles to draw out the significance of an event or a trend is what makes writing interesting to read.

CONCLUSION

What you have been doing in the reading and writing assignments in this chapter amounts to a kind of cultural analysis of rap music. The assignments have asked you not only to read what other writers have said about rap but also to think about the writers' purposes and how they have developed their own positions on the issues. In this sense, you have been analyzing how writers seek to shape public opinion and how the media represents what is happening in American culture. This amounts to a cultural analysis of the role of the media and the press in American life. As you have read and written about rap music, you have also encountered a series of related issues about popular music, race, class, the representation of women, censorship, and cultural values. In the following chapters, we will be presenting further opportunities to do this kind of cultural analysis—to read and write your way into the cultural meanings of contemporary life in America.

CHAPTER 2

GENERATIONS

"This is not your father's Oldsmobile.
This is the new generation — of Olds."

— 1990 television commercial
for Oldsmobile

A merica is a nation of immigrants, and it is common to distinguish between first and second generations—between those who first traveled to and settled in the United States from Europe, Asia, Africa, or Latin America and their children who were born here. The two generations, of course, are biologically related to each other as well as to older generations of grandparents, great-grandparents, and great great-grandparents, as far back as people can trace their ancestry. Yet, first-generation and second-generation Americans often differ in the way they live their lives, in the hopes they have for themselves and their children, and in the ties they feel to the traditions and customs of their places of ancestry.

Individuals grow up as part of a biological generation that comes along every twenty years to continue their family's line. At the same time, however, individuals are also members of a historical generation. In cultural terms, generations are not only produced through biological descent. They are also formed out of a common history and the common experiences people have growing up with others their age. To be a member of a generation, then, is to belong not only to a family. It also means belonging to a generation of people to whom you are historically related.

In this chapter, we will be asking you to read, think, and write about what it means to be a member of and a participant in your historical generation. Whether you are straight out of high school or returning to college, it can be valuable to consider how your own personal experience has been shaped by growing up at a particular moment in a particular historical generation.

The term *generation* denotes change. It suggests new life and new growth—new styles, new values, new ways of living. Americans hear generational voices all the time in everyday conversation, when young people tell their parents not to be "so old-fashioned" and their parents reply "it wasn't like that when we were growing up." Sportswriters and fans talk about how Shaquille O'Neal is ushering in a new generation of basketball players for the 1990s, now that Michael Jordan has retired. And advertising, too, as the Oldsmobile commercial at the beginning of this chapter indicates, likes to make us believe that the new generation of goods—not only cars but stereos, computers, household appliances—is smarter, better designed, and more high tech than its predecessors.

Each generation differs from those that came before. Cultural historian Raymond Williams says that "no generation speaks quite the same language as its predecessor." Each generation produces its own way of speaking and its own forms of cultural expression. Young people, for example, use slang to recognize friends, to distinguish between insiders and outsiders, to position themselves in relation to the older generation. Whether you say things are "icy" or "far out," the kind of music you like to listen to, the way you dance, your style of dress, where you go to hang out—all these things reveal something about you and your relation to the constantly changing styles of youth culture in contemporary America.

People's tastes in popular entertainment and their participation in fads, styles, and trends, of course, are not just personal matters, though they are often deeply felt by individuals. They also, quite literally, date individuals by tying people's personal experience to a particular time, when they first heard a song or saw a movie. How a generation looks at itself is inevitably entangled in the decisive historical events and the geopolitical changes of its day. The Depression, World War II, the Vietnam War, and the Reagan years have each influenced a generation profoundly. To understand what it means to belong to your generation, you will need to locate your experience growing up as a member of your generation in its historical times—to see how your generation has made sense of its place in American history and its relation to past generations.

From the invention of the American teenager and juvenile delinquency in movies like *Rebel Without a Cause* and *The Wild One* in the 1950s to grunge rock and MTV in the 1990s, American media has been fascinated by each new generation of young people. In America, a generation is always in part a media event, and to think about your generation, you will want to look at how the media have represented your generation and how these media representations have entered into your generation's conception of itself. Each generation seems to have its own characteristic mood or identity that the press and the media try to capture in a label—whether the "lost" generation of the Jazz Age in the 1920s or the "silent" generation of the Eisenhower years in the 1950s. When people use these labels or refer to the "sixties" generation of activists and hippies or the "yuppies" of the 1980s or the "slackers" of the 1990s, they are not only referring to particular groups of people. They are also calling up a set of values, styles, and images, a collective feeling in the air.

This is not to say that everyone in the same generation has the same experience and the same feelings. A generation is not, after all, a monolithic thing. In fact, every generation is divided along the same lines of race, class, gender, and ethnicity that divide the wider society. But a generation is not simply a composite of individuals either. To think about the mood of your generation—the sensibility that suffuses its lived experience—you will need to consider how the character of your generation distinguishes it from generations of the past, even if that character is contradictory or inconsistent.

READING THE CULTURE OF GENERATIONS

We begin this chapter with three reading selections that present various writing strategies to characterize the relationship between generations. In the first, a chapter called "Kiswana Browne" from the novel *The Women of Brewster Place,* Gloria Naylor uses fiction to explore the relationship between generations in a single family, emphasizing both differences and continuities between an African American mother and daughter. In the next selection, the personal essay "The New Lost Generation," David Leavitt draws on his own experience to represent what it was like to be a member of the generation of young people that grew up "in between" the activists of the 1960s and the yuppies of the 1980s. The next reading, "Youth and American Identity," taken from Lawrence Grossberg's longer study *It's a Sin,* takes a broader, more analytical perspective on the way post-World War II America invested its hopes in the younger generation as the living symbol of national identity and the American Dream.

The next three selections—Laura Zinn's "Move Over, Boomers: The Busters Are Here—And They're Angry," Michael Oreskes' "Profiles of Today's Youth: They Couldn't Care Less," and Neil Howe and William Strauss's "The New Generation Gap"—offer examples of how journalists have written for the popular press about the current generation of young people in America. These articles raise a number of questions worth considering. For one thing, you will notice how each selection attempts to characterize this generation by locating it in relation to the baby-boom generation that came of age in the 1960s and early 1970s. The various labels applied to this generation—whether "busters," "slackers," "Generation X," or "Thirteeners"—point to key generational differences. Just as important, the use of such labels raises the issue of how the press and the media represent young people and what cultural forces and attitudes shape these representations.

As you read, think, talk, and write about the interpretations presented in this chapter, you should begin to consider how you would characterize the meaning of your own generation. How is your generation portrayed in the media? What styles of cultural expression mark your generation from those that preceded it? What is your generation's sense of itself? These are some of the questions you will ask as you work your way through this chapter. Perhaps when you have completed your work, you will find a way to define the particular mood and character of your generation.

Gloria Naylor

KISWANA BROWNE

Gloria Naylor's highly acclaimed novel *The Women of Brewster Place* (1980) tells the stories of a number of African American women who live in a housing project in an unnamed city. We have selected the chapter "Kiswana Browne" because it presents a powerful account of the encounter between a mother and daughter that explores both their generational differences and the aspirations they hold in common. Naylor's story reveals how the much-publicized generation gap of the 1960s is never simply a matter of differences in politics and life-style but rather is complicated by the intersecting forces of race, class, and gender. The cultural shift signified by Kiswana's change of name represents both a break with the past and, as Kiswana discovers, a continuation of her family's resistance to racial oppression.

Suggestion for Reading

- As you read, underline and annotate the passages where the story establishes conflict between the two characters and where (or whether) it resolves the conflict.

F rom the window of her sixth-floor studio apartment, Kiswana could see over the wall at the end of the street to the busy avenue that lay just north of Brewster Place. The late-afternoon shoppers looked like brightly clad marionettes as they moved between the congested traffic, clutching their packages against their bodies to guard them from sudden bursts of the cold autumn wind. A portly mailman had abandoned his cart and was bumping into indignant window-shoppers as he puffed behind the cap that the wind had snatched from his head. Kiswana leaned over to see if he was going to be successful, but the edge of the building cut him off from her view.

A pigeon swept across her window, and she marveled at its liquid movements in the air waves. She placed her dreams on the back of the bird and fantasized that it would glide forever in transparent silver circles until it ascended to the center of the universe and was swallowed up. But the wind died down, and she watched with a sigh as the bird beat its wings in awkward, frantic movements to land on the corroded top of a fire escape on the opposite building. This brought her back to earth.

Humph, it's probably sitting over there crapping on those folks' fire escape, she thought. Now, that's a safety hazard. . . . And her mind was busy again, creating flames and smoke and frustrated tenants whose escape was being hindered because they were slipping and sliding in pigeon shit. She watched their cussing, haphazard descent on the fire escapes until they had all reached the bottom. They were milling around, oblivious to their burning apartments, angrily planning to march on the mayor's office about the pigeons. She materialized placards and banners for them, and they had just reached the corner, boldly sidestepping fire hoses and broken glass, when they all vanished.

A tall copper-skinned woman had met this phantom parade at the corner, and they had dissolved in front of her long, confident strides. She plowed through the re- mains of their faded mists, unconscious of the lingering wisps of their presence on her leather bag and black fur-trimmed coat. It took a few seconds for this transfer from one realm to another to reach Kiswana, but then suddenly she recognized the woman.

"Oh, God, it's Mama!" She looked down guiltily at the forgotten newspaper in her lap and hurriedly circled random job advertisements.

By this time Mrs. Browne had reached the front of Kiswana's building and was checking the house number against a piece of paper in her hand. Before she went into the building she stood at the bottom of the stoop and carefully inspected the condition of the street and the adjoining property. Kiswana watched this meticulous inventory with growing annoyance but she involuntarily followed her mother's slowly rotating head, forcing herself to see her new neighborhood through the older woman's eyes. The brightness of the unclouded sky seemed to join forces with her mother as it high-lighted every broken stoop railing and missing brick. The afternoon sun glittered and cascaded across even the tiniest fragments of broken bottle, and at that very moment the wind chose to rise up again, sending unswept grime flying into the air, as a stray tin can left by careless garbage collectors went rolling noisily down the center of the street.

Kiswana noticed with relief that at least Ben wasn't sitting in his usual place on the old garbage can pushed against the far wall. He was just a harmless old wino, but Kiswana knew her mother only needed one wino or one teenager with a reefer within a twenty-block radius to decide that her daughter was living in a building seething with dope factories and hang-outs for derelicts. If she had seen Ben, nothing would have made her believe that practically every apartment contained a family, a Bible, and a dream that one day enough could be scraped from those meager Friday night paychecks to make Brewster Place a distant memory.

As she watched her mother's head disappear into the building, Kiswana gave silent thanks that the elevator was broken. That would give her at least five minutes' grace to straighten up the apartment. She rushed to the sofa bed and hastily closed it without smoothing the rumpled sheets and blanket or removing her nightgown. She felt that somehow the tangled bedcovers would give away the fact that she had not slept alone last night. She silently apologized to Abshu's memory as she heartlessly crushed his spirit between the steel springs of the couch. Lord, that man was sweet. Her toes curled involuntarily at the passing thought of his full lips moving slowly over her instep. Abshu was a foot man, and he always started his lovemaking from the bottom up. For that reason Kiswana changed the color of the polish on her toenails every week. During the course of their relationship she had gone from shades of red to brown and was now into the purples. I'm gonna have to start mixing them soon, she thought aloud as she turned from the couch and raced into the bathroom to remove any traces of Abshu from there. She took up his shaving cream and razor and threw them into the bottom drawer of her dresser beside her diaphragm. Mama wouldn't dare pry into my drawers right in front of me, she thought as she slammed the drawer shut. Well, at least not the *bottom* drawer. She may come up with some sham excuse for opening the top drawer, but never the bottom one.

When she heard the first two short raps on the door, her eyes took a final flight over the small apartment, desperately seeking out any slight misdemeanor that might have to be defended. Well, there was nothing she could do about the crack in the wall over that table. She had been after the landlord to fix it for two months now. And there had been no time to sweep the rug, and everyone knew that off-gray always looked dirtier than it really was. And it was just too damn bad about the kitchen. How was she expected to be out job-hunting every day and still have time to keep a kitchen that looked like her mother's, who didn't even work and still had someone come in twice a month for general cleaning. And besides . . .

Her imaginary argument was abruptly interrupted by a second series of knocks, accompanied by a penetrating, "Melanie, Melanie, are you there?"

Kiswana strode toward the door. She's starting before she even gets in here. She knows that's not my name anymore.

She swung the door open to face her slightly flushed mother. "Oh, hi, Mama. You know, I thought I heard a knock, but I figured it was for the people next door, since no one hardly ever calls me Melanie." Score one for me, she thought.

"Well, it's awfully strange you can forget a name you answered to for twenty-three years," Mrs. Browne said, as she moved past Kiswana into the apartment. "My, that was a long climb. How long has your elevator been out? Honey, how do you manage with your laundry and groceries up all those steps? But I guess you're young, and it wouldn't bother you as much as it does me." This long string of questions told Kiswana that her mother had no intentions of beginning her visit with another argument about her new African name.

"You know I would have called before I came, but you don't have a phone yet. I didn't want you to feel that I was snooping. As a matter of fact, I didn't expect to find you home at all. I thought you'd be out looking for a job." Mrs. Browne had mentally covered the entire apartment while she was talking and taking off her coat.

"Well, I got up late this morning. I thought I'd buy the afternoon paper and start early tomorrow."

"That sounds like a good idea." Her mother moved toward the window and picked up the discarded paper and glanced over the hurriedly circled ads. "Since when do you have experience as a fork-lift operator?"

Kiswana caught her breath and silently cursed herself for her stupidity. "Oh, my hand slipped—I meant to circle file clerk." She quickly took the paper before her mother could see that she had also marked cutlery salesman and chauffeur.

"You're sure you weren't sitting here moping and day-dreaming again?" Amber specks of laughter flashed in the corner of Mrs. Browne's eyes.

Kiswana threw her shoulders back and unsuccessfully tried to disguise her embarrassment with indignation.

"Oh, God, Mama! I haven't done that in years—it's for kids. When are you going to realize that I'm a woman now?" She sought desperately for some womanly thing to do and settled for throwing herself on the couch and crossing her legs in what she hoped looked like a nonchalant arc.

"Please, have a seat," she said, attempting the same tones and gestures she'd seen Bette Davis use on the late movies.

Mrs. Browne, lowering her eyes to hide her amusement, accepted the invitation and sat at the window, also crossing her legs. Kiswana saw immediately how it should have been done. Her celluloid poise clashed loudly against her mother's quiet dignity, and she quickly uncrossed her legs. Mrs. Browne turned her head toward the window and pretended not to notice.

"At least you have a halfway decent view from here. I was wondering what lay beyond that dreadful wall—it's the boulevard. Honey, did you know that you can see the trees in Linden Hills from here?"

Kiswana knew that very well, because there were many lonely days that she would sit in her gray apartment and stare at those trees and think of home, but she would rather have choked than admit that to her mother.

"Oh, really, I never noticed. So how is Daddy and things at home?"

"Just fine. We're thinking of redoing one of the extra bedrooms since you children have moved out, but Wilson insists that he can manage all that work alone. I told him that he doesn't really have the proper time or energy for all that. As it is, when he gets home from the office, he's so tired he can hardly move. But you know you can't tell your father anything. Whenever he starts complaining about how stubborn you are, I tell him the child came by it honestly. Oh, and your brother was by yesterday," she added, as if it had just occurred to her.

So that's it, thought Kiswana. That's why she's here.

Kiswana's brother, Wilson, had been to visit her two days ago, and she had borrowed twenty dollars from him to get her winter coat out of layaway. That son-of-a-bitch probably ran straight to Mama—and after he swore he wouldn't say anything. I should have known, he was always a snotty-nosed sneak, she thought.

"Was he?" she said aloud. "He came by to see me, too, earlier this week. And I borrowed some money from him because my unemployment checks hadn't cleared in the bank, but now they have and everything's just fine." There, I'll beat you to that one.

"Oh, I didn't know that," Mrs. Browne lied. "He never mentioned you. He had just heard that Beverly was expecting again, and he rushed over to tell us."

Damn. Kiswana could have strangled herself.

"So she's knocked up again, huh?" she said irritably.

Her mother started. "Why do you always have to be so crude?"

"Personally, I don't see how she can sleep with Willie. He's such a dishrag."

Kiswana still resented the stance her brother had taken in college. When everyone at school was discovering their blackness and protesting on campus, Wilson never took part; he had even refused to wear an Afro. This had outraged Kiswana because, unlike her, he was dark-skinned and had the type of hair that was thick and kinky enough for a good "Fro." Kiswana had still insisted on cutting her own hair, but it was so thin and fine-textured, it refused to thicken even after she washed it. So she had to brush it up and spray it with lacquer to keep it from lying flat. She never forgave Wilson for telling her that she didn't look African, she looked like an electrocuted chicken.

"Now that's some way to talk. I don't know why you have an attitude against your brother. He never gave me a restless night's sleep, and now he's settled with a family and a good job."

"He's an assistant to an assistant junior partner in a law firm. What's the big deal about that?"

"The job has a future, Melanie. And at least he finished school and went on for his law degree."

"In other words, not like me, huh?"

"Don't put words into my mouth, young lady. I'm perfectly capable of saying what I mean."

Amen, thought Kiswana.

"And I don't know why you've been trying to start up with me from the moment I walked in. I didn't come here to fight with you. This is your first place away from home, and I just wanted to see how you were living and if you're doing all right. And I must say, you've fixed this apartment up very nicely."

"Really, Mama?" She found herself softening in the light of her mother's approval.

"Well, considering what you had to work with." This time she scanned the apartment openly.

"Look, I know it's not Linden Hills, but a lot can be done with it. As soon as they come and paint, I'm going to hang my Ashanti print over the couch. And I thought a big Boston Fern would go well in that corner, what do you think?"

"That would be fine, baby. You always had a good eye for balance."

Kiswana was beginning to relax. There was little she did that attracted her mother's approval. It was like a rare bird, and she had to tread carefully around it lest it fly away.

"Are you going to leave that statue out like that?"

"Why, what's wrong with it? Would it look better somewhere else?"

There was a small wooden reproduction of a Yoruba goddess with large protruding breasts on the coffee table.

"Well," Mrs. Browne was beginning to blush, "it's just that it's a bit suggestive, don't you think? Since you live alone now, and I know you'll be having male friends stop by, you wouldn't want to be giving them any ideas. I mean, uh, you know, there's no point in putting yourself in any unpleasant situations because they may get the wrong impressions and uh, you know, I mean, well. . ." Mrs. Browne stammered on miserably.

Kiswana loved it when her mother tried to talk about sex. It was the only time she was at a loss for words.

"Don't worry, Mama." Kiswana smiled. "That wouldn't bother the type of men I date. Now maybe if it had big feet. . . " And she got hysterical, thinking of Abshu.

Her mother looked at her sharply. "What sort of gibberish is that about feet? I'm being serious, Melanie."

"I'm sorry, Mama." She sobered up. "I'll put it away in the closet," she said, knowing that she wouldn't.

"Good," Mrs. Browne said, knowing that she wouldn't either. "I guess you think I'm too picky, but we worry about you over here. And you refuse to put in a phone so we can call and see about you."

"I haven't refused, Mama. They want seventy-five dollars for a deposit, and I can't swing that right now."

"Melanie, I can give you the money."

"I don't want you to be giving me money—I've told you that before. Please, let me make it by myself."

"Well, let me lend it to you, then."

"No!"

"Oh, so you can borrow money from your brother, but not from me."

Kiswana turned her head from the hurt in her mother's eyes. "Mama, when I borrow from Willie, he makes me pay him back. You never let me pay you back," she said into her hands.

"I don't care. I still think it's downright selfish of you to be sitting over here with no phone, and sometimes we don't hear from you in two weeks—anything could happen—especially living among these people."

Kiswana snapped her head up. "What do you mean, *these people*. They're my people and yours, too, Mama—we're all black. But maybe you've forgotten that over in Linden Hills."

"That's not what I'm talking about, and you know it. These streets—this building—it's so shabby and rundown. Honey, you don't have to live like this."

"Well, this is how poor people live."

"Melanie, you're not poor."

"No, Mama, *you're* not poor. And what you have and I have are two totally different things. I don't have a husband in real estate with a five-figure income and a home in Linden Hills—*you* do. What I have is a weekly unemployment check and an overdrawn checking account at United Federal. So this studio on Brewster is all I can afford."

"Well, you could afford a lot better," Mrs. Browne snapped, "if you hadn't dropped out of college and had to resort to these dead-end clerical jobs."

"Uh-huh, I knew you'd get around to that before long." Kiswana could feel the rings of anger begin to tighten around her lower backbone, and they sent her forward onto the couch. "You'll never understand, will you? Those bourgie schools were counterrevolutionary. My place was in the streets with my people, fighting for equality and a better community."

"Counterrevolutionary!" Mrs. Browne was raising her voice. "Where's your revolution now, Melanie? Where are all those black revolutionaries who were shouting and demonstrating and kicking up a lot of dust with you on that campus? Huh? They're sitting in wood-paneled offices with their degrees in mahogany frames, and they won't even drive their cars past this street because the city doesn't fix potholes in this part of town."

"Mama," she said, shaking her head slowly in disbelief, "how can you—a black woman—sit there and tell me that what we fought for during the Movement wasn't important just because some people sold out?"

"Melanie, I'm not saying it wasn't important. It was damned important to stand up and say that you were proud of what you were and to get the vote and other social opportunities for every person in this country who had it due. But you kids thought you were going to turn the world upside down, and it just wasn't so. When all the smoke had cleared, you found yourself with a fistful of new federal laws and a country still full of obstacles for black people to fight their way over—just because they're black. There was no revolution, Melanie, and there will be no revolution."

"So what am I supposed to do, huh? Just throw up my hands and not care about what happens to my people? I'm not supposed to keep fighting to make things better?"

"Of course, you can. But you're going to have to fight within the system, because it and these so-called 'bourgie' schools are going to be here for a long time. And that means that you get smart like a lot of your old friends and get an important job where you can have some influence. You don't have to sell out, as you say, and work for some corporation, but you could become an assemblywoman or a civil liberties lawyer or open a freedom school in this very neighborhood. That way you could really help the community. But what help are you going to be to these people on Brewster while you're living hand-to-mouth on file-clerk jobs waiting for a revolution? You're wasting your talents, child."

"Well, I don't think they're being wasted. At least I'm here in day-to-day contact with the problems of my people. What good would I be after four or five years of a lot of white brainwashing in some phony, prestige institution, huh? I'd be like you and Daddy and those other educated blacks sitting over there in Linden Hills with a terminal case of middle-class amnesia."

"You don't have to live in a slum to be concerned about social conditions, Melanie. Your father and I have been charter members of the NAACP for the last twenty-five years."

"Oh, God!" Kiswana threw her head back in exaggerated disgust. "That's being concerned? That middle-of-the-road, Uncle Tom dumping ground for black Republicans!"

"You can sneer all you want, young lady, but that organization has been working for black people since the turn of the century, and it's still working for them. Where are all those radical groups of yours that were going to put a Cadillac in every garage and Dick Gregory in the White House? I'll tell you where."

I knew you would, Kiswana thought angrily.

"They burned themselves out because they wanted too much too fast. Their goals weren't grounded in reality. And that's always been your problem."

"What do you mean, my problem? I know exactly what I'm about."

"No, you don't. You constantly live in a fantasy world—always going to extremes—turning butterflies into eagles, and life isn't about that. It's accepting what is and working from that. Lord, I remember how worried you had me, putting all that lacquered hair spray on your head. I thought you were going to get lung cancer—trying to be what you're not."

Kiswana jumped up from the couch. "Oh, God, I can't take this anymore. Trying to be something I'm not—trying to be something I'm not, Mama! Trying to be proud of my heritage and the fact that I was of African descent. If that's being what I'm not, then I say fine. But I'd rather be dead than be like you—a white man's nigger who's ashamed of being black!"

Kiswana saw streaks of gold and ebony light follow her mother's flying body out of the chair. She was swung around by the shoulders and made to face the deadly stillness in the angry woman's eyes. She was too stunned to cry out from the pain of the long fingernails that dug into her shoulders, and she was brought so close to her mother's face that she saw her reflection, distorted and wavering, in the tears that stood in the older woman's eyes. And she listened in that stillness to a story she had heard from a child.

"My grandmother," Mrs. Browne began slowly in a whisper, "was a full-blooded Iroquois, and my grandfather a free black from a long line of journeymen who had lived in Connecticut since the establishment of the colonies. And my father was a Bajan who came to this country as a cabin boy on a merchant mariner."

"I know all that," Kiswana said, trying to keep her lips from trembling.

"Then, know this." And the nails dug deeper into her flesh. "I am alive because of the blood of proud people who never scraped or begged or apologized for what they were. They lived asking only one thing of this world—to be allowed to be. And I learned through the blood of these people that black isn't beautiful and it isn't ugly—black is! It's not kinky hair and it's not straight hair—it just is.

"It broke my heart when you changed your name. I gave you my grandmother's name, a woman who bore nine children and educated them all, who held off six white men with a shotgun when they tried to drag one of her sons to jail for 'not knowing his place.' Yet you needed to reach into an African dictionary to find a name to make you proud.

"When I brought my babies home from the hospital, my ebony son and my golden daughter, I swore before whatever gods would listen—those of my mother's people or those of my father's people—that I would use everything I had and could ever get to see that my children were prepared to meet this world on its own terms, so that no one could sell them short and make them ashamed of what they were or how they looked—whatever they were or however they looked. And Melanie, that's not being white or red or black—that's being a mother."

Kiswana followed her reflection in the two single tears that moved down her mother's cheeks until it blended with them into the woman's copper skin. There was nothing and then so much that she wanted to say, but her throat kept closing up every time she tried to speak. She kept her head down and her eyes closed, and thought, Oh, God, just let me die. How can I face her now?

Mrs. Browne lifted Kiswana's chin gently. "And the one lesson I wanted you to learn is not to be afraid to face anyone, not even a crafty old lady like me who can outtalk you." And she smiled and winked.

"Oh, Mama, I . . . " and she hugged the woman tightly.

"Yeah, baby." Mrs. Browne patted her back. "I know."

She kissed Kiswana on the forehead and cleared her throat. "Well, now, I better be moving on. It's getting late, there's dinner to be made, and I have to get off my feet—these new shoes are killing me."

Kiswana looked down at the beige leather pumps. "Those are really classy. They're English, aren't they?"

"Yes, but, Lord, do they cut me right across the instep." She removed the shoe and sat on the couch to massage her foot.

Bright red nail polish glared at Kiswana through the stockings. "Since when do you polish your toenails?" she gasped. "You never did that before."

"Well. . . " Mrs. Browne shrugged her shoulders, "your father sort of talked me into it, and, uh, you know, he likes it and all, so I thought, uh, you know, why not, so. . . " And she gave Kiswana an embarrassed smile.

I'll be damned, the young woman thought, feeling her whole face tingle. Daddy's into feet! And she looked at the blushing woman on her couch and suddenly realized that her mother had trod through the same universe that she herself was now traveling. Kiswana was breaking no new trails and would eventually end up just two feet away on that couch. She stared at the woman she had been and was to become.

"But I'll never be a Republican," she caught herself saying aloud.

"What are you mumbling about, Melanie?" Mrs. Browne slipped on her shoe and got up from the couch.

She went to get her mother's coat. "Nothing, Mama. It's really nice of you to come by. You should do it more often."

"Well, since it's not Sunday, I guess you're allowed at least one lie."

They both laughed.

After Kiswana had closed the door and turned around, she spotted an envelope sticking between the cushions of her couch. She went over and opened it up; there was seventy-five dollars in it.

"Oh, Mama, darn it!" She rushed to the window and started to call to the woman, who had just emerged from the building, but she suddenly changed her mind and sat down in the chair with a long sight that caught in the upward draft of the autumn wind and disappeared over the top of the building.

SUGGESTIONS FOR DISCUSSION

1. Gloria Naylor tells this story from Kiswana Browne's point of view. How would the story be different if Naylor had chosen to tell it from Kiswana's mother's point of view? What would be gained? What lost?
2. Consider how Naylor has organized this story—how she establishes a central conflict, leads up to the story's climax, and finally resolves the conflict. Does this kind of plot seem familiar? Does the story achieve a kind of closure or does it seem open-ended? What kinds of satisfaction do readers derive from plots like this one? What, if anything, do such plots leave out or ignore?
3. Is Naylor making a judgment, whether implicit or explicit, of her characters? Explain your answer.

SUGGESTIONS FOR WRITING

1. Take the perspective of either Kiswana Browne or her mother and write an essay that explains how the character you have chosen sees the other. If you wish, write the essay in the voice of the character. Or you may choose to comment on the character's perceptions of the other and their generational differences in your own voice. In either case, be specific in your use of detail to define generational differences between the two women.
2. On one level, the chapter "Kiswana Browne" seems to be concerned with a "generation gap" between Kiswana and her mother. At the same time, other factors—race, class, and gender—affect the way generational differences are played out between the two characters. Write an essay that explains to what extent the chapter presents a version of the generation gap and to what extent other factors determine what happens between Kiswana and her mother. Do Kiswana and her mother

have things in common, as well as generational differences? How do these factors influence the outcome of the story?

3. "Kiswana Browne" tells of the encounter between a young woman and her family and explores generational differences that have to do with issues such as life-style, names, and politics. Can you think of an encounter you have had with your parents or someone you know has had with his or her parents that involves such telling generational conflicts? (The conflict, of course, should be something that highlights differences in generational attitudes, values, or styles—not just "normal" disagreements about using the car or what time curfew should be.) Write an essay that explores such a conflict and explains what generational differences are at stake.

David Leavitt

THE NEW LOST GENERATION

David Leavitt is a fiction writer, essayist, and AIDS activist who has published a number of novels and short story collections, including *The Lost Language of Cranes* and *Family Dancing*. His essay "The New Lost Generation" appeared in *Esquire* in May 1985 and offers a good illustration of what an essay is—in the sense of its etymological root *essai*, an attempt, a trial, a weighing out. "The New Lost Generation" represents David Leavitt's attempt to locate the characteristic mood of his generation and to give it a name. By positioning young people his age as "somewhere in between" the movement activists of the 1960s and the yuppies of the 1980s, Leavitt pictures his generation as "partially what came before and partially what followed." Because of this "in between" position, Leavitt sees young people characterized by a kind of ironic detachment mixed with a desire for "stability, neatness, entrenchment." The essay's title relies on the image of the Lost Generation of the 1920s—F. Scott Fitzgerald's beautiful but rootless youth and Ernest Hemingway, Gertrude Stein, and the American expatriates in Paris. But at the same time, Leavitt updates his title, making it new by using these literary associations to produce a portrait of a new generation and its place in history.

Suggestion for Reading

• As you read, you will notice that David Leavitt has divided his essay into seven sections. Each of these sections could be read as a mini-essay in its own right, and yet at the same time readers expect the parts will eventually combine to form a whole essay. This is a normal expectation readers bring to essays, that the essay will make and support one main point or in some fashion create one dominant impression. In this essay, Leavitt is making certain demands of his readers to take the seven sections and to put them together. As you read, write a brief summary note—anywhere from a word or two to a sentence—at the end of each of the seven sections. This will help you see where Leavitt has been and where he is going. Then, when you have finished reading the complete essay, you can refer to these summary notes to think about how (or if) the seven sections combine to make one dominant impression on you as a reader.

◆

My generation has always resisted definition. The younger siblings of the Sixties, we watched riots from a distance, sneaked peeks at the *Zap Comix* lying around our older siblings' bedrooms, grew our hair long, and in prepubescent droves campaigned door to door for McGovern. When I was ten I played the guitar and wanted to be like Joni Mitchell. A friend of my sister's, a fellow who must have fancied himself a Bill Graham in the making, arranged for me to sing my own compositions in a series of little concerts given in the communal dining hall of Columbae House. By the time I was old enough to take part in any real way, disillusion had set in, people had given up, cocaine was the drug of choice. Tail end. We have always been the tail end—of the Sixties, of the baby boom. We hit our stride in an age of burned-out, restless, ironic disillusion. With all our much-touted youthful energy boiling inside us, where were we supposed to go? What were we supposed to do?

Now the Rainbows and the Moon Units of the world (conceived at love-ins, "birthed" in birthing rooms) are hitting their teens. They are computer-literate. They own their own Apple Macintoshes. They watch MTV on VCRs. Those with an artistic inclination rent video cameras, make their own films, and proclaim that written language will soon degenerate until it serves as a vehicle for nostalgia, eclipsed by the shot—videotape and its new alphabet of images.

My generation is somewhere in between. Born too late and too early, we are partially what came before us and partially what followed. But we can make certain claims. We are the first generation, for instance, that is younger than television. We knew the Vietnam War as something about as real as the *Mannix* episodes it seemed to interrupt so often. We learned stealth by figuring out how to get around our parents' efforts to ration the number of hours we watched each day. And we are the first generation whose members usually cannot remember their first plane trip. And the first in recent history that has never seen its friends missing in action or lost in combat or living and working in Canada.

It should have been perfect, the perfect time and place. As our parents always reminded us, we had so much they had not even been able to imagine as children. So little harm came to us. And yet, on those bright afternoons of my childhood, when I sat indoors, watching sunlight reflect off the face of *Speed Racer* on the television, I was already aware that rips were being made in the fabric of perfection. When my parents shouted at each other, their voices sounded like fabric ripping. My friends sat in the cafeteria of our middle school reading brightly colored books with titles like *The Kids' Book of Divorce*. On television the Brady Bunch and the Partridge Family continued on their merry ways. Sometimes I closed my eyes and tried to will myself through the television's scrim of glass and into their world. It was, in its own way, as appealing and as inaccessible as the world of the folk dancers, of my brothers and sisters, who went to college and were free of the big house with its burden of memories. But I knew that if I broke through the television, I wouldn't instantly emerge in that magical community of Sherman Oaks, with its homecoming dances, ice-cream floats, and wise maids. Instead I'd find circuits and wires, the complicated brainworks of the famous "tube."

In the real world, real parents were splitting up, moving out, questioning and in some cases rejecting the commandment to marry and have a family, commandments that had been the foundation of their parents' lives. In my family it was happening against our wishes. In a community where the divorce rate had reached a record high, and every family seemed to have at least one child in prison, or in a hospital, or dead of an overdose, my parents had never even separated. Still, there were sharp words, often, and a sense of desperate effort and hard, unrewarded labor through it all. We felt it in the politics of playing records, of who did the dishes, and who really cared around here, and who had slaved for whom for how long. Sometimes it seemed to me that we walked around the house opened up and bleeding, yet talking, laughing, smiling, like actors in a horror movie who, during a break in the shooting, simply forget to remove the prop knives from their backs or mop up the imitation blood. In this case the blood was real, though we pretended it wasn't.

I watched. During *Star Trek* my mother brought me dinner on a tray. Sometimes, after watching for hours and hours, I would have to get very close to the screen in order to focus, even though I knew it was bad for my eyes. Sometimes I'd see how close I could get, let the lenses of my eyes touch the hot lens of the television, soak in the pure light.

• • •

When my brother and sister were my age, they had already seen much more of the world than I will probably ever see. They'd gone to India, Guatemala, Cuba, Hong Kong. They'd worked in prisons, and organized striking farm workers, and driven across the country half a dozen times each. They'd read Kerouac, Castaneda, *Zen and the Art of Motorcycle Maintenance.* And when, as a child, I'd ask them about their lives, they'd tell me about the movement. Movement. It seemed an appropriate word, since they moved all the time, driven by exploratory wanderlust into the vast American wilderness. I possess no similar desire whatsoever, and neither, I think, do most members of my generation. Rather than move, we burrow. We are interested in stability, neatness, entrenchment. We want to stay in one place and stay in one piece, establish careers, establish credit. We want good apartments, fulfilling jobs, nice boy/girl friends. We want American Express Gold Cards. Whereas my brother and sister, at the same age, if asked, would probably have said that their goals were to expand their minds, see the world, and encourage revolutionary change.

I've never thought of myself as naive; I've never imagined that I might lead a sheltered life. I am, after all, "sophisticated," have been to Europe, understand dirty jokes and the intricacies of sexually transmitted diseases. This is my milieu, the world I live in, and I have almost never stepped beyond its comfortable borders. A safety net surrounds my sophisticated life, and the question is, of course, how did it get there? Did I build it myself? Was it left for me? Sometimes I feel as if I live in a room with mirrored walls, imagining that the tiny space I occupy is in fact endless, and constitutes a real world. I remember when I first moved to New York, and I was looking for work, I dropped my résumé off with the manager of the Oscar Wilde Memorial Bookshop—a political gay book store—and he asked me to tell him about my "movement experience." For a few seconds I blanked out. I thought he was talking about a dance.

• • •

Last year I went with three friends to see the film *Liquid Sky,* which was enjoying a cult following in lower Manhattan. The film portrays a culture of young people who live in lower Manhattan, dress in outlandish costumes, and spend most of their nights in wildly decorated clubs—a culture of young people very much like the young people in the theater that night watching the film. Margaret, the heroine, explains that she has moved beyond the suburban dream of having a husband, and also moved beyond the middle-urban dream of having an agent (and hence a career), and has now recognized the pointlessness of striving for anything. Her new dream lover is an alien creature that thrives on the chemicals released in the brain during orgasm and that will ultimately devour Margaret in the course of a final, quite literally cosmic climax. Perhaps the moment in the film that stuck most to my ribs is the one in which Margaret's ex-lover and ex-acting teacher, a man in his late forties, accuses her of dressing like a whore. She retaliates with a childish sneer that his jeans (throwbacks to his own heyday) are just as much a costume as her push-up bras and red leather skirts. Of her peers, she says something like, "At least we don't pretend we aren't wearing costumes."

At least we don't pretend we aren't wearing costumes? Well, yes, I guess they don't, I thought. For Margaret, to pretend one isn't wearing a costume is contemptible. She rejects the idea that the way one dresses might represent a claim made about the world today, or project an idea for the world tomorrow. Hell, there probably won't be a world tomorrow. Clothes have to do with what we aren't, not what we are. Screw art, let's dance.

And yet Margaret lets something slip when she makes this claim. She implicates herself by referring to her friends, her cronies, as "we." The "we" in *Liquid Sky* is disloyal, backstabbing, bitchy, and violent. But it is still a "we"; it is a group, defined by its belief in its own newness, its own green youthfulness; it is a generation. In performance spaces, bars that double as art galleries, clubs with names like 8B.C. or Save the Robots, on the darkest and most dangerous streets of New York, a culture is being born out of the claim that there is no culture—that it's all mere dress-up, mere fakery, mere whooping-it-up-before-the-plague. This culture is downtown. It basks in the limelight of the present moment. It avoids tall buildings. Poverty is its kin, its company, and sometimes its reality, but it draws the curious rich like flies. Then real estate possibilities emerge out of nowhere: tenements turn into town houses, yet another chic colorful neighborhood for the new rich emerges. Sometimes I wonder whether my generation's lunatic fringe of trendsetters keep moving into more and more dangerous parts because the gentrified keep pushing them out of the neighborhoods they've pioneered, or because they're attracted to the hopeless edge of the city, where the future means finding food and drugs to get you through tomorrow. That is about as far as you can get from long-term investments. And the irony is, of course, that where they have gone, the rich young future-mongers of the generation ahead have followed, attracted by the scent of potential development. Farther east, and farther down, their worlds keep moving. It is some-times decadent, destructive, dangerous. It is sometimes gloriously, extraordinarily fun.

I've seen that world. Good yuppie that I am, I've even dipped my toe in its freez-ing waters on select Saturday nights and Sunday mornings when an urge to dance came over me like an itch. When I was an undergraduate I was friends with a couple of women who became lovers and took to walking around the campus with dog collars around their necks connected by a link chain. And I remember going with them once to have tea at the home of one of their mothers—a big brownstone in the East Sixties, on the same block where Nixon used to live. They marched defiantly through the foyer, their very entrance a calculated affront, me following meekly, while the mother strove not to notice the white-blond tint of her daughter's hair, or the double nose ring (she had pierced the nostril herself in the bathroom), and offered to take my jacket. "So how is school going, honey?" the mother said. In the course of tea she made a valiant effort to call her daughter "Max," as Max currently insisted. (Her real name was Elizabeth.) And a year later, in New York, I walked home from a party one night with an NYU stu-dent and her friend, a boy dressed like Boy George—eyeliner, dreadlocks, lipstick. And they were going to steal the boy's sister's food stamps so they could get something to eat. They said this matter-of-factly. And when I expressed amazement that the girl's af-fluent parents didn't send her enough money to buy food, she said equally matter-of-factly, "Oh, they send me plenty of money, but I use it all up on booze and drugs." Without a trace of self-consciousness she said it; but with more than a trace of self-pity.

It was Saturday night and we were going to a party. It was always Saturday night and we were always going to a party. Someone was stoned. Someone was drunk, lying snoring on the big sofa in the library. Someone was wearing Salada tea-bag fortunes as earrings. In their rooms, the boys were experimenting with eye makeup. In their rooms, the girls were experimenting with mushrooms. It was Saturday night and we were going to a dress party (everyone had to wear a dress), to a gender-transcendence party, to a party supporting the women's center, supporting the Marxist Literary Group, support-ing the Coalition Against Apartheid. My friends were not active in these organizations; we expressed our support by giving the parties. For days beforehand we'd trade twelve-inch singles, mix them on our stereos, compete to produce the greatest dance tape ever, the one that would bring the dancers to the floor in an orgiastic heap.

The favorite songs that year, I think, were "Dancing With Myself," by Billy Idol, and "I Wanna Be Sedated," by the Ramones. But "Rock Lobster" seemed to turn up on every tape, as did "We Got the Beat" and "I Love a Man in a Uniform."

A photographer friend of mine used to come to all the parties that year, throw her camera out into the pulsating dark as arbitrarily as Richard Misrach, who was known for blindly aiming his camera out into the dark Hawaiian jungle. It became a kind of joke, Jennie's presence at every party. You could count on seeing yourself a few days later, stoned or drunk or vomiting, or making out with someone you didn't recognize on a sofa you couldn't remember. In the photographs bodies were frozen in the midst of flight, heads shook in beady haloes of light and sweat, clothes flew and were sus-pended, forever revealing small patches of white skin. There was a quality of ecstasy. But when I see those pictures these days, I think *I was mad.*

I don't remember ever feeling as much joy as I did that year, when, on any Saturday night, on a crowded dance floor I'd hear my favorite song begin. It was as if my body itself had become an instrument, pulled and plucked and wrenched by the music, thrown beyond itself. This was no love-in of the Sixties, no drug-hazed ritual of communion. We were dancing with ourselves. Someone joked that each of us could have had on his own individual Walkman.

The mornings after such evenings always began around two in the afternoon. Exhausted and hung over, we would go back to the big rooms where the parties had taken place to confront the hundreds of empty beer cans and cigarette stubs, the little clots of lost sweaters stuffed into corners, forgotten, never to be retrieved. Sunlight streamed in. While the guests slept in late, and Jennie toiled in her darkroom, frenzied with creation, the partygivers took out their mops.

• • •

Like our older brothers and sisters, my generation belongs to gyms. We find Nautilus equipment consoling. Nothing gets in your way when you're bench pressing, or swimming, or running, not even the interfering subconscious that tended to muck up all those Seventies efforts at psychological self-improvement. Muscles appear as a manifestation of pure will.

In contrast to our older brothers and sisters, however, the fact that we believe in health does not necessarily mean that we believe in the future. The same bright young person who strives for physical immortality also takes for granted the imminence of his destruction. At Brown University, students voted last October on a referendum to stock poison tablets in the school infirmary, so that in the event of a nuclear catastrophe, they could commit suicide rather than die of fallout. As if nuclear disaster, rather than being a distant threat, were a harsh reality, an immediacy, something to prepare for. I am reminded of Grace Paley's description of an eighteen-year old in her story "Friends." "His friends have a book that says a person should, if properly nutritioned, live forever . . . He also believes that the human race, its brains and good looks, will end in his time."

Brains and good looks. Last year I went dancing at Area for the first time, arguably the choicest dance club in New York. (A friend of mine who is more of an expert than I in these matters insists that the club called Save the Robots is choicer, since it is frequented by the people who work at the Area and does not open until after Area has closed.) At this point Area was dressed in its nuclear holocaust garb. On our way in, we passed tableaux vivants of people in Karen Silkwood suits, peeling lurid green candy off sheets on a conveyor belt. Women danced inside fantastic, menacing pseudo-reactors. Signs reading DANGER-RADIOACTIVE MATERIAL glowed above the dance floor. Later, at the bar, I was introduced to an artist who had been asked to create a work of art in support of the nuclear freeze, and was thinking of carving a mushroom cloud out of a block of ice. It was hard for me to keep from wondering about the famed holocaust anxiety of my postnuclear generation. The world after the bomb, it seemed to me, had become a cliché, incorporated into our dialogue and our culture with an alarming thoughtlessness. Do most of us dream, like Eddie Albert as the President in the movie *Dreamscape,* of a parched postholocaust landscape, peopled by weird half-human monsters and scared children wailing, "It hurts! It hurts!" I doubt it. I think we purport to worry about the world ending much more than we actually do.

Because the terror of knowing the world could end at any moment haunts them so vividly, older people seem to believe that it must be ten times worse for the young.

The realization that nuclear disaster is not only possible, but possibly imminent, writes the noted essayist Lewis Thomas, "is bad enough for the people in my generation. We can put up with it, I suppose, since we must. We are moving along anyway. . . . What I cannot imagine, what I cannot put up with. . . . is what it would be like to be young. How do the young stand it? How can they keep their sanity?"

Well, I want to say, we do. Indeed, I think we are more sane and less hysterical about the issue of nuclear holocaust than are the generations ahead of us. We do not go crazy, because for us the thought of a world with no future—so terrifying to Dr. Thomas—is completely familiar; is taken for granted; is nothing new.

I have tried time and again to explain this to people who are older than I. I tell them that no matter how hard I try—and I have closed my eyes tightly, concentrated, tried to will my mind to do it—I simply cannot muster an image of myself fifty, or twenty, or even ten years in the future. I go blank. I have no idea where or what or even if I'll be. Whereas my parents, when they were young, assumed vast and lengthy futures for themselves, a series of houses, each larger than the one before, and finally the "golden years" of retirement, knitting by fires, bungalows in Florida. I think we have inserted into our minds the commercialized image of the mushroom cloud and the world in flames in order to justify a blind spot in us—an inability to think beyond the moment, or conceive of any future at all, which makes us immune to the true horror felt by older people. This blind spot has more to do with our attitude toward the nuclear family than with nuclear disaster—with the fact that our parents, as they now reach the golden years they once looked forward to, are finding themselves trapped in unhappy marriages or divorced, are too bitter to ever consider loving again, or are desperate to find a new mate with whom they can share those last happy years that they were promised, that they worked so hard for, that they were so unfairly cheated out of.

And we—well, we aren't going to make the same mistakes they did. Alone at least, we're safe—from pain, from dependency, from sexually transmitted disease. Those who belong to no one but themselves can never be abandoned.

• • •

It is 1983. I have just graduated from college and, like most of my friends, lead the sort of life that makes a good biographical note in the back of a literary magazine— "living and working in Manhattan." Most mornings, I have to get up at 7:30 A.M.— unnaturally early for someone like me, who finds it hard to fall asleep before 3:00. I don't eat breakfast, I shower in three minutes, timed. From inside my apartment, where it is warm, I head out into the cold, begin the long trek to the subway. My station is famous for its poor design. If I have a token, I must run down one staircase and up another to get to the train. Sometimes the train doors close on my nose. Other times I'm lucky. I squeeze in, find a space to stand. The train begins to move, and there are newspapers in my eyes, painted fingernails, noses, the smell of toothpaste and coffee everywhere around me. People are nodding, falling asleep on their feet. For six months now, this subway ride in the morning and afternoon has been the closest I have come physically to another human being.

I arrive at my office. For the length of the morning, I work, taking frequent breaks. I visit the cookie lady in publicity. I visit the water cooler. I gossip with friends on the phone, thinking about lunch.

I used to think there was something gloriously romantic about the nine-to-five life. I used to imagine there could be no greater thrill than being part of the crush riding the escalator down from the Pan Am building into Grand Central at 5:00. The big station ceiling, with its map of stars, would unfold above you, the escalator would slip down under your feet—you, so small, so anonymous in all that hugeness and strangeness. Yet you'd know you were different. Light on your feet at rush hour, you'd dodge and cut through the throng, find your way fast to the shuttle. Like the north-or-south-going Zax in Doctor Seuss, you'd have one direction, and no choice but to move in it.

Ha, as the old woman who has worked forty years in accounting says to everyone. *Ha-ha.*

It's 5:30. Outside the sun has set. Inside other people are still typing, still frenzied. Everyone works harder than you, no matter how hard you work. Everyone makes more than you do, no matter how much you make. You slip out silently, guilty to be leaving only a half hour late, wondering why you're not as ambitious as they are, why you don't have it in you to make it.

But when you get outside, the wind is cold on your face, the streets are full of people herding toward the subway. You put on your Walkman. You think that tonight you might like to go dancing. Then the Pointer Sisters come on, and you realize that, like John Travolta tripping down the streets of Brooklyn in *Saturday Night Fever,* you already are.

• • •

A few years after I stopped going, the Saturday night folk-dancing ritual at Stanford ceased. Lack of interest, I suppose. The women wrapped in gypsy fabric and the boys with dirty feet were getting cleaned up and prepping for their GMATs. Today they are baby-boomers. They are responsible, says a *People* magazine ad, for "the surge in microchips, chocolate chips, and a host of special services to help Boomers run their two-career households." They work, live, love in offices. They have "drive."

My generation, in the meantime, still trots outside their circle, eager to learn the steps. In every outward way we are perfect emulators. We go to work in corporations right out of college. We look good in suits. But we also have haircuts that are as acceptable at East Village early-hours clubs as they are at Morgan Stanley. And (of course) at least we don't pretend we're not wearing costumes.

There are advantages to growing up, as we did, on the cusp of two violently dislocated ages; advantages to becoming conscious just as one decade is burning out, and another is rising, phoenixlike, from the ashes of its dissolution—or disillusion. If the Sixties was an age of naive hope, then the Eighties is an age of ironic hopelessness—its perfect counterpart, its skeptical progeny. We are the children of that skepticism. We go through all the motions. But if we tried then to learn the steps from our brothers and sisters because we believed in what they were doing, we follow in their footsteps now for almost the opposite reason—to prove that we can sell out just as well as they can, and know it too.

I remember, as a child, listening to my mother talk about fashions. "Once you've seen stiletto heels come and go three times, you'll realize how little any of it means," she said. I don't think I knew yet what a stiletto heel was, but I understood already and perfectly how little any of it meant. It came to me very early, that ironic and distanced view on things, and it's stayed.

The voice of my generation is the voice of David Letterman, whose late-night humor—upbeat, deadpan, more than a little contemptuous—we imitate because, above all else, we are determined to make sure everyone knows that what we say might not be what we mean. Consider these words from Brett Duval Fromson, in an op-ed piece for *The New York Times:* "Yuppies, if we do anything at all, respect those who deliver the goods. How else are we going to afford our Ferragamo pumps, Brooks Brothers suits, country houses, European cars, and California chardonnays?" The balance of the irony is perfect—between self-mockery and straight-faced seriousness, between criticism and comfy self-approval. "If we do anything at all," Fromson writes, leaving open the possibility that we don't. Certainly, he acknowledges, during the recession we "didn't give much thought to those who wouldn't make it." And now I am thinking about a headline I read recently in *The Village Voice,* above one of a series of articles analyzing Reagan's victory last November. It read DON'T TRUST ANYONE UNDER THIRTY.

Mine is a generation perfectly willing to admit its contemptible qualities. But our self-contempt is self-congratulatory. The buzz in the background, every minute of our lives, is that detached, ironic voice telling us: At least you're not faking it, as they did, at least you're not pretending as they did. It's okay to be selfish as long as you're up-front about it. Go ahead. "Exercise your right to exercise." Other people are dying to defend other people's right to speak, to vote, and to live, but at least you don't pretend you're not wearing a costume.

What is behind this bitterness, this skepticism? A need, I think, for settledness, for security, for home. Our parents imagined they could satisfy this urge by marrying and raising children; our older brothers and sisters through community and revolution. We have seen how far those alternatives go. We trust ourselves, and money. Period.

Fifteen years ago you weren't supposed to trust anyone over thirty. For people in my generation, the goal seems to be to get to thirty as fast as possible, and stay there. Starting out, we are eager, above all else, to be finished. If we truly are a generation without character, as is claimed, it is because we have seen what has happened to generations with character. If we are without passion or affect, it is because we have decided that passion and affect are simply not worth the trouble. If we stand crouched in the shadows of a history in which we refuse to take part, it is because that's exactly where we've chosen to stand.

Characterlessness takes work. It is defiance and defense all at once.

• • •

During my freshman year in college I remember going to see Mary Tyler Moore as a woman paralyzed from the neck down in *Whose Life Is It Anyway?* At intermission I ran into a friend from school who was practically in tears. "You don't know what it's like for me to see her like that," he said. "Mary's a metaphor for my youth. And looking at her on that stage, well, I can't help but feel that it's my youth lying paralyzed up there." Later, a woman I know told me in all earnestness, "When I'm in a difficult situation, a real bind, I honestly think to myself, 'What would Mary have done?' I really do." I know people who significantly altered the shape of their lives so that they could stay up every weeknight for a 2:30 to 4:00 A.M. Mary tripleheader on Channel 4 in New York. Even John Sex, the East Village's reigning club maven, is famous for his early-morning rendition, at the Pyramid club, of the Mary theme.

Remember those words? "Who can take the world on with her smile? Who can take a nothing day and suddenly make it all seem worthwhile?" And of course, at the end of the opening credits, there is the famous epiphany, the throw of the hat. "You're gonna make it after all," sings Sonny Curtis, who faded quickly into obscurity, but whose dulcet voice will live forever in reruns, and in our hearts. She throws the red cap into the air; the frame freezes, leaving Mary's hat perpetually aloft, and Mary perpetually in the bloom of youthful anticipation. The great irony of that shot, underscoring the show's tender, melancholy tone, is that as the seasons wore on, and new images of a shorter-haired Mary were spliced into the opening credit sequence, it always remained the same. So that even in the last, saddest season with Mary pushing forty and wanting a raise and still not married, we are still given a glimpse of Mary as she used to be, young Mary, full of youthful exuberance, and that image of Mary and her hat and her hope gently plays against the truth of what her life has given her. The fact is that Mary's life stinks. She is underpaid in a second-rate job at a third-rate television station. Her best friends, Rhoda and Phyllis, have both left her to fail in spin-offs in other cities, and she doesn't even have a boyfriend. That's Mary's life, and even the clever tactic of changing the last line of the theme song from "You're gonna make it after all" to "Look's like you've made it after all" fails to convince us that it's anything but rotten.

But Mary presses on, and the great epic film, which all episodes of the Mary show comprise, ends as it began—with Mary not getting married. The camaraderie of the newsroom has provided her less with a bond of strength than with a buffer against sorrow. Mary and her friends share one another's loneliness, but they don't cure it. The station closes down, the lights go out, and still young Mary throws her hat.

I see Marys often these days; the other day I saw one going into a deli on Third Avenue in the Eighties, just after work. She's younger, a bit fatter, better paid, so she wears silk blouses with ruffles and bows. And because she lives in New York, she's a bit more desperate, the pain is a little closer to the surface. It's 9:00, and she's just gotten off from work. She buys herself dinner—chicken hot dogs, Diet Coke, Haagen-Dazs—and heads home to the tiny apartment, with a bathtub in the kitchen, for which she pays far too much. And I can't help but think that, even as a child, when the going-ons in that Minneapolis newsroom were the high point of her week, she knew she was going to end up here. Remember the episodes where Mary and Lou quit in order to protest how little money they make? Mary is forced to borrow from Ted. Nothing upsets her more than the realization that, for the first time in her life, she's in debt. She never asked for more than a room to live in, after all, and someplace to go each day, and perhaps a little extra money for a new dress now and then.

Here in New York, all the prime-time shows of my childhood have found their way, like memories or dreams, to the darkest part of the night. First there's *Star Trek* and the familiar faces of the *Enterprise* crew. Tonight they are confronted with an android that has become human because it has felt the first pangs of love. Once again, no woman can win Kirk, because he's already married to the most beautiful woman of them all—his ship. At 1:00 *The Twilight Zone* comes on, another lost astronaut wanders a blank landscape, the world before or after man. At 1:30, only an hour before Mary begins, I watch the *Independent News*. I am, by this time, on the floor, and close to sleep. The newscaster's voice clucks amicably, telling us that Mary Tyler Moore has checked herself into the Betty Ford Center. She has bravely admitted to having a problem, and she is battling it.

I leap up. I stare at the screen. The image has already passed, the newscaster moved on to another story. And I think, how sad that Mary's life has come to this. And yet, how good that she is bravely admitting to having a problem, and battling it. And I wonder if Mary Tyler Moore sat and looked at herself in the mirror before she made the decision; sat and looked at herself in the mirror and asked herself, "What would Mary do?"

Mary would do the right thing. And that is a comfort to me, this dark night, as I drag myself from the living room floor and click the television into silence. We have learned a few things from Mary. We have learned, on a day-to-day basis, how to do the right thing. We have learned to be kind and patient with one another, to give comfort. We have learned how to be good and generous friends.

It is late. The apartment is close and quiet. Tonight I am alone, but this weekend I will be with my friends. Like the folks in Mary's newsroom or the crew of the *Enterprise* bridge, we are a gang. We go dancing, and afterward, to an all-night deli for babkas and French toast, our clothes permeated with the smell of cigarettes. We walk five abreast, arm-in-arm, so that other people must veer into the street to avoid hitting us. When we decide the time has come to head back uptown, we pile into a cab, sometimes five or six of us, and sit on each other's laps and legs, and feel happy that we have friends, because it means we can take cabs for less than the price of the subway. It is nearly dawn, and a few sour-looking prostitutes are still marching the sidewalks of the West Side Highway in the cold. In a moment when we're not looking a sun will appear, small and new and fiery, as if someone had thrown it into the air.

SUGGESTIONS FOR DISCUSSION

1. David Leavitt has titled his essay "The New Lost Generation." Is this is an apt title? What evidence does Leavitt use to support his title? To what extent is his generation "lost"? What makes it "new"?

2. Leavitt cites a line from the film *Liquid Sky*, "At least we don't pretend we aren't wearing costumes," as a particularly significant insight into his generation. Why do you think Leavitt has picked out this line? He doesn't really explain its meaning, but clearly it is meant to have a good deal of weight in his essay. How would you explain its meaning for the context in which Leavitt presents it?

3. Leavitt closes his essay with an extended meditation on the Mary Tyler Moore Show. What is the point Leavitt is making? How does this section fit into the essay as a whole? In what sense does it or does it not provide a satisfying ending?

SUGGESTIONS FOR WRITING

1. Throughout "The New Lost Generation," David Leavitt uses representative examples—films, songs, Walkmen, health clubs, dancing, television shows, and so on—to stand as symbols of his generation. Pick something out of your own experience to use as a representative example. Write an essay that explains why you consider the example to be representative of your generation and what it symbolizes.

2. Leavitt writes, "It was Saturday night and we were going to a dress party (everyone had to wear a dress), to a gender-transcendence party." Leavitt doesn't really develop the idea, but he implies here nonetheless that sexual orientation has become more fluid within his generation—that homosexuality, bisexuality, and experiments with gender identity are facts of life instead of cultural taboos no one should talk about. There is no question that gay and lesbian culture is more visible in American life. For Leavitt, of course, as a gay man, this is simply part of the cultural landscape, but for others, the issue of homosexuality is still a problematic and deeply troubling one—witness, for example, the resistance to lifting the ban on gays and lesbians in the military or the controversies surrounding gays and lesbians adopting children. Write an essay on how gays and lesbians are portrayed in the American media. Pick a particular instance (a film, television show, magazine or newspaper article) to analyze how the media presents homosexuality to the American public. You might end the essay with your own thoughts about the meaning to American culture of the heightened visibility of gays and lesbians.

3. Use Leavitt's essay as a model to compose a written collage of separate but associated sections. Write an essay about your generation that uses this technique.
Write four or five separate sections, each focusing on a particular aspect of your
generation. Then decide on the order you want them to appear in your essay.
Taken together, the sections should resonate with each other and create a dominant impression.

Lawrence Grossberg

YOUTH AND AMERICAN IDENTITY

This selection from *It's a Sin: Essays on Postmodernism, Politics, and Culture*
(1988) is part of Lawrence Grossberg's longer examination of the political
swing toward conservatism in the 1980s. Grossberg is a cultural critic and professor of speech communication at the University of Illinois who is interested in
the connections between politics and culture during the Reagan years and the
rise of what he calls the New Right alliance of free-market neo-liberals, moral
traditionalists, and nationalistic neo-conservatives. According to Grossberg,
Reaganism and the New Right represent a new strategy for influencing public
opinion and winning national leadership that extends beyond conventional politics into the realm of popular culture. Grossberg argues that the New Right has
sought to articulate a new consensus about America's self-image—what he calls
the "national popular"—by undermining the "meanings and investments we
have made in youth" as the embodiment of the American Dream. In the selection we have chosen, Grossberg explains how young people came to be seen
following World War II as a living symbol of a unified national identity.

Suggestion for Reading

- As you read, notice that Lawrence Grossberg has organized this section from
his longer essay in a problem-and-solution format. To follow Grossberg's line
of thought, underline and annotate the passages where Grossberg defines
what he sees as the problem of American national identity and where he explains how American young people were represented as the solution in the
post-World War II period.

---◆---

T he meaning of "America" has always been a problem. Except for rare moments, Americans have rarely had a shared sense of identity and unity.
Rather, the United States has always been a country of differences without a
center. The "foreign" has always been centrally implicated in our identity
because we were and are a nation of immigrants. (Perhaps that partly explains why Americans took up anti-communism with such intensity—here at least was an "other," a defi-

nition of the foreign, which could be construed as non-American, as a threatening presence which defied integration.) It is a nation without a tradition, for its history depends upon a moment of founding violence which almost entirely eradicated the native population, thereby renouncing any claim to an identity invested in the land. And despite various efforts to define some "proper" ethnic and national origin, it is precisely the image of the melting pot, this perpetual sense of the continuing presence of the other within the national identity, that has defined the uniqueness of the nation. It is a nation predicated upon differences, but always desperately constructing an imaginary unity. The most common and dominant solution to this in its history involved constituting the identity of the United States in the future tense; it was the land of possibility, the "beacon on the hill," the new world, the young nation living out its "manifest destiny." Perhaps the only way in which the diversity of populations and regions could be held together was to imagine itself constantly facing frontiers. It is this perpetual ability to locate and conquer new frontiers, a sense embodied within "the American dream" as a recurrent theme, that has most powerfully defined a national sense of cultural uniqueness.

After what the nation took to be "its victory" in the second world war it anxiously faced a depressing contradiction. On the one hand, the young nation had grown up, taking its "rightful" place as the leader of the "free world." On the other hand, what had defined its victory—its very identity—depended upon its continued sense of difference from the "grown-up" (i.e., corrupt, inflexible, etc.) European nations. It was America's openness to possibility, its commitment to itself as the future, its ability to reforge its differences into a new and self-consciously temporary unity, that had conquered the fascist threat to freedom. The postwar period can be described by the embodiments of this contradiction: it was a time of enormous conservative pressure (we had won the war protecting the American way; it was time to enjoy it and not rock the boat) and a time of increasingly rapid change, not only in the structures of the social formation but across the entire surface of everyday life. It was a time as schizophrenic as the baby boom generation onto which it projected its contradictions. Resolving this lived dilemma demanded that America still be located in and defined by a future, by an American dream but that the dream be made visible and concrete. If the dream had not yet been realized, it would be shortly. Thus, if this dream were to effectively define the nation in its immediate future, if there was to be any reality to this vision, it would have to be invested, not just in some abstract future, but in a concrete embodiment of America's future, i.e., in a specific generation. Hence, the American identity was projected upon the children of those who had to confront the paradox of America in the postwar years. But if the dream was to be real for them, and if it were to be immediately realizable, people would have to have children and have children they did! And they would have to define those children as the center of their lives and of the nation; the children would become the justification for everything they had done, the source of the very meaning of their lives as individuals and as a nation.

The baby-boom created an enormous population of children by the mid-fifties, a population which became the concretely defined image of the nation's future, a future embodied in a specific generation of youth who would finally realize the American dream and hence become its living symbol. This was to be "the best fed, best dressed, best educated generation" in history, the living proof of the American dream, the realisation of the future in the present. The American identity slid from a contentless image of the future to a powerful, emotionally invested image of a generation. America found itself by identifying its meaning with a generation whose identity was articulated by the meanings and promises of youth. Youth, as it came to define a generation, also came to define America itself. And this generation took up the identification as its own fantasy. Not only was its own youthfulness identified with the perpetual youthfulness of the nation, but its own generational identity was defined by its necessary and continued youthfulness. But youth in this equation was not measured simply in terms of age; it was an ideological and cultural signifier, connected to utopian images of the future and of this generation's ability to control the forces of change and to make the world over in its own images. But it was also articulated by economic images of the teenager as consumer, and by images of the specific sensibilities, styles and forms of popular culture which this generation took as its own (hence, the necessary myth that rock and roll was made by American youth). Thus, what was placed as the new defining center of the nation was a generation, an ideological commitment to youth, and a specific popular cultural formation. Obviously, this "consensus" constructed its own powerfully selective frontier: it largely excluded those fractions of the population (e.g., black) which were never significantly traversed by the largely white middle class youth culture. Nevertheless, for the moment, the United States had an identity, however problematic the very commitment to youth was and would become, and it had an apparently perpetually renewable national popular; it had a culture which it thought of as inherently American and which it identified with its own embodied image of itself and its future.

But this was, to say the least, a problematic solution to America's search for an identity, not merely because any generation of youth has to grow up and, one assumes, renounce their youthfulness, but also because "youth" was largely, even in the fifties, an empty signifier. As [Carolyn] Steedman says, "children are always episodes in someone else's narratives, not their own people, but rather brought into being for someone else's purpose." Youth has no meaning except perhaps its lack of meaning, its energy, its commitment to openness and change, its celebratory relation to the present, and its promise of the future. Youth offers no structure of its own with which it can organize and give permanence to a national identity. That is, youth itself, like America, can only be defined apparently in a forever receding future. How could this generation possibly fulfill its own identity and become the American dream—become a future which is always as yet unrealized and unrealizable? How could a generation hold on to its own self-identity as youthful, and at the same time, fulfill the responsibility of its identification with the nation? What does it mean to have constructed a concrete yet entirely mobile center for a centerless nation? Perhaps this rather paradoxical position explains the sense of failure that characterizes the postwar generations, despite the fact that they did succeed in reshaping the cultural and political terrain of the United States.

SUGGESTIONS FOR DISCUSSION

1. Define the problem of American national identity as Grossberg poses it early in this selection. How and in what sense did American young people become a "solution" to this "problem" in the post-World War II period?

2. Grossberg says that after World War II America faced a "depressing contradiction." Explain what he sees as this contradiction. Why does he call the time of the baby-boom generation a "schizophrenic" one?

3. At the end of this selection, Grossberg suggests that youth is a "problematic solution to America's search for identity." What makes the solution a problematic one? What is the "sense of failure that characterizes the postwar generations, despite the fact that they did succeed in reshaping the cultural and political terrain of the United States"?

SUGGESTIONS FOR WRITING

1. Lawrence Grossberg quotes Carolyn Steedman's remark that "children are always episodes in someone else's narratives, not their own people, but rather brought into being for someone else's purposes." Apply this quote to your own experience growing up. Write an essay that explains how your life might be seen as an "episode" in "someone else's narrative." You will need to take into account the hopes your parents and other significant adults invested in you and your future.

2. Grossberg opens this selection by saying that "the United States has always been a country of differences without a center." He describes American national identity as one "predicated upon differences, but always desperately constructing an imaginary unity." Write an essay that explains how you would describe America's national identity. To do this, you will need to consider whether you see a "shared sense of identity and unity" or whether, as Grossberg suggests, American identity should be characterized according to its diversity and the "continuing presence of the other within the national identity."

3. Gloria Naylor in "Kiswana Browne," David Leavitt in "The New Lost Generation," and Lawrence Grossberg in "Youth and American Identity" have each written of the issue of generational identity, though in quite different ways. Naylor has written a fictional account, which is a chapter in her novel *The Women of Brewster Place,* while Leavitt has written a personal essay that draws on his own experience and the selection from Grossberg's book *It's a Sin* takes an analytical perspective on the emotional and cultural investments made in American youth in the post-World War II period. Since each of these writers uses such a different writing strategy, they are likely to have somewhat different effects on their readers. Write an essay that compares the writing strategies. What do you see as the advantages and disadvantages of each writer's attempt to address the issue of generational identity? What effects are the writers' various strategies likely to have on readers?

Laura Zinn

MOVE OVER, BOOMERS: THE BUSTERS ARE HERE—AND THEY'RE ANGRY

"Move Over, Boomers" was originally published as the cover story for *Business Week* magazine, December 14, 1992. Staff writer Laura Zinn, with help from research assistants and bureau reports, profiled the "46 million Americans, aged 18 to 29, who make up the vanguard of the next generation" for her readers in the business community. Characterized as the "twentysomethings, Generation X, slackers, busters," this generation, Zinn suggests, now constitutes a large but "virtually invisible sub-culture" that defines itself, at least in part, in opposition to the baby-boom generation that came of age in the 1960s and early 1970s.

Suggestion for Reading

- Notice the subtitle of this article is "The Busters Are Here—And They're Angry." As you read, underline passages where Zinn explains what she sees as the sources of the busters' anger. When you are finished, you can then consider whether Zinn's explanations are persuasive ones.

◆

"The guy who has the job I want is 34 and has a wife and kids. So he's not leaving."
—Amy Ross, 24, who has a master's degree from Cornell University and now works as a traveling fabric salesperson

"I'm very cynical about the Sixties: 'Peace, love, groovy, let's get high'—and look what happened. These people turned out to be worse than the people they rebelled against. They're materialistic hypocrites."
—Blan Holman, 23, free-lance environmental writer

Hear that, baby boomers? That's the sound of the future coming up behind you. It's the sound of the 46 million Americans, aged 18 to 29, who make up the vanguard of the next generation.

Face it, you're not the future anymore. The idea will take some getting used to. As the largest demographic cohort in history moved through the years, boomers shaped much of postwar America—how it dressed, what it watched, read, listened to. Now, as they move into offices both corner and Oval, boomers will determine how America manages and governs.

But for the shape of things to come, look not at the boomers but at their successors. Call them by any of the many names they have already been saddled with—twentysomethings, Generation X, slackers, busters—they are entering the mainstream of American life. They're the ones who are studying on our campuses, slogging through first jobs—or just hoping to land a job, any job.

For all the talk of the baby bust, this is no small bunch. Compared to those born from 1951 through 1962—the core of the baby boom—this current crop of 18-to-29-year-olds is the second-largest group of young adults in U.S. history. They're already starting to set tastes in fashion and popular culture. They're the ones who will vote you into office, buy your products, and work in your factories. They will give birth to your grandchildren, nieces, and nephews.

TATTOOED AND PIERCED

So far, this group is having a tough time. Busters are the first generation of latchkey children, products of dual-career households, or, in some 50% of cases, of divorced or separated parents. They have been entering the work force at a time of prolonged downsizing and downturn, so they're likelier than the previous generation to be unemployed, underemployed, and living at home with Mom and Dad. They're alienated by a culture that has been dominated by boomers for as long as they can remember. They're angry as they look down a career path that's crowded with thirty- and fortysomethings who are in no hurry to clear the way. And if they're angry and alienated, they dress the part, with aggressively unpretty fashions, pierced noses, and tattoos.

At the same time, though, they're more ethnically diverse, and they're more comfortable with diversity than any previous generation. Many of them don't give a hoot for the old-fashioned war between the sexes, either, but instead tend to have lots of friends of the opposite sex. Furthermore, as a generation that's been bombarded by multiple media since their cradle days, they're savvy—and cynical—consumers.

To many older Americans, the Generation Xers have been a virtually invisible subculture. They have been largely ignored by U.S. media, businesses, and public institutions, which have spent years coveting the baby boomers as audience, market, and constituency. "Marketers have been distracted by boomers going through their household formations," says Scott L. Kauffman, 36, vice-president for marketing, promotion, and development at *Entertainment Weekly*. "Busters don't feel like anyone's paying attention to them."

Magic Number

But that will have to change. For one thing, despite their many hardships, consumers in their late teens and their twenties already wield annual spending power of some $125 billion, according to a survey by Roper Organization Inc. And the baby busters are essential to the success of many major categories, such as beer, fast food, cosmetics, and electronics. More important, within this decade, these consumers will be entering their peak earning years. With all the boomers blocking the road ahead, it may take the busters longer than some previous generations. But soon enough, they'll be setting up households by the millions, having families, and buying refrigerators, cars, homes—all the big-ticket items that drive an economy.

Indeed, it could well be the busters who lead the country out of recession, according to the theory of the 25-year-old's powerful purse strings. Richard Hokenson, a demographer at Donaldson Lufkin & Jenrette in New York, has been studying 25-year-olds' purchasing power back to the 1950s. His theory: When a large number of young adults turn 25 at the same time, they buy a lot of consumer goods, pumping money into the economy and so stimulating demand across the board. Take 1986, when an unprecedented number of Americans turned 25. It was the best year for housing in the 1980s: 1.8 million units were built. And 1986 was also a record year for cars, with sales of 15.1 million cars and light trucks.

Big Gap

Beginning next year, a bulge of 13 million kids who were born between October, 1968, and March, 1971, will start turning 25. They'll be the largest group of 25-year-olds since 1986. If Hokenson is right, then for three years starting next October, busters will be buying enough houses and durable goods to ignite a healthy recovery.

So who are these folks who will shape our destiny? The boomers who increasingly dominate the Establishment they once rebelled against will make a big mistake if they assume that the busters are just like they were at that age. "Most marketers today are boomers and much more likely to impose their values on this generation, to the point where busters are invisible," says Peter Kim, U.S. director for strategic planning at J. Walter Thompson North America.

At a recent convention of magazine publishers and editors, Karen Ritchie, a senior vice-president at ad agency McCann-Erickson in Detroit, told the largely boomer audience that they were in danger of losing busters forever if they didn't pay attention to them now. "I told them that the media were not treating the next generation very well," says Ritchie. "They have never been addressed in any significant way and have very real reasons to be hostile."

And hostile they are. Busters resent the boomers, whom they see as having partied through the 1970s and 1980s, sticking the younger generation with the check. "It will be me and my children that pay off the deficit," says Laura Ramis, 23, a part-time bank teller and Ohio State University graduate who would like to be a journalist. "I blame the generations before us."

'McJobs'

Many busters find they have graduated from high school and college into unemployment or underemployment. Unlike the trailing edge of baby boomers, who easily entered the expanding job market of the mid-1980s, busters often have to settle for what Douglas Coupland, thirtysomething author of the novel *Generation X,* calls "McJobs"—mundane and marginally challenging work that provides a paycheck and little else. Take Kristi Doherty, 22, a graduate of Lewis & Clarke College. She wants to be an anthropologist, but she's clerking in a clothing store in Portland, Ore., and taking on babysitting jobs. "We were told since we were kids that if we worked hard, we would be successful." Instead, she says. "I worked hard. I had a high grade-point average, and I am 100% overqualified for my job."

This is the generation of diminished expectations—polar opposites of the baby boomers, who grew up thinking anything was possible. In a general survey commissioned by Shearson Lehman Hutton Holdings Inc., 18-to-29-year-olds were the only age group to evaluate their own economic class as lower than their parents'. Of course, that's partly because they're early in their careers, says Sara Lipson, director of business development and market research at Shearson. "But the answer also reflects the sense that affluence is going to be harder to achieve, that the window of opportunity is closing on this generation." According to the Center for Labor Market Studies at Northeastern University, the current median income for households headed by adults under 30 is $24,500. That's a 21% drop in constant dollars from 1973.

Boomer Castoffs

And as if a bleak economic situation wasn't enough, busters don't have much emotional security, either. Boomers grew up in the post-Eisenhower era of the working dad and homemaker mom. "Boomers were told as kids, 'You're wonderful, you're the center of the universe,'" says Susan Hayward, senior vice-president of market research firm Yankelovich Partners Inc. "And boomers will feel that way until they're 90." Meanwhile, the busters' world became progressively gloomier. "The economy began to fall apart, safety nets began to unravel, the loan guarantees were gone by the time they went to college, and they didn't have their mothers at home," says Hayward.

And where baby boomers had the sexual revolution, busters are growing up in the age of AIDS. "People our age were forming their sexual identity with the understanding that we could die for our actions," says Adam Glickman, 26, co-founder of Condomania, a Los Angeles-based chain of eight condom stores. "No other generation has had to deal with this at this stage of our lives."

All this insecurity has created a painful paradox. "There's a strong desire to be Establishment, but the recession is making it very hard to attain that," says Bradford Fay, 27, a research director at Roper. "The ironic thing is that the baby-boom generation had everything for the taking and at first rejected it. Here's a generation that very much wants those things but is having a very hard time getting them."

Except for their collective sense of foreboding, busters have little in common with each other. Where boomers were united by pivotal events, such as the Vietnam War and Watergate, busters have been left largely unmoved by their era's low-cal war, Operation Desert Storm, and scandal-lite, Iran-*contra*.

They're also a racially diverse group, with 14% blacks, 12.3% Hispanics, and 3.9% Asians, compared with 12.4%, 9.5%, and 3.3%, respectively, for the entire population. This diversity isn't always accepted—witness the rash of racial brawls on campuses. But the greater prevalence of minorities in this generation heavily influences the language, music, and dress that it adopts. And marketers use black cultural idioms such as hip hop—dance-oriented street music—as a kind of semaphore to reach Xers. "You see the African-American segment of the youth market leading the way," says Thomas Burrell, chairman of Burrell Advertising Inc. in Chicago, which does ads for McDonald's Corp. in African-American publications. "The groups aren't coming together physically, but you see the signals picked up through the media." Adds Keith Clinkscales, 28, publisher and editor-in-chief of *Urban Profile,* a magazine for black college students: "The mainstream has expanded. Now you have Madison Avenue copywriters enjoying the fruits of hip hop and other parts of black culture."

Busters are also creating their own pop culture by borrowing discarded boomer icons and mocking them while making them their own. Witness the renewed enthusiasm among young cable viewers for reruns of vapid TV shows made about two decades or more ago—*Gilligan's Island, The Brady Bunch,* and *The Dick Van Dyke Show.* It's all fascinating for trend-watchers. "This derisive viewing of *The Brady Bunch* is not just motivated by a need to feel superior," says Mark Crispin Miller, professor of media studies at Johns Hopkins University. "It's also motivated by a longing for the more stable world of *The Brady Bunch.*"

Busters' passion for boomer castoffs is also creeping into fashion. This fall, the '70s-inspired "grunge" look has influenced some of Seventh Avenue's younger designers. What's grunge? You're showing your age. Grunge is slovenly, asexual, antifashion fashion. The style has even surfaced in *Vogue.* In a special spread in the magazine's December issue, a cast of waiflike models sports long, lank hair, faded flannel shirts, clunky work boots, ripped sweaters, old jeans and corduroys, long flowing skirts, pierced noses, and a bleak "Fine, fire me, I don't care" look. "Grunge speaks to a narrow band and to the exclusion of boomers," says *Entertainment Weekly's* Kauffman.

Jolt-Fueled 'Raves'

Grunge music is similarly anomie-riddled and angry. Grunge stars include Kurt Cobain and his group, Nirvana, whose 1991 album *Nevermind* sold 4.5 million copies in the U.S. Even harsher are Soundgarden and Mudhoney. Then there are the spontaneous dance marathons on the West Coast, called "raves," where music from such groups as Nine Inch Nails makes up in speed what it lacks in melody. Ravers take over vast warehouses or parking lots, where they dance wildly in huge crowds, often fueled by super-caffeinated Jolt cola, "smart drinks" of caffeine and protein mixers, and Ecstasy, a combination of mild hallucinogens and speed. Busters also dive into new magazines, such as *Details, Urban Profile, Spin,* and *YSB (Young Sisters & Brothers),* that most boomers have probably never heard of.

Grunge, anger, cultural dislocation, a secret yearning to belong: They add up to a daunting cultural anthropology that marketers have to confront if they want to reach twentysomethings. But it's worth it. Busters do buy stuff: CDs, sweaters, jeans, boots, soda, beer, cosmetics, electronics, cars, fast food, personal computers, mountain bikes, and Rollerblades. In part because so many live at home—54% of 18-to-24-year olds in 1991, vs. 48% in 1980—they have lots of discretionary income. Their brand preferences haven't yet been entirely established, unlike those of aging boomers who are already set in their ways. And like any group, they will appreciate being courted—if the wooing is done right.

Finding the right tone can be tricky. For one thing, Xers were often exposed to the temptations of consumer culture at an even more tender age than boomers. Since so many busters grew up with working parents, they were given early shopping chores. Says Linda Cohen, publisher of *Sassy* magazine: "They're used to deciding what stereo is best, what car is cool, what vacation to go on. They are very savvy consumers."

That's good and bad for marketers. It's good because busters are accustomed to shopping, bad because it means they are far more knowledgeable about and suspicious of advertising than earlier generations passing through their twenties. "Today's teens are media maniacs," says *Sassy's* Cohen. "Generation X has been brought up in the most overcommunicated society in the world." Adds James Truman, editor-in-chief of *Details,* whose readers' median age is 26: "They're tremendously cynical because they know the media is most often talking to them to sell them something."

'Hey, We Know'

That combination of cynicism and responsibility even shows up among supposedly carefree college students. Gary Flood, a vice-president for marketing at MasterCard International Inc., was surprised at how knowingly focus groups of students talked about getting a good credit rating. "Try some frivolous approach in selling them a credit card, or tell them to have a good time with the card with their friends, and it turns them off." Flood says. Instead. MasterCard is providing seminars or handling credit responsibly. Similarly, in a move that shows an understanding of buster concerns in the dour 1990s. MC Communications Corp. has planned a promotion around a brochure it is publishing on the dos and don'ts of finding a first job.

At the same time, busters are turned off by marketing pitches that take themselves too seriously. Not for them the 1980s-style yuppie ads that treat luxury cars or expensive cosmetics so reverentially. Busters respond best to messages that take a self-mocking tone. What works, says market researcher Judith Langer, is "advertising that is funny and hip and says, 'Hey, we know.'"

So how do you show you know? In one television ad for Maybelline Inc.'s Expert Eyes Shadow, model Christy Turlington is shown looking coolly glamorous against a moonlit sky. A voice-over says: "Was it a strange celestial event . . . that gave her such bewitching eyes?" Then, Turlington, magically transported to her living room sofa, laughs and says: "Get over it." Says Sheri Colonel, executive vice-president at Maybelline's ad agency, Lintas New York: "We found we had to be irreverent, sassy, and surprising with this age group."

Another cosmetics maker, Revlon Inc., has ditched the gauzy, worshipful ad approach in favor of a pitch that plays to diversity. In ads for its Charlie perfume, Revlon shows supermodel Cindy Crawford playing basketball with a racially mixed group of young men.

Taco Bell Worldwide also figured it had to use a playful approach to pursue busters. The fast-food chain did a lot of market research to determine the right tone, says Tim Ryan, senior vice-president for marketing. His discovery: Busters "love music, they love to party, and they love irreverence." Taco Bell's ad agency, Foote, Cone & Belding, created a campaign that incorporates rockabilly music and MTV-style shots of musicians playing in the desert.

Marketers also figure that busters like to think that they live life on the edge. So one sure sign of an ad aimed at this group is imagery of wild, death-defying stunts. "You're dealing with a group that really feels like it's seen it all," says Ann Glover, brand manager for PepsiCo Inc.'s regular and Diet Mountain Dew soft drinks. "So the challenge is how do you create a commercial that breaks through to this person who thinks he knows everything?" Recent TV ads for the $275 million Diet Dew brand attempt to reach 20-to-29-year-old men by showing their ilk rollerblading down a volcano or kayaking over a waterfall. Diet Dew advertises aggressively on MTV and on Fox Broadcasting Co. shows such as *Melrose Place* and *In Living Color* intended for busters.

HONESTY POLICY

Buster cynicism about blatant product pitches has also shaped Nike Inc.'s marketing. Says Kate Bednarski, global marketing manager for the footwear maker's women's division: "That's one of the reasons we decided to be as honest as possible, even though we are a brand name and trying to sell a product."

Nike's ads for women's athletic shoes are all soft sell, showing little footwear or apparel. Instead, they feature a lot of text and depict women running, walking, or doing aerobics—always resolving with an exhortation to go do some self-improving fitness activity—sort of a consciousness raising session in print. "I always read Nike ads from start to finish," says Abby Levine, 23, a junior retail executive in New York City. "They always have some words of encouragement."

Busters also resent all the lecturing they have gotten from boomers, who, as Ritchie of McCann-Erickson notes, have grown increasingly restrictive and reactionary as they approach middle age, despite their revered memories of free love and political protest. "The repressiveness of the baby boomers has really come to the fore in the last 10 years," Ritchie says.

Recent TV ads for the Isuzu Rodeo off-road vehicle tap into busters' feelings of rebellion. One begins with a little girl in a classroom being urged by her teacher to color only between the lines. In the next shot, she's a twentysomething who abandons the traffic lanes and roars off the highway onto a dirt road. As a result of the campaign and its success with busters, the average age of Rodeo buyers has dropped into the low 30s, and overall sales have increased 60%, to 5,000 a month.

Not that busters don't have their own orthodoxies. They're concerned about the environment: Ice cream maker Ben & Jerry's Homemade Inc. sells this point by informing customers of how it recycles packaging and buys blueberries from Indians in Maine.

BYE-BYE, BIMBOS

And while they respond to sexy advertising, they're repelled by anything that smacks of sexism. When August A. Busch IV became brand manager for Budweiser in July, 1991, the then-27-year-old told Anheuser-Busch Cos. wholesalers that research showed the typical bouncing-bimbo-filled beer ad "just doesn't cut through" to the 21-to-27-year-old drinkers he wanted to reach. Busch launched a campaign that displayed the kind of nonsexist irreverence that appeals to many Xers. One ad shows a granny teaching a rocker how to play his guitar better. Another series has busters receiving a slightly tongue-in-cheek lesson about the glorious tradition of Bud from older barmates. Busch's father, CEO August A. Busch III, was skeptical. "But he's looking through younger eyes," the father admitted. "He was right, and I was wrong." Through September, Anheuser-Busch posted a 1.3% gain in barrel shipments; the industry showed a 0.3% gain.

Marketers who get their messages right may be in for a pleasant surprise. Like other demographers, Hokenson of Donaldson, Lufkin & Jenrette believes that a population cohort's size has a big influence on its standard of living. Today's baby-bust generation, large as it is, still runs smaller than the boomer generation. That means it may not face the heavy competition boomers now encounter from their numerous brethren.

So, despite their struggles, busters may yet end up living better than the boomers. That would be a rich irony: the overlooked generation ultimately beating out the Me Generation in the race for prosperity.

SUGGESTIONS FOR DISCUSSION

1. This article not only relies on drawing a distinction between "boomers" and "busters," it also assumes that there are very real tensions between the two generations. What evidence does Zinn offer to explain the "busters'" anger? Does her analysis correspond to your own sense of the relations between the two generations? What, if anything, does she leave out or ignore?
2. This article appeared in *Business Week*, and it treats the "buster" generation as a potential market, as well as a cultural phenomenon, and offers advice to American businesses and advertising firms on how to tap this market. Identify passages in the article where Zinn characterizes the sensibility or mood of 18- to 29-year-olds in marketing terms. What kinds of advertising messages does she suggest "busters" are most responsive to? How does her emphasis on advertising affect the way she represents this generation? Are there aspects of this generation's experience and identity that thereby get lost or ignored?

3. In "Youth and American Identity," Lawrence Grossberg argues that in the post-World War II period, Americans invested their hopes for the future in the younger generation. In "Move Over, Boomers," however, Zinn says that young people today are a "generation of diminished expectations—polar opposites of the baby-boomers, who grew up thinking everything was possible." Do you agree with Zinn? Is this an era and a generation of "diminished expectations"? Have attitudes toward the future and the American Dream changed from the baby-boom to the current generation? If so, what do you see as the implications?

SUGGESTIONS FOR WRITING

1. Zinn points to representative examples that she thinks express something about the anger, cynicism, and alienation of the current generation of young people—grunge rock, Douglas Coupland's novel *Generation X,* ripped jeans, pierced noses, tatoos, "rave" dance marathons, watching TV reruns. Write an essay that explains how a particular form of cultural expression you associate with 18- to 29-year-olds—whether in music, fashion (or antifashion), hair style, film, books, television shows, or any other popular entertainment or pastime—reveals something significant about this generation's mood or sensibility. Don't feel you need to limit yourself here to anger, cynicism, or alienation. You may find other structures of feeling revealed through the form of cultural expression you are analyzing.

2. Zinn offers examples of a number of advertisements that she believes capture the mood or tone of the "busters" generation—ads from cosmetic makers, Nike, soft-drink and beer companies. Pick an ad that you think appeals to 18- to 29-year-olds and write an essay that explains how the ad constructs the mood of the "busters" and what this reveals about how the media represents the younger generation. The issue here is not whether the ad represents young people accurately but rather what characteristics the ad attributes to them and why.

3. A number of the writers in this chapter have commented on the relation between youth and the future. Lawrence Grossberg notes how Americans in the post-World War II period sought a form of national unity by projecting their hopes into the future of the new generation. On the other hand, both David Leavitt and Zinn suggest that things have changed, that the future looks very different today from the way it did in the 1950s and 1960s when the baby-boom generation was growing up. What do you make of this shift in sensibility? Write an essay that considers how an era of diminished expectations has changed the way both the media and young people represent the identity and the future of this generation.

Michael Oreskes

PROFILES OF TODAY'S YOUTH: THEY COULDN'T CARE LESS

The following is a news feature that appeared in the *New York Times* on July 28, 1990. Michael Oreskes, the news writer, summarizes the results of two national studies of the attitudes of young people, aged 18 to 29, toward public affairs, conducted by the Times Mirror Center for the People and the Press and by People for the American Way. He also draws upon interviews of 24 young people in Columbus, Ohio. The profile he draws of young people in America is one of "indifference," "disengagement," and a lack of participation in electoral politics. This news article raises some interesting questions about how the media represent today's young people.

Suggestion for Reading

- Survey results appear to possess a kind of objectivity that puts them beyond question and above criticism. As you read, notice how you respond to the results of the polls as Oreskes reports them. Do you accept the results or do you find yourself wanting to talk back to the pollsters? Annotate as you read, recording your reactions to the article.

———————————————◆———————————————

J ohn Karras, 28 years old, was in a card shop the other day as the radio, which provides the soundtrack for his generation, offered a report on the dead and missing in the floods that had just flashed through southeastern Ohio.

The cashier, a man a bit younger than Mr. Karras, looked up at the radio and said: "I wish they'd stop talking about it. I'm sick of hearing about it."

Mr. Karras, a doctoral student in education at Ohio State, recalled this incident to illustrate what he sees as a "pervasive" attitude among the members of his generation toward the larger world: the typical young person doesn't want to hear about it "unless it's knocking on my door."

The findings of two national studies concur. The studies, one released today and the other late last year, paint a portrait of a generation of young adults, from 18 to 29 years of age, who are indifferent toward public affairs. It is a generation that, as the Times Mirror Center for the People and the Press put it in a report released today, "knows less, cares less, votes less, and is less critical of its leaders and institutions than young people in the past."

Caught in the backwash of the baby boom, whose culture and attitudes still dominate American discourse, members of the "baby bust" seem almost to be rebelling against rebellion. Anyone who was hoping that the energy of this new generation would snap the nation out of its political lethargy, as young people helped awaken the nation from the quiescent 1950's, will probably be disappointed.

"My teacher told me: 'Always question authority,'" said Paul Grugin, 22, one of two dozen young people interviewed this week by *The New York Times* in this mid-size city in the middle of the country. "You can question authority, but you can burden authority. Let them authoritate."

The indifference of this generation—to politics, to government, even to news about the outside world—is beginning to affect American politics and society, the reports suggest, helping to explain such seemingly disparate trends as the decline in voting, the rise of tabloid television and the effectiveness of negative advertising.

While apathy and alienation have become a national plague, the disengagement seems to run deeper among young Americans, those 18 to 29, setting them clearly apart from earlier generations.

No one has yet offered a full explanation for why this should be so. The lack of mobilizing issues is part of the answer, as are the decline of the family and the rise of television.

Young people themselves mention the weakness of their civics education, and they talk incessantly of stress—their preoccupation with getting jobs or grades and their concern about personal threats like AIDS and drugs. "There are a lot more pressures on them than there were on us," said 48-year-old Ron Zeller, who talked about the differences along with his 22-year-old daughter, Susan, and his 18-year-old son, John.

The study by Times Mirror, a public opinion research center supported by Times Mirror Co., looked at 50 years of public opinion data and concluded, "Over most of the past five decades, younger members of the public have been at least as well informed as older people. In 1990 that is no longer the case."

This concern was echoed in a second report, prepared last year by People for the American Way, a liberal lobby and research organization, which concluded that there is "a citizenship crisis" in which "America's youth are alarmingly ill-prepared to keep democracy alive in the 1990's and beyond."

Susan Zeller, 22, who is about to enter Case Western law school, agreed. "I don't think many people my age group are very concerned," she said. "They're only concerned about issues that affect them. When the drinking age went up, quite a few people were upset."

The decline in voting is one illustration of how what seems to be a general problem is, in fact, most heavily concentrated among the young. Surveys by the census bureau show that since 1972 almost all of the decline in voting has been among those under 45, and that the sharpest drop is among those between 18 and 25. Among the elderly, voting has risen, according to the census bureau surveys.

Older people, more settled than the young, have always participated more in elections. But the gap has widened substantially. In 1972, half of those between 18 and 24 said they voted, as did 71 percent of those 45 to 64, a gap of 21 percentage points. In 1988, 36 percent of the 18- to 24-year-olds and 68 percent of the 45- to 64-year-olds said they voted, a gap of 32 percentage points.

Shonda Wolfe, 24, who has waited tables since dropping out of college, said she had voted only once, when she was 18 and still living at home. "I guess my mom was there to push me," she said.

Now, she said, she does not pay much attention to politics or to the news. "I try to avoid it—all the controversy," she said. "It just doesn't interest me at this point in my life. I'd rather be outside doing something, taking a walk."

Young people have always had to worry about getting started in life, beginning a career and a family. But this young generation, for whom Vietnam is a history lesson and Watergate a blurry childhood memory, seems to have adopted the cynicism of parents and older siblings without going through the activism and disappointments that produced that cynicism.

Not one of the young people interviewed in Columbus, at the Street Scene Restaurant and the Short North Tavern, had a good word to say about politics or politicians. But unlike older people, who often express anger about news about sloth or corruption in government, these young people seem simply to be reporting it as a well-known fact. "Most politicians are liars," said Deborah Roberts, a 29-year-old secretary.

People for the American Way, in its report, noted that young people seemed to have a half-formed understanding of citizenship, stressing rights but ignoring responsibilities.

When asked to define citizenship, Shonda Wolfe said it meant the right not to be harassed by the police. She cited as an intrusion on her rights the security guards' insistence at a concert that she and her boyfriend stop turning on their cigarette lighters.

Nancy Radcliffe-Spurgeon, 24, a student at Ohio State, said she thought that many of the attitudes of her generation were based on feeling safe. "It's easy to isolate yourself when you think things are going pretty well for you, so you don't rock the boat."

Occasionally, someone in the interview would mention voting. None of the young people when asked about citizenship included in their definition of good citizenship running for office, attending a community board meeting, studying an issue, signing a petition, writing a letter to the governor, or going to a rally.

These young people are aware that some of their attitudes are a product of different times. Young people protesting the war in Vietnam were also engaged by an issue that affected them, but one that the rest of the country also accepted as being of central importance. "When people your age were our age, there was a lot more strife," Jeff Brodeur, a 22-year-old senior at Ohio State, told a 36-year-old visitor.

Certain issues do get their attention, almost always involving government interference in personal freedoms. They generally favor access to abortion, and a few of the young people were upset by efforts to cut off Federal funds for art work deemed obscene.

Their concern about the arts was not surprising because in the interviews the young people showed that their main contact with the larger world was through culture. Mr. Brodeur, for example, said he first became aware of apartheid in South Africa through the song "Biko," written by Peter Gabriel about Steve Biko, a prominent anti-apartheid leader in South Africa of the 1970's.

But Mr. Brodeur's research seems more the exception than the rule. Andrew Kohut, director of surveys for Times Mirror, said there was a new generation gap, in which those under 30 were separated by their lack of knowledge and interest from those over 30.

People in their 30's and 40's are disenchanted with the world, but remain aware, said Mr. Kohut. But those under 30, he said, "are not so much disillusioned as disinterested."

The Times Mirror analysis was based on its own public opinion polling as well as comparisons with polling conducted by other organizations over the past 50 years.

Deborah Roberts, the secretary, says she still reads a newspaper, sort of. "There's more bad news on the front page," she said, explaining why she skips over it. "I like to go to the local news; it's the fun news."

"Attitudes like this are having a considerable effect on the news media," Mr. Kohut said. The number of people who read newspapers is declining, in general, but that number has plunged among the young. And not simply because they have turned to television, according to surveys. Viewing of traditional television news by the young is also shown to be down, although they do watch the new types of shows that concentrate on scandal and celebrity.

"The generation gap in news and information is playing out in politics in very significant ways," Mr. Kohut added.

"The 30-second commercial spot is a particularly appropriate medium for the MTV generation," he continued.

"At the conclusion of the 1988 campaign, Times Mirror's research showed that young voters, who began the campaign knowing less than older voters, were every bit as likely to recall advertised political themes such as pollution in Boston Harbor, Willie Horton and the flag.

"Sound bites and symbolism, the principal fuel of modern political campaigns, are well suited to young voters who know less and have limited interest in politics and public policy. Their limited appetites and aptitudes are shaping the practice of politics and the nature of our democracy."

SUGGESTIONS FOR DISCUSSION

1. Do you think the reports by Times Mirror and the People for the American Way present an accurate profile of 18- to -29-year-old Americans? If so, why? If not, why not? Do you think voting is a good measure of concern for public affairs? Are there other ways to interpret the lack of participation on election day? Explain your answer.
2. Oreskes cites a number of possible explanations for the "alienation and apathy" of young people. These include the "[l]ack of mobilizing issues," "the decline of the family, and the rise of television." To what extent are these useful explanations? What assumptions does each of these explanations make? What do they leave out or ignore?
3. Is Oreskes' article an instance of what Laura Zinn in "Move Over, Boomers" sees as "boomers'" lecturing to "busters"?

SUGGESTIONS FOR WRITING

1. Is there, as the People for the American Way put it, a "citizenship crisis" in America today? Do you think "America's youth are alarmingly ill-prepared to keep democracy alive in the 1990s and beyond"? Write an essay that presents your answers to these questions. First, summarize the conclusions of the report from the People for the American Way. Then present your own position. To do this, you will need to define for yourself what the term "citizenship" means before you can decide whether it is in crisis.
2. Write a letter to the editor of the New York Times that responds to "Profiles of Today's Youth: They Couldn't Care Less." Decide whether you want a) to defend young people against the implied criticism in this article or b) to use the article to draw out the larger consequences of young people's apathy toward public affairs. Take into account the extent to which the results of the polls and interviews capture accurately the mood of 18- to 29-year-old Americans and the extent to which they leave out something crucial.
3. David Leavitt, Laura Zinn, and Michael Oreskes each point, at least in passing, to how changes in the American family have shaped the mood of young people today. Zinn, for example, notes this is "the first generation of latchkey children, products of dual-career households, or, in some 50% of cases, of divorced or separated parents." These changes are undeniable, but their effects have yet to be fully calculated. Zinn says that "busters don't have much emotional security," and Oreskes attributes "apathy and alienation" in part to the "decline of the family." These are possible interpretations but not the only ones. Write an essay that begins with Zinn's description of changes in the family, and then draw your own conclusions. Use your own experience, as Leavitt does, if you wish, but remember

the point of the essay is not simply to describe your experience but to interpret it—
to show what it reveals about the effects of changes in the American family on
young people today.

Neil Howe and William Strauss

THE NEW GENERATION GAP

This selection originally appeared as part of a longer essay in the *Atlantic Monthly* (December 1992). Neil Howe and William Strauss seek to account for what they see as a "new generation gap" in American life, where "two world views, reflecting fundamentally different visions of society and self, are moving into conflict in the America of the 1990s." What Howe and Strauss call the "Thirteeners" in the following selection refers to the thirteenth generation of Americans, those young people born between 1961 and 1981, the age cohort that followed the baby-boomers, born between 1943 and 1960. Howe and Strauss have gone on to publish a book-length study, *Generations,* in which they offer a sweeping interpretation of generational clashes in American history, in which "missionary" generations devoted to social and moral crusades alternate with "lost" generations who feel they have somehow been ruined by the generation that preceded them. Whether you accept this cyclic view of American history or not, Howe and Strauss's essay nonetheless poses interesting questions about relations between the generations in the 1990s.

Suggestion for Reading

• As you read, keep in mind the two previous selections, Laura Zinn's "Move Over, Busters" and Michael Oreskes' "Profiles of Today's Youth." Annotate passages that seem to comment in one way or another on issues that Zinn and Oreskes have already raised.

A quarter century ago kids called older people names. These days, the reverse is true. For the past decade Thirteeners have been bombarded with study after story after column about how dumb, greedy, and just plain bad they supposedly are. They can't find Chicago on a map. They don't know when the Civil War was fought. They watch too much TV, spend too much time shopping, seldom vote (and vote for shallow reasons when they do), cheat on tests, don't read newspapers, and care way too much about cars, clothes, shoes, and money. Twenty years ago Boomers cautioned one another not to trust anyone over thirty; now the quip is "Don't *ask* anyone *under* thirty." "How can kids today be so dumb?" Tony Korn-

heiser, of *The Washington Post,* recently wondered. "They can't even make change unless the cash register tells them exactly how much to remit. Have you seen their faces
when your cheeseburger and fries comes to $1.73, and you give them $2.03? They
freeze, thunderstruck. They have absolutely no comprehension of what to do next."

Amidst this barrage, Thirteeners have become (in elders' eyes) a symbol of an
America in decline. Back in the 1970s social scientists looked at the American experience over the preceding half century and observed that each new generation, compared
with the last, traveled another step upward on the Maslovian scale of human purpose,
away from concrete needs and toward higher, more spiritual aspirations. Those due to
arrive after the Boomers, they expected, would be even more cerebral, more learned,
more idealistic, than any who came before. No chance—especially once Boomers
started to sit in judgment and churn out condemnatory reports on the fitness of their
generational successor. To fathom this Boom-defined Thirteener, this creature of pleasure and pain—this "Last Man" of history, driven only by appetites and no longer by
ideas or beliefs—you can wade through Francis Fukuyama's commentary on Nietzsche.
Or you can just imagine a TV-glued Thirteener audience nodding in response to Jay
Leno's line about why teenagers eat Doritos: "Hey, kids! We're not talkin' brain cells
here. We're talkin' taste buds."

Over the past decade Boomers have begun acting on the assumption that
Thirteeners are "lost"—reachable by pleasure-pain conditioning perhaps, but closed to
reason or sentiment. In the classroom Boomers instruct the young in "emotional literacy"; in the military they delouse the young with "core values" training; on campus they
drill the young in the vocabulary of "political correctness." The object is not to get
them to understand—that would be asking too much—but to get them to behave.
Back in the era of Boomers' youth, when young people did things that displeased older
people—when they drank beer, drove fast, didn't study, had sex, took drugs—the nation had an intergenerational dialogue, which, if nasty, at least led to a fairly articulate
discourse about values and social philosophy. Today the tone has shifted to monosylla-
bles ("Just say no"). The lexicon has been stripped of sentiment ("workfare" and "wed-
fare" in place of "welfare"). And the method has shifted to brute survival tools: prophy-
laxis or punishment.

This generation—more accurately, this generation's *reputation*—has become a
Boomer metaphor for America's loss of purpose, disappointment with institutions, despair over the culture, and fear for the future. Many Boomers are by now of the settled
opinion that Thirteeners are—front to back—a disappointing bunch. This attitude is
rooted partly in observation, partly in blurry nostalgia, partly in self-serving sermoniz-
ing, but the very fact that it is becoming a consensus is a major problem for today's
young people. No one can blame them if they feel like a demographic black hole whose
only elder-anointed mission is somehow to pass through the next three quarters of a
century without causing too much damage to the nation during their time.

To date Thirteeners have seldom either rebutted their elders' accusations or
pressed their own countercharges. Polls show them mostly agreeing that, yes, Boomer
kids probably were a better lot, listened to better music, pursued better causes, and
generally had better times on campus. So, they figure, why fight a rap they can't beat?
And besides, why waste time and energy arguing? Their usual strategy, in recent years
at least, has been to keep their thoughts to themselves. On campus Thirteeners chat
pleasantly in P.C. lingo with their "multiculti" prof or dean and then think nothing of

spoofing the faculty behind their backs (they can't be totally serious, right?) or play-fully relaxing with headphones to the racist lyrics of Ice Cube or Guns N' Roses. But among friends they talk frankly about how to maneuver in a world full of self-righteous ideologues.

Every phase and arena of life has been fine, even terrific, when Boomers entered it—and a wasteland when they left. A child's world was endlessly sunny in the 1950s, scarred by family chaos in the 1970s. Most movies and TV shows were fine for adolescents in the 1960s, unfit in the 1980s. Young-adult sex meant free love in the 1970s, AIDS in the 1990s. Boomers might prefer to think of their generation as the leaders of social progress, but the facts show otherwise. Yes, the Boom *is* a generation of trends, *but all those trends are negative.* The eldest Boomers (those born in the middle 1940s) have had relatively low rates of social pathology and high rates of academic achievement. The youngest Boomers (born in the late 1950s) have had precisely the opposite: high pathology, low achievement.

Again and again America has gotten fed up with Boom-inspired transgressions. But after taking aim at the giant collective Boomer ego and winding up with a club to bash Boomers for all the damage they did, America has swung late, missed, and (*pow!*) hit the next bunch of saps to come walking by. Constantly stepping into post-Boom desertscapes and suffering because of it, Thirteeners see Boomers as a generation that was given everything—from a *Happy Days* present to a Tomorrowland future—and then threw it all away.

Many a Thirteener would be delighted never to read another commemorative article about Woodstock, Kent State, or the Free Speech Movement. Or to suffer through what Coupland calls "legislated nostalgia"—the celebration of supposedly great events in the life cycle of people one doesn't especially like. Thirteeners fume when they hear Boomers taking credit for things they didn't do (starting the civil-rights movement, inventing rock-and-roll, stopping the Vietnam War) and for supposedly having been the most creative, idealistic, morally conscious youth in the history of America, if not the world. Even among Thirteeners who admire what young people did back in the sixties, workaholic, values-fixated Boomers are an object lesson in what not to become in their thirties and forties.

Put yourself in Thirteener shoes. Watching those crusaders gray in place just ahead of you—ensconced in college faculties, public-radio stations, policy foundations, and trendy rural retreats—you notice how Boomers keep redefining every test of idealism in ways guaranteed to make you fail. You're expected to muster passions against political authority you've never felt, to search for truth in places you've never found useful, to solve world problems through gestures you find absurd. As you gaze at the seamy underside of grand Boomer causes gone bust, you turn cynical. Maybe you stop caring. And the slightest lack of interest on your part is interpreted as proof of your moral blight. No matter that it was the crusaders' own self-indulgence that let the system fall apart. The "decade of greed" is *your* fault. "Compassion fatigue" is *your* fault. The "age of apathy" has *your* monosyllabic graffiti splattered all over it.

What Thirteeners want from Boomers is an apology mixed in with a little generational humility. Something like: "Hey, guys, we're sorry we ruined everything for you. Maybe we're not such a super-duper generation, and maybe we can learn something from you." Good luck. A more modest Thirteener hope is that Boomers will lighten up, look at their positive side, and find a little virtue in the "Just do it" motto written on their sneaker pumps.

Like two neighbors separated by a spite fence, Boomers and Thirteeners have grown accustomed to an uneasy adjacence.

SUGGESTIONS FOR DISCUSSION

1. Neil Howe and William Strauss suggest that "Boomers" blame "Thirteeners" for a "decade of greed," "compassion fatigue," and an "age of apathy" in the 1990s. They imply that these things are not the fault of the Thirteeners, but, at the same time, they don't really explain why these things happened, though Howe and Strauss do seem to believe they have indeed taken place in American life. Are these things—"decade of greed," "compassion fatigue," and an "age of apathy"— fair characterizations of the mood of American culture in the 1990s? How would you explain their occurrence?
2. Laura Zinn's "Move Over, Boomers," Michael Oreskes' "Profiles of Today's Youth," and Howe and Strauss's "The New Generation Gap" all assume that there are con-sequential differences between the baby-boom generation of the 1960s and young people today, whether you call them "busters," "slackers," "Thirteeners," or "Generation X." Is this a reasonable appraisal? What similarities or continuities be-tween the generations do these portraits of intergenerational conflict and tension ignore or suppress?
3. Howe and Strauss say, in passing, that "young-adult sex meant free love in the 1970s, AIDS in the 1990s." How, in your view, has the AIDS epidemic affected young people?

SUGGESTIONS FOR WRITING

1. A number of the selections in this chapter seem to emphasize intergenerational con-flict, but at least one, Gloria Naylor's "Kiswana Browne," also suggests that there are continuities and shared concerns between generations. Write an essay in which you locate the generation in which you grew up in relation to the generation that preceded you. To what extent were (or are) the generations in conflict? To what extent is there continuity?
2. Taken together, the last three selections—Laura Zinn's "Move Over, Boomers," Michael Oreskes' "Profiles of Today's Youth," and Howe and Strauss's "The New Generation Gap"—suggest that young people today are portrayed by the media as, in Howe and Strauss's words, a "Boomer metaphor for America's loss of pur-pose, disappointment with institutions, despair over the culture, and fear for the fu-ture." Pick an example of how today's younger generation is represented in the me-dia—in a film, television show, or book—and write an essay that analyzes how young people are portrayed. The point of the essay is not to judge whether the portrayal is accurate but to examine the cultural meanings that are attributed to young people and to explain why.
3. Write your own essay on today's generation of young people. Begin your essay by locating your own views in relation to one or more of the writers whose work you have read in this chapter. Use their ideas to develop your own—to agree with and extend their analysis or to disagree and give a counteranalysis.

FOR FURTHER EXPLORATION

As you have seen in this chapter, Americans are fascinated by the emergence of new generations—and apparently obsessed by the desire to label and characterize each new generation. To explore some of the issues that arise from this fascination, you might investigate the emergence of a new genera-tion in American life, such as the "lost generation" of the 1920s, the Beat gen-eration of the 1950s, the hippies and the New Left of the 1960s, or the yup-pies of the 1980s. Or you might want to look at how one writer marks the passage from one generation to the next in memoirs such as Richard Rodriguez's *The Hunger of Memory*, Richard Wright's *Black Boy*, or Patricia Hampl's *Romantic Education*.

C H A P T E R   3

SCHOOLING

I wish first that we should recognize that education is ordinary;
that is, before everything else, the process of giving to the ordinary
members of society its full common meanings, and the skills that will
enable them to amend these meanings, in the light of their personal
and common experience.

– Raymond Williams,
"Culture Is Ordinary"

B y the time you read this chapter it is quite likely that you will have already spent a considerable amount of time in school. Most Americans between the ages of five and seventeen or eighteen are full-time students whose daily lives revolve around their schooling. From the moment individuals enter school until they drop out, leave temporarily, graduate from high school, or go on to college, their intellectual and cultural growth is intimately connected to going to school and learning how to be students. Because so much of growing up takes place in them, schools are key agents of acculturation in America, the place where the younger generation not only learns how to read, write, and do mathematics but also gets its upbringing in literature, history, and civics. One of the purposes of all this schooling is to transmit bodies of knowledge from one generation to the next, and classrooms are the place where this intergenerational communication normally occurs, from teacher to student.

Americans have always put a lot of faith in educating the younger generation, to prepare them for the work of the future and to teach them what it means to be an American, a good citizen, and a productive member of society. But it is precisely because Americans put so much faith—and invest so many resources—in schooling that they worry and argue incessantly about what the schools are—or should be—accomplishing. Over the past decade, there has been mounting dissatisfaction with and criticism of the American education system at all levels, elementary, secondary, and college. Educational reformers have noted a variety of problems—ranging from declining standardized test scores and the "literacy crisis" to unimaginative teaching, passive learning, and outdated or irrelevant curriculum to skyrocketing college costs and the loss of careers in science, engineering, and mathematics. Critics have called attention to male biases in the curriculum and the neglect of race, ethnicity, and class in the study of history, culture, and literature. Others have argued that the way schools test and reward achievement favors middle-class students over working-class and poor students, white over black, males over females.

As a student, you are at the center of much of this controversy, and you are in a unique position to comment upon schooling in your life and in the lives of others. The purpose of this chapter is to offer you opportunities to read, think, and write about the role of schooling in America today. You will be asked in the reading and writing assignments in this chapter to recall classroom episodes from your past and observe classroom life in the present. You will be asked to work your way from the everyday practices of schooling to the mission and function of education in contemporary America. We want to invite you to explore the world of schooling in order to identify how it has influenced you as a student, a learner, and a person. The writers we have gathered in this chapter will give you an idea of some of the questions educators are currently asking about schooling in America. By engaging the educational issues raised by the reading and writing assignments in this chapter, you can begin to develop your own analysis of the role of schooling in America.

One way to begin an investigation of the role of schooling is to ask what sounds like a very simple and innocent question: What did you learn in school? The answers you might get, however, may not be simple at all. You would need, for one thing, to consider the **formal curriculum** you studied—the subjects you took, the teachers who instructed you, and the knowledge you acquired. You would want to think about why American schools teach what they do, why academic subjects are organized as they are, and what assumptions about the nature and function of education have shaped the formal curriculum.

The experience of going to school, of course, involves more than just learning the content of the courses. For students, schooling is not just a matter of the subjects they study. It is a way of life that shapes their sense of themselves and their life chances. Many people remember their first day in school because it marks, quite literally, the transition from home and play to classroom life and the world of schoolwork. The kind of knowledge students acquire when they learn how to be students and go to school forms what educators call the **hidden curriculum.** This part of the curriculum is just as structured as the lessons students study in the formal curriculum. The difference is that in the hidden curriculum the content remains unstated and gets acted out in practice instead. The hidden curriculum, that is, refers to all the unspoken beliefs and procedures that regulate classroom life, the rules of the game no one writes down but that both teachers and students have internalized in their expectations about each other.

Students learn the hidden curriculum from the early grades on, when they learn how to sit still, to pay attention, to raise their hands to be called on, to follow directions, to perform repetitive tasks, and to complete work on time. Students learn what pleases teachers and what doesn't, what they can say to teachers and what they ought to keep to themselves. One of the functions of American schools has always been to instill the habits of discipline, punctuality, hard work, and the wise use of time in the younger generation—to teach them, as the old adage goes, that "there is a time for work and a time for play." We might describe the hidden curriculum as a training ground where students learn to work for grades and other symbolic rewards, to take tests and believe in their accuracy and fairness.

Examining the hidden curriculum offers a useful way to look at classroom life, in part because it demands that you research and bring into view the kinds of things that take place in school that both teachers and students seem to take for granted. Bringing the familiar and the habitual into view can help generate questions about what you might otherwise accept without question. Why, for example, is the school day divided as it is, and what is the effect of moving from subject to subject in fifty-minute intervals? Why do students sit in rows? Who has the right to speak in class? Who gets called on by the teacher? Why do teachers ask questions when they already know the answer? You will be asked in the reading and writing assignments in this chapter to research questions such as these, to bring the hidden curriculum's unstated norms to light and to assess their effects on students and on the role schooling plays in American culture.

READING THE CULTURE OF SCHOOLING

The reading and writing assignments in this chapter will ask you to draw on your memories of schooling and your current position as a student, to be a participant-observer of the education you are currently experiencing. The opening selections in the chapter— "What High School Is," Theodore R. Sizer's critical analysis of the typical high school day, and "The Classroom World," Robert B. Everhart's study of junior high student culture—offer some interesting leads to think about your own junior high and high school years. But the questions they raise about the goals of education and the meaning of work in school can also be applied to college. From different perspectives, Sizer and

Everhart pose some basic issues about the role of schooling. Sizer is interested in the formal curriculum and what students actually study, while Everhart is interested in how students make sense of the world of school and the work they are asked to do.

In the next two selections, Mike Rose and Myra and David Sadker look at particular educational practices—testing and reciting in class—and how they structure the success and failure of individual students. In "Crossing Boundaries," Mike Rose recounts the struggles and aspirations of returning adult learners and raises troubling questions about how the education system uses test performances to measure and certify success and failure. Rose makes us aware of how schooling labels and stigmatizes individuals as intellectually deficient—blaming the victim, as it were, for school failure that has deeper social and political roots. In the following selection, "Sexism in the Schoolroom," Myra and David Sadker are also interested in the social and political roots of school performance, in particular the constraints imposed upon and internalized by female students not to talk too much in class, not to be too aggressive, not to risk popularity by achieving too much.

The final two selections offer considerably different perspectives on the formal curriculum. E. D. Hirsch, Jr., has become one of the leading spokespersons for a curriculum that transmits a shared body of knowledge about American national culture. His approach—and the assumptions he makes about the nature of schooling and literacy—in "Cultural Literacy and the Schools" contrasts sharply with June Jordan's account of a class she taught on Black English in "Nobody Mean More to Me Than You and the Future Life of Willie Jordan." Taken together, these two essays explore in quite different ways what it means to learn to read and write and what it means to be literate in contemporary America.

What may begin to emerge from the reading and writing assignments in this chapter is a picture of schooling as a way of life that sorts out students to prepare them for their future roles in society. How this sorting out takes place—how tracking assigns some students to college prep and others to vocational programs, how some students learn to be successful in school while others fail, how schooling confirms or undermines individual students' self-confidence and sense of self-worth—these are some of the questions you will be invited to explore in this chapter. Your position as a participant-observer gives you a useful vantage point to raise such questions from the inside, to ask about the meaning of your own education and about the role of schooling in American culture.

Theodore R. Sizer

WHAT HIGH SCHOOL IS

Theodore R. Sizer has been chairman of the Education Department at Brown University, headmaster of Phillips Academy, Andover, and Dean of the

Graduate School of Education at Harvard. The following selection is a chapter from *Horace's Compromise*, Sizer's book-length study of American high schools. Sizer's book takes a critical look at high schools—at overworked teachers, undermotivated students, and the "assembly-line" educational practices that process people rather than educate them. Originally published in 1984, Sizer's study was one of a number of national reports that appeared in the 1980s raising serious questions about the quality of American education. We have selected the opening chapter of *Horace's Compromise* because it looks at how the school day is organized and what it means to students to "take subjects."

Suggestion for Reading

- As you read, notice that Sizer gives a full account of Mark's day before he steps back to generalize about its significance. Underline and annotate this selection to indicate where Sizer begins to analyze the meaning of Mark's day and how Sizer goes on to develop a critical analysis of the typical high school day.

———————————◆———————————

Mark, sixteen and a genial eleventh-grader, rides a bus to Franklin High School, arriving at 7:25. It is an Assembly Day, so the schedule is adapted to allow for a meeting of the entire school. He hangs out with his friends, first outside school and then inside, by his locker. He carries a pile of textbooks and notebooks; in all, it weighs eight and a half pounds.

From 7:30 to 8:19, with nineteen other students, he is in Room 304 for English class. The Shakespeare play being read this year by the eleventh grade is *Romeo and Juliet.* The teacher, Ms. Viola, has various students in turn take parts and read out loud. Periodically, she interrupts the (usually halting) recitations to ask whether the thread of the conversation in the play is clear. Mark is entertained by the stumbling readings of some of his classmates. He hopes he will not be asked to be Romeo, particularly if his current steady, Sally, is Juliet. There is a good deal of giggling in class, and much attention paid to who may be called on next. Ms. Viola reminds the class of a test on this part of the play to be given next week.

The bell rings at 8:19. Mark goes to the boys' room, where he sees a classmate who he thinks is a wimp but who constantly tries to be a buddy. Mark avoids the leech by rushing off. On the way, he notices two boys engaged in some sort of transaction, probably over marijuana. He pays them no attention. 8:24. Typing class. The rows of desks that embrace big office machines are almost filled before the bell. Mark is uncomfortable here: typing class is girl country. The teacher constantly threatens what to Mark is a humiliatingly girl future: "Your employer won't like these erasures." The minutes during the period are spent copying a letter from a handbook onto business stationery. Mark struggles to keep from looking at his work; the teacher wants him to watch only the material from which he is copying. Mark is frustrated, uncomfortable, and scared that he will not complete his letter by the class's end, which would be embarrassing.

Nine tenths of the students present at school that day are assembled in the auditorium by the 9:18 bell. The dilatory tenth still stumble in, running down aisles.

Annoyed class deans try to get the mob settled. The curtains part; the program is a concert by a student rock group. Their electronic gear flashes under the lights, and the five
boys and one girl in the group work hard at being casual. Their movements on stage are
studiously at three-quarter time, and they chat with one another as though the tu-
multuous screaming of their schoolmates were totally inaudible. The girl balances on a
stool; the boys crank up the music. It is very soft rock, the sanitized lyrics surely cleared
with the assistant principal. The girl sings, holding the mike close to her mouth, but
can scarcely be heard. Her light voice is tentative, and the lyrics indecipherable. The
guitars, amplified, are tuneful, however, and the drums are played with energy.

The students around Mark—all juniors, since they are seated by class—alternately slouch in their upholstered, hinged seats, talking to one another, or sit forward,
leaning on the chair backs in front of them, watching the band. A boy near Mark
shouts noisily at the microphone-fondling singer, "Bite it . . . ohhh," and the area
around Mark explodes in vulgar male laughter, but quickly subsides. A teacher walks
down the aisle. Songs continue, to great applause. Assembly is over at 9:46, two minutes early.

9:53 and biology class. Mark was at a different high school last year and did not
take this course there as a tenth-grader. He is in it now, and all but one of his classmates are a year younger than he. He sits on the side, not taking part in the chatter that
goes on after the bell. At 9:57, the public address system goes on, with the announcements of the day. After a few words from the principal ("Here's today's cheers and
jeers. . ." with a cheer for the winning basketball team and a jeer for the spectators who
made a ruckus at the gymnasium), the task is taken over by officers of ASB (Associated
Student Bodies). There is an appeal for "bat bunnies." Carnations are for sale by the
Girls' League. Miss Indian American is coming. Students are auctioning off their services (background catcalls are heard) to earn money for the prom. Nominees are
needed for the ballot for school bachelor and school bachelorette. The announcements
end with a "thought for the day. When you throw a little mud, you lose a little
ground."

At 10:04 the biology class finally turns to science. The teacher, Mr. Robbins, has
placed one of several labeled laboratory specimens—some are pinned in frames, other
swim in formaldehyde—on each of the classroom's eight laboratory tables. The three or
so students whose chairs circle each of these benches are to study the specimen and
make notes about it or drawings of it. After a few minutes each group of three will move
to another table. The teacher points out that these specimens are of organisms already
studied in previous classes. He says that the period-long test set for the following day
will involve observing some of these specimens—then to be without labels—and writing an identifying paragraph on each. Mr. Robbins points out that some of the printed
labels ascribe the specimens names different from those given in the textbook. He explains that biologists often give several names to the same organism.

The class now falls to peering, writing, and quiet talking. Mr. Robbins comes over
to Mark, and in whispered words asks him to carry a requisition form for science department materials to the business office. Mark, because of his "older" status, is usually
chosen by Robbins for this kind of errand. Robbins gives Mark the form and a green
hall pass to show to any teacher who might challenge him, on his way to the office, for
being out of a classroom. The errand takes Mark four minutes. Meanwhile Mark's

group is hard at work but gets to only three of the specimens before the bell rings at 10:42. As the students surge out, Robbins shouts a reminder about a "double" laboratory period on Thursday.

Between classes one of the seniors asks Mark whether he plans to be a candidate for schoolwide office next year. Mark says no. He starts to explain. The 10:47 bell rings, meaning that he is late for French class.

There are fifteen students in Monsieur Bates's language class. He hands out tests taken the day before: *"C'est bien fait, Etienne . . . c'est mieux, Marie . . . Tch, tch, Robert. . . "* Mark notes his C+ and peeks at the A− in front of Susanna, next to him. The class has been assigned seats by M. Bates; Mark resents sitting next to prissy, brainy Susanna. Bates starts by asking a student to read a question and give the correct answer. *"James, question un."* James haltingly reads the question and gives an answer that Bates, now speaking English, says is incomplete. In due course: *"Mark, question cinq."* Mark does his bit, and the sequence goes on, the eight quiz questions and answers filling about twenty minutes of time.

"Turn to page forty-nine. *Maintenant, lisez après moi. . . "* and Bates reads a sentence and has the class echo it. Mark is embarrassed by this and mumbles with a barely audible sound. Others, like Susanna, keep the decibel count up, so Mark can hide. This I-say-you-repeat drill is interrupted once by the public address system, with an announcement about a meeting for the cheerleaders. Bates finishes class, almost precisely at the bell, with a homework assignment. The students are to review these sentences for a brief quiz the following day. Mark takes notes of the assignment, because he knows that tomorrow will be a day of busywork in French class. Much though he dislikes oral drills, they are better than the workbook stuff that Bates hands out. Write, write, write, for Bates to throw away, Mark thinks.

11:36. Down to the cafeteria, talking noisily, hanging out, munching. Getting to Room 104 by 12:17: U.S. history. The teacher is sitting crosslegged on his desk when Mark comes in, heatedly arguing with three students over the fracas that had followed the previous night's basketball game. The teacher, Mr. Suslovic, while agreeing that the spectators from their school certainly were provoked, argues that they should neither have been so obviously obscene in yelling at the opposing cheerleaders nor have allowed Coke cans to be rolled out on the floor. The three students keep saying that "it isn't fair." Apparently they and some others had been assigned "Saturday mornings" (detentions) by the principal for the ruckus.

At 12:34, the argument appears to subside. The uninvolved students, including Mark, are in their seats, chatting amiably. Mr. Suslovic climbs off his desk and starts talking: "We've almost finished this unit, chapters nine and ten. . . ." The students stop chattering among themselves and turn toward Suslovic. Several slouch down in their chairs. Some open notebooks. Most have the five-pound textbook on their desks.

Suslovic lectures on the cattle drives, from north Texas to railroads west of St. Louis. He breaks up this narrative with questions ("Why were the railroad lines laid largely east to west?"), directed at nobody in particular and eventually answered by Suslovic himself. Some students take notes. Mark doesn't. A student walks in the open door, hands Mr. Suslovic a list, and starts whispering with him. Suslovic turns from the class and hears out this messenger. He then asks, "Does anyone know where Maggie Sharp is?" Someone answers, "Sick at home"; someone else says, "I thought I saw her at lunch." Genial consternation. Finally Suslovic tells the messenger, "Sorry, we can't help you," and returns to the class: "Now, where were we?" He goes on for some minutes. The bell rings. Suslovic forgets to give the homework assignment.

1:11 and Algebra II. There is a commotion in the hallway: someone's locker is rumored to have been opened by the assistant principal and a narcotics agent. In the five-minute passing time, Mark hears the story three times and three ways. A locker had been broken into by another student. It was Mr. Gregory and a narc. It was the cops, and they did it without Gregory's knowing. Mrs. Ames, the mathematics teacher, has not heard anything about it. Several of the nineteen students try to tell her and start arguing among themselves. "O.K., that's enough." She hands out the day's problem, one sheet to each student. Mark sees with dismay that it is a single, complicated "word" problem about some train that, while traveling at 84 mph, due west, passes a car that was going due east at 55 mph. Mark struggles: Is it $d = rt$ or $t = rd$? The class becomes quiet, writing, while Mrs. Ames writes some additional, short problems on the blackboard. "Time's up." A sigh; most students still writing. A muffled "Shit." Mrs. Ames frowns. "Come on, now." She collects papers, but it takes four minutes for her to corral them all.

"Copy down the problems from the board." A minute passes. "William, try number one." William suggests an approach. Mrs. Ames corrects and cajoles, and William finally gets it right. Mark watches two kids to his right passing notes; he tries to read them but the handwriting is illegible from his distance. He hopes he is not called on, and he isn't. Only three students are asked to puzzle out an answer. The bell rings at 2:00. Mrs. Ames shouts a homework assignment over the resulting hubbub.

Mark leaves his books in his locker. He remembers that he has homework, but figures that he can do it during English class the next day. He knows that there will be an in-class presentation of one of the *Romeo and Juliet* scenes and that he will not be in it. The teacher will not notice his homework writing, or won't do anything about it if she does.

Mark passes various friends heading toward the gym, members of the basketball teams. Like most students, Mark isn't an active school athlete. However, he is associated with the yearbook staff. Although he is not taking "Yearbook" for credit as an English course, he is contributing photographs. Mark takes twenty minutes checking into the yearbook staff's headquarters (the classroom of its faculty adviser) and getting some assignments of pictures from his boss, the senior who is the photography editor. Mark knows that if he pleases his boss and the faculty adviser, he'll take that editor's post for the next year. He'll get English credit for his work then.

After gossiping a bit with the yearbook staff, Mark will leave school by 2:35 and go home. His grocery market bagger's job is from 4:45 to 8:00, the rush hour for the store. He'll have a snack at 4:30, and his mother will save him some supper to eat at 8:30. She will ask whether he has any homework, and he'll tell her no. Tomorrow, and virtually every other tomorrow, will be the same for Mark, save for the lack of the assembly; each period then will be five minutes longer.

• • •

Most Americans have an uncomplicated vision of what secondary education should be. Their conception of high school is remarkably uniform across the country, a striking fact, given the size and diversity of the United States and the politically decentralized character of the schools. This uniformity is of several generations' standing. It has, however, two appearances, each quite different from the other, one of words and the other of practice, a world of political rhetoric and Mark's world.

A California high school's general goals, set out in 1979, could serve equally well most of America's high schools, public and private. This school had as its ends:

- Fundamental scholastic achievement . . . to acquire knowledge and share in the traditionally accepted academic fundamentals . . . to develop the ability to make decisions, to solve problems, to reason independently, and to accept responsibility for self-evaluation and continuing self-improvement.

- Career and economic competence . . .

- Citizenship and civil responsibility . . .

- Competence in human and social relations . . .

- Moral and ethical values . . .

- Self-realization and mental and physical health . . .

- Aesthetic awareness . . .

- Cultural diversity . . .

In addition to its optimistic rhetoric, what distinguished this list is its comprehensiveness. The high school is to touch most aspects of an adolescent's existence—mind, body, morals, values, career. No one of these areas is given especial prominence. School people arrogate to themselves an obligation to all.

An example of the wide acceptability of these goals is found in the courts. Forced to present a detailed definition of "thorough and efficient education," elementary as well as secondary, a West Virginia judge sampled the best of conventional wisdom and concluded that

> there are eight general elements of a thorough and efficient system of education: (a) Literacy, (b) The ability to add, subtract, multiply, and divide numbers, (c) Knowledge of government to the extent the child will be equipped as a citizen to make informed choices among persons and issues that affect his own governance, (d) Self-knowledge and knowledge of his or her total environment to allow the child to intelligently choose life work—to know his or her options, (e) Work-training and advanced academic training as the child may intelligently choose, (f) Recreational pursuits, (g) Interests in all creative arts such as music, theater, literature, and the visual arts, and (h) Social ethics, both behavioral and abstract, to facilitate compatibility with others in this society.

That these eight—now powerfully part of the debate over the purpose and practice of education in West Virginia—are reminiscent of the influential list, "The Seven Cardinal Principles of Secondary Education," promulgated in 1918 by the National

Education Association, is no surprise. The rhetoric of high school purpose has been uniform and consistent for decades. Americans agree on the goals for their high schools.

That agreement is convenient, but it masks the fact that virtually all the words in these goal statements beg definition. Some schools have labored long to identify specific criteria beyond them; the result has been lists of daunting pseudospecificity and numbing earnestness. However, most leave the words undefined and let the momentum of traditional practice speak for itself. That is why analyzing how Mark spends his time is important: from watching him one uncovers the important purposes of education, the ones that shape practice. Mark's day is similar to that of other high school students across the country, as similar as the rhetoric of one goal statement to others'. Of course, there are variations, but the extent of consistency in the shape of school routine for a large and diverse adolescent population is extraordinary, indicating more graphically than any rhetoric the measure of agreement in America about what one does in high school, and, by implication, what it is for.

The basic organizing structures in schools are familiar. Above all, students are grouped by age (that is, freshman, sophomore, junior, senior), and all are expected to take precisely the same time—around 720 school days over four years, to be precise—to meet the requirements for a diploma. When one is out of his grade level, he can feel odd, as Mark did in his biology class. The goals are the same for all, and the means to achieve them are also similar.

Young males and females are treated remarkably alike; the schools' goals are the same for each gender. In execution, there are differences, as those pressing sex discrimination suits have made educators intensely aware. The students in metalworking classes are mostly male; those in home economics, mostly female. But it is revealing how much less sex discrimination there is in high schools than in other American institutions. For many young women, the most liberated hours of their week are in school.

School is to be like a job: you start in the morning and end in the afternoon, five days a week. You don't get much of a lunch hour, so you go home early, unless you are an athlete or are involved in some special school or extracurricular activity. School is conceived of as the children's workplace, and it takes young people off parents' hands and out of the labor market during prime-time work hours. Not surprisingly, many students see going to school as little more than a dogged necessity. They perceive the day-to-day routine, a Minnesota study reports, as one of "boredom and lethargy." One of the students summarizes: School is "boring, restless, tiresome, puts ya to sleep, tedious, monotonous, pain in the neck."

The school schedule is a series of units of time: the clock is king. The base time block is about fifty minutes in length. Some schools, on what they call modular scheduling, split that fifty-minute block into two or even three pieces. Most schools have double periods for laboratory work, especially in the sciences, or four-hour units for small numbers of students involved in intensive vocational or other work-study programs. The flow of all school activity arises from or is blocked by these time units. "How much time do I have with my kids" is the teacher's key question.

Because there are many claims for those fifty-minute blocks, there is little time set aside for rest between them, usually no more than three to ten minutes, depending on how big the school is and, consequently, how far students and teachers have to walk from class to class. As a result, there is a frenetic quality to the school day, a sense of sustained restlessness. For the adolescents, there are frequent changes of room and fellow students, each change giving tempting opportunities for distraction, which are stoutly resisted by teachers. Some schools play soft music during these "passing times," to quiet the multitude, one principal told me.

Many teachers have a chance for a coffee break. Few students do. In some city schools where security is a problem, students must be in class for seven consecutive periods, interrupted by a heavily monitored twenty-minute lunch period for small groups, starting as early as 10:30 A.M. and running to after 1:00 P.M. A high premium is placed on punctuality and on "being where you're supposed to be." Obviously, a low premium is placed on reflection and repose. The student rushes from class to class to collect knowledge. Savoring it, it is implied, is not to be done much in school, nor is such meditation really much admired. The picture that these familial patterns yield is that of an academic supermarket. The purpose of going to school is to pick things up, in an organized and predictable way, the faster the better.

What is supposed to be picked up is remarkably consistent among all sorts of high schools. Most schools specifically mandate three out of every five courses a student selects. Nearly all of these mandates fall into five areas—English, social studies, mathematics, science, and physical education. On the average, English is required to be taken each year, social studies and physical education three out of the four high school years, and mathematics and science one or two years. Trends indicate that in the mid-eighties there is likely to be an increase in the time allocated to these last two subjects. Most students take classes in these four major academic areas beyond the minimum requirements, sometimes in such special areas as journalism and "yearbook," offshoots of English departments.

Press most adults about what high school is for, and you hear these subjects listed. *High school? That's where you learn English and math and that sort of thing.* Ask students, and you get the same answers. High school is to "teach" these "subjects."

What is often absent is any definition of these subjects or any rationale for them. They are just there, labels. Under those labels lie a multitude of things. A great deal of material is supposed to be "covered"; most of these courses are surveys, great sweeps of the stuff of their parent disciplines.

While there is often a sequence *within* subjects—algebra before trigonometry, "first-year" French before "second-year" French—there is rarely a coherent relationship or sequence *across* subjects. Even the most logically related matters—reading ability as a precondition for the reading of history books, and certain mathematical concepts or skills before the study of some physics—are only loosely coordinated, if at all. There is little demand for a synthesis of it all; English, mathematics, and the rest are discrete items, to be picked up individually. The incentive for picking them up is largely through tests and, with success at these, in credits earned.

Coverage within subjects is the key priority. If some imaginative teacher makes a proposal to force the marriage of, say, mathematics and physics or to require some culminating challenges to students to use several subjects in the solution of a complex problem, and if this proposal will take "time" away from other things, opposition is usually phrased in terms of what may be thus forgone. If we do that, we'll have to give up colonial history. We won't be able to get to programming. We'll not be able to read *Death of a Salesman.* There isn't time. The protesters usually win out.

The subjects come at a student like Mark in random order, a kaleidoscope of worlds: algebraic formulae to poetry to French verbs to Ping-Pong to the War of the

Spanish Succession, all before lunch. Pupils are to pick up these things. Tests measure whether the picking up has been successful.

The lack of connection between stated goals, such as those of the California high school cited earlier, and the goals inherent in school practice is obvious and, curiously, tolerated. Most striking is the gap between statements about "self-realization and mental and physical growth" or "moral and ethical values"—common rhetoric in school documents—and practice. Most physical education programs have neither the time nor the focus really to ensure fitness. Mental health is rarely defined. Neither are ethical values, save at the negative extremes, such as opposition to assault or dishonesty. Nothing in the regimen of a day like Mark's signals direct or implicit teaching in this area. The "schoolboy code" (not ratting on a fellow student) protects the marijuana pusher, and a leechlike associate is shrugged off without concern. The issue of the locker search was pushed aside, as not appropriate for class time.

Most students, like Mark, go to class in groups of twenty to twenty-seven students. The expected attendance in some schools, particularly those in low-income areas, is usually higher, often thirty-five students per class, but high absentee rates push the actual numbers down. About twenty-five per class is an average figure for expected attendance, and the actual numbers are somewhat lower. There are remarkably few students who go to class in groups much larger or smaller than twenty-five.

A student such as Mark sees five or six teachers per day; their differing styles and expectations are part of his kaleidoscope. High school staffs are highly specialized; guidance counselors rarely teach mathematics, mathematics teachers rarely teach English, principals rarely do any classroom instruction. Mark, then, is known a little bit by a number of people, each of whom sees him in one specialized situation. No one may know him as a "whole person"—unless he becomes a special problem or has special needs.

Save in extracurricular or coaching situations, such as in athletics, drama, or shop classes, there is little opportunity for sustained conversation between student and teacher. The mode is a one-sentence or two-sentence exchange: *Mark, when was Grover Cleveland president?* Let's see, was 1890 . . . or something . . . wasn't he the one . . . he was elected twice, wasn't he? . . . *Yes . . . Gloria, can you get the dates right?* Dialogue is strikingly absent, and as a result the opportunity of teachers to challenge students' ideas in a systematic and logical way is limited. Given the rushed, full quality of the school day, it can seldom happen. One must infer that careful probing of students' thinking is not a high priority. How one gains (to quote the California school's statement of goals again) "the ability to make decisions, to solve problems, to reason independently, and to accept responsibility for self-evaluation and continuing self-improvement" without being challenged is difficult to imagine. One certainly doesn't learn these things merely from lectures and textbooks.

Most schools are nice places. Mark and his friends enjoy being in theirs. The adults who work in schools generally like adolescents. The academic pressures are limited, and the accommodations to students are substantial. For example, if many members of an English class have jobs after school, the English teacher's expectations for them are adjusted, downward. In a word, school is sensitively accommodating, as long as students are punctual, where they are supposed to be, and minimally dutiful about picking things up from the clutch of courses in which they enroll.

This characterization is not pretty, but it is accurate, and it serves to describe the vast majority of American secondary schools. "Taking subjects" in a systematized, conveyer-belt way is what one does in high school. That this process is, in substantial respects, not related to the rhetorical purposes of education is tolerated by most people, perhaps because they do not really either believe in those ill-defined goals or, in their heart of hearts, believe that schools can or should even try to achieve them. The students are happy taking subjects. The parents are happy, because that's what they did in high school. The rituals, the most important of which is graduation, remain intact. The adolescents are supervised, safely and constructively most of the time, during the morning and afternoon hours, and they are off the labor market. That is what high school is all about.

SUGGESTIONS FOR DISCUSSION

1. The portrait of Mark that begins in this selection, as Sizer notes, is "made up." It is a composite blending of a number of real students and real high schools—"somewhere," Sizer says, "between precise journalism and nonfiction fiction." As a composite of real students in real high schools, Sizer's portrait of Mark's school day must appear to be typical and recognizable for it to be persuasive and credible. Does Sizer's portrait achieve the kind of typicality he is trying for? Draw on your own experience and observations in high school to decide whether this is a fair portrait and what, if anything, it leaves out.
2. Sizer says, "Press most adults about what high school is for, and you hear these subjects listed. 'High school? That's where you learn English and math and that sort of thing.'" How does Sizer answer his question, what is high school for? How would you answer it? Explain how you would account for differences and similarities between Sizer's answer and your own.
3. Do you agree with Sizer that there is a "lack of connection between stated goals" of high school education and "the goals inherent in school practice?" Sizer gives some examples of stated goals, such as the general goals for California high schools and the goals presented by a West Virginia judge, but he doesn't really say what the "goals inherent in school practice" might be. To answer this question you will need to decide what these unstated goals are and how they determine what actually takes place in the daily routines of American high schools.

SUGGESTIONS FOR WRITING

1. At the end of this selection, Sizer says, "'Taking subjects' in a systematized, conveyer-belt way is what one does in high school." A few lines later he says, "Students are happy taking subjects." Do you agree with Sizer? Are high school students, in your experience, happy "taking subjects," or do they feel something is missing? Write an essay that develops your own position. Begin by summarizing what Sizer views as "conveyer-belt" education. Then explain to what extent and why you agree or disagree with his sense that students are happy "taking subjects."
2. Sizer says, "Most schools are nice. . . . The academic pressures are limited, and the accommodations to students are substantial. For example, if many members of an English class have jobs after school, the English teacher's expectations for them are adjusted, downward." Write an essay that describes the expectations of teachers in the high school you attended and explains what influence those expectations have had on you as a student, a learner, and a person. Take into account whether teachers' expectations varied and whether they held the same expectations for all students.

3. Use Sizer's composite portrait of Mark's school day as a model to write a portrait of a typical school day at the high school you attended. Draw on your own experiences and memories of schooling, but remember the point of this portrait is not really autobiographical. You want to capture what is typical of high school students, not what is special to individuals.

Robert B. Everhart

THE CLASSROOM WORLD

Robert B. Everhart is an educational ethnographer who studies life in school much as an anthropologist would study the customs, belief systems, and everyday practices of traditional cultures. The following selection is taken from the chapter "The Classroom World" that appeared in Everhart's book-length study of a junior high school, *Reading, Writing, and Resistance: Adolescence and Labor in a Junior High School* (1983). Everhart spent two years in the junior high, going to classes with students, eating lunch with them, and generally "hanging out." As an ethnographer, Everhart studies how students make sense of their own experience in school and, as the following selection indicates, how they interpret the "work" teachers ask them to do in school. We have chosen this selection because Everhart is interested not so much in the curriculum and educational goals (as Theodore Sizer is in the preceding selection) but instead in "the distinctive way of life that students lived" and the "student-generated belief system" that defines student culture.

Suggestion for Reading

• In the following selection, Everhart uses the notion of "work" repeatedly as a key term to discuss students' attitudes toward their activities in school and toward their teachers. As you read, underline passages where Everhart derives the meaning of "work" from what students say they do in school and what they say about their teachers.

---◆---

'Then if this is true,' I said, 'our belief about these matters must be this, that the nature of education is not really as some say it is; as you know, they say that there is not understanding

in the soul, but they put it in as if they were putting sight into
blind eyes.'
—Plato, *The Republic,* Book VII.

T he typical day begins with the yellow buses rolling up to the breeze-way in front of the school at about 8:10 A.M. By 8:25—only five minutes before the first class—some students have already filed into their first-period class and are sitting on the desks or standing around in groups talking to each other. Others stand around in the hall outside the classroom, talking to friends who are going to other classes. At 8:30, the shrill electronic pitch of the bell pierces throughout the school, and at that instant those still left in the halls and outside corridors scurry into their first-period class; those in the rooms proceed to their assigned seats. The halls are empty and quiet as doors to the classrooms are shut. It is time for the schoolday to begin "officially."

The first-period class starts as students listen to the notices for the day. Following these announcements, the class settles down and students begin the work which the teacher has planned for that period. The bell rings at the end of the fifty-five minute period and students flood into the halls to go to their second-period class. The second period proceeds much as the first with some variations occurring depending on the class, be it shop, PE, art or the typical "academic" courses such as English, math, social studies or science. In the middle of the day, students go to the cafeteria for one of three thirty-minute lunch periods during which time they eat lunch and talk to each other. More classes follow lunch until 3:00 P.M. when the students who had arrived on the buses pile back on to them for the return trip home while others take to the streets and roads and walk home. Various students remain for athletic practices, club meetings, detention, and other activities of a required or optional nature.

To the casual observer, the student day seems fairly typical and not unlike those schooldays they may have experienced five, ten, maybe thirty years ago. But beneath this rather pallid veneer is a distinctive way of life that students lead: this life reflects their confrontation and interpretation of a given environment and the meaning they draw from it.

WORK

As a result of structured interviews with students I was able to construct a composite map of what students said they did in school. When I asked this question of them a typical response was "we work."

I became intrigued with the notion of work for two reasons. First, in my two years within the school I was somewhat puzzled by the relative infrequency with which it was discussed by students among themselves. Quite simply, the subject of schoolwork rarely was entertained during student chatter, and I wondered why. Second, when it was mentioned, I noticed what appeared to be subtle distinctions between activities assigned to the notion of "work" and those that were discussed as "non-work." As I explored more fully how students saw work in the school, I began to understand their perspectives within the ongoing regularities of the classroom environment.

Table 1   Work and Non-work Activities

Work	Writing Having to write on paper Read so many pages in so much time Do assignments Things teachers make you do Films if there is a quiz or notes to take Piling it on Doing questions at the end of the chapter Graded assignments Doing the same thing over and over Memorizing Something you have to do alone Do exercises
Non-work	Experiments Listening Extra credit Art Science Going at your own speed Things where you can get away with doing other things Things assigned I never do Watching films Easy work $\begin{cases} \text{Just reading stuff you already know} \\ \text{Assignments with lots of time} \end{cases}$ Chorus

Toward the end of the seventh grade, I asked Don and Steve, Chris, Bill, and John and a number of other students what type of activities constituted work. From what they told me, the list reflected in Table 1 was generated.

The students, by their categorization, were telling me that work was something that characteristically came from teachers. Of course, not all things that teachers did in class constituted work, but then most of what came to be seen as work emanated from the teacher. This distinction became clear after I talked to three girls, Sharon, Susan and Anna, about work in school. I asked them what activities constituted work.

"Assignments."

"You know, sentences, stupid stuff."

"Yeah, I forgot to do mine today too," Sharon replied.

I asked them if work was the same in all classes or if it differed from class to class. "Like how about social studies, what kind of work do you do in social studies?"

"Write down different stuff about a story . . . watching a film."

"Is watching a film work?" I asked.

"It's boring, it's not work."

"Where does work come from?" I asked.

"Teachers," replied Anna.

I continued in a somewhat different vein. "But what if you write a story yourself; for example I noticed you were writing a story about your horse the other day in Creadley's class. Was that work?"

"Oh no," Anna replied emphatically. "That was extra credit. I was doing that for English class. You get extra credit on your grade for doing that."

Thus for these girls (and for most of the students to whom I talked) "work" or "doing work" did not depend so much on the type of activity being done as much as on whether or not the person in authority required it be done. Anna made this clear by emphasizing that writing things down about a story was considered work because it was *required* in Richards's class, but writing a story in English class was not envisioned as work because Anna herself had *initiated* the writing of the story. Without the imperative of the teacher standing over her telling her she had to do it, she saw what was essentially the same activity in a different light.

The notion of requirements—having to do something stated by the teacher—helps to distinguish analytically between what were considered "work" and "non-work" activities. In this respect, a film could be perceived as 'work,' or 'non-work,' depending upon whether the students needed to pay attention in order to fulfill the expectations of the teacher. Thus, a film might be considered work if students had to watch it to pass a test, but be considered non-work if they could ignore it.

Another criterion, already alluded to, that made work distasteful and which tended to be a definer of work was that it was something you did alone. The preponderance of activities listed under work were those where the students had to sit at their seats, pay attention to the lesson that the teacher had arranged for them, and do what was required by themselves. On the other hand, most of the activities classified as 'non-work' were those in which some semblance of social interaction could go on while the activity was being performed. Science and art were the two classes where students could usually do what was required of them and discuss personal subjects at the same time, and these two classes appeared most frequently on the "non-work" list; no other specific classes appeared with any regularity on the "work" list.

The perception of work as a required activity coming from someone in a position of authority and an activity the product of which had an exchange-value (usually by the submission of a paper indicating the satisfactory completion of the work) made sense in the world of the student at Harold Spencer. Work itself was something done not so much because of its intrinsic interest or value, but rather as it was commensurate with the student role that demanded students selling labor power (or the physical and mental capabilities of a person used through labor) in exchange for some symbolic reward. Such a role helps explain the location in Table 1 of such activities as "doing exercises," "memorizing," "doing the same thing over and over again," "doing questions at the end of the chapter" and similar activities listed under the rubric of work. These activities all were congruent with the position of the student as a recipient of knowledge—as one who not so much created knowledge as consumed it. Classrooms were dominated by the teacher. These mandatory activities were subsequently evaluated by the teacher and a grade assigned to them. Such activities were not "individualized" but were required of the entire class to be done at approximately the same time. Work then developed a negative connotation because work, rather than something emanating from within students themselves, was something that controlled them.

Students' views of my role further illustrate their over-all perspective on work. To them, I was not working most of the time I was in the school. "You get paid for this?" was a comment. I replied that I did, and their response was to ask who was crazy enough to pay someone to sit around in school all day with junior high students. But what made my role one of non-work was the students' perceptions of my liberties to come and go as I pleased and to decide for myself what needed attention. Since I was in the school almost every day of the first year, my infrequent absences were noticeable and many wondered how I could work and still "skip" from the location of my work—the school. The fact that I could choose which classes to attend, which lunch to go to, which students to hang around—all were conditions simply not connected with work. To the students, work meant having to do something, being regulated, the presence of tight parameters and the like. They had come to see work as the absence of control over the conditions of their own labor.

TEACHERS AND TEACHING

Parallel with students' perspective on work were the visions they carried with them on teachers and what teachers did. I should note here that, like the subject of work, characteristics of teachers were not frequently discussed either. As students filed from classes, they immediately began or continued their conversations relating to their personal interests with few comments on either how interesting or boring the class had been. Minimal discussion does not mean that students did not construct certain perspectives on teachers and the teaching process, for they obviously did. Yet these perspectives must be placed in context, for other activities were far more important and occupied a much more pre-eminent space in the student's cognitive framework than did any discussion of work or the teachers who parceled out the work.

Table 2 is an arrangement of the comments made regarding teachers throughout the year, gathered mostly by my being with the students when the subject was raised but also during formal interviews which I held with a number of students near the end of the seventh grade. Generally, students believed that teachers could be divided into two groups, those labeled "teachers with negative attributes" and "teachers with positive attributes." It is interesting to note the distinction that the students made between the two groups.

Two conditions characterized teachers with negative attributes. The first centered around *physical or personal characteristics* and included such characterizations as "bastards," "screwy," "weirdo," "fairies," "hard to get along with teachers," "fish," "those that think they're funny," "crabs," or "snappers." There was not uniform agreement on what every one of these terms meant as distinguished from the other, but it was obvious that certain ones were reserved for specific people. The term "bastard," for example, was usually reserved for teachers who carried on in ways that were seen as unfair or demeaning. Don and Steve, for example, thought Richards was a bastard because "he's always yelling, standing up there getting red in the face, making a fool out of himself." "Treating us like kids," was another of Richards's attributes.

Table 2 Kinds of Teachers

Teachers with negative attributes	Strict Those with favorites Those that hate the whole class Bastards Screwy Fairies Femmies Busters Mean Those who don't communicate Worse teachers Narcs Hard to get along with teachers Fish Pick n'flicks Those that think they're funny Those that do the same thing over and over Slave drivers Crabs Snappers
Teachers with positive attributes	Nice { They respect us / They trust us / They listen to us Those that let you chew gum Neat teachers Cool teachers

Terms like "screwy," "weirdo," "fairies," "fish," "pick and flick" related to personal habits such as voice inflections, mannerisms of walking and other movements, and dress. Discussions frequently occurred over whether Mr. Bruce was "queer" simply because he had a high voice, dressed fairly well, and bounced a little while he walked. A few students even debated the same issue about Mr. Charles simply because he called people "honey" or "sweetheart," and because often he put his arm on a student's shoulders while helping him with a math problem.

Personal appearance, too, often served as a basis for student's discriminations among teachers. Mrs. Ansel was considered "weird" because she wore what students considered to be mismatched clothing. Students usually picked on Mr. Von Hoffman because of his short haircut, a butch cut from the 1950s. Mr. Franks was considered "screwy" because he wore old ties and was reputed to pick the wax out of his ears and flick it across the room while talking, an act that I never personally observed although Steve and others swore a hunk of wax once landed on their science book. Mr. Hackett, who often had bloodshot eyes, was suspected of being a heavy drinker; the students never placed much credence in the fact that he wore contact lenses and held down a part-time job in the evenings, a combination that, I imagined, would give anyone bloodshot eyes.

The *specific actions* of teachers in the classroom was a second criterion used to assign negative attributes to teachers. Such attributes as "strictness," "those with favorites," "those that hate the whole class," "those that think they're funny," "those that do the same things over and over," and "slave drivers" were included. These conditions often overlapped and many were assigned to the same teacher as an over-all negative indictment.

Negative attributes connected with specific actions usually were connected with the notion of "teachers who don't communicate." Chris decided this during a discussion about Von Hoffman. "I don't think he communicates with kids. Like he's giving a spelling test and the word is supposed to be 'entered,' like 'He entered the door quickly.' He pronounced it 'innard' so I said out loud, 'You mean entered.' He just says, 'Look buddy, you have a detention slip.' He's one of the most self-conscious persons I have ever met, he's always worried about another person looking at him . . . you see him talking to himself a lot and doing things like pointing and hitting his fist and maybe frowning and hitting the table and you think 'What's going through that guy's mind?'"

The characterization of "hard to get along with teachers' was another category that included a variety of descriptors and that reflected the overall flexibility of the teacher in the school. I once asked Chris and John what a hard-to-get-along-with teacher was.

"They're the ones who have been at Harold Spencer since the first year . . . they've seen year after year of kids come through here and I think it just gives them the impression when a new group of students comes in that 'Oh man, here comes another group of those brats,' and they think that they have to push their thumb on someone completely and if they let half their thumb off the class is going to go wild." To many students, these teachers were inflexible, and students had to meet them on their terms, which meant "doing the same thing over and over." Barry and John, both good students, commented that their English teacher was hard to get along with because they did the same thing in class over and over again: "prepositional phrases, prepositional phrases, just do it over everyday, do assignments three and four times, and it gets so boring, you just sit there. Everyday I hate to go to that class because I know we are going to do the same things again."

Hard-to-get-along-with teachers, in other words, were like bad bosses—they extracted the most from the students and viewed work as an exchange process that operated on the basis of the controllers of production having authority over the means of production.

To understand characteristics about teachers that students did not like is also to understand the characteristics of the teachers they viewed positively. I found surprisingly little disagreement among the students when they specified what it was about a teacher that made them, in their terms, "nice," "neat," or "cool." John said that most of the kids thought Mr. Creadley was the best teacher in the school. "He just says, 'Okay, we have some work to do, let's do it and keep the talking down.' He gives you work and he expects you to have it done. It's not that it's that hard, he just gives you a little incentive."

Chris added, "He's the only teacher I know who gives you an opportunity to go ahead and do other things. Like with Mr. Franks, he just wants you to answer the questions and then you sit around waiting for everyone else to finish but Mr. Creadley encourages you to do things other than just answer the questions."

While John and Chris mentioned some ways in which Creadley ran his class, it was Creadley's style and personality rather than what they learned in class that appealed most to them. Most of the other students like him because he treated the students "fairly," was not "uptight," did not "yell a lot," and so on. When most students talked about 'cool' or 'neat' teachers, these seemed to be the attributes to which they were referring.

Also common were comments such as "they respect us," or "they listen to us." In their more reflective moments, many of the students could tell what they saw in teachers they valued positively, and usually had little to do with how or what they taught, but rather how they interacted with the students as people. One boy who spent considerable time in the office for minor discipline problems told me he thought the vice-principal, Mr Pall, was really quite fair and that "at least he usually listens to you." He could not speak as highly of his other teachers for, as he saw them, "they don't look at you as an individual, they look at you as a group like they want you to be. In fact a lotta times the only time a teacher remembers your name is if you're always getting into trouble or if you're especially good, but if you're just sort of average they don't notice you."

Most teachers fell between what students perceived to be completely positive and negative attributes when they did talk about teachers, but I never felt that this signified a real resentment against most of the teachers.

What teachers did in the school appeared, at least on the surface, in conflict with what the students thought was best or desirable, as shown in Table 3, wherein I have presented the students' belief about what the teachers did. This list dramatizes that students saw themselves as passive and the adults as the active member of the relationship. In the area of what I have called "interaction with students" students portrayed a picture of themselves as being less than or below adults. Students saw many adults in terms of authority hierarchies where the adults interacted with students on the basis of the authority vested in their office. Thus, when teachers interacted with students, the students perceived they were underestimated and treated "like third-graders" through a simplification of work and assignments. Students also thought they were talked down to and that little allowance was made for their input as individuals.

The tendency of the teachers to give out work and the students to do it is clear in Table 3. Teachers "pile it [work] on" and then turn around and "write," "sit at their desk," "correct papers," and "grade us." If there were problems with the class, teachers "scream," "watch people," and "be strict." From the student point of view, there was little else involved in what teachers did in the classroom other than that represented in this simple "factory model" of learning, that is, the teachers pouring in the facts and the students pouring them back in the form of papers and tests. Students had little, if any, conception of teachers planning lessons, debating alternatives of what to teach, agonizing over grading, the treatment of a student, wondering if their teaching had an effect, or anything like that. The student picture of teachers provided little room for emotion, with the exception of that associated with student violation of school standards. The teacher's world, in the student's eyes, was straightforward and linear, hardly complex at all.

Table 3 Things Teachers Do

Interaction with students	Simplify things like third-graders Don't treat us as individuals Don't listen to us Not congratulate you Embarrass us Take for granted you know what to do Try to build a reputation with students Sit around and expect you to learn by yourself
Duties	Run projector Sit Talk ⎰ to us ⎱ to each other Pile it on Read papers Correct papers Sit at desk Give work Tap pencils Grade us Write Read stories Give detention
Discipline	Catch people smoking Study people's jaws Scream Watch people Argue Tell us to stop talking Eye you Be strict Stare at the girls Send us to the office Cuss Nag Give hacks Give sentences Throw people out
Actions	Be self-conscious Act like commandos Try to be cool ⎰ Dumb jokes to us ⎱ Dirty jokes to each other ⎱ Don't take things seriously.

Such viewpoints on teachers—their characteristics and what they do, confirms the presence of a separate student culture—one poised at odds with the adult culture in the school. First, students saw their academic activities consisting mostly of "work" and it was the teacher who so defined their task, thereby providing students with little formal control over their own labor. Second, upon examining student-held beliefs about teachers, we see that teachers were viewed negatively owing to the extent to which they maintained tight control over student activities in the classroom; teachers who were viewed more positively were those who provided some greater degree of self-determination, although this did not necessarily mean that these teachers might be less demanding. Finally, students' beliefs about what teachers "did" was remarkably congruous to their own conception of what they, as students, did. Accordingly, the student-generated belief system held that the teacher's job consisted mostly of handing out work and enforcing the standards by which work was done. Most social interaction with students by teachers existed from a position of authority, making even sharper the divisions between the adult and student way of understanding the junior high school.

SUGGESTIONS FOR DISCUSSION

1. Reread Table 1. Explain the distinction between "work" and "non-work" activities. What criteria does Everhart use to make this distinction? Does his table correspond to the way students in the junior high or high school you attended thought of "work" and "non-work"?
2. Reread Table 2. Notice the terms that students use to characterize various teachers. How did students in the junior high or high school you attended talk about their teachers? What criteria did students use to ascribe negative and positive attributes to teachers? What do these criteria reveal about the belief systems of students?
3. Both Sizer and Everhart use a kind of industrial language to describe what goes on in school. Sizer talks about "taking subjects" in a "systematized, conveyor-belt way," and Everhart describes "simple 'factory model' of learning." To what extent is this kind of language helpful to describe schooling? What, if anything, does it leave out? Do you agree with Everhart that schooling demands that students "sell labor power (or the physical and mental capabilities of a person used through labor) in exchange for some symbolic reward"?

SUGGESTIONS FOR WRITING

1. In the beginning of this selection, Everhart suggests that "beneath [the] veneer" of the typical school day is a "distinctive way of life that students lead." Later in the selection, Everhart expands on this statement when he says that there is a "separate student culture—one poised at odds with the adult culture in school." Write an essay that explores this statement in light of your own experience in high school (or college, if you wish). Is there a "separate student culture," and if so, is it "at odds with adult culture"? Use the essay to explain your response.
2. Everhart draws a distinction between activities that are *required* by teachers and those that are *initiated* by students. Think of a particularly important learning experience you have had in school. To what extent was the activity required and controlled by a teacher? To what extent did you initiate it or control its development yourself? Write an essay that explores why and how the learning took place. Don't limit yourself to just describing what happened and what you learned. Take into account who controlled the learning experience and how the matter of control affected the experience. You might end your essay by discussing what the experience reveals about you as a student and a learner.
3. Write an essay about a teacher you have had in the past. The teacher might be a particularly effective or inspiring one or a particularly ineffective and uninspiring one. The point of this assignment, however, is not just to express your personal likes and dislikes about teachers. Use the essay to develop your own position about what constitutes good teaching and how it affects students.

Mike Rose

CROSSING BOUNDARIES

Mike Rose is a professor of education at UCLA. He has worked for the past twenty years teaching and tutoring children and adults from what he calls America's "educational underclass"—working-class children, poorly educated Vietnam vets, underprepared college students, adults in basic literacy programs. We have taken the following selection from the chapter "Crossing Boundaries" in Rose's award-winning book, *Lives on the Boundary* (1989). This book is an intensely personal account of Rose's own life growing up in a Los Angeles ghetto and his struggles as an educator to make schooling more accessible to children and adults labeled "remedial," "illiterate," and "intellectually deficient." As the following selection indicates, throughout *Lives on the Boundary* Rose is especially interested in the "politics and sociology of school failure."

Suggestion for Reading

- You will notice that the following selection is separated into three parts. To help you think about how these parts combine to form a whole (or whether they do) underline and annotate as you read, noting the focus of each section and how it provides a commentary on the other sections.

◆

> I myself I thank God for the dream to come back to school
> and to be able to seek the dream I want, because I know this
> time I will try and make my dream come true.

E ach semester the staff of the Bay Area literacy program we're about to visit collects samples of their students' writing and makes books for them. You can find an assortment on an old bookshelf by the coordinator's desk. The booklets are simple: mimeographed, faint blue stencil, stapled, dog-eared. There are uneven drawings on the thin paper covers: a bicycle leaning against a tree, the Golden Gate Bridge, an Aubrey Beardsley sketch. The stories are about growing up, raising children, returning—sadly or with anticipation—to hometowns, to Chicago or St. Louis or to a sweep of rural communities in the South. Many of the stories are about work: looking for work, losing work, wanting better work. And many more are about coming back to school. Coming back to school. Some of these writers haven't been in a classroom in thirty years.

The stories reveal quite a range. Many are no longer than a paragraph, their sentences simple and repetitive, tenuously linked by *and* and *then* and *anyway*. There are lots of grammar and spelling errors and problems with sentence boundaries—in a few essays, periods come where commas should be or where no punctuation is needed at all:

"It was hard for me to stay in school because I was allway sick. and that was verry hard for me." Or, "I sound better. now that my boys are grown." Papers of this quality are written, for the most part, by newcomers, people at the end of their first semester. But other papers—quite a few, actually—are competent. They tend to come from those who have received a year or more of instruction. There are still problems with grammar and sentence fragments and with spelling, since the writers are using a wider, more ambitious vocabulary. Problems like these take longer to clear up, but the writers are getting more adept at rendering their experience in print, at developing a narrative, at framing an illustration, at turning a phrase in written language:

> The kitchen floor was missing some of its tiles and had not been kissed with water and soap for a long time.

> The [teacher] looked for a moment, and then said, "All the students wishing to be accounted for, please be seated."

> A minute went by, then a tough looking Mexican boy got up, and walked to the teacher with a knife in his hand. When he got to the desk he said, "I'm here teacher! My name is Robert Gomez." With that he put the knife away, and walked over and found a seat.

> Back in the jaws of dispair, pain, and the ugly scars of the defeated parents he loved. Those jaws he had struggled free of when he had moved out and away when he was eighteen years old.
> . . . the wind was howling, angry, whirling.

A few new students also created such moments, indicators of what they'll be able to do as they become more fluent writers, as they develop some control over and confidence in establishing themselves on paper:

> [I used to have] light, really light Brown eyes, like Grasshopper eyes. which is what some peoples used to call me. Grasshopper, or Grasshopper eyes. . . . I decided one Day to catch a Grasshopper. and look at its eye to be sure of the color.

> It was early in the morning just before dawn. Big Red, the sun hasen't showed its face in the heaven. The sky had that midnight blue look. The stars losing their shine.

There are about eight or ten of these stapled collections, a hundred and fifty or so essays. Five years' worth. An archive scattered across an old bookcase. There's a folding chair close by. I've been sitting in it for some time now, reading one book, then another, story after story. Losing track. Drifting in and out of lives. Wondering about grasshopper eyes, about segregated schools, wanting to know more about this journey to the West looking for work. Slowly something has been shifting in my perception: the errors—the weird commas and missing letters, the fragments and irregular punctuation—they are ceasing to be slips of the hand and brain. They are becoming part of the stories themselves. They are the only fitting way, it seems, to render dislocation—

shacks and field labor and children lost to the inner city—to talk about parents you long for, jobs you can't pin down. Poverty has generated its own damaged script, scars manifest in the spelling of a word.

This is the prose of America's underclass. The writers are those who got lost in our schools, who could not escape neighborhoods that narrowed their possibilities, who could not enter the job market in any ascendent way. They are locked into unskilled and semiskilled jobs, live in places that threaten their children, suffer from disorders and handicaps they don't have the money to treat. Some have been unemployed for a long time. But for all that, they remain hopeful, have somehow held onto a deep faith in education. They have come back to school. Ruby, the woman who wrote the passage that opens this section, walks unsteadily to the teacher's desk—the arthritis in her hip goes unchecked—with a paper in her hand. She looks over her shoulder to her friend, Alice: "I ain't givin' up the ship this time," she says and winks, "though, Lord, I might drown with it." The class laughs. They understand.

It is very iffy thing, this schooling. But the participants put a lot of stock in it. They believe school will help them, and they are very specific about what they want: a high school equivalency, or the ability to earn seven dollars an hour. One wants to move from being a nurse's aide to a licensed vocational nurse, another needs to read and write and compute adequately enough to be self-employed as a car painter and body man. They remind you of how fundamentally important it is—not just to your pocket but to your soul as well—to earn a decent wage, to have a steady job, to be just a little bit in control of your economic life. The goals are specific, modest, but they mean a tremendous amount for the assurance they give to these people that they are still somebody, that they can exercise control. Thus it is that talk of school and a new job brings forth such expansive language, as soaring as any humanist's testament to the glory of the word: "I thank God to be able to seek the dream I want. . . ." For Ruby and her classmates the dream deferred neither dried up like a raisin in the sun, nor has it exploded. It has emerged again—for it is so basic—and it centers on schooling. "I admire and respect knowledge and thoes that have it are well blessed," writes another student. "My classmates are a swell group because they too have a dream and they too are seeking knowledge and I love them for that."

Sitting in the classroom with Ruby, Alice, and the rest, you think, at times, that you're at a revival meeting. There is so much testifying. Everybody talks and writes about dreams and goals and "doing better for myself." This is powerful, edifying—but something about it, its insistence perhaps, is a little bit discordant. The exuberance becomes jittery, an almost counterphobic boosting and supporting. It is no surprise, then, that it alternates with despair. In their hearts, Ruby and her classmates know how tenuous this is, how many times they've failed before. Somebody says something about falling down. Sally says, "I've felt that too. Not falling down on my legs or knees, but falling down within me." No wonder they sermonize and embrace. It's not just a few bucks more a week that's at stake; literacy, here, is intimately connected with respect, with a sense that they are not beaten, the mastery of print revealing the deepest impulse to survive.

• • •

When they entered the program, Ruby and Alice and Sally and all the rest were given several tests, one of which was a traditional reading inventory. The test had a section on comprehension—relatively brief passages followed by multiple-choice questions—and a series of sections that tested particular reading skills: vocabulary, syllabication, phonics, prefixes and roots. The level of the instrument was pretty sophisticated, and the skills it tested are the kind you develop in school: answering multiple-choice questions, working out syllable breaks, knowing Greek and Latin roots, all that. What was interesting about this group of test takers was that— though a few were barely literate—many could read and write well enough to get along, and, in some cases, to help those in their communities who were less skilled. They could read, with fair comprehension, simple news articles, could pay bills, follow up on sales and coupons, deal with school forms for their kids, and help illiterate neighbors in their interactions with the government. Their skills were pretty low-level and limited profoundly the kinds of things they could read or write, but they lived and functioned amid print. The sad thing is that we don't really have tests of such naturally occurring competence. The tests we do have, like the one Ruby and the others took, focus on components of reading ability tested in isolation (phonetic discrimination, for example) or on those skills that are school-oriented, like reading a passage on an unfamiliar topic unrelated to immediate needs: the mating habits of the dolphin, the Mayan pyramids. Students then answer questions on these sorts of passages by choosing one of four or five possible answers, some of which may be purposely misleading.

To nobody's surprise, Ruby and her classmates performed miserably. The tasks of the classroom were as unfamiliar as could be. There is a good deal of criticism of these sorts of reading tests, but one thing that is clear is that they reveal how well people can perform certain kinds of school activities. The activities themselves may be of questionable value, but they are interwoven with instruction and assessment, and entrance to many jobs is determined by them. Because of their centrality, then, I wanted to get some sense of how the students went about taking the tests. What happened as they tried to meet the test's demands? How was it that they failed?

My method was simple. I chose four students and had each of them take sections of the test again, asking them questions as they did so, encouraging them to talk as they tried to figure out an item.

The first thing that emerged was the complete foreignness of the task. A sample item in the prefixes and roots section (called Word Parts) presented the word "unhappy," and asked the testtaker to select one of four other words "which gives the meaning of the underlined part of the first word." The choices were *very, glad, sad, not.* Though the person giving the test had read through the instructions with the class, many still could not understand, and if they chose an answer at all, most likely chose *sad,* a synonym for the whole word *unhappy.*

Nowhere in their daily reading are these students required to focus on parts of words in this way. The multiple-choice format is also unfamiliar—it is not part of day-to-day literacy—so the task as well as the format is new, odd. I explained the directions again—read them slowly, emphasized the sample item—but still, three of the four students continued to fall into the test maker's trap of choosing synonyms for the target word rather than zeroing in on the part of the word in question. Such behavior is common among those who fail in our schools, and it has led some commentators to posit that students like these are cognitively and linguistically deficient in some fundamental way: They process language differently, or reason differently from those who succeed in school, or the dialect they speak in some basic way interferes with their processing of Standard Written English.

Certainly in such a group—because of malnourishment, trauma, poor health care, environmental toxins—you'll find people with neurolinguistic problems or with medical difficulties that can affect perception and concentration. And this group—ranging in age from nineteen to the mid-fifties—has a wide array of medical complications: diabetes, head injury, hypertension, asthma, retinal deterioration, and the unusual sleep disorder called narcolepsy. It would be naive to deny the effect of all this on reading and writing. But as you sit alongside these students and listen to them work through a task, it is not damage that most strikes you. Even when they're misunderstanding the test and selecting wrong answers, their reasoning is not distorted and pathological. Here is Millie, whose test scores placed her close to the class average—and average here would be very low just about anywhere else.

Millie is given the word "kilometer" and the following list of possible answers:

a. thousand

b. hundred

c. distance

d. speed

She responds to the whole word—*kilometer*—partially because she still does not understand how the test works, but also, I think, because the word is familiar to her. She offers *speed* as the correct answer because: "I see it on the signs when I be drivin'." She starts to say something else, but stops abruptly. "Whoa, it don't have to be 'speed'—it could be 'distance.'"

"It could be 'distance,' couldn't it?" I say.

"Yes, it could be one or the other."

"Okay."

"And then again," she says reflectively, "it could be a number."

Millie tapped her knowledge of the world—she had seen *kilometer* on road signs—to offer a quick response: *speed*. But she saw just as quickly that her knowledge could logically support another answer (*distance*), and, a few moments later, saw that what she knew could *also* support a third answer, one related to number. What she lacked was specific knowledge of the Greek prefix *kilo*, but she wasn't short on reasoning ability. In fact, reading tests like the one Millie took are constructed in such a way as to trick you into relying on commonsense reasoning and world knowledge—and thereby choosing a *wrong* answer. Take, for example, this item:

Cardiogram

a. heart

b. abnormal

c. distance

d. record

Millie, and many others in the class, chose *heart*. To sidestep that answer, you need to know something about the use of *gram* in other such words (versus its use as a metric weight), but you need to know, as well, how these tests work.

After Millie completed five or six items, I had her go back over them, talking through her answers with her. One item that had originally given her trouble was "extraordinary": a)"beyond"; b) "acute"; c) "regular"; d) "imagined." She had been a little rattled when answering this one. While reading the four possible answers, she stumbled on "imagined": "I . . . im . . . "; then, tentatively, "imaged"; a pause again, then "imagine," and, quickly, "I don't know that word."

I pronounce it.

She looks up at me, a little disgusted: "I said it, didn't I?"

"You did say it."

"I was scared of it."

Her first time through, Millie had chosen *regular,* the wrong answer—apparently locking onto *ordinary* rather than the underlined prefix *extra*—doing just the opposite of what she was supposed to do. It was telling, I thought, that Millie and two or three others talked about words scaring them.

When we came back to "extraordinary" during our review, I decided on strategy. "Let's try something," I said. "These tests are set up to trick you, so let's try a trick ourselves." I take a pencil and do something the publishers of the test tell you not to do: I mark up the test booklet. I slowly begin to circle the prefix *extra,* saying, "This is the part of the word we're concerned with, right?" As soon as I finish she smiles and says "beyond," the right answer.

"Did you see what happened there?" I said. "As soon as I circled the part of the word, you saw what it meant."

"I see it," she says. "I don't be thinking about what I'm doing."

I tell her to try what I did, to circle the part of the word in question, to remember that trick, for with tests like this, we need a set of tricks of our own.

"You saw it yourself," I said.

"Sure did. It was right there in front of me—'cause the rest of them don't even go with 'extra.'"

I had been conducting this interview with Millie in between her classes, and our time was running out. I explained that we'd pick this up again, and I turned away, checking the wall clock, reaching to turn off the tape recorder. Millie was still looking at the test booklet.

"What is this word right here?" she asked. She had gone ahead to the other, more difficult, page of the booklet and was pointing to "egocentric."

I take my finger off the recorder's STOP button. "Let's circle it," I say. "What's that word? Say it."

"Ego."

"What's that mean?"

"Ego. Oh my." She scans the four options—*self, head, mind, kind*—and says "self."

"Excellent!"

"You know, when I said 'ego,' I tried to put it in a sentence: 'My ego,' I say. That's *me*."

I ask her if she wants to look at one more. She goes back to "cardio<u>gram</u>," which she gets right this time. Then to "<u>therm</u>ometer," which she also gets right. And "<u>bi</u>focal," which she gets right without using her pencil to mark the prefix. Once Millie saw and understood what the test required of her, she could rely on her world knowledge to help her reason out some answers. Cognitive psychologists talk about task representation, the way a particular problem is depicted or reproduced in the mind. Something shifted in Millie's conception of her task, and it had a powerful effect on her performance.

• • •

It was common for nineteenth-century American educators to see their mission with the immigrant and native-born urban poor as a fundamentally moral one. Historian Michael Katz quotes from the Boston school committee's description of social and spiritual acculturation:

> . . . taking children at random from a great city, undisciplined, uninstructed, often with inveterate forwardness and obstinacy, and with the inherited stupidity of centuries of ignorant ancestors; forming them from animals into intellectual beings, and . . . from intellectual beings into spiritual beings; giving to many their first appreciation of what is wise, what is true, what is lovely and what is pure.

In our time, educators view the effects of poverty and cultural dislocation in more enlightened ways; though that moralistic strain still exists, the thrust of their concern has shifted from the spiritual to the more earthly realm of language and cognition. Yet what remains is the disturbing tendency to perceive the poor as *different* in some basic way from the middle and upper classes—the difference now being located in the nature of the way they think and use language. A number of studies and speculations over the past twenty-five years has suggested that the poor are intellectually or linguistically deficient or, at the least, different: They lack a logical language or reason in ways that limit intellectual achievement or, somehow, process information dysfunctionally. If we could somehow get down to the very basic loops and contours of their mental function, we would find that theirs are different from ours. There's a huge literature on all this and, originating with critics like linguist William Labov, a damning counterliterature. This is not the place to review that work, but it would be valuable to consider Millie against the general outlines of the issue.

Imagine her in a typical classroom testing situation. More dramatically, imagine her in some university laboratory being studied by one or two researchers—middle class and probably white. Millie is a strong woman with a tough front, but these would most likely be uncomfortable situations for her. And if she were anxious, her performance would be disrupted: as it was when she didn't identify *imagined*—a word she pronounced and knew—because she was "scared of it." Add to this the fact that she is very much adrift when it comes to school-based tests: She simply doesn't know how to do them. What would be particularly damning for her would be the fact that, even with repeated instruction and illustration, she failed to catch on to the way the test worked.

You can see how an observer would think her unable to shift out of (inadequate) performance, unable to understand simple instructions and carry them out. Deficient or different in some basic way: nonlogical, nonrational, unable to think analytically. It would be from observations like this that a theory of fundamental cognitive deficiency or difference would emerge.

We seem to have a need as a society to explain poor performance by reaching deep into the basic stuff of those designated as other: into their souls, or into the deep recesses of their minds, or into the very ligature of their language. It seems harder for us to keep focus on the politics and sociology of intellectual failure, to keep before our eyes the negative power of the unfamiliar, the way information poverty constrains performance, the effect of despair on cognition.

"I was so busy looking for 'psychopathology,'. . . " says Robert Coles of his early investigations of childhood morality, "that I brushed aside the most startling incidents, the most instructive examples of ethical alertness in the young people I was getting to know." How much we don't see when we look only for deficiency, when we tally up all that people can't do. Many of the students in this book display the gradual or abrupt emergence of an intellectual acuity or literate capacity that just wasn't thought to be there. This is not to deny that awful limits still exist for those like Millie: so much knowledge and so many procedures never learned; such a long, cumbersome history of relative failure. But this must not obscure the equally important fact that if you set up the right conditions, try as best you can to cross class and cultural boundaries, figure out what's needed to encourage performance, that if you watch and listen, again and again there will emerge evidence of ability that escapes those who dwell on differences.

Ironically, it's often the reports themselves of our educational inadequacies— the position papers and media alarms on illiteracy in America—that help blind us to cognitive and linguistic possibility. Their rhetorical thrust and their metaphor conjure up disease or decay or economic and military defeat: A malignancy has run wild, an evil power is consuming us from within. (And here reemerges that nineteenth-century moral terror.) It takes such declamation to turn the moneyed wheels of government, to catch public attention and entice the givers of grants, but there's a dark side to this political reality. The character of the alarms and, too often, the character of the responses spark in us the urge to punish, to extirpate, to return to a precancerous golden age rather than build on the rich capacity that already exists. The reports urge responses that reduce literate possibility and constrain growth, that focus on pathology rather than on possibility. Philosophy, said Aristotle, begins in wonder. So does education.

SUGGESTIONS FOR DISCUSSION

1. What motivates students like Ruby, Alice, Sally, and Millie to return to school? What assumptions do they seem to make about the effects of education? Are these assumptions realistic? How do they compare to the assumptions you and your classmates make about the effects of education? Explain what you see as differences and similarities.

2. How does Rose explain poor performance and failure in school? Don't settle for generalizations such as "poverty and cultural dislocation." Look closely at how Rose analyzes Millie's experience with questions on a reading comprehension test. Do you find Rose's explanations persuasive? What do these explanations imply about the nature and function of schooling in America?

3. Rose says that "nineteenth-century American educators" looked at their "missions" as a "fundamentally moral one." Later he suggests that such a "moralistic strain still exists" in the way Americans think about education and that it can "spark in us the urge to punish, to extirpate, to return to a precancerous golden age." What is the nature of the "moral terror" Rose talks about? Do you agree with him? Draw upon your experience in school to respond to this question.

SUGGESTIONS FOR WRITING

1. Write an essay that explains what Mike Rose sees as the causes of failure in school. Compare his explanation to your own views on what causes students to fail. Draw on your own experience and what you have observed.

2. Most students have been "punished" at some point or another during their schooling. Write an essay that tells the story of a time when you (or someone you know) were "punished" in school. What did you do? Did you break a rule? Was the rule fair? Was the "punishment" just or unjust? Your story should tell about what happened and how you felt about it. Then use the story to reflect on what the incident reveals about life in school and how students encounter and deal with the "rules" of schooling.

3. Testing is intimately connected to the reward system in American education. Students take tests in elementary school, high school, and college in order to get grades. High school students take the SATs to get into college. Some colleges and universities give incoming students placement tests to assign them to classes in composition, mathematics, and foreign languages. By this point in your education, you have probably been tested frequently. Write an essay that explores the effects of testing on you as a student, a learner, and a person. Use this essay as an occasion to think about your responses to being tested. But also use it to generalize about the kinds of knowledge and skills testing measures and rewards. What does testing reveal about the reward system in American education—in particular about who and what kinds of performances get rewarded?

Myra and David Sadker

SEXISM IN THE SCHOOLROOM

Myra and David Sadker are professors of education at American University. "Sexism in the Schoolroom" was published in *Psychology Today* (March 1985). In this article as well as in their recent book-length study, *Failing at*

Fairness: How America's Schools Cheat Girls (1993), the Sadkers report their own and others' research on how patterns of classroom communication work to the disadvantage of female students. As the Sadkers note, despite the assumption that classroom sexism disappeared in the 1970s, teachers still continue to treat and respond to male students differently from the way they treat and respond to female students, largely in subtle and unconscious ways. As you will see, the Sadkers raise important questions about how classroom life determines success and failure in school.

Suggestion for Reading

• As you read, notice how the Sadkers have integrated research findings into their article. To help you see how the Sadkers develop their overall argument, use underlining and annotating to distinguish passages that report research findings from passages that present the conclusions the Sadkers draw from this research.

———————————◆———————————

I f a boy calls out in class, he gets teacher attention, especially intellectual attention. If a girl calls out in class, she is told to raise her hand before speaking. Teachers praise boys more than girls, give boys more academic help and are more likely to accept boys' comments during classroom discussions. These are only a few examples of how teachers favor boys. Through this advantage boys increase their chances for better education and possibly higher pay and quicker promotions. Although many believe that classroom sexism disappeared in the early '70s, it hasn't.

Education is not a spectator sport. Numerous researchers, most recently John Goodlad, former dean of education at the University of California at Los Angeles and author of *A Place Called School,* have shown that when students participate in classroom discussion they hold more positive attitudes toward school, and that positive attitudes enhance learning. It is no coincidence that girls are more passive in the classroom and score lower than boys on SAT's.

Most teachers claim that girls participate and are called on in class as often as boys. But a three-year study we recently completed found that this is not true; vocally, boys clearly dominate the classroom. When we showed teachers and administrators a film of a classroom discussion and asked who was talking more, the teachers overwhelmingly said the girls were. But in reality, the boys in the film were outtalking the girls at a ratio of three to one. Even educators who are active in feminist issues were unable to spot the sex bias until they counted and coded who was talking and who was just watching. Stereotypes of garrulous and gossipy women are so strong that teachers fail to see this communications gender gap even when it is right before their eyes.

Field researchers in our study observed students in more than a hundred fourth-, sixth- and eighth-grade classes in four states and the District of Columbia. The teachers and students were male and female, black and white, from urban, suburban and rural communities. Half of the classrooms covered language arts and English—subjects in which girls traditionally have excelled; the other half covered math and science—traditionally male domains.

We found that at all grade levels, in all communities and in all subject areas, boys dominated classroom communication. They participated in more interactions than girls did and their participation became greater as the year went on.

Our research contradicted the traditional assumption that girls dominate classroom discussion in reading while boys are dominant in math. We found that whether the subject was language arts and English or math and science, boys got more than their fair share of teacher attention.

Some critics claim that if teachers talk more to male students, it is simply because boys are more assertive in grabbing their attention—a classic case of the squeaky wheel getting the educational oil. In fact, our research shows that boys are more assertive in the classroom. While girls sit patiently with their hands raised, boys literally grab teacher attention. They are eight times more likely than girls to call out answers. However, male assertiveness is not the whole answer.

Teachers behave differently, depending on whether boys or girls call out answers during discussions. When boys call out comments without raising their hands, teachers accept their answers. However, when girls call out, teachers reprimand this "inappropriate" behavior with messages such as, "In this class we don't shout out answers, we raise our hands." The message is subtle but powerful: Boys should be academically assertive and grab teacher attention; girls should act like ladies and keep quiet.

Teachers in our study revealed an interaction pattern that we called a "mind sex." After calling on a student, they tended to keep calling on students of the same sex. While this pattern applied to both sexes, it was far more pronounced among boys and allowed them more than their fair share of airtime.

It may be that when teachers call on someone, they continue thinking of that sex. Another explanation may be found in the seating patterns of elementary, secondary and even postsecondary classrooms. In approximately half of the classrooms in our study, male and female students sat in separate parts of the room. Sometimes the teacher created this segregation, but more often, the students segregated themselves. A teacher's tendency to interact with same-sex students may be a simple matter of where each sex sits. For example, a teacher calls on a female student, looks around the same area and then continues questioning the students around this girl, all of whom are female. When the teacher refocuses to a section of the classroom where boys are seated, boys receive the series of questions. And because boys are more assertive, the teacher may interact with their section longer.

Girls are often shortchanged in quality as well as in quantity of teacher attention. In 1975 psychologists Lisa Serbin and K. Daniel O'Leary, then at the State University of New York at Stony Brook, studied classroom interaction at the preschool level and found that teachers gave boys more attention, praised them more often and were at least twice as likely to have extended conversations with them. Serbin and O'Leary also found that teachers were twice as likely to give male students detailed instructions on how to do things for themselves. With female students, teachers were more likely to do it for them instead. The result was that boys learned to become independent, girls learned to become dependent.

Instructors at the other end of the educational spectrum also exhibit this same "let me do it for you" behavior toward female students. Constantina Safilios-Rothschild, a sociologist with the Population Council in New York, studied sex desegregation at the Coast Guard Academy and found that the instructors were giving detailed instructions on how to accomplish tasks to male students, but were doing the jobs and operating the equipment for the female students.

Years of experience have shown that the best way to learn something is to do it yourself; classroom chivalry is not only misplaced, it is detrimental. It is also important to give students specific and direct feedback about the quality of their work and answers. During classroom discussion, teachers in our study reacted to boys' answers with dynamic, precise and effective responses, while they often gave girls bland and diffuse reactions.

Teachers' reactions were classified in four categories: praise ("Good answer"); criticism ("That answer is wrong"); help and remediation ("Try again—but check your long division"); or acceptance without any evaluation or assistance ("OK" "Uh-huh").

Despite caricatures of school as a harsh and punitive place, fewer than 5 percent of the teachers' reactions were criticisms, even of the mildest sort. But praise didn't happen often either, it made up slightly more than 10 percent of teachers' reactions. More than 50 percent of teachers' responses fell into the "OK" category.

Teachers distributed these four reactions differently among boys than among girls. Here are some of the typical patterns.

Teacher: "What's the capital of Maryland? Joel?"

Joel: "Baltimore."

Teacher: "What's the largest city in Maryland, Joel?"

Joel: "Baltimore."

Teacher: "That's good. But Baltimore isn't the capital. The capital is also the location of the U.S. Naval Academy. Joel, do you want to try again?"

Joel: "Annapolis."

Teacher: "Excellent. Anne, what's the capital of Maine?"

Anne: "Portland."

Teacher: "Judy, do you want to try?"

Judy: "Augusta."

Teacher: "OK."

In this snapshot of a classroom discussion, Joel was told when his answer was wrong (criticism); was helped to discover the correct answer (remediation); and was praised when he offered the correct response. When Anne was wrong, the teacher, rather than staying with her, moved to Judy, who received only simple acceptance for her correct answer. Joel received the more specific teacher reaction and benefited from a longer, more precise and intense educational interaction.

Too often, girls remain in the dark about the quality of their answers. Teachers rarely tell them if their answers are excellent, need to be improved or are just plain wrong. Unfortunately, acceptance, the imprecise response packing the least educational punch, gets the most equitable sex distribution in classrooms. Active students receiving precise feedback are more likely to achieve academically. And they are more likely to be boys. Consider the following:

- Although girls start school ahead of boys in reading and basic computation, by the time they graduate from high school, boys have higher SAT scores in both areas.

- By high school, some girls become less committed to careers, although their grades and achievement-test scores may be as good as boys'. Many girls' interests turn to marriage or stereotypically female jobs. Part of the reason may be that some women feel that men disapprove of their using their intelligence.

- Girls are less likely to take math and science courses and to participate in special or gifted programs in these subjects, even if they have a talent for them. They are also more likely to believe that they are incapable of pursuing math and science in college and to avoid the subjects.

- Girls are more likely to attribute failure to internal factors, such as ability, rather than to external factors, such as luck.

The sexist communication game is played at work, as well as at school. As reported in numerous studies it goes like this:

- Men speak more often and frequently interrupt women.

- Listeners recall more from male speakers than from female speakers, even when both use a similar speaking style and cover identical content.

- Women participate less actively in conversation. They do more smiling and gazing; they are more often the passive bystanders in professional and social conversations among peers.

- Women often transform declarative statements into tentative comments. This is accomplished by using qualifiers ("kind of" or "I guess") and by adding tag questions ("This is a good movie, isn't it?"). These tentative patterns weaken impact and signal a lack of power and influence.

Sexist treatment in the classroom encourages formation of patterns such as these, which give men more dominance and power than women in the working world. But there is a light at the end of the educational tunnel. Classroom biases are not etched in stone, and training can eliminate these patterns. Sixty teachers in our study received four days of training to establish equity in classroom interactions. These trained teachers succeeded in eliminating classroom bias. Although our training focused on equality, it improved overall teaching effectiveness as well. Classes taught by these trained teachers had a higher level of intellectual discussion and contained more effective and precise teacher responses for all students.

There is an urgent need to remove sexism from the classroom and give women the same educational encouragement and support that men receive. When women are treated equally in the classroom, they will be more likely to achieve equality in the workplace.

SUGGESTIONS FOR DISCUSSION

1. The Sadkers cite a number of studies that conclude teachers treat and respond to male and female students in different ways. Do these findings correspond to your own experience in the classroom? Compare your answer to those of classmates.

Do men and women answer this question in the same way? If there are differences in response, how would you account for them?

2. The Sadkers suggest that female students sometimes worry that men will disapprove of women using their intelligence in school. Is there a kind of subtle pressure in student culture, where women trade off academic success for popularity with males? What stereotypes about femininity might encourage both men and women to think that intellectual work is not women's work?

3. Toward the end of the article, the Sadkers cite studies that suggest men and women have different conversational styles. Men not only talk more in mixed groups, they also interrupt more often and exert more control over the direction of the conversation. Women, on the other hand, listen more, are more supportive, and have greater skills in sustaining conversation. Do these findings correspond to your experience in mixed-company conversations? Do men and women in your class answer this question in the same way? If they differ, how would you account for the differences?

SUGGESTIONS FOR WRITING

1. The Sadkers suggest that female students sometimes experience a conflict between academic success and their image of femininity. Write an essay that begins with the Sadkers' view and goes on to explain how—or whether—in your view, the conflict between success and images of femininity plays itself out in female students' lives. Draw on your own experience and what you have observed in school to develop your position. But don't be content just to offer anecdotes. You will need to consider how the reward system in schooling defines success and whether it favors boys over girls and in what ways.

2. Pay attention to how conversations take place in mixed company over a period of time. Notice whether men or women talk more, whether men interrupt and direct the conversation, and whether women participate less actively and in more tentative ways, as the Sadkers suggest. Then write an essay that summarizes your findings and draws out the implications you see in the patterns of communication in conversations among men and women. How do these patterns of communication define gender roles?

3. One suggested method to deal with sexism in the classroom is all-women colleges. In fact, there is currently renewed interest and rising applications to historically women's colleges, such as Smith, Bryn Mawr, Wellesley, Mount Holyoke, and Mills. Write an essay that develops your own position on the advantages and disadvantages of single-sex education for women. Use the knowledge you have acquired about how college fosters or inhibits women's development as students, learners, and persons. What criteria should women use to decide whether a co-ed or a single-sex college is best for them?

June Jordan

Nobody Mean More to Me Than You[1] and the Future Life of Willie Jordan

June Jordan is a poet, playwright, essayist, and professor of English at the State University of New York at Stony Brook. The following selection, "Nobody Mean More to Me Than You and the Future Life of Willie Jordan," opens *On Call*, a collection of Jordan's political essays, published in 1985. In this essay, Jordan weaves two stories together, one concerning a class she taught on Black English and the other concerning Willie Jordan, a young black student in the class trying to come to terms with injustice in South Africa while facing the death of his brother through police brutality at home in Brooklyn. Jordan's story of how her students discovered the communicative power and clarity of Black English forms the backdrop for Willie Jordan's struggle to articulate his own understanding of oppressive power.

Suggestion for Reading

- Notice that there are many voices speaking in this essay—not just June Jordan the essayist and teacher, but also Alice Walker in *The Color Purple*, Jordan's students studying and translating Black English, and Willie Jordan in the essay that closes the selection. Underline and annotate passages in this essay to indicate who is speaking and where the voice shifts.

---◆---

Black English is not exactly a linguistic buffalo; as children, most of the thirty-five million Afro-Americans living here depend on this language for our discovery of the world. But then we approach our maturity inside a larger social body that will not support our efforts to become anything other than the clones of those who are neither our mothers nor our fathers. We begin to grow up in a house where every true mirror shows us the face of somebody who does not belong there, whose walk and whose talk will never look or sound "right," because that house was meant to shelter a family that is alien and hostile to us. As we learn our way around this environment, either we hide our original word habits, or we completely surrender our own voice, hoping to please those who will never respect anyone different from themselves: Black English is not exactly a linguistic buffalo, but we should understand its status as an endangered species, as a perishing, irreplaceable sys-

---

[1] Black English aphorisms crafted by Monica Morris, a junior at S.U.N.Y., Stony Brook, October, 1984.

tem of community intelligence, or we should expect its extinction, and, along with that, the extinguishing of much that constitutes our own proud, and singular, identity.

What we casually call "English," less and less defers to England and its "gentlemen." "English" is no longer a specific matter of geography or an element of class privilege; more than thirty-three countries use this tool as a means of "intranational communication."[2] Countries as disparate as Zimbabwe and Malaysia, or Israel and Uganda, use it as their non-native currency of convenience. Obviously, this tool, this "English," cannot function inside thirty-three discrete societies on the basis of rules and values absolutely determined somewhere else, in a thirty-fourth other country, for example.

In addition to that staggering congeries of non-native users of English, there are five countries, or 333,746,000 people, for whom this thing called "English" serves as a native tongue.[2] Approximately 10 percent of these native speakers of "English" are Afro-American citizens of the U.S.A. I cite these numbers and varieties of human beings dependent on "English" in order, quickly, to suggest how strange and how tenuous is any concept of "Standard English." Obviously, numerous forms of English now operate inside a natural, an uncontrollable, continuum of development. I would suppose "the standard" for English in Malaysia is not the same as "the standard" in Zimbabwe. I know that standard forms of English for Black people in this country do not copy that of Whites. And, in fact, the structural differences between these two kinds of English have intensified, becoming more Black, or less White, despite the expected homogenizing effects of television[3] and other mass media.

Nonetheless, White standards of English persist, supreme and unquestioned, in these United States. Despite our multi-lingual population, and despite the deepening Black and White cleavage within that conglomerate, White standards control our official and popular judgments of verbal proficiency and correct, or incorrect, language skills, including speech. In contrast to India, where at least fourteen languages co-exist as legitimate Indian languages, in contrast to Nicaragua, where all citizens are legally entitled to formal school instruction in their regional or tribal languages, compulsory education in America compels accommodation to exclusively White forms of "English." White English, in America, is "Standard English."

This story begins two years ago. I was teaching a new course, "In Search of the Invisible Black Woman," and my rather large class seemed evenly divided among young Black women and men. Five or six White students also sat in attendance. With unexpected speed and enthusiasm we had moved through historical narration of the 19th century to literature by and about Black women, in the 20th. I then assigned the first forty pages of Alice Walker's *The Color Purple,* and I came, eagerly, to class that morning:

"So!" I exclaimed, aloud. "What did you think? How did you like it?"

The students studied their hands, or the floor. There was no response. The tense, resistant feeling in the room fairly astounded me.

---

[2] *English Is Spreading, But What Is English?* A presentation by Professor S. N. Sridhar, Department of Linguistics, S.U.N.Y., Stony Brook, April 9, 1985: Dean's Convocation Among the Disciplines.

[3] *New York Times,* March 15, 1985, Section One, p. 14: Report on Study by Linguists at the University of Pennsylvania.

At last, one student, a young woman still not meeting my eyes, muttered something in my direction:

"What did you say?" I prompted her.

"Why she have them talk so funny. It don't sound right."

"You mean the language?"

Another student lifted his head: "It don't look right, neither. I couldn't hardly read it."

At this, several students dumped on the book. Just about unanimously, their criticisms targeted the language. I listened to what they wanted to say and silently marvelled at the similarities between their casual speech patterns and Alice Walker's written version of Black English.

But I decided against pointing to these identical traits of syntax, I wanted not to make them self-conscious about their own spoken language—not while they clearly felt it was "wrong." Instead I decided to swallow my astonishment. Here was a negative Black reaction to a prize-winning accomplishment of Black literature that White readers across the country had selected as a best seller. Black rejection was aimed at the one irreducibly Black element of Walker's work: the language—Celie's Black English. I wrote the opening lines of *The Color Purple* on the blackboard and asked the students to help me translate these sentences into Standard English:

You better not never tell nobody but God. It'd kill your mommy.

Dear God,

I am fourteen years old. I have always been a good girl. Maybe you can give me a sign letting me know what is happening to me.

Last spring after Little Lucious come I heard them fussing. He was pulling on her arm. She say it too soon, Fonso. I aint well. Finally he leave her alone. A week go by, he pulling on her arm again. She say, Naw, I ain't gonna. Can't you see I'm already half dead, an all of the children.[4]

Our process of translation exploded with hilarity and even hysterical, shocked laughter: The Black writer, Alice Walker, knew what she was doing! If rudimentary criteria for good fiction include the manipulation of language so that the syntax and diction of sentences will tell you the identity of speakers, the probable age and sex and class of speakers, and even the locale—urban/rural/southern/western—then Walker had written, perfectly. This is the translation into Standard English that our class produced:

Absolutely, one should never confide in anybody besides God. Your secrets could prove devastating to your mother.

---

[4] Alice Walker. *The Color Purple* (New York: Harcourt Brace Jovanovich, 1982), p. 11.

Dear God,

I am fourteen years old. I have always been good. But now, could you help me to understand what is happening to me?

Last spring, after my little brother, Lucious, was born, I heard my parents fighting. My father kept pulling at my mother's arm. But she told him, "It's too soon for sex, Alfonso. I am still not feeling well." Finally, my father left her alone. A week went by, and then he began bothering my mother, again: Pulling her arm. She told him, "No, I won't! Can't you see I'm already exhausted from all of these children?"

(Our favorite line was "It's too soon for sex, Alfonso.")

Once we could stop laughing, once we could stop our exponentially wild improvisations on the theme of Translated Black English, the students pushed to explain their own negative first reactions to their spoken language on the printed page. I thought it was probably akin to the shock of seeing yourself in a photograph for the first time. Most of the students had never before seen a written facsimile of the way they talk. None of the students had ever learned how to read and write their own verbal system of communication: Black English. Alternatively, this fact began to baffle or else bemuse and then infuriate my students. Why not? Was it too late? Could they learn how to do it, now? And, ultimately, the final test question, the one testing my sincerity: Could I teach them? Because I had never taught anyone Black English and, as far as I knew, no one, anywhere in the United States, had ever offered such a course, the best I could say was "I'll try."

• • •

He looked like a wrestler.

He sat dead center in the packed room and, every time our eyes met, he quickly nodded his head as though anxious to reassure, and encourage me.

Short, with strikingly broad shoulders and long arms, he spoke with a surprisingly high, soft voice that matched the soft bright movement of his eyes. His name was Willie Jordan. He would have seemed even more unlikely in the context of Contemporary Women's Poetry, except that ten or twelve other Black men were taking the course, as well. Still, Willie was conspicuous. His extreme fitness, the muscular density of his presence underscored the riveted, gentle attention that he gave to anything anyone said. Generally, he did not join the loud and rowdy dialogue flying back and forth, but there could be no doubt about his interest in our discussions. And, when he stood to present an argument he'd prepared, overnight, that nervous smile of his vanished and an irregular stammering replaced it, as he spoke with visceral sincerity, word by word.

That was how I met Willie Jordan. It was in between "In Search of the Invisible Black Women" and "The Art of Black English." I was waiting for departmental approval and I supposed that Willie might be, so to speak, killing time until he, too, could study Black English. But Willie really did want to explore contemporary women's poetry and, to that end, volunteered for extra research and never missed a class.

Towards the end of that semester, Willie approached me for an independent study project on South Africa. It would commence the next semester. I thought Willie's writing needed the kind of improvement only intense practice will yield. I knew his intelligence was outstanding. But he'd wholeheartedly opted for "Standard English" at a rather late age, and the results were stilted and frequently polysyllabic, simply for the sake of having more syllables. Willie's unnatural formality of language seemed to me consistent with the formality of his research into South African apartheid. As he projected his studies, he would have little time, indeed, for newspapers. Instead, more than 90 percent of his research would mean saturation in strictly historical, if not archival, material. I was certainly interested. It would be tricky to guide him into a more confident and spontaneous relationship both with language and apartheid. It was going to be wonderful to see what happened when he could catch up with himself, entirely, and talk back to the world.

September, 1984: Breezy fall weather and much excitement! My class, "The Art of Black English," was full to the limit of the fire laws. And in Independent Study, Willie Jordan showed up weekly, fifteen minutes early for each of our sessions. I was pretty happy to be teaching, altogether!

I remember an early class when a young brother, replete with his ever-present porkpie hat, raised his hand and then told us that most of what he'd heard was "all right" except it was "too clean." "The brothers on the street," he continued, "they mix it up more. Like 'fuck' and 'motherfuck.' Or like 'shit.'" He waited. I waited. Then all of us laughed a good while, and we got into a brawl about "correct" and "realistic" Black English that led to Rule 1.

Rule 1: *Black English is about a whole lot more than mothafuckin.*

As a criterion, we decided, "realistic" could take you anywhere you want to go. Artful places. Angry places. Eloquent and sweetalkin places. Polemical places. Church. And the local Bar & Grill. We were checking out a language, not a mood or a scene or one guy's forgettable mouthing off.

It was hard. For most of the students, learning Black English required a fallback to patterns and rhythms of speech that many of their parents had beaten out of them. I mean *beaten.* And, in a majority of cases, correct Black English could be achieved only by striving for *incorrect* Standard English, something they were still pushing at, quite uncertainly. This state of affairs led to Rule 2.

Rule 2: *If it's wrong in Standard English it's probably right in Black English, or, at least, you're hot.*

It was hard. Roommates and family members ridiculed their studies, or remained incredulous, "You *studying* that shit? At school?" But we were beginning to feel the companionship of pioneers. And we decided that we needed another rule that would establish each one of us as equally important to our success. This was Rule 3.

Rule 3: *If it don't sound like something that come out somebody mouth then it don't sound right. If it don't sound right then it ain't hardly right. Period.*

This rule produced two weeks of compositions in which the students agonizingly tried to spell the sound of the Black English sentence they wanted to convey. But Black English is, preeminently, an oral/spoken means of communication. *And spelling don't talk.* So we needed Rule 4.

Rule 4: *Forget about the spelling. Let the syntax carry you.*

Once we arrived at Rule 4 we started to fly, because syntax, the structure of an idea, leads you to the world view of the speaker and reveals her values. The syntax of a sentence equals the structure of your consciousness. If we insisted that the language of Black English adheres to a distinctive Black syntax, then we were postulating a profound difference between White and Black people, *per se.* Was it a difference to prize or to obliterate?

There are three qualities of Black English—the presence of life, voice, and clarity—that intensify to a distinctive Black value system that we became excited about and self-consciously tried to maintain.

1. Black English has been produced by a pre-technocratic, if not anti-technological, culture. More, our culture has been constantly threatened by annihilation or, at least, the swallowed blurring of assimilation. Therefore, our language is a system constructed by people constantly needing to insist that we exist, that we are present. Our language devolves from a culture that abhors all abstraction, or anything tending to obscure or delete the fact of the human being who is here and now/the truth of the person who is speaking or listening. Consequently, *there is no passive voice construction possible in Black English.* For example, you cannot say, "Black English is being eliminated." You must say, instead, "White people eliminating Black English." The assumption of the presence of life governs all of Black English. Therefore, overwhelmingly, *all action takes place in the language of the present indicative.* And every sentence assumes the living and active participation of at least two human beings, the speaker and the listener.

2. A primary consequence of the person-centered values of Black English is the delivery of voice. If you speak or write Black English, your ideas will necessarily possess that otherwise elusive attribute, *voice.*

3. One main benefit following from the person-centered values of Black English is that of *clarity.* If your idea, your sentence, assumes the presence of at least two living and active people, you will make it understandable, because the motivation behind every sentence is the wish to say something real to somebody real.

As the weeks piled up, translation from Standard English into Black English or vice versa occupied a hefty part of our course work.

Standard English (hereafter S.E.): "In considering the idea of studying Black English those questioned suggested—"

(What's the subject? Where's the person? Is anybody alive in here, in that idea?)

Black English (hereafter B.E.): "I been asking people what you think about somebody studying Black English and they answer me like this:"

But there were interesting limits. You cannot "translate" instances of Standard English preoccupied with abstraction or with nothing/nobody evidently alive, into Black English. That would warp the language into uses antithetical to the guiding perspective of its community of users. Rather you must first change those Standard English sentences, themselves, into ideas consistent with the person-centered assumptions of Black English.

Guidelines for Black English

1. Minimal number of words for every idea: This is the source for the aphoristic and/or poetic force of the language; eliminate every possible word.
2. Clarity: If the sentence is not clear it's not Black English.
3. Eliminate use of the verb *to be* whenever possible. This leads to the deployment of more descriptive and, therefore, more precise verbs.
4. Use *be* or *been* only when you want to describe a chronic, ongoing state of things.
    He *be* at the office, by 9. (He is always at the office by 9.)
    He *been* with her since forever.
5. Zero copula: Always eliminate the verb *to be* whenever it would combine with another verb, in Standard English.
    S.E.: She is going out with him.
    B.E.: She going out with him.
6. Eliminate *do* as in:
    S.E.: What do you think? What do you want?
    B.E.: What you think? What you want?

Rules number 3, 4, 5, and 6 provide for the use of the minimal number of verbs per idea and, therefore, greater accuracy in the choice of verb.

7. In general, if you wish to say something really positive, try to formulate the idea using emphatic negative structure.
    S.E.: He's fabulous.
    B.E.: He bad.
8. Use double or triple negatives for dramatic emphasis.
    S.E.: Tina Turner sings out of this world.
    B.E.: Ain nobody sing like Tina.
9. Never use the *ed* suffix to indicate the past tense of a verb.
    S.E.: She closed the door.
    B.E.: She close the door. Or, she have close the door.
10. Regardless of intentional verb time, only use the third person singular, present indicative, for use of the verb *to have,* as an auxiliary.
    S.E.: He had his wallet then he lost it.
    B.E.: He have him wallet then he lose it.
    S.E.: We had seen that movie.
    B.E.: We seen that movie. Or, we have see that movie.
11. Observe a minimal inflection of verbs. Particularly, never change from the first person singular forms to the third person singular.
    S.E.: Present Tense Forms: He goes to the store.
    B.E.: He go to the store.

S.E.: Past Tense Forms: He went to the store.

B.E.: He go to the store. Or, he gone to the store. Or, he been to the store.

12. The possessive case scarcely ever appears in Black English. Never use an apostrophe ('s) construction. If you wander into a possessive case component of an idea, then keep logically consistent: *ours, his, theirs, mines.* But, most likely, if you bump into such a component, you have wandered outside the underlying world view of Black English.

S.E.: He will take their car tomorrow.

B.E.: He taking they car tomorrow.

13. Plurality: Logical consistency, continued: If the modifier indicates plurality then the noun remains in the singular case.

S.E.: He ate twelve doughnuts.

B.E.: He eat twelve doughnut.

S.E.: She has many books.

B.E.: She have many book.

14. Listen for, or invent, special Black English forms of the past tense, such as: "He losted it. That what she felted." If they are clear and readily understood, then use them.

15. Do not hesitate to play with words, sometimes inventing them: e.g. "astropotomous" means huge like a hippo plus astronomical and, therefore, signifies real big.

16. In Black English, unless you keenly want to underscore the past tense nature of an action, stay in the present tense and rely on the overall context of your ideas for the conveyance of time and sequence.

17. Never use the suffix -*ly* form of an adverb in Black English.

S.E.: The rain came down rather quickly.

B.E.: The rain come down pretty quick.

18. Never use the indefinite article an in Black English.

S.E.: He wanted to ride an elephant.

B.E.: He wanted to ride him a elephant.

19. Invariant syntax: in correct Black English it is possible to formulate an imperative, an interrogative, and a simple declarative idea with the same syntax:

B.E.: You going to the store?

You going to the store.

You going to the store!

Where was Willie Jordan? We'd reached the mid-term of the semester. Students had formulated Black English guidelines, by consensus, and they were now writing with remarkable beauty, purpose, and enjoyment:

I ain hardly speakin for everybody but myself so understan that.

—Kim Parks

Samples from student writings:

Janie have a great big ole hole inside her. Tea Cake the only thing that fit that hole. . . .

That pear tree beautiful to Janie, especial when bees fiddlin with the blossomin pear there growin large and lovely. But personal speakin, the love she get from starin at that tree ain the love what starin back at her in them relationship. (Monica Morris)

Love a big theme in, *They Eye Was Watching God.* Love show people new corners inside theyself. It pull out good stuff and stuff back bad stuff . . . Joe worship the doing uh his own hand and need other people to worship him too. But he ain't think about Janie that she a person and ought to live like anybody common do. Queen life not for Janie. (Monica Morris)

In both life and writin, Black womens have varietous experience of love that be cold like a iceberg or fiery like a inferno. Passion got for the other partner involve, man or women, seem as shallow, ankle-deep water or the most profoundest abyss. (Constance Evans)

Family love another bond that ain't never break under no pressure. (Constance Evans)

You know it really cold/When the friend you/Always get out the fire/Act like they don't know you/When you in the beat. (Constance Evans)

Big classroom discussion bout love at this time. I never take no class where us have any long arguin for and against for two or three day. New to me and great. I find the class time talkin a million time more interestin than detail bout the book. (Kathy Esseks)

As these examples suggest, Black English no longer limited the students, in any way. In fact, one of them, Philip Garfield, would shortly "translate" a pivotal scene from Ibsen's *A Doll's House,* as his final term paper.

Nora: I didn't gived no shit. I thinked you a asshole back then, too, you make it so hard for me save mines husband life.

Krogstad: Girl, it clear you ain't any idea what you done. You done exact what I once done, and I losed my reputation over it.

Nora: You asks me believe you once act brave save you wife life?

Krogstad: Law care less why you done it.

Nora: Law must suck.

Krogstad: Suck or no, if I wants, judge screw you wid dis paper.

Nora: No way, man. (Philip Garfield)

But where was Willie? Compulsively punctual, and always thoroughly prepared with neat typed compositions, he had disappeared. He failed to show up for our regularly scheduled conference, and I received neither a note nor a phone call of explanation. A whole week went by. I wondered if Willie had finally been captured by the extremely current happenings in South Africa: passage of a new constitution that did not enfranchise the Black majority, and militant Black South African reaction to that affront. I wondered if he'd been hurt, somewhere. I wondered if the serious workload of weekly readings and writings had overwhelmed him and changed his mind about independent study. Where was Willie Jordan?

One week after the first conference that Willie missed, he called: "Hello, Professor Jordan? This is Willie. I'm sorry I wasn't there last week. But something has come up and I'm pretty upset. I'm sorry but I really can't deal right now."

I asked Willie to drop by my office and just let me see that he was okay. He agreed to do that. When I saw him I knew something hideous had happened. Something had hurt him and scared him to the marrow. He was all agitated and stammering and terse and incoherent. At last, his sadly jumbled account let me surmise, as follows: Brooklyn police had murdered his unarmed, twenty-five-year-old brother, Reggie Jordan. Neither Willie nor his elderly parents knew what to do about it. Nobody from the press was interested. His folks had no money. Police ran his family around and around, to no point. And Reggie was really dead. And Willie wanted to fight, but he felt helpless.

● ● ●

With Willie's permission I began to try to secure legal counsel for the Jordan family. Unfortunately, Black victims of police violence are truly numerous, while the resources available to prosecute their killers are truly scarce. A friend of mine at the Center for Constitutional Rights estimated that just the preparatory costs for bringing the cops into court normally approaches $180,000. Unless the execution of Reggie Jordan became a major community cause for organizing and protest, his murder would simply become a statistical item.

Again, with Willie's permission, I contacted every newspaper and media person I could think of. But the Bastone feature article in *The Village Voice* was the only result from that canvassing.

Again, with Willie's permission, I presented the case to my class in Black English. We had talked about the politics of language. We had talked about love and sex and child abuse and men and women. But the murder of Reggie Jordan broke like a hurricane across the room.

There are few "issues" as endemic to Black life as police violence. Most of the students knew and respected and liked Jordan. Many of them came from the very neighborhood where the murder had occurred. All of the students had known somebody close to them who had been killed by police, or had known frightening moments of gratuitous confrontation with the cops. They wanted to do everything at once to avenge death. Number One: They decided to compose a personal statement of condolence to Willie Jordan and his family, written in Black English. Number Two: They decided to compose individual messages to the police, in Black English. These should be prefaced by an explanatory paragraph composed by the entire group. Number Three: These individual messages, with their lead paragraph, should be sent to *Newsday*.

The morning after we agreed on these objectives, one of the young women students appeared with an unidentified visitor, who sat through the class, smiling in a peculiar, comfortable way.

Now we had to make more tactical decisions. Because we wanted the messages published, and because we thought it imperative that our outrage be known by the police, the tactical question was this: Should the opening, group paragraph be written in Black English or Standard English?

I have seldom been privy to a discussion with so much heart at the dead beat of it. I will never forget the eloquence, the sudden haltings of speech, the fierce struggle against tears, the furious throwaway, and useless explosions that this question elicited.

That one question contained several others, each of them extraordinarily painful to even contemplate. How best to serve the memory of Reggie Jordan? Should we use the language of the killer—Standard English—in order to make our ideas acceptable to those controlling the killers? But wouldn't what we had to say be rejected, summarily, if we said it in our own language, the language of the victim, Reggie Jordan? But if we sought to express ourselves by abandoning our language wouldn't that mean our suicide on top of Reggie's murder? But if we expressed ourselves in our own language wouldn't that be suicidal to the wish to communicate with those who, evidently, did not give a damn about us/Reggie/police violence in the Black community?

At the end of one of the longest, most difficult hours of my own life, the students voted, unanimously, to preface their individual messages with a paragraph composed in the language of Reggie Jordan. *"At least we don't give up nothing else. At least we stick to the truth: Be who we been. And stay all the way with Reggie."*

It was heartbreaking to proceed, from that point. Everyone in the room realized that our decision in favor of Black English had doomed our writings, even as the distinctive reality of our Black lives always has doomed our efforts to "be who we been" in this country.

I went to the blackboard and took down this paragraph dictated by the class:

YOU COPS!

WE THE BROTHER AND SISTER OF WILLIE JORDAN, A FELLOW STONY BROOK STUDENT WHO THE BROTHER OF THE DEAD REGGIE JORDAN. REGGIE, LIKE MANY BROTHER AND SISTER, HE A VICTIM OF BRUTAL RACIST POLICE, OCTOBER 25, 1984. US APPALL, FED UP, BECAUSE THAT ANOTHER SENSELESS DEATH WHAT OCCUR IN OUR COMMUNITY. THIS WHAT WE FEEL, THIS, FROM OUR HEART, FOR WE AIN'T STAYIN' SILENT NO MORE.

With the completion of this introduction, nobody said anything. I asked for comments. At this invitation, the unidentified visitor, a young Black man, ceaselessly smiling, raised his hand. He was, it so happens, a rookie cop. He had just joined the force in September and, he said, he thought he should clarify a few things. So he came forward and sprawled easily into a posture of barroom, or fire-side, nostalgia:

"See," Officer Charles enlightened us, "Most times when you out on the street and something come down you do one of two things. Over-react or under-react. Now, if you under-react then you can get yourself kilt. And if you over-react then maybe you kill somebody. Fortunately it's about nine times out of ten and you will over-react. So the brother got kilt. And I'm sorry about that, believe me. But what you have to understand is what kilt him: Over-reaction. That's all. Now you talk about Black people and White police but see, now, I'm a cop myself. And (big smile) I'm Black. And just a couple months ago I was on the other side. But it's the same for me. You a cop, you the ultimate authority: the Ultimate Authority. And you on the street, most of the time you can only do one of two things: over-react or under-react. That's all it is with the brother. Over-reaction. Didn't have nothing to do with race."

That morning Officer Charles had the good fortune to escape without being boiled alive. But barely. And I remember the pride of his smile when I read about the fate of Black policemen and other collaborators, in South Africa. I remember him, and I remember the shock and palpable feeling of shame that filled the room. It was as though that foolish, and deadly, young man had just relieved himself of his foolish, and deadly, explanation, face to face with the grief of Reggie Jordan's father and Reggie Jordan's mother. Class ended quietly. I copied the paragraph from the blackboard, collected the individual messages and left to type them up.

Newsday rejected the piece.

The Village Voice could not find room in their "Letters" section to print the individual messages from the students to the police.

None of the TV news reporters picked up the story.

Nobody raised $180,000 to prosecute the murder of Reggie Jordan.

Reggie Jordan is really dead.

I asked Willie Jordan to write an essay pulling together everything important to him from that semester. He was still deeply beside himself with frustration and amazement and loss. This is what he wrote, unedited, and in its entirety:

Throughout the course of this semester I have been researching the effects of oppression and exploitation along racial lines in South Africa and its neighboring countries. I have become aware of South African police brutalization of native Africans beyond the extent of the law, even though the laws themselves are catalyst affliction upon Black men, women and children. Many Africans die each year as a result of the deliberate use of police force to protect the white power structure.

Social control agents in South Africa, such as policemen, are also used to force compliance among citizens through both overt and covert tactics. It is not uncommon to find bold-faced coercion and cold-blooded killings of Blacks by South African police for undetermined and/or inadequate reasons. Perhaps the truth is that the only reasons for this heinous treatment of Blacks rests in racial differences. We should also understand that what is conveyed through the media is not always accurate and may sometimes be construed as the tip of the iceberg at best.

I recently received a painful reminder that racism, poverty, and the abuse of power are global problems which are by no means unique to South Africa. On October 25, 1984 at approximately 3:00 p.m. my brother, Mr. Reginald Jordan, was shot and killed by two New York City policemen from the 75th precinct in the East New York section of Brooklyn. His life ended at the age of twenty-five. Even up to this current point in time the Police Department has failed to provide my family, which consists of five brothers, eight sisters, and two parents, with a plausible reason for Reggie's death. Out of the many stories that were given to my family by the Police Department, not one of them seems to hold water. In fact, I honestly believe that the Police

Department's assessment of my brother's murder is nothing short of AB-SOLUTE BULLSHIT, and thus far no evidence had been produced to alter perception of the situation.

Furthermore, I believe that one of three cases may have occurred in this incident. First, Reggie's death may have been the desired outcome of the police officer's action, in which case the killing was premeditated. Or, it was a case of mistaken identity, which clarifies the fact that the two officers who killed my brother and their commanding parties are all grossly incompetent. Or, both of the above cases are correct, i.e., Reggie's murderers intended to kill him and the Police Department behaved insubordinately.

Part of the argument of the officers who shot Reggie was that he had attacked one of them and took his gun. This was their major claim. They also said that only one of them had actually shot Reggie. The facts, however, speak for themselves. According to the Death Certificate and autopsy report, Reggie was shot eight times from point-blank range. The Doctor who performed the autopsy told me himself that two bullets entered the side of my brother's head, four bullets were sprayed into his back, and two bullets struck him in the back of his legs. It is obvious that unnecessary force was used by the police and that it is extremely difficult to shoot someone in his back when he is attacking or approaching you.

After experiencing a situation like this and researching South Africa I believe that to a large degree, justice may only exist as rhetoric. I find it difficult to talk of true justice when the oppression of my people both at home and abroad attests to the fact that inequality and injustice are serious problems whereby Blacks and Third World people are perpetually short-changed by society. Something has to be done about the way in which this world is set up. Although it is a difficult task, we do have the power to make a change.

—Willie J. Jordan, Jr.
EGL 487, Section 58, November 14, 1984

It is my privilege to dedicate this book to the future life of Willie J. Jordan, Jr., August 8, 1985.

SUGGESTIONS FOR DISCUSSION

1. How does June Jordan intertwine the story of her class on Black English and the story of Willie Jordan? Would these stories have the same impact if they were presented separately? What if anything does Jordan accomplish by weaving them together?
2. Reread the passages where Jordan's students translate the opening of *The Color Purple* into Standard English and the scene from *A Doll's House* into Black English.

Describe the qualities of Black expression that get lost in the first case and added in the second.

3. What are the advantages and disadvantages of Jordan's students' decision to write the preface to their individual messages to the police in Black English?

SUGGESTIONS FOR WRITING

1. Write an essay that explains the point June Jordan is making about the relationship between Black English and Standard English and what she thinks ought to be taught in school and why. Compare what Jordan says to your own views on how language should be taught in American schools.

2. Write an essay that explains what you see as the advantages and disadvantages of Jordan's students' decision to compose the introduction to their letters to the police in Black English. You will want to arrive at your own evaluation of their decision, but before you do, it may help to explain how and in what sense the decision they had to make was a difficult one.

3. Choose a passage of dialogue in a novel or play you are familiar with, in which the speakers are speaking Standard English. Use Phil Garfield's translation of a scene from *A Doll's House* into Black English as a model. Translate the passage into some form of non-Standard English—whether the spoken language of your neighborhood, the vernacular of youth culture, or the dialect of a region.

E. D. Hirsch, Jr.

CULTURAL LITERACY AND THE SCHOOLS

E. D. Hirsch, Jr., is William R. Kenan Professor of English at the University of Virginia and a prominent literary critic whose books *The Aims of Interpretation* and *The Validity of Interpretation* have become standard works. Over the past ten years, Hirsch has turned his attention away from literary studies and has developed a keen interest in the problems of literacy and American education. His book *Cultural Literacy* was a bestseller when it was published in 1987. It contains what has since become a controversial proposal to base the elementary and secondary curriculum on a list of "essential facts and words" required to be culturally literate. The following selection is an article Hirsch published in 1985, shortly before *Cultural Literacy* appeared. "Cultural Literacy and the Schools" is a fair summary of Hirsch's views on education and literacy.

Suggestion for Reading

- Notice that Hirsch has divided his article into eleven sections. As you read, annotate each section to help you keep track of how Hirsch defines the problem he is addressing in this article and how he proposes and explains his solution to the problem.

◆

L et me begin with a picture of what I mean by true literacy. It is good to start with our national educational goals, because unless we can agree upon our goals, we cannot deal forthrightly with the political and ideological issues that public education must always entail. Let me depict our educational goal as a social one, using the unforgettable vision of Martin Luther King, Jr. in his speech "I Have a Dream." Those of you who heard that speech or teach it will know what I am thinking. King had a vision in which the children of former slave owners sit down at the table of equality with the children of former slaves, a vision of an America where men and women deal with each other as equals and judge each other on their character rather than their origins. King had a dream of a classless society. To help us share his dream, he quoted from our most traditional texts, from Jefferson, the Bible, and patriotic and religious songs. We all know those traditional passages and songs. King reminded us that his dream has been shared and cherished by all Americans of good will.

The dream of Thomas Jefferson and Martin Luther King, Jr. carries a very specific educational implication in the modern world: No modern society can think of becoming a classless society except on the basis of universal literacy. Never mind for the moment the various utilitarian and humanistic arguments in favor of literacy. I am considering now an even more basic principle that sponsored our Jeffersonian system of public education in the first place. It is the principle that people in a democracy can be left free to think and decide things for themselves because they can all communicate with each other. Universal communication is the canvas for King's vision as well as Jefferson's. And universal communication is possible in our modern world only on the basis of universal literacy. Americans must be able to talk to each other not just in person or by telephone but across time and space through reading and writing. We can add to that traditional democratic imperative to literacy the well-known economic imperative that has been brought by the technological age. Today, only someone who reads well can adjust to changes in technology and the job market or can participate in our cultural and political life. From these very elementary considerations, it is obvious that genuine literacy must be a paramount and minimal goal of a high school education.

But what, more specifically, does that goal mean for the curriculum? That depends on what we mean by literacy. I would define literacy in this way: To be truly literate, a high school graduate must be able to grasp the meaning of written materials in any field or subject, provided that those materials are addressed to a general reader. High school graduates should be able to read serious newspapers, for instance. Remember what Jefferson said about reading newspapers:

> Were it left to me to decide whether we should have a government without newspapers, or newspapers without a government, I should not hesitate a moment to prefer the latter. But I should mean that every man should receive those papers and be capable of reading them.

That last comment of Jefferson's is often omitted. But it is the crucial one. Every American should be able to read serious books, newspapers, and articles addressed to the general reader. And our high school graduates should also be able to convey information in writing to a general readership. Universal literacy means that every citizen must be able to give as well as receive written information.

● ● ●

Literacy in this fundamental sense requires not just technical proficiency but also "cultural literacy." What I mean by this term may become clear in a provisional way as I describe a recent experience.

A few years ago, I was conducting some experiments at the University of Virginia to measure the effectiveness of a piece of writing when it is read by ordinary audiences. We were measuring the actual effects of writing rather than mere opinions of its quality. Our readers in the experiment (who were mainly university students) performed just as we expected them to as long as we kept the topics simple and familiar. Then, one memorable day we transferred our experiments from the university to a community college, and my complacency about adult literacy was forever shattered. This community college was located in Richmond, Virginia, and the irony of the location will appear in a moment. Our first experiments went well, because we began by giving the students a paper to read on the topic of friendship. When reading about friendship, these young men and women showed themselves to be, on the average, just as literate as university students. The evidence showed that, based on the usual criteria of speed and accurate recall, the community college and university groups were equally skilled readers. But that evidence changed with the next piece of writing we asked them to read. It was a comparison of the characters of Ulysses S. Grant and Robert E. Lee, and the students' performance on that task was, to be blunt, illiterate. Our results showed that Grant and Lee were simply not familiar names to these young adults in the capital of the Confederacy. The students' speed and recall declined because they had to continually backtrack through the unfamiliar material to test out different hypotheses about what was meant or referred to.

Shortly after that disorienting experience, I discovered that Professor Richard Anderson of the Center for Reading Research at the University of Illinois and other researchers in psycholinguistics had reached firm conclusions about the importance of background knowledge in reading. For instance, in one experiment, Anderson and his colleagues discovered that an otherwise literate audience in India could not properly read a simple text about an American wedding. But, by the same token, an otherwise literate audience in America could not properly read a simple text about an Indian wedding. Why not? Structurally speaking, the texts were similar and the audiences were similar. It wasn't a matter of vocabulary or phonics or word recognition; it was a matter of cultural literacy. Anderson and others showed that to read a text with understanding one needs to have the background knowledge that the author has tacitly assumed the reader to have. This tacit knowledge is fundamental to literacy.

What these experiments demonstrate is that the idea that reading is a general, transferable skill unrelated to subject matter is essentially wrong, containing only the following grain of truth. Reading is a general skill only with regard to its rather elementary aspects, those involving phonics, parsing strategies, guessing strategies, eye habits, and so on. While these elementary skills are important, normally endowed students, once they acquire the rudiments, need not be continually drilled in them. Such skills are always being used, and every reading task will automatically exercise, improve, and automate them. With that single elementary exception, then, the usual picture of reading as a general skill is wrong. Reading skill varies from task to task, because reading skill depends on specific background knowledge.

• • •

To illustrate the dependency of literacy on cultural literacy, I shall quote a recent snippet from *The Washington Post:*

> A federal appeals panel today upheld an order barring foreclosure on a Missouri farm, saying that U.S. Agriculture Secretary John R. Block has reneged on his responsibilities to some debt-ridden farmers. The appeals panel directed the USDA to create a system of processing loan deferments and of publicizing them as it said Congress had intended. The panel said that it is the responsibility of the agriculture secretary to carry out this intent "not as a private banker, but as a public broker."

Imagine that item being read by persons who have been trained to read but are as culturally illiterate as were my community college students. They might possibly know words like foreclosure, but they would surely not understand the text as a whole. Who gave the order that the federal panel upheld? What is a federal appeals panel? Even if culturally illiterate readers bothered to look up individual words, they would not have much idea of the reality being referred to. Nor, in reading other texts, would they understand references to such things as, say, the equal protection clause or Robert E. Lee, no matter how well they could read a text on friendship. But a truly literate American does understand references to the equal protection of the laws and Robert E. Lee and newspaper reports like the one I just quoted. As a practical matter, newspaper reporters and writers of books cannot possibly provide detailed background information on every occasion. Think, if they did, how much added information would be needed even in the short item that I quoted from *The Washington Post.* Every sentence would need a dozen sentences of explanation! And each of those sentences would need a dozen more.

Writers work with an idea of what their audiences can be expected to know. They assume, they must assume, a "common reader" who knows the things that are known by other literate persons in the culture.

When I say that these writers must assume such background knowledge, I am affirming a fact about language use that sociolinguists and psycholinguists have known for twenty years: The explicit words of a text are just the tip of the iceberg in a linguistic transaction. In order to understand even the surface of a text, a reader must have the sort of background knowledge that was assumed, for example, in *The Washington Post* report that I quoted.

To understand that paragraph, literate readers would know in the backs of their minds that the American legal system allows a judgment at a lower level to be reversed at a higher level. They would know that a judge can tell the executive branch what it can or cannot do to farmers and other citizens, and they would know a lot more that is relevant. But none of their knowledge would have to be highly detailed. They wouldn't need to know, for instance, whether an appeals panel is the final level before the Supreme Court. In general, readers need to share a cloudy but still accurate sense of the *realities* that are being referred to in a piece of writing. This allows them to make the necessary associations.

Besides this topic-determined knowledge, the reader needs to know less explicit and less topic-defined matters, such as culturally shared attitudes, values, conventions, and connotations that the writer assumes the reader to have. The writer cannot start from ground zero, even in a children's reader designed for the first grade. The subtlety and complexity of written communication is directly dependent upon a shared background.

• • •

To an ill-informed adult who is unaware of what literate persons are expected to know, the assumption by writers that their readers possess cultural literacy could be regarded as a conspiracy of the literate against the illiterate for the purpose of keeping them out of the club. Although newspaper reporters, writers of books, and the framers of the verbal SAT necessarily make assumptions about the things literate persons know, no one ever announces what that body of information is. So, although we Americans object to pronouncements about what we all should know, there is a body of information that literate people *do* know. And this creates a kind of silent, *de facto* dictating from on high about the things adults should know in order to be truly literate.

Our silence about the explicit contents of cultural literacy leads to the following result, observable in the sociology of the verbal SAT. This exam is chiefly a vocabulary test, which, except for its omission of proper names and other concrete information, constitutes a test of cultural literacy. Hence, when young people from deprived backgrounds ask how they can acquire the abilities tested on the verbal SAT, they are told, quite correctly under present circumstances, that the only way to acquire that knowledge is through wide reading in many domains over many years. That is advice that deprived students already in high school are not in a position to take. Thus there remains a strong correlation between the verbal SAT score and socioeconomic status. Students from middle-class and upper-middle-class backgrounds get their knowledge for the verbal SAT not just from reading, but through the pores, from talk at home and social chitchat.

• • •

What follows from this situation goes to the heart of the school curriculum. It means nothing less than the whole conceptual basis of the curriculum as inculcating skills independently of specific content has been wrong—and not just a little wrong, but fundamentally so. The influence of this mistaken educational formalism upon our policies has been, in my opinion, a chief cause of our educational failures in the domain of literacy.

The skills orientation to education has assumed that the particular contents of the curriculum can be arbitrary.

Any good content will develop the skill of reading, but on the contrary, the information that is taken for granted between literate people is not arbitrary. Although quite fuzzy at the edges, this information is known to be central by every truly literate person in our culture. I stress *our* literate culture, because the information shared by literate Americans is different from the information shared by literate Germans or Russians. Literacy in every nation depends on a specifically national literate culture.

Of course, no literate national culture makes absolute sense. Although Shakespeare might be better than Racine in absolute terms, we don't tell the French that they should abandon Racine for Shakespeare. For purposes of national education in America or France, neither Shakespeare nor Racine could be replaced in their respective cultures as necessary background knowledge for literacy and communication. Although we may admire our traditional culture for its own sake, it is mainly for these instrumental reasons (that is, to achieve true literacy and widescale communication) that our central traditional materials must continue to be taught and learned.

If our high school graduates are to be literate, our school curriculum must ensure, at a minimum, that students acquire those facts of cultural literacy that are requisite to true literacy. To accomplish this, the school curriculum needs significant improvement, particularly in grades K through ten. By *improvement,* I do not suggest that it must be completely overhauled. And I do not say that we need what is usually meant by the term "core curriculum." The proposal to introduce a substantial core curriculum in literature whereby every child reads *Silas Marner, Julius Caesar,* and *A Tale of Two Cities* is, I think, lacking in appropriate subtlety. A core of shared information must indeed be learned. But the means by which it is conveyed may vary a good deal. The destination is one, but the routes are many. No educational reform can succeed if it fails to keep students and teachers motivated and interested. Different pupils require different materials, and so do different teachers. For that reason alone, we need to keep diversity and local judgment at the heart of the curriculum. But we also need to be sure that our students get the ABCs of knowledge in the earlier grades. How, then, can we keep a desirable flexibility in the curriculum and also ensure that our students get the core knowledge they need in order to become literate Americans?

• • •

In broaching a solution to this problem, let me make a distinction between two kinds of knowledge taught in school. The two kinds are both necessary, but they are quite distinct. I call them "extensive" and "intensive" knowledge. I'll describe extensive knowledge first. It tends to be broad, but superficial. It is often learned by rote. It is mainly enumerative. It consists of atomic facts and categories. It does not put things together. It's the kind of knowledge possessed by the Major General in Gilbert and Sullivan's *Pirates of Penzance:*

I am the very model of a modern Major General,
I've information vegetable, animal, and mineral,
I know the kings of England, and I quote the fights historical,
From Marathon to Waterloo in order categorical;
I'm very well acquainted too with matters mathematical,
I understand equations, both the simple and quadradical,
About binomial theorem I'm teeming with a lot o' news—
With many cheerful facts about the square of the hypotenuse.

This was comic because these cheerful facts were *all* the Major General knew, and they offered him no help in military strategy. Everybody in his audience also knew those same facts, which were part of the intellectual baggage that every schoolboy acquired in nineteenth-century Britain. It was clear to Gilbert and Sullivan's audience that this knowledge was just a lot of isolated, schoolboy facts that the Major General couldn't put together in any useful way.

Understanding how to put things together is the contribution of *intensive* study. Suppose that instead of just being able to list the fights historical, the Major General wanted to learn something about war and strategy. To gain that knowledge, he would have to study at least a battle or two in some detail. Yet it might not greatly matter which battle he studied carefully. It could be the battle of Austerlitz or the battle of Waterloo. But in order to gain a coherent idea of nineteenth-century warfare, General Stanley would have needed to study specific examples of warfare. Thereafter, any new fact about it that he encountered could be grafted upon or accommodated to the model-idea that he had gained from, say, the battle of Austerlitz. To generalize from this illustration, if we want to make isolated facts fit together in some coherent way, we must acquire models of how they do so from detailed, intensive study and experience.

The school curriculum should foster this intensive learning as much as possible. Indeed, it should be the chief substance of the school curriculum, particularly in the later grades. At the same time, intensive study is also the most flexible part of the school curriculum. For building mental models, it doesn't greatly matter whether the Shakespeare play read in ninth grade is *Macbeth* or *Julius Caesar*. What does matter is whether our idea of Shakespeare is formed on an actual, concrete experience of a Shakespearian play. Such intensive learning is necessary, because the mental model we get from the detailed study of an example lets us connect our atomic facts together and build a coherent picture of reality. On the other hand, since the chief function of intensive study is to get examples for such models, our choice of examples can vary with circumstances and should depend on students' knowledge and interest. That is why a lock-step core curriculum is both unnecessary and undesirable for the intensive part of the curriculum. On the other hand, there is a limit to the flexibility of the intensive curriculum. A play by Neil Simon or George Chapman is no effective substitute for a play by Shakespeare.

• • •

Although we must gain intensive knowledge to make coherent sense out of facts, we must also gain a store of particular, widely shared background facts in order to make sense of what we read. This extensive part of the curriculum, the part that is crucial to shared knowledge and literacy, has been neglected.

The best time to get this extensive background information is before tenth grade, and the earlier the better. In early grades, children are fascinated by straightforward information. Our official modern distaste for old-fashioned memorization and rote learning seems more pious than realistic. Young children are eager to master the materials essential for adult life, and if they believe in the materials they will proudly soak them up like sponges and never forget them. There is a tremendous weight of human tradition across many cultures to support this view. At about age thirteen, young Catholics get confirmed, having memorized the materials they must know in adult life. At the same age, young Jews get bar mitzvahed. At around the same age, young tribal boys and girls must show that they have mastered the rites of passage into the tribe.

There are good reasons why these universal traditions of early acculturation should have come into being. They correspond to something that seems almost biological in its appropriateness and necessity. Human beings function in the world only by becoming members of a culture. The human species survives through social and cultural organizations, not through instinct. Young children have an urge to become acculturated into the adult world by learning the facts of the tribe long before they can make sense out of them.

But in neglecting the extensive part of the school curriculum, we have forsaken the responsibility that rests with the adult members of any tribe. For many decades, we have followed educational theories and ideologies that have now turned out to be inadequate. We have forgotten the acculturative responsibilities of the earlier grades. In a larger historical perspective, we can see that we lost touch with our earlier educational traditions, and, as a consequence, whole generations of schoolchildren lost touch with earlier traditions of our national culture. But those decades did not and could not signal a permanent change in American education, because the failure to include schoolchildren in our literate traditions is in conflict with some of the root purposes of national education.

A lot of us are beginning to recognize our earlier mistakes. That is one of the meanings of the current educational reform movement. We are beginning to see that educational formalism—the idea that we can teach reading and writing as formal skills only—is not sound and has not worked. We have also seen the superficiality of believing that a literate nation can abandon its traditions and remake its literate culture from scratch according to some new ideology. That is a mistake not in moral terms, but in practical terms. When the national languages were fixed in the eighteenth century, some of the cultural baggage that went with each language also became fixed. The two elements, language and cultural baggage, cannot be disentangled. If one believes in literacy, one must also believe in *cultural* literacy.

A great deal is at stake in understanding and acting on these truths as soon as possible. For most children, the opportunity of acquiring cultural literacy, once lost in the early grades, is lost for good. That is most likely to be true with children of parents who have not themselves mastered the literate national culture. To deprive these children of cultural literacy in the early grades is to deprive most of them forever. By contrast, children from literate families may get at home what the schools have failed to provide. It is the neediest, therefore, who suffer most from our failure to live up to our educational responsibility to teach the traditional extensive curriculum.

• • •

What are the specific contents of that extensive curriculum? Let me be quite specific about goals, even if not about the contents of each grade level. I said that the extensive curriculum consists of broad, often superficial information that is taken for granted in writings directed to a mature general reader. Let me now list some of that information under appropriate categories. American readers are assumed to know vaguely who the following pre-1865 people were (I give just the briefest beginning of an alphabetical list, stopping with H.): John Adams, Benedict Arnold, Daniel Boone, John Brown, Aaron Burr, John C. Calhoun, Henry Clay, James Fenimore Cooper, Lord Cornwallis, Davy Crockett, Emily Dickinson, Stephen A. Douglas, Frederick Douglass, Jonathan Edwards, Ralph Waldo Emerson, Benjamin Franklin, Robert Fulton, Ulysses S. Grant, Alexander Hamilton, and Nathaniel Hawthorne. Most of us know rather little about most of these names, but that little is of crucial importance because it enables writers to assume a foundation from which they can treat in detail whatever they wish to focus upon.

Here is another alphabetical list: Antarctic Ocean, Arctic Ocean, Atlantic Ocean, Baltic Sea, Black Sea, Caribbean Sea, Gulf of Mexico, North Sea, Pacific Ocean, Red Sea. It has a companion list: Alps, Appalachians, Himalayas, Rocky Mountains, Mt. Everest, Mt. Vesuvius, the Matterhorn. Because writers mention these things without explanation, readers need to have them as part of their intellectual baggage.

Another category is the large realm of allusion that belongs to our literary and mythic heritage. These traditional myths enable writers to say complex things compactly and to use the emotive and ironic values of allusion. Here is a sampling of such taken-for-granted materials from the literature that one often gets in childhood: Adam and Eve, Cain and Abel, Noah and the Flood, David and Goliath, the 23rd Psalm, Humpty Dumpty, Jack Sprat, Jack and Jill, Little Jack Horner, Cinderella, Jack and the Beanstalk, Mary Had a Little Lamb, The Night Before Christmas, Peter Pan, Pinocchio, The Princess and the Pea.

Here are some patriotic songs that are generally known: The Battle Hymn of the Republic; Columbia, the Gem of the Ocean; My Country, 'Tis of Thee; America the Beautiful; The Star-Spangled Banner; This Land Is Your Land; Yankee Doodle.

At random I will add (alphabetically) such personages as Achilles, Adonis, Aeneas, Agamemnon, Antigone, and Apollo. Not to mention Robin Hood, Paul Bunyan, Satan, Sleeping Beauty, Sodom and Gomorrah, the Ten Commandments, and Tweedledum and Tweedledee.

Obviously you don't expect me to give the whole list of cultural literacy here. But perhaps it would surprise you to learn that I could do so if I had the time and you had the patience. In fact, such a list was compiled, after much consultation, by a historian, a natural scientist, and myself. It represents background knowledge that people need to have by the time they graduate from high school. Although the list is 131 pages long, it could be cut down by about a third for the pre-tenth-grade age group. Perhaps its most important feature is its limited character. It represents a specific, finite body of superficial knowledge, which, if taught to youngsters in the context of a good *intensive* curriculum, would enable them to understand serious materials directed to a general reader.

• • •

Any such list is of course open to objections like the following: Why aren't there more women on the list? Why isn't there more representation of Chicano culture? Doesn't your list simply certify and perpetuate the existing WASP, establishment culture? Must this status quo, traditional material be the only method of achieving universal literacy? Won't this return to traditional materials make our culture even more static, dull and monolithic than it already is?

My reply is that the various movements that have been resisting such cultural dominance have been working reasonably effectively and will continue to do so. Also, as Catherine Stimpson, the well-known feminist literary critic and former editor of the feminist journal *Signs,* recently observed, we must distinguish between people who are actively trying to change our literate culture and those who are trying to make a useful dictionary of its current structure. Unless the two functions are kept separate, the dictionary makers like me, who are trying to make a serviceable list, will lose their credibility and usefulness.

Stimpson's shrewd observation describes a situation that teachers always find themselves in. Although we are citizens who want to work for social and political ends, such as a more pluralistic culture, we are also professionals whose personal politics must stop at the classroom door. In our roles as teachers, we have an obligation to be descriptive lexicographers, to tell our students what they currently need in order to be literate. If we disapprove of the current literate culture and want to change some of its elements, we should pursue outside the classroom the sort of cultural politics that Catherine Stimpson pursues. But until we succeed in changing the literate culture, we must not misinform our students by pretending that its contents are just what we wish them to be. Of course, we also have an obligation to explain to our students why it is, for example, that a pre-1865 list of Americans whom a culturally literate person might be expected to know of would not include many blacks. The content of a society's cultural literacy bears witness to its sins as well as its successes.

• • •

I mentioned feminism as an example of cultural change because it has succeeded in altering our collective usages. It has made us self-conscious about gender words and gender attitudes. Similarly, the civil rights movement succeeded in changing our usages in such ways as effectively removing the word "nigger" from the English language—a beneficent change, indeed! This kind of change goes on all the time, for both good and ill. As a result, the content of cultural literacy is always changing, as is obvious to everyone in the case of such words as *DNA* and *software.*

What may not be obvious is that the *central* content of cultural literacy has not changed very much in the last hundred years. What changes is at the periphery, not at the center. These days, writers can assume their readers know who Gerald Ford is, but thirty years from now they probably won't make that assumption. On the other hand, thirty years from now writers will continue to assume that George Washington could not tell a lie and that Scrooge hated Christmas. Of course, no single item of cultural literacy has any importance by itself. But the bulk of such items, taken together, are as important as anything we teach.

In the technological age, Washington and the Cherry Tree, and Scrooge and Christmas, the fights historical, the oceans geographical, the beings animalculus, and all the other shared materials of literate culture have become more, not less, important. The more we become computerized, the more we need not just shared scientific knowledge but also shared fairy tales, Greek myths, historical images, and so on. Let me explain this paradox. The more specialized and technical our civilization becomes, the harder it is for nonspecialists to participate in the decisions that deeply affect their lives. The growing power of the technological class will create, according to experts, more and more distance between the rest of us and the ruling cadre of technicians who control the systems. The technicians with their arcane specialties will not be able to communicate with us, nor we with them. This contradicts the basic principles of democracy and must not be allowed to happen.

The only antidote to this problem of specialization was put forward many centuries ago by Cicero. He said that each of us should be trained to communicate our special knowledge to the rest of our society in the language of ordinary people. That this Ciceronian ideal *can* be achieved is proven by those literate scientists who are able to write for a general literate public. But such a literate culture can only be achieved if all of us, including technicians, share enough traditional background material to enable complex communication to occur.

• • •

In conclusion, I want to stress again that the only skills that train for life are those knowledge-based activities that continue specifically to be used in life. Reading and writing, of course, continue to be used. Everyone knows they are absolutely central to productive membership in our society and to the ability to acquire new knowledge-based skills when needed. Reading and writing at the high levels required for such future flexibility are skills that are based on a large, complex system of world knowledge that I have called cultural literacy. Imparting this knowledge to our students, through the study of the humanities and the sciences, is the chief responsibility of our educational system.

Our schools have not imparted these essential facts and words, because in recent times we have not been willing as a nation to decide what the essential facts and words are. Despite our national virtues of diversity and pluralism, our failure to decide upon the core content of cultural literacy has created a positive barrier to adult literacy in this country, and thus to full citizenship and full acculturation into our society. We Americans need to be decisive and explicit about the background information that a citizen should know in order to be literate in the 1980s. Access to this democratic literate culture is not only a proper goal of our curriculum but is also the only possible way of realizing the dream of Jefferson and King.

SUGGESTIONS FOR DISCUSSION

1. Hirsch begins his article by citing the "dream of Thomas Jefferson and Martin Luther King, Jr." and its "very specific educational implication." Why do you think Hirsch has cited Jefferson and King in the opening of the essay? What authority do they bring to the article? What exactly is the "dream" and what are its "educational implications"?

2. Look at the list Hirsch offers in section eight of the article as an example of what the "extensive" curriculum might look like. What seems to be Hirsch's principle of selection? Are there kinds of knowledge that do not appear on Hirsch's list that you think are valuable?

3. What does Hirsch see as the objections to his list? How does he respond to these objections? Do you find his response persuasive? Are there objections you can think of that Hirsch does not address?

SUGGESTIONS FOR WRITING

1. Hirsch suggests that reading is not a "general, transferable skill unrelated to subject matter." Instead, according to Hirsch, reading "varies from task to task, because reading skill depends on specific background knowledge." Write an essay that explores your own experience as a reader to test Hirsch's assertion. Be specific here by focusing on actual episodes of reading and how the background knowledge you bring to reading affects the way you read and how you comprehend.

2. Write an essay that explains what Hirsch means by the term *cultural literacy* and compares it to what you have learned in and out of school. Offer an example of a body of knowledge you have acquired (whether it is through collecting comic books, learning to cook Chinese food, or knowing how to build houses) that is not on Hirsch's list and explain what you see as the value of being literate in a field Hirsch does not include under the term *cultural literacy.*

3. June Jordan and E. D. Hirsch, Jr., offer quite different perspectives on what it means to be literate. Write an essay that compares their views on the meanings and purposes of literacy. You will need, of course, to describe their ideas as accurately as you can, but don't limit your essay to just summarizing. Use the differences you identify between Jordan and Hirsch to develop your own ideas about the value of literacy to individuals and groups in contemporary America. You may find yourself in agreement with either Jordan or Hirsch about the goals of literacy or you may find yourself staking out a third position in relation to them.

FOR FURTHER EXPLORATION

School reform has been a persistent theme in American public life over the past decade, and you can find many issues for further exploration. Much has been written, for example, about the merits and shortcomings of ability-group tracking, of parental choice and the use of vouchers, and of single-sex education. The successful struggle of women students to keep Mills College single-sex is an interesting case study. Or you might look at the role of historically black colleges or the debate over bilingual education. Another possibility is to investigate why women are underrepresented in the physical sciences and engineering. A number of the selections in this chapter are taken from book-length studies (Theodore Sizer's *Horace's Compromise*, Robert B. Everhart's *Reading, Writing, and Resistance*, and Mike Rose's *Lives on the Boundary*). To explore these writers' ideas, you might read their work and some of the reviews that responded to their book.

CHAPTER 4

IMAGES

Every day we move through a visual world of advertisements and
newspapers, photographs and magazines, cinema and television:
an optical empire that is regularly criticized for its power to shape our
lives. This visual collage, accompanying us from morning to night, is a
product of the three giant forces of the contemporary world:
industrialization, capitalism, and urbanization. And the power of the
images that these processes have produced . . . is inescapable. They are a
part of daily vision, contributing to the way we look at and understand
our world. We continually select images from the cinema, from fashion,
from magazines, from adverts, from television. They stand in for 'reality,'
become a reality; the signs of experience, of self.

– Iain Chambers, *Popular Culture:*
The Metropolitan Experience

A s Iain Chambers' statement suggests, you already know quite a bit about images because you cannot easily escape them. Even if you do not watch much television or see many movies, you are surrounded by images every time you go into a small town or a large city, every time you pick up a magazine or newspaper, every time you ride down the highway. These images ask you to buy products or give to charities or vote for candidates or decide on issues of importance. They might be as easily read as an ad of a new car speeding down the highway or as enigmatic as a pair of hands reaching out to empty space. No matter. Every image has the capacity to send a message.

Advertisers, in particular, count on the public being able to read very quickly a few generalized images. For example, a commercial that opens with a child in bed, covers drawn up to her chin, and a parent bending over her is likely selling some cold remedy. The visual details are familiar: child, parent, cover, bed. Because such scenes are so easily recognizable, advertisers are able to use just a few words ("sniffling, sneezing, aching, nighttime relief medicine") to get their message across. As you read this chapter, you will be asked to look at and read such messages and others like them—messages that rely on pictures more than on words.

Like words, nonverbal images are symbols or signs that relay meanings that have come to be attached to them through historic use, through association with things familiar, and through such media as books, television, film, magazines, and billboards. That is not to say that visual meaning is unchanging or that everyone who sees these signs reads precisely the same message. In fact, visual language, like any language, continually shifts with time, circumstance, and use. Still, the most quickly read messages are often those that carry with them expressions of common cultural meanings or ideals, images that act as a kind of visual shorthand.

Take, for example, the following poster depicting a gagged George Washington. Even without the words beneath this picture, most individuals schooled in the United States are likely to read it as a message about the right to speak. The Gilbert Stuart portrait of Washington from which this picture is drawn is the image most often copied when Americans want to portray the first president of the United States. It appears on dollar bills, on postage stamps, and in elementary schoolrooms across the country. Moreover, Washington's image has come to be closely associated with issues of the American Revolution such as freedom of speech and the right of the people to determine their own form of government. The gagged mouth suggests forceful suppression of speech, perhaps by outlaws or thugs. Thus, even without the text, "Let Washington Speak. Congressional Voting Rights for Washington, D.C.," the image has within it the possibility of conveying a powerful message. The text works to anchor a common reading of this image. It tells readers that this poster is about a particular issue in a particular political struggle. The text, then, helps limit the ways in which the image, on its own, might be read.

What the cultural shorthand cannot control is the additional meaning that individuals are able to generate with an image such as this one. In the early seventies, for example, the "Keep America Beautiful" campaign made use of a close-up of an American Indian's face, a tear streaming down one cheek, to sell Americans on picking up their litter. The message was a potent one: Americans had managed to pollute the land its indigenous peoples had lived in, worked in, and revered. In the nineties one

trash bag company has rewritten that antilitter ad to draw again upon the image of the "vanishing American," an Indian who watches a group of children putting trash into plastic bags, smiles, then literally vanishes from the screen. Embedded in both ads are additional messages expressing cultural forms or ideals. One of the most obvious is the non-Indian notion of American Indians as a vanished culture, a notion that today's tribes work hard to correct. Naturally, then, American Indians are likely to find meanings in those ad campaigns that readers oblivious to the stereotype will miss.

The "Let Washington Speak" poster works in much the same way. Though the artist who created this poster very likely wanted to persuade voters that a vote against congressional voting rights for the District of Columbia was a vote against the principles upon which this nation was founded, a reader could conceivably look at the image and feel that it is about time that the bigwigs of this country were finally gagged. That reader would be one who did not feel strongly persuaded by the image of Washington as a symbol of freedom but instead might see Washington as the first in a long line of patri-archal authority figures. Both readers are likely to understand the message about free-dom of speech and constitutional rights, but their response to that message would dif-fer depending on particular circumstances that may be determined by differences in politics, social, ethnic, or economic background or even by gender. Visual meaning, like all meaning, is dependent on both the message being sent and the receiver of that message.

Cultural meanings need not refer to patriotism or ethnic stereotypes, however. Advertisers take advantage of cultural meanings every time they present an image as if it were representative of what everyone desires. A recent advertisement for Aramis men's cologne for example, links the product with the idea that all men want to be he-roes. The ad is more image than text, but the text is quite provocative. In a corner be-neath the picture of a young businessman walking through a door are the words, "An American Hero. The impact never fades." Of course, this text is meant to apply both to the cologne and the man pictured in the ad. More than that, the text is meant to apply to any man who uses this cologne and, by extension, any man who uses this cologne can be the man in this ad: An American Hero.

To read the Aramis ad as the advertisers intend, you simply look at the ad quickly, perhaps identify with the fellow at the door (maybe wish you or your best friend were like him), and link Aramis cologne with the attractiveness the ad portrays. Reading the ad critically takes a bit more time because it means paying very close atten-tion to visual details and thinking about what those details mean in an ad like this one. The details work together to help you read what the advertisers are telling us is the American Hero. The pinstriped suit, expensive glasses, and *Wall Street Journal* all seem to indicate that this is a young man on the rise in a corporate, urban world. He carries a racquet and tosses an orange indicating that he is health-conscious—perhaps he'll eat the orange for lunch and use his break to play racquetball on the company court. This entire scenario is set with just a few carefully chosen details that tell a story and portray a life-style. It is a life-style not easily available to all, though it seems so very accessible in this ad—as accessible as a small bottle of men's cologne.

The assuredness with which the Aramis cologne ad sells a life-style and a new kind of American hero is precisely what bothers many people when they look at ad-vertising. Knowing that most people simply let ads go by without reading them closely, at least one group of artists and activists has taken to writing over ads so that the public at large might more easily see the alternative meanings possible in any ad campaign. This group of graffitists, who call themselves Billboard Using Graffitists Against Unhealthy Promotion (BUGAUP), changed the text of the following Marlboro ad to accomplish just that purpose. This billboard originally looked like most Marlboro ads. The text of the original billboard reads, "New. Mild. And Marlboro." By contrast, the BUGAUP group sees the original ad as one for an un-healthy product, so it uses the original text to rewrite the advertiser's message in order to send a message of their own making.

The reading/rewriting by the BUGAUP group disrupts the ad's meanings by transforming "Mild" into "Vile" and "Marlboro" into "A Bore," thus challenging the Marlboro Man's image as well as the text that tries to reconcile cigarette smoking with health and independence. The tombstone drawn by BUGAUP onto the billboard uses a traditional sign of the Western legend—Boot Hill—to subvert the code of the Western and to turn the text into a warning in the name of health. Writing and rewriting, in the hands of BUGAUP, thus becomes a forceful tool of resistance.

READING IMAGES

Many of the images you encounter daily are likely to be television, film, or advertising images. Because these kinds of images are the ones most immediately available, we open this chapter with Stuart and Elizabeth Ewen's "In the Shadow of the Image," an article that dramatizes just how much our lives are affected by a daily barrage of popular images. As you read the Ewens' article you might begin to gather and think about images from your own surroundings. The first writing assignments from this chapter will ask you to do just that, collect as much from your daily life as you can so that you have something on which to base later judgments.

In the next selection, Jean Kilbourne argues the importance of understanding advertising images as conveying cultural meaning. Because most of us read ads in the way that they are meant to be read—quickly, without much thought—we normally do not spend the kind of time that a writer like Kilbourne spends in working out how ads take on meaning and how that meaning reflects cultural ideals.

You may discover, though, that an ad becomes more interesting when you attempt to read it more closely than its advertisers may have intended. A good example of how that might work occurred in 1993 for readers of *Premiere Magazine*. Diesel Jeans company ran an ad apparently meant to be sarcastic, even satiric. In a full two-page spread the ad was, like much magazine advertising, more image than text. The background of the ad was taken up by the repeated black-and-white image of a man pointing a handgun toward the camera and toward the full-color image of a woman standing in front of him, looking out at the camera. For many readers, this was an image of violence and threatened rape. The ad copy attempted to satirize contemporary

attitudes toward women, men, and violence by challenging readers to teach their children to "blast the brains out of their neighbors." The very next issue (June 1993) of *Premiere Magazine* carried the following letter from the magazine's editor to its readers:

> To Our Readers:
> We received an enormous number of letters and telephone calls about the Diesel jeans advertisement that ran in our April issue. We have since concluded that the ad was inappropriate for this magazine, and it will not appear in these pages again. Many advertisers today are using the element of shock to distinguish themselves from their competitors and, in some cases, to generate discussion about contemporary topics. I believe. Diesel thought its ad was in that tradition. But *Premiere* has been, and will always be, edited for its readers . . . and when you find the time to write us about something you hate—or love—in the magazine, we will respond.
>
> Susan Lyne
>
> Editor/publication director

What this editor's response suggests is that your ability to read and pay attention even to advertisements makes a difference. Advertisers are particularly sensitive to the demands of their customers because their business is to persuade. If they offend or miss the mark, they lose business. That is precisely what writers like Jean Kilbourne want you to do—understand what is being said or sold to you through contemporary advertising.

Kilbourne argues that we must pay attention to meaning because, as she points out, Americans see over 2,000 ads a day, and advertising is intended to persuade. As you examine the ads in this chapter and those that occur in your daily life, take the time to examine what you are being persuaded to do, how you are being persuaded to look, to feel, and to think about yourself and others.

Kilbourne focuses her attention on advertising's impact on women, but you can, if you wish, go beyond women's issues, for advertising makes promises to all consumers regardless of gender, race, class, or ability to spend.

Once you have collected images that interest you, where do you go next? It is easy, for example, to attack the values represented by an ad that tells you how you should look, what you should wear, and who you should be. It is much more difficult to understand how those images take on meaning or to explain why such simplistic images have power in a complex culture. In a chapter from one of Arthur Asa Berger's many discussions of how meaning is conveyed in popular culture, Berger reads a specific kind of advertising image and offers a checklist of what to look for as you write your own visual analysis.

The final selections in this chapter extend our discussion of visual meaning to a discussion of the ways in which other issues are often affected by the culture of the image. In an essay on how environmental concerns can be influenced by pictures, Joel Connelly explains how potent the visual image has been in environmental campaigns. Advertising campaigns for environmental movements are especially provocative in the context of cultural meaning because they must draw on cultural ideals about land use and wilderness, ideals that are perpetuated by much of the advertising that we see throughout magazines and on billboards across the nation.

Danny Duncan Collum and bell hooks take the discussion of images even further by suggesting that even the way we understand history and the way we understand cultural events and major historical and political figures may be influenced by film and advertising images. Their articles on film and advertising's influence on our image of Malcolm X raise these issues quite forcefully. Their concerns may lead you to consider how images affect much of your knowledge about events in American history or the men and women we have called our heroes, our models, or our villains.

After you have read others' interpretations of images and collected images yourself, you will be asked to write your own interpretation of the visual image as a rich medium of cultural meaning. Keep in mind how skillful you already are at interpreting those images, many of which will hold at least some meaning for you. Ask yourself how real-seeming the image is. Is it a reflection of something you have experienced, or does it seem to be a fiction?

Advertising is perhaps the most prolific medium of communication today. Companies bet profits or predict losses based on ad campaigns that succeed or fail. Those campaigns succeed when consumers buy into the image. Just what that image is telling us about ourselves is, you may discover, worth investigating.

Stuart and Elizabeth Ewen

In the Shadow of the Image

Elizabeth and Stuart Ewen have written several books and articles on the history and meaning of popular culture. Cultural scholar Stuart Ewen's work includes *All Consuming Images: The Politics of Style in Contemporary Culture* and *Captains of Consciousness.* Historian Elizabeth Ewen's work includes *Immigrant Women in the Land of Dollars. Channels of Desire,* from which the following selection is taken, is their first full-length collaboration. In *Channels of Desire,* written in 1982, the Ewens argue that much of what Americans understand self-image to be is actually a reflection of mass media images. As the opening essay reprinted here illustrates, we are a culture that lives in the shadow of the image, especially the advertising image. Everywhere we go, we see images created for mass consumption but seemingly aimed at individuals. We measure our looks against the looks in the ads, and we measure our aches and pains against the aches and pains depicted in those same ads.

Suggestion for Reading

- In the final paragraphs of "In the Shadow of the Image," the Ewens sum up the point they are trying to make. If you begin to lose track of what is going on in this selection, read those last few paragraphs and then go back and finish reading through the vignettes.

———————————◆———————————

Maria Aguilar was born twenty-seven years ago near Mayagüez, on the island of Puerto Rico. Her family had lived off the land for generations. Today she sits in a rattling IRT subway car, speeding through the iron-and-rock guts of Manhattan. She sits on the train, her ears dazed by the loud outcry of wheels against tracks. Surrounded by a galaxy of unknown fellow strangers, she looks up at a long strip of colorful signboards placed high above the bobbing heads of the others. All the posters call for her attention.

Looking down at her, a blond-haired lady cabdriver leans out of her driver's side window. Here is the famed philosopher of this strange urban world, and a woman she can talk to. The tough-wise eyes of the cabby combine with a youthful beauty, speaking to Maria Aguilar directly:

Estoy sentada 12 horas al dia.

Lo último que necesito son hemorroides.

(I sit for twelve hours a day. The last thing I need are hemorrhoids.)

Under this candid testimonial lies a package of Preparation H ointment, and the promise "Alivia dolores y picasonas. Y ayuda a reducir la hinchazón." (Relieves pain and itching. And helps reduce swelling.) As her mind's eye takes it all in, the train sweeps into Maria's stop. She gets out; climbs the stairs to the street; walks to work where she will spend her day sitting on a stool in a small garment factory, sewing hems on pretty dresses.

• • •

Every day, while Benny Doyle drives his Mustang to work along State Road Number 20, he passes a giant billboard along the shoulder. The billboard is selling whisky and features a woman in a black velvet dress stretching across its brilliant canvas.

As Benny Doyle downshifts by, the lounging beauty looks out to him. Day after day he sees her here. The first time he wasn't sure, but now he's convinced that her eyes are following him.

• • •

The morning sun shines on the red-tan forehead of Bill O'Conner as he drinks espresso on his sun deck, alongside the ocean cliffs of La Jolla, California. Turning through the daily paper, he reads a story about Zimbabwe.

"Rhodesia," he thinks to himself.

The story argues that a large number of Africans in Zimbabwe are fearful about black majority rule, and are concerned over a white exodus. Two black hotel workers are quoted by the article. Bill puts this, as a fact, into his mind.

Later that day, over a business lunch, he repeats the story to five white business associates, sitting at the restaurant table. They share a superior laugh over the ineptitude of black African political rule. Three more tellings, children of the first, take place over the next four days. These are spoken by two of Bill O'Conner's luncheon companions; passed on to still others in the supposed voice of political wisdom.

• • •

Barbara and John Marsh get into their seven-year-old Dodge pickup and drive twenty-three miles to the nearest Sears in Cedar Rapids. After years of breakdowns and months of hesitation they've decided to buy a new washing machine. They come to Sears because it is there, and because they believe that their new Sears machine will be steady and reliable. The Marshes will pay for their purchase for the next year or so.

Barbara's great-grandfather, Elijah Simmons, had purchased a cream-separator from Sears, Roebuck in 1897 and he swore by it.

• • •

When the clock-radio sprang the morning affront upon him, Archie Bishop rolled resentfully out of his crumpled bed and trudged slowly to the john. A few moments later he was unconsciously squeezing toothpaste out of a mess of red and white Colgate packaging. A dozen scrubs of the mouth and he expectorated a white, minty glob into the basin.

Still groggy, he turned on the hot water, slapping occasional palmfuls onto his gray face.

A can of Noxzema shave cream sat on the edge of the sink, a film of crud and whiskers across its once neat label. Archie reached for the bomb and filled his left hand with a white creamy mound, then spread it over his beard. He shaved, then looked with resignation at the regular collection of cuts on his neck.

Stepping into a shower, he soaped up with a soap that promised to wake him up. Groggily, he then grabbed a bottle of Clairol Herbal Essence Shampoo. He turned the tablet-shaped bottle to its back label, carefully reading the "Directions."

"Wet hair."

He wet his hair.

"Lather."

He lathered.

"Rinse."

He rinsed.

"Repeat if necessary."

Not sure whether it was altogether necessary, he repeated the process according to directions.

Late in the evening, Maria Aguilar stepped back in the subway train, heading home to the Bronx after a long and tiring day. This time, a poster told her that "The Pain Stops Here!"

She barely noticed, but later she would swallow two New Extra Strength Bufferin tablets with a glass of water from a rusty tap.

• • •

Two cockroaches in cartoon form leer out onto the street from a wall advertisement. The man cockroach is drawn like a hipster, wearing shades and a cockroach zoot-suit. He strolls hand-in-hand with a lady cockroach, who is dressed like a floozy and blushing beet-red. Caught in the midst of their cockroach-rendezvous, they step sinfully into a Black Flag Roach Motel. Beneath them, in Spanish, the words:

Las Cucarachas entran . . . pero non pueden salir.
(In the English version: Cockroaches check in . . . but they don't check out.)

• • •

The roaches are trapped; sin is punished. Salvation is gauged by one's ability to live roach-free. The sinners of the earth shall be inundated by roaches. Moral tales and insects encourage passersby to rid their houses of sin. In their homes, sometimes, people wonder whether God has forsaken them.

• • •

Beverly Jackson sits at a metal and tan Formica table and looks through the *New York Post*. She is bombarded by a catalog of horror. Children are mutilated . . . subway riders attacked. . . . Fanatics are marauding and noble despots lie in bloody heaps. Occasionally someone steps off the crime-infested streets to claim a million dollars in lottery winnings.

Beverly Jackson's skin crawls; she feels a knot encircling her lungs. She is beset by immobility, hopelessness, depression.

Slowly she walks over to her sixth-floor window, gazing out into the sooty afternoon. From the empty street below, Beverly Jackson imagines a crowd yelling "Jump! . . . Jump!"

• • •

Between 1957 and 1966 Frank Miller saw a dozen John Wayne movies, countless other westerns and war dramas. In 1969 he led a charge up a hill without a name in Southeast Asia. No one followed; he took a bullet in the chest.

Today he sits in a chair and doesn't get up. He feels that images betrayed him, and now he camps out across from the White House while another movie star cuts benefits for veterans. In the morning newspaper he reads of a massive weapons buildup taking place.

• • •

Gina Concepcion now comes to school wearing the Jordache look. All this has been made possible by weeks and weeks of afterschool employment at a supermarket checkout counter. Now, each morning, she tugs the decorative denim over her young legs, sucking in her lean belly to close the snaps.

These pants are expensive compared to the "no-name" brands, but they're worth it, she reasons. They fit better, and she fits better.

• • •

The theater marquee, stretching out over a crumbling, garbage-strewn sidewalk, announced "The Decline of Western Civilization." At the ticket window a smaller sign read "All seats $5.00."

• • •

It was ten in the morning and Joyce Hopkins stood before a mirror next to her bed. Her interview at General Public Utilities, Nuclear Division, was only four hours away and all she could think was "What to wear?"

A half hour later Joyce stood again before the mirror, wearing a slip and stockings. On the bed, next to her, lay a two-foot-high mountain of discarded options. Mocking the title of a recent bestseller, which she hadn't read, she said aloud to herself, "Dress for Success. . . . What *do* they like?"

At one o'clock she walked out the door wearing a brownish tweed jacket; a cream-colored Qiana blouse, full-cut with a tied collar; a dark beige skirt, fairly straight and hemmed (by Maria Aguilar) two inches below the knee; shear fawn stockings, and simple but elegant reddish-brown pumps on her feet. Her hair was to the shoulder, her look tawny.

When she got the job she thanked her friend Millie, a middle manager, for the tip not to wear pants.

• • •

Joe Davis stood at the endless conveyor, placing caps on a round-the-clock parade of automobile radiators. His nose and eyes burned. His ears buzzed in the din. In a furtive moment he looked up and to the right. On the plant wall was a large yellow sign with THINK! printed on it in bold type. Joe turned back quickly to the radiator caps.

Fifty years earlier, in another factory, in another state, Joe's grandfather, Nat Davis, had looked up and seen another sign:

A *Clean* Machine Runs Better.

Your Body is a Machine.

KEEP IT CLEAN.

Though he tried and tried, Joe Davis' grandfather was never able to get the dirt out from under his nails. Neither could his great-grandfather, who couldn't read.

• • •

In 1952 Mary Bird left her family in Charleston to earn money as a maid in Philadelphia suburb. She earned thirty-five dollars a week, plus room and board, in a dingy retreat of a ranch-style tract house.

Twenty-eight years later she sits on a bus, heading toward her small room in North Philly. Across from her, on an advertising poster, a sumptuous meal is displayed. Golden fried chicken, green beans glistening with butter and flecked by pimento, and a fluffy cloud of rice fill the greater part of a calico-patterned dinner plate. Next to the plate sit a steaming boat of gravy, and an icy drink in an amber tumbler. The plate is on a quilted blue placemat, flanked by a thick linen napkin and colonial silverware.

As Mary Bird's hungers are aroused, the wording on the placard instructs her: *"Come Home to Carolina."*

• • •

Shopping List

paper towels
milk
eggs
rice crispies
chicken
snacks for kids (twinkies, chips, etc.)
potatoes
coke, ginger ale, plain soda
cheer
brillo
peanut butter
bread
ragu (2 jars)
spaghetti
saran wrap
salad
get cleaning, bank, *must pay electric!!!*

• • •

On his way to Nina's house, Sidney passed an ad for Smirnoff vodka. A sultry beauty with wet hair and beads of moisture on her smooth, tanned face looked out at him. *"Try a Main Squeeze."* For a teenage boy the invitation transcended the arena of drink; he felt a quick throb-pulse at the base of his belly and his step quickened.

• • •

In October of 1957, at the age of two and a half, Aaron Stone was watching television. Suddenly, from the black screen, there leaped a circus clown, selling children's vitamins, and yelling "Hi! boys and girls!" He ran, terrified, from the room, screaming.

For years after, Aaron watched television in perpetual fear that the vitamin clown would reappear. Slowly his family assured him that the television was just a mechanical box and couldn't really hurt him, that the vitamin clown was harmless.

Today, as an adult, Aaron Stone takes vitamins, is ambivalent about clowns, and watches television, although there are occasional moments of anxiety.

These are some of the facts of our lives; disparate moments, disconnected, dissociated. Meaningless moments. Random incidents. Memory traces. Each is an unplanned encounter, part of day-to-day existence. Viewed alone, each by itself, such spaces of our lives seem insignificant, trivial. They are the decisions and reveries of survival; the stuff of small talk; the chance preoccupations of our eyes and minds in a world of images—soon forgotten.

Viewed together, however, as an ensemble, an integrated panorama of social life, human activity, hope and despair, images and information, another tale unfolds from these vignettes. They reveal a pattern of life, the structures of perception.

As familiar moments in American life, all of these events bear the footprints of a history that weighs upon us, but is largely untold. We live and breathe an atmosphere where mass images are everywhere in evidence; mass produced, mass distributed. In the streets, in our homes, among a crowd, or alone, they speak to us, overwhelm our vision. Their presence, their messages are given; unavoidable. Though their history is still relatively short, their prehistory is, for the most part, forgotten, unimaginable.

The history that unites the seemingly random routines of daily life is one that embraces the rise of an industrial consumer society. It involves explosive interactions between modernity and old ways of life. It includes the proliferation, over days and decades, of a wide, repeatable vernacular of commercial images and ideas. This history spells new patterns of social, productive, and political life.

This book, in its various essays, attempts to plumb the social history that stands behind the apparent immortality of a consumer society; its universe of commodities; its priorities; its social forms. The pages that follow offer some historical suggestions aimed at telling some of the story by which these disparate events, these "insignificant" details and occurrences, took hold as the facts of life.

SUGGESTIONS FOR DISCUSSION

1. How well would you say this series of vignettes represents your own daily experience of images?
2. Most of these vignettes seem to deal with the trivial decisions consumers make about buying one kind of product over another. A few of the vignettes also include references to daily news stories. What would you say is the purpose of interspersing references to news stories with those advertisement vignettes?
3. Consider the products you buy that are brand name products. How often would you say your own or your family's buying habits are influenced by advertisements?

SUGGESTIONS FOR WRITING

1. Write an essay in which you compare your own experience with advertising to that represented by the vignettes in "In the Shadow of the Image." In your essay, you should examine how frequently your own or your family's buying habits seem to be influenced by all of the advertising you see daily.
2. Near the end of their essay, the Ewens write, "The history that unites the seemingly random routines of daily life is one that embraces the rise of an industrial consumer society. It involves explosive interactions between modernity and old ways of life. It includes the proliferation, over days and decades, of a wide, repeatable vernacular of commercial images and ideas. This history spells new patterns of social, productive, and political life." Write an explanation of what you understand the authors to be saying in that statement. In your explanation, provide examples from your own experience or reading that might help make the meaning clear.
3. Make a list of ad images that you see on most days. The list might include posters, billboards, commercials, magazine and newspaper ads, anything that carries with it an ad image. Keep the images that you think are the most effective in conveying one particular argument that you would like to make about advertising images and their role in our daily lives. Eliminate the others. Then,

write an essay in which you describe the kinds of images you encounter daily and what cultural meanings those images seem to be conveying in the details of the ads. How, for example, are women, men, lawyers, repair people, and so on represented in these ads?

Jean Kilbourne

BEAUTY . . . AND THE BEAST OF ADVERTISING

Jean Kilbourne is a filmmaker and lecturer whose work focuses primarily on alcohol and cigarette advertising and on images of women in advertising. She is the creator of the award-winning *Still Killing Us Softly*, a film which examines images of women in advertising. In the selection that follows, Kilbourne explains why it is important that we pay attention to the ways in which gender is portrayed in advertising today. This article originally appeared as an essay in 1989 in the media action magazine *Media & Values* as a segment of a two-part series of articles on images of men and women in the media.

Suggestion for Reading

• Early in this article Kilbourne writes, "ads sell a great deal more than products. They sell values, images and concepts of success and worth, love and sexuality, popularity and normalcy. They tell us who we are and who we should be. Sometimes they sell addictions." In the margins of your text, annotate this essay with your own examples of ads that sell more than just the product.

---◆---

ou're a Halston woman from the very beginning," the advertisement proclaims. The model stares provocatively at the viewer, her long blonde hair waving around her face, her bare chest partially covered by two curved bottles that give the illusion of breasts and a cleavage.

The average American is accustomed to blue-eyed blondes seductively touting a variety of products. In this case, however, the blonde is about five years old.

Advertising is an over $100 billion a year industry and affects all of us throughout our lives. We are each exposed to over 2,000 ads a day, constituting perhaps the most powerful educational force in society. The average adult will spend one and one-half years of his/her life watching television commercials. But the ads sell a great deal more than products. They sell values, images and concepts of success and worth, love and sexuality, popularity and normalcy. They tell us who we are and who we should be. Sometimes they sell addictions.

Advertising's foundation and economic lifeblood is the mass media, and the primary purpose of the mass media is to deliver an audience to advertisers, just as the primary purpose of television programs is to deliver an audience for commercials.

Adolescents are particularly vulnerable, however, because they are new and inexperienced consumers and are the prime targets of many advertisements. They are in the process of learning their values and roles and developing their self-concepts. Most teenagers are sensitive to peer pressure and find it difficult to resist or even question the dominant cultural messages perpetuated and reinforced by the media. Mass communication has made possible a kind of nationally distributed peer pressure that erodes private and individual values and standards.

But what does society, and especially teenagers, learn from the advertising messages that proliferate in the mass media? On the most obvious level they learn the stereotypes. Advertising creates a mythical, WASP-oriented world in which no one is ever ugly, overweight, poor, struggling or disabled either physically or mentally (unless you count the housewives who talk to little men in toilet bowls, animated germs in drains or muscle-bound giants clad in white clothing). And it is a world in which people talk only about products.

HOUSEWIVES OR SEX OBJECTS

The aspect of advertising most in need of analysis and change is the portrayal of women. Scientific studies and the most casual viewing yield the same conclusion: Women are shown almost exclusively as housewives or sex objects.

The housewife, pathologically obsessed by cleanliness and lemonfresh scents, debates cleaning products with herself and worries about her husband's "ring around the collar."

The sex object is a mannequin, a shell. Conventional beauty is her only attribute. She has no lines or wrinkles (which would indicate she had the bad taste and poor judgment to grow older), no scars or blemishes—indeed, she has no pores. She is thin, generally tall and long-legged, and, above all, she is young. All "beautiful" women in advertisements (including minority women), regardless of product or audience, conform to this norm. Women are constantly exhorted to emulate this ideal, to feel ashamed and guilty if they fail, and to feel that their desirability and lovability are contingent upon physical perfection.

CREATING ARTIFICIALITY

The image is artificial and can only be achieved artificially (even the "natural look" requires much preparation and expense). Beauty is something that comes from without; more than one million dollars is spent every hour on cosmetics. Desperate to conform to an ideal and impossible standard, many women go to great lengths to manipulate and change their faces and bodies. A woman is conditioned to view her face as a mask and her body as an object, as *things* separate from and more important than her real self, constantly in need of alteration, improvement, and disguise. She is made to feel dissatisfied with and ashamed of herself, whether she tries to achieve "the look" or not. Objectified constantly by others, she learns to objectify herself. (It is interesting to note that one in five college-age women have an eating disorder.)

"When *Glamour* magazine surveyed its readers in 1984, 75 percent felt too heavy and only 15 percent felt just right. Nearly half of those who were actually underweight reported feeling too fat and wanting to diet. Among a sample of college women, 40 percent felt overweight when only 12 percent actually were too heavy," according to Rita Freedman in her book *Beauty Bound.*

There is evidence that this preoccupation with weight begins at ever-earlier ages for women. According to a recent article in *New Age Journal,* "even grade-school girls are succumbing to sticklike standards of beauty enforced by a relentless parade of wasp-waisted fashion models, movie stars and pop idols." A study by a University of California professor showed that nearly 80 percent of fourth-grade girls in the Bay Area are watching their weight.

A recent *Wall Street Journal* survey of students in four Chicago-area schools found that more than half the fourth-grade girls were dieting and three-quarters felt they were overweight. One student said, "We don't expect boys to be that handsome. We take them as they are." Another added, "But boys expect girls to be perfect and beautiful. And skinny."

Dr. Steven Levenkron, author of *The Best Little Girl in the World,* the story of an anorexic, says his blood pressure soars every time he opens a magazine and finds an ad for women's fashions. "If I had my way," he said, "every one of them would have to carry a line saying, 'Caution: This model may be hazardous to your health.'"

Women are also dismembered in commercials, their bodies separated into parts in need of change or improvement. If a woman has "acceptable" breasts, then she must also be sure that her legs are worth watching, her hips slim, her feet sexy, and that her buttocks look nude under her clothes ("like I'm not wearin' nothin' "). This image is difficult and costly to achieve and impossible to maintain (unless you buy the product)—no one is flawless and everyone ages. Growing older is the great taboo. Women are encouraged to remain little girls ("because innocence is sexier than you think"), to be passive and dependent, never to mature. The contradictory message—"sensual, but not too far from innocence"—places women in a double bind; somehow we are supposed to be both sexy and virginal, experienced and naïve, seductive and chaste. The disparagement of maturity is, of course, insulting and frustrating to adult women, and the implication that little girls are seductive is dangerous to real children.

INFLUENCING SEXUAL ATTITUDES

Young people also learn a great deal about sexual attitudes from the media and from advertising in particular. Advertising's approach to sex is pornographic; it reduces people to objects and de-emphasizes human contact and individuality. This reduction of sexuality to a dirty joke and of people to object is the real obscenity of the culture. Although the sexual sell, overt and subliminal, is at a fevered pitch in most commercials, there is at the same time a notable absence of sex as an important and profound human activity.

There have been some changes in the images of women. Indeed, a "new woman" has emerged in commercials in recent years. She is generally presented as superwoman, who manages to do all the work at home and on the job (with the help of a product, of course, not of her husband or children or friends), or as the liberated woman, who owes her independence and self-esteem to the products she uses. These new images do not represent any real progress but rather create a myth of progress, an illusion that reduces complex sociopolitical problems to mundane personal ones.

Advertising images do not cause these problems, but they contribute to them by creating a climate in which the marketing of women's bodies—the sexual sell and dismemberment, distorted body image ideal and children as sex objects—is seen as acceptable.

This is the real tragedy, that many women internalize these stereotypes and learn their "limitations," thus establishing a self-fulfilling prophecy. If one accepts these mythical and degrading images, to some extent one actualizes them. By remaining unaware of the profound seriousness of the ubiquitous influence, the redundant message and the subliminal impact of advertisements, we ignore one of the most powerful "educational" forces in the culture—one that greatly affects our self-images, our ability to relate to each other, and effectively destroys any awareness and action that might help to change that climate.

SUGGESTIONS FOR DISCUSSION

1. In her article, Kilbourne asks, "But what does society, and especially teenagers, learn from the advertising messages that proliferate in the mass media?" How would you answer that question?
2. Kilbourne objects to the "new woman" presented in advertising as much as she does to the old stereotype. With your classmates, list ads that represent this "new woman." In your judgment, why is this stereotype also so offensive to Kilbourne? What is your response to this stereotype?
3. With your classmates, make a list of current ads that use sexism to sell the product. What image of the product is each ad attempting to project?

SUGGESTIONS FOR WRITING

1. Write a brief explanation of how cultural ideals are promoted through advertising. Use examples from your own experience of seeing and reading ads and buying into or rejecting the images projected by those ads.
2. Kilbourne writes that "the aspect of advertising most in need of analysis and change is the portrayal of women." Write an essay in which you examine the portrayal of women in ads promoting the same type of product (e.g., cleaning supplies, office supplies, hair products, makeup, etc.). These ads should represent different brand names. Pay attention to how the women are portrayed in these ads, what they look like, and what the ads seem to be saying about women in this culture.
3. Gather together a collection of ten to fifteen printed ads that seem to convey a particular cultural meaning. This meaning might be about gender or status or beauty or age, though you need not limit your choices to these. (For example, some ads project a cultural ideal of motherhood in which the mother is represented as the caretaker, the person worried over "ring around the collar," toilet bowl stains, and shinny linoleum.) From the ads you have collected, choose three to five that you feel most comfortable discussing, and write an essay in which you explain what cultural meaning the ads seem to convey. In order to write about the ideas of the ads, you will have to pay attention to visual details. Your purpose in this essay will be to practice reading meaning from specific visual detail. When you write in this way, you are doing more than simply describing the ads; you are analyzing or examining the basic assumptions upon which the ads are constructed.

Arthur Asa Berger

SEX AS SYMBOL IN FASHION ADVERTISING AND ANALYZING SIGNS AND SIGN SYSTEMS

Arthur Asa Berger is a Professor of Broadcast Communication Arts at San Francisco State University. His work on popular culture includes *The Comic Stripped American, The TV-Guided American,* and *Television as an Instrument of Terror.* Throughout his career, Berger has attempted to make accessible the language of media analysis and cultural critique. In the following selections taken from two book-length discussions of media analysis, published in 1982 and 1984, Berger provides an analysis of fashion advertisements and a checklist of what to look for when you analyze a visual image.

Suggestion for Reading

- Like Elizabeth and Stuart Ewen, Arthur Asa Berger suggests that much of advertising functions on an unconscious level. Note in the margins of your text what issues seem to be raised by that suggestion. Consider why ads must function on this level in order for them to be most effective.

Sex as Symbol in Fashion Advertising

◆

While reading an issue of *Vogue* recently, I noticed that I was, somehow, taken by a number of the advertisements for fashions and cosmetics. Many of these advertisements contained striking photographs and suggestive (and in some cases rather overt) copy. I found myself absorbed by the advertisements. They had a remarkable power over me—to seize my attention and to stimulate, if only for a moment, fantasies of an erotic nature. It was not only the physical characteristics of the models that affected me; rather it was a kind of gestalt effect. There was the element of graphic design, of color, of light, and a host of other matters that "conspired" to excite me.

"What's going on?" I asked myself. That question led me to consider how magazine advertising works to stimulate desire and sell clothes, cosmetics, and everything else that is connected with beauty (in this case) or any product.

In analyzing an advertisement there are a number of factors that we must consider, such as the ambience, the design, the use of white space, the significant images and symbols, the use of language, the type faces used, and the item itself (and its role and function in society). We can also consider how the advertisement attempts to "sell" us and what roles it offers us to imitate, as well as examine how social phenomena might be reflected, indirectly. (Here I'm thinking about such things as alienation, boredom, conformism, generational conflict, and so on.) We can use whatever concepts we have at our command from history, psychology, sociology, anthropology, and any other disciplines to help us "dissect" the advertisement. In applying all of the above it is important to keep one cardinal principle in mind: The creators of any advertisement are trying to generate some kind of an effect or emotional response. So we must start with the effect and work backwards. What is the fantasy? And how is it induced?

Selling Magic

I will answer these questions by examining some of the advertisements in the April 1978 issue of *Vogue* magazine. I've selected advertisements that, for some reason, caught my attention for a moment and that I think are interesting and worth examining closely.

Let me start with a double-page advertisement by Revlon for its Formula 2 cleanser and moisturizer. The left-hand page of the advertisement is devoted to an extreme close-up of a woman's face, but the face is rendered by using quarter-inch squares of various colors. We are, in fact, given an optical illusion. If we squint, or place the magazine fifteen feet away from us, the squares merge together and form a face. But at arm's length, the face is somewhat distorted and out of focus. It is also larger than life in size. From there we move over to the right-hand page, which has a great deal of white space and is formally designed, approximating axial balance. Generally speaking, large amounts of white space and axial balance (and formality) are associated with quality and "class" in most people's mind.

The copy of the ad stresses science and technology as opposed to nature. We find the following suggestive words and phrases in the advertisement:

> Revlon Research Group
> skincare system
> natural electricity
> formula
> skincare that's simple, scientific
> precision tip
> beauty technology
> hygiene
> principle

All of these terms are signifiers for science and technology; we are led to think of scientists in laboratories discovering remarkable things that lead to "the New-Face Hygiene" and "beautiful life for your skin." A smaller photograph on this page shows two medicinal-looking bottles, in which the future-age Formula 2 cleanser and moisturizer are packaged.

Though this is something of a generalization, there seems to be a polar opposition in the public's mind that posits a world divided between culture (and with it science and technology) and nature. Thus the people who created the Revlon advertisement had two possibilities: to stress nature and all that's suggested by it, or to stress culture, in this case, science and technology. They chose the latter course and offered their readers a minicourse in science and technology: *This* principle leads to *those* results.

Ultimately what is being sold here—and what is being sold in most cosmetics ads—is magic, and that is where the large rendering of the woman's face comes in. It is an optical illusion that has two functions: First, it catches our attention because when we look at the face we see that it is really only a huge patchwork of squares. At first glance it seems out of focus and strange. But, if we squint or stare at it, magically it becomes a face, just the same way that Revlon Formula 2's "beauty technology of the future" gives you the gift of "life" (for your skin). Just as the law of closure forces us to complete that which is unfinished, we find ourselves obliged to make sense of the picture, and we visualize the woman's face even more completely than we find it. This act of visualization is what is asked of patrons or purchasers of the product. From the bits and pieces of their old faces they are asked (almost forced) to envision the new faces they will have with Formula 2.

Now that the face is taken care of, let us "finish off" the job (the law of closure once again) and take care of the entire body. For this we can use Benandré, which says it "will do for your body what a facial does for your face." This single-page advertisement has, like the Revlon advertisement, axial balance and a considerable amount of white space. It shows a woman in a glass bathtub bathing herself in "Mediterranean blue" water. A bit of greenery signifies the Mediterranean here. The woman's face is clearly shown, in profile, but her body is not. We see only a diffused figure in blue-green water. Benandré promises that its special form of collagen (a protein contained in the connective tissues and bones, which yields gelatin on boiling) helps the body retain moisture and helps it to restore moisture it loses during the day.

This matter of keeping the skin (and body) moist is interesting. A great deal of cosmetic advertising stresses wetness, moisture, and related concepts, as if the body were in danger of becoming an arid desert, devoid of life, dry, uninteresting, and infertile. These ads suggest that women fear, or should fear, losing their body fluids, which becomes the equivalent of losing their capacity to reproduce. This, in turn, is connected with sexuality and desirability. Anxiety over the body as a kind of wasteland is implicit in appeals in advertisements about retaining and restoring moisture. Dehydration is a metaphor for loss of sexual attractiveness and capacity, that is, desexualization.

Dry skin becomes, then, a sign of a woman who is all dried up and who is not sexually responsive—and who may also be sterile. This is because water is connected, in our psyches, with birth. It is also tied to purity, as in baptismal rites when sin is cleansed from a person. All of this suggests that words and images that picture a body of a woman as being dehydrated and losing water have great resonance.

In *Man and His Symbols,* Carl Jung (1968: 29) writes:

Every concept in our conscious mind, in short, has its own psychic associations. While such associations may vary in intensity . . . they are capable of changing the "normal" character of that concept. It may even become something quite different as it drifts below the level of consciousness.

These subliminal aspects of everything that happens to us may seem to play very little part in our daily lives. But in dream analysis, where the psychologist is dealing with expressions of the unconscious, they are very relevant, for they are the almost invisible roots of our conscious thoughts. That is why commonplace objects or ideas can assume such powerful psychic significance in a dream.

If we substitute "advertisements" for "dreams" in the above quotation, we can understand why and how we are affected so profoundly by images and words.

The copy in the Benandré ad is full of purple prose indicating power and luxury. Some of the more interesting words and phrases appear below:

lavished
unique
expensive
luxury
rare oils
prefer
enriching
treat yourself
beneficial
beauty treatment

This product is sold as a kind of indulgence for women. The copy hints at sex ("You'll make the skin of your body as nice to touch as the skin on your face. Just ask the one who touches you most."), which is always a strong selling point for beauty aids. But the pictorial element is connected with symbols of innocence—baptism, cleanliness, and so on. And the towel in the lower right-hand corner of the ad is a chaste white. From a psychoanalytic perspective, there is also something regressive about all this. It is almost as if the woman emerges with the skin of a baby. She also is quite undefined sexually; we are certain we are seeing a woman, but her sexuality has been subdued a great deal, which is in keeping with "class" as we have been taught to think of it.

Next let us move on to some clothes for our moist and soft-skinned beauty: Danskins. The advertisement for Danskins shows three female bodies lying down on a blue-green piece of fabric that may also be water—it is hard to say. What is interesting is the arrangement of the bodies, all horizontal and jammed together. Two of the models are lying with their heads on the left and the third is between them with her head to the right side of the picture. Although they touch one another, each seems unaware of any of the others—they all stare off into space in separate directions.

The Danskin ad is extremely simple and formal. It has three elements: a headline, the photograph of the three women, and an element containing six lines of copy, all in capitals. The product advertised is a "freestyle" leotard/swimsuit that comes in various "sensuous styles and colors." The large element of white space contrasts with the crowding in the photograph, a crowding that a Marxist would say reflects a diffuse alienation among the women, who are touching one another but do not seem to be aware of each other. They are all, we must assume, pursuing their private fantasies.

Finally, let us move on to an ad depicting a fully dressed woman in Calvin Klein separates. Here we find a model with her right hand on her hip, her left hand behind her head, and her left knee bent (in the "bashful knee pose") and prominently displayed. The background is gray and there is hardly any text. The shirt the model wears has a plunging neckline, but there is no cleavage showing, and there is a slit in the skirt, which enables her to display her knee.

We are given little textual information: the designer, Calvin Klein; the store where the outfit can be purchased, I. Magnin; and the fabric manufacturer, the Ideacomo group.

The model has long, curly hair. She has a rather cold look on her face, a look that is commonly seen in high-fashion advertising. And she is posed in a way that emphasizes her arms and legs rather than her breasts and hips. Thus attention is focused on her appendages, which are sexually undifferentiated. Yet there is something of a sexually alluring quality about this pose, which shows a lot of upper leg. It may have something to do with the tilt of the hips, the twist of the torso, and the neckline. Perhaps the unnaturalness of the pose is important, also.

BREAKING THE ADVERTISING CODE

The codes of simplicity, white space and formality, appear in the Calvin Klein advertisement just as they did in all the other advertisements discussed to this point. These "couture" codes are learned by people, who are taught, by advertisers, to associate simplicity, spaciousness, and formal structure with "class." In the same manner, we are taught the "meanings" of various typefaces and kinds of images. Soft focus signifies dream-like states, formal structure or design implies "classic" (whatever that means), and so on. All of these associations are carried around in our heads, so that all the advertiser has to do is "activate" us by striking the appropriate responsive chord. As Tony Schwartz (1974: 24–25) writes in *The Responsive Chord:*

> The critical task is to design our package of stimuli so that it resonates with information already stored with the individual and thereby induces the desired learning or behavioral effect. Resonance takes place when the stimuli put into our communication evoke *meaning* in a listener or viewer. That which we put into the communication has no meaning in itself. The meaning of our communication is what a listener or viewer *gets out* of his experience with the communicator's stimulus.

Culture, and "couture," which is part of culture, is a collection of codes we learn that provide us with meaning in the world. But how, specifically, do these codes work, and how do we find meaning in advertisements (as well as other forms of communication)?

In a magazine (or other form of print) advertisement there are two ways that information is communicated—through the text and through pictorial and design elements. We can examine the text to determine what appeals are being pressed forward and what means are used to lead the reader/viewer to desire the product. Anxiety may be provoked. There may be inducements to self-gratifications of varying natures. Snobbery may be invoked. Any number of techniques of persuasion can be used here. And in the pictorial material there is also a "language" that may be employed to generate the desired feelings and fantasies. I have mentioned some of these techniques: design, size, color, grain, focus, and so on. And I have suggested that we learn to associate certain kinds of advertisements with certain kinds of fashions.

Can we take matters a step further? Can we explain how these associations are made and how the various signs and symbols generate the meanings they do? In some cases, yes. To do so we must expand our vocabulary of analysis. I would like to reintroduce some terms from semiology at this point:

metaphor: relationship by analogy (example: my love is a red rose)
metonymy: relationship by association (example: rich people and mansions)
icon: relationship by resemblance (example: photograph of an object)
index: relationship by implication (example: smoke implies fire)
symbol: relationship by convention (example: Star of David and Jews)

There is a problem in differentiating between metonymy and symbol that I find hard to solve. Neither are motivated or natural, but relationships by association seem to be stronger than relationships by convention. Anything can be a symbol once people learn to accept it as such. But the association between wealth and large mansions seems quite logical. Wealthy people, people with "class," tend to live in large houses, have a great deal of land and space for themselves, and are powerful. Thus spatiality becomes associated with wealth and class indirectly, through the matter of living space found in large homes.

In metonymy, then, the relationships are stronger than in symbols. One important form of metonymy is synecdoche, in which a part stands for a whole or vice versa. Monoca (1977: 135) in *How to Read a Film* suggests that in film "close shots of marching feet to represent an army" is synecdochic and "falling calendar pages" to indicate the passing of time are metonymic, and that it is through metonymy and synecdoche that Hollywood and films in general are able to communicate with people so quickly and powerfully. Thus, for example, sweat is an index of body heat (or nervous anxiety) that functions metonymically since "associated details invoke an abstract idea."

Magazine advertisements function in much the same way, using whatever devices they can to signify "abstract ideas"—what we call signifieds—such as passion, love, romance, and so on. Because these advertisements can use language, they can use metaphor, but more often they also wish to imply or suggest things (fantasies of exotic love, hopes for beauty) through pictorial elements that make use of the devices described above in various combinations.

With these terms we can do more than simply say that signs and symbols work on the basis of associations that people learn and that become codes by which they interpret the world and function in it. For example, let us consider our first advertisement, the one for Revlon's Formula 2 cleanser and moisturizer. Although there are many things going on in this advertisement it seems to me that the most important thing in the ad is the way it forces the reader to turn the optical illusion into a face, which suggests, perhaps subliminally, *magic.* Most cosmetic advertisements involve a belief in magic, but usually the appeals are verbal. In this advertisement, however, we are forced to do a great deal of work, work that "convinces" us that it is logical to believe in magic. Why not? We've just done something magical. We've seen that magic works, with our own eyes.

I see this process as indexical. The Revlon products promise beauty by magic just the way the square patches hold the promise of a face, once we learn how to see the patches correctly. The implication is that Revlon is magic and it will work for you the way your eyes work to figure out the optical illusion. There may also be an element of suggesting that beauty is an illusion and is attainable by all who can employ the correct magic. The picture of the woman in the ad is indexical, but the bottles are symbolic and rely upon the conventional look of medicinal products for their power. The stylishness of the advertisement, with its use of white space and simplicity, is also symbolic. There is nothing natural or logical about our associating white space and simplicity with "class." It is historical, part of our culture, and something that most of us learn.

In the Revlon advertisement and in all advertisements we find a kind of chain reaction taking place. The verbal and pictorial elements in the advertisement function as signifiers that generate feelings and beliefs or signifieds for those who look at and read the advertisement. These feelings and beliefs (and, we might add, hopes, fantasies, and the like) are based on codes (structured belief systems), which, in turn, operate via metaphor, metonymy, icon, index, and symbols in various combinations. Thus, in order to determine how advertisements and other forms of visual–verbal communication generate meaning, we can move beyond the notion of codes and see how the codes themselves function.

It is a fascinating business taking advertisements apart to see how they function and determining what they reflect about society. It is also a perilous business, for there is always the possibility that we are not examining society's fantasies, or those of the creators of the advertisements, but our own. In *The Strategy of Desire,* Ernest Dichter (1960: 11), one of the founding fathers of motivation research, writes:

> Human desire is the raw material we are working with. The strategy of desire is the tool of shaping the human factor, the most important aspect of our worldly arsenal. Human progress is a conquest of the animal within us. No conquest is possible without strategy.

Whether or not advertising and other tools of persuasion are leading us to higher levels of development is questionable. One thing seems quite evident—knowing the strategies used by the people who work at creating and shaping our desire is important, for then we can make more rational decisions and avoid manipulation. The person who is a slave to fashion is often also a slave to his or her own emotions—emotions that can be manipulated by the fashion advertising industry. But escape is possible.

Analyzing Signs and Sign Systems

I would like to offer a check-list for analyzing photographs, advertisements, and frames from films in addition to less complicated signs. I am concerned with the various kinds of signs being used, how they generate meaning, how they relate to one another, what they reflect about our society and culture, and the problems they pose for the semiologist or other "interpreters" of signs.

Let us assume we are dealing with an advertisement in a magazine. We should be concerned with some or all of the following matters:

A. What is the general ambience of the advertisement? What mood does it create? How does it do this?

B. What is the design of the advertisement? Does it use axial balance or some other form? How are the basic components or elements of the advertisement arranged?

C. What is the relationship that exists between pictorial elements and written material and what does this tell us?

D. What is the spatiality in the advertisement? Is there a lot of "white space" or is the advertisement full of graphic and written elements (that is, "busy")?

E. What signs and symbols do we find? What role do the various signs and symbols play in the advertisement?

F. If there are figures (men, women, children, animals) in the advertisement, what are they like? What can be said about their facial expressions, poses, hairstyle, age, sex, hair color, ethnicity, education, occupation, relationships (of one to the other), and so on?

G. What does the background tell us? Where is the action in the advertisement taking place and what significance does this background have?

H. What action is taking place in the advertisement and what significance does this action have? (This might be described as the plot of the advertisement.)

I. What theme or themes do we find in the advertisement? What is the advertisement about? (The plot of an advertisement may involve a man and a woman drinking but the theme might be jealousy, faithlessness, ambition, passion, etc.)

J. What about the language used in the advertisement? Does it essentially provide information or generate some kind of an emotional response? Or both? What techniques are used by the copywriter: humor, alliteration, "definitions" of life, comparisons, sexual innuendo, and so on?

K. What typefaces are used and what impressions do these typefaces convey?

L. What is the item being advertised and what role does it play in American culture and society?

M. What about aesthetic decisions? If the advertisement is a photograph, what kind of a shot is it? What significance do long shots, medium shots, close-ups have? What about the lighting, use of color, angle of the shot?

N. What sociological, political, economic or cultural attitudes are indirectly reflected in the advertisement? An advertisement may be about a pair of blue jeans but it might, indirectly, reflect such matters as sexism, alienation, stereotyped thinking, conformism, generational conflict, loneliness, elitism, and so on.

SUGGESTIONS FOR DISCUSSION

1. Choose one of the ads in the following section. What does the ad seem to be selling besides the product being advertised? Pay attention to visual cues. Is there a great deal of white space, for example? Berger has written elsewhere that white space denotes high class, elegance, and money. Is the picture fuzzy (perhaps suggesting a dream or a time gone by) or sharp (suggesting the precision of modern technology)? Notice the setting, the models, the clothing, even the furniture or other accessories. Does the ad seem to propose a particular standard that a reader might apply to beauty, body type, gender roles, parenting, or other cultural ideals?
2. Collect an assortment of ads on your own. What values or ideals are portrayed in these ads?
3. After reading about advertising and looking at the ads in this section and the ads you have gathered, how much would you say Americans are influenced by the value systems presented in advertisements?

SUGGESTIONS FOR WRITING

1. Choose one ad from the selection reprinted in this text. Use Berger's checklist to help you write an analysis of the ad which specifies at least some of the cultural meanings that are conveyed and how they are conveyed.
2. Elizabeth and Stuart Ewen, Jean Kilbourne, and Arthur Asa Berger all write about the power of advertising in this culture. Generally, much of what they say about advertising is similar. In order for you to understand their separate arguments, however, you will need to identify not only what is similar but also what differs in their analysis. Write an essay that compares the three discussions presented here, identifying what they have in common and how they differ in what they argue about advertising images.
3. Art historian John Berger argues that advertising "proposes to each of us that we transform ourselves, or our lives, by buying something more." Choose any one of the ads presented in this section and write a brief essay in which you explain how the ad proposes to transform us with the purchase of the product being advertised. Be sure to pay attention to both the visual and textual details of the ad.

A Gallery of Ads

For Bill Demby, the difference means getting another shot.

When Bill Demby was in Vietnam, he used to dream of coming home and playing a little basketball with the guys.

A dream that all but died when he lost both his legs to a Viet Cong rocket.

But then, a group of researchers discovered that a remarkable Du Pont plastic could help make artificial limbs that were more resilient, more flexible, more like life itself.

Thanks to these efforts, Bill Demby is back. And some say, he hasn't lost a step.

At Du Pont, we make the things that make a difference.

Better things for better living.

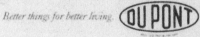

General Motors has found a way to keep people in their seats without using seat belts.

We do it with quality television programming. Over the past decade General Motors has been presenting the kind of programs that can bring a family together—the kind that can earn broadcasting's most prestigious awards. GM Mark of Excellence Presentations.

First aired in 1981, *A Christmas Special with Luciano Pavarotti* became a holiday tradition on PBS. *The Verdi Requiem's* debut on public television, and *Vivaldi: The Four Seasons* played on the ABS cable network. *The Kennedy Center Honors* gala annually pays tribute to America's greatest performing artists, and it has won three Emmy Awards in the process.

Peabody Awards for broadcast excellence went to *Bill Moyers: In Search of the Constitution* and to the mini-series *George Washington*. GM completed this rare look at America's first presidency with the sequel, *George Washington: The Forging of a Nation*, And we premiered Bill

Moyers' unprecedented interview of retiring Chief Justice Warren Burger.

In every project, for commercial television of PBS, GM looks for excellence in concept, script, talent, and production, just as we care about excellence throughout our automobiles.

This year, Mark of Excellence Presentations include *American Playwrights Theater* on ABC. Three Emmy-winning programs return: *American Film Institute's Life Achievement Award* on ABC, *The Kennedy Center Honors* on CBS, and the *Live From Lincoln Center* series on PBS. NBC is carrying *The Old Man and the Sea*, with Anthony Quinn. Also on PBS are the Peabody Award-winning weekly series *A World of Ideas with Bill Moyers*, and the 30-hour Ken Burns documentary *The Civil War*.

General Motors Mark of Excellence Presentations. They are our way of bringing your family quality television as well as quality cars and trucks.

General Motors Mark of Excellence Presentations

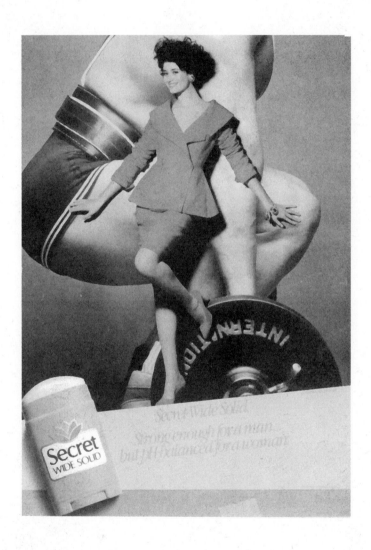

Decanters by Fabergé.   *Lamp by Deusta.*

Screen by the Kyoto School.

Gourmet Cat Food by Fancy Feast.

GET REAL.

TRETORN

Joel Connelly

A GROWING AWARENESS: ENVIRONMENTAL GROUPS AND THE MEDIA

Joel Connelly works as the National Correspondent for the *Seattle Post Intelligencer*. The essay included here first appeared in 1990 in a special wilderness issue of the photography journal *Aperture*. In it Connelly provides a history of how the environmental movement has skillfully drawn upon the power of pictures to advertise past and potential environmental disasters. He writes, particularly, of three possible ways in which the image has had an impact on the environmental movement: advertising, news reports, and film, video, or photographic essays.

Suggestion for Reading

•Underline those passages in this text in which Connelly supports his contention that "In the world of the 1990s . . . political and societal change flow through the lens of a camera."

---◆---

A half century ago, Mao Zedong taught his followers that political power grows out of the barrel of a gun. In the world of the 1990s, however, political and societal change flow through the lens of a camera. Environmentalists learned this lesson long ago. These days the "green lobby" packs political clout in many countries. In its infancy, however, the movement found that the only way to save species and preserve wild places was to arouse the public with visual images. Some of these images, both the brutal and the beautiful, will remain in our memories for a long time.

A pioneer in the use of visual images to alert the public to environmental threats was Dr. Fred Darvill, a Mt. Vernon, Washington, family doctor. Darvill was among the first to deploy images of sublime places followed by the horrors that awaited them. Over twenty years ago, Darvill flew to New York armed only with a painting of Image Lake, a 10,000-foot-high tarn in Washington's Glacier Peak Wilderness Area, some slides, and three shares in the Kennecott Copper Company. He was bound for the annual meeting of the multinational mining company, which proposed to build a half-mile-wide open-pit copper mine in the wilderness area. Kennecott had the legal right to do so, in the form of a mining claim that predated the Wilderness Act. Darvill set out to test the company's will. "The Sierra Club had alerted the wire services," he recalls. "I showed the painting of Image Lake, and explained what a mine would do in the area. I mentioned that it would be so big it could be seen through a telescope from the moon."

The presentation received nationwide publicity. It also attracted the eye of David Brower, then executive director of the Sierra Club and a man who pioneered the use of visual images in conservation battles. A full-page ad appeared in the *New York Times* under the heading: "AN OPEN PIT LARGE ENOUGH THAT IT CAN BE SEEN FROM THE MOON." Readers were presented with a picture of alpine glory beside one of a gouged-out open-pit mine in Utah.

In the end Kennecott never touched the wilderness. Brower would later deploy the same sorts of imagery—in a style described by John McPhee as "Early Paul Revere"—to stop two planned dams in the Grand Canyon. Above a canyon sunset picture was the classic headline: "WOULD YOU FLOOD THE SISTINE CHAPEL SO TOURISTS COULD GET CLOSER TO THE CEILING?" The Sierra Club lost its tax-exempt status, but the Grand Canyon was saved. Congressman Morris Udall of Arizona later paid grudging tribute to Brower's genius for capturing public attention, and for stopping an unwise project that Udall at the time had supported.

A prime goal of conservationists, according to Brock Evans of the National Audubon Society, has been to nationalize and even internationalize key battles. "Visual images are the key for us," says Evans. "They've kept ancient forests standing and oil rigs out of the Arctic Refuge." Cameras connect the global village. Viewers thousands of miles away can watch pictures of thousand-year-old Sitka spruce trees falling under a logger's chain saw. They can see oil-covered otters being lifted from Prince William Sound. They can feel the fear of those on a Greenpeace zodiac boat as Soviet whalers fire a harpoon over its bow to mortally wound one of the world's largest marine mammals. Such pictures can generate thousands of words in citizen anger, enough to sway Congress or force the new president of Brazil to name an environmentalist to his cabinet.

When the *Exxon Valdez* fouled Prince William Sound, it disrupted a slick campaign aimed at persuading Congress to allow oil drilling in Alaska's Arctic National Wildlife Refuge. Oil lobbyists had effectively argued the necessity of reducing dependence on foreign petroleum. Environmentalists had been unable to sway the public with pretty pictures of caribou. But images of oil-soaked beaches, birds, and seals triggered outrage. Alaska Senator Ted Stevens put it best: the *Exxon Valdez* spill had set drilling back at least two years. Asked when it would resurface, he replied: "When the oil spill is no longer news."

Direct action has proven a potent way to focus the camera on environmental events. "The Fox" was its prophet. This anonymous ecological saboteur stalked Chicago in the late 1960s. He never showed his face, but publicized his deeds with calls to TV stations and explained his outrage to columnist Mike Royko. Refineries found their outfalls plugged. Banners were hung from smokestacks. The Fox even invaded the executive offices of a steel company to dump smelly effluent on its carpets.

Over twenty years later, the Fox is frequently copied. Greenpeace protestors recently decorated a stack at the Longview Fiber Company pulp mill in Washington, on the Columbia River. When the press arrived, the activists were ready with documentation of dioxin dumping into one of North America's great rivers.

Direct action is sometimes condemned by mainstream environmentalists who stress action through Congress and the courts. But confrontations can purchase time. In rain forests along the Northwest coast, the radical environmental group Earth First! has plunked down protesters in ancient trees marked for logging. When hauled down and arrested, they've given such names as "Doug Fir" and "Bobcat." These tree-ins have generated nationwide attention and slowed the pace of logging.

A daring, filmed protest can focus attention on activities that some might wish to remain unnoticed. The Greenpeace Foundation was formed in Vancouver, British Columbia, in 1971, an outgrowth of protests aimed at planned U.S. nuclear tests in Alaska's Aleutian Islands. In 1973 Greenpeace began stalking bigger game—atmospheric nuclear tests being conducted by the French. Greenpeace vessels were boarded by the French navy, and crew members beaten. But the protesters kept sailing into test zones, and kept arguing that radiation posed a danger to peoples of the South Pacific. In 1986 French commandos sank a Greenpeace ship as it prepared to sail from a New Zealand harbor. One crew member was killed. The resulting uproar strained French relations with New Zealand, drove the French defense minister to resign, and cast France in the role of international outlaw.

Greenpeace has chosen the camera lens as its weapon for a variety of environmental crusades. "We go to the scene of a crime and bring back images of what's going on," says Alan Reichman, ocean ecology director for Greenpeace International. "In that way we mobilize public concern and pressure. We're not talking abstractions and descriptions. We're showing a factory ship which cuts up whales. We're showing marine mammals trapped in nets. We're showing what comes out of pulp mills." Reichman has helped create memorable images. He was part of a flotilla of zodiac boats that tried to stop a supertanker test run up the Strait of Juan de Fuca between British Columbia and Washington. Airborne photographers had a field day as the tiny craft buzzed around the 185,000-ton oil ship. A maneuverability test by the U.S. Coast Guard was turned into a political confrontation over whether to permit supertankers in sensitive West Coast estuaries.

A Greenpeace photo service makes pictures available to news sources, and engages in visual lobbying on Capitol Hill. Members of Congress, aides, and press gathered in a Longworth Building office last year to watch films of dolphins and birds entangled in the thick mesh of driftnet fishing lines. The seventy-mile-long driftnets are set on the North Pacific by Japanese and Taiwanese fishermen, supposedly to catch tuna and squid. In real life, they snare thousands of birds, marine mammals, and salmon. Congress has since pressed a reluctant Bush administration to support a worldwide ban on driftnet fishing.

The media savvy of such groups as Greenpeace has reached the environmental mainstream. The Natural Resources Defense Council has generally stayed far removed from visual imagery: its battles have been fought in court, notably with suits that have forced the U.S. Department of Energy to abide by the nation's environmental laws in operating its nuclear weapons plants. On February 26, 1989, though, NRDC entered the court of public opinion. It gave CBS's "60 Minutes" a study entitled "Intolerable Risk: Pesticides in Our Children's Food." One of the pesticides in the report was daminozide (trade name Alar), a chemical sprayed on apples to improve their color, crispness, and shelf life. In its study, NRDC predicted that Alar might cause one case of cancer for every 4,200 preschool children—a rate of risk 240 times the standard considered acceptable by the Environmental Protection Agency.

Although written by scientists, "Intolerable Risk" translated well to the TV screen. "60 Minutes" focused on Alar. Americans saw apples being sprayed in fields. They watched those apples going into baby food. And a day later, Oscar-winning actress (and parent) Meryl Streep went before a Senate hearing to argue the case for a ban on Alar. During the week following the "60 Minutes" report, apple sales fell fourteen percent, and industry losses were estimated at over $100 million. A few months later, Uniroyal Chemical, Inc., announced it was taking the product off the market.

The media determines what is seen, and often what is saved. Photographs taken in a remote corner of northwest Wyoming helped create Yellowstone National Park over a century ago. Pictures can also lift politicians' sights up from ledger sheets. The U.S. Forest Service urged a veto of 1976 legislation creating a 393,000-acre Alpine Lakes Wilderness Area in Washington, arguing that it would cost too much to acquire private lands. Washington Governor Dan Evans, an avid backpacker, carried a picture book into an Oval Office meeting with President Gerald Ford. Evans turned to photos of the Enchantment Lakes region and told of guiding his three young sons over rugged, 7,800-foot Aasgard Pass during a violent storm. "Dan, we've got to save it," said Ford. He signed the bill.

As a writer I hate to admit it, but the camera's lens can be more powerful than the writer's pen. A physical confrontation convinced me. The state had let a logging contract on one of the few stands of old-growth trees left on Whidbey Island in Washington's scenic Puget Sound. Island environmentalists vowed to block the logging. I stood at the end of a narrow logging track with Mark Anderson, a young photographer with KING-TV in Seattle. A logging rig rumbled into view; protesters sat down in its path, and Anderson began filming. The truck stopped. After much waving of arms, the loggers retreated. A few hours later, KING carried an unforgettable film of trucks and bodies. It followed up with a film of the undisturbed forest. Birds chirped and sunlight wafted through 500-year-old trees. Anderson grew up in a logging town and knew the difference between a natural scene and a "working forest." Logging plans were promptly suspended.

The lawyering over Whidbey's forest was long and tedious. Not long ago, however, I enjoyed a walk among those same ancient trees, now—thanks at least in part to the powerful images presented by KING-TV and others—part of South Whidbey State Park.

SUGGESTIONS FOR DISCUSSION

1. How would you describe most of the environmental advertising you have seen? When do you think environmental advertising is most effective? When is it, for you, least effective?

2. Although news images and some publicity photos take as their subject environmental disasters, much of the publicity we see (in calendars, slick magazines, and many ads) depicts the wilderness as unspoiled. Under what circumstances would you consider it more effective to use pictures of unspoiled nature rather than of toxic waste dumps in attempts to persuade the public?

3. List ways in which the media determines "what is seen, and often what is saved" in the environment, as Connelly tells us it does?

SUGGESTIONS FOR WRITING

1. Connelly tells us that many environmentalists would rather have good media coverage than participate in direct action against polluters. Write an essay in which you explain what you perceive is the current media image of environmentalists.
2. Choose one ad that is currently in use for an environmental group or about an environmental issue. Use the techniques of analysis described by Berger to write an analysis of how that ad makes its appeal and what the ad is selling besides the movement or group itself.
3. In an article on the contemporary landscape photographer Richard Misrach, writer Rebecca Solnit says the following of this culture's understanding of "wilderness": "Wilderness is the quixotic American myth of an ideal landscape, a white myth of a place unknown, unnamed, and unpossessed. It has also been largely a male myth, in which words like 'pure' and 'unsullied' recur, of a place to be encountered in heroic journeys." Write an essay in which you describe the image of the American wilderness or American West that has been popularized by advertising images (including car ads, vacation ads, cigarette ads, and others). How is that myth pictured in popular advertising? What would you say that myth omits of historical, social, and environmental realities? Choose at least three ads for specific reference in your discussion.

Danny Duncan Collum

BUY ANY MEANS NECESSARY

Danny Duncan Collum writes a cultural criticism column called "Eyes and Ears" for *Sojourners Magazine.* In it Collum examines film, television, advertising, current events—anything that might give us a clue about the temper of our times. In the selection reprinted here from the March 1993 issue of *Sojourners,* Collum examines the selling of a major historical and political figure, Malcolm X. He argues that the pressures of the marketplace can change forever the ways we understand our past and our political present.

Suggestion for Reading

• Before you begin your reading, write a brief summary of what you know or think you know about Malcolm X. Think about where or how you got your information. Keep that writing in mind as you read Collum's article.

ay back in the 1950s, before the invention of the microchip or the fiber optic cable, the French Situationists—a bohemian clique of artists and anti-intellectual intellectuals—became the first to peg the essential nature of post-modern, post-industrial Information Age capitalism. According to the Situationist credo, we were entering, even then, an age in which capital would become so concentrated that it would transmute into pure image.

That's happened. Increasingly we live, think, and feel in terms of "pure image": thought and feeling are more and more divorced from action and substance, or from what we once quaintly called "life itself." You could call it a process of disincarnation.

The process of producing image-commodities is relentless and all-consuming. No one is exempt, and no culture or subculture will long go ignored. Where there is a single living human soul there is, after all, at least a potential market. It's a process of cultural colonization at least as relentless as the geographic one of centuries past.

So, we have Malcolm X, the cap, the T-shirt, the air freshener (yeah, really . . . in the shape of an "X"), and the all-round Christmas-Kwaanza political action figure. In fact, at this early December writing, the Malcolm X phenomenon has already resulted in some new marketing scams from some unlikely sources. In the first week of December 1992, CBS News ran an hour-long special, hosted by Dan Rather, titled *The Real Malcolm X.*

The show did a fair job of recapping Malcolm's life, even admitting the possibility that the FBI and/or CIA may have had some hand in his February 21, 1965 assassination (or the events leading up to it). The segment on what Malcolm X means today was pretty lame, but that only reflects the general level of public discourse on the topic.

Overall the show was not bad for network TV, I thought. "But why did they bother?" I wondered. The answer came at the end with an on-screen notice of how you could buy a video-cassette copy of the program. Then two days later my subscriber copy of *Premiere* magazine landed in the mailbox. *Premiere* is a monthly film mag with a circulation way into six figures, and there, prominently displayed in the magazine's video section, was an advertisement for *The Real Malcolm X* on home video, complete with a distribution deal with Twentieth Century Fox. Dan Rather goes straight to video.

The point is that the CBS News piece was not conceived as a news piece. That ad in a monthly magazine must have been purchased months before the documentary aired, and the deal with Fox cut long before that. *The Real Malcolm X* was conceived as a home video commodity to cash in on the Malcolm X craze. (At least CNN waited until the war was over to hawk its Desert Storm home video series.)

That example from the highest levels of corporate America only serves to illustrate what is obvious on the American streets. By now the visage and voice of Malcolm X is an image-commodity. Like denim, leather jackets, baggy jeans, backwards baseball caps, or the flannels and hightops of rock-and-roll grunge, the wearing and brandishing of Malcolm X is now a consumption choice signifying a passive and vaguely defined politico-cultural attitude. It is simply another case of advertisers pushing the idealism button and/or the black pride button in the same way that they more usually push the human sex or envy buttons.

Simple as that, we might say, and we could be tempted to leave the matter there. But things are not really all *that* simple. For one thing, the real Malcolm X was himself a media figure from the get-go. That was his genius, and perhaps his vocation. In his short life, he built no organization and left behind no institution. Maybe he would have if he'd lived—but maybe not. What Malcolm X did do, and do brilliantly, was make speeches and gestures. He made an image—a vibrant and startling new image of the African American—and he struck that image across the sensory hearts and minds of America, black and white.

The making and striking of that image mattered. Even simply as image. Spike Lee, as a film artist and mythmaker, understands that an image is never just an image. Despite the commodity trappings and the trivialization, what we wear on top of our head, or see on the screen, can also define new territory inside the cranial cavity.

Certainly it is better for young people to be identifying themselves, however superficially, with Malcolm X than with an NFL football team. Surely Malcolm X makes a more positive and progressive image of African America than did the last omnipresent black media figure, Michael Jackson. In fact, Malcolm the Commodity can be seen as a necessary counterweight to the global marketing of Jackson's bleached, trimmed, and straightened persona.

This is simply to say that images, as mental-emotional-spiritual creatures of the imagination, are part of real life. The problem comes when an image, like that of Malcolm X, is disincarnated from the flesh of real life and from the possibility of real human transformation.

As we noted at the outset, that separation process is perhaps the core operating function of the business system today. It is up to real people, living real lives—be they Hollywood actors, artist-intellectuals, religious leaders, educators, business professionals, street kids, or even mall rats—to take the image of transformation and liberation represented by Malcolm X and reincarnate it in the communal life of America, African and otherwise.

SUGGESTIONS FOR DISCUSSION

1. What do you think it means for, as Collum says, "capital" to "become so concentrated that it would transmute into pure image"? How has that happened with Malcolm X or other figures like him?
2. Why would you say Collum is concerned about the selling of Malcolm X's image? Is any coverage better than none?
3. What other figures can you name who have become commodified in the way Malcolm X has? How do you think commodification has altered or affected the way we understand these men and women?

SUGGESTIONS FOR WRITING

1. Write a brief summary of Collum's argument.
2. Throughout this chapter, you have read about images of women and men, even images of the environment. Collum suggests that our culture's need to cash in on what is popular also drives image-making. Consider the Malcolm X products Collum mentions or those products you know of first hand and write an analysis of what you consider to be the image of Malcolm X that is projected through such promotional products.

3. Collum writes, "It is up to real people, living real lives—be they Hollywood actors, artist-intellectuals, religious leaders, educators, business professionals, street kids, or even mall rats—to take the image of transformation and liberation represented by Malcolm X and reincarnate it in the communal life of America, African and otherwise." In a two- to three-page response to Collum, write a proposal for how real people might do that.

bell hooks

MALCOLM X: CONSUMED BY IMAGES

bell hooks, professor of English at Oberlin College, is a poet, teacher, and activist who writes a regular column, "Sisters of the Yam," for *Z Magazine*. Throughout her career, she has written extensively on the politics of race, class, and gender, including the books *Talking Back: Thinking Feminist, Thinking Black, Feminist Theory: From Margin to Center,* and *Black Looks: Race and Representation.* In the following article, first printed in *Z Magazine,* hooks reviews Spike Lee's film biography of Malcolm X. In her review, she argues that African Americans must look critically at the images they create themselves of their history and their legends, especially when those images are created in Hollywood, the center of white mainstream American film making. The Malcolm X who emerges from Spike Lee's film, hooks argues, is a benign figure resembling only faintly the radical she remembers.

Suggestion for Reading

- Because hooks is writing both about Spike Lee's film biography and about an African American film maker working in Hollywood, her argument can seem difficult to follow. As you read, underline and annotate those passages that seem to be about mainstream film making and separate them from hooks's discussion of the film biography itself.

---◆---

Shortly after the brutal assassination of Malcolm X, Bayard Rustin predicted, "White America, not the Negro people, will determine Malcolm X's role in history." At the time this statement seemed ludicrous. White Americans appeared to have no use for Malcolm X, not even a changed Malcolm, no longer fiercely advocating racial separation. Today market forces in white supremacist capitalist patriarchy have found a way to use Malcolm X. The field of representation—where black images are concerned—has always been a plantation culture. Malcolm X is turned into a "hot" commodity, his militant black nationalist, anti-imperialist, anti-capitalist politics diffused and undermined by a process of objectification. In his essay, "On Malcolm X, His Message and Meaning," Manning Marable warns: "There is a tendency to drain the radical message of a dynamic, living activist into an abstract icon, to replace radical content with pure image." Politically progressive black folks and our allies in struggle recognize that the power of Malcolm X's political thought is threatened when his image and ideas are commodified and sold by conservative market forces that strip the work of all radical and/or revolutionary content.

Understanding the power of mass media images to determine how we see ourselves and how we choose to act, Malcolm X admonished black folks: "Never accept images that have been created for you by someone else. It is always better to form the habit of learning how to see things for yourself: then you are in a better position to judge for yourself."

Interpreted narrowly, this admonition refers only to images of black folks created in the white imagination. Broadly speaking, it urges us to look with a critical eye at all images. Malcolm X promoted and encouraged the development of a critical black gaze, one that would be able to move beyond passive consumption and be fiercely confronting, challenging, interrogating.

This critical militancy must be re-invoked in all serious discussions of Spike Lee's latest film *Malcolm X*. Celebrated and praised in mainstream media, this joint project by white producers and black filmmaker risks receiving no meaningful cultural critique. More often than not black admirers of Lee and his work, both from the academic front and the street, seek to censor, discrediting any view of the film that is not unequivocally celebratory. Black folks who subject the film to rigorous critique risk being seen as traitors to the race, as petty competitors who do not want to see another black person succeed, or as having personal enmity towards Spike Lee. Filmmaker Marlon Riggs emphasizes the dangers of such silencing in a recent interview in *Black Film Review*. Riggs stresses that we cannot develop a body of black cultural criticism as long as all rigorous critique is censored: "There's also a crying desire for representation. That's what you see when audiences refuse to allow any critique of artists. I've witnessed this personally. At one forum, Spike Lee was asked several questions by a number of people, myself included, about his representations in his movies. The audience went wild with hysterical outbursts to 'shut up,' 'sit down,' 'make your own goddamn movies,' 'who are you, this man is doing the best he can, and he is giving us dignified images, he is doing positive work, why should you be criticizing him?' I admit that there is often trashing just for the sake of trashing. But even when it is clear that the critique is trying to empower and trying to heal certain wounds within our communities, there is not any space within our communities, there is not any space within our culture to constructively critique. There is an effort simply to shut people up in order to reify these gods, if you will, who have delivered some image of us which seems to affirm our existence in this world. As if they make up for the lack, but, in fact, they don't. They can become part of the hegemony."

This is certainly true of Spike Lee. Despite the hype that continues to depict him as an outsider in the white movie industry, constantly struggling to produce work against the wishes and desires of a white establishment, Lee is an insider. He was able to use his power to compel Warner to choose him instead of white director Norman Jewison to make the film. In the business to make money, Warner was probably not moved by Spike's narrow identity politics (he insisted that having a white man directing Malcolm would be "wrong with a capital W"), but rather by the recognition that his presence as a director would likely draw the biggest crossover audience and thus ensure financial success.

Committed to making a mega-hit, Spike Lee had to create a work that would address the needs and desires of a consuming audience that is predominantly white. Ironically, to achieve this end his film had to be similar to other Hollywood epic dramas, especially fictional biographies, hence there is nothing in *Malcolm X* that would indicate that a white director could not have made this film. This seems especially tragic since Spike Lee's brilliance as a filmmaker surfaces most when he provides us with insightful representations of blackness and black life that emerge from the privileged standpoint of familiarity. No such familiarity surfaces in *Malcolm X*. His representation of Malcolm has more in common with Stephen Spielberg's representation of Mister in the film version of *The Color Purple* than with real life portraits of Malcolm X.

In her essay on *The Color Purple*, "Blues For Mr. Spielberg," Michele Wallace asserts: "The fact is there's a gap between what blacks would like to see in movies about themselves and what whites in Hollywood are willing to produce. Instead of serious men and women encountering consequential dilemmas, we're almost always minstrels, more than a little ridiculous; we dance and sing without continuity, as if on the end of a string." Sadly, these comments could be describing the first half of *Malcolm X*. With prophetic vision Wallace continues: "I suspect that backs who wish to make their presence known in American movies will have to seek some middle ground between the stern seriousness of black liberation and the tap dances of Mr. Bojangles and Aunt Jemima." Clearly, Spike Lee attempts to negotiate this middle ground in *Malcolm X*, but unsuccessfully.

The first half of the film moves back and forth from neo-minstrel spectacle to tragic scenes. Yet the predominance of spectacle, of the coon show, whether an accurate portrayal of this phase of Malcolm's life or not, undermines the pathos the tragic scenes (flash backs of childhood incidents of racial oppression and discrimination) should, but do not, evoke. By emphasizing Malcolm as street hustler (critics of Lee's project, like Baraka, predicted that this would be the central focus so as to entertain white audiences), Spike Lee can highlight Malcolm's romantic and sexual involvement with the white woman Sophia, thereby exploiting the voyeuristic obsession this culture has with inter-racial sex. While his relationship with Sophia was clearly important to Malcolm for many years, it is portrayed with the same shallowness of vision that characterizes Lee's vision of inter-racial romance between black men and white women in *Jungle Fever*. Unwilling and possibly unable to imagine that any bond between a white woman and a black man could be based on ties other than pathological ones, Lee portrays Malcolm's desire for Sophia as rooted solely in racial competition between white and black men. Yet Malcolm continued to feel affection for her even as he acquired a radical critique of race, racism, and sexuality.

Without the stellar performance of actor Delroy Lindo playing West Indian Archie, the first half of *Malcolm X* would have been utterly facile. The first character that appears is not Malcolm, as audiences anticipate, but a comic Spike Lee in the role of Shorty. Lee's presence in the film intensifies the sense of spectacle and his comic antics easily upstage the Little character who appears awkward and stupid. Denzel Washington, a box office draw, never stops being Denzel Washington giving us his version of Malcolm X. No degree of powerful acting by Washington can convey the issues around skin color that were so crucial to Malcolm's development of racial consciousness and identity. Lacking his stature and his light hue, Denzel never comes across as a "threatening" physical presence. Washington's real life persona as everybody's "nice guy" makes it particularly difficult for him to convey the seriousness and intensity of a black man consumed with rage. By choosing him, white producers were already deciding that Malcolm should appear less militant if white audiences were to identify with him.

Since so much of the movie depicts Malcolm's days as Detroit Red, the remainder is a skeletal, imagistic outline of his later political changes solely in regard to issues of racial separatism. None of his powerful critiques of capitalism and colonialism are dramatized in this film. Early in the second part, the prison scenes raise crucial questions about Lee's representation of Malcolm. No explanations have been given to clarify why Lee chose not to portray Malcolm's brother and sister leading him to Islam, but instead created a fictional older black male prisoner, Blaines (played by Albert Hall), as tutor and mentor to Malcolm Little, educating him for critical consciousness and leading him to Islam. This is the kind of distortion and misrepresentation that can occur in fictional biographies and which ultimately violates the integrity of the life portrayed. Indeed, throughout the film Malcolm X's character is constructed as being without family, even though some member of his family was always present in his life. By presenting him symbolically as an "orphan," Lee erases the complex relations Malcolm had to black women in his life—his mother and his older sister—making it appear that the only important women are sexual partners. He also makes Malcolm a lone "heroic" figure and, by so doing, is able to re-inscribe him within a Hollywood tradition of heroism that effaces his deep emotional engagement with family and community.

Lee insists, along with the white producer Worth, that there is no revisionism in this film, that as Worth puts it, "We're not playing games with making up our opinion of the truth. We're doing *The Autobiography of Malcolm X*." Yet the absence of family members and the insertion of fictional characters does indeed revise and distort the representation of Malcolm. That mis-representation is not redeemed by Lee's use of actual speeches or the placing of them in chronological order. Lee has boasted that this film will "teach" folks about Malcolm. In *By Any Means Necessary*, the book that describes the behind the scenes production of the film, he asserts: "I want our people to be all fired up for this. To get inspired by it. This is life and death we're dealing with. This is a mindset, this is what Black people in America have come through." To ensure that *Malcolm X* would not be a "regular bullshit Hollywood movie," Lee could have insisted on accuracy. But to do so, he would have had to make sacrifices, relinquishing complete control, allowing more folks to benefit from the project if need be. He would have to face the reality that masses of people, including black folks, will see this film who will never know the "true story" because they do not read or write, and that mis-representations of Malcolm's life and work could permanently distort their understanding.

Knowing that he had to answer to a militant Nation of Islam, Spike Lee was much more careful in the construction of the character of Elijah Mohammed (portrayed by Al Freeman, Jr.), preserving the integrity of his spirit and work. It is sad that the same intensity of care was not given to either the Malcolm character or the fictional portrait of his widow Betty Shabazz. Although the real life Shabazz shared with Spike Lee that she and Malcolm did not argue, no doubt because what was most desirable in a Nation of Islam wife was obedience, the film shows her "reading" him in the same bitchified way that all black female characters in previous films by Lee talk to mates. Nor was Shabazz as assertive in romantic pursuit of Malcolm as the film depicts. As with the white woman character Sophia, certain stereotypical sexist-defined images of black women emerge in this film. Women are either virgins or whores, Madonnas or prostitutes—and that's Hollywood.

If Lee's version of Malcolm's life becomes the example all other such films must follow, then it will remain equally true that there is no place for black male militant political rage in Hollywood. For it is, finally, Malcolm's political militancy that this film erases, largely because it is not the politically revolutionary Malcolm X that Lee identifies with. Lee is primarily fascinated by Malcolm's fierce critique of white racism and his early obsession with viewing racism as being solely about masculinist phallocentric struggle for power between white men and black men. It is this aspect of Malcolm's politics that most resembles Lee's, not the critique of racism in conjunction with imperialism and colonialism, and certainly not the critique of capitalism. It is not surprising, then, that the film's most powerful portrayal of political resistance shows Malcolm galvanizing men in the Nation of Islam to face off with white men around the issue of police brutality. Malcolm is portrayed in these scenes as a Hitler type leader who rules with an iron fist. Deflecting away from the righteous resistance to police brutality that was the catalyst for this confrontation, the film makes it "a dick thing"—yet another "shoot out at the OK corral"—and that's Hollywood.

The closing scenes of *Malcolm X* highlight Lee's cinematic conflict: his desire to make a black epic drama that would compete with and yet mirror white Hollywood epics made by white male directors he perceives as great, and his longing to preserve and convey the spirit and integrity of Malcolm's life and work. In the finale viewers are bombarded with images—stirring documentary footage, compelling testimony, and the use of schoolchildren and Nelson Mandela to show that Malcolm's legacy is still important and has global impact. Tragically, all knowledge of Malcolm as militant black revolutionary has been erased, consumed by images. Gone is the icon who represents our struggle for black liberation, for militant resistance, and in its place we are presented with a de-politicized image with little substance or power. The Malcolm we see at the end of Spike Lee's film is tragically alone, with only a few followers, suicidal, maybe even losing his mind. The didacticism of this image suggests only that it is foolhardy and naive to think that there can be meaningful political revolution—that truth and justice will prevail. In no way subversive, Malcolm X re-inscribes the black image within a colonizing framework.

The underlying political conservatism of Lee's film will be ignored by those seduced by the glitter, glamor, and the spectacle. Like many other bad Hollywood movies with powerful subject matter, *Malcolm X* touches the hearts and minds of folks who bring their own meaning to the film and connect it with their own social experience. That is why young black folks can brag about the way the fictional Malcolm courageously confronts white folks, even as young white folks leave the theater pleased and relieved that the Malcolm they see is such a good guy, and not the threatening presence they have heard about. Spike Lee's focus on Malcolm follows in the wake of a sustained and/or renewed interest in his life and work generated by hip-hop, by progressive contemporary cultural criticism, political writings, and various forms of militant activism. These counter hegemonic voices are needed resistance opposing conservative commodifications of Malcolm's life and work.

Just as these forms of commodification freeze and exploit the image of Malcolm X while simultaneously undermining the power of his work to radicalize and educate for critical consciousness, they strip him of icon status. This gives rise to an increase in cultural attacks, especially in the mainstream mass media. One of the most powerful attacks has been that by white writer Bruce Perry. Though Malcolm lets any reader know in his auto-biography that during his hustling days he did "unspeakable" acts (the nature of which should be obvious to anyone familiar with the street culture of cons, drugs, sexual hedo-nism, etc.), yet Perry assumes that his naming of these acts exposes Malcolm as a fraud. This is the height of white supremacist patriarchal arrogance. No doubt his work shocks and surprises many folks who need to believe their icons are saints but no information Perry reveals (much of it gleaned from interviews with Malcolm's enemies and detractors) diminishes the power of Malcolm's role in the struggle to end white supremacy.

Perry's work has received a boost in media attention since the opening of Spike Lee's movie and is rapidly acquiring authoritative status. Writing in *The Washington Post* Perry claims to be moved by the film even as he insists that Lee's version of Malcolm "is largely a myth," the assumption being that Perry's version is "truth." Magazines like *The New Yorker,* which rarely focus on black life, have highlighted their anti-Malcolm pieces. The December issue of *Harpers* has a piece by black scholar Gerald Early "Their Malcolm, My Problem" that also aims to diminish the power of his life and work. Usually when black folks are attempting to denounce Malcolm, they gain in the white press. Unless there is serious critical intervention, Rustin's dire pre-diction that non-progressive white folks will determine how Malcolm is viewed histor-ically may very well come to pass. Those of us who respect and revere Malcolm as teacher, political mentor, and comrade must focus on his political contribution to black liberation struggle and the global fight for freedom and justice for all.

Spike Lee's film biography shows no abiding connection between Malcolm's per-sonal rage at racism and his compassionate devotion to alleviating the sufferings of all black people. Significantly, Spike Lee's *Malcolm X* does not compel audiences to expe-rience the pain, sorrow, and suffering of black life in white supremacist patriarchal cul-ture. Nothing in the film conveys an anguish and grief so intense as to overwhelm emotionally. Nothing that would help folks understand the necessity of rage and resis-tance. Nothing that would let them see why, after working all day long, Malcolm would walk the streets for hours thinking "about what terrible things have been done to our people here in the United States." While the early footage of the brutal beating of Rodney King is a graphic reminder of "the terrible things," the pathos that this im-age evokes is quickly displaced by the neo-minstrel show that entertains and titillates.

As sentimental, romanticized drama *Malcolm X* seduces by encouraging us to for-get the brutal reality that created black rage and militancy. The film does not compel viewers to confront, challenge, and change. It embraces and rewards passive response—inaction. It encourages us to weep but not to fight. In James Baldwin's powerful essay "Everybody's Protest Novel" he reminds readers that "Sentimentality, the ostentatious parading of excessive and spurious emotion, is the mark of dishonesty, the inability to feel: the wet eyes of the sentimentalist betray his aversion to experience, his fear of life, his arid heart; and it is always, therefore, the signal of secret and violent inhumanity, the mask of cruelty." As Wallace warned, there is no place in Hollywood movies for the "seriousness of black liberation." Spike Lee's film is no exception. To take liberation se-riously we must take seriously the reality of black suffering. Ultimately, it is this reality the film denies.

SUGGESTIONS FOR DISCUSSION

1. What did Bayard Rustin mean when he said, "White America, not the Negro people, will determine Malcolm X's role in history"? How has that been true or not true?
2. Hooks writes, "There is nothing in *Malcolm X* that would indicate that a white director could not have made this film." What does she mean by that? How would you expect a white director's representation to differ from an African American director's representation of Malcolm?
3. Do you believe, as Michele Wallace states, there is no place in Hollywood movies for "the seriousness of black liberation"? If that is true, why is it true? If you disagree, explain your position.

SUGGESTIONS FOR WRITING

1. Summarize bell hooks's argument, making sure to separate out what she says about the film from what she says about Hollywood and from what she says about our culture's willingness to represent political difference.
2. Early in her article, hooks quotes Malcolm X as saying, "Never accept images that have been created for you by someone else. It is always better to form the habit of learning how to see things for yourself: then you are in a better position to judge for yourself." For African Americans, American Indians, Asian Americans, Latinos, gay rights activists, and many others, this warning must ring true. Write an exploratory response to this passage in which you examine what it might mean for a group not in the mainstream of American media to begin creating its own images. Think about how advertising, television, film, and other visual representations might change if they were not all emanating from a common source.
3. Film biographies have become extremely popular in the United States today. In the same year that *Malcolm X* was produced, for example, Hollywood also offered biographies of John F. Kennedy and former Teamster leader Jimmy Hoffa. Take time to look at one or more of these film biographies and write your own critique of its representation of the title figure. Keep in mind the way bell hooks links her discussion to events of the past, other possible ways of understanding Malcolm, and concerns of contemporary representation of history.

FOR FURTHER EXPLORATION

Many of the issues raised in this chapter were first raised by John Berger in his book *Ways of Seeing.* You may wish to read that book and compare his discussion of images with the more traditional approach taken by someone like art historian Kenneth Clark in his classic book-length study, *The Nude: A Study in Ideal Form.* If you are interested in popular culture images, you might begin with Susan Willis's *A Primer for Everyday Life,* and Ward Churchill's *Fantasies of the Master Race* is a good introduction to images of American Indians in popular culture. If you are interested in doing any further work in advertising images, you might look at the magazine *Media & Values,* a magazine devoted to images in television, film, and advertising.

Other topics raised by the writers in this chapter include:

- The life and work of Malcolm X
- The role of advertising and the "green" market
- Images of class, race, and gender in film
- Film as history (especially in the lives of past leaders or cultural heroes)

CHAPTER 5

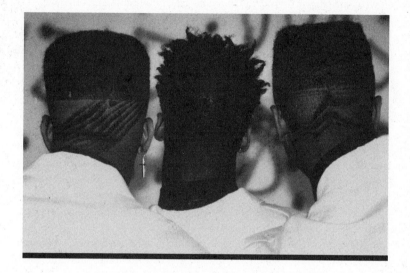

STYLE

"I have been at odds with the hair on my head for most of my life."

– Susan Brownmiller, *femininity*

A mericans live in a style-conscious culture in which even elementary school children know the difference between Air Jordans and the generic imitations. That the label means so much even to children may seem surprising until you consider how often all of us characterize people in terms of their clothing, their hair, or their body type. Of course, just as we judge others, we are judged by others on what sociologist Erving Goffman has called our daily "performance." Like the actors in a stage play, we present ourselves to the public each day. Some, Goffman claims, are taken in by their own performance. They present themselves in the way that seems right for their group or social position without being conscious of how their choices are influenced by the style and manner of those around them. Others are more cynical. They know they are dressing up or dressing down; their style is calculated for the effect it will have on the people they meet.

Although style might refer to many things—the way you present yourselves to others, your writing, your speech—we will limit our discussion of style to matters of personal appearance. The essays in this chapter focus on the body types that many try to emulate, the hair styles we select, and the ways we choose to dress, because those personal preferences in style are among the first choices individuals make as they decide who they are and how they want to appear to others. The hair on their heads, the length of their skirts, the tightness of their jeans—all of these choices can somehow absorb people whether they will them to or not.

Of course, in many ways a concern for appearance or "stylishness" is trivial. After all, what does it really matter whether clothes or hair or automobiles or homes are up-to-date or old-fashioned? Why should anyone care? That is difficult to say, and yet somehow many Americans do care. They care a great deal. The entire cosmetics and fashion industries thrive on such caring. Fashion designers, for example, depend on American consumers caring enough to change styles periodically. Sometimes it even seems that manufacturers make those changes on their own and determine what the rest of us will buy, but style is not simply a product of manufacturers. Consumers make choices that have to do with everything from comfort and cost to status and tradition. In our own time, style has been at the center of animal rights controversies, a key to counterculture identities, the statement of teenagers wishing to declare themselves independent of their parents, and, always, a guide to economic and social class. Style identifies.

Through close attention to style and the details of dress and look, men and women become visual objects themselves. Furthermore, we have in our cultural consciousness a measure by which we might judge those details. Any one of us standing before the mirror can only evaluate the look reflected by measuring it against a more general look or style popular or unpopular in the culture at the time. Think of how often you judge others based on their clothing or hair style or makeup. Such a judgment can only be made if you already have an idea of what the person *ought* to look like in a given situation. How *ought* a high school teacher or a business executive or a rock singer dress? Of course, not everyone will answer that question in the same way, but most of us have had many of the same visual experiences that have shaped attitudes about personal as well as public styles.

Many of those shared visual experiences are media images, particularly advertising, film, and television images that generalize a look that privileges certain segments of our society while suppressing others. As actress Linda Evans reminds us in one of her hair color commercials, "He said he liked my hair in its original color, but I noticed that both of his wives were blond."

Because media images are so pervasive, they can easily become prototypes of style, class, or even profession. That is why viewers recognize the upscale dress of the kids on *Beverly Hills, 90210,* or the working-class look of *Roseanne* and *Married . . . with Children.* You may or may not be familiar with these particular television shows, but if you were to see them, you could easily identify the economic class or social status of the people by the way in which they are dressed.

For many Americans today, it is the label that signals class, and so the most style-conscious shop not simply for look or quality but for designer names. The designer name labels the wearer as someone who can afford *Guess* jeans or Air Jordan shoes. The label promises acceptance. For the clothing industry, then, it is the label that determines cost, not the heft of the denim. For others, the look is to seem as uninterested in fashion as possible while still remaining hip or stylish. Grunge does just that. Torn, worn jeans, jackets, and vests layered over rumpled second-hand shirts is one style that cuts across class lines and has many serious shoppers wandering through second-hand clothing stores.

You might well feel that you do not want to be told how to dress or whom to impress. You might have already established what you think of as a style that is yours, not your parents' style or even the style worn by the "fashionable" people you know. Even the most personal style, however, originates from the culture in which it is created. Even those styles that are outright rejections of that culture define themselves in reference to dominant styles. Some groups do position themselves outside the values of the dominant culture. These subcultures see themselves as offering alternatives to dominant ways of thinking and acting. Punks used dress, hair, makeup, language, music, and dance to declare a separateness. Still, much of what begins as a subculture's style—punked-out hair, rivet-laden jackets, makeup for men as well as women—often enters the fashion market later as popular, stylish dress. "Distressed" or torn jeans, for example, are no longer a symbol of poverty or defiance but a marker of wealth or hipness. Subculture styles that are incorporated into dominant culture fashion are most often incorporated without the politics that motivated them. When that happens, the fashion generated by the subculture no longer carries with it the power of difference.

READING STYLE

As you read through the selections in this chapter, you will be asked to write your own commentary on style and stylishness. Your initial commentary will, undoubtedly, be influenced by what you already think of this topic. As you read, however, your writing will be informed by others who have also written about style and choice.

It is true that concern for style and fashion can seem foolish, but those concerns are also at the heart of some of the most serious issues in this culture. The first selections in this chapter, Margaret Atwood's "The Female Body" and bell hooks's "Straightening Our Hair," begin our discussion on style and its connection with the ways we see and treat our own bodies because these choices can become political as well as personal ones. Women in particular are concerned about these issues because two of the most serious psychological and physical disturbances among young women today are anorexia and bulimia, devastating eating disorders that can lead to severe depression, illness, and death. Even those women who do not have eating disorders are likely to be affected by style's insistence on thinness, perfection, and ageless beauty. In "Straightening Our Hair," bell hooks eloquently reveals how choices that ought to be simple (hair style, in this case) are rarely uncomplicated, especially for those whose looks do not conform. Both Atwood and hooks raise questions about cultural dominance and personal choice. In your writing assignments, you will be asked to consider what it means in this or any culture to look different, not to conform to the standard model because of those things you cannot control—ethnicity, race, body type, or even the way you have been raised.

The selections that follow, John Molloy's "Dress for Success," Dick Hebdige's "Style in Revolt: Revolting Style," Wendy Chapkis's "Dress as Success: Joolz," and Franz Lidz's "Black Is Golden," explore the role fashion plays in determining how people are received by those in power or by what we might call the mainstream. Molloy's text, for example, assumes that we all want to look upper middle class and that, to succeed, we *must* look upper middle class. Hebdige, whose work also assumes that people judge each other on the basis of appearance, raises the issue of what it means when certain groups decide to position themselves outside the mainstream. In his study of punk fashions, Hebdige examines the way in which those who wish to defy dominant orders express their defiance through style. Chapkis provides a kind of testimony to punk style in her interview with Joolz, the woman who dresses for a different kind of success than Molloy would identify.

As you read through and study the positions of writers like Margaret Atwood, John Molloy, Dick Hebdige, Wendy Chapkis, and Franz Lidz, you will be asked to reconsider and rewrite your own position on this topic. By keeping in mind your experiences with and observations on style and consumption as a way of declaring your own identity or determining the identity of others, you can explore the meaning of dress, the concept of stylishness, and the ways in which style affects your judgments of others.

As in the chapter on images, you will be asked to pay particular attention to visual detail and to choices that you make as you dress or buy a particular product or create a "look" for yourself. You can begin by paying more careful attention than you normally would to such choices. Even if you have made a decision to ignore stylishness, you are making a decision about style and what it means in the larger culture. Why do you buy one pair of jeans and not another? Why do you wear your hair the way you do? Do you see models (the word, of course, means *example* or *prototype*) that you want to emulate? Even if you don't, do you see others emulating those models? Do you want to be thinner, taller, fuller, darker—anything but what you are? Your answers to questions like these can help you sort out some of your own already held notions about style and stylishness in this culture. You can very easily begin with yourself when you ask questions about style, but you need not remain focused on yourself for long. In fact, the questions become even more interesting when you ask them about entire groups or when you place them in more serious political contexts.

By the conclusion of this chapter, you will have had the chance to make observations of your own, to discuss these observations and ideas with your classmates, and to formulate your own position on the topic of style and its place in American culture. Your final essays will be informed by both the reading you do in this chapter and by the remarks of friends and classmates as you talk through the topic.

That style is a powerful motivator in this culture ought to be obvious from such recent phenomena as the boom in the designer jeans market or the push even in some public schools to adopt a school uniform, thus avoiding some of the schoolyard wars that are waged over one kind of athletic shoe or another. But jeans, shoes, and uniforms are simply the most recent and most obvious manifestations of our obsession with style. The significance of this obsession must be understood in terms of its connection to an entire culture, not just one group of consumers.

Margaret Atwood

THE FEMALE BODY

Margaret Atwood is a Canadian-born writer whose fiction includes the novels *The Handmaid's Tale* and *Cat's Eye*. In the following selection, written for a special edition on the female body of *Michigan Quarterly Review*, Atwood draws on her skills as a poet and novelist to create a poetic commentary on the subject. In it, Atwood touches on stereotypes, outrages, reactions, fears, ironies, and humor. Her response to the female body as a topic provides a suitable beginning to a chapter on style since so much of what we talk of as style is centered on current ideals of the body.

Suggestion for Reading

- "The Female Body" has been anthologized in *The Best American Essays: 1991*, yet it does not take the form we normally think of as an essay form. Instead, it is made up of seven separate sections that seem, at first, unconnected and impressionistic. Annotate each section in an attempt to understand what each section is about separately, and then use your annotations to write a summary statement of what Atwood seems to be saying about the female body with the entire essay.

———————————◆———————————

. . . entirely devoted to the subject of "The Female Body."
Knowing how well you have written on this topic . . . this
capacious topic . . .
—letter from *Michigan Quarterly Review*

1.

I agree, it's a hot topic. But only one? Look around, there's a wide range. Take my own, for instance.

I get up in the morning. My topic feels like hell. I sprinkle it with water, brush parts of it, rub it with towels, powder it, add lubricant. I dump in the fuel and away goes my topic, my topical topic, my controversial topic, my capacious topic, my limping topic, my nearsighted topic, my topic with back problems, my badly behaved topic, my vulgar topic, my outrageous topic, my aging topic, my topic that is out of the question and anyway still can't spell, in its oversized coat and worn winter boots, scuttling along the sidewalk as if it were flesh and blood, hunting for what's out there, an avocado, an alderman, an adjective, hungry as ever.

2.

The basic Female Body comes with the following accessories: garter belt, panti-girdle, crinoline, camisole, bustle, brassiere, stomacher, chemise, virgin zone, spike heels, nose ring, veil, kid gloves, fishnet stockings, fichu, bandeau, Merry Widow, weepers, chokers, barrettes, bangles, beads, lorgnette, feather boa, basic black, compact, Lycra stretch one-piece with modesty panel, designer peignoir, flannel nightie, lace teddy, bed, head.

3.

The Female Body is made of transparent plastic and lights up when you plug it in. You press a button to illuminate the different systems. The circulatory system is red, for the heart and arteries, purple for the veins; the respiratory system is blue; the lymphatic system is yellow; the digestive system is green, with liver and kidneys in aqua. The nerves are done in orange and the brain is pink. The skeleton, as you might expect, is white.

The reproductive system is optional, and can be removed. It comes with or without a miniature embryo. Parental judgment can thereby be exercised. We do not wish to frighten or offend.

4.

He said, I won't have one of those things in the house. It gives a young girl a false notion of beauty, not to mention anatomy. If a real woman was built like that she'd fall on her face.

She said, If we don't let her have one like all the other girls she'll feel singled out. It'll become an issue. She'll long for one and she'll long to turn into one. Repression breeds sublimation. You know that.

He said, It's not just the pointy plastic tits, it's the wardrobes. The wardrobes and that stupid male doll, what's his name, the one with the underwear glued on.

She said, Better to get it over with when she's young. He said, All right, but don't let me see it.

She came whizzing down the stairs, thrown like a dart. She was stark naked. Her hair had been chopped off, her head was turned back to front, she was missing some toes and she'd been tattooed all over her body with purple ink in a scrollwork design. She hit the potted azalea, trembled there for a moment like a botched angel, and fell.

He said, I guess we're safe.

5.

The Female Body has many uses. It's been used as a door knocker, a bottle opener, as a clock with a ticking belly, as something to hold up lampshades, as a nutcracker, just squeeze the brass legs together and out comes your nut. It bears torches, lifts victorious wreaths, grows copper wings and raises aloft a ring of neon stars; whole buildings rest on its marble heads.

It sells cars, beer, shaving lotion, cigarettes, hard liquor; it sells diet plans and diamonds, and desire in tiny crystal bottles. Is this the face that launched a thousand products? You bet it is, but don't get any funny big ideas, honey, that smile is a dime a dozen.

It does not merely sell, it is sold. Money flows into this country or that country, flies in, practically crawls in, suitful after suitful, lured by all those hairless pre-teen legs. Listen, you want to reduce the national debt, don't you? Aren't you patriotic? That's the spirit. That's my girl.

She's a natural resource, a renewable one luckily, because those things wear out so quickly. They don't make 'em like they used to. Shoddy goods.

6.

One and one equals another one. Pleasure in the female is not a requirement. Pair-bonding is stronger in geese. We're not talking about love, we're talking about biology. That's how we all got here, daughter.

Snails do it differently. They're hermaphrodites, and work in threes.

7.

Each Female Body contains a female brain. Handy. Makes things work. Stick pins in it and you get amazing results. Old popular songs. Short circuits. Bad dreams.

Anyway: each of these brains has two halves. They're joined together by a thick cord; neural pathways flow from one to the other, sparkles of electric information washing to and fro. Like light on waves. Like a conversation. How does a woman know? She listens. She listens in.

The male brain, now, that's a different matter. Only a thin connection. Space over here, time over there, music and arithmetic in their own sealed compartments. The right brain doesn't know what the left brain is doing. Good for aiming though, for hitting the target when you pull the trigger. What's the target? Who's the target? Who cares? What matters is hitting it. That's the male brain for you. Objective.

This is why men are so sad, why they feel so cut off, why they think of themselves as orphans cast adrift, footloose and stringless in the deep void. What void? she asks.

What are you talking about? The void of the universe, he says, and she says Oh and looks out the window and tries to get a handle on it, but it's no use, there's too much going on, too many rustlings in the leaves, too many voices, so she says, Would you like a cheese sandwich, a piece of cake, a cup of tea? And he grinds his teeth because she doesn't understand, and wanders off, not just alone but Alone, lost in the dark, lost in the skull, searching for the other half, the twin who could complete him.

Then it comes to him: he's lost the Female Body! Look, it shines in the gloom, far ahead, a vision of wholeness, ripeness, like a giant melon, like an apple, like a metaphor for "breast" in a bad sex novel; it shines like a balloon, like a foggy noon, a watery moon, shimmering in its egg of light.

Catch it. Put it in a pumpkin, in a high tower, in a compound, in a chamber, in a house, in a room. Quick, stick a leash on it, a lock, a chain, some pain, settle it down, so it can never get away from you again.

SUGGESTIONS FOR DISCUSSION

1. What do you think Atwood is saying about the female body in her essay? What is her attitude toward this topic?
2. Where do you think Atwood's thoughts about the female body come from? Are you familiar with any of them? Would you add any of your own?
3. Why would any journal devote an entire issue to the female body?

SUGGESTIONS FOR WRITING

1. Choose any one of the seven sections from this article and write a one- to two-page explanation of and response to what you believe that section to be about.
2. Many critics of fashion today argue that the ideal female form is excessively thin and childlike. Margaret Atwood evokes a wide range of responses to the female form in her essay. Write a response to Atwood's essay in which you explore how popular notions of the ideal female body affect our ideas about what is stylish and what is not.
3. Imitate Atwood's essay form and write your own essay on the male body.

bell hooks

STRAIGHTENING OUR HAIR

A professor of English at Oberlin College, bell hooks is a poet, teacher, and activist who writes a regular column, "Sisters of the Yam," for *Z Magazine*. Throughout her career, she has written extensively on the politics of race, class, and gender including the books *Talking Back: Thinking Feminist, Thinking Black, Feminist Theory: From Margin to Center*, and *Black Looks: Race and Representation*. In the following article, published in 1988, hooks writes of her decision, during the Black Power Movement of the sixties, to stop straightening her hair, even though it took her a long time to feel comfortable with nonprocessed hair. Her discussion of the politics of African American women straightening their hair is one that must be read with that historical and political context in mind. She made her decision when it was the decision that seemed most honest for her to make.

hooks opens her essay with a memory of her own childhood in a family of six daughters who spent every Saturday morning in the intimacy of the kitchen where women straightened each other's hair. She then expands that memory to the questions of race, gender, beauty, and political dominance. In that way, her essay serves to present both a personal story and an extended discussion of broader political issues.

Suggestion for Reading

• As you read, you may notice that bell hooks writes of a dilemma that is at once a very private and public one. Underline those passages in her essay in which hooks touches on this issue of the political nature of private choices.

O n Saturday mornings we would gather in the kitchen to get our hair fixed, that is straightened. Smells of burning grease and hair, mingled with the scent of our freshly washed bodies, with collard greens cooking on the stove, with fried fish. We did not go to the hairdresser. Mama fixed our hair. Six daughters—there was no way we could have afforded hairdressers. In those days, this process of straightening black women's hair with a hot comb (invented by Madame C.J. Waler) was not connected in my mind with the effort to look white, to live out standards of beauty set by white supremacy. It was connected solely with rites of initiation into womanhood. To arrive at that point where one's hair could be straightened was to move from being perceived as child (whose hair could be neatly combed and braided) to being almost a woman. It was this moment of transition my sisters and I longed for.

Hair pressing was a ritual of black women's culture—of intimacy. It was an exclusive moment when black women (even those who did not know one another well) might meet at home or in the beauty parlor to talk with one another, to listen to the talk. It was as important a world as that of the male barber shop—mysterious, secret. It was a world where the images constructed as barriers between one's self and the world were briefly let go, before they were made again. It was a moment of creativity, a moment of change.

I wanted this change even though I had been told all my life that I was one of the "lucky" ones because I had been born with "good hair"—hair that was fine, almost straight—not good enough but still good. Hair that had no nappy edges, no "kitchen," that area close to the neck that the hot comb could not reach. This "good hair" meant nothing to me when it stood as a barrier to my entering this secret black woman world. I was overjoyed when mama finally agreed that I could join the Saturday ritual, no longer looking on but patiently waiting my turn. I have written of this ritual: "For each of us getting our hair pressed is an important ritual. It is not a sign of our longing to be white. There are no white people in our intimate world. It is a sign of our desire to be women. It is a gesture that says we are approaching womanhood . . . Before we reach the appropriate age we wear braids, plaits that are symbols of our innocence, our youth, our childhood. Then, we are comforted by the parting hands that comb and braid, comforted by the intimacy and bliss. There is a deeper intimacy in the kitchen on Saturdays when hair is pressed, when fish is fried, when sodas are passed around, when soul music drifts over the talk. It is a time without men. It is a time when we work as women to meet each other's needs, to make each other feel good inside, a time of laughter and outrageous talk."

Since the world we lived in was racially segregated, it was easy to overlook the relationship between white supremacy and our obsession with hair. Even though black women with straight hair were perceived to be more beautiful than those with thick, frizzy hair, it was not overtly related to a notion that white women were a more appealing female group or that their straight hair set a beauty standard black women were struggling to live out. While this was probably the ideological framework from which the process of straightening black women's hair emerged, it was expanded so that it became a real space of black woman bonding through ritualized, shared experience. The beauty parlor was a space of consciousness raising, a space where black women shared life stories—hardship, trials, gossip; a place where one could be comforted and one's spirit renewed. It was for some women a place of rest where one did not need to meet the demands of children or men. It was the one hour some folk would spend "off their feet," a soothing, restful time of meditation and silence. These positive empowering implications of the ritual of hair pressing mediate but do not change negative implications. They exist alongside all that is negative.

Within white supremacist capitalist patriarchy, the social and political context in which the custom of black folks straightening our hair emerges, it represents an imitation of the dominant white group's appearance and often indicates internalized racism, self-hatred, and/or low self-esteem. During the 1960s black people who actively worked to critique, challenge, and change white racism pointed to the way in which black people's obsession with straight hair reflected a colonized mentality. It was at this time that the natural hairdo, the "afro," became fashionable as a sign of cultural resistance to racist oppression and as a celebration of blackness. Naturals were equated with political militancy. Many young black folks found just how much political value was placed on straightened hair as a sign of respectability and conformity to societal expectations when they ceased to straighten their hair. When black liberation struggles did not lead to revolutionary change in society the focus on the political relationship between appearance and complicity with white racism ceased and folks who had once sported afros began to straighten their hair.

In keeping with the move to suppress black consciousness and efforts to be self-defining, white corporations began to acknowledge black people and most especially black women as potential consumers of products they could provide, including hair-care products. Permanents specially designed for black women eliminated the need for hair pressing and the hot comb. They not only cost more but they also took much of the economy and profit out of black communities, out of the pockets of black women who had previously reaped the material benefits (see Manning Marable's *How Capitalism Underdeveloped Black America*, South End Press). Gone was the context of ritual, of black woman bonding. Seated under noisy hair dryers black women lost a space for dialogue, for creative talk.

Stripped of the positive binding rituals that traditionally surrounded the experience, black women straightening our hair seemed more and more to be exclusively a signifier of white supremacist oppression and exploitation. It was clearly a process that was about black women changing their appearance to imitate white people's looks. This need to look as much like white people as possible, to look safe, is related to a desire to succeed in the white world. Before desegregation black people could worry less about what white folks thought about their hair. In a discussion with black women about beauty at Spelman College, students talked about the importance of wearing straight hair when seeking jobs. They were convinced and probably rightly so that their chances of finding good jobs would be enhanced if they had straight hair. When asked to elaborate they focused on the connection between radical politics and natural hairdos, whether natural or braided. One woman wearing a short natural told of purchasing a straight wig for her job search. No one in the discussion felt black women were free to wear our hair in natural styles without reflecting on the possible negative consequences. Often older black adults, especially parents, respond quite negatively to natural hairdos. I shared with the group that when I arrived home with my hair in braids shortly after accepting my job at Yale my parents told me I looked disgusting.

Despite many changes in racial politics, black women continue to obsess about their hair, and straightening hair continues to be serious business. It continues to tap into the insecurity black women feel about our value in this white supremacist society. Talking with groups of women at various college campuses and with black women in our communities there seems to be general consensus that our obsession with hair in general reflects continued struggles with self-esteem and self-actualization. We talk about the extent to which black women perceive our hair as the enemy, as a problem we must solve, a territory we must conquer. Above all it is a part of our black female body that must be controlled. Most of us were not raised in environments where we learned to regard our hair as sensual or beautiful in an unprocessed state. Many of us talk about situations where white people ask to touch our hair when it is unprocessed then show surprise that the texture is soft or feels good. In the eyes of many white folks and other non-black folks, the natural afro looks like steel wool or a helmet. Responses to natural hairstyles worn by black women usually reveal the extent to which our natural hair is perceived in white supremacist culture as not only ugly but frightening. We also internalize that fear. The extent to which we are comfortable with our hair usually reflects on our overall feelings about our bodies. In our black women's support group, *Sisters of the Yam,* we talk about the ways we don't like our bodies, especially our hair. I suggested to the group that we regard our hair as though it is not part of our body but something quite separate—again a territory to be controlled. To me it was important for us to link this need to control with sexuality, with sexual repression. Curious about what black women who had hot-combed or had permanents felt about the relationship between straightened hair and sexual practice I asked whether people worried about their hairdo, whether they feared partners touching their hair. Straightened hair has always seemed to me to call attention to the desire for hair to stay in place. Not surprisingly many black women responded that they felt uncomfortable if too much attention was focused on their hair, if it seemed to be too messy. Those of us who have liberated our hair and let it go in whatever direction it seems fit often receive negative comments.

Looking at photographs of myself and my sisters when we had straightened hair in high school I noticed how much older we looked than when our hair was not processed. It is ironic that we live in a culture that places so much emphasis on women looking young, yet black women are encouraged to change our hair in ways that make us appear older. This past semester we read Toni Morrison's *The Bluest Eye* in a black women's fiction class. I ask students to write autobiographical statements which reflect their thoughts about the connection between race and physical beauty. A vast majority of black women wrote about their hair. When I asked individual women outside class why they continued to straighten their hair, many asserted that naturals don't look good on them, or that they required too much work. Emily, a favorite student with very short hair, always straightened it and I would tease and challenge her. She explained to me convincingly that a natural hairdo would look horrible with her face, that she did not have the appropriate forehead or bone structure. Later she shared that during spring break she had gone to the beauty parlor to have her perm and as she sat there waiting, thinking about class reading and discussion, it came to her that she was really frightened that no one else would think she was attractive if she did not straighten her hair. She acknowledged that this fear was rooted in feelings of low self-esteem. She decided to make a change. Her new look surprised her because it was so appealing. We talked afterwards about her earlier denial and justification for wearing straightened hair. We talked about the way it hurts to realize connection between racist oppression and the arguments we use to convince ourselves and others that we are not beautiful or acceptable as we are.

• • •

In numerous discussions with black women about hair one of the strongest factors that prevent black women from wearing unprocessed hairstyles is the fear of losing other people's approval and regard. Heterosexual black women talked about the extent to which black men respond more favorably to women with straight or straightened hair. Lesbian women point to the fact that many of them do not straighten their hair, raising the question of whether or not this gesture is fundamentally linked to heterosexism and a longing for male approval. I recall visiting a woman friend and her black male companion in New York years ago and having an intense discussion about hair. He took it upon himself to share with me that I could be a fine sister if I would do something about my hair (secretly I thought mama must have hired him). What I remember is his shock when I calmly and happily asserted that I like the touch and feel of unprocessed hair.

When students read about race and physical beauty, several black women describe periods of childhood when they were overcome with longing for straight hair as it was so associated with desirability, with being loved. Few women had received affirmation from family, friends, or lovers when choosing not to straighten their hair and we have many stories to tell about advice we receive from everyone, including total strangers, urging to understand how much more attractive we would be if we would fix (straighten) our hair. When I interviewed for my job at Yale, white female advisers who had never before commented on my hair encouraged me not to wear braids or a large natural to the interview. Although they did not say straighten your hair, they were suggesting that I change my hairstyle so that it would most resemble theirs, so that it would indicate a certain conformity. I wore braids and no one seemed to notice. When I was offered the job I did not ask if it mattered whether or not I wore braids. I tell this story to my students so that they will know by this one experience that we do not always need to surrender our power to be self defining to succeed in an endeavor. Yet I have found the issue of hairstyle comes up again and again with students when I give lectures. At one conference on black women and leadership I walked into a a packed auditorium, my hair unprocessed wild and all over the place. The vast majority of black women seated there had straightened hair. Many of them looked at me with hostile contemptuous stares. I felt as though I was being judged on the spot as someone out on the fringe, an undesirable. Such judgments are made particularly about black women in the United States who choose to wear dreadlocks. They are seen and rightly so as the total antithesis of straightening one's hair, as a political statement. Often black women express contempt for those of us who choose this look.

• • •

Ironically, just as the natural unprocessed hair of black women is the subject of disregard and disdain we are witnessing return of the long dyed, blonde look. In their writing my black women students described wearing yellow mops on their heads as children to pretend they had long blonde hair. Recently black women singers who are working to appeal to white audiences, to be seen as crossovers, use hair implanting and hair weaving to have long straight hair. There seems to be a definite connection between a black female entertainer's popularity with white audiences and the degree to which she works to appear white, or to embody aspects of white style. Tina Turner and Aretha Franklin were trend setters; both dyed their hair blonde. In everyday life we see more and more black women using chemicals to be blonde. At one of my talks focusing on the social construction of black female identity within a sexist and racist society, a black woman came to me at the end of the discussion and shared that her seven-year-old daughter was obsessed with blonde hair, so much so that she had made a wig to imitate long blonde curls. This mother wanted to know what she was doing wrong in her parenting. She asserted that their home was a place where blackness was affirmed and celebrated. Yet she had not considered that her processed straightened hair was a message to her daughter that black women are not acceptable unless we alter our appearance or hair texture. Recently I talked with one of my younger sisters about her hair. She uses bright colored dyes, various shades of red. Her skin is very dark. She has a broad nose and short hair. For her these choices of straightened dyed hair were directly related to feelings of low self-esteem. She does not like her features and feels that the hairstyle transforms her. My perception was that her choice of red straightened hair actually called attention to the features she was trying to mask. When she commented that this look receives more attention and compliments, I suggested that the positive feedback might be a direct response to her own projection of a higher level of self-satisfaction. Folk may be responding to that and not her altered looks. We talked about the messages she is sending her dark-skinned daughters—that they will be most attractive if they straighten their hair.

A number of black women have argued that straightened hair is not necessarily a signifier of low self-esteem. They argue that it is a survival strategy; it is easier to function in this society with straightened hair. There are fewer hassles. Or as some folk stated, straightened hair is easier to manage, takes less time. When I responded to this argument in our discussion at Spelman by suggesting that perhaps the unwillingness to spend time on ourselves, caring for our bodies, is also a reflection of a sense that this is not important or that we do not deserve such care. In this group and others, black women talked about being raised in households where spending too much time on appearance was ridiculed or considered vanity. Irrespective of the way individual black women choose to do their hair, it is evident that the extent to which we suffer from racist and sexist oppression and exploitation affects the degree to which we feel capable of both self-love and asserting an autonomous presence that is acceptable and pleasing to ourselves. Individual preferences (whether rooted in self-hate or not) cannot negate the reality that our collective obsession with straightening black hair reflects the psychology of oppression and the impact of racist colonization. Together racism and sexism daily reinforce to all black females via the media, advertising, etc. that we will not be considered beautiful or desirable if we do not change ourselves, especially our hair. We cannot resist this socialization if we deny that white supremacy informs our efforts to construct self and identity.

Without organized struggles like the ones that happened in the 1960s and early 1970s, individual black women must struggle alone to acquire the critical consciousness that would enable us to examine issues of race and beauty, our personal choices, from a political standpoint. There are times when I think of straightening my hair just to change my style, just for fun. Then I remind myself that even though such a gesture could be simply playful on my part, an individual expression of desire, I know that such a gesture would carry other implications beyond my control. The reality is: straightened hair is linked historically and currently to a system of racial domination that impresses upon black people, and especially black women, that we are not acceptable as we are, that we are not beautiful. To make such a gesture as an expression of individual freedom and choice would make me complicit with a politic of domination that hurts us. It is easy to surrender this freedom. It is more important that black women resist racism and sexism in every way; that every aspect of our self-representation be a fierce resistance, a radical celebration of our care and respect for ourselves.

Even though I have not had straightened hair for a long time, this did not mean that I am able to really enjoy or appreciate my hair in its natural state. For years I still considered it a problem. (It wasn't naturally nappy enough to make a decent interesting afro. It was too thin.) These complaints expressed my continued dissatisfaction. True liberation of my hair came when I stopped trying to control it in any state and just accepted it as it is. It has been only in recent years that I have ceased to worry about what other people would say about my hair. It has been only in recent years that I could feel consistent pleasure washing, combing, and caring for my hair. These feelings remind me of the pleasure and comfort I felt as a child sitting between my mother's legs feeling the warmth of her body and being as she combed and braided my hair. In a culture of domination, one that is essentially anti-intimacy, we must struggle daily to remain in touch with ourselves and our bodies, with one another. Especially black women and men, as it is our bodies that have been so often devalued, burdened, wounded in alienated labor. Celebrating our bodies, we participate in a liberatory struggle that frees mind and heart.

SUGGESTIONS FOR DISCUSSION

1. Review the opening and closing moments of hooks's essay and then discuss why she begins and ends with references to her own and others' experiences with hair styles. What would you say she is getting at by providing these experiences?
2. Most people probably think of hair style as a trivial concern, yet hooks connects hair style with serious political choices. Discuss why it is that hooks tells us that,

though she has not straightened her hair for many years, it took her a very long time to actually take pleasure from leaving her hair in its natural state.

3. Hooks's essay suggests that hair style, especially for African Americans, plays a substantial role in presenting a public image. In a discussion of what importance this culture, in general, places on an individual's hair style, consider how that general bias toward hair style reflects what hooks is saying about the choices she has had to make.

SUGGESTIONS FOR WRITING

1. Near the end of her essay, hooks writes the following: "Individual preferences (whether rooted in self-hate or not) cannot negate the reality that our collective obsession with straightening black hair reflects the psychology of oppression and the impact of racist colonization. Together racism and sexism daily reinforce to all black females via the media, advertising, etc. that we will not be considered beautiful or desirable if we do not change ourselves, especially our hair." Review this essay especially with that passage in mind, and then write a one- to two-page explanation of what hooks is getting at in this passage. Consider supporting your discussion with examples from your own experience with or your own observations on mainstream attitudes toward beauty and race.

2. Bell hooks asks her classes to write "autobiographical statements which reflect their thoughts about the connection between race and physical beauty." Write your own autobiographical position statement. In it you should begin with a memory or a personal observation. Then use that memory or observation to develop your own position on the connection between beauty and race in the American media. Remember that your experience with style, beauty, and race may be very different from hooks's experience, just as your attitude toward processed hair may be very different from hers, because of your age or experience or politics or personal preference.

3. One of the points bell hooks makes in her article is that hair styles have cultural meanings that we often overlook or take for granted. Pick a hair style and write a short essay in which you describe the style, identify who commonly wears that style, and explain what the style seems to represent in this culture.

John Molloy

DRESS FOR SUCCESS

John Molloy made his reputation in the late seventies with the publication of his widely read and extraordinarily popular self-help book *Dress for Success*, first published in 1975. In it, Molloy claimed to have found a no-miss formula for dressing guaranteed to impress the corporate boss and to give the prospective job seeker the advantage over the competition. In the following selection from the book's introduction, Molloy describes his methods for studying the concept of dressing for success and presents some of his conclusions from that study. Molloy's study began with particular assumptions about dress and most people's response to dress. He assumed that dress was an important indicator of social and economic class. He further assumed that most white collar employers judge potential employees by their dress. His experiments on dressing for success are built on those assumptions. Molloy was just as triumphant with his woman's guide to dressing for success, but the men's guide was one of the many self-help books that became a best-seller in the eighties. Self-help books became a popular genre in the seventies and eighties. They addressed such problems as dieting, quitting smoking, changing personal relationships, and feeling less guilt. Like others in the genre, Molloy's book promotes a quick fix for a complex problem.

Suggestion for Reading

- Underline and annotate those passages in which Molloy develops his thesis about the importance of dress as a signal of class.

◆

THE PROOF: WHAT WORKS AND WHAT DOESN'T

Since I had very early on discovered that the socioeconomic value of a man's clothing is important in determining his credibility with certain groups, his ability to attract certain kinds of women and his acceptance to the business community, one of the first elements I undertook to research was the socioeconomic level of all items of clothing.

Take the raincoat, for example. Most raincoats sold in this country are either beige or black; those are the two standard colors. Intuitively I felt that the beige raincoat was worn generally by the upper-middle class and black by the lower-middle class.

First I visited several Fifth Avenue stores that cater almost exclusively to upper-middle-class customers and attempted to ascertain the number of beige raincoats versus black raincoats being sold. The statistical breakdown was approximately four to one in favor of beige. I then checked stores on the lower-middle-class level and found that almost the reverse statistic applied. They sold four black raincoats to each beige raincoat.

This indicated that in all probability my feeling was correct, but recognizing that there were many variables that could discredit such preliminary research, I set the second stage in motion. On rainy days, I hired responsible college students to stand outside subway stations in determinable lower-middle-class neighborhoods and outside determinable upper-middle-class suburban commuter-stations, all in the New York area. The students merely counted the number of black and beige raincoats. My statistics held up at approximately four to one in either case, and I could now say that in the New York area, the upper-middle class generally wore beige raincoats and the lower-middle class generally wore black ones.

My next step was to take a rainy-day count in the two different socioeconomic areas in Chicago, Los Angeles, Dallas, Atlanta and six equally widespread small towns. The research again held up; statistics came back from the cities at about four to one and from the small towns at about two-and-a-half to three to one. (The statistics were not quite that clear cut, but averaged out into those ranges.)

From these statistics I was able to state that in the United States, the beige raincoat is generally worn by members of the upper-middle class and the black raincoat generally worn by members of the lower-middle class. From this, I was able to hypothesize that since these raincoats were an intrinsic part of the American environment, they had in all probability conditioned people by their predominance in certain classes, and automatic (Pavlovian) reactions could be expected.

In short, when someone met a man in a beige raincoat, he was likely to think of him as a member of the upper-middle class, and when he met a man in a black raincoat, he was likely to think of him as a member of the lower-middle class. I then had to see if my hypothesis would hold up under testing.

My first test was conducted with 1362 people—a cross section of the general public. They were given an "extrasensory perception" test in which they were asked to guess the answers to a number of problems to which the solutions (they were told) could only be known through ESP. The percentage of correct answers would indicate their ESP quotient. Naturally, a participant in this type of test attempts to get the right answer every time and has no reason to lie, since he wants to score high.

In this test, among a group of other problems and questions, I inserted a set of almost identical "twin pictures." There was only one variable. The twin pictures showed the same man in the same pose dressed in the same suit, the same shirt, the same tie, the same shoes. The only difference was the raincoat—one black, one beige. Participants were told that the pictures were of twin brothers, and were asked to identify the most prestigious of the two. Over 87 percent, or 1118 people, chose the man in the beige raincoat.

I next ran a field test. Two friends and I wore beige raincoats for one month, then switched to black raincoats the following month. We attempted to duplicate our other clothing during both months. At the end of each month, we recorded the general attitude of people toward us—waiters, store clerks, business associates, etc. All three of us agreed that the beige raincoat created a distinctly better impression upon the people we met.

Finally, I conducted one additional experiment alone. Picking a group of business offices at random, I went into each office with a *Wall Street Journal* in a manila envelope and asked the receptionist or secretary to allow me to deliver it personally to the man in charge. When wearing a black raincoat, it took me a day and a half to deliver twenty-five papers. In a beige raincoat, I was able to deliver the same number in a single morning.

The impression transmitted to receptionists and secretaries by my black raincoat and a nondescript suit, shirt and tie clearly was that I was a glorified delivery boy, and so I had to wait or was never admitted. But their opinion of me was substantially altered by the beige raincoat worn with the same other clothes. They thought I might be an associate or friend of the boss because that is what I implied, and they had better let me in. In short, they reacted to years of preconditioning and accepted the beige raincoat as a symbol of authority and status while they rejected the black raincoat as such.

This study was conducted in 1971. And although more and more lower-middle class men are wearing beige raincoats each year (basically because of improved wash-and-wear methods that make them much less expensive to keep clean), the results of the study remain valid and will continue to be for years to come. You cannot wear a black raincoat, and you must wear a beige raincoat—if you wish to be accepted as a member of the upper-middle class and treated accordingly (among all other raincoat colors, only dark blue tests as acceptable).

I continue to test the beige raincoat each year in my multiple-item studies. In the field of clothing, multiple-item studies are those that incorporate an entire look: the upper-middle-class look, the lower-middle class look, etc. These studies usually are not geared to test people's responses to specific items, but if a particular item is not consistent with the rest, it will destroy the effectiveness of the study because the incongruous item spoils the total look.

In one multiple-item study, I sent a twenty-five-year-old male college graduate from an upper-middle-class midwestern background to 100 offices. To fifty of them he wore an outfit made up entirely of garments that had been previously tested as having lower-middle class characteristics; to the remaining fifty he wore an outfit of garments that had been previously tested as having upper-middle-class characteristics. Prior to his arrival at each office, I had arranged for the man in charge to tell his secretary that he had hired an assistant, and to instruct her to show the young man around. The executive also made sure that his secretary would not be going to lunch, would not be going home, and would not be overworked at the time of my man's arrival.

After being shown through the offices, which took anywhere from fifteen minutes to an hour, depending on the secretary and the office, the young man made a series of requests. He first asked for something simple like letterhead stationery or a pencil and pad. The responses of the secretaries to these requests had no statistical significance, although the young man did note that there was a substantial difference in attitude. In upper-middle-class garb, he received the requested item with no comment, but pejorative comments or quizzical looks were directed toward him at least one-third of the time when he wore lower-middle class clothing.

Once the first request sequence was completed, the young man gave each secretary a standardized order. Before going to each office, he had been given the names of three people in the files of the office. These names were written on a card, and his procedure was always the same. Putting the card on the secretary's desk, he would say, "Miss (always using her name) Jones, please get these files for me; I will be at Mr. Smith's desk." He would then walk away, trying not to give the secretary a chance to answer him verbally. The results were quite significant.

In upper-middle-class garb, he received the files within ten minutes forty-two times. In lower-middle class garb, he received the files only twelve times. Pejorative comments were directed at him twelve times while wearing upper-middle-class clothes, and eight times while wearing lower-middle class clothes. This means that he received positive responses only four times out of fifty while wearing lower-middle class garb; but he received positive responses thirty times out of fifty when he was wearing upper-middle-class garb.

From this experiment and many others like it, I was able to conclude that in upper-middle-class clothes, a young man will be more successful in giving orders to secretaries.

The experiment will give you an idea of why I have spent so many years and so much of my clients' money in determining what constitutes upper-middle-class dress. It is obvious from the experiment that secretaries, who generally were not members of the upper-middle-class, did in fact recognize upper-middle-class clothing, if not consciously then at least subconsciously, and they did react to it. The reactions of the secretaries indicate that dress is neither trivial nor frivolous, but an essential element in helping a man to function in the business world with maximum effectiveness.

But does everyone react as the secretaries did?

For years, some companies have been attempting to increase the efficiency of employees by prescribing dress and establishing dress codes. Most of these schemes have proved ineffective because they have been created by amateurs who don't understand the effect clothing has on the work environment. Dress codes *can* work, as I will show later, but the assumption that clothing has a major, continuing impact on the wearer is erroneous. True, you may feel shabby when you wear shabby clothes, and your morale may perk up a bit when you splurge on an expensive tie. But clothing most significantly affects the people whom the wearer meets and, in the long run, affects the wearer only indirectly because it controls the reaction of the world to him. My research shows that in most business situations the wearer is not directly affected by his clothing, and that the effect of clothing on other people is mainly controlled by the socioeconomic level of the clothing.

Let me say it straight out: We all wear uniforms and our uniforms are clear and distinct signs of class. We react to them accordingly. In almost any situation where two men meet, one man's clothing is saying to the other man: "I am more important than you are, please show respect"; or "I am your equal and expect to be treated as such"; or "I am not your equal and I do not expect to be treated as such."

How 100 Top Executives Described Successful Dress

Over the years I have conducted literally thousands of studies, experiments and tests to aid my corporate and individual clients in using clothing better and as an indispensable tool of business life. Immediately prior to beginning this book, and specifically for this book, I asked several series of questions of 100 top executives in either medium-sized or major American corporations. The first series was to establish the most up-to-date attitudes on corporate dress.

I showed the executives five pictures of men, each of them wearing expensive, well-tailored, but high-fashion clothing. I asked if this was a proper look for the junior business executive. Ninety-two of the men said no, eight said yes.

I showed them five pictures of men neatly dressed in obvious lower-middle-class attire and asked if these men were dressed in proper attire for a young executive. Forty-six said yes, fifty-four said no.

I next showed them five pictures of men dressed in conservative upper-middle-class clothing and asked if they were dressed in proper attire for the young executive. All one hundred said yes.

I asked them whether they thought the men in the upper-middle-class garb would succeed better in corporate life than the men in the lower-middle-class uniform. Eighty-eight said yes, twelve said no.

I asked if they would choose one of the men in the lower-middle-class dress as their assistant. Ninety-two said no, eight said yes.

I next showed them pictures of four young men. The first had a very short haircut; the second had a moderate haircut with moderate sideburns; the third had a moderate haircut, but with fairly long sideburns; and the fourth had very long hair. I asked which haircut was the most profitable for a young man to wear. Eighty-two of them picked the moderate haircut with moderate sideburns; three picked the very short cut; and fifteen picked the moderate cut with long sideburns. No one picked the long hair.

I next asked if they would hire the man with long hair. Seventy-four said no.

To 100 other top executives of major corporations, I submitted the following written questions:

1. Does your company have a written or an unwritten dress code? Ninety-seven said yes. Three said no. Only two had a written dress code.

2. Would a number of men at your firm have a much better chance of getting ahead if they knew how to dress? Ninety-six said yes, four said no.

3. If there were a course in how to dress for business, would you send your son? All 100 said yes.

4. Do you think employee dress affects the general tone of the office? All 100 said yes.

5. Do you think employee dress affects efficiency? Fifty-two said yes, forty-eight said no.

6. Would you hold up the promotion of a man who didn't dress properly? Seventy-two said yes, twenty-eight said no.

7. Would you tell a young man if his dress was holding him back? Eighty said no, twenty said yes.

8. Does your company at present turn down people who show up at job interviews improperly dressed on that basis alone? Eighty-four said yes, sixteen said no.

9. Would you take a young man who didn't know how to dress as your assistant? Ninety-two said no, eight said yes.

10. Do you think there is a need for a book that would explain to a young man how to dress? Ninety-four said yes, six said no.

11. Do you think there is a need for a book to tell people in business how to dress? One hundred said yes.

Keep reading, fellows, you got it.

SUGGESTIONS FOR DISCUSSION

1. Although he uses the terms frequently, Molloy doesn't give readers many specific details of upper middle class and lower middle class dress. What examples of dress (besides Molloy's raincoats) can you think of that signal class? Do you think class is easily spotted by dress?
2. Review Molloy's description of his raincoat experiment. He calls the results of this experiment "the proof of what works and what doesn't." Do you find the results to be convincing? What, if anything, do they leave out?
3. John Molloy equates success in this culture with upward movement in corporations. What assumptions is he making about the nature of success in contemporary America?

SUGGESTIONS FOR WRITING

1. Write an essay in which you consider whether, as Molloy claims, dress is a marker of social class. Use examples from your own experience and from your observations of others.
2. Molloy's work suggests that we think about the clothes we own in terms of the effect those clothes have on the people around us. Write an essay in which you describe what you wear (or would want to wear) when you are trying to impress someone. Give examples of how or if your style changes depending on who it is you want to impress.
3. Spend some time in the local mall, the campus cafeteria, or any other public space that offers opportunities for people watching. Pay attention to the way the people around you dress and how they wear their hair. From your observations, what would you say clothing or hair styles tell you about the people who wear them? Write an essay that explains how you identify people by their clothes and hair styles. What details do you use in your judgments?

Dick Hebdige

STYLE IN REVOLT: REVOLTING STYLE

Dick Hebdige is a lecturer in Communication at Goldsmith College, University of London. His research in such articles as "Reggae, Rastas and Rudies" has primarily focused on subcultures, those men and women who create their own culture of speaking, acting, and dressing outside and against mainstream society's more accepted ways. The following selection is excerpted from Hebdige's 1979 book-length study *Subculture: The Meaning of Style,* in which he examines the political and cultural importance of the British punk movement. In this short segment from his study of style in subcultures, Hebdige examines the punk movement's use of style as a tool of disruption and revolt. The punk movement, originally a British subculture, made style a primary means of rebellion, threatening the stability of mainstream culture with images of violence and with a profound disrespect for all things conventional.

Suggestion for Reading

- As you read, notice the range of evidence Hebdige produces to develop his characterization of punk culture. Underline passages in which he makes general points about that culture.

———————◆———————

Nothing was holy to us. Our movement was neither mystical,
communistic nor anarchistic. All of these movements had
some sort of programme, but ours was completely nihilistic.
We spat on everything, including ourselves. Our symbol was
nothingness, a vacuum, a void.
—George Grosz on Dada

We're so pretty, oh so pretty . . . vac-unt.
—The Sex Pistols

A lthough it was often directly offensive (T-shirts covered in swear words) and threatening (terrorist/guerilla outfits) punk style was defined principally through the violence of its "cut ups." Like Duchamp's "ready mades"—manufactured objects which qualified as art because he chose to call them such, the most unremarkable and inappropriate items—a pin, a plastic clothes peg, a television component, a razor blade, a tampon—could be brought within the province of punk (un)fashion. Anything within or without reason could be turned into part of what Vivien Westwood called "confrontation dressing" so long as the rupture between "natural" and constructed context was clearly visible (i.e., the rule would seem to be: if the cap doesn't fit, wear it).

Objects borrowed from the most sordid of contexts found a place in the punks' ensembles: lavatory chains were draped in graceful arcs across chests encased in plastic bin-liners. Safety pins were taken out of their domestic "utility" context and worn as gruesome ornaments through the cheek, ear or lip. "Cheap" trashy fabrics (PVC, plastic, lurex, etc.) in vulgar designs (e.g., mock leopard skin) and "nasty" colours, long discarded by the quality end of the fashion industry as obsolete kitsch, were salvaged by the punks and turned into garments (fly boy drainpipes, "common" mini-skirts) which offered self-conscious commentaries on the notions of modernity and taste. Conventional ideas of prettiness were jettisoned along with the traditional feminine lore of cosmetics. Contrary to the advice of every woman's magazine, make-up for both boys and girls was worn to be seen. Faces became abstract portraits: sharply observed and meticulously executed studies in alienation. Hair was obviously dyed (hay yellow, jet black, or bright orange with tufts of green or bleached in question marks), and T-shirts and trousers told the story of their own construction with multiple zips and outside seams clearly displayed. Similarly, fragments of school uniform (white brinylon shirts, school ties) were symbolically defiled (the shirts covered in graffiti, or fake blood; the ties left undone) and juxtaposed against leather drains or shocking pink mohair tops. The perverse and the abnormal were valued intrinsically. In particular, the illicit iconography of sexual fetishism was used to predictable effect. Rapist masks and rubber wear, leather bodices and fishnet stockings, implausibly pointed stiletto heeled shoes, the whole paraphernalia of bondage—the belts, straps and chains—were exhumed from the boudoir, closet and the pornographic film and placed on the street where they retained their forbidden connotations. Some young punks even donned the dirty raincoat—that most prosaic symbol of sexual "kinkiness"—and hence expressed their deviance in suitably proletarian terms.

Of course, punk did more than upset the wardrobe. It undermined every relevant discourse. Thus dancing, usually an involving and expressive medium in British rock and mainstream pop cultures, was turned into a dumbshow of blank robotics. Punk dances bore absolutely no relation to the desultory frugs and clinches which Geoff Mungham describes as intrinsic to the respectable working-class ritual of Saturday night at the Top Rank or Mecca.[1] Indeed, overt displays of heterosexual interest were generally regarded with contempt and suspicion (who let the BOF/wimp[2] in?) and conventional courtship patterns found no place on the floor in dances like the pogo, the pose and the robot. Though the pose did allow for a minimum sociability (i.e. it could involve two people) the "couple" were generally of the same sex and physical contact was ruled out of court as the relationship depicted in the dance was a "professional" one. One participant would strike a suitable cliché fashion pose while the other would fall into a classic "Bailey" crouch to snap an imaginary picture. The pogo forebade even this much interaction, though admittedly there was always a good deal of masculine jostling in front of the stage. In fact the pogo was a caricature—*a reductio ad absurdum* of all the solo dance styles associated with rock music. It resembled the "anti dancing" of the "Leapniks" which Melly describes in connection with the trad boom (Melly, 1972). The same abbreviated gestures—leaping into the air, hands clenched to the sides, to head an imaginary ball—were repeated without variation in time to the strict mechanical rhythms of the music. In contrast to the hippies' languid, free-form dancing, and the "idiot dancing" of the heavy metal rockers, the pogo made improvisation redundant: the only variations were imposed by changes in the tempo of the music—fast numbers being "interpreted" with manic abandon in the form of frantic on-the-spots, while the slower ones were pogoed with a detachment bordering on the catatonic.

The robot, a refinement witnessed only at the most exclusive punk gatherings, was both more "expressive" and less "spontaneous" within the very narrow range such terms acquired in punk usage. It consisted of barely perceptible twitches of the head and hands or more extravagant lurches (Frankenstein's first steps?) which were abruptly halted at random points. The resulting pose was held for several moments, even minutes, and the whole sequence was as suddenly, as unaccountably, resumed and re-enacted. Some zealous punks carried things one step further and choreographed whole evenings, turning themselves for a matter of hours, like Gilbert and George,[3] into automata, living sculptures.

The music was similarly distinguished from mainstream rock and pop. It was uniformly basic and direct in its appeal, whether through intention or lack of expertise. If the latter, then the punks certainly made a virtue of necessity ("We want to be amateurs"—Johnny Rotten). Typically, a barrage of guitars with the volume and treble turned to maximum accompanied by the occasional saxophone would pursue relentless (un)melodic lines against a turbulent background of cacophonous drumming and screamed vocals. Johnny Rotten succinctly defined punk's position on harmonics: "We're into chaos not music."

The names of the groups (the Unwanted, the Rejects, the Sex Pistols, the Clash, the Worst, etc.) and the titles of the songs: "Belsen was a Gas," "If You Don't Want to Fuck Me, Fuck Off," "I Wanna Be Sick on You," reflected the tendency towards willful desecration and the voluntary assumption of outcast status which characterized the whole punk movement. Such tactics were, to adapt Levi-Strauss's famous phrase, "things to whiten mother's hair with." In the early days at least, these "garage bands" could dispense with musical pretensions and substitute, in the traditional romantic terminology, "passion" for "technique," the language of the common man for the arcane posturings of the existing élite, the now familiar armoury of frontal attacks for the bourgeois notion of entertainment or the classical concept of "high art."

It was in the performance arena that punk groups posed the clearest threat to law and order. Certainly, they succeeded in subverting the conventions of concert and nightclub entertainment. Most significantly, they attempted both physically and in terms of lyrics and life-style to move closer to their audiences. This in itself is by no means unique: the boundary between artist and audience has often stood as a metaphor in revolutionary aesthetics (Brecht, the surrealists, Dada, Marcuse, etc.) for that larger and more intransigent barrier which separates art and the dream from reality and life under capitalism.[4] The stages of those venues secure enough to host "new wave" acts were regularly invaded by hordes of punks, and if the management refused to tolerate such blatant disregard for ballroom etiquette, then the groups and their followers could be drawn closer together in a communion of spittle and mutual abuse. At the Rainbow Theatre in May 1977 as the Clash played "White Riot," chairs were ripped out and thrown at the stage. Meanwhile, every performance, however apocalyptic, offered palpable evidence that things could change, indeed were changing: that performance itself was a possibility no authentic punk should discount. Examples abounded in the music press of "ordinary fans" (Siouxsie of Siouxsie and the Banshees, Sid Vicious of the Sex Pistols, Mark P of *Sniffin Glue,* Jordan of the Ants) who had made the symbolic crossing from the dance floor to the stage. Even the humbler positions in the rock hierarchy could provide an attractive alternative to the drudgery of manual labour, office work or a youth on the dole. The Finchley Boys, for instance, were reputedly taken off the football terraces by the Stranglers and employed as roadies.

If these "success stories" were, as we have seen, subject to a certain amount of "skewed" interpretation in the press, then there were innovations in other areas which made opposition to dominant definitions possible. Most notably, there was an attempt, the first by a predominantly working-class youth culture, to provide an alternative critical space within the subculture itself to counteract the hostile or at least ideologically inflected coverage which punk was receiving in the media. The existence of an alternative punk press demonstrated that it was not only clothes or music that could be immediately and cheaply produced from the limited resources at hand. The fanzines (*Sniffin Glue, Ripped and Torn,* etc.) were journals edited by an individual or a group, consisting of reviews, editorials and interviews with prominent punks, produced on a small scale as cheaply as possible, stapled together and distributed through a small number of sympathetic retail outlets.

The language in which the various manifestoes were framed was determinedly "working class" (i.e., it was liberally peppered with swear words) and typing errors and grammatical mistakes, misspellings and jumbled pagination were left uncorrected in the final proof. Those corrections and crossings out that were made before publication were left to be deciphered by the reader. The overwhelming impression was one of urgency and immediacy, of a paper produced in indecent haste, of memos from the front line.

This inevitably made for a strident buttonholing type of prose which, like the music is described, was difficult to "take in" in any quantity. Occasionally a written, more abstract item—what Harvey Garfinkel (the American ethnomethodologist) might call an "aid to sluggish imaginations"—might creep in. For instance, *Sniffin Glue*, the first fanzine and the one which achieved the highest circulation, contained perhaps the single most inspired item of propaganda produced by the subculture—the definitive statement of punk's do-it-yourself philosophy—a diagram showing three finger positions on the neck of a guitar over the caption: "Here's one chord, here's two more, now form your own band."

Even the graphics and typography used on record covers and fanzines were homologous with punk's subterranean and anarchic style. The two typographic models were graffiti which was translated into a flowing "spray can" script, and the ransom note in which individual letters cut up from a variety of sources (newspapers, etc.) in different type faces were pasted together to form an anonymous message. The Sex Pistols' "God Save the Queen" sleeve (later turned into T-shirts, posters, etc.) for instance incorporated both styles: the roughly assembled legend was pasted across the Queen's eyes and mouth which were further disfigured by those black bars used in pulp detective magazines to conceal identity (i.e., they connote crime or scandal). Finally, the process of ironic self abasement which characterized the subculture was extended to the name "punk" itself which, with its derisory connotations of "mean and petty villainy," "rotten," "worthless," etc. was generally preferred by hardcore members of the subculture to the more neutral 'new wave'.[5]

References

1. In his P.O. account of the Saturday night dance in an industrial town, Mungham (1976) shows how the constricted quality of working-class life is carried over into the ballroom in the form of courtship rituals, masculine paranoia and an atmosphere of sullenly repressed sexuality. He paints a gloomy picture of joyless evenings spent in the desperate pursuit of "booze and birds" (or "blokes and a romantic bus-ride home") in a controlled setting where "spontaneity is regarded by managers and their staff—principally the bouncers—as the potential hand-maiden of rebellion".

2. BOF = Boring old Fart
Wimp = "wet"

3. Gilbert and George mounted their first exhibition in 1970 when, clad in identical conservative suits, with metallized hands and faces, a glove, a stick and a tape recorder, they won critical acclaim by performing a series of carefully controlled and endlessly repeated movements on a dais while miming to Flanagan and Allen's "Underneath the Arches." Other pieces with titles like "Lost Day" and "Normal Boredom" have since been performed at a variety of major art galleries throughout the world.

4. Of course, rock music had always threatened to dissolve these categories, and rock performances were popularly associated with all forms of riot and disorder—from the slashing of cinema seats by teddy boys through Beatlemania to the hippy happenings and festivals where freedom was expressed less aggressively in nudity, drug taking and general "spontaneity." However, punk represented a new departure.

5. The word "punk," like the black American "funk" and "superbad" would seem to form part of that "special language of fantasy and alienation" which Charles Winick describes (1959), "in which values are reversed and in which 'terrible' is a description of excellence."

See also Wolfe (1969) where he describes the "cruising" scene in Los Angeles in the mid-60s—a subculture of custom-built cars, sweatshirts and "high-piled, perfect coiffure" where "rank" was a term of approval:

> Rank! Rank is just the natural outgrowth of Rotten . . . Roth and Schorsch grew up in the Rotten Era of Los Angeles teenagers. The idea was to have a completely rotten attitude towards the adult world, meaning, in the long run, the whole established status structure, the whole system of people organising their lives around a job, fitting into the social structure embracing the whole community. The idea in Rotten was to drop out of conventional status competition into the smaller netherworld of Rotten Teenagers and start one's own league.

SUGGESTIONS FOR DISCUSSION

1. What would you say is Hebdige's attitude toward the punk movement? Point to passages that best convey that attitude.
2. Hebdige's work is primarily about British styles. Is there a mainstream culture, a minority culture, a subculture, or several variations of those in your own community? How do you recognize each? What of Hebdige's discussion might seem to apply to the way these different groups express themselves?
3. Notice that Hebdige quite often compares punk fashion and punk actions to art movements and the artists in those movements. These artists, and the movements like Dada which he mentions, all rejected mainstream art values in order to create an art of their own which would surprise and shock a mass audience. What point is Hebdige attempting to make by comparing punks with such movements in the art world?

SUGGESTIONS FOR WRITING

1. Hebdige explains how punks use common objects or forms of dress in new ways. Write an essay on how a group that you know about uses objects or styles in ways that depart from their originally intended uses. What new meanings are invested in the style they create?
2. Write an essay that compares Hebdige's and Molloy's analyses of style. What do you think they might agree on? In what ways do their perspectives differ?
3. Write an essay that describes how a group or an individual in your school or local community uses style of dress as part of its group identity. What would you say are the key markers of this group's style? Explain how the group uses style to distinguish itself from other groups.

Wendy Chapkis

DRESS AS SUCCESS: JOOLZ

Wendy Chapkis began writing a journal to deal with the attacks she often experienced on the street. Men and children, in particular, felt comfortable laughing at or commenting on the fact that she has a "moustache." A woman, we all know, is not supposed to have a moustache. Through that experience, Chapkis began the book *Beauty Secrets: Women and the Politics of Appearance,* published in 1986, from which the following selection is taken. In her book, Chapkis writes of how cultural ideals of beauty are passed on to us through film, advertising, and even such self-help books as John Molloy's *Dress for Success.* The book also includes interviews with women who do not fit the customary idea of beauty. Joolz, the woman in the following interview, talks of what it meant to her to wear punk fashions.

Suggestion for Reading

- As you read, keep in mind that this is an excerpt from an interview. The speaker is not analyzing punk fashion. Instead, she is relating her own experience with it.

◆

JOOLZ

"Punks are rejecting their class position but you have to be
there before you can reject it"

I was nineteen when I married a man who became a Satan's Slave. During the time I was with him, I looked pretty normal. Bikers don't like outrageous looking girls—at all. They do like "nice-looking" girls, though. And they prefer it if you have long hair. It fits with the heavy metal image.

You aren't to wear too much make-up or anything like that, and you wear jeans or trousers because you are on the bike so much. Though some of the girls did wear miniskirts which I always thought pretty stupid under the circumstances. The men clearly liked very girly girls. Oh, and they preferred blondes!

I never paid too terribly much attention to how I was supposed to look. I wore my hair short. It was more comfortable under the helmet. And I used to walk around in boy's clothes all the time. It was a bit of a problem for my husband in the club. But eventually they accepted me because they decided I was artistic and if I was an artist I was allowed to be eccentric. In general, the women were expected to be very domestic and they were.

The club is a close tribal community. Because my background had been so insecure, I found it very reassuring in the beginning. But after five years, I left. It had become too restrictive.

Even before I left my husband, I already had become interested in the punk image. I had already dyed my hair pink—something which didn't go down well in the club.

To dye your hair this color, you've got to first bleach it absolutely white, to strip it right down to the roots. I've had it this way for four years now. Pink was an easy first choice; it was a fashionable color, if you remember. Shocking pink and fluorescent green, those were the colors associated with punk. Nowadays, I have it colored a bright scarlet, Fire Red.

Even when I was a child I wanted colored hair. I remember wanting waist-length green hair because there was this puppet in a children's show on television, a mermaid who never spoke but was extremely beautiful and had long green hair.

I've always tended toward fantasy, the fantastic. In fact my image may have more to do with fantasy than punk in the pure sense. Punk started off anti-fashion. So you set out to make yourself look as anti-pretty as possible. But I've always been too insecure to do it properly. I worry too much about what I actually look like.

My mother is very beautiful—feminine, small and pretty in the magazine style. I take after my father who is big. When I was a child, my mother was very disappointed in me and was always trying to make me more presentable. Other people's mothers used to shout at them for wearing make-up; my mother used to shout at me for not wearing any.

When I was an adolescent, I suffered very badly from acne. I was also overweight. So I was sort of a tall, fat, spotty teenager. I had good teeth though. My mother used to tell me "you have good teeth; smile, it's your best feature."

Having been a hideous adolescent, I've always been too insecure to intentionally make myself more hideous. I tend to sort of go to the "glam" side of punk rather than the anarchy end. I always wanted a Mohican, but I never quite had the nerve to shave my head. I did have very, very short hair at one point, and I looked like a dog. And being big as well I was mistaken for a boy all the time. There are lots of things I wish I had the nerve to do with myself, but I just can't.

It's relative, of course. I suppose the way I look appears pretty outrageous to other people. Something like having a pierced nose I don't even think about anymore. But a lot of people seem to find it shocking.

My tattoos draw a lot of attention too. I got tattooed for the first time when I was about nineteen. I had one on my wrist and another around my ankles. I thought they were alright at the time—a sort of bracelet of flowers. But I only recently met a really good tattooist and have had new tattoos done over the old ones. These are in the Celtic style and are much better and much more extensive. Tattoos and tattooing fascinate me.

There are moments, though, when you get tired of it all. Everybody who looks this different feels that ways sometimes, even if they don't admit it. There are mornings when I wake up and know I have to go down to the shops and wish that I looked like a perfectly ordinary person. But they are not often enough for me to want to change anything.

Not too long ago, for a giggle, I borrowed a plain brown wig off a friend and put it on. It looked pretty convincing. I didn't put on much make-up and went to a gig that way. People who have known me for months and months didn't recognize me.

It was tremendous. But after a while, I didn't find it tremendous at all. I found it extremely unpleasant. I actually entered a state of panic. I was so relieved to take the wig off and be myself again. I felt I had lost my whole personality. My whole statement was gone and I really hated it.

The tattoos are the big thing actually. The scarlet hair you can just cut off if you get tired of it. But when you take the step of having big tattoos so close to the hands, you really make a permanent statement, especially as a woman.

I always wear long skirts and I always wear black. I don't wear jeans anymore because I wore them for so long when I was biking that I just got sick of them. They feel constricting to me. Same with underwear.

Despite all the black and the tattoos and the skull rings, some of my stage costumes, made of lycra and sequins, are extremely glam. I love feather boas and fans. But always with studs; say a studded belt at the waist. It is the combination that appeals to me. To be too completely glam would be tiresome. I like to confuse the eye.

The most important statement I am making through what I look like is one of strength. I have a strong personality and want to indicate that straight away. Especially in the business I am in, it is important to have a strong image. Not just from the point of selling your records, but more importantly so that from the moment you walk into a venue you are noticed by the sound crew, the security men, everyone. They've got to know right away you are not someone to be messed with. This is particularly true for a woman. The rock business is totally sexist. If you are not a strong person, they will walk all over you.

Of course sometimes the way I look frightens people I have no reason to want to impress with my strength. I was taking a train recently that was absolutely full—people were standing in the corridors—and there was an empty seat next to me but nobody would sit in it. People will often stare, but they don't want to get too close and only rarely will they try to make contact.

Sometimes it seems that people feel that if you look "odd" it is a license for them to abuse you or threaten you; it's as if the normal rules of politeness in society don't apply anymore. You've given up straight looks, therefore you've given up any right to be treated with respect.

A lot of people, particularly middle class people, look at punk and think it is a working class thing. But actually there are few working class punk rockers. Only children of the middle class can afford to look ragged. It *is* a class statement, but not in the way people tend to assume. Punks are rejecting their class position, but you have to be there before you can reject it. And I am not saying that rejecting everything that's expected of you is easy.

It is, in fact, very difficult to actually put yourself outside of society; to appear so different that you are beyond the normal relationships most women have. I don't blame girls who are secretaries during the day and backcomb their hair a bit at night to come to the clubs. For those girls, punk is just fashion.

In a way, I am jealous of them because, in the end, they can become normal. They can submerge themselves in the great stream of weddings and tumble dryers. But I also think that, somewhere inside them, they're disappointed. They know they have experienced a failure of nerve.

I have my hair done by a woman named Lorraine. She works in a very small salon in the suburbs. Every time I go in there, I see this row of ladies with The Perm under the dryers just having had The Cut—which ever one it is at the time. I once asked Lorraine "don't you ever get tremendously sick of doing this?" And she said "If another woman comes in who wants that Perm I'll scream and go mad!" But of course she'd then go and start rolling up the next woman's hair . . .

The clients watch her working on me and they are fascinated. They'll come over and feel my hair and ask questions. It must be tremendously tempting for them to say "the hell with it; make mine scarlet too!"

SUGGESTIONS FOR DISCUSSION

1. What would Molloy and Hebdige say about Joolz?
2. Much of the writing in this chapter is about changing our styles in order to be accepted. It seems that Joolz was not after acceptance at all. What was she after?
3. What kinds of fashion do you think adults find shocking today? What kinds of fashion do you find shocking? Why?

SUGGESTIONS FOR WRITING

1. Joolz tells us, "Sometimes it seems that people feel that if you look 'odd' it is a license for them to abuse you or threaten you; it's as if the normal rules of politeness in society don't apply anymore. You've given up straight looks, therefore you've given up any right to be treated with respect." Write an essay in which you respond to this phenomenon. If you have witnessed this happening, you might want to use that event as a way to begin your essay. In the essay speculate about why some people feel free to attack others who don't conform to mainstream styles.
2. Joolz claims that punk is rarely, any longer, a working-class image. "Only children of the middle class can afford to look ragged. It *is* a class statement, but not in the way people tend to assume." The same might be said for grunge. Write an essay in which you explain what kind of a class statement middle-class or upper-middle-class kids make when they dress in grunge or look punk.
3. After rereading and thinking about the issues raised by the writers in this chapter, write your own politics of style for the nineties. How should we dress, wear our hair, treat our bodies? In your statement, think about all of the consequences of the choices you make. Don't simply go for the easy sweeping conclusion that people should just do what they want. What determines what we want?

Franz Lidz

BLACK IS GOLDEN

Franz Lidz is a writer for *Sports Illustrated*. This article, which appeared in the April 1993 issue of that magazine, details the recent sports fashion phenomenon of using team caps, shirts, and jackets (all in black and silver or white) as status markers. The fashion, dubbed "black rage," also raises issues of racial tension and gang affiliation that this fashion is sometimes connected with.

SUGGESTION FOR READING

• Before you read this essay, review Hebdige's essay on subculture fashion. As you read Lidz, annotate his essay with notes that help you connect what he says about the new fashion with subculture styles in general.

———————◆———————

That's gospel in the lucrative world of sports marketing, in
which sales for pro teams featuring black in logos and
uniforms are red hot
—Franz Lidz
I'll try to carry off a little darkness on my back,
Until things are brighter, I'm the man in black.
—Johnny Cash

Scoobie Johnson is sporting a hip-hop version of stygian cruise wear: black baggy breeches, black Los Angeles King T-shirt, black King jacket and boots that appear to have been cobbled out of a black reptile. Perched at a jaunty angle atop his pyramid—a high-rise 'do clipped with box-hedge precision—is a King cap in bleakest black. For the boys in Johnson's L.A. 'hood, *black rage* has a new shade of meaning. "The fact I'm in black's got nothing to do with hockey sticks or Wayne Gretzky," he says. "It's like black is the shadow of everything that's on it. It's like black's got a nice villain approach to it. Ninjas, they wear black. Cat burglars, they wear black. It's like, black makes you look nasty and mean, and if you're already mean, you look meaner. It's a fashion thing, a black thing."

A red-hot black thing. Black is back—in the streets, in the shops, in the stadiums. The top-selling team merchandise in each major sport—that of the Los Angeles Raiders, the Chicago Bulls, the Chicago White Sox and the San Jose Sharks—features black. Black-and-silver caps, shirts and jackets adorned with the Raider emblem account for 17% of all NFL gear sales. When the White Sox turned black at the end of the 1990 season, the South Siders catapulted from 18th to first in baseball's licensed-apparel standings. Michael Jordan's Bulls do as well in the malls as they do on the floor. And while the two-year-old Sharks are floundering in the deep waters of the NHL, they've fueled a feeding frenzy among consumers, outselling every team in the league. In the licensed-apparel business, the color of money is not green.

Nowadays everyone seems to be looking for that old black magic. Following the lead of the black-and-silver Kings, the Minnesota North Stars went black in 1990, the same year Jerry Glanville's Atlanta Falcons returned to their original black regalia. This season the New Jersey Devils ditched red, white and green for red, white and black, joining the expansion Ottawa Senators and Tampa Bay Lightning on the list of hockey's nine black-bearing teams. The Florida Marlins and the Colorado Rockies, both fledgling teams, put black into their color schemes and now rank eighth and fourth, respectively, in baseball merchandising.

It seems league licensees can't put out a product and paint it black fast enough. The purple-and-gold Los Angeles Laker insignia appears on black caps and jackets. Ditto that of the green-and-white Philadelphia Eagles, the red-and-white Cincinnati Reds, the Los Angeles Dodgers—Dodger black? Indeed, one wonders how long it will be before things look black for blue-white-and-silver Dallas Cowboy gear, which, the NFL says, is selling briskly in the wake of the team's 1993 Super Bowl victory.

The binge began in 1985, soon after the Raiders defected from Oakland, when members of the emerging rap group NWA—Niggers With Attitude—swaggered into the L.A. office of the team's marketing director at the time, Michael Orenstein. "I was a little nervous," recalls Orenstein. "There were six of them, and they looked like a gang." He was relieved to learn that all they wanted were team caps and jackets. "The group promised to perform in Raider gear," says Orenstein. "So I gave them eight boxes of stuff. I didn't know what rap was. I figured they'd be onstage in front of 20 people and the exposure would be good for us."

What happened next is the stuff marketing directors have built careers on. Rap artists—young, black and vocal—became the Raiders' ultimate sales team. Thanks to all-powerful MTV, Raider fashion was beamed around the country, molding a teenage subculture. Since then the black look has asserted itself everywhere, from halfway houses to houses of haute couture.

You don't have to be a colorphobe to love back. "It's the color against which other colors are set," says Danny Noble, a Philadelphia-based designer whose clothes are sold throughout the country. "It slims you, doesn't show dirt and you can hide behind it. Plus, if your wardrobe is all black, everything matches."

No team has exploited the anger and protest symbolized by black more success-fully than the Raiders. Their very insignia—a one-eyed pirate with crossed cutlasses jut-ting from behind his helmet—is an implied threat. "Kids wear Raider jackets because they want to have that look of control about them," says Raider defensive tackle Bob Golic. "It's part of the Raider mystique."

That mystique draws heavily on the allure of black, the color that cancels out all others. "Black has always been—and may always be—associated with the diabolical, the supremely sinister, that which is most greatly feared," says black activist Harry Edwards, a special consultant to the San Francisco 49ers. "On one hand there's the white dove of peace; on the other, the black raven of Poe. Black compels and it terrorizes."

And when it comes to inducing terror, no team mascot beats San Jose's shark. Massive, toothy and jet black, it explodes out of a black triangle to chomp on a hockey stick. The implication is that a hockey player is next in the food chain. "You look at that shark and sense it's not a happy camper," says Shark defenseman Doug Wilson. "It's very menacing, and the black intensifies the menace."

The Shark management wasn't interested in the sort of carefree, well-fed creature you might see swimming about the languid pools of Sea World. "We had in mind a phantasmagorical shark that conveyed speed, danger, relentlessness," says Matt Levine, the Sharks' marketing whiz. "A predator that would remind you of *Jaws* and attacks on surfers." (But not so fearsome that parents wouldn't buy it.)

In a sport that traditionally lags far behind football, baseball and basketball in merchandising, retail sales of Sharkabilia in 1992 topped $150 million. That's about a third of the NHL's total merchandising sales. Much of it was through mail orders—the team puts out a color catalog featuring 155 items, from stuffed sharks to a toilet-seat-shaped foam hat called Puckhead. "From a marketing standpoint our problem was that we were an expansion team, an unknown commodity with little chance of winning," Levine says. "We had to count on our merchandise to sell the team."

So in the winter of 1990, a full five months before San Jose was officially awarded an NHL franchise, Levine began market research. Over the next 17 months he considered hundreds of ideas, consulted fashion experts and held focus groups. He surveyed 1,400 hockey fans and weighed their responses to artwork, color combinations and lettering.

A contest was run to select the name of the team. Nearly 6,000 entries came in from as far away as Genoa, Italy (the Genoese suggested the Barracudas and the Blade Runners). Other suggestions included Yodeling Yams, Aftershocks, Technopolitans, Screaming Squids and San Jose Cansecos. The most popular name, the Blades, was discarded because it was closely identified with gangs. Ironically, Sharks is the name of one of the gangs in *West Side Story*. When the Winnipeg Jets are in town, you half expect to see players face off in choreographed violence as the goalies belt out *Maria*.

Team colors took a year to sort out. The question was never what colors to use in the logo, but what colors to use with black. The Sharks tried black, turquoise, orange and white, but people said the color combination looked too much like that of the Miami Dolphins. Similarly, black, royal blue, silver and white conjured up the Detroit Lions. "Fans were saying, 'Give us our own colors,'" says Levine. "So we decided to use a watercolor to deliver a shark." Pacific teal was appropriated from the Charlotte Hornets, who are second overall in NBA product sales. "Teal appeals strongly to women and doesn't turn off men when combined with black," says Levine. "Grandmothers are buying Shark gear because it's cute, and teenagers buy it because it's tough."

The three young Dutchmen cruising the aisles of the X store, a sporting-goods store in Amsterdam's New Market district, look like outlaw bikers just in from Marin County on their Harleys. They're wearing steel-tipped boots, black leather jackets and elaborate tattoos. The big guy has a belly that reaches far enough out over his belt to qualify him for the presidency of the Hell's Angels.

They shuffle past the rack of Los Angeles Raider jackets. They pass under the huge San Jose Shark pennant hanging from the ceiling. They stop at the wall of black baseball caps. The big guy tries on one with a White Sox insignia.

"Before I buy, there is something I must know," he tells a visitor from America. "What is Sox, and how does it look?"

That all depends on which Sox he means. The White Sox have changed uniform designs 57 times since 1900, five times in the last 15 years. The Bermuda shorts that Sox players donned briefly in 1976 were not one of the fashion industry's sublime achievements. Still, the team's greatest stylistic outrage may have been the retina-searing red-white-and-blue ensemble it adopted in 1983. Children wept when they saw it. Dogs howled. Sox outfielder Greg Luzinski complained that he felt like a box of cereal.

The White Sox faded to black and silver at the end of the 1990 season. New colors and a new stadium helped boost in-park product sales from $200,000 in 89 to $4.5 million in '91, when the new gear was introduced. The black sea of hats that now floods Comiskey Park's bleachers suggests a convocation of Greek widows. "Black uniforms were the key to reenfranchising the disenfranchised Sox fans," says Rob Gallas, White Sox marketing director. "For years people hadn't been proud to wear our merchandise."

Sales of White Sox caps were so brisk that two summers ago New Era, the official milliner of baseball, ran out of stock. "New Era had to shut down normal operations for three weeks and just make White Sox caps," Gallas says. "And after the three weeks were up, they still had a backlog of 200,000 orders."

Of course, it didn't hurt that the Sox started winning game after game—and that they had enlisted the services of an ex-Raider named Bo. "I wonder if Bo chose us because of the colors," says Gallas.

Street gangs seem to have, Black team caps and jackets have spread like wildfire in the inner cities. "Black and silver are not just popular gang colors," Gallas protests. "They're a popular combination, period." Yet black-clad teams are being accused of contributing to gang violence. "It's not like we're arming people!" says Golic. "I mean, it takes a sick mind to watch a guy in a Raider cap and jacket getting fried in the electric chair on a show like *America's Most Wanted* and then say, 'Gee, his clothes were nice; I think I'll buy the same outfit.'"

The word on the streets of Inglewood, Calif., is Don't look black. A Raider or a King jacket may identify the wearer—wittingly or not—as a gang member. Two years ago, concern for student safety prompted Oak Street Elementary principal Yolanda Mendoza to bar all clothes with Raider and King logos from the school. "Is it helping?" she says. "Probably not very much. But I've got 1,200 kids toeing the mark. I know it sounds stupid, but by eliminating the symbols, we no longer have so many discipline problems. And I no longer worry about my kids getting jumped for their jackets after school."

Raider executive assistant Al LoCasale thinks that instead of playing clothes cop, schools should address the social and economic pressures that lead kids to see gangs as their only families in a bleak and uncaring world. "Banning Raider jackets is like putting a Band-Aid on a crack in the Hoover Dam," he says. "It's a simplistic shortcut. These are deep-seated problems that have nothing to do with sports. You're not going to solve them by taking a kid's hat or jacket and putting him in a strawberry patch T-shirt. Besides, of the 90,000 gang members in Los Angeles, there can't be one percent that wears Raider clothes."

Nevertheless, whatever the percentage is, it is particularly noticeable. A 19-year-old laborer and gang member was blown away by rival gang members last winter at a Culver City, Calif., gas station. Police say that the Raider jacket he was wearing may have marked him for death. "I was totally devastated," says Marie Marden, a friend of the slain youth. One week later Marden's young nephew was shot at while wearing his Dodger jacket; he was not a member of a gang. "I never would have believed team clothing could get you killed. I finally felt I had to do something." Marden and a friend formed a company called Peace In Time, which puts out an embroidered emblem that proclaims I'M A SPORTS FAN. GANGS AREN'T MY GAME. They have sold more than 10,000 iron-on patches to schools and youth programs throughout California.

Even LoCasale is disturbed by TV-news footage of kids in Raider gear getting busted. "All that does is reaffirm an image we're trying to dispel," he says. "By the same token. I remember once staring at the *Mona Lisa* in the Louvre when this guy stepped in front of me wearing a Raider sweatshirt. I tell you, our fans are everywhere."

So who's to blame? White marketers who cannily package fan loyalty with urban black rage? "What's sad," says Mendoza, a consummate Raider fan, "is that we have taken teams that we honor and respect and turned their emblems into something negative."

Edwards believes that the Black Rush reflects both the rising anarchy of neighborhoods and the volatile climate of the day. "Hard times generate hard responses in the population," he says. "People wear black if for no other reason than to perpetuate the illusion of coping and surviving. As circumstances in society begin to turn up economically and the tension between races lessens, you'll see movement away from this black imagery. Understand: We're living in some very, very dark times."

SUGGESTIONS FOR DISCUSSION

1. How does "black rage" compare to punk fashion as Hebdige explains its social or political function?
2. How do you respond to the anecdote Lidz tells of marketing director Michael Orenstein's initial reaction to the rap group NWA approaching him in his office?
3. Lidz mentions the negative connotations the color black has traditionally held in our culture. Does the new fashion change people's attitudes toward the color black?

SUGGESTIONS FOR WRITING

1. Write a response to Lidz's article in which you explore your own knowledge of and attitudes toward "black" fashion.
2. Write an essay in which you explain how a style or a fashion can unite a group. You may wish to draw on the work of bell hooks, Dick Hebdige, and Wendy Chapkis for your discussion.
3. Some schools, even some public schools, are considering instituting dress codes to keep fashion wars at a minimum. Write an essay in which you take a position about dress codes. You may wish to review the writers in this chapter and draw on some of their work for your essay.

FOR FURTHER EXPLORATION

One way of doing further research on any one of the issues or topics included in this chapter is to go to the original sources from which many of these selections have been excerpted. Wendy Chapkis's *Beauty Secrets*, Dick Hebdige's *Subculture: The Meaning of Style*, and John Molloy's *Dress for Success* or his *Women's Dress for Success* all offer much more complete arguments for how style works in modern culture. You might instead be more interested in some of the political issues raised by this chapter. In that case, you will want to find more out about one or more of the following:

- Bulimia and anorexia
- The Black Pride movement of the sixties
- The origin of grunge, punk, and hip-hop fashions
- The Men's Movement

CHAPTER 6

TELEVISION CULTURE

"I'm not a doctor, but I play one on TV."

— actor Peter Bergman, who played
Dr. Cliff Warner on *All My
Children,* speaking for a popular
cough medication.

Since its inception, television has prided itself on bringing the world into America's living rooms. In fact, one commercial for an upcoming CBS fall season featured a man watching television alone in a darkened room when suddenly the CBS characters appeared in the room with him, some even perching on the arms of his easy chair. It is this promise, that television is a link with the rest of the world, an intimate encounter with the lives of others, that makes television so different from other media.

Yet, for all of its immediacy, television brings us only a distorted version of the rest of the world. Prime time television, in particular, offers up a primarily white, upper middle class, comfortable, fashionable, articulate, and healthy cast of characters. Marginalized groups in America—African Americans, Hispanics, Asians, American Indians, the impoverished of all races—tend to appear as extras, "buddies," or villains; only rarely do they figure into storylines as central characters. This monocultural version of the world is common in popular film as well, but television is such an immediate and accessible medium that cultural depictions, even comedic ones, are often taken by viewers as real.

Consider, for example, how television has depicted one common television professional, the doctor. The television doctor has traditionally promised what our own doctors could not: a quick solution, a quicker cure. Dr. Welby, Dr. Kildare, and even the staff at St. Elsewhere (an eighties "reality" version of hospital drama) seemed smarter and more compassionate than the doctors viewers lined up for in real waiting rooms across the country. The typical narrative pattern in the old series *Marcus Welby, M.D.* provides a good example: A friend visits Dr. Welby; Dr. Welby notices that something "isn't right"; Dr. Welby diagnoses the rare disease with the help of his private medical library; Dr. Welby cures the friend in the next fifty minutes.

Viewers, of course, recognized that this was all a fiction. Yet, when Robert Young retired from his role as Dr. Marcus Welby, he went straight into his role as promoter of Sanka brand coffee, reminding the audience that he was no real doctor but that real doctors recommend decaffeinated coffee. The advertiser's hope, naturally, was that consumers would continue to remember the kindly Dr. Welby who knew so much, cared so deeply, and never lost a patient. Like the ad with actor Peter Bergman, who is not a doctor but plays one on TV, this one linked the television professional with reality, the character with the actor. And, in doing so, both the Sanka and the cough medicine advertisements drew on the medical profession as a cultural ideal constructed, in part, through the stories and characters common in television programming.

Of course, television realism is not isolated to prime time drama. In fact, some of the most popular cultural constructions are evident in situation comedies, those programs that offer quick, funny slices of life in half-hour segments throughout the week. Classic sitcoms—*M*A*S*H, Mary Tyler Moore, All in the Family, Family Ties, The Cosby Show,* and *Cheers,* to name a few of the most popular—have built their audiences in the same way that prime time dramas have built theirs. They rely on real-seeming characters in real-seeming situations. Perhaps that is why, even though they are comedies, these shows have often come under careful scrutiny for the way in which they portray American life, portrayals that have also contributed to culturally constructed ideals.

From their beginnings, sitcoms have been more than simple comedies. No one ever believed that Ozzie and Harriet could exist, and yet the Nelsons were, after all, really the Nelsons. Theirs wasn't a made-up family like the one on *Father Knows Best*. It really was Ozzie, Harriet, David, and Ricky who lived such an even life in such a clean house with so few real worries. The blur between fantasy and reality was broad. Because sitcoms build upon the lives of real-seeming families in real-seeming situations, television analysts pay particular attention to how these shows construct cultural ideals. Such shows project very particular attitudes about American family life, the look of American middle-class homes, the goals of American youth, and more. Except for the Fox Network's counter-image of the American family (with such shows as *The Simpsons* and *Married . . . With Children*), sitcoms are remarkably alike whether the family is Anglo, African American, Latino, Asian American, or American Indian, or even if it has two mothers or two fathers rather than the more traditional combination.

READING THE CULTURE OF TELEVISION

You do not have to be a television critic or historian to read the culture that is projected over the airwaves. Most Americans know a good deal about television, and, as with any topic that you investigate, you will want to begin with what you do know. Think about the television programming you currently watch and programming you watched while you were growing up. It is that programming that probably gave you your idea of what you liked to watch on TV, what you thought was dull, and what you thought was important. Most children, for example, have seen at least some children's programming, probably *Sesame Street, Mr. Rogers' Neighborhood,* or Saturday morning cartoons. Those programs have just as much power to project cultural ideals as any soap opera, prime time drama, or popular sitcom. Mr. Rogers tells his viewers about the things he likes and teaches them about tidiness and obedience and honesty. The Muppets on *Sesame Street* provide some of those same lessons and add lessons in reading, arithmetic, geography, and foreign language. These programs and others like them help children construct such ideals as fairness, goodness, or helpfulness. They also project cultural meanings for such concepts as bad, lazy, or sloppy. In other words, even while you were singing "Rubber Ducky" with Ernie on *Sesame Street,* you were picking up values and learning about cultural ideals.

We open this chapter with three articles that address issues of the creation of cultural ideals and television realism. In "What a Waste of (Prime) Time" media critic Walter Shapiro raises important questions about what most Americans see when they submit to a steady diet of prime time. He calls this a world "tinged with escapism and societal wish fulfillment." Michael Ventura's "Report from El Dorado" analyzes the role television has played in constructing an idea of who Americans believe they are and what they believe their world to be. In his discussion of television culture, Ventura insists that Americans must pay attention to the meanings that are presented on television, for television has the power to rewrite history, to establish political positions, and to determine how viewers feel about everyday reality. Ventura equates media culture with a culture of desire—wanting to have a life that doesn't exist but that seems so very real and attainable. Henry Gates, Jr., in "TV's Black World Turns—But Stays Unreal" writes of the changing image of African Americans in television history. Gates's essay, in particular, raises issues of mainstream and minority cultural representations in a medium that is, as we suggested earlier, an astoundingly limited one in which certain ethnic and racial groups continue to remain marginalized or idealized.

The selections that follow suggest ways of understanding and commenting on the constructed world of television. Michael Arlen's "More Greenery, Less Garage" provides a narrative of the making of AT&T's most popular commercial campaign ("Reach Out and Touch Someone"), uncovering the extent to which a producer can go to create a world that looks very real but that is entirely created. John Leland's report on the recently popular MTV cartoon *Beavis and Butt-head* opens to examination the kind of hip cynicism that is popular with many young viewers today. Bill McKibben's "In the Age of Missing Information" is a part of McKibben's diary of a single day's television fare on ninety-three cable stations in Fairfax, Virginia. We conclude with a short story by Lucy Honig, "English as a Second Language," which may be the strongest statement yet of the odd relationship television has to lived experience.

Your own examination of television ideals can extend from your memories of popular shows into an analysis of how mainstream and marginalized groups are portrayed in popular television. In this chapter, you will be asked to move from thinking, remembering, and writing about television reality, to reading and writing about stereotypes and other social constructions typical of television, to considering television as a political force. The writers in this chapter demonstrate that you can look at even the most mundane details of television to understand why this medium seems to have such an impact on the marketplace, on our images of ourselves, and even on the ways in which some Americans shape their daily lives. Above all, these writers ask you to think seriously about a subject that most Americans simply accept without question as a small part of the modern world.

Walter Shapiro

WHAT A WASTE OF (PRIME) TIME

Walter Shapiro is a media critic for *Time* magazine from which the following article, published in 1990, was excerpted. In it, he takes a look at the world that is projected in prime time programming, the evening hours during which most Americans watch television. Shapiro does not suggest that Americans believe everything they see. Instead, he argues, viewers do understand unrealistic characters like Doogie Howser, but they may not so easily dismiss Doogie's affluence or the family setting that is the mark of television reality.

Suggestion for Reading

- Shapiro writes that in his survey of prime time television "the results were depressing, not only in the obvious vast-wasteland sense but also more seriously as a reminder of the insidious ways in which prime-time TV distorts America's sense of itself." Underline passages in which Shapiro explains that thesis.

———————◆———————

Picture an America where friendly, funky, Cub-fan-fanatic Chicago is the only inhabited spot between New York City and Twin Peaks. Imagine that this mythical U.S. has become so awash in racial sensitivity and tolerance that even drug dealers practice affirmative action, yet, strangely enough, intergalactic aliens are a far more visible minority group than Hispanics. In this youth-obsessed culture, where children of all races automatically come equipped with loving families, the stork must have supplanted traditional biology, for there are virtually no pregnant women.

Other oddities abound. How can the economy remain prosperous when half the work force lazes around luncheonettes and broadcast studios swapping dirty-word-free double entendres, while the other half consists of overworked and underappreciated cops? And why are all these people so hazy about their history? Is it not peculiar that no one ever refers to an event that predates Elvis' appearing on *Ed Sullivan?*

If such through-the-looking-glass images of an alternative America seem eerily familiar, the reason is probably that they are an impressionistic synopsis of a recent week's worth of prime-time TV watching on all four broadcast networks. Why would anyone voluntarily subject himself to nearly 50 hours of sex-and-sass sitcoms, puerile police procedurals and yuppie yammering about the meaning of life? Call it a census of sorts, a time-slot-by-time-slot canvass of the nation's nightly fantasy life, a solitary journey up the lazy river of the collective consciousness armed only with VCR and fast-forward button. The goal was to view television through the eyes of an outsider and to pretend to encounter the Huxtables, Roseanne and, yes, even the Simpsons for the first time. Alas, the results were depressing, not only in the obvious vast-wasteland sense but also more seriously as a reminder of the insidious ways in which prime-time TV distorts America's sense of itself.

Make no mistake, not even the most credulous couch potato believes that, say, 16-year-old Doogie Howser, M.D., is for real. But the easy affluence that is the birthright of Doogie's family might seem representative enough, especially when on the following ABC show (*The Marshall Chronicles*) the TV father was dressed in a tuxedo for an evening of Manhattan night life. Despite the pseudo-lower-middle-class realism of *Roseanne* and *Married . . . with Children,* the implicit message in much of prime time remains almost effortless economic entitlement. For while most of the nation resides in what bicoastal types call "the great flyover," TV characters are never rooted in Toledo or Omaha; instead, most spring to life magically equipped with sprawling houses and apartments in glamorous cities like New York and Los Angeles.

• • •

Take last Monday night's prime-time schedule. *Murphy Brown* and *Capital News* depict journalistic superstars strutting down the corridors of power in Washington. *Working Girl* is climbing her way into the upper echelons of New York corporate life; next maybe Tess will be dating Donald Trump. In Atlanta the *Designing Women* are even less likely than Scarlett O'Hara ever to be hungry again. *Newhart* is living the yuppie fantasy of owning a Vermont country inn. Even the downwardly mobile Philadelphia lawyer of *Shannon's Deal* can still manage to take a first date out for a $172 restaurant meal. Yes, one of *My Two Dads* did abandon an oversize New York apartment during reruns but only because he left his heart in San Francisco.

On television, most real work is done by just four occupational groups: cops, lawyers, gravediggers (funerals are a dramatic staple) and the staffs of hospital intensive-care units who are constantly battling to keep characters like MacGyver alive. Everyone else is on a perpetual coffee break. Most of the cast of *Wings* hangs out in the airport restaurant. The office scenes in *Working Girl* and *Open House* were all devoted to the workaday rigors of party planning.

What scant vigor remains in American capitalism is mostly due to the indestructible J.R. Ewing, who is still spouting business maxims like "He's my kind of man—bribable." Only *thirtysomething* tries to replicate the real-life stress of middle management, the ulcer-producing anxiety normally reserved for commercials hawking business phone systems and airlines. At a time when America needs role models of scientists, engineers and factory managers striving to keep ahead of the Japanese, all prime time offered were Elliot's self-indulgent efforts to direct a public service spot worthy of Fellini.

But the treatment of most social problems on the networks cannot avoid being tinged with escapism and societal wish fulfillment. With the best of post-Cosby intentions, television seems determined to become the only place in the nation where the black middle class is growing exponentially. Most black sitcoms are like old-fashioned white ones except with better music. On *Family Matters,* the Winslows all joined together to perform in a rap video to help Eddie win a contest. The kids enjoying a beach vacation on *A Different World* may be black, but their primary identity seems to be boisterous middle-class college students. Symbolically, of course, it is indeed a different world when sitcom characters routinely wear T shirts that proclaim, MARTIN, MALCOLM, MANDELA, ME.

But in their zeal to do the right thing, the architects of prime time are largely masking the strains in race relations and the social isolation of the black underclass. On most shows, blacks are portrayed either as work buddies or in comfortable middle-class roles like an art-gallery owner on *Father Dowling Mysteries.* As a result, prejudice becomes an abstraction to be preached against and overt bigotry all but limited to a bizarrely menacing alliance between American Nazis and skinheads on *21 Jump Street.* So too does TV breezily dismiss the crisis of the black family. On *Bagdad Cafe,* Whoopi Goldberg plays a recently jettisoned wife whose son's only adjustment problem is that working in the restaurant kitchen interferes with his ambition to be a classical pianist. This atypical dilemma is resolved in 1950s-sitcom style: Henry Mancini decrees that the kid has real talent.

• • •

Crime is the one arena where prime time drops its Panglossian pose to pander to public hysteria. This is not to argue that the narcotics squad on *Nasty Boys* should instead pursue jaywalkers or that the cops on *Hunter* should stop shouting, "Freeze. Police. Drop the gun!" O.K., so you cannot have detective shows without serious crime. But why are sitcoms also menaced by a crime wave that resembles New York City during a blackout? In this single week, there was an interracial team of angry drug dealers on *A Different World,* a psychotic killer rudely intruding on an office camping trip on *Perfect Strangers,* and that laugh riot—a berserk gun-wielding bus-boy—on *Sugar and Spice.* Even when Suzanne and Julia of *Designing Women* jetted off on vacation to Japan, probably the world's safest nation, their luggage was promptly stolen in Tokyo's Narita Airport. The thieves, of course, belonged to a criminal class that now exists only on shows determined not to offend anyone's sensibilities: American hippies.

After seven days of total immersion in such prime-time platitudes, other smaller, less socially significant mysteries remain. Why was Grace, the tall, blond judge on *L.A. Law,* the only person allowed to voice the all-American sentiment that she hates her job? What happened to all the neighbors who used to drop by for coffee on all the sitcoms, and why have they been replaced by work groups? Why are there so few good meals and so many bad restaurants on television? Why are there no nostalgia shows reprising the '50s or '70s? And how about the biggest puzzle: What ever happened to all those car chases?

SUGGESTIONS FOR DISCUSSION

1. What seems to bother Shapiro most about the version of American culture that is projected on prime time television?
2. Shapiro is particularly critical of television's representation of the economy. Why might the economic level of television families be an important issue in relation to television realism?
3. Make a list of programs that you remember watching as a child. What version of American culture did these programs project? How would you compare them to today's programs?

SUGGESTION FOR WRITING

1. Shapiro writes, "on television most real work is done by just four occupational groups: cops, lawyers, gravediggers . . . and the staffs of hospital intensive-care units who are constantly battling to keep characters like MacGyver alive." Choose an occupational group that you have frequently seen depicted on television and write an essay in which you characterize that group according to the way it is represented on television. Use specific television characters or programs to develop your essay.
2. Shapiro charges that television seems to know nothing of the middle part of this nation and that cities like New York and Los Angeles are glamorized in television programming. Write an essay in which you compare your knowledge either of these cities or of the Midwest with the image that you see on television of that area.
3. Make a list of the programs you remember watching while you were growing up. From that list, choose one and write an essay in which you explain how American life was depicted in that program. How does that depiction compare to your own knowledge of this culture?

Michael Ventura

REPORT FROM EL DORADO

Michael Ventura writes a column on popular culture and ideas for the *L.A. Weekly.* Some of these articles are collected in the 1985 book *Shadow Dancing in the U.S.A.* For many Americans, watching television is simply a way to block out the daily stress of work or school or personal problems. It might seem, then, that analyzing such a medium is to give it too much credit. It is, in fact, easy to dismiss most television programming as mere entertainment, but Ventura argues in the following article that we must pay attention to this medium, because "It *means* something to watch so much TV."

Suggestion for Reading

- In order to follow Ventura's argument in this essay, it may help to mark those passages that clearly set forth his discussion of television and its role in our culture. Annotate those passages by noting how you respond to Ventura's assertions or by writing out examples of your own that seem to develop the same argument about the role television plays in the lives of Americans who watch so much of it.

---◆---

o go from a job you don't like to watching a screen on which others live more intensely than you . . . is American life, by and large.

This is our political ground. This is our artistic ground. This is what we've done with our immense resources. We have to stop calling it "entertainment" or "news" or "sports" and start calling it what it is: our most immediate environment.

This is a very, very different America from the America that built the industrial capacity to win the Second World War and to surge forward on the multiple momentums of that victory for thirty years. That was an America that worked at mostly menial tasks during the day (now we work at mostly clerical tasks) and had to look at each other at night.

I'm not suggesting a nostalgia for that time. It was repressive and bigoted to an extent that is largely forgotten today, to cite only two of its uglier aspects. But in that environment America meant *America:* the people and the land. The land was far bigger than what we'd done with the land.

This is no longer true. Now the environment of America is media. Not the land itself, but the image of the land. The focus is not on the people so much as it is on the interplay between people and screens. What we've done with the land is far more important now than the land—we're not even dealing with the land anymore, we're dealing with our manipulation and pollution of it.

And what we've done with the very concept of "image" is taking on far more importance for many of us than the actual sights and sounds of our lives.

For instance: Ronald Reagan stands on a cliff in Normandy to commemorate the day U.S. Army Rangers scaled those cliffs in the World War II invasion. Today's Rangers reenact the event while some of the original Rangers, in their sixties now, look on. Except that it is the wrong cliff. The cliff that was actually scaled is a bit further down the beach, but it's not as photogenic as this cliff, so this cliff has been chosen for everybody to emote over. Some of the old Rangers tell reporters that the historical cliff is over yonder, but the old Rangers are swept up (as well they might be) in the ceremonies, and nobody objects enough. This dislocation, this choice, this stance that the real cliff is not important, today's photograph is more important, is a media event. It insults the real event, and overpowers it. Multiplied thousands of times over thousands of outlets of every form and size, ensconced in textbooks as well as screenplays, in sales presentations as well as legislative packages, in religious revivals as well as performance-art pieces, this is the process that has displaced what used to be called "culture."

• • •

"I'm not even sure it's a culture anymore. It's like this careening hunger splattering out in all directions."

Jeff Nightbyrd was trying to define "culture" in the wee hours at the Four Queens in Las Vegas. It was a conversation that had been going on since we'd become friends working on the *Austin Sun* in 1974, trying to get our bearings now that the sixties were *really over.* He'd spent that tripletime decade as an SDS organizer and editor of *Rat,* and I'd hit Austin after a few years of road-roving, commune-hopping, and intensive (often depressive) self-exploration—getting by, as the song said, with a little help from my friends, as a lot of us did then. This particular weekend Nightbyrd had come to Vegas from Austin for a computer convention, and I had taken off from my duties at the *L.A. Weekly* for some lessons in craps (at which Jeff is quite good) and to further our rap. The slot machines clattered around us in unison, almost comfortingly, the way the sound of a large shaky air-conditioner can be comforting in a cheap hotel room when you're trying to remember to forget. We were, after all, trying to fathom an old love: America.

There are worse places to indulge in this obsession than Las Vegas. It is the most American, the most audacious, of cities. Consuming unthinkable amounts of energy in the midst of an unlivable desert (Death Valley is not far away), its decor is based on various cheap-to-luxurious versions of a 1930s Busby Berkeley musical. Indeed, no studio backlot could ever be more of a set, teeming with extras, people who come from all over America, and all over the world, to see the topless, tasteless shows, the Johnny Carson guests on parade doing their utterly predictable routines, the dealers and crap-table croupiers who combine total boredom with ruthless efficiency and milk us dry—yet at least these tourists are risking something they genuinely value: money. It's a quiz show turned into a way of life, where you can get a good Italian dinner at dawn. Even the half-lit hour of the wolf doesn't faze Las Vegas. How could it, when the town has survived the flash of atom bombs tested just over the horizon?

The history books will tell you that, ironically enough, the town was founded by
Mormons in 1855. Even their purity of vision couldn't bear the intensity of this desert,
and they abandoned the place after just two years. But they had left a human imprint,
and a decade later the U.S. Army built a fort here. The settlement hung on, and the
railroad came through in 1905. During the Second World War the Mafia started to
build the city as we know it now. Religious zealots, the Army, and the Mafia—quite a
triad of founding fathers.

Yet one could go back even further, some 400 years, when the first Europeans discovered the deserts of the American West—Spaniards who, as they slowly began to believe that there might be no end to these expansive wilds, became more and more certain that somewhere, somewhere to the north, lay El Dorado—a city of gold.
Immeasurable wealth would be theirs, they believed, and eternal youth. What would
they have thought if they had suddenly come upon modern Las Vegas, lying as it does
in the midst of this bleached nowhere, glowing at night with a brilliance that would
have frightened them? We have built our desert city to their measure—for they were
gaudy and greedy, devout and vicious, jovial and frenzied, like this town. They had just
wasted the entire Aztec civilization because their fantasies were so strong they couldn't
see the ancient cultural marvels before their eyes. The Aztecs, awed and terrified, believed they were being murdered by gods; and in the midst of such strangeness, the
Spaniards took on godlike powers even in their own eyes. As many Europeans would in
America, they took liberties here they would never have taken within sight of their
home cathedrals. Their hungers dominated them, and in their own eyes the New
World seemed as inexhaustible as their appetites. So when Nightbyrd described our
present culture as "a careening hunger splattering out in all directions," he was also, if
unintentionally, speaking about our past. Fittingly, we were sitting in the midst of a
city that had been fantasized by those seekers of El Dorado 400 years ago. In that sense,
America had Las Vegas a century before it had Plymouth Rock. And our sensibility has
been caught between the fantasies of the conquistadors and the obsessions of the
Puritans ever since.

Yes, a fitting place to try to think about American culture.

"There are memories of culture," Nightbyrd was saying, "but the things that have
given people strength have dissolved. And because they're dissolved, people are into distractions. And distractions aren't culture."

Are there even memories? The media have taken over our memories. That day
Nightbyrd had been driving through the small towns that dot this desert, towns for
which Vegas is only a dull glow to the southwest. In a bar in one of those towns, "like
that little bar in *The Right Stuff*," he'd seen pictures of cowboys on the wall. "Except
that they weren't cowboys. They were movie stars. Guys who grew up in Glendale
[John Wayne] and Santa Monica [Robert Redford]." Surely this desert had its own heroes once, in the old gold-mining towns where a few people still hang on, towns like
Goldfield and Tonopah. Remembering those actual heroes would be "culture."
Needing pictures of movie stars for want of the real thing is only a nostalgia for culture.

Nostalgia is not memory. Memory is specific. One has a relationship to a memory, and it may be a difficult relationship, because a memory always makes a demand upon the present. But nostalgia is vague, a sentimental wash that obscures memory and acts as a narcotic to dull the importance of the present.

Media as we know it now thrives on nostalgia and is hostile to memory. In a television bio-pic, Helen Keller is impersonated by Mare Winningham. But the face of Helen Keller was marked by her enormous powers of concentration, while the face of Mare Winningham is merely cameo-pretty. A memory has been stolen. It takes a beauty in you to see the beauty in Helen Keller's face, while to cast the face of a Mare Winningham in the role is to suggest, powerfully, that one can come back from the depths unscathed. No small delusion is being sold here. Yet this is a minor instance in a worldwide, twenty-four-hour-a-day onslaught.

An onslaught that gathers momentum every twenty-four hours. Remember that what drew us to Las Vegas was a computer fair. One of these new computers does interesting things with photographs. You can put a photograph into the computer digitally. This means the photograph is in there without a negative or print, each element of the image stored separately. In the computer, you can change any element of the photograph you wish, replacing it or combining it with elements from other photographs. In other words, you can take composites of different photographs and put them into a new photograph of your own composition. Combine this with computer drawing, and you can touch up shadows that don't match. When it comes out of the computer the finished product bears no evidence of tampering with any negative. The possibilities for history books and news stories are infinite. Whole new histories can now be written. Events which never happened can be fully documented.

The neo-Nazis who are trying to convince people that the Holocaust never happened will be able to show the readers of their newsletter an Auschwitz of well-fed, happy people being watched over by kindly S.S. men while tending gardens. And they will be able to make the accusation that photographs of the *real* Auschwitz were created in a computer by manipulative Jews. The Soviet Union can rewrite Czechoslovakia and Afghanistan, the United States can rewrite Vietnam, and atomic weapons proponents can prove that the average resident of Hiroshima was unharmed by the blast. On a less sinister, but equally disruptive, level, the writers of business prospectuses and real-estate brochures can have a field day.

Needless to say, when any photograph can be processed this way then all photographs become suspect. It not only becomes easier to lie, it becomes far harder to tell the truth.

But why should this seem shocking when under the names of "entertainment" and "advertising" we've been filming history, and every facet of daily life, in just this way for nearly a century now? It shouldn't surprise us that the ethics of our entertainment have taken over, and that we are viewing reality itself as a form of entertainment. And, as entertainment, reality can be rewritten, transformed, played with, in any fashion.

These considerations place us squarely at the center of our world—and we have no choice, it's the only world there is anymore. *Electronic media has done for everyday reality what Einstein did for physics:* everything is shifting. Even the shifts are shifting. And a fact is not so crucial anymore, not so crucial as the process that turns a fact into an image. For we live now with images as much as facts, and the images seem to impart more life than facts *precisely because they are so capable of transmutation, of transcendence, able to transcend their sources and their uses.* And all the while the images goad us on, so that we become partly images ourselves, imitating the properties of images as we surround ourselves with images.

This is most blatant in our idea of "a vacation"—an idea only about 100 years old. To "vacation" is to enter an image. Las Vegas is only the most shrill embodiment of this phenomenon. People come here not so much to gamble (individual losses are comparatively light), nor for the glittery entertainment, but to step into an image, a daydream, a filmlike world where "everything" is promised. No matter that the Vegas definition of "everything" is severely limited, what thrills tourists is the sense of being surrounded in "real life" by the same images that they see on TV. But the same is true of the Grand Canyon, or Yellowstone National Park, or Yosemite, or Death Valley, or virtually any of our "natural" attractions. What with all their roads, telephones, bars, cable-TV motels, the visitors are carefully protected from having to *experience* the place. They view its image, they camp out in its image, ski down or climb up its image, take deep breaths of its image, let its image give them a tan. Or, when they tour the cities, they ride the quaint trolley cars of the city's image, they visit the Latin Quarter of its image, they walk across the Brooklyn Bridge of its image—our recreation is a *re-*creation of America into one big Disneyland.

And this is only one way we have stripped the very face of America of any content, any reality, concentrating only on its power as image. We also elect images, groom ourselves as images, make an image of our home, our car, and now, with aerobics, of our very bodies. For in the aerobics craze the flesh becomes a garment, susceptible to fashion. So it becomes less *our* flesh, though the exercise may make it more serviceable. It becomes "my" body, like "my" car, "my" house. What, within us, is saying "my"? What is transforming body into image? We shy away from asking. In this sense it can be said that after the age of about twenty-five we no longer *have* bodies anymore—we have possessions that are either more or less young, which we are constantly trying to transform and through which we try to breathe.

It's not that all this transformation of realities into un- or non- or supra-realities is "bad," but that it's unconscious, compulsive, reductive. We rarely make things more than they were; we simplify them into less. Though surely the process *could*—at least theoretically—go both ways. Or so India's meditators and Zen's monks say. But that would be to *increase* meaning, and we seem bent on the elimination of meaning. We're Reagan's Rangers, climbing a cliff that *is* a real cliff, except it's not the cliff we say it is, so that the meaning of both cliffs—not to mention of our act of climbing—is reduced.

As I look out onto a glowing city that is more than 400 years old but was built only during the last forty years, as I watch it shine in blinking neon in a desert that has seen the flash of atom bombs, it becomes more and more plain to me that America is at war with meaning. America is form opposed to content. Not just form *instead* of content. Form opposed. Often violently. There are few things resented so much among us as the suggestion that what we do *means*. It *means* something to watch so much TV. It *means* something to be obsessed with sports. It *means* something to vacation by indulging in images. It means something, and therefore it has consequences. Other cultures have argued over their meanings. We tend to deny that there is any such thing, insisting instead that what you see is what you get and that's *it*. All we're doing is having a *good time,* all we're doing is making a buck, all we're doing is enjoying the spectacle, we insist. So that when we export American culture what we are really exporting is an attitude toward content. Media is the American war on content with all the stops out, with meaning in utter rout, frightened nuances dropping their weapons as they run.

• • •

"Media is the history that forgives," my friend Dave Johnson told me on a drive through that same desert a few months later. We love to take a weekend every now and again and just *drive*. Maybe it started with reading *On the Road* when we were kids, or watching a great old TV show called *Route 66* about two guys who drove from town to town working at odd jobs and having adventures with intense women who, when asked who they were, might say (as one did), "Suppose I said I was the Queen of Spain?" Or maybe it was all those rock 'n' roll songs about "the road"—the road, where we can blast our tape-decks as loud as we want, and watch the world go by without having to touch it, a trip through the greatest hologram there is, feeling like neither boys nor men but both and something more, embodiments of some ageless, restless principle of movement rooted deep in our prehistory. All of which is to say that we're just as stuck with the compulsion to enter the image as anybody, and that we love the luxuries of fossil fuel just as much as any other red-blooded, thickheaded Americans.

Those drives are our favorite time to talk, and, again, America is our oldest flame. We never tire of speaking of her, nor of our other old girlfriends. For miles and miles of desert I thought of what Dave had said.

"Media is the history that forgives." A lovely way to put it, and quite un-Western. We Westerners tend to think in sets of opposites: good/bad, right/wrong, me/you, past/present. These sets are often either antagonistic (East/West, commie/capitalist, Christian/heathen) or they set up a duality that instantly calls out to be bridged (man/woman). But Dave's comment sidesteps the dualities and suggests something more complex: a lyrical impulse is alive somewhere in all this media obfuscation. It is the impulse to redeem the past—in his word, to *forgive* history—by presenting it as we would have most liked it to be.

It is one thing to accuse the media of lying. They are, and they know it, and they know we know, and we know they know that we know, and nothing changes. It is another to recognize the rampant lying shallowness of our media as a massive united longing for . . . innocence? For a sheltered childlike state in which we need not know about our world or our past. We are so desperate for this that we are willing to accept ignorance as a substitute for innocence. For there can be no doubt anymore that this society *knowingly* accepts its ignorance as innocence—we have seen so much in the last twenty years that now we know what we *don't* see. Whenever a TV show or a movie or a news broadcast leaves out crucial realities for the sake of sentimentality, we pretty much understand the nature of what's been left out and why.

But American media *forgives* the emptiness and injustice of our daily life by presenting our daily life as innocent. Society, in turn, forgives American media for lying because if we accept the lie as truth then we needn't *do* anything, we needn't change.

I like Dave's line of thought because it suggests a motive—literally, a motive force—for these rivers of glop that stream from the screens and loudspeakers of our era. Because, contrary to popular belief, profit is *not* the motive. That seems a rash statement to make in the vicinity of Las Vegas, but the profit motive merely begs the question: *why* is it profitable? Profit, in media, is simply a way of measuring attention. Why does what we call "media" attract so much attention?

The answer is that it is otherwise too crippling for individuals to bear the strain of accepting the unbalanced, unrewarding, uninspiring existence that is advertised as "normal daily life" for most people who have to earn a living every day.

Do those words seem too strong? Consider: to go to a job you don't value in itself but for its paycheck, while your kids go to a school that is less and less able to educate them; a large percentage of your pay is taken by the government for defenses that don't defend, welfare that doesn't aid, and the upkeep of a government that is impermeable to the influence of a single individual; while you are caught in a value system that judges you by what you own, in a society where it is taken for granted now that children can't communicate with their parents, that old people have to be shut away in homes, and that no neighborhood is *really* safe; while the highest medical costs in the world don't prevent us from having one of the worst health records in the West (for instance, New York has a far higher infant mortality rate than Hong Kong), and the air, water, and supermarket food are filled with God-knows-what; and to have, at the end of a busy yet uneventful life, little to show for enduring all this but a comfortable home if you've "done well" enough; yet to *know* all along that you're living in the freest, most powerful country in the world, though you haven't had time to exercise much freedom and don't personally have any power—this is to be living a life of slow attrition and maddening contradictions.

Add to this a social style that values cheerfulness more than any other attribute, and then it is not so strange or shocking that the average American family watches six to eight hours of network television a day. It is a cheap and sanctioned way to partake of this world without having actually to live in it.

Certainly they don't watch so much TV because they're bored—there's far too much tension in their lives to call them bored, and, in fact, many of the products advertised on their favorite programs feature drugs to calm them down. Nor is it because they're stupid—a people managing the most technically intricate daily life in history can hardly be written off as stupid; nor because they can't entertain themselves—they are not so different from the hundreds of generations of their forebears who entertained themselves very well as a matter of course. No, they are glued to the TV because one of the most fundamental messages of television is: "It's all right."

Every sitcom and drama says: "It's all right." Those people on the tube go through the same—if highly stylized—frustrations, and are exposed to the same dangers as we are, yet they reappear magically every week (every day on the soap operas) ready for more, always hopeful, always cheery, never questioning the fundamental premise that this is the way a great culture behaves and that all the harassments are the temporary inconveniences of a beneficent society. It's going to get even *better*, but even now *it's all right*. The commercials, the Hollywood movies, the universal demand in every television drama or comedy that no character's hope can ever be exhausted, combine in a deafening chorus of: *It's all right*.

As a screenwriter I have been in many a film production meeting, and not once have I heard any producer or studio executive say, "We have to lie to the public." What I have heard, over and over, is, "They have to leave the theater feeling good." This, of course, easily (though not always) translates into lying—into simplifying emotions and events so that "it's all right." You may measure how deeply our people know "it" is *not* all right, not at all, by how much money they are willing to pay to be ceaselessly told that it is. The more they feel it's not, the more they need to be told it is—hence Mr. Reagan's popularity.

Works that don't say "It's all right" don't get much media attention or make much money.

The culture itself is in the infantile position of needing to be assured, every day, all day, that this way of life is good for you. Even the most disturbing news is dispensed in the most reassuring package. As world news has gotten more and more disturbing, the trend in broadcast journalism has been to get more and more flimflam, to take it less seriously, to keep up the front of "It's really quite all right." This creates an enormous tension between the medium and its messages, because everybody knows that what's on the news is *not* all right. That is why such big money is paid to a newscaster with a calm, authoritative air who, by his presence alone, seems to resolve the contradictions of his medium. Walter Cronkite was the most popular newscaster in broadcast history because his very presence implied: "As long as I'm on the air, you can be sure that, no matter what I'm telling you, *it's still all right.*"

Which is to say that the media has found it profitable to do the mothering of the mass psyche. But it's a weak mother. It cannot nurture. All it can do is say it's all right, tuck us in, and hope for the best.

Today most serious, creative people exhaust themselves in a sideline commentary on this state of affairs, a commentary that usually gets sucked up into the media and spewed back out in a format that says "It's all right. What this guy's saying is quite all right, what this woman's singing is all right, all right." This is what "gaining recognition" virtually always means now in America: your work gets turned inside out so that its meaning becomes "It's all right."

Of course, most of what exists *to make media of,* to make images of, is more and more disorder. Media keeps saying, "It's all right" while being fixated upon the violent, the chaotic, and the terrifying. So the production of media becomes more and more schizoid, with two messages simultaneously being broadcast: "It's all right. We're dying. It's all right. We're all dying." The other crucial message—"We're dying"—runs right alongside *It's all right.*

Murder is the crux of much media "drama." But it's murder presented harmlessly, with trivial causes cited. Rare is the attempt, in all our thousands of murder dramas, to delve below the surface. We take for granted now, almost as an immutable principle of dramatic unity, that significant numbers of us want to kill significant numbers of the rest of us. And what are all the murders in our media but a way of saying "We are being killed, we are killing, we are dying"? Only a people dying and in the midst of death would need to see so much of it in such sanitized form *in order to make death harmless.* This is the way we choose to share our death.

Delete the word "entertainment" and say instead, North Americans devote an enormous amount of time to the ritual of sharing death. If this were recognized as a ritual, and if the deaths were shared with a respect for the realities and the mysteries of death, this might be a very useful thing to do. But there is no respect for death in our death-dependent media, there is only the compulsion to display death. As for the consumers, they consume these deaths like sugar pills. Their ritual goes on far beneath any level on which they'd be prepared to admit the word "ritual." So we engage in a ritual we pretend isn't happening, hovering around deaths that we say aren't real.

It is no coincidence that this practice has thrived while the Pentagon uses the money of these death watchers to create weapons for death on a scale that is beyond the powers of human imagination—the very same human imagination that is stunting itself by watching ersatz deaths, as though intentionally crippling its capacity to envision the encroaching dangers. It is possible that the Pentagon's process could not go on without the dulling effects of this "entertainment."

When we're not watching our screens, we're listening to music. And, of course, North Americans listen to love songs at every possible opportunity, through every possible orifice of media. People under the strain of such dislocating unrealities need to hear "I love you, I love you," as often as they can. "I love you" or "I used to love you" or "I ought to love you" or "I need to love you" or "I want to love you." It is the fashion of pop-music critics to discount the words for the style, forgetting that most of the world's cultures have had songs about *everything,* songs about work, about the sky, about death, about the gods, about getting up in the morning, about animals, about children, about eating, about dreams—about everything, along with love. These were songs that everybody knew and sang. For a short time in the late sixties we moved toward such songs again, but that was a brief digression; since the First World War the music that most North Americans listen to has been a music of love lyrics that rarely go beyond adolescent yearnings. Either the song is steeped in the yearnings themselves, or it is saturated with a longing for the days when one could, shamelessly, feel like an adolescent. The beat has changed radically from decade to decade, but with brief exceptions that beat has carried the same pathetic load. (The beat, thankfully, has given us other gifts.)

It can't be over-emphasized that these are entertainments of a people whose basic imperative is the need not to think about their environment. The depth of their need may be measured by the hysterical popularity of this entertainment; it is also the measure of how little good it does them.

• • •

Media is not experience. In its most common form, media substitutes a fantasy of experience or (in the case of news) an abbreviation of experience for the living fact. But in our culture the absorption of media has become a substitute for experience. We absorb media, we don't live it—there is a vast psychological difference, and it is a difference that is rarely brought up.

For example, in the 1940s, when one's environment was still one's *environment,* an experience to be lived instead of a media-saturation to be absorbed, teenagers like Elvis Presley and Jerry Lee Lewis didn't learn their music primarily from the radio. Beginning when they were small boys they sneaked over to the black juke joints of Louisiana and Mississippi and Tennessee, where they weren't supposed to go, and they listened and learned. When Lewis and Presley began recording, even though they were barely twenty they had tremendous authority because they had experience—a raw experience of crossing foreign boundaries, of streets and sounds and peoples, of the night-to-night learning of ways that could not be taught at home.

This is very different from young musicians now who learn from a product, not a living ground. Their music doesn't get to them till it's been sifted through elaborate corporate networks of production and distribution. It doesn't smack of the raw world that exists before "product" can even be thought of.

The young know this, of course. They sense the difference intensely, and often react to it violently. So white kids from suburban media culture invented slam dancing (jumping up and down and slamming into each other) while black kids from the South Bronx, who have to deal with realities far more urgent than media, were elaborating the astounding graces of break dancing.

Slam dancing was a dead end. Break dancing, coming from a living ground, goes out through media but becomes ultimately transformed into another living ground—the kids in the elementary school down the street in Santa Monica break dance. Which is to say, a grace has been added to their lives. A possibility of grace. With the vitality that comes from having originated from a living ground. The media here is taking its proper role as a channel, not as a world in itself. It's possible that these kids are being affected more in their bodies and their daily lives by the South Bronx subculture than by high-gloss films like *Gremlins* or *Indiana Jones and the Temple of Doom.* Even through all this static, life can speak to life.

Of course, break dancing inevitably gets hyped, and hence devalued, by the entertainment industry, the way Elvis Presley ended up singing "Viva Las Vegas" as that town's most glamorous headliner. He went from being the numinous son of a living ground to being the charismatic product of a media empire—the paradigm of media's power to transform the transformers. The town veritably glows in the dark with the strength of media's mystique.

We do not yet know what life *is* in a media environment. We have not yet evolved a contemporary culture that can supply the definition—or rather, supply the constellation of concepts in which that definition would live and grow. These seem such simple statements, but they are at the crux of the American dilemma now. An important aspect of this dilemma is that we've barely begun a body of thought and art which is focused on what is really *alive* in the ground of a media-saturated daily life. For culture always proceeds from two poles: one is the people of the land and the street; the other is the thinker. You see this most starkly in revolutions: the ground swell on the one hand, the thinker (the Jefferson, for instance) on the other. Or religiously, the ground swell of belief that is articulated by a Michelangelo or a Dante. The two poles can exist without each other but they cannot be effective without each other.

Unless a body of thought connects with a living ground, there is no possibility that this era will discover itself within its cacophony and create, one day, a post-A.D. culture. It is ours to attempt the thought and seek the ground—for all of us exist between those poles. We are not only dying. We are living. And we are struggling to share our lives, which is all, finally, that "culture" means.

SUGGESTIONS FOR DISCUSSION

1. In his conversation with Jeff Nightbyrd, Ventura tells us about a bar in a small western town that had pictures of famous cowboys all over its walls. The cowboys, however, weren't real cowboys at all but movie cowboys. What point would you say he is trying to make with this anecdote? Why do you suppose the bar owner might not consider replacing his movie cowboys with pictures of the actual men and women who settled in that area?

2. Discuss what you think Ventura is getting at when he says, "It takes beauty in you to see the beauty in Helen Keller's face, while to cast the face of a Mare Winningham

in the role is to suggest, powerfully, that one can come back from the depths un-scathed. No small delusion is being sold here. Yet this is a minor instance in a worldwide, twenty-four-hour-a-day onslaught." What does this example have to do with the impact television has made on our lives?

3. In his discussion of television's version of history, Ventura says, "It is one thing to accuse the media of lying. They are, and they know it, and they know we know, and we know they know that we know, and nothing changes. It is another to rec-ognize the rampant lying shallowness of our media as a massive united longing for . . . innocence?" Discuss times when you do know that the media is lying (or, at least, not telling the entire story). If Ventura is right and we just don't want all of the bad news, what do we want from television news?

SUGGESTIONS FOR WRITING

1. Like others in this chapter, Ventura accuses television of ignoring important issues in favor of entertainment. At one point in this essay he writes, "American media *for-gives* the emptiness and injustice of our daily life by presenting our daily life as in-nocent. Society, in turn, forgives American media for lying because if we accept the lie as truth then we needn't *do* anything, we needn't change." Write an essay in which you discuss how American television presents our daily lives as innocent and in what ways American society accepts the lies of television.

2. Write an essay in which you compare the following statement about how Americans watch television to the way in which you or a friend or family member uses televi-sion: "yet to know all along that you're living in the freest, most powerful country in the world, though you haven't had time to exercise much freedom and don't person-ally have any power—this is to be living a life of slow attrition and maddening con-tradictions. Add to this a social style that values cheerfulness more than any other at-tribute, and then it is not so strange or shocking that the average American family watches six to eight hours of network television a day. It is a cheap and sanctioned way to partake of this world without having actually to live in it."

3. Michael Ventura writes that it "*means* something" that Americans watch so much television. Considering what you have read in this chapter, the discussions you have had with your classmates, and the writing you have done in response to the questions raised throughout the chapter, write an essay in which you explain what it means that Americans watch so much television.

Henry Louis Gates, Jr.

TV's Black World Turns—But Stays Unreal

Henry Louis Gates, Jr., is the John Spencer Bassett Professor of English at Duke University. He has written and spoken widely about the representation of African Americans in popular culture. His book-length studies include *The Signifying Monkey* and *Figures in Black: Words, Signs & the Racial Self.* In the following article, published in 1989 in the *New York Times* "Lifestyle" sec-tion, Gates traces the African American image through its history in popular television. His is both an analysis of contemporary representations of African Americans on television and a history of their image in television programming. He uses history to examine what seems to be the trend in television's representations of African Americans today.

Suggestion for Reading

- Gates presents *The Cosby Show* as well as *Amos 'n' Andy* as programs he likes. At the same time, he understands the problems both of those programs pose if we are to take them as representative of African American life and culture. As you read, underline those passages in the article in which Gates discusses stereotypes and role models as they have appeared throughout television history and in these programs in particular.

There is a telling moment in the 1986 film "Soul Man" when a young man explains to a friend why he has decided to down a bottle of tanning pills and turn himself black. The friend is skeptical: What's it actually going to be like, being black? "It's gonna be great," the hero assures him. "These are the 80's, man. This is the 'Cosby' decade. America *loves* black people."

Alas, he soon discovers the gulf that separates the images of black people he sees on television and the reality that blacks experience every day.

Even black Americans sometimes need to be reminded about the deceptiveness of television. Blacks retain their fascination with black characters on TV: Many of us buy *Jet* magazine primarily to read its weekly television feature, which lists *every* black character (major or minor) to be seen on the screen that week. Yet our fixation with the presence of black characters on TV has blinded us to an important fact that "Cosby," which began in 1984, and its offshoots over the years demonstrate convincingly: There is very little connection between the social status of black Americans and the fabricated images of black people that Americans consume each day. Moreover, the representations of blacks on TV is a very poor index to our social advancement or political progress.

But the young man is right about one thing: This is the "Cosby" decade. The show's unprecedented success in depicting the lives of affluent blacks has exercised a profound influence on television in the last half of the 80's. And, judging from the premiere of this season's new black series—"Family Matters," "Homeroom" and "Snoops," as well as "Generations," an interracial soap opera—"Cosby's" success has led to the flow of TV sitcoms that feature the black middle class, each of which takes its lead from the "Cosby" show.

Historically, blacks have always worried aloud about the image that white Americans harbor of us, first because we have never had control of those images and, second, because the greater number of those images have been negative. And given television's immediacy, and its capacity to reach so many viewers so quickly, blacks, at least since "Amos 'n' Andy" back in the early 50's, have been especially concerned with our images on the screen. I can remember as a child sitting upstairs in my bedroom and hearing my mother shout at the top of her voice that someone "*colored . . . colored!*" was on TV and that we had all better come downstairs at once. And, without fail, we did, sitting in front of our TV, nervous, full of expectation and dread, praying that our home girl or boy would not let the race down.

"WHITE" MONEY VS. "COLORED" MONEY

Later, when American society could not successfully achieve the social reformation it sought in the 60's through the Great Society, television solved the problem simply by inventing symbols of that transformation in the 80's, whether it was Cliff Huxtable—whom we might think of as the grandson of Alexander Scott (played by Mr. Cosby in "I Spy," 1965–68)—or Benson (1979–86), the butler who transforms himself into a lieutenant governor.

Today, blacks are doing much better on TV than they are in real life, an irony underscored by the use of black public figures (Mr. Cosby, Michael Jackson, Michael Jordan, Bobby McFerrin) as spokesmen for major businesses. When Mr. Cosby, deadpan, faces the camera squarely and says, "B.F. Hutton. Because it's my money," the line blurs between Cliff Huxtable's successful career and Mr. Cosby.

This helps to explain why "Cosby" makes some people uncomfortable: As the dominant representation of blacks on TV, it suggests that blacks are solely responsible for their social conditions, with no acknowledgement of the severely constricted life opportunities that most black people face. What's troubling about the phenomenal success of "Cosby," then, is what was troubling about the earlier popularity of "Amos 'n' Andy": it's not the representation itself (Cliff Huxtable, a child of college-educated parents, is altogether believable), but the role it begins to play in our culture, the status it takes on as being, well, truly representative.

As long as *all* blacks were represented in demeaning or peripheral roles, it was possible to believe that American racism was, as it were, indiscriminate. The social vision of "Cosby," however, reflecting the minuscule integration of blacks into the upper middle class (having "white money," my mother used to say, rather than "colored" money) reassuringly throws the blame for black poverty back onto the impoverished.

• • •

This is the subliminal message of America's weekly dinner date with the Huxtables, played out to a lesser extent in other weekly TV encounters with middle-class black families, such as "227," "A Different World," "Amen" (Sherman Helmsley is a lawyer), and with isolated black individuals, such as the dashing Blair Underwood on "L.A. Law" and Philip Michael Thomas on "Miami Vice." One principal reason for the failure of Flip Wilson's "Charlie & Company" was the ambiguity of his class status; Wilson's character, Charlie Richmond, was an office worker at the Department of Highways, his wife (Gladys Knight) a schoolteacher. Wilson once joked, acidly, that he was the star of the black version of "The Cosby Show," which may have been true in ways that he did not intend.

THE GREAT "AMOS 'N' ANDY" DEBATE

In 1933, Sterling Brown, the great black poet and critic, divided the full range of black character types in American literature into seven categories: the contented slave; the wretched freeman; the comic Negro; the brute Negro; the tragic mulatto; the local color Negro; and the exotic primitive. It was only one small step to associate our public negative image in the American mind with the public negative social roles that we were assigned and to which we were largely confined. "If only they could be exposed to the *best* of the race," the sentiment went, "then they would see that we were normal human beings and treat us better."

Such a burdensome role for the black image led, inevitably, to careful monitoring and, ultimately, to censorship of our representations in literature, film, radio and later television. The historian W. E. B. Du Bois summarized this line of thinking among blacks: "We want," he said in 1925, "everything that is said about us to tell of the best and highest and noblest in us. We insist that our Art and Propaganda be one. We fear that the evil in us will be called racial while in others it is viewed as individual. We fear that our shortcomings are not merely human but foreshadowings and threatenings of disaster and failure." And the genre about which we were most sensitive, Du Bois wrote, was comedy. "The more highly trained we become," he wrote in 1921, "the less we can laugh at Negro comedy."

One of my favorite pastimes is screening episodes of "Amos 'n' Andy" for black friends who think that the series was both socially offensive and politically detrimental. After a few minutes, even hardliners have difficulty restraining their laughter. "It's still racist," is one typical comment, "but it was funny."

The performance of those great black actors—Tim Moore, Spencer Williams and Ernestine Wade—transformed racist stereotypes into authentic black humor. The dilemma of "Amos 'n' Andy," however, was that these were the *only* images of blacks that Americans could see on TV. The political consequences for the early civil rights movement were thought to be threatening. The N.A.A.C.P. helped to have the series killed.

• • •

What lies behind these sorts of arguments is a belief that social policies affecting black Americans were largely determined by our popular images in the media. But the success of the "Cosby" show has put the lie to that myth: "Cosby" exposes more white Americans than ever before to the most nobly idealized blacks in the history of entertainment, yet social and economic conditions for the average black American have not been bleaker in a very long time.

To make matters worse, "Cosby" is also one of the most popular shows in apartheid South Africa, underscoring the fact that the relationship between how whites treat us and their exposure to "the best" in us is far from straightforward. (One can hear the Afrikaaner speaking to his black servants: "When you people are like Cliff and Clare, *then* we will abandon apartheid.")

There are probably as many reasons to like the "Cosby" show as there are devoted viewers—and there are millions of them. I happen to like it because my daughters (ages 9 and 7) like it, and I enjoy watching them watch themselves in the depictions of middle-class black kids, worrying about school, sibling rivalries and family tradition. But I also like "Cosby" because its very success has forced us to rethink completely the relation between black social progress and the images of blacks that American society fabricates, projects and digests.

But the "Cosby" vision of upper-middle-class blacks and their families is comparatively recent. And while it may have constituted the dominant image of blacks for the last five years, it is a direct reaction against the lower-class ghetto comedies of the 70's, such as "Sanford and Son" (1972–77), "Good Times" (1974–79), "That's My Mama" (1974–75) and "What's Happening!!" (1976–79). The latter three were single-mother-dominated sitcoms. Although "Good Times" began with a nuclear family, John Amos—who had succeeded marvelously in transforming the genre of the black maternal household—was soon killed off, enabling the show to conform to the stereotype of a fatherless black family.

Even "The Jeffersons" (1975–85) conforms to this mold. George and Louise began their TV existence as Archie Bunker's working-class neighbors, saved their pennies, then "moved on up," as the theme song says, to Manhattan's East Side. "The Jeffersons" also served as a bridge between sitcoms depicting the ghetto and those portraying the new black upper class.

In fact, in the history of black images on television, character types have distinct pasts and, as is also the case with white shows, series seem both to lead to other series and to spring from metaphorical ancestors.

Pure Street in a Brooks Brothers Suit

Let's track the evolution of the "Cosby" type on television. While social engineering is easier on the little screen than in the big city, Sterling Brown's list of black stereotypes in American literature proves quite seviceable as a guide to the images TV has purveyed for the last two decades. Were we writing a new sitcom using these character types, our cast might look like this—contented slave: Andy, Fred Sanford, J.J. ("Good Times"); wretched freeman: George Jefferson; comic Negro: Flip Wilson; brute Negro: Mr. T ("The A-Team"), Hawk ("Spencer: for Hire"); tragic mulatto: "Julia," Elvin ("Cosby"), Whitley ("A Different World"); local color Negro: Meschach Taylor ("Designing Women"); exotic primitive: Link ("Mod Squad" 1968–73); most black characters on MTV. If we add the category of Noble Negro (Cliff Huxtable, Benson), our list might be complete.

We can start with George Jefferson, who we might think of as a Kingfish ("Amos 'n' Andy") or as a Fred Sanford ("Sanford and Son") who has finally made it. Jefferson epitomized Richard Nixon's version of black capitalism, bootstrap variety, and all of its terrifying consequences. Jefferson was anything but a man of culture: Unlike the "Cosby" living room, his East Side apartment had no painting by Jacob Lawrence or Charles White, Romare Bearden or Varnette Honeywood. Despite his new-found wealth, Jefferson was pure street, draped in a Brooks Brothers suit. You did not want to live next to a George Jefferson, and you most certainly did not want your daughter to marry one.

"The Jeffersons" was part of a larger trend in television in the depiction of black men. We might think of this as their domestication, in direct reaction to the questing, macho images of black males shown in the 60's news clips of the civil rights movement, the Black Panthers and the black power movement. While Jefferson (short, feisty, racist, rich, vulgar) represents one kind of domestication, a more curious kind was the cultural dwarfism represented by "Diff'rent Strokes" (1978–86) and "Webster" (1983–87), in which small black "boys" (arrested adolescents who were much older than the characters they played) were adopted by tall, successful white males. These establishment figures represented the myth of the benevolent paternalism of the white upper class, an American myth as old as the abolitionist movement.

• • •

Indeed, one central motif of 19th-century American art is a sculpted tall white male (often Lincoln) towering above a crouched or kneeling adult or adolescent slave, in the act of setting them free. "Webster" and "Diff'rent Strokes" depict black orphans who are rescued from blackness and poverty, adopted and raised just like any other upper-middle-class white kid, prep schools and all. These shows can be thought of as TV's fantasy of Lyndon Johnson's "Great Society" and the war on poverty rolled into one.

The formula was not as successful with a female character: An attempt to use the same format with a black woman, Shirley Hemphill ("One in a Million," 1980) lasted only six months. "The White Shadow" (1978–81) was a variation of this paternal motif, in which wild and unruly ghetto kids were tamed with a basketball.

These small black men signaled to the larger American audience that the very idea of the black male could be, and had been, successfully domesticated. Mr. T—whose 1983–87 "A-Team" run paralleled that of "Webster"—might appear to be an exception. We are forced to wonder, however, why such an important feature of his costume—and favorite fetish—was those dazzling gold chains, surely a subliminal suggestion of bondage.

This process of paternal domestication, in effect, made Cliff Huxtable's character a logical next step. In fact, I think of the evolution of the Huxtable character, generationally, in this way: imagine if George Jefferson owned the tenement building in which Florida and her family from "Good Times" lived. After John Amos dies, Jefferson evicts them for nonpayment of rent. Florida, destitute and distraught, tries to kill George. The state puts her children up for adoption.

They are adopted by Mr. Drummond ("Diff'rent Strokes") and graduate from Dalton, Exeter and Howard. Gary Coleman's grandson becomes an obstetrician, marries a lovely lawyer named Clare, and they move to Brooklyn Heights. And there you have it: the transformation of the character type of the black male on television.

And while Clare Huxtable is a refreshingly positive depiction of an intelligent, successful black woman, she is clearly a descendant of "Julia" (1968–71), though a Julia with sensuality and sass. The extent of typecasting of black women as *mammy* figures, descended from the great Hollywood "Mammy" of "Gone With the Wind," is astonishing: Beulah, Mama in "Amos 'n' Andy," Geraldine ("Flip Wilson," 1970–75), Florida, Nell in "Gimme a Break" (1981–88), Louise ("The Jeffersons"), Eloise ("That's My Mama," 1974–75).

Is TV Depicting a Different World?

And what is the measure of the Huxtables' nobility? One of the reasons "Cosby" and its spin-off, "A Different World," are so popular is that the black characters in them have finally become, in most respects, just like white people.

While I applaud "Cosby's" success at depicting (at long last) the everyday concerns of black people (love, sex, ambition, generational conflicts, work and leisure) far beyond reflex responses to white racism, the question remains: Has TV managed to depict a truly "different world?" As Mark Crispin Miller puts it, "By insisting that blacks and whites are entirely alike, television denies the cultural barriers that slavery necessarily created; barriers that have hardened over years and years, and that still exist"—barriers that produced different cultures, distinct worlds.

And while "Cosby" is remarkably successful at introducing most Americans to traditional black cultural values, customs and norms, it has not succeeded at introducing America to a truly different world. The show that came closest—that presented the fullest range of black character types—was the 1987–88 series "Frank's Place," starring Tim Reid and his wife Daphne Maxwell Reid and set in a Creole restaurant in New Orleans.

Unfortunately, Mr. Reid apparently has learned his lesson: His new series, "Snoops," in which his wife also stars, is a black detective series suggestive of "The Thin Man." The couple is thoroughly middle class: He is a professor of criminology at Georgetown; she is head of protocol at the State Department. "Drugs and murder and psychotic people," Mr. Reid said in a recent interview. "I think we've seen enough of that in real life."

But it is also important to remember that the early 70's ghetto sitcoms ("Good Times" and "Sanford") were no more realistic than "Cosby" is. In fact, their success made the idea of ghetto life palatable for most Americans, robbing it of its reality as a place of exile, a place of rage, and frustration, and death. And perhaps with "Cosby's" success and the realization that the very structure of the sitcom (in which every character is a type) militates against its use as an agent of social change, blacks will stop looking to TV for our social liberation. As a popular song in the early 70's put it, "The revolution will not be televised."

SUGGESTIONS FOR DISCUSSION

1. Make a list of television shows that include African American characters. Use that list to discuss how these characters are depicted. How might Henry Gates's discussion of stereotypes help you explain these characters?
2. At the end of his analysis, Gates argues that we are asking too much of situation comedy when we ask it to model behavior. Why do you think he says that? To what extent do you think sitcoms model behavior or living conditions?
3. African Americans are one of the many groups marginalized in television programming. Make a list of other groups that have been marginalized in the culture of television. Identify ways in which these other groups have been depicted on television or in the movies.

SUGGESTIONS FOR WRITING

1. Gates argues against the notion that if television is ever to combat racism, it must show the public the "best and the brightest" of a race. In fact, he tells us, that is what the Cosby show does. The result, however, is not the elimination of racism but the overwhelming impression that the failure of the majority of African Americans to be Cliff and Clare Huxtable is a result of individual weaknesses rather than a facet of social and institutional racism. Write an essay in which you explain your reaction to Gates's position as he states it.
2. Choose any current program or rerun on television that includes minority characters as a part of its regular cast. Describe the role the characters play and write an analysis of those characters' status on the show. In your analysis, explain what cultural ideals or stereotypes are conveyed in the program. As you write, you should examine all of the characters in relation to each other. For example, who is the hero? Who is the clown?

Who is the faithful partner? Who is the love interest? It is only by examining these other roles that you will be able to discuss the role any individual character plays.

3. It is often helpful to begin any thinking about a topic by mining your own memory for what you already know. Write an essay in which you describe the characters you remember most from television programs you watched, movies you saw, or books you read as a child. Did any of the really memorable characters represent minority groups? What minority characters do you remember from your television watching? What would you say is your overwhelming impression of minorities in popular American culture as they are depicted in the media that you remember?

Michael Arlen

MORE GREENERY, LESS GARAGE

Television critic Michael Arlen has written several books on television, including *The Livingroom War* and *The Camera Age*. Arlen has also written television criticism for *The New Yorker*. In the mid-seventies, Arlen followed the advertising firm N W Ayers while they created the popular AT&T commercial campaign, "Reach Out and Touch Someone." In the book *Thirty Seconds*, which appeared in 1979, Arlen used several of the conversations he recorded during production meetings and actual shootings to recreate a narrative of the making of a television commercial. The following excerpt from that book records a meeting concerning the choice of settings for a number of the vignettes, including one to take place at a racetrack, one at a rodeo, and a double vignette the production team has taken to calling the white yoga and the black yoga.

Suggestion for Reading

• Arlen does not use commentary to argue his position. Instead, he reports real conversations as if they were typical moments in the production of the AT&T ad campaign. As you read, underline and annotate what seem to you the most telling passages of conversation.

E arly in May, Steve Horn returns from Florida, muttering about bad weather in the Sunshine State, various delays, and a recalcitrant child actor, and asks the Ayer people to come by for a meeting at five in the afternoon. Once again, the group assembles in Horn's basement conference room, whose oak table is once again laden with Perrier, soft drinks, fruit, and cheese. Horn, with his gray silk scarf around his neck, sits at the head of the table, eating grapes. Linda, as usual, is on his left, with a large accordion folder beside her that contains the files on various shooting locations: the files are ordinary manila folders whose inside surfaces are covered with Polaroid snapshots of locations—mainly interiors—with numerical information penciled in about light and exposure angles.

At the moment, a suburban-house folder is being passed around for consideration as one of the locations for the yoga vignette.

Steve says: "I like this house. It's a little upscale, but it photographs very well."

Gaston says: "We could do the white yoga here."

Linda says: "Wouldn't the black yoga be better?"

Jerry says: "I'm not sure it reads black."

Steve says: "Don't worry. We can fix the downstairs room like a black girl's apartment, whatever that is. You know, give it a condominium look."

Gaston is meanwhile looking through another house folder. "There's a nicer house here," he says.

Linda says: "That's the Zacharia house. We've used that a lot. I know it almost as well as I know my own house."

Jerry says: "We have a black scene, but I don't know if this looks like a black house, either."

Steve says: "Let's take a look. I like this house, too. This room here has a very nice quality of light."

Gaston says: "I think we could do the white yoga here."

Jerry says: "It's a good house, but it's awfully up-scale."

Steve says: "You know what I could do in this house? I could do the kid tap dancing."

Linda says: "I thought we were going to do the tap dancing in the Lawrence house."

Steve says: "Well, that's a good one, too, but I like this one better. It says tap dancing to me."

Gaston and Jerry have been looking at still another folder, and now they pass it to Linda.

Linda says: "I know *this* house as well as I know my own house."

Steve says: "You say that about every house."

Linda says: "That's not true. Just this one and maybe a couple of others. This one is a real dirty, low-down house, but we can make it look young again."

Steve says: "We could put some frills around, right?"

Linda says: "We could clean it up."

Jerry says: "Where do we need a young house?"

Steve says: "I'd like a young house for the toothless kid, but I don't think this is it."

Gaston passes him another folder. "What about this for white yoga?"

Steve looks at it in silence for a moment. Then: "You know, I could make it rain there."

Gaston says: "I don't think we're utilizing rain."

Steve says: "But I can utilize it here. I love rain. Visually, it's one of the best things. We could do something very nice in soft focus."

Jerry says: "Not too soft."

Steve says: "I mean normal soft focus."

Linda says: "You don't want to make it look too period."

Steve says: "I wasn't talking about period, I was talking about soft focus. Normal soft focus, nothing special."

Gaston says: "Maybe we should talk about the backstage vignette."

Steve says: "Let's use the Beacon Theatre."

Linda says: "I think we used it on the Rhonda Fleming shot."

Alayne produces a folder from a pile in front of her and gives it to Steve.

Steve opens it and examines the pictures with an increasingly perplexed expression. "Hell, this isn't the Beacon, this is the Lotos Club."

Linda says: "I like the Lotos Club. Remember? We used it for Paine Webber."

Steve says: "But it's not a theater."

Now Alayne hands him the Beacon folder and takes back the Lotos Club.

"Here we are," he says. "This is old-timey as hell."

Jerry says: "Maybe we should go with it."

Linda says: "We were hoping for the City Center, but there's a ballet there."

Gaston says: "Does it bother you to go back to the same location?"

Steve says: "Nobody knows if you go back. Besides, I hardly ever shoot wide-angle."

Now the group turns to a discussion of race-track locations for the jockey vignette. In the course of the past ten days, Ray Guarino, Steve Horn's location scout, has been checking on race tracks within a hundred miles of New York and has brought back at least fifty different Polaroid views. But as soon as Jerry and Gaston start looking at them it is apparent that something is wrong.

Jerry says: "The problem I'm having with these locations is that they don't say race track to me, they say garage."

Ray says: "I Polaroided every track and paddock in the area."

Steve says: "I agree about this bunch, but I think we could use that area out at Roosevelt Raceway."

Gaston says: "If this is Roosevelt I'm looking at, it has an awful lot of concrete. It looks like a car-racing place."

Steve says: "A while ago, we shot a race-track thing for 7Up in California. We brought in all sorts of trees and grass to make it look right."

Jerry says: "I don't see how we can make Roosevelt look right."

Gaston says: "I'd say we need more greenery, less garage."

Ray says: "I think they're all like that. I checked out every track in the area."

Steve says: "Maybe we should check farther away. Maybe we should even cheat a little—you know, go for the greenery and prop the track effect."

Finally, there is a discussion of locations for the rodeo vignette, which Ray has been scouting in what might seem unlikely areas of New Jersey and Pennsylvania. The generally favored location is in New Jersey, but it apparently presents a difficulty.

Gaston says: "I think we have a phone problem."

Steve says: "What kind of a phone problem?"

Gaston says: "Well, this is a phone-company ad. We have to have a phone there somewhere."

Steve says: "Well, we can just put one in, like we do everywhere else."

Linda says: "The point is, you can't just put a phone *anywhere* in a rodeo corral."

Steve says: "Well, I didn't mean we'd put it *anywhere*. We could stick a phone on one of the posts."

Linda says: "What's a phone doing on a post?"

Jerry says: "I don't think the phone problem is going to be so hard to solve. I think our main problem is getting a place that says rodeo."

Steve says: "Yes, we have to be careful it doesn't say farm."

Jerry says: "Something rustic and rundown."

Steve says: "Definitely not farm."

Gaston says: "So where do we put the phone?"

Jerry says: "The phone problem isn't major. Trust me."

SUGGESTIONS FOR DISCUSSION

1. With a group of your classmates, discuss what Steve Horn's production team might have meant with their observation that a house is "awfully upscale" or doesn't "read" black or "says tap dancing."
2. Near the end of this chapter, producer Steve Horn directs his staff to make a rodeo scene that "doesn't say farm." What would viewers need to see to identify a scene as rodeo and not farm?
3. In many ways, "More Greenery, Less Garage" is about how television constructs places so that most viewers recognize them without much thought. With a group of your classmates, choose a place that might typically be generalized on television (school, church, farm, grandparents' house, city neighborhood, upscale bar, working class bar, etc.) and discuss how you think television would depict the place. Make a list of those objects or details an ad firm like N W Ayers would use to make the place look like their ideal.

SUGGESTIONS FOR WRITING

1. Because Arlen allows the dialogue to make his commentary for him, this chapter from *Thirty Seconds* relies on readers to draw their own conclusions. As readers, we get to "listen in" on this discussion. Write an essay that explains what you think Arlen is getting at by recording this discussion. What does the conversation he reports reveal about the making of television ads and programs?
2. Write an essay in which you describe any setting that you think would be easily recognized on television. This might be home, church, farm, school, playgrounds, any setting that seems to have become a part of our cultural imagination. What visual clues do you use to identify the place and what it is meant to represent? Refer to specific ads or programs to develop your description. How do these television places compare to their counterparts outside television?
3. The "Reach Out" campaign that Arlen followed is no longer played on national television. Look for AT&T's most recent campaign, and write an essay in which you describe how these most recent commercials reflect today's political or social concerns.

Bill McKibben

IN THE AGE OF MISSING INFORMATION

Best known as a nature writer, Bill McKibben wrote *In the Age of Missing Information,* from which the following selection is excerpted, as a kind of diary of television life. As an experiment, McKibben taped one day's worth of viewing (May 3, 1990) from ninety-three cable television channels in Fairfax, Virginia. He then sat down to watch and respond to what he saw. As a counterpoint to his viewing experience, McKibben then spent twenty-four hours in the Adirondacks simply camping, watching, listening, and writing his thoughts. His aim was to discover what seems to be missing in what seems to be an overwhelming amount of information flooding over us through our television sets. From McKibben's point of view, he learned much more in twenty-four hours in the mountains than in over one thousand hours of television programming.

Suggestion for Reading

- Keep in mind that this excerpt begins with a long catalogue of the kinds of "information" McKibben found in his many hours of viewing. Not until the second half of this excerpt does McKibben begin to explain what the catalogue of information is all about.

7:00 A.M.

That's Beverly, who leads Christian calisthenics on channel 116, Family Net. "If you used someone else's lip balm, I could see that. But not your own." *So much happens* between seven and eight in the morning on the 93 stations of the Fairfax, Virginia, cable system, until recently the largest in the world. On *Good Morning America,* Joel, the movie critic, says, "I learned something about England. For sore throats, the actors of Shakespeare's time used to take a live frog and lower the frog by its foot into their mouths. They figured that would keep the juices going. That's where the expression 'a frog in your throat' comes from." Since seaweed grows "in the nutrient-rich ocean", it comes as no surprise to anyone in the Annushka cosmetics organization that it attacks and destroys cellulite. An Amtrak train has gone off the rails in Iowa, according to CNN, and American companies will now be allowed to sell laptop computers in Eastern Europe. Kevin Johnson of the Phoenix Suns, so racked with the flu he had to be fed intravenously, nonetheless tallied 29 points and 12 assists in last night's game. Meanwhile, a robot surgeon has successfully replaced a dog's arthritic hip with an artificial joint. On the Fox affiliate, a cartoon Mr. Wilson is *sure* that's Dennis (the Menace) in the gorilla suit, so he uses a pair of pliers on the snout; entertainingly, however, it's an actual gorilla escaped from the zoo. The Infiniti Q-45 goes 0 to 60 in 6.9 seconds—"'Wow' is an involuntary response of pure pleasure." Type A personalities are five times as likely to have a *second* heart attack, according to Otto Wahl, the psychiatry professor at George Mason University. Following vertical roasting on the Spanik Vertical Roaster, a chicken can be—is—carved with a carrot. In Czechoslovakia, Ambassador Rita Klimova tells C-SPAN, the newly emerging democracy has spawned dozens of political parties, including one for beer drinkers. Sesame Street is brought to you this morning by L, S, and 6. Only 11 percent of Americans feel the penny should be banned. Mr. Wizard is ripping apart fireworks to get at the chemicals inside. "Finally one of my favorites—strontium chloride," he exults. In Japan an exchange has opened to trade memberships in golf clubs as if they were stocks—they are already accepted as collateral by banks. Margie Grant now uses Dove soap: "I had this revelation. It's about time for me to start paying more attention to my skin, my face. Because you just don't realize how fast time passes." The Travel Channel provides the Lisbon forecast (high of 77) and then a documentary about Austria, a country you "may encounter on the far shores of the world, wherever humanity is striving to improve life." For instance, "airport passengers in Los Angeles may be driven to the terminal by airport buses made in Austria." The Hobel, a machine from nearby West Germany, is featured on *Breakthroughs.* It transforms food preparation from a tedious routine into an exciting event, and is top-rack-dishwasher-safe. Precision-minted pewter medallions celebrating former President Reagan are available for $10 on the Nashville Network. "Tums tastes like chalk," proclaims an ex-Tums user. On *McHale's Navy,* all leaves have been cancelled until annoying enemy pilot Washing Machine Charlie can be silenced, much to McHale's disgust. ("If he's a menace, I'm a ring-tailed goony bird," he declares.) Hans, a Dutch national, prepares a creamy Gouda sauce to drizzle over cauliflower for the A & E audience. A harrowing documentary on the Howard University station documents the British genocide of Tasmanian aboriginals, right down to the last man, whose skeleton hangs in the Oxford Museum. Richard Simmons introduces his brother, who used to weigh 205 pounds: "Here I was only 42 and I felt 52, maybe 62." There's terrible flooding in Texas—on the *Today* show, a woman is plucked off the roof of her submerged car by a helicopter. Richard Nixon tells Bryant Gumbel that while it's true his resignation from the presidency may continue to cloud his record, "the main point is to live life to the hilt, all the time you possibly can, and to continue to give it your best shot to the end." Owning a firearm is a deeply personal decision, says a young woman in a checkered suit appearing on behalf of the NRA. "Whistle at me, will you, you shirttail cousin to a piccolo!" declares Wally Gator, "the swinging navigator in the swamp." A preacher is explaining something on the Inspirational Network—"As long as you're holding on to cash, you can't do anything with it. And if God tries to give you more, what happens?" He demonstrates—the bills bounce off your closed fist and fall to the floor. On the CBS morning news a "controversial Milwaukee alderman" says that unless a $100 million minority jobs program is created soon, "revolutionary violence will be committed against the city of Milwaukee." Newly released hostage Frank Reed declares from his hospital balcony that he is looking forward to a three pound Maine lobster. A man named Delvin Miller has been harness racing for eight decades, not including a stretch in World War I where he trained mules to deliver medicine in Burma for General "Vinegar Joe" Stilwell. The members of singing group Wilson Phillips remark that people tell them their name makes them sound like a law firm or a type of screwdriver. Fairfax County residents are encouraged to burlap-band their trees for gypsy-moth detection and control. "The reason I'll always make a big deal about three-quarter sleeves is that you always used to have to push up your sleeves," says an announcer on the J.C. Penney Channel. Hamstrings work in opposition to quadriceps, according to an exercise instructor on the Lifetime Channel, who adds "the adductor muscles are too tight in most of the population." More CEOs of Fortune 500 companies were born under Taurus than any other sign; also, age-based sizing for children's clothing is out-of-date because children are larger than they were when the sizing was devised. A National Family Opinion Research survey discussed on Channel 34 found that most consumers "aren't shy about testing out beds in retail showrooms." On MTV, Bruce Dickinson of Iron Maiden describes his new solo album, which has songs about how there are "all those people at the cocktail party with their little masks on, and all the businessmen in their suits and ties and they're just stabbing each other in the back all the time." (Adds Dickinson, "We've got a real rip-your-head-off direction in Maiden, and we're very proud of that direction. But with the solo stuff I can do stuff that's a little more varied.") Research from the University of Wisconsin indicates that hamburger may contain certain substances that inhibit skin cancer. Congressman Donald (Bux) Lukens, who was convicted of having sex with a 16 year-old, said he had made a "dumb mistake" but that he would run for re-election anyway.

By Now It's Nearly Eight

We believe that we live in the "age of information", that there has been an information "revolution." While in a certain narrow sense this is the case, in many important ways just the opposite is true. We also live at a moment of deep ignorance, when vital knowledge that humans have always possessed about who we are and where we live seems beyond our reach. An unenlightenment. An age of missing information.

This account of that age takes the form of an experiment—a contrast between two days. One day, May 3, 1990, lasted well more than a thousand hours—I collected on videotape nearly every minute of television that came across the enormous Fairfax cable system from one morning to the next, and then I watched it all. The other day, later that summer, lasted the conventional 24 hours. A mile from my house, camped on a mountaintop by a small pond, I awoke, took a day hike up a neighboring peak, returned to the pond for a swim, made supper, and watched the stars till I fell asleep.

If climbing the mountain was easy, assembling a video record of May 3, 1990, was not. No machine exists that can tape nearly a hundred channels simultaneously; instead, you need a hundred people with videocassette recorders who will simultaneously do you a favor. With their help I compiled what I think is a unique snapshot of American culture—a sort of video Doomsday that for 24 hours captures the images and voices that normally vanish like birdcalls on the breeze. For even in the age of the VCR, the invisible ink effect of television is amazing. One day last year, for instance, a reporter for *The New York Times* needed to find out how the local ABC affiliate had covered a story the previous night. He failed, reporting only that a spokesman "could not release what was said on Sunday night's newscast without the permission of William Applegate, the news director, and Mr. Applegate did not respond to repeated requests left with his secretary for a transcript." In other words, the most powerful newspaper in the world could not get its hands on a newscast watched by millions only hours before. So I was pleased with my archive of tape, even if there were hours blanked out here and there, and MTV was nothing but snow so I had to retape it and a few others a couple of days later, and several hours of CBS were in black and white.

I chose Fairfax solely because of the astounding size of the system, which in 1990 was roughly 40 percent larger than its nearest competitor. There were five Christian channels, four shopping channels, two country music video channels, even a channel that broadcasts all the arrival and departure information off the Dulles and National airport screens. Its *Cable Guide* lists nearly 1,000 movies each month; in May 1990 they ranged from *About Last Night* (1986, romantic comedy. A young man and woman find themselves confused, frustrated, enthralled) to *Zombie* (1964, horror. Friends vacationing on a remote island find it inhabited by disfigured ghouls), with everything in between from *Slumber Party Massacre II* to *The Son of Hercules Versus Medusa* to *It Happened One Night* to *Bonzo Goes to College* to *Sagebrush Law* to *Shaft* (and *Shaft in Africa*) to *Watchers* (1988, science fiction. A dog, the subject of experiments in fostering superintelligence, escapes from a CIA compound). For those who want *more,* a six-channel pay-per-view setup offers first-run films—on May 3: *Lethal Weapon 2; Honey, I Shrunk the Kids; Welcome Home; Field of Dreams; Alienator* ("She's programmed to kill anything in her path"); and *Enraptured.* Two comedy channels, nine public-access and government channels, a national sports channel and a local one, two weather channels, even a unique "four-in-one" channel that splits your screen into quarters and lets you watch the three networks and PBS simultaneously. Before the '90s are out, technology could permit 600 channels per set, but even with a 100 stations you can watch virtually every national TV program aired in America on Fairfax Cable. On a single day you can hear about virtually every topic on earth.

Two thirds of Americans tell researchers they get "most of their information" about the world from television, and the other statistics are so familiar we hardly notice them—more American homes have TVs than plumbing and they're on an average of seven hours a day; children spend more time watching TV than doing anything else save sleeping; on weekday evenings in the winter, half the American population is sitting in front of television; as many as 12 percent of adults (that is, one in eight) feel they are physically addicted to the set, watching an average of 56 hours a week; and so on. The industry works hard to make this absorption seem glamorous: the Fairfax system runs an around-the-clock Cable Welcome Channel for instance, which tells viewers how to operate their systems ("If you can't get a picture on your TV, make sure it is plugged in"), but mainly congratulates them endlessly on "being part of a complete communications system that puts the whole world at your fingertips, from the far reaches of outer space to the heart of Fairfax." Outer space! Satellites! Fiber optics! Data! The final installment of an A & E series called *The Romantic Spirit* gushes, "Computers and satellites and silicon chips signal that we are in sight of a post-Romantic Age, of a fresh start." Communications are now "almost instantaneous", a documentary on the computer age explains. "Communications are the currency we trade in, the currency of the information age."

SUGGESTIONS FOR DISCUSSION

1. What do you think McKibben is trying to say about television with that long list of bits of information that takes up the first part of this excerpt?
2. McKibben tells us that two thirds of Americans say they get most of their information from television. Where do you get most of your information? What are the problems associated with getting most information from television?
3. What point is McKibben making by contrasting his day in the Adirondacks with his hours of television viewing?

SUGGESTIONS FOR WRITING

1. Spend one morning, one afternoon, or one evening watching two to three hours of television programming and write a diary response to what you see.
2. Although two thirds of Americans say they get most of their information from television, most college students say they have no time for television. Many also say they feel cut off from world events even though they are attending college. For the next week, keep a record of where you get your information, what kind of information it is, and why it is important or not important to you. Reread McKibben and write a summary report of your week in which you compare the kinds of information you get and its usefulness to the kinds of information McKibben writes of from his experiment.
3. Thus far, the writers in this chapter have focused their attention on what is missing on television. Shapiro tells us that prime time is a waste. Gates writes that, despite changes, depictions of African Americans are still fake. Arlen demonstrates how unreal all of television advertising is. Ventura and McKibben report a kind of emptiness of meaning in television. Write an essay in which you take a position on this question of television and meaning. In your mind what should television be doing? Does it accomplish that? Why? Keep in mind what the writers in this chapter have said, but don't feel you have to agree entirely or even at all. Write your own position on what television is or can be.

John Leland

BATTLE FOR YOUR BRAIN

John Leland is a reporter and feature writer for such news magazines as *Newsweek,* where the following article first appeared in 1993. As of this writing, the MTV cartoon characters Beavis and Butt-head are, for teenagers and college students, two of the most popular commentators on contemporary taste on television today. Their popularity has taken the place of the attention paid to such Fox cable shows as *The Simpsons* and *Married . . . with Children,* programs that often sneer at middle-class American values and at television taboos. Beavis and Butt–head seem to recognize no taboos. In his examination of the show's popularity, Leland attempts to explain how *Beavis and Butt-head* and characters like them reflect the temperament of what has come to be called Generation X.

Suggestion for Reading

- If you haven't seen an episode of *Beavis and Butt-head,* try watching one before you read this article, or talk to a friend or classmate who has seen the show.

------------------◆------------------

Stupidity, served with knowing intelligence, is now TV's answer to real smarts. And no one serves it like the crude and rude Beavis and Butt-head.

I t is television at its most redeeming. A whale swims gracefully across the screen as the narrator mourns its imminent destruction. Watching in their living room, two boys, about 14, are visibly moved. Their eyes widen, their nostrils twitch uncomfortably. One boy's lips stiffen around his wire braces. The only hope, the narrator says, "is that perhaps the young people of today will grow up more caring, more understanding, more sensitive to the very special needs of the creatures of the earth." It is a rich moment, ripe with television's power to make remote events movingly immediate. The boys can watch idly no longer. Finally one turns to the other and asks, "Uh, did you fart?"

The boys are Beavis and Butt-head, two animated miscreants whose adventures at the low end of the food chain are currently the most popular program on MTV. Caught in the ungainly nadir of adolescence, they are not nice boys. They torture animals, they harass girls and sniff paint thinner. They like to burn things. They have a really insidious laugh: *huh-huh huh-huh.* They are the spiritual descendants of the semi-sentient teens from "Wayne's World" and "Bill and Ted's Excellent Adventure," only dumber and meaner. The downward spiral of the living white male surely ends here: in a little pimple named Butt-head whose idea of an idea is, "Hey, Beavis, let's go over to Stuart's house and light one in his cat's butt."

For a generation reminded hourly of its diminished prospects, these losers have proven remarkably embraceable. "Why do I like 'Beavis and Butt-head'?" asks Warren Lutz, 26, a journalism major at San Francisco State. "You're asking me to think, dude." Created by beginner animator Mike Judge, 30, for a festival of "sick and twisted" cartoons last year, Beavis and Butt-head have become a trash phenomenon. T shirts, hats, key rings, masks, buttons, calendars, dolls are all working their way to malls: a book, a comic book, a movie, a CD and a Christmas special are in the works. David Letterman drops a Beavis and Butt-head joke almost nightly; later this fall the pair will become a semiregular feature on his program. As their notoriety reached Fort Lewis College in Durango, Colo., archeology students have started calling Jim Judge, Mike's father, Dr. Butt-head. "Whenever any . . . 8- to 12-year-olds find out I'm related to Beavis and Butt-head," he says, "I become a god to them." Beavis and Butt-head, whose world divides into "things that suck" and "things that are cool," are clearly the new morons in town.

They are also part of a much wider TV phenomenon, one that drives not just stupid laughs but the front-page battle now being waged for control of Paramount Pictures. It is the battle to play road hog on the Information Highway. As cable technology continues to expand our range of viewing options, the old boundaries of propriety and decency no longer apply. Beavis and Butt-head join a growing crowd of characters who have found a magic formula: nothing cuts through the clutter like a slap of bracing crudity. Nothing stops a channel surfer like the word "sucks."

Stupidity, served with a knowing intelligence, has become the next best thing to smarts. Letterman's signature "Stupid Pet Tricks" bit, now 11 years running, introduced a new voice to television: ironic, self-aware, profoundly interested in the ingrained dumbness of the tube. Instead of dumbing down, it made smart comedy out of the process of dumbing down—and it clicked. Barry Diller successfully built Fox into the fourth network on a shockingly *lumpen* cartoon family, the Simpsons, and an even more *lumpen* real one, the Bundys of "Married . . . With Children." Nickelodeon's cartoon "The Ren & Stimpy Show," the highest rated original series on cable, follows the scatological adventures of a Chihuahua and a cat, sometimes not getting much farther than the litter box. The network's new contender, "Rocko's Modern World," wallows down a similarly inspired low road. Its first episode, in which a home-shopping channel called "Lobot-o-shop" pitched items like tapeworm farms for kids, beat "Ren & Stimpy" in the ratings. And the widely loved and hated radio host Howard Stern has taken his act to E! Entertainment Television. "There's a purity to [this] kind of ignorance," says "Beavis and Butt-head" writer David Felton, at 53 MTV's oldest staff member. "Going back to the basic point where thinking begins. And staying there."

But they are not just any losers, this lineage of losers. They are specifically *our* losers, totems of an age of decline and nonachievement. One in five people who graduated from college between 1984 and 1990 holds a job that doesn't require a college education. If this is not hard economic reality for a whole generation, it is psychological reality. Loser television has the sense to play along; it taps the anxiety in the culture and plays it back for laughs. Homer Simpson works in a nuclear power plant. Al Bundy sells shoes. Beavis and Butt-head work at Burger World and can't even visualize the good life. In one episode, as an act of community service, they get jobs in a hospital. Sucking on IV bags, planning to steal a cardiac patient's motorized cart, they agree: "It doesn't get any better than this, dude."

The shows also all share a common language. When "Beavis and Butt-head" producer John Andrews, 39, needed to put together a writing staff, he first called Letterman head writer Rob Burnett for suggestions. "Most of this stuff is done by overeducated guys who grew up reading Mad magazine, National Lampoon, and watching 'Animal House' and 'Saturday Night Live'," says Matt Groening, creator of the Simpsons. "Scripts are based on what comes out of the collective memory of the writers, which is mostly memories of sitting in front of a TV set growing up." More than just throwbacks to the intelligently dumb television of the Three Stooges and Ernie Kovacs, the current shows are broad immersions in pop culture, satirical and multitiered. They address an audience that can view reruns of "Gilligan's Island" and "I Dream of Jeannie" half as camp, half as the fabric of shared experience. "The smarter you are, the more you see single events on different levels simultaneously," says Fernanda Moore, 25, who likes "The Simpsons," "Ren & Stimpy" and "Beavis and

Butt-head." A doctoral candidate at Stanford, Moore is the daughter we all crave and perhaps fear. "Dumb people I know," she says, "aren't self-referential."

Of course, this is only one way to watch the shows. Lars Ulrich, drummer in the band Metallica, was delighted one day to spot Beavis wearing a Metallica T shirt. Yet he was also alarmed. "I would have to say—as little as I want to say it—that I think there are people like that. I'm not sure dumb is the right word. I would go more in the direction of the word ignorant." Either way, as the channels open up, the ship of fools is now sailing at full capacity.

At MTV's offices in New York last week, the ship was running through some rough waters. MTV from the inside is a Marshall McLuhan rec room, a place where precociously creative young people invent cool ways to frame ugly heavy-metal videos. In the production area of "Beavis and Butt-head," these young people had a problem. "I don't know," said the show's creator, Mike Judge, in a voice hauntingly close to Butt-head's (Judge does the voices for most of the characters). The staff was watching an unfinished episode in which Bill Clinton visits Beavis and Butt-head's high school, and something just didn't feel real. As MTV political reporter Tabitha Soren introduced the president to the assembly on screen, Judge's face just lost its air. "Do you really think she could hear [Butt-head] fart from across the gym?" he asked. It was a pressing question; the show was set to air in less than a week. The staff was hushed. Finally someone offered, "If it was a big one she could." Judge considered. "No way."

The fast success of the show, along with the rapid production pace, has been a shock to Judge. Since he moved to New York from Dallas in February, he says, he hasn't met anyone except the people he works with. His office at MTV is spare, the walls empty except for a few pictures of Beavis and Butt-head and a snapshot of his daughter, Julia, almost 2. In his locker is a stuffed Barney dinosaur, a bottle of Jack Daniel's and a Gap jacket. "You know what's weird?" he says, with a gentle Southwestern accent. "Every now and then I'll say, 'Well, that's pretty cool,' and I can't tell if that's something I would have said before or if I'm doing Butt-head." In a file on his desk, he keeps a drawing of a black Beavis and Butt-head, renamed Rufus and Tyrone. At the moment he has no plans for them. For all their anti-P.C. offensiveness, Beavis and Butt-head have yet to cross the line into race humor. "Actually," says Kimson Albert, 22, one of four African-American artists on the show's staff, "the creator and producer are the most P.C. people."

Judge grew up in Albuquerque, N.M., by his own description "just the most awkward, miserable kid around." He played trumpet in the area youth symphony and competed on the swim team and made honor roll at St. Pius X High School. For kicks, he and his friends used to set fires, just to see how many they could keep going at once and still be able to stomp them out. Three years ago, after working at a couple of unhappy engineering jobs, Judge bought himself a $200 animation kit. His first short, "Office Space," aired on last month's season première of "Saturday Night Live." His third, completed in January 1992, introduced the characters Beavis and Butt-head. It was about torturing animals. He called it "Frog Baseball."

"I was a total animal lover," he says. "When I did the storyboard, I didn't want people to see what I was working on. I thought, 'I don't want to show this to anybody; why am I doing this?'" Even now Judge looks back on "Frog Baseball" with mixed feelings: "I never thought that's what I'd be known for."

Gwen Lipsky, 34, is MTV's vice president of research and planning. When she tested "Beavis and Butt-head" before a target audience last October, she noticed something peculiar. "The focus group was both riveted and hysterical from the moment they saw it. After the tape was over, they kept asking to see it again. Then, after they had seen it again, several people offered to buy it from me." Almost without exception, she says, the group members said Beavis and Butt-head reminded them of people they knew. "Interestingly, the people in the focus group who seem the most like Beavis and Butt-head themselves never acknowledge that the characters are them."

Susan Smith-Pinelo, 24, knows them well. A graduate of Oberlin, she is an artist working at what "Generation X" writer Douglas Coupland calls a McJob, as a receptionist at the Sierra Legal Defense Fund. "People laugh at Beavis and Butt-head, Wayne and Garth," she says. "Our generation can relate to this lunatic fringe of teenagers who have fallen out of society, live in a world of TV . . . It's kind of sick, but we like to laugh at them and say, 'I'm not a loser'."

Dick Zimmermann is not a twentysomething and is not amused. A retired broadcasting executive from Larkspur, Calif., Zimmermann, 44, won a state lottery worth nearly $10 million in 1988. Early last summer, while channel surfing, he caught Beavis and Butt-head in the infamous cat episode—touchy ground for anyone involved with the show. Even today it makes Judge uneasy. "They never did this thing with the cat." he says, defensively. "They just made a joke about it: what if you put a firecracker in Stuart's cat's butt." Five days after the show ran, when a cat was found killed by a firecracker in nearby Santa Cruz, Zimmermann put up a $5,000 reward and went to the press. The cause of death, he told Larkspur's Independent Journal in a front-page story, was "Beavis and Butt-head." Opening a hot line, he mounted a one-man campaign against the program. "I admit that shows like 'Cops' are obviously very violent," he told NEWSWEEK, "but at least there is the element of good triumphing over evil. The thing about 'Beavis and Butt-head' that caught my eye was the total lack of redeemability. [They] engage in arson, petty theft, shoplifting, auto theft, credit-card fraud, cruelty to animals and insects—not to mention their attitude toward women."

The infamous cat episode will never air again. Three other episodes are also out of circulation, and the show has softened considerably this season. All involved are particularly sensitive because the show runs in family hours: at 7 and 11 p.m. weekdays, and in the afternoon on Saturdays. "The sniffing-paint-thinner we probably shouldn't have done," Judge concedes. "But I'm new to this. I thought of this show as going on at 11, no one's ever going to see it. I think it should run once at 11. We have toned it down."

Gwen Lipsky contends that young kids don't watch the show, that 90 percent of the audience is over 12. But part of the show's appeal is that, yes, these are dangerous, irresponsible messages. "They'll do stuff that we want to do but don't have the guts to do," says Alex Chriss, 14, who dropped his karate classes to watch "Beavis and Butt-head." "On one episode they stole a monster truck and ran over a hippie guy singing save-the-earth songs. We go around mimicking them—not what they say, but how they say it."

Of course, such mimicry is not always harmless, and it is here that we probably need some parental caution. Beavis and Butt-head don't have it; confronted with an image of a nuclear family at the table, Butt-head asks, "Why's that guy eating dinner with those old people?" But other children do. Bill Clinton likes to watch "American

Gladiators" with Chelsea; they enjoy the camp value together. And there are lessons to be learned, even from television that prides itself on not doling out lessons. "The whole point of [Beavis and Butt-head] is that they don't grow up," says Lisa Bourgeault, an eighth grader at Marblehead Middle School in Marblehead, Mass. "That's what's hip and cool. But *we* will."

Let's hope so. As our former vice president once put it, with an eloquence few scripted TV characters could match, "What a waste it is to lose one's mind, or not to have a mind." To which, like Beavis and Butt-head, we can only reply, "Huh-huh. Huh-huh. Cool."

With Carey Monserrate and Danzy Senna in New York, Carl Holcombe in San Francisco, Tim Pryor and Mark Miller in Los Angeles and bureau reports

SUGGESTIONS FOR DISCUSSION

1. From what you have read and what you have seen or heard of the show, how would you describe the characters Beavis and Butt-head?
2. Why do you suppose this program has become so popular with young viewers? Is there a real subculture message here? If so, what is it?
3. Toward the end of his article, Leland mentions Dick Zimmermann's attempt to get *Beavis and Butt-head* off the air. Besides the obvious concern that some of what passes for humor on this show might give very young viewers new ideas for destructive behavior, what might be other reasons that some viewers would want the show off the air? Do you agree with MTV's decision to tone down the show rather than cancel? What might toning down the show do for its original appeal?

SUGGESTIONS FOR WRITING

1. After reading this article, write a letter to an adult in your life who you know would not approve of this show or one like it. In your letter explain what you think the appeal is of such a show. If you don't like the show or the idea of the show yourself, you can still (as does Leland) attempt to understand what it is that seems to appeal to young people about it.
2. When it first appeared on the air, *The Simpsons* was heralded as the great counterculture cartoon, a "family" show with the not-so-perfect family. According to some television critics, however, *The Simpsons* is just as much a family show as *Leave it to Beaver* was in its time. That would suggest that even shows that attempt to offer something contrary to the norm end up telling the same stories and passing on the same values as mainstream offerings. Write an essay in which you explain why this seems to happen on television. You might consider thinking about programming that breaks patterns, such as Beavis and Butt-head, as well as programs that easily conform to those patterns.
3. In a July 30, 1990, article for *Newsweek*, columnist George Will wrote that America was sliding into the sewer with its taste in violent rap lyrics and the general degradation of popular taste. If we can judge by that column, we might guess that *Beavis and Butt-head* might not appeal to someone like George Will, who would like us to upgrade our standards. In his column, Will said, "Certainty: the coarsening of a community, the desensitizing of a society will have behavioral consequences." Considering what you have read or watched of this program and the programming that is currently popular with young people today, write a response to Will's charge that the coarsening of standards has behavioral consequences.

Lucy Honig

ENGLISH AS A SECOND LANGUAGE

Novelist and short story writer Lucy Honig lives in upstate New York where she teaches English as a Second Language (ESL), directs a local human rights commission, and writes fiction. According to Honig, the story reprinted below came from her experience teaching ESL in New York. Her students, she writes, "were struggling to live, struggling to be understood, and grasping for insider tips on how to fit in in America." "English as a Second Language" is the story of a Guatemalan woman and her attempts to understand American culture through its language and its media.

Suggestion for Reading

- As Maria moves through her day, her thoughts are often broken up by memories of escaping from Guatemala. It may help you to trace the events of both stories if you mark off those passages which are clearly memories. When you have finished reading and marking, go back through the story and notice how those memories help illuminate Maria's confusion about what she sees and experiences in her new home.

I nside Room 824, Maria parked the vacuum cleaner, fastened all the locks and the safety chain and kicked off her shoes. Carefully she lay a stack of fluffy towels on the bathroom vanity. She turned the air conditioning up high and the lights down low. Then she hoisted up the skirt of her uniform and settled all the way back on the king-sized bed with her legs straight out in front of her. Her feet and ankles were swollen. She wriggled her toes. She threw her arms out in each direction and still her hands did not come near the edges of the bed. From here she could see, out the picture window, the puffs of green treetops in Central Park, the tiny people circling along the paths below. She tore open a small foil bag of cocktail peanuts and ate them very slowly, turning each one over separately with her tongue until the salt dissolved. She snapped on the TV with the remote control and flipped channels.

The big mouth game show host was kissing and hugging a woman playing on the left-hand team. Her husband and children were right there with her, and *still* he encircled her with his arms. Then he sidled up to the daughter, a girl younger than her own Giuliette, and *hugged* her and kept *holding* her, asking questions. None of his business, if this girl had a boyfriend back in Saginaw!

"Mama, you just don't understand." That's what Jorge always said when she watched TV at home. He and his teenaged friends would sit around in their torn blue-jeans dropping potato chips between the cushions of her couch and laughing, writhing with laughter while she sat like a stone.

Now the team on the right were hugging each other, squealing, jumping up and down. They'd just won a whole new kitchen—refrigerator, dishwasher, clothes washer, microwave, *everything!* Maria could win a whole new kitchen too, someday. You just spun a wheel, picked some words. She could do that.

She saw herself on TV with Carmen and Giuliette and Jorge. Her handsome children were so quick to press the buzzers the other team never had a chance to answer first. And they got every single answer right. Her children shrieked and clapped and jumped up and down each time the board lit up. They kissed and hugged that man whenever they won a prize. That man put his hands on her beautiful young daughters. That man pinched and kissed *her*, an old woman, in front of the whole world! Imagine seeing *this* back home! Maria frowned, chewing on the foil wrapper. There was nobody left at home in Guatemala, nobody to care if a strange man squeezed her wrinkled flesh on the TV.

"Forget it, Mama. They don't let poor people on these programs," Jorge said one day.

"But poor people need the money, they can win it here!"

Jorge sighed impatiently. "They don't give it away because you *need* it!"

It was true, she had never seen a woman with her kids say on a show: My husband's dead. Jorge knew. They made sure before they invited you that you were the right kind of people and you said the right things. Where would she put a new kitchen in her cramped apartment anyway? No hookups for a washer, no space for a two-door refrigerator . . .

She slid sideways off the bed, carefully smoothed out the quilted spread, and squeezed her feet into her shoes. Back out in the hall she counted the bath towels in her cart to see if there were enough for the next wing. Then she wheeled the cart down the long corridor, silent on the deep blue rug.

• • •

Maria pulled the new pink dress on over her head, eased her arms into the sleeves, then let the skirt slide into place. In the mirror she saw a small dark protrusion from a large pink flower. She struggled to zip up in back, then she fixed the neck, attaching the white collar she had crocheted. She pinned the rhinestone brooch on next. Shaking the pantyhose out of the package, she remembered the phrase: the cow before the horse, wasn't that it? She should have put these on first. Well, so what. She rolled down the left leg of the nylons, stuck her big toe in, and drew the sheer fabric around her foot, unrolling it up past her knee. Then she did the right foot, careful not to catch the hose on the small flap of scar.

• • •

The right foot bled badly when she ran over the broken glass, over what had been the only window of the house. It had shattered from gunshots across the dirt yard. The chickens dashed around frantically, squawking, trying to fly, spraying brown feathers into the air. When she had seen Pedro's head turn to blood and the two oldest boys dragged away, she swallowed every word, every cry, and ran with the two girls. The fragments of glass stayed in her foot for all the days of hiding. They ran and ran and ran and somehow Jorge caught up and they were found by their own side and smuggled out. And still she was silent, until the nurse at the border went after the glass and drained the mess inside her foot. Then she had sobbed and screamed, "Aaiiiee!"

• • •

"Mama, stop thinking and get ready," said Carmen.

"It is too short, your skirt," Maria said in Spanish. "What will they say?"

Carmen laughed. "It's what they all wear, except for you old ladies."

"Not to work! Not to school!"

"Yes, to work, to school! And Mama, you are going for an award for your English, for all you've learned, so please speak English!"

Maria squeezed into the pink high heels and held each foot out, one by one, so she could admire the beautiful slim arch of her own instep, like the feet of the American ladies on Fifth Avenue. Carmen laughed when she saw her mother take the first faltering steps, and Maria laughed too. How much she had already practiced in secret, and still it was so hard! She teetered on them back and forth from the kitchen to the bedroom, trying to feel steady, until Carmen finally sighed and said, "Mama, quick now or you'll be late!"

• • •

She didn't know if it was a good omen or a bad one, the two Indian women on the subway. They could have been sitting on the dusty ground at the market in San _____, selling corn or clay pots, with the bright-colored striped shawls and full skirts, the black hair pulled into two braids down each back, the deeply furrowed square faces set in those impassive expressions, seeing everything, seeing nothing. They were exactly as they must have been back home, but she was seeing them *here*, on the downtown IRT from the Bronx, surrounded by businessmen in suits, kids with big radio boxes, girls in skin-tight jeans and dark purple lipstick. Above them, advertisements for family planning and TWA. They were like stone-age men sitting on the train in loincloths made from animal skins, so out of place, out of time. Yet timeless. Maria thought, they are timeless guardian spirits, here to accompany me to my honors. Did anyone else see them? As strange as they were, nobody looked. Maria's heart pounded faster. The boys with the radios were standing right over them and never saw them. They were invisible to everyone but her: Maria was utterly convinced of it. The spirit world had come back to life, here on the number 4 train! It was a miracle!

"Mama, look, you see the grandmothers?" said Carmen.

"Of course I see them," Maria replied, trying to hide the disappointment in her voice. So Carmen saw them too. They were not invisible. Carmen rolled her eyes and smirked derisively as she nodded in their direction, but before she could put her derision into words, Maria became stern. "Have respect," she said. "They are the same as your father's people." Carmen's face sobered at once.

• • •

She panicked when they got to the big school by the river. "Like the United Nations," she said, seeing so much glass and brick, an endless esplanade of concrete.

"It's only a college, Mama. People learn English here, too. And more, like nursing, electronics. This is where Anna's brother came for computers."

"Las Naciones Unidas," Maria repeated, and when the guard stopped them to ask where they were going, she answered in Spanish: to the literacy award ceremony.

"*English,* Mama!" whispered Carmen.

But the guard also spoke in Spanish: take the escalator to the third floor.

"See, he knows," Maria retorted.

"That's not the point," murmured Carmen, taking her mother by the hand.

• • •

Every inch of the enormous room was packed with people. She clung to Carmen and stood by the door paralyzed until Cheryl, her teacher, pushed her way to them and greeted Maria with a kiss. Then she led Maria back through the press of people to the small group of award winners from other programs. Maria smiled shakily and nodded hello.

"They're all here now!" Cheryl called out. A photographer rushed over and began to move the students closer together for a picture.

"Hey Bernie, wait for the Mayor!" someone shouted to him. He spun around, called out some words Maria did not understand, and without even turning back to them, he disappeared. But they stayed there, huddled close, not knowing if they could move. The Chinese man kept smiling, the tall black man stayed slightly crouched, the Vietnamese woman squinted, confused, her glasses still hidden in her fist. Maria saw all the cameras along the sides of the crowd, and the lights, and the people from television with video machines, and more lights. Her stomach began to jump up and down. Would she be on television, in the newspapers? Still smiling, holding his pose, the Chinese man next to her asked, "Are you nervous?"

"Oh yes," she said. She tried to remember the expression Cheryl had taught them. "I have worms in my stomach," she said.

• • •

He was a much bigger man than she had imagined from seeing him on TV. His face was bright red as they ushered him into the room and quickly through the crowd, just as it was his turn to take the podium. He said hello to the other speakers and called them by their first names. The crowd drew closer to the little stage, the people standing farthest in the back pushed in. Maria tried hard to listen to the Mayor's words. "Great occasion . . . pride of our city . . . ever since I created the program . . . people who have worked so hard . . . overcoming hardship . . . come so far." Was that them? Was he talking about them already? Why were the people out there all starting to laugh? She strained to understand, but still caught only fragments of his words. "My mother used to say . . . and I said, Look, Mama . . . " He was talking about *his* mother now; he called her Mama, just like Maria's kids called *her.* But everyone laughed so hard. At his mother? She forced herself to smile; up front, near the podium, everyone could see her. She should seem to pay attention and understand. Looking out into the crowd she felt dizzy. She tried to find Carmen among all the pretty young women with big eyes and dark hair. There she was! Carmen's eyes met Maria's; Carmen waved. Maria beamed out at her. For a moment she felt like she belonged there, in this crowd. Everyone was smiling, everyone was so happy while the Mayor of New York stood at the podium telling jokes. How happy Maria felt too!

• • •

"Maria Perez grew up in the countryside of Guatemala, the oldest daughter in a family of 19 children," read the Mayor as Maria stood quaking by his side. She noticed he made a slight wheezing noise when he breathed between words. She saw the hairs in his nostrils, black and white and wiry. He paused. "Nineteen children!" he exclaimed, looking at the audience. A small gasp was passed along through the crowd. Then the Mayor looked back at the sheet of paper before him. "Maria never had a chance to learn to read and write, and she was already the mother of five children of her own when she fled Guatemala in 1980 and made her way to New York for a new start."

It was her own story, but Maria had a hard time following. She had to stand next to him while he read it, and her feet had started to hurt, crammed into the new shoes. She shifted her weight from one foot to the other.

"At the age of 45, while working as a chambermaid and sending her children through school, Maria herself started school for the first time. In night courses she learned to read and write in her native Spanish. Later, as she was pursuing her G.E.D. in Spanish, she began studying English as a Second Language. This meant Maria was going to school five nights a week! Still she worked as many as 60 hours cleaning rooms at the Plaza Hotel.

"Maria's ESL teacher, Cheryl Sands, says—and I quote—'Maria works harder than any student I have ever had. She is an inspiration to her classmates. Not only has she learned to read and write in her new language, but she initiated an oral history project in which she taped and transcribed interviews with other students, who have told their stories from around the world.' Maria was also one of the first in New York to apply for amnesty under the 1986 Immigration Act. Meanwhile, she has passed her enthusiasm for education to her children: her son is now a junior in high school, her youngest daughter attends the State University, and her oldest daughter, who we are proud to have with us today, is in her second year of law school on a scholarship."

• • •

Two older sons were dragged through the dirt, chickens squawking in mad confusion, feathers flying. She heard more gunshots in the distance, screams, chickens squawking. She heard, she ran. Maria looked down at her bleeding feet. Wedged tightly into the pink high heels, they throbbed.

• • •

The Mayor turned toward her. "Maria, I think it's wonderful that you have taken the trouble to preserve the folklore of students from so many countries." He paused. Was she supposed to say something? Her heart stopped beating. What was folklore? What was preserved? She smiled up at him, hoping that was all she needed to do.

"Maria, tell us now, if you can, what was one of the stories you collected in your project?"

This was definitely a question, meant to be answered. Maria tried to smile again. She strained on tiptoes to reach the microphone, pinching her toes even more tightly in her shoes. "Okay," she said, setting off a high-pitched ringing from the microphone.

The Mayor said, "Stand back," and tugged at her collar. She quickly stepped away from the microphone.

"Okay," she said again, and this time there was no shrill sound. "One of my stories, from Guatemala. You want to hear?"

The Mayor put his arm around her shoulder and squeezed hard. Her first impulse was to wriggle away, but he held tight. "Isn't she wonderful?" he asked the audience. There was a low ripple of applause. "Yes, we want to hear!"

She turned and looked up at his face. Perspiration was shining on his forehead and she could see by the bright red bulge of his neck that his collar was too tight. "In my village in Guatemala," she began, "the mayor did not go along—get along—with the government so good."

"Hey, Maria," said the Mayor, "I know exactly how he felt!" The people in the audience laughed. Maria waited until they were quiet again.

"One day our mayor met with the people in the village. Like you meet people here. A big crowd in the square."

"The people liked him, your mayor?"

"Oh, yes," said Maria. "Very much. He was very good. He tried for more roads, more doctors, new farms. He cared very much about his people."

The Mayor shook his head up and down. "Of course," he said, and again the audience laughed.

Maria said, "The next day after the meeting, the meeting in the square with all the people, soldiers come and shoot him dead."

For a second there was total silence. Maria realized she had not used the past tense and felt a deep, horrible stab of shame for herself, shame for her teacher. She was a disgrace! But she did not have more than a second of this horror before the whole audience began to laugh. What was happening? They couldn't be laughing at her bad verbs? They couldn't be laughing at her dead mayor! They laughed louder and louder and suddenly flashbulbs were going off around her, the TV cameras swung in close, too close, and the Mayor was grabbing her by the shoulders again, holding her tight, posing for one camera after another as the audience burst into wild applause. But she hadn't even finished! Why were they laughing?

"What timing, huh?" said the Mayor over the uproar. "What d'ya think, the Republicans put her here, or maybe the Board of Estimate?" Everyone laughed even louder and he still clung to her and cameras still moved in close, lights kept going off in her face and she could see nothing but the sharp white poof! of light over and over again. She looked for Carmen and Cheryl, but the white poof! poof! blinded her. She closed her eyes and listened to the uproar, now beginning to subside, and in her mind's eye saw chickens trying to fly, chickens fluttering around the yard littered with broken glass.

He squeezed her shoulders again and leaned into the microphone. "There are ways to get rid of mayors, and ways to get rid of mayors, huh Maria?"

The surge of laughter rose once more, reached a crescendo, and then began to subside again. "But wait," said the Mayor. The cameramen stepped back a bit, poising themselves for something new.

"I want to know just one more thing, Maria," said the Mayor, turning to face her directly again. The crowd quieted. He waited a few seconds more, then asked his question. "It says here 19 children. What was it like growing up in a house with 19 children? How many *bathrooms* did you have?"

Her stomach dropped and twisted as the mayor put his hand firmly on the back of her neck and pushed her toward the microphone again. It was absolutely quiet now in the huge room. Everyone was waiting for her to speak. She cleared her throat and made the microphone do the shrill hum. Startled, she jumped back. Then there was silence. She took a big, trembling breath.

"We had no bathrooms there, Mister Mayor," she said. "Only the outdoors."

The clapping started immediately, then the flashbulbs burning up in her face. The Mayor turned to her, put a hand on each of her shoulders, bent lower and kissed her! Kissed her on the cheek!

"Isn't she terrific?" he asked the audience, his hand on the back of her neck again, drawing her closer to him. The audience clapped louder, faster. "Isn't she just the greatest?"

She tried to smile and open her eyes, but the lights were still going off—poof! poof!—and the noise was deafening.

• • •

"Mama, look, your eyes were closed *there,* too," chided Jorge, sitting on the floor in front of the television set.

Maria had watched the camera move from the announcer at the studio desk to her own stout form in bright pink, standing by the Mayor.

"In my village in Guatemala," she heard herself say, and the camera showed her wrinkled face close up, eyes open now but looking nowhere. Then the mayor's face filled the screen, his forehead glistening, and then suddenly all the people in the audience, looking ahead, enrapt, took his place. Then there was her wrinkled face again, talking without a smile. ". . . soldiers come and shoot him dead." Maria winced, hearing the wrong tense of her verbs. The camera shifted from her face to the Mayor. In the brief moment of shamed silence after she'd uttered those words, the Mayor drew his finger like a knife across his throat. And the audience began to laugh.

"Turn it off!" she yelled to Jorge. "Off! This minute!"

• • •

Late that night she sat alone in the unlighted room, soaking her feet in Epson salts. The glow of the television threw shadows across the wall, but the sound was off. The man called Johnny was on the screen, talking. The people in the audience and the men in the band and the movie stars sitting on the couch all had their mouths wide open in what she knew were screams of laughter while Johnny wagged his tongue. Maria heard nothing except brakes squealing below on the street and the lonely clanging of garbage cans in the alley.

She thought about her English class and remembered the pretty woman, Ling, who often fell asleep in the middle of a lesson. The other Chinese students all teased her. Everyone knew that she sewed coats in a sweatshop all day. After the night class she took the subway to the Staten Island Ferry, and after the ferry crossing she had to take a bus home. Her parents were old and sick and she did all their cooking and cleaning late at night. She struggled to keep awake in class; it seemed to take all her energy simply to smile and listen. She said very little and the teacher never forced her, but she fell further and further behind. They called her the Quiet One.

One day just before the course came to an end the Quiet One asked to speak. There was no reason, no provocation—they'd been talking informally about their summer plans—but Ling spoke with a sudden urgency. Her English was very slow. Seeing what a terrible effort it was for her, the classmates all tried to help when she searched for words.

"In my China village there was a teacher," Ling began. "Man teacher." She paused. "All children love him. He teach mathematic. He very—" She stopped and looked up toward the ceiling. Then she gestured with her fingers around her face.

"Handsome!" said Charlene, the oldest of the three Haitian sisters in the class.

Ling smiled broadly. "Handsome! Yes, he very handsome. Family very rich before. He have sister go to Hong Kong who have many, many money."

"*Much* money," said Maria.

"Much, much money," repeated Ling thoughtfully. "Teacher live in big house."

"In China? Near you?"

"Yes. Big house with much old picture." She stopped and furrowed her forehead, as if to gather words inside of it.

"Art? Paint? Pictures like that?" asked Xavier.

Ling nodded eagerly. "Yes. In big house. Most big house in village."

"But big house, money, rich like that, bad in China," said Fu Wu. "Those year, Government bad to you. How they let him do?"

"In *my* country," said Carlos, "government bad to you if you got *small* house, *no* money."

"Me too," said Maria.

"Me too," said Charlene.

The Chinese students laughed.

Ling shrugged and shook her head. "Don't know. He have big house. Money gone, but keep big house. Then I am little girl." She held her hand low to the floor.

"I *was* a little girl," Charlene said gently.

"I *was*," said Ling. "Was, was." She giggled for a moment, then seemed to spend some time in thought. "We love him. All children love—all children did loved him. He giving tea in house. He was—was—so handsome!" She giggled. All the women in the class giggled. "He very nice. He learn music, he go . . . he went to school far away."

"America?"

Ling shook her head. "Oh no, no. You know, another . . . west."

"Europa!" exclaimed Maria proudly. "Espain!"

"No, no, another."

"France!" said Patricia, Charlene's sister. "He went to school in France?"

"Yes, France," said Ling. Then she stopped again, this time for a whole minute. The others waited patiently. No one said a word. Finally she continued. "But big boys in more old school not like him. He too handsome."

"Oooh!" sang out a chorus of women. "Too handsome!"

"The boys were jealous," said Carlos.

Ling seized the word. "Jealous! Jealous! They very jealous. He handsome, he study France, he very nice to children, he give tea and cake in big house, he show picture on wall." Her torrent of words came to an end and she began to think again, visibly, her brow furrowing. "Big school boys, they . . . " She stopped.

"Jealous!" sang out the others.

"Yes," she said, shaking her head "no." "But more. More bad. Hate. They hate him."

"That's bad," said Patricia.

"Yes, very bad." Ling paused, looking at the floor. "And they heat."

"Hate."

"No, they heat."

All the class looked puzzled. Heat? Heat? They turned to Cheryl.

The teacher spoke for the first time. "Hit? Ling, do you mean hit? They hit him?" Cheryl slapped the air with her hand.

Ling nodded, her face somehow serious and smiling at the same time. "Hit many time. And also so." She scooted her feet back and forth along the floor.

"Oooh," exclaimed Charlene, frowning. "They kicked him with the feet."

"Yes," said Ling. "They kicked him with the feet and hit him with the hands, many many time they hit, they kick."

"Where this happened?" asked Xavier.

"In the school. In classroom like . . . " She gestured to mean their room.

"In the school?" asked Xavier. "But other people were they there? They say stop, no?"

"No. Little children in room. They cry, they . . . " She covered her eyes with her hand, then uncovered them. "Big boys kick and hit. No one stop. No one help."

Everyone in class fell silent. Maria remembered: they could not look at one another then. They could not look at their teacher.

Ling continued. "They break him, very hurt much place." She stopped. They all fixed their stares on Ling, they could bear looking only at her. "Many place," she said. Her face had not changed, it was still half smiling. But now there were drops coming from her eyes, a single tear down each side of her nose. Maria would never forget it. Ling's face did not move or wrinkle or frown. Her body was absolutely still. Her shoulders did not quake. Nothing in the shape or motion of her eyes or mouth changed. None of the things that Maria had always known happen when you cry happened when Ling shed tears. Just two drops rolled slowly down her two pale cheeks as she smiled.

"He very hurt. He *was* very hurt. He blood many place. Boys go away. Children cry. Teacher break and hurt. Later he in hospital. I go there visit him." She stopped, looking thoughtful. "I went there." One continuous line of wetness glistened down each cheek. "My mother, my father say don't go, but I see him. I say, 'You be better?' But he hurt. Doctors no did helped. He alone. No doctor. No nurse. No medicine. No family." She stopped. They all stared in silence for several moments.

Finally Carlos said, "Did he went home?"

Ling shook her head. "He go home but no walk." She stopped. Maria could not help watching those single lines of tears moving down the pale round face. "A year, more, no walk. Then go."

"Go where?"

"End."

Again there was a deep silence. Ling looked down, away from them, her head bent low.

"Oh, no," murmured Charlene. "He died."

Maria felt the catch in her throat, the sudden wetness of tears on her own two cheeks, and when she looked up she saw that all the other students, men and women both, were crying too.

Maria wiped her eyes. Suddenly all her limbs ached, her bones felt stiff and old. She took her feet from the basin and dried them with a towel. Then she turned off the television and went to bed.

SUGGESTIONS FOR DISCUSSION

1. At the beginning of this story, Maria is watching a game show, perhaps *Family Feud*. What bothers her about what she sees on television? What is it that, as her son tells her, she just doesn't understand?
2. Go through this story and reread the memory passages. What do those memory passages tell you about Maria, about what she has been through, and about what she is experiencing now? Why does she have the children turn off the news story?
3. At the end of this story, Maria is watching television and remembering a story from her ESL class. Why does Honig leave us with this story? What is it about, and how does it help you understand what Maria and other immigrants experience as they struggle to learn a new language and a new culture and learn to live with memories of what they left behind?

SUGGESTIONS FOR WRITING

1. Write a brief explanation of how television in this story conveys cultural meaning to someone like Maria and, by extension, to all of us.
2. Choose a scene from this story that moves you or that you think is particularly important for understanding what the story is about, then write an essay in which you explain what that scene tells you about the characters, actions, or meaning of this story.
3. Throughout this chapter, writers have asked questions about television and its ability to reveal or illuminate reality. Lucy Honig's short story raises many of these same questions in a much more dramatic and moving manner. Write an essay in which you explain how television and real-life experience are contrasted in this story. In your essay you might wish to explore Maria's confusion and her frustration at trying to understand what is on television and what is in the mayor's questions as well as her eagerness to be a part of this new world.

FOR FURTHER EXPLORATION

Television has been at the center of several controversies since its beginnings. For some background on television news coverage, you might wish to read Michael Arlen's *The Livingroom War*, about television's role in influencing the public's attitude toward Vietnam. In connection with that research, you might also look for information on television's role during the war in Grenada, the Panama action in which Manuel Noriega was targeted, and the Gulf War.

Television has also been a shaping force for Americans' images of family. Ella Taylor's *Prime Time Families* offers a good history of television's changing image of the family.

Other topics you can explore relating to television include the following:

- Docudramas and their role in teaching history
- The popularity and appeal of daytime soap operas
- Daytime television talk shows and the way they shape issues
- Freedom of access or community access to television signals

C H A P T E R   7

PUBLIC SPACE

The rhythm is so dynamic that a "slice of life" seen from a
cafe terrace is a spectacle. The most diverse elements collide and jostle one
another there. The interplay of contrasts is so violent that there is
always exaggeration in the effect you glimpse.

On the boulevards two men are carrying some immense
gilded letters in a handcart; the effect is so unexpected that everyone
stops and looks. *There is the origin of the modern spectacle.* The
shock of the surprise effect....

Objects, lights, the colors that used to be fixed and
restrained have become alive and mobile.

> – Fernand Leger, "The Spectacle:
> Light, Color, Moving Image,
> Object-Spectacle"

"When you go up to the city, you better have some cash,
'Cause the people in the city don't mess around with trash"

> – Traditional blues lyric

One way of examining how a culture lives and what it values is to look at its public spaces—its streets, parks, sports arenas, shopping malls, museums—all those places where people gather to do business and play and loiter. Such spaces are abundant in countrysides and suburbs as well as in cities. Megamalls and fast food restaurants line the highway system as a result of urban sprawl, and in small towns and rural areas, the fairgrounds, town halls, county arenas, and churches still function as public gathering spots. In fact, in this century, even America's wilderness areas have become places where the public gathers, with tourists traveling to catch a glimpse of the Grand Canyon, to picnic in Yellowstone, and to hike in the Adirondacks.

Of course, most public spaces are designed to be simply functional, which is why much of what you see every day is remarkable only for its similarity to nearly everything else you see. Office buildings that seem to pop up from the pavement overnight look like every other office building in the city. The new wing of a local hospital looks tacked on to the old wing—a highrise box of rooms and corridors. One grocery store looks like all the others, schools look like schools, and doctors' offices look like doctors' offices. A popular motel chain even tried for a while to capitalize on its across-the-continent sameness. Holiday Inn ads promised "no surprises," apparently assuming that most Americans are uncomfortable with anything too flashy or too different. Perhaps that is why it is so easy to take most public spaces for granted. It is only when a place looks different—newer, flashier, stranger—that most visitors stop to look. In a world crowded with so much to look at, it takes an effort, a real spectacle, to get people's attention.

Certainly, if you think of the most famous or infamous public spaces in contemporary America it is very easy to think of them as constituting spectacle above all else. From the Mall of America to Epcot Center, this country sometimes seems designed as one continuous spectacle, each new space vying to be the biggest and most expensive. Such spaces compete for attention, inviting visitors to look, to linger, and to buy. These are public spaces turned spectacle, and these are the spaces that characterize at least one impulse in a consumer economy—the impulse to sell.

In America, perhaps the purest example of public space as spectacle is the Las Vegas casino strip. Writer Tom Wolfe once described Vegas as "the only town in the world whose skyline is made up of neither buildings, like New York, nor of trees, like Wilbraham, Massachusetts, but of signs. . . . But such signs! They tower. They revolve, they oscillate, they soar in shapes before which the existing vocabulary of art history is helpless." As a place of spectacle, Las Vegas is pure flash, pure appearance—spectacle for its own sake.

Even that characterization is misleading, however, for the spectacle that is Las Vegas hardly exists for its own sake; it is there for the sake of the sale. In an era in which advertising is one of the most prolific forms of communication, spectacle emerges as a natural manifestation of the sales pitch. In this age of the automobile and the highway system, spectacle caters to a moving public, a public that hasn't time for a lengthy meal or a complex ad. Bright lights, motion, glitter, surprise—this is the landscape that modern Americans drive past in their motor homes.

Public space turned spectacle, then, is the space that is designed deliberately to attract attention and seduce the senses. In that way, Las Vegas may seem the purest example of public space as spectacle, but it is hardly the only one. As artist Fernand Leger tells us, modern spectacle has its origins in the world of movement, light, color, sparkle, and surprise. Today, however, it is probably much more difficult to surprise you with dazzling lights than it was earlier generations. Since the fifties, Americans have been surrounded by the magic of neon—lights that seemed to dance, to form and reform themselves for *Ronnie's Drive-In* or *Joe's Bar & Grill* or the *First National Bank.* Today, travelers in Chicago's O'Hare International Airport can ride a people mover beneath the light and sound show of a pulsing, ever-changing light sculpture. Yet, if you were to watch these travelers, you would notice that only a few pause to look up. Even fewer turn back for a second ride. The show is there to keep travelers amused, perhaps, or distracted, but the very fact that it is set in a busy place of travel beneath a machine that keeps observers moving away prohibits the amount of time most people are likely to spend simply looking. More than ever, spectacle must rely on the wizardry of electronic gadgets, the charge of supersaturated colors, and the excitement of media hype to make a real impression.

Whether you live in the city, the suburbs, or the country, if you have visited historical monuments, spent time in New York or Los Angeles, attended a ball game, watched a parade, shopped in a mall, eaten in a fast food restaurant, played for a day in an amusement park, or simply attended a church bazaar or school dance, you already know a good deal about how public space is organized in contemporary America, and you probably make more judgments about public spaces than you think.

READING THE CULTURE OF PUBLIC SPACE

As you read and talk about the public spaces that constitute the "look" of modern America, you will be asked to write your own impressions of and draw your own meaning from those spaces. One way to look at public space in America is to recall the immediate impressions you have had of places you have seen. As you explore these memories, you may begin to understand how you form your own judgments of places. We open this chapter, then, with first-person accounts of place. Garrison Keillor's story "State Fair," based on memories of the young boy traveling to the Minnesota State Fair, tells of the dazzle of the unexpected, the excitement of being away from home, away from the familiar. It offers the outsider's view, a view you probably already understand from your own experience of places that are new and exciting, places that promise a different kind of life than the one you know well. Edward Abbey's description of Arches National Monument raises questions about America's wilderness areas. In *Desert Solitaire,* Edward Abbey presents his position on wilderness and its value in this culture. Abbey's argument that progress can mean leaving things the way they are, not trying to make them into something bigger, better, flashier, or more marketable, is one that you might consider as you think about the role of public lands in the way America characterizes itself. What the Abbey selection might also suggest for you as a writer and thinker is that writing about place need not merely be a matter of describing what is there, as if it were natural or normal or inevitable. You can, instead, take a position on the meaning and value of that place.

The selections that follow offer examples of how the most ordinary and extraordinary places in America—retirement communities and shopping malls—might be described and interpreted. These are the kinds of places with which Americans are most familiar, places where people live and eat and spend leisure time. Frances FitzGerald's "Sun City," David Guterson's "Enclosed. Encyclopedic. Endured. One Week at the Mall of America," and John Fiske's "Shopping for Pleasure: Malls, Power, and Resistance" each offer cultural interpretations of places that are so much a part of the American landscape that they seem quintessentially American. In their essays, these writers suggest that you look at such places as emerging from the meanings and values of the culture within which they were created. Fiske, in particular, is insistent that, though the malls, for example, may represent a powerful pull to the senses, most consumers are not duped by the hype. Instead, most of us are able to use these spaces to meet our own needs, even or especially when those uses directly contradict the carefully planned-for use of the developers. Thus, teenagers become mall rats, hanging out but rarely shopping in those megamalls that seem so seductive.

The chapter concludes with two selections that demonstrate the difference between impression and analysis. Jean Baudrillard's *America* and Mike Davis's "Fortress Los Angeles" both examine life in contemporary major U.S. cities. The short selection from Baudrillard's postcard portrait serves as a telling example of how one writer collects quick and vivid impressions and puts them into short, highly imagistic prose. Baudrillard's reaction to New York is that of the visitor, the newcomer who has heard much about this great city, a city of excitement and spectacle. Davis, on the other hand, goes much beyond impression to examine the ways in which Los Angeles resembles a controlled, armed camp. He particularly looks at the loss of public space as one indicator of the changed American city.

The kind of work proposed in this chapter always begins with observation and memory. What you write depends very much on what you have already experienced and what you already think about the topic. Take your time at the beginning of your reading to mine your memory, for it is your memory that will be your most important initial resource here.

Garrison Keillor

STATE FAIR

From 1974 to 1987, Garrison Keillor hosted National Public Radio's *A Prairie Home Companion*, a live radio program originating from St. Paul, Minnesota, that featured music, comedy sketches, and his own storytelling. Keillor's stories portray life in Lake Wobegon ("the little town that time forgot

and that the decades cannot improve"). Each story began with the same introduction: "It has been a quite week in Lake Wobegon. . . ." From that beginning, Keillor entered, in a more or less direct way, the lives of the people in
this mythic midwestern town. Though now collected in the volume *Leaving
Home*, which appeared in 1987, these stories, Keillor tells us, "were written
for performance on the radio, on 'A Prairie Home Companion,' as you may
see from the tone of them. They were written for my voice, which is flat and
slow. There are long pauses in them and sentences that trail off into the raspberry bushes." The story that follows is one that Keillor told. In it, he relives the
wonder of the Minnesota State Fair, a spectacle of contrasts and fantasy. If
you have the opportunity, you might first try reading the story aloud as Keillor
did when he recited it for his audiences.

Suggestion for Reading

• Unlike many descriptions that focus on surface detail, Keillor gets at place
through story. This means that he begins with an event and people, then
sets his story in a place, in this case the Minnesota State Fair. The events
and characters are not meant to distract from the place; they are meant to
be a part of what the place is, what it means. As you read, you may wish to
keep track of the several different characters and stories Keillor introduces
and make note of how they come together to convey what the State Fair
seems to mean to the man telling the story.

I t has been a quiet week in Lake Wobegon and it's a great pleasure to be here at
the Minnesota State Fair. I've come every year since I was five, and that's more
than twenty years. Every August my mother said, "Well, I don't know if I care
to go to the Fair this year or not." Nobody had so much as mentioned the Fair,
we were too busy canning vegetables and perishing of the heat and the steam from the
pressure cooker—a burning hot day and us stripping skins off tomatoes, slaving to put
up a hundred or so quarts of a vegetable we were rapidly losing our appetite for. She
said, "There's too much work to do and we can't afford it, it's too crowded, and anyway
it's the same as last year. I don't see how we can do it. I'm sorry."

It was her way of lending drama to the trip. So we'd come to the Fair, the roar of
engines and the smell of grease, and Mother marched around the Home Activities
building looking at competitive cakes and jams. One year we shook hands with Senator
Ed Thye, and another time we won a roll of linoleum by guessing the number of agates
in a toilet bowl. One year we wandered into the Education building and saw a demon-
stration of television, an interesting invention: people stood in a crowd and looked at a
picture of themselves on a screen. When they moved the picture moved—interesting.
Hard to see why you'd want one if you had a mirror, but it was entertaining for a few
minutes.

I came with Mother and Dad, and because we were Christians we gave a wide
berth to the Midway, where ladies danced and did other things at the Persian Palms
and Harlem Revue tent shows. We avoided sin, but it was exciting for me to be so close
to it and see flashing pink lights and hear barkers say, in a voice like a talking dog's,

"See Miss Roxanne just inside the gate, just beyond that tent flap, she's waiting in there for you, she wants to show you a *good* time," and I tried to see beyond the flap, not wanting Miss Roxanne to be disappointed by my lack of interest in her. It was exciting to hear bands playing slow raunchy dance tunes and to walk past the freak show with the two-headed boy, where the gypsy ticketseller looked at me with a haughty look that said, *I know things you'll never know, what I've seen you'd never understand.*

I loved the Fair, the good and the bad. It was good to get out of our quiet town into a loud place with bad food and stink, music and sex blaring—listen—it's gorgeous. Dad gave me three dollars and I walked around not spending it, just gaping at the sights. Once I saw a sad midget stand and smoke a cigarette, holding his dog's leash, a big dog. Once I saw a man necking with a fat lady behind the Tilt-A-Whirl. He was running the ride. People were getting tossed around like eggs in a blender, and he was putting his hands up her shirt. Once I saw the newspaper columnist Olson Younger sitting in a booth under the sign MEET OLSON YOUNGER. He was puffier than his picture in the paper and more dejected. He sat drinking coffee after coffee and scrawling his autograph on free paper visors. He led a fairy-tale life in his column, meeting stars of stage and screen, eating meals with them, and even dancing once with Rita Hayworth, and he shared these wonderful moments with us through "The Olson Younger Column." The bad part was that I had to wear fundamentalist clothes to the Fair, white rayon shirt, black pants, black shoes, narrow tie, because we had to sing in the evening at the Harbor Light gospel tent near the Midway gate. We sang "Earnestly, tenderly, Jesus is calling, calling for you and for me," and fifty feet away a man said, "Yes, she is absolutely naked as the day she was born, and she's inside, twenty-five cents, two bits, the fourth part of a dollar." I held the hymnbook high so nobody would see me. I wanted to be cool and wear a T-shirt. In the pioneer days before polyester, a rayon shirt was like wearing waxed paper.

When the service was over, we got one ride on the ferris wheel, rising up over the bright lights into the dark night toward the stars, and falling back into our real lives. On the long ride home I slept, and when I woke up I was in a classroom that smelled of floor wax; Mrs. Mortenson was asking me to explain the Smoot-Hawley Act.

In 1955 my uncle Earl saw an ad for the $2,000 Minnesota State Fair Cake Baking Sweepstakes, sponsored by Peter Pan Flour, and he entered my aunt Myrna. He didn't mention this to her because he didn't want to upset her. She was a nervous person, easily startled by a sudden hello, and he was right, she made the greatest chocolate angel-food cake on the face of the earth. (To call it devil's food would give Satan encouragement so we didn't.) She also kept the cleanest kitchen in the Christian world. I liked to walk in, say hello, and when she recovered, she sat me down and fed me chocolate angel-food cake. As I ate it, she hovered overhead and apologized for it.

"*Oh,*" she sighed. "I don't know. I ought to throw this out for the dog. It's not very good. I don't know where my mind was—I lost track of how many eggs I put in, and I was all out of the kind of brown sugar I always use." I looked up at her in a trance, confused by the pure transcendent beauty of it, and she cut me a second, larger piece. "My mother was the one who could make a chocolate cake," she said, and then she allowed herself one taste of cake. And frowned. "It's gummy," she said. "It's like pudding."

"No," I said. "It's the best chocolate cake I ever tasted."

"Oh," she said, "your mother makes cake just as good as that."

Once my mother heard that and smiled at me, hopefully, but all my life I've tried to tell the truth, and I replied honestly, "Sometimes she does, but not often."

Aunt Myrna was one of the few truly slender women in town. She set an impossible standard for the others. "She's small-boned," they said, but the truth is that she was so critical of her cooking, which was head and shoulders above everyone else's, that food didn't satisfy her. She was supernatural that way, like an angel. Angels who visit earth don't feed on corn dogs and pizza. Heavenly creatures have low metabolism, a little bite of something perfect is more than enough. Like her cake. An angel visiting Minnesota to do research on sweet corn could go for a week on one thin sliver of Aunt Myrna's chocolate cake.

When, in early August, Uncle Earl got an invitation from the Peter Pan Flour people, none of us was surprised she was chosen, she was so good. She was mad at him when he broke the news; she said, "I can't bake in front of a hundred people. Stand up and make a cake and have them stare at me like I was some kind of carnival freak. I won't do it."

He considered that for a minute. "I was thinking of it," he said, "as an opportunity to witness for the Lord. If you win the bake-off, I'm certain that you get to make a speech. You could give that Scripture recipe, 'Take four cups of 1 Corinthians 13 and three cups of Ephesians 4:32, four quarts of Hebrews 11:1....'"

"I don't know if I would be up to it...."

"I can do all things through Christ which strengtheneth me. Phillipians 4:13."

She practiced for two weeks and baked about forty cakes, most of them barely edible. She was experimenting with strange ingredients, like maple syrup and peanut butter, marshmallows, cherry bits. "You can't just stand up in front of a crowd and bake an ordinary chocolate cake," she said, but we convinced her that hers was good enough. She baked two of them that Friday, both champs. On the big Saturday she packed her ingredients, cake pans, mixer, and utensils in a cardboard box and covered it with a cloth, and they drove to the Cities, stopping on account of car trouble in Anoka and transferring from the Dodge to the bus. The bake-off was at three o'clock.

They arrived at two-thirty. She had assumed the bake-off was in the Home Activities building and then she discovered it was here at the grandstand. Peter Pan Flour had gone all out. The bake-off was part of the afternoon grandstand program, which also included high-wire acts, a big band playing Glenn Miller tunes, and Siberian tigers jumping through hoops of fire. She and twelve other women would stand on stage and bake cakes, and while the cakes were in the oven, Joey Chitwood's Thrill Show would perform daredevil stunts on the dirt track, and Olson Younger the newspaper columnist would judge the contest and award the prize. We helped Aunt Myrna to the stage. She was weak and moist. "Good luck," we said.

I stand here and look up at the grandstand and can see how nervous she must've been. I remember sitting up there in the forty-ninth row, under the pavilion, looking down at my tiny aunt in the green dress to the left of the saxophones while Joey Chitwood's Thrill Show drivers did flips and rolls, roaring around in white Fords. She stood at a long table whipping mix in a silver bowl, my aunt Myrna making a cake. She was mine, my relative, and I was so proud.

And then the cakes came out of the oven. The State Fair orchestra put down their newspapers and picked up their horns and played something from opera, and the radio-announcer emcee said that now the moment had come, and Olson Younger pranced around. He wore a green suit and orange tie and he waved to us with both hands. It was his moment of glory, and he sashayed from one entrant to the next, kissing her, rolling his eyes, and tasting her cake. When he tasted Myrna's cake, she shrank back from his embrace. She said a few words to him and I knew she was saying, "I don't know. I just can't seem to make em as rich as I used to—this isn't very good at all. It's gummy." It was the greatest chocolate cake in the world but he believed her. So she came in tenth.

A woman in white pedal pushers won because, Younger said, her cake was richer and moister. He had a hard time getting the words out. You could see the grease stains from her cake, beads of grease glittered in the sun. Uncle Earl said, "That's not cake, that's pudding he gave a prize to. This is a pudding contest he's running. He wouldn't know chocolate cake if it came up and ate him." And he was right. When Younger waltzed over to give Aunt Myrna her prize, a bowl, you could see he didn't know which way was north. It wasn't fair. She was the best. We waited for her in front of the grandstand. We both felt bad.

But when we saw her coming, she was all smiles. She hugged us both. She hardly seemed like herself. She threw her head back and said, "Oh, I'm glad it's over. But it was fun. I was so scared. And then I just forgot to be."

"But it wasn't fair," I said. She said, "Oh, he was drunk. It was all whiskey cake to him. But it doesn't matter. It was so much fun." I never saw her so lighthearted and girlish.

That night an old man came forward at the Harbor Light gospel meeting. He was confused and may have been looking for the way out, but we latched onto him and prayed for him. When he left, he seemed relieved. He was our first convert and we were thrilled. A soul hanging in the balance, there in our tent. Heaven and hell his choice, and he chose heaven, with our help, and then Dad lent him busfare.

That night, I said to my mother, "This is the last time I wear a rayon shirt, I hate them." She said, "All right, that's fine." I said, "You're not mad?" She said, "No, I thought you liked them, that's all."

I went up in the ferris wheel for a last ride before being thrown into seventh grade. It went up into the stars and fell back to earth and rose again, and I had a magnificent vision, or think I did, though it's hard to remember if it was that year with the chocolate cake or the next one with the pigs getting loose. The ferris wheel is the same year after year. It's like all one ride to me: we go up and I think of people I knew who are dead and I smell fall in the air, manure, corn dogs, and we drop down into blazing light and blaring music. Every summer I'm a little bigger, but riding the ferris wheel, I feel the same as ever, I feel eternal. The combination of cotton candy, corn dogs, diesel smoke, and sawdust, in a hot dark summer night, it never changes, not an inch. The wheel carries us up high, high, high, and stops, and we sit swaying, creaking, in the dark, on the verge of death. You can see death from here. The wind blows from the northwest, from the farm school in Saint Anthony Park, a chilly wind with traces of pigs and sheep in it. This is my vision: little kids holding on to their daddy's hand, and he is me. He looks down on them with love and buys them another corn dog. They are worried they will lose him, they hang on to his leg with one hand, eat with the other. This vision is unbearably wonderful. Then the wheel brings me down to the ground. We get off and other people get on. Thank you, dear God, for this good life and forgive us if we do not love it enough.

SUGGESTIONS FOR DISCUSSION

1. Keillor tells us that his audience was important to him as he performed his stories. How might the performance have affected the way this story is written? Are there passages that seem to be written for oral performance?
2. Keillor makes use of several contrasts throughout the story to describe the State Fair and its particular allure. For example, as his choir is singing, the barker just a few feet away is advertising the naked lady in the tent next door. What do these and other contrasts like them tell us about the world of the State Fair?
3. What would you say the story of Aunt Myrna's chocolate cake has to do with the narrator's experience of the State Fair?

SUGGESTIONS FOR WRITING

1. We might say of spectacle that it is a grand appearance that makes a promise, a promise of excitement or newness or of something better to come. Write an essay in which you explain what you think the State Fair promises for the boy in this story.
2. Some readers have criticized Keillor's stories as being too moralistic; others read a measure of irony in his voice. Which of these voices is, for you, strongest in this story? Write an essay in which you explain your position with reference to events or passages in the story.
3. Make a list of places that, for you, hold special meaning. From that list choose one and write an essay in which you narrate an event that occurred there so that the meaning of this place becomes apparent for your audience. If you wish, use one of the postcard descriptions you wrote earlier as the starting point for your essay.

Edward Abbey

THE FIRST MORNING AND LABOR DAY

Edward Abbey was a novelist, naturalist, activist, and iconoclast. Throughout his life he fought the predominant notion in this country that "progress" means building something new. In response to an interviewer's question Abbey once said that the Southwest's biggest enemy was "expansion, development, commercial greed, industrial growth. That kind of growth which has become a pathological condition in our society. That insatiable demand for more and more; the urge to dominate and consume and destroy." In 1968 Abbey wrote *Desert Solitaire,* from which the following selections were excerpted, as "not a travel guide but an elegy. A memorial." For two years in the mid-fifties, Abbey was a park ranger in Arches National Monument, at that time an undeveloped national park in southeastern Utah. For those two years, he kept a journal from which *Desert Solitaire* was written. In the two selections that follow, Abbey writes of why he treasures the park and what he sees as the foremost threat to its beauty.

Suggestion for Reading

- As you read, underline those passages that seem best to convey Abbey's attitude toward growth and expansion.

◆

The First Morning

This is the most beautiful place on earth.

There are many such places. Every man, every woman, carries in heart and mind the image of the ideal place, the right place, the one true home, known or unknown, actual or visionary. A houseboat in Kashmir, a view down Atlantic Avenue in Brooklyn, a gray gothic farmhouse two stories high at the end of a red dog road in the Allegheny Mountains, a cabin on the shore of a blue lake in spruce and fir country, a greasy alley near the Hoboken waterfront, or even, possibly, for those of a less demanding sensibility, the world to be seen from a comfortable apartment high in the tender, velvety smog of Manhattan, Chicago, Paris, Tokyo, Rio or Rome—there's no limit to the human capacity for the homing sentiment. Theologians, sky pilots, astronauts have even felt the appeal of home calling to them from up above, in the cold black outback of intersteller space.

For myself I'll take Moab, Utah. I don't mean the town itself, of course, but the country which surrounds it—the canyonlands. The slickrock desert. The red dust and the burnt cliffs and the lonely sky—all that which lies beyond the end of the roads.

The choice became apparent to me this morning when I stepped out of a Park Service housetrailer—my caravan—to watch for the first time in my life the sun come up over the hoodoo stone of Arches National Monument.

I wasn't able to see much of it last night. After driving all day from Albuquerque—450 miles—I reached Moab after dark in cold, windy, clouded weather. At park headquarters north of town I met the superintendent and the chief ranger, the only permanent employees, except for one maintenance man, in this particular unit of America's national park system. After coffee they gave me a key to the housetrailer and directions on how to reach it; I am required to live and work not at headquarters but at this one-man station some twenty miles back in the interior, on my own. The way I wanted it, naturally, or I'd never have asked for the job.

Leaving the headquarters area and the lights of Moab, I drove twelve miles farther north on the highway until I came to a dirt road on the right, where a small wooden sign pointed the way: Arches National Monument Eight Miles. I left the pavement, turned east into the howling wilderness. Wind roaring out of the northwest, black clouds across the stars—all I could see were clumps of brush and scattered junipers along the roadside. Then another modest signboard:

WARNING: QUICKSAND

DO NOT CROSS WASH

WHEN WATER IS RUNNING

The wash looked perfectly dry in my headlights. I drove down, across, up the other side and on into the night. Glimpses of weird humps of pale rock on either side, like petrified elephants, dinosaurs, stone-age hobgoblins. Now and then something alive scurried across the road: kangaroo mice, a jackrabbit, an animal that looked like a cross between a raccoon and a squirrel—the ringtail cat. Farther on a pair of mule deer started from the brush and bounded obliquely through the beams of my lights, raising puffs of dust which the wind, moving faster than my pickup truck, caught and carried ahead of me out of sight into the dark. The road, narrow and rocky, twisted sharply left and right, dipped in and out of tight ravines, climbing by degrees toward a summit which I would see only in the light of the coming day.

Snow was swirling through the air when I crossed the unfenced line and passed the boundary marker of the park. A quarter-mile beyond I found the ranger station—a wide place in the road, an informational display under a lean-to shelter, and fifty yards away the little tin government housetrailer where I would be living for the next six months.

A cold night, a cold wind, the snow falling like confetti. In the lights of the truck I unlocked the housetrailer, got out bedroll and baggage and moved in. By flashlight I found the bed, unrolled my sleeping bag, pulled off my boots and crawled in and went to sleep at once. The last I knew was the shaking of the trailer in the wind and the sound, from inside, of hungry mice scampering around with the good news that their long lean lonesome winter was over—their friend and provider had finally arrived.

This morning I awake before sunrise, stick my head out of the sack, peer through a frosty window at a scene dim and vague with flowing mists, dark fantastic shapes looming beyond. An unlikely landscape.

I get up, moving about in long underwear and socks, stooping carefully under the low ceiling and the lower doorways of the housetrailer, a machine for living built so efficiently and compactly there's hardly room for a man to breathe. An iron lung it is, with windows and venetian blinds.

The mice are silent, watching me from their hiding places, but the wind is still blowing and outside the ground is covered with snow. Cold as a tomb, a jail, a cave; I lie down on the dusty floor, on the cold linoleum sprinkled with mouse turds, and light the pilot on the butane heater. Once this thing gets going the place warms up fast, in a dense unhealthy way, with a layer of heat under the ceiling where my head is and nothing but frigid air from the knees down. But we've got all the indispensable conveniences: gas cookstove, gas refrigerator, hot water heater, sink with running water (if the pipes aren't frozen), storage cabinets and shelves, everything within arm's reach of everything else. The gas comes from two steel bottles in a shed outside; the water comes by gravity flow from a tank buried in a hill close by. Quite luxurious for the wilds. There's even a shower stall and a flush toilet with a dead rat in the bowl. Pretty soft. My poor mother raised five children without any of these luxuries and might be doing without them yet if it hadn't been for Hitler, war and general prosperity.

Time to get dressed, get out and have a look at the lay of the land, fix a breakfast. I try to pull on my boots but they're stiff as iron from the cold. I light a burner on the stove and hold the boots upside down above the flame until they are malleable enough to force my feet into. I put on a coat and step outside. In the center of the world, God's navel, Abbey's country, the red wasteland.

The sun is not yet in sight but signs of the advent are plain to see. Lavender clouds sail like a fleet of ships across the pale green dawn; each cloud, planed flat on the wind, has a base of fiery gold. Southeast, twenty miles by line of sight, stand the peaks of the Sierra La Sal, twelve to thirteen thousand feet above sea level, all covered with snow and rosy in the morning sunlight. The air is dry and clear as well as cold; the last fogbanks left over from last night's storm are scudding away like ghosts, fading into nothing before the wind and the sunrise.

The view is open and perfect in all directions except to the west where the ground rises and the skyline is only a few hundred yards away. Looking toward the mountains I can see the dark gorge of the Colorado River five or six miles away, carved through the sandstone mesa, though nothing of the river itself down inside the gorge. Southward, on the far side of the river, lies the Moab valley between thousand-foot walls of rock, with the town of Moab somewhere on the valley floor, too small to be seen from here. Beyond the Moab valley is more canyon and tableland stretching away to the Blue Mountains fifty miles south. On the north and northwest I see the Roan Cliffs and the Book Cliffs, the two-level face of the Uinta Plateau. Along the foot of those cliffs, maybe thirty miles off, invisible from where I stand, runs U.S. 6–50, a major east-west artery of commerce, traffic and rubbish, and the main line of the Denver-Rio Grande Railroad. To the east, under the spreading sunrise, are more mesas, more canyons, league on league of red cliff and arid tablelands, extending through purple haze over the bulging curve of the planet to the ranges of Colorado—a sea of desert.

Within this vast perimeter, in the middle ground and foreground of the picture, a rather personal demesne, are the 33,000 acres of Arches National Monument of which I am now sole inhabitant, usufructuary, observer and custodian.

What are the Arches? From my place in front of the housetrailer I can see several of the hundred or more of them which have been discovered in the park. These are natural arches, holes in the rock, windows in stone, no two alike, as varied in form as in dimension. They range in size from holes just big enough to walk through to openings large enough to contain the dome of the Capitol building in Washington, D.C. Some resemble jug handles or flying buttresses, others natural bridges but with this technical distinction: a natural bridge spans a watercourse—a natural arch does not. The arches were formed through hundreds of thousands of years by the weathering of the huge sandstone walls, or fins, in which they are found. Not the work of a cosmic hand, nor sculptured by sand-bearing winds, as many people prefer to believe, the arches came into being and continue to come into being through the modest wedging action of rainwater, melting snow, frost, and ice, aided by gravity. In color they shade from off-white through buff, pink, brown and red, tones which also change with the time of day and the moods of the light, the weather, the sky.

Standing there, gaping at this monstrous and inhuman spectacle of rock and cloud and sky and space, I feel a ridiculous greed and possessiveness come over me. I want to know it all, possess it all, embrace the entire scene intimately, deeply, totally, as a man desires a beautiful woman. An insane wish? Perhaps not—at least there's nothing else, no one human, to dispute possession with me.

The snow-covered ground glimmers with a dull blue light, reflecting the sky and the approaching sunrise. Leading away from me the narrow dirt road, an alluring and primitive track into nowhere, meanders down the slope and toward the heart of the labyrinth of naked stone. Near the first group of arches, looming over a bend in the road, is a balanced rock about fifty feet high, mounted on a pedestal of equal height; it looks like a head from Easter Island, a stone god or a petrified ogre.

Like a god, like an ogre? The personification of the natural is exactly the tendency I wish to suppress in myself, to eliminate for good. I am here not only to evade for a while the clamor and filth and confusion of the cultural apparatus but also to confront, immediately and directly if it's possible, the bare bones of existence, the elemental and fundamental, the bedrock which sustains us. I want to be able to look at and into a juniper tree, a piece of quartz, a vulture, a spider, and see it as it is in itself, devoid of all humanly ascribed qualities, anti-Kantian, even the categories of scientific description. To meet God or Medusa face to face, even if it means risking everything human in myself. I dream of a hard and brutal mysticism in which the naked self merges with a non-human world and yet somehow survives still intact, individual, separate. Paradox and bedrock.

Well—the sun will be up in a few minutes and I haven't even begun to make coffee. I take more baggage from my pickup, the grub box and cooking gear, go back in the trailer and start breakfast. Simply breathing, in a place like this, arouses the appetite. The orange juice is frozen, the milk slushy with ice. Still chilly enough inside the trailer to turn my breath to vapor. When the first rays of the sun strike the cliffs I fill a mug with steaming coffee and sit in the doorway facing the sunrise, hungry for the warmth.

Suddenly it comes, the flaming globe, blazing on the pinnacles and minarets and balanced rocks, on the canyon walls and through the windows in the sandstone fins. We greet each other, sun and I, across the black void of ninety-three million miles. The snow glitters between us, acres of diamonds almost painful to look at. Within an hour all the snow exposed to the sunlight will be gone and the rock will be damp and steaming. Within minutes, even as I watch, melting snow begins to drip from the branches of a juniper nearby; drops of water streak slowly down the side of the trailerhouse.

I am not alone after all. Three ravens are wheeling near the balanced rock, squawking at each other and at the dawn. I'm sure they're as delighted by the return of the sun as I am and I wish I knew the language. I'd sooner exchange ideas with the birds on earth than learn to carry on intergalactic communications with some obscure race of humanoids on a satellite planet from the world of Betelgeuse. First things first. The ravens cry out in husky voices, blue-black wings flapping against the golden sky. Over my shoulder comes the sizzle and smell of frying bacon.

That's the way it was this morning.

◆

Labor Day

N ow here comes another clown with a scheme for the utopian national park: Central Park National Park, Disneyland National Park. Look here, he says, what's the matter with you fellows?—let's get cracking with this dump. Your road is bad; pave it. Better yet, build a paved road to every corner of the park; better yet, pave the whole damned place so any damn fool can drive anything anywhere—is this a democracy or ain't it? Next, charge a good stiff admission fee; you can't let people in free; that leads to socialism and regimentation. Next, get rid of all these homely rangers in their Smokey the Bear suits. Hire a crew of pretty girls, call them rangerettes, let them sell the tickets and give the campfire talks. And advertise, for godsake, advertise! How do you expect to get people in here is you don't advertise? Next, these here Arches—light them up. Floodlight them, turn on colored, revolving lights—jazz it up, man, it's dead. Light up the whole place, all night long, get on a 24-hour shift, keep them coming, keep them moving, you got two hundred million people out there waiting to see your product—is this a free country or what the hell is it? Next your campgrounds, you gotta do something about your campgrounds, they're a mess. People can't tell where to park their cars or which spot is whose—you gotta paint lines, numbers, mark out the campsites nice and neat. And they're still building fires on the ground, with wood! Very messy, filthy, wasteful. Set up little grills on stilts, sell charcoal briquettes, better yet hook up with the gas line, install jets and burners. Better yet do away with the campgrounds altogether, they only cause delay and congestion and administrative problems—these people want to see America, they're not going to see it sitting around a goddamned campfire; take their money, give them the show, send them on their way—that's the way to run a business. . . .

I exaggerate. Slightly. Was he real or only a bad dream? Am I awake or sleeping? Will Tuesday never come? No wonder they call it Labor Day.

SUGGESTIONS FOR DISCUSSION

1. Much of Edward Abbey's anger toward developers was aimed at those developers who wanted to "improve" places like Arches National Monument by putting in roads and running water and convenience stores. What does Abbey see are the issues raised by development, growth, expansion, and "progress"? How does his position compare to your own?
2. Abbey calls the Arches "this monstrous and inhuman spectacle of rock and cloud and space." How does Abbey's use of the term spectacle differ from other uses of the term that you are familiar with?
3. What would you say are the assumptions about how human beings ought to live (or their relation to the natural world) that underlie Abbey's thinking? What are your own assumptions about how we ought to live?

SUGGESTIONS FOR WRITING

1. Write a portrait of a typical tourist at some place that you have visited or vacationed.
2. Write an essay about a place that you know well that you have seen change. Use the change to explain your own attitude toward progress or development.
3. Write a description of a place that you think should be preserved as it is and explain why you take that position.

Frances FitzGerald

SUN CITY

Frances FitzGerald received the National Book Award and the Pulitzer Prize for *Fire in the Lake* and is the author of *America Revised,* a study of history textbooks in America. The following selection, taken from *Cities on a Hill,* a study of ideal communities, is a description of Sun City Center, a planned retirement community near Tampa. FitzGerald chose this community, she tells us, because "most Sun Citians were well enough off so that settling in the town—and staying there—was a matter of choice rather than one of necessity. Even more important, it was a true community—a social unit; founded in 1960, it had, like any small town evolved its own institutions and customs. . . . Belonging to the first generation to reach old age en masse, in good health, and with the resources to live independently of their children, [Sun City residents] were people for whom society had as yet no set of expectations and no vision. They were people who had to invent, and along with others of their generation, they were creating a conception of how their stage in life should be led. They were, I thought, pioneers on the frontier of age." *Cities on a Hill* also includes studies of Liberty Village, a fundamentalist community, The Castro, a San Francisco gay community, and Rancho Rajneesh, a guru-inspired commune. The title for this text, taken from a speech by John Winthrop to his fellow founders of the Massachusetts Bay Colony, links these modern experimental communities with a tradition of ideal communities in our history. "We must consider that we shall be a City Upon a Hill," he told his people, "the eyes of all people are upon us."

Suggestion for Reading

• Frances FitzGerald has written both a description and an analysis of this community. As you read, underline passages in which she is clearly analyzing the community rather than simply describing it.

————————————◆————————————

On Route 301 south of Tampa, billboards advertising Sun City Center crop up every few miles, with pictures of Cesar Romero and slogans that read FLORIDA'S RETIREMENT COMMUNITY OF THE YEAR, 87 HOLES OF GOLF, THE TOWN TOO BUSY TO RETIRE. According to a real-estate brochure, the town is "sensibly located . . . comfortably removed from the crowded downtown areas, the highway clutter, the tourists and the traffic." It is twenty-five miles from Tampa, thirty miles from Bradenton, thirty-five miles from Sarasota, and eleven miles from the nearest beach on the Gulf Coast. Route 301, an inland route—to be taken in preference to the coast road, with its lines of trucks from the phosphate plants—passes through a lot of swampland, some scraggly pinewoods, and acre upon acre of strawberry beds covered with sheets of black plastic. There are fields where hairy, tough-looking cattle snatch at the grass between the palmettos. There are aluminum warehouses, cinder-block stores, and trailer homes in patches of dirt with laundry sailing out behind. There are Pentecostal churches and run-down cafés and bars with rows of pickup trucks parked out front.

Turn right with the billboards onto Route 674 and there is a green-and-white suburban-looking resort town. Off the main road, white asphalt boulevards with avenues of palm trees give onto streets that curve pleasingly around golf courses and small lakes. White ranch-style houses sit back from the streets on small, impeccably manicured lawns. A glossy four-color map of the town put out by a real-estate company shows cartoon figures of golfers on the fairways and boats on the lakes, along with drawings of churches, clubhouses, and curly green trees. The map is a necessity for the visitor, since the streets curve around in maze fashion, ending in culs-de-sac or doubling back on themselves. There is no way in or out of Sun City Center except by the main road bisecting the town. The map, which looks like a child's board game (Snakes and Ladders or Uncle Wiggily), shows a vague area—a kind of no-man's-land—surrounding the town. As the map suggests, there is nothing natural about Sun City Center. The lakes are artificial, and there is hardly a tree or a shrub or a blade of grass that has any correspondence in the world just beyond it. At the edges of the development, there are houses under construction, with the seams still showing in the transplanted lawns. From there, you can look out at a flat brown plain that used to be a cattle ranch. The developer simply scraped the surface off the land and started over again.

Sun City Center is an unincorporated town of about eighty-five hundred people, almost all of whom are over the age of sixty. It is a self-contained community, with stores, banks, restaurants, and doctors' offices. It has the advertised eighty-seven holes of golf; it also has tennis courts, shuffleboard courts, swimming pools, and lawn-bowling greens. In addition to the regular housing, it has a "life-care facility"—a six-story apartment building with a nursing home in one wing. "It's a strange town," a clinical psychologist at the University of South Florida, in Tampa, told me before I went. "It's out there in the middle of nowhere. It has a section of private houses, where people go when they retire. Then it has a section of condos and apartments, where people go when they can't keep up their houses. Then it has a nursing home. Then it has a cemetery." In fact, there is no cemetery in Sun City Center, but the doctor was otherwise correct. . . .

• • •

. . . Twenty-five miles from Tampa, the nearest city, Sun City Center has become a world unto itself. Over the years, the town attracted a supermarket and all the stores and services necessary to the maintenance of daily life. Now, in addition, it has a golf-cart dealer, two banks, three savings and loan associations, four restaurants, and a brokerage firm. For visitors, there is the Sun City Center Inn. The town has a post office. Five churches have been built by the residents, and a sixth is under construction. A number of doctors have set up offices in the town, and a Bradenton hospital recently opened a satellite hospital with 112 beds. There is no school, of course. The commercial establishments all front on the state road running through the center of town, but, because most of them are more expensive than those in the neighboring towns, the people from the surrounding area patronize only the supermarket, the laundromat, and one or two others. The local farmers and the migrant workers they employ, many of whom are Mexican, have little relationship to golf courses or to dinner dances with organ music. Conversely, Sun Citians are not the sort of people who would go to bean suppers in the Pentecostal churches or hang out at raunchy bars where gravel-voiced women sing "Satin Sheets and Satin Pillows." The result is that Sun Citians see very little of their Florida neighbors. They take trips to Tampa, Bradenton, and Sarasota, but otherwise they rarely leave the green-and-white developments, with their palm-lined avenues and artificial lakes. In the normal course of a week, they rarely see anyone under sixty. . . .

• • •

. . . Sun City Center has age restrictions, of course. For a family to be eligible to live in Sun City, at least one member must be fifty, and neither there nor in Kings Point can residents have children under eighteen. But with one exception no Sun Citian I talked to said he or she had chosen the town because of the age restrictions. When I asked Mrs. Krauch why she and her husband had chosen an age-segregated community she looked startled. "Oh, I didn't feel I would just be with a lot of older people," she said. "And Sun City Center isn't like that!" Sun Citians would certainly be horrified to know that some retirees in St. Petersburg and Tampa look upon their town as an old-age ghetto. When Sun Citians speak of a "retirement community," what they usually mean is a life-care center or a nursing home. They came to Sun City Center for all the amenities spelled out in the advertising brochures and for a homogeneity that had little to do with age. In a country where class is rarely discussed, they had found their own niche like homing pigeons. And once they were home they were happy. "Lots of fine people," one resident told the community newspaper. "This is a cross section of the better people in the nation."

The notion that Sun Citians do not care about past professional status is a thought often articulated in Sun City. Sun City boosters—and most Sun Citians are boosters when they talk to an outsider—say it almost as regularly as they say that they are always active and on the go. The fact that the Sun City membership directory—it is actually the phone book—lists the residents' past professions along with their addresses suggests, however, that the notion is less a description of the community than a doctrine belonging to it. (Some people list the company or service they worked for, others their calling—"educator," say—and a very few put nothing at all.) Most people, like Mrs. Krauch and Mrs. Smith, have a fairly exact idea of the professional standing of their neighbors. The less exacting say, "We have some doctors and lawyers. We have some millionaires, too." Sun Citians will very often praise the company they are in by saying, "They're people of achievement—people with prestige." That most Sun Citians have the same set of achievements and the same sort of prestige does not seem to worry them; indeed, the contrary is true. . . .

• • •

. . . Certainly it is fortunate that Sun Citians can discern the differences between the houses in their development, for an outsider walking or driving around Sun City finds the experience akin to sensory deprivation. The curving white streets—with names like La Jolla Avenue and Pebble Beach Boulevard—lead only back upon themselves, and since the land is flat they give no vistas on the outside world. Turning through the points of the compass, the visitor comes to another lake, another golf course, another series of white houses. The houses are not identical—the developer always gives buyers several models to choose from—but they are all variations on the same theme: white ranch house. Then, too, the whole town looks as if it had been landscaped by the same landscape gardener. Every house has a Bermuda-grass lawn, a tree surrounded by white gravel, and a shrubbery border set off by white stones. Some owners have put white plaster statues of cupids or wading birds in the shrubs. In the newer sections, each house has a wrought-iron fixture with a carriage lamp and a sign reading THE JONESES OR THE SMITHS (there are twenty-eight Smiths in Sun City Center, and fifteen Joneses), and, under that, "Bob and Betty" or "Bill and Marge." No toys litter the pathways. The streets and the sidewalks are so clean they look scrubbed.

The developers have created this world, but they have made no mistakes. Sun Citians maintain it, and they like it as it is. One woman told me that she had come there at least in part because of the neatness of the lawns. "But I'm afraid I don't take as good care of my lawn as I should," she said. "When the wind blows hard, a palm frond will often blow down, and the next day my neighbor will be angry at me for not picking it up. He wants me to cut the tree down. I don't think I will." Kings Point people often sit outside their houses; Sun City people rarely do, perhaps because they require more privacy, perhaps because they're loath to disturb such perfection.

Sun Citians keep their houses with the same fanatical tidiness: the fibers in the carpets are stiff from vacuuming; the tables reflect one's face. One woman I visited had put a plastic runner across her new white carpeting; another apologized for the mess in her workroom when there was only a pencil and a sheet of paper out of place. But the interiors of Sun City houses are not anonymous, for Sun Citians are collectors; their houses are showcases for family treasures and the bric-a-brac collected over a lifetime. On the walls are oil paintings of bucolic landscapes, pastel portraits of children, Thai rubbings, or Chinese lacquer panels inlaid with cherry blossoms. Almost every living room has a cabinet filled with pieces of antique china and gold-rimmed glass. On the tables are ship models, sports trophies, carved animals, china figurines, or trees made of semiprecious stones. In a week in Sun City, I visited only one house where there was no bric-a-brac to speak of and where the owners lived in a comfortable disarray of newspapers, usable ashtrays, and paperback books. In most Sun City living rooms, the objects seem to rule. China birds, wooden horses, or ivory elephants parade resolutely across coffee tables and seem to have an independent life and purpose of their own.

For all this cleanliness and order, there is something childlike about Sun City. In part, it's that so many people have collections of puppets, animals, pillows, or dolls. In part, it's that everyone is so talkative, so pleasant, so eager to please. The impression also comes from the warm air, the pastel colors, the arbitrary curving of the streets, the white plaster ducks on the lawns and the real ducks that parade undisturbed among them on their way from lake to lake. The very absence of children contributes to this atmosphere, since the people riding around on three-wheelers or golf carts seem to have no parents. Then, too, one associates uniformity of age with camp or school. . . .

SUGGESTIONS FOR DISCUSSION

1. Taking into account the way in which FitzGerald describes Sun City, what would you say is her attitude about the place? Point to passages in which this attitude is best expressed.
2. FitzGerald notes how very much alike everything seems to be in Sun City. Can you think of other public spaces that seem to convey that impression as well? What reasons can you think of for a developer to make a public space that looks so uniform?
3. Ours is often called an ageist culture, meaning that we discriminate against the aged in our society. How does that seem to be true or not true in places like Sun City Center?

SUGGESTIONS FOR WRITING

1. Write an essay in which you explain what attitude FitzGerald seems to convey toward Sun City and its residents. Consider, in your essay, what she might mean when she states "the eyes of all the people are upon" the residents.
2. Sun City Center is a place built specifically for a homogeneous group of people, people who are generally alike. Write an essay in which you explain why you would prefer either a homogeneous or a heterogeneous place. As you write, you might develop your response by describing places that you know which are created for homogeneous sets of people—places that seem to suggest a particular lifestyle or social or economic class simply by their appearance. How do you feel about such places?
3. Though it is most common to think of spectacle as Leger defines it—surprise, lights, flash—FitzGerald's analysis of Sun City can suggest yet another way of thinking about public space as spectacle. In its own way, Sun City might be read as the spectacle of having made it in America. It is a vision of successful retirement in which everyone makes it to the same economic stage as represented by the very appearance of their houses, lawns, and streets. Write an essay in which you describe and comment on a place that, like Sun City, seems to convey the image of having made it in America.

David Guterson

ENCLOSED. ENCYCLOPEDIC. ENDURED. ONE WEEK AT THE MALL OF AMERICA

Writer and cultural critic David Guterson is the author of *Family Matters: Why Home Schooling Makes Sense*. His description of the Mall of America is based on personal observation and interpretations, but you will notice that Guterson observes the Mall much in the way Baudrillard (in a later selection in this chapter) looks at New York. To Guterson, the Mall of America is like a foreign country. He spent one week there taking observation notes and trying, he tells us, to answer the question, "If the Mall of America was part of America, what was that going to mean?"

Suggestion for Reading

- Before you read this article, write down your own interpretations of "mall culture." In other words, how do you think malls function in American culture? What do they suggest about what we value and how we live?

———————————————◆———————————————

L ast April, on a visit to the new Mall of America near Minneapolis, I carried with me the public-relations press kit provided for the benefit of reporters. It included an assortment of "fun facts" about the mall: 140,000 hot dogs sold each week, 10,000 permanent jobs, 44 escalators and 17 elevators, 12,750 parking places, 13,300 short tons of steel, $1 million in cash disbursed weekly from 8 automatic-teller machines. Opened in the summer of 1992, the mall was built on the 78-acre site of the former Metropolitan Stadium, a five-minute drive from the Minneapolis–St. Paul International Airport. With 4.2 million square feet of floor space—including twenty-two times the retail footage of the average American shopping center—the Mall of America was "the largest fully enclosed combination retail and family entertainment complex in the United States."

Eleven thousand articles, the press kit warned me, had already been written on the mall. Four hundred trees had been planted in its gardens, $625 million had been spent to build it, 350 stores had been leased. Three thousand bus tours were anticipated each year along with a half-million Canadian visitors and 200,000 Japanese tourists. Sales were projected at $650 million for 1993 and at $1 billion for 1996. Donny and Marie Osmond had visited the mall, as had Janet Jackson and Sally Jesse Raphael, Arnold Schwarzenegger, and the 1994 Winter Olympic Committee. The mall was five times larger than Red Square and twenty times larger than St. Peter's Basilica; it incorporated 2.3 miles of hallways and almost twice as much steel as the Eiffel Tower. It was also home to the nation's largest indoor theme park, a place called Knott's Camp Snoopy.

On the night I arrived, a Saturday, the mall was spotlit dramatically in the manner of a Las Vegas casino. It resembled, from the outside, a castle or fort, the Emerald City or Never-Never Land, impossibly large and vaguely unreal, an unbroken, windowless multi-storied edifice the size of an airport terminal. Surrounded by parking lots and new freeway ramps, monolithic and imposing in the manner of a walled city, it loomed brightly against the Minnesota night sky with the disturbing magnetism of a mirage.

I knew already that the Mall of America had been imagined by its creators not merely as a marketplace but as a national tourist attraction, an immense zone of entertainments. Such a conceit raised provocative questions, for our architecture testifies to our view of ourselves and to the condition of our souls. Large buildings stand as markers in the lives of nations and in the stream of a people's history. Thus I could only ask myself: Here was a new structure that had cost more than half a billion dollars to erect—what might it tell us about ourselves? If the Mall of America was part of America, what was that going to mean?

• • •

I passed through one of the mall's enormous entranceways and took myself inside. Although from a distance the Mall of America had appeared menacing—exuding the ambience of a monstrous hallucination—within it turned out to be simply a shopping mall, certainly more vast than other malls but in tone and aspect, design and feel, not readily distinguishable from them. Its nuances were instantly familiar as the generic features of the American shopping mall at the tail end of the twentieth century: polished stone, polished tile, shiny chrome and brass, terrazzo floors, gazebos. From third-floor vistas, across vaulted spaces, the Mall of America felt endlessly textured—glass-enclosed elevators, neon-tube lighting, bridges, balconies, gas lamps, vaulted skylights—and densely crowded with hordes of people circumambulating in an endless promenade. Yet despite the mall's expansiveness, it elicited claustrophobia, sensory deprivation, and an unnerving disorientation. Everywhere I went I spied other pilgrims who had found, like me, that the straight way was lost and that the YOU ARE HERE landmarks on the map kiosks referred to nothing in particular.

Getting lost, feeling lost, being lost—these states of mind are intentional features of the mall's psychological terrain. There are, one notices, no clocks or windows, nothing to distract the shopper's psyche from the alternate reality the mall conjures. Here we are free to wander endlessly and to furtively watch our fellow wanderers, thousands upon thousands of milling strangers who have come with the intent of losing themselves in the mall's grand, stimulating design. For a few hours we share some common ground—a fantasy of infinite commodities and comforts—and then we drift apart forever. The mall exploits our acquisitive instincts without honoring our communal requirements, our eternal desire for discourse and intimacy, needs that until the twentieth century were traditionally met in our marketplaces but that are not met at all in giant shopping malls.

• • •

On this evening a few thousand young people had descended on the mall in pursuit of alcohol and entertainment. They had come to Gators, Hooters, and Knuckleheads, Puzzles, Fat Tuesday, and Ltl Ditty's. At Players, a sports bar, the woman beside me introduced herself as "the pregnant wife of an Iowa pig farmer" and explained that she had driven five hours with friends to "do the mall party scene together." She left and was replaced by Kathleen from Minnetonka, who claimed to have "a real shopping thing—I can't go a week without buying new clothes. I'm not fulfilled until I buy something."

Later a woman named Laura arrived, with whom Kathleen was acquainted. "I *am* the mall," she announced ecstatically upon discovering I was a reporter. "I'd move in here if I could bring my dog," she added. "This place is heaven, it's a *mecca*."

"We egg each other on," explained Kathleen, calmly puffing on a cigarette. "It's like, sort of, an addiction."

"You want the truth?" Laura asked. "I'm constantly suffering from megamall withdrawal. I come here all the time."

Kathleen: "It's a sickness. It's like cocaine or something; it's a drug."

Laura: "Kathleen's got this thing about buying, but I just need to *be* here. If I buy something it's an added bonus."

Kathleen: "She buys stuff all the time; don't listen."

Laura: "Seriously, I feel sorry for other malls. They're so small and *boring*."

Kathleen seemed to think about this: "Richdale Mall," she blurted finally. She rolled her eyes and gestured with her cigarette. "Oh, my God, Laura. Why did we even *go* there?"

● ● ●

There is, of course, nothing naturally abhorrent in the human impulse to dwell in marketplaces or the urge to buy, sell, and trade. Rural Americans traditionally looked forward to the excitement and sensuality of market day; Native Americans traveled long distances to barter and trade at sprawling, festive encampments. In Persian bazaars and in the ancient Greek agoras the very soul of the community was preserved and could be seen, felt, heard, and smelled as it might be nowhere else. All over the planet the humblest of people have always gone to market with hope in their hearts and in expectation of something beyond mere goods—seeking a place where humanity is temporarily in ascendance, a palette for the senses, one another.

But the illicit possibilities of the marketplace also have long been acknowledged. The Persian bazaar was closed at sundown; the Greek agora was off-limits to those who had been charged with certain crimes. One myth of the Old West we still carry with us is that market day presupposes danger; the faithful were advised to make purchases quickly and repair without delay to the farm, lest their attraction to the pleasures of the marketplace erode their purity of spirit.

In our collective discourse the shopping mall appears with the tract house, the freeway, and the backyard barbecue as a product of the American postwar years, a testament to contemporary necessities and desires and an invention not only peculiarly American but peculiarly of our own era too. Yet the mall's varied and far-flung predecessors—the covered bazaars of the Middle East, the stately arcades of Victorian England, Italy's vaulted and skylit galleries, Asia's monsoon-protected urban markets—all suggest that the rituals of indoor shopping, although in their nuances not often like our own, are nevertheless broadly known. The late twentieth-century American contribution has been to transform the enclosed bazaar into an economic institution that is vastly profitable yet socially enervated, one that redefines in fundamental ways the human relationship to the marketplace. At the Mall of America—an extreme example—we discover ourselves thoroughly lost among strangers in a marketplace intentionally designed to serve no community needs.

In the strict sense the Mall of America is not a marketplace at all—the soul of a community expressed as a *place*—but rather a tourist attraction. Its promoters have peddled it to the world at large as something more profound than a local marketplace and as a destination with deep implications. "I believe we can make Mall of America stand for all of America," asserted the mall's general manager, John Wheeler, in a promotional video entitled *There's a Place for Fun in Your Life.* "I believe there's a shopper in all of us," added the director of marketing, Maureen Hooley. The mall has memorialized its opening-day proceedings by producing a celebratory videotape: Ray Charles singing "America the Beautiful," a laser show followed by fireworks, "The Star-Spangled Banner" and "The Stars and Stripes Forever," the Gatlin Brothers, and Peter Graves. "Mall of America. . . ," its narrator intoned. "The name alone conjures up images of greatness, of a retail complex so magnificent it could only happen in America."

Indeed, on the day the mall opened, Miss America visited. The mall's logo—a red, white, and blue star bisected by a red, white, and blue ribbon—decorated everything from the mall itself to coffee mugs and the flanks of buses. The idea, director of tourism Colleen Hayes told me, was to position America's largest mall as an institution on the scale of Disneyland or the Grand Canyon, a place simultaneously iconic and totemic, a revered symbol of the United States and a mecca to which the faithful would flock in pursuit of all things purchasable.

• • •

On Sunday I wandered the hallways of the pleasure dome with the sensation that I had entered an M. C. Escher drawing—there was no such thing as up or down, and the escalators all ran backward. A 1993 Ford Probe GT was displayed as if popping out of a giant packing box; a full-size home, complete with artificial lawn, had been built in the mall's rotunda. At the Michael Ricker Pewter Gallery I came across a miniature tableau of a pewter dog peeing on a pewter man's leg, at Hologram Land I pondered 3-D hallucinations of the Medusa and Marilyn Monroe. I passed a kiosk called The Sportsman's Wife; I stood beside a life-size statue of the Hamm's Bear, carved out of pine and available for $1,395 at a store called Minnesot-ah! At Pueblo Spirit I examined a "dream catcher"—a small hoop made from deer sinew and willow twigs and designed to be hung over its owner's bed as a tactic for filtering bad dreams. For a while I sat in front of Glamour Shots and watched while women were groomed and brushed for photo sessions yielding high-fashion self-portraits at $34.95 each. There was no stopping, no slowing down. I passed Mug Me, Queen for a Day, and Barnyard Buddies, and stood in the Brookstone store examining a catalogue: a gopher "eliminator" for $40 (it's a vibrating, anodized-aluminum stake), a "no-stoop" shoehorn for $10, a nose-hair trimmer for $18. At the arcade inside Knott's Camp Snoopy I watched while teenagers played Guardians of the 'Hood, Total Carnage, Final Fight, and Varth Operation Thunderstorm; a small crowd of them had gathered around a lean, cool character who stood calmly shooting video cowpokes in a game called Mad Dog McCree. Left thumb on his silver belt buckle, biceps pulsing, he banged away without remorse while dozens of his enemies crumpled and died in alleyways and dusty streets.

At Amazing Pictures a teenage boy had his photograph taken as a bodybuilder—his face smoothly grafted onto a rippling body—then proceeded to purchase this pleasing image on a poster, a sweatshirt, and a coffee mug. At Painted Tipi there was wild rice for sale, hand-harvested from Leech Lake, Minnesota. At Animalia I came across a polyresin figurine of a turtle retailing for $3,200. At Bloomingdale's I pondered a denim shirt with its sleeves ripped away, the sort of thing available at used-clothing stores (the "grunge look," a Bloomingdale's employee explained), on sale for $125. Finally, at a gift shop in Knott's Camp Snoopy, I came across a game called Electronic Mall Madness, put out by Milton Bradley. On the box, three twelve-year-old girls with good features happily vied to beat one another to the game-board mall's best sales.

At last I achieved an enforced self-arrest, anchoring myself against a bench while the mall tilted on its axis. Two pubescent girls in retainers and braces sat beside me sipping coffees topped with whipped cream and chocolate sprinkles, their shopping bags gathered tightly around their legs, their eyes fixed on the passing crowds. They came, they said, from Shakopee—"It's nowhere," one of them explained. The megamall, she added, was "a buzz at first, but now it seems pretty normal. 'Cept my parents are like Twenty Questions every time I want to come here. 'Specially since the shooting."

On a Sunday night, she elaborated, three people had been wounded when shots were fired in a dispute over a San Jose Sharks jacket. "In the *mall*," her friend reminded me. "Right here at megamall. A shooting."

"It's like nowhere's safe," the first added.

They sipped their coffees and explicated for me the plot of a film they saw as relevant, a horror movie called *Dawn of the Dead,* which they had each viewed a half-dozen times. In the film, they explained, apocalypse had come, and the survivors had repaired to a shopping mall as the most likely place to make their last stand in a poisoned, impossible world. And this would have been perfectly all right, they insisted, except that the place had also attracted hordes of the infamous living dead—sentient corpses who had not relinquished their attraction to indoor shopping.

I moved on and contemplated a computerized cash register in the infant's section of the Nordstrom store: "The Answer Is Yes!!!" its monitor reminded clerks. "Customer Service Is Our Number One Priority!" Then back at Bloomingdale's I contemplated a bank of televisions playing incessantly an advertisement for Egoïste, a men's cologne from Chanel. In the ad a woman on a wrought-iron balcony tossed her black hair about and screamed long and passionately, then there were many women screaming passionately, too, and throwing balcony shutters open and closed, and this was all followed by a bottle of the cologne displayed where I could get a good look at it. The brief, strange drama repeated itself until I could no longer stand it.

• • •

America's first fully enclosed shopping center—Southdale Center, in Edina, Minnesota—is a ten-minute drive from the Mall of America and thirty-six years its senior. (It is no coincidence that the Twin Cities area is such a prominent player in mall history: Minnesota is subject to the sort of severe weather that makes climate-controlled shopping seductive.) Opened in 1956, Southdale spawned an era of fervid mall construction and generated a vast new industry. Shopping centers proliferated so rapidly that by the end of 1992, says the National Research Bureau, there were nearly 39,000 of them operating everywhere across the country. But while malls recorded a much-ballyhooed success in the America of the 1970s and early 1980s, they gradually became less profitable to run as the exhausted and overwhelmed American worker inevitably lost interest in leisure shopping. Pressed for time and short on money, shoppers turned to factory outlet centers, catalogue purchasing, and "category killers" (specialty stores such as Home Depot and Price Club) at the expense of shopping malls. The industry, unnerved, re-invented itself, relying on smaller and more convenient local centers—especially the familiar neighborhood strip mall—and building far fewer large regional malls in an effort to stay afloat through troubled times. With the advent of cable television's Home Shopping Network and the proliferation of specialty catalogue retailers (whose access to computerized market research has made them, in the Nineties, powerful competitors), the mall industry reeled yet further. According to the International Council of Shopping Centers, new mall construction in 1992 was a third of what it had been in 1989, and the value of mall-construction contracts dropped 60 percent in the same three-year period.

Anticipating a future in which millions of Americans will prefer to shop in the security of their living rooms—conveniently accessing online retail companies as a form of quiet evening entertainment—the mall industry, after less than forty years, experienced a full-blown mid-life crisis. It was necessary for the industry to re-invent itself once more, this time with greater attentiveness to the qualities that would allow it to endure relentless change. Anxiety-ridden and sapped of vitality, mall builders fell back on an ancient truth, one capable of sustaining them through troubled seasons they discovered what humanity had always understood, that shopping and frivolity go hand in hand and are inherently symbiotic. *If you build it fun, they will come.*

The new bread-and-circuses approach to mall building was first ventured in 1985 by the four Ghermezian brothers—Raphael, Nader, Bahman, and Eskander—builders of Canada's $750 million West Edmonton Mall, which included a water slide, an artificial lake, a miniature-golf course, a hockey rink, and forty-seven rides in an amusement park known as Fantasyland. The complex quickly generated sales revenues at twice the rate per square foot of retail space that could be squeezed from a conventional outlet mall, mostly by developing its own shopping synergy: people came for a variety of reasons and to do a variety of things. West Edmonton's carnival atmosphere, it gradually emerged, lubricated pocketbooks and inspired the sort of impulse buying on which malls everywhere thrive. To put the matter another way, it was time for a shopping-and-pleasure palace to be attempted in the United States.

After selling the Mall of America concept to Minnesotans in 1985, the Ghermezians joined forces with their American counterparts—Mel and Herb Simon of Indianapolis, owners of the NBA's Indiana Pacers and the nation's second-largest developers of shopping malls. The idea, in the beginning, was to outdo West Edmonton by building a mall far larger and more expensive—something visionary, a wonder of the world—and to include such attractions as fashionable hotels, an elaborate tour de force aquarium, and a monorail to the Minneapolis–St. Paul airport. Eventually the project was downscaled substantially: a million square feet of floor space was eliminated, the construction budget was cut, and the aquarium and hotels were never built (reserved, said marketing director Maureen Hooley, for "phase two" of the mall's development). Japan's Mitsubishi Bank, Mitsui Trust, and Chuo Trust together put up a reported $400 million to finance the cost of construction, and Teachers Insurance and Annuity Association (the majority owner of the Mall of America) came through with another $225 million. At a total bill of $625 million, the mall was ultimately a less ambitious project than its forebear up north on the Canadian plains, and neither as large nor as gaudy. Reflecting the economy's downturn, the parent companies of three of the mall's anchor tenants—Sears, Macy's, and Bloomingdale's—were battling serious financial trouble and needed substantial transfusions from mall developers to have their stores ready by opening day.

The mall expects to spend millions on marketing itself during its initial year of operation and has lined up the usual corporate sponsors—Ford, Pepsi, US West—in an effort to build powerful alliances. Its public relations representatives travel to towns such as Rapid City, South Dakota, and Sioux City, Iowa, in order to drum up interest within the Farm Belt. Northwest Airlines, another corporate sponsor, offers package deals from London and Tokyo and fare adjustments for those willing to come from Bismarck, North Dakota; Cedar Rapids, Iowa; and Kalamazoo or Grand Rapids,

Michigan. Calling itself a "premier tourism destination," the mall draws from a primary tourist market that incorporates the eleven Midwest states (and two Canadian provinces) lying within a day's drive of its parking lots. It also estimates that in its first six months of operation, 5.3 million out of 16 million visitors came from beyond the Twin Cities metropolitan area.

The mall has forecast a much-doubted figure of 46 million annual visits by 1996—four times the number of annual visits to Disneyland, for example, and twelve times the visits to the Grand Canyon. The number, Maureen Hooley explained, seems far less absurd when one takes into account that mall pilgrims make far more repeat visits—as many as eighty in a single year—than visitors to theme parks such as Disneyland. Relentless advertising and shrewd promotion, abetted by the work of journalists like myself, assure the mall that visitors will come in droves—at least for the time being. The national media have comported themselves as if the new mall were a place of light and promise, full of hope and possibility. Meanwhile the Twin Cities' media have been shameless: on opening night Minneapolis's WCCO-TV aired a one-hour mall special, hosted by local news anchors Don Shelby and Colleen Needles, and the *St. Paul Pioneer Press* (which was named an "official" sponsor of the opening) dedicated both a phone line and a weekly column to answering esoteric mall questions. Not to be outdone, the *Minneapolis Star Tribune* developed a special graphic to draw readers to mall stories and printed a vast Sunday supplement before opening day under the heading A WHOLE NEW MALLGAME. By the following Wednesday all perspective was in eclipse: the local press reported that at 9:05 A.M., the mall's Victoria's Secret outlet had recorded its first sale, a pair of blue/green silk men's boxer shorts; that mall developers Mel and Herb Simon ate black-bean soup for lunch at 12:30 P.M.; that Kimberly Levis, four years old, constructed a rectangular column nineteen bricks high at the mall's Lego Imagination Center, and that mall officials had retained a plumber on standby in case difficulties arose with the mall's toilets.

From all of this coverage—and from the words you now read—the mall gains status as a phenomenon worthy of our time and consideration: place as celebrity. The media encourage us to visit our megamall in the obligatory fashion we flock to *Jurassic Park*—because it is there, all glitter and glow, a piece of the terrain, a season's diversion, an assumption on the cultural landscape. All of us will want to be in on the conversation and, despite ourselves, we will go.

• • •

Lost in the fun house I shopped till I dropped, but the scale of the mall eventually overwhelmed me and I was unable to make a purchase. Finally I met Chuck Brand on a bench in Knott's Camp Snoopy; he was seventy-two and, in his personal assessment of it, had lost at least 25 percent of his mind. "It's fun being a doozy," he confessed to me. "The security cops got me figured and keep their distance. I don't get hassled for hanging out, not shopping. Because the deal is, when you're seventy-two, man, you're just about all done shopping."

After forty-seven years of selling houses in Minneapolis, Chuck comes to the mall every day. He carries a business card with his picture on it, his company name and phone number deleted and replaced by his pager code. His wife drops him at the mall at 10:00 A.M. each morning and picks him up again at six; in between he sits and watches. "I can't sit home and do nothing," he insisted. When I stood to go he assured me he understood: I was young and had things I had to do. "Listen," he added, "thanks for talking to me, man. I've been sitting in this mall for four months now and nobody ever said nothing."

The next day I descended into the mall's enormous basement, where its business offices are located. "I'm sorry to have to bring this up," my prearranged mall guide, Michelle Biesiada, greeted me. "But you were seen talking to one of our housekeepers— one of the people who empty the garbage?—and really, you aren't supposed to do that."

Later we sat in the mall's security center, a subterranean computerized command post where two uniformed officers manned a bank of television screens. The Mall of America, it emerged, employed 109 surveillance cameras to monitor the various activities of its guests, and had plans to add yet more. There were cameras in the food courts and parking lots, in the hallways and in Knott's Camp Snoopy. From where we sat, it was possible to monitor thirty-six locations simultaneously; it was also possible, with the use of a zoom feature, to narrow in on an object as small as a hand, a license place, or a wallet.

While we sat in the darkness of the security room, enjoying the voyeuristic pleasures it allowed (I, for one, felt a giddy sense of power), a security guard noted something of interest occurring in one of the parking lots. The guard engaged a camera's zoom feature, and soon we were given to understand that a couple of bored shoppers were enjoying themselves by fornicating in the front seat of a parked car. An officer was dispatched to knock on their door and discreetly suggest that they move themselves along; the Mall of America was no place for this. "If they want to have sex they'll have to go elsewhere," a security officer told me. "We don't have anything against sex, per se, but we don't want it happening in our parking lots."

I left soon afterward for a tour of the mall's basement, a place of perpetual concrete corridors and home to a much-touted recyclery. Declaring itself "the most environmentally conscious shopping center in the industry," the Mall of America claims to recycle up to 80 percent of its considerable refuse and points to its "state-of-the-art" recycling system as a symbol of its dedication to Mother Earth. Yet Rick Doering of Browning-Ferris Industries—the company contracted to manage the mall's 700 tons of monthly garbage—described the on-site facility as primarily a public-relations gambit that actually recycles only a third of the mall's tenant waste and little of what is discarded by its thousands of visitors; furthermore, he admitted, the venture is unprofitable to Browning-Ferris, which would find it far cheaper to recycle the mall's refuse somewhere other than in its basement.

A third-floor "RecycleNOW Center," located next to Macy's and featuring educational exhibits, is designed to enhance the mall's self-styled image as a national recycling leader. Yet while the mall's developers gave Macy's $35 million to cover most of its "build-out" expenses (the cost of transforming the mall's basic structure into finished, customer-ready floor space), Browning-Ferris got nothing in build-out costs and operates the center at a total loss, paying rent equivalent to that paid by the mall's retailers. As a result, the company has had to look for ways to keep its costs to a minimum, and the mall's garbage is now sorted by developmentally disabled adults working a conveyor belt in the basement. Doering and I stood watching them as they picked at a stream of paper and plastic bottles; when I asked about their pay, he flinched and grimaced, then deflected me toward another supervisor, who said that wages were based on daily productivity. Did this mean that they made less than minimum wage? I inquired. The answer was yes.

Upstairs once again, I hoped for relief from the basement's oppressive, concrete gloom, but the mall felt densely crowded and with panicked urgency I made an effort to leave. I ended up instead at Knott's Camp Snoopy—the seven-acre theme park at the center of the complex—a place intended to alleviate claustrophobia by "bringing the outdoors indoors." Its interior landscape, the press kit claims, "was inspired by Minnesota's natural habitat—forests, meadows, riverbanks, and marshes. . . ." And "everything you see, feel, smell and hear adds to the illusion that it's summertime, seventy degrees and you're outside enjoying the awesome splendor of the Minnesota woods."

Creators of this illusion had much to contend with, including sixteen carnival-style midway rides, such as the Pepsi Ripsaw, the Screaming Yellow Eagle, Paul Bunyan's Log Chute by Brawny, Tumbler, Truckin', and Huff 'n' Puff; fifteen places for visitors to eat, such as Funnel Cakes, Stick Dogs and Campfire Burgers, Taters, Pizza Oven, and Wilderness Barbecue; seven shops with names like Snoopy's Boutique, Joe Cool's Hot Shop, and Camp Snoopy Toys; and such assorted attractions as Pan for Gold, Hunter's Paradise Shooting Gallery, the Snoopy Fountain, and the video arcade that includes the game Mad Dog McCree.

As if all this were not enough to cast a serious pall over the Minnesota woods illusion, the theme park's designers had to contend with the fact that they could use few plants native to Minnesota. At a constant temperature of seventy degrees, the mall lends itself almost exclusively to tropical varieties—orange jasmine, black olive, oleander, hibiscus—and not at all to the conifers of Minnesota, which require a cold dormancy period. Deferring ineluctably to this troubling reality, Knott's Camp Snoopy brought in 526 tons of plants—tropical rhododendrons, willow figs, buddhist pines, azaleas—from such places as Florida, Georgia, and Mississippi.

Anne Pryor, a Camp Snoopy marketing representative, explained to me that these plants were cared for via something called "integrated pest management," which meant the use of predators such as ladybugs instead of pesticides. Yet every member of the landscape staff I spoke to described a campaign of late-night pesticide spraying as a means of controlling the theme park's enemies—mealybugs, aphids, and spider mites. Two said they had argued for integrated pest management as a more environmentally sound method of controlling insects but that to date it had not been tried.

Even granting that Camp Snoopy is what it claims to be—an authentic version of Minnesota's north woods tended by environmentally correct means—the question remains whether it makes sense to place a forest in the middle of the country's largest shopping complex. Isn't it true that if people want woods, they are better off not going to a mall?

• • •

On Valentine's Day last February—cashing in on the promotional scheme of a local radio station—ninety-two couples were married en masse in a ceremony at the Mall of America. They rode the roller coaster and the Screaming Yellow Eagle and were photographed beside a frolicking Snoopy, who wore an immaculate tuxedo. "As we stand here together at the Mall of America," presiding district judge Richard Spicer declared, "we are reminded that there is a place for fun in your life and you have found it in each other." Six months earlier, the Reverend Leith Anderson of the Wooddale Church in Eden Prairie conducted services in the mall's rotunda. Six thousand people had congregated by 10:00 A.M., and Reverend Anderson delivered a sermon entitled "The Unknown God of the Mall." Characterizing the mall as a "direct descendant" of the ancient Greek agoras, the reverend pointed out that, like the Greeks before us, we Americans have many gods. Afterward, of course, the flock went shopping, much to the chagrin of Reverend Delton Krueger, president of the Mall Area Religious Council, who told the *Minneapolis Star Tribune* that as a site for church services, the mall may trivialize religion. "A good many people in the churches," said Krueger, "feel a lot of the trouble in the world is because of materialism."

● ● ●

But a good many people in the mall business today apparently think the trouble lies elsewhere. They are moving forward aggressively on the premise that the dawning era of electronic shopping does not preclude the building of shopping-and-pleasure palaces all around the globe. Japanese developers, in a joint venture with the Ghermezians known as International Malls Incorporated, are planning a $400 million Mall of Japan, with an ice rink, a water park, a fantasy-theme hotel, three breweries, waterfalls, and a sports center. We might shortly predict, too, a Mall of Europe, a Mall of New England, a Mall of California, and perhaps even a Mall of the World. The concept of shopping in a frivolous atmosphere, concocted to loosen consumers' wallets, is poised to proliferate globally. We will soon see monster malls everywhere, rooted in the soil of every nation and offering a preposterous, impossible variety of commodities and entertainments.

The new malls will be planets unto themselves, closed off from this world in the manner of space stations or of science fiction's underground cities. Like the Mall of America and West Edmonton Mall—prototypes for a new generation of shopping centers—they will project a separate and distinct reality in which an "outdoor café" is not outdoors, a "bubbling brook" is a concrete watercourse, and a "serpentine street" is a hallway. Safe, surreal, and outside of time and space, they will offer the mind a potent dreamscape from which there is no present waking. This carefully controlled fantasy— now operable in Minnesota—is so powerful as to inspire psychological addiction or to elicit in visitors a catatonic obsession with the mall's various hallucinations. The new malls will be theatrical, high-tech illusions capable of attracting enormous crowds from distant points and foreign ports. Their psychology has not yet been tried pervasively on the scale of the Mall of America, nor has it been perfected. But in time our marketplaces, all over the world, will be in essential ways interchangeable, so thoroughly divorced from the communities in which they sit that they will appear to rest like permanently docked space-ships against the landscape, windowless and turned in upon their own affairs. The affluent will travel as tourists to each, visiting the holy sites and taking photographs in the catacombs of far-flung temples.

Just as Victorian England is acutely revealed beneath the grandiose domes of its overwrought train stations, so is contemporary America well understood from the upper vistas of its shopping malls, places without either windows or clocks where the temperature is forever seventy degrees. It is facile to believe, from this vantage point, that the endless circumambulations of tens of thousands of strangers—all loaded down with the detritus of commerce—resemble anything akin to community. The shopping mall is not, as the architecture critic Witold Rybczynski has concluded, "poised to become a real urban place" with "a variety of commercial and noncommercial functions." On the contrary, it is poised to multiply around the world as an institution offering only a desolate substitute for the rich, communal lifeblood of the traditional marketplace, which will not survive its onslaught.

Standing on the Mall of America's roof, where I had ventured to inspect its massive ventilation units, I finally achieved a full sense of its vastness, of how it overwhelmed the surrounding terrain—the last sheep farm in sight, the Mississippi River incidental in the distance. Then I peered through the skylights down into Camp Snoopy, where throngs of my fellow citizens caroused happily in the vast entrails of the beast.

SUGGESTIONS FOR DISCUSSION

1. Compare your own interpretations of mall culture with Guterson's interpretation of the Mall of America. How do they compare? How do your classmates' interpretations compare with yours and with Guterson's?
2. What is it about a place like the Mall of America that might interest cultural critics? After all, isn't it just another place to shop?
3. In what ways might Guterson's impressions of the Mall of America be compared with FitzGerald's impressions of Sun City or Keillor's impressions of the Minnesota State Fair?

SUGGESTIONS FOR WRITING

1. Write a brief summary of Guterson's impressions and interpretations of the Mall of America.
2. Write a description of a place, any place, that you think does or should represent American values and concerns. Explain, in your description, what it is about the place that is an important representation of what you think America is all about.
3. Guterson begins by asking what the Mall of America means about America. He compares it to a Las Vegas casino and the Emerald City in *The Wizard of Oz*. From what you know about this place and other places like it (you might include places like Disneyland, Epcot Center, or any other megamall that tries to do more than simply enclose shops), write an essay in which you attempt to answer Guterson's question. You may well agree with some of his assessments and disagree with others. Take into account the writing you have done thus far in which you have considered how any place might represent cultural values. You should consider talking to family members and friends who did not grow up with the megamall phenomenon.

John Fiske

SHOPPING FOR PLEASURE: MALLS, POWER, AND RESISTANCE

John Fiske is a Professor of Communication at the University of Wisconsin–Madison. He is among the many scholars today who make use of the artifacts of daily life to interpret modern culture. Although much of his work has focused on reading television, he has written on a wide range of cultural phenomena, including beaches and shopping malls. For Fiske as well as others engaging in cultural studies, the analysis of popular culture can help reveal how a society produces meaning from its social experience. The following selection, taken from *Reading the Popular*, written in 1989, is one example of how these phenomena we take for granted in our everyday lives (shopping malls) are a part of that cultural production of meaning.

Suggestion for Reading

- You will notice, as you read, that Fiske makes reference to other studies from which he has drawn ideas, interpretations, and information. He uses those references both to give scholarly weight to his argument and to acknowledge his use of others' work in building his own interpretation. If you are not familiar with the names (he nearly always uses last names only), don't let that stop your reading. The context in which the name is used can usually give you enough information to allow you to continue. As you read, underline passages in which Fiske distinguishes his own view from that of those other scholars.

—————————————◆—————————————

Shopping malls are cathedrals of consumption—a glib phrase that I regret the instant it slides off my pen. The metaphor of consumerism as a religion, in which commodities become the icons of worship and the rituals of exchanging money for goods become a secular equivalent of holy communion, is simply too glib to be helpful, and too attractive to those whose intentions, whether they be moral or political, are to expose the evils and limitations of bourgeois materialism. And yet the metaphor *is* both attractive and common precisely because it does convey and construct *a* knowledge of consumerism; it does point to one set of "truths," however carefully selected a set.

Truths compete in a political arena, and the truths that the consumerism-as-contemporary-religion strives to suppress are those that deny the difference between the tenor and vehicle of the metaphor. Metaphor always works within that tense area within which the forces of similarity and difference collide, and aligns itself with those of similarity. Metaphor constructs similarity out of difference, and when a metaphor becomes a cliché, as the shopping mall-cathedral one has, then a resisting reading must align itself with the differences rather than the similarities, for clichés become clichés only because of their centrality to common sense: the cliché helps to construct the commonality of common sense.

So, the differences: the religious congregation is powerless, led like sheep through the rituals and meanings, forced to "buy" the truth on offer, all the truth, not selective bits of it. Where the interests of the Authority on High differ from those of the Congregation down Low, the congregation has no power to negotiate, to discriminate: all accommodations are made by the powerless, subjugated to the great truth. In the U.S. marketplace, 90 percent of new products fail to find sufficient buyers to survive (Schudson 1984), despite advertising, promotions, and all the persuasive techniques of the priests of consumption. In Australia, Sinclair (1987) puts the new product failure rate at 80 percent—such statistics are obviously best-guesstimates: what matters is that the failure rate is high. The power of consumer discrimination evidenced here has no equivalent in the congregation: no religion could tolerate a rejection rate of 80 or 90 percent of what it has to offer.

Religion may act as a helpful metaphor when our aim is to investigate the power of consumerism; when, however, our focus shifts to the power of the consumer, it is counter-productive. . . . Shopping is the crisis of consumerism: it is where the art and tricks of the weak can inflict most damage on, and exert most power over, the strategic interests of the powerful. The shopping mall that is seen as the terrain of guerrilla warfare looks quite different from the one constructed by the metaphor of religion.

Pressdee (1986), in his study of unemployed youth in the South Australian town of Elizabeth, paints a clear picture of both sides in this war. The ideological practices that serve the interests of the powerful are exposed in his analysis of the local mall's promotional slogan, which appears in the form of a free ticket: "Your ticket to a better shopping world: ADMITS EVERYONE." He comments:

> The words "your" and "everyone" are working to socially level out class distinction and, in doing so, overlook the city's two working class groups, those who have work and those who do not. The word "admits" with a connotation of having to have or be someone to gain admittance is cancelled out by the word "everyone"—there are no conditions of admittance; everyone is equal and can come in.

This pseudoticket to consumerism denies the basic function of a ticket—to discriminate between those who possess one and those who do not—in a precise moment of the ideological work of bourgeois capitalism with its denial of class difference, and therefore of the inevitability of class struggle. The equality of "everyone" is, of course, an equality attainable only by those with purchasing power: those without are defined out of existence, as working-class interests (derived from class *difference*) are defined out of existence by bourgeois ideology. "The ticket to a better shopping world does not say 'Admits everyone with at least some money to spend'. . . ; money and the problems associated with getting it conveniently disappear in the official discourse" (Pressdee 1986:10–11).

Pressdee then uses a variation of the religious metaphor to sum up the "official" messages of the mall:

> The images presented in the personal invitation to all in Elizabeth is then that of the cargo cult. Before us a lightshaft beams down from space, which contains the signs of the "future"; "Target", "Venture"—gifts wrapped; a table set for two. But beamed down from space they may as well be, because . . . this imagery can be viewed as reinforcing denial of the production process—goods are merely beamed to earth. The politics of their production and consumption disappear.

Yet his study showed that 80 percent of unemployed young people visited the mall at least once a week, and nearly 100 percent of young unemployed women were regular visitors. He comments on these uninvited guests:

> For young people, especially the unemployed, there has been a congregating within these cathedrals of capitalism, where desires are created and fulfilled and the production of commodities, the very activity that they are barred from, is itself celebrated on the alter of consumerism. Young people, cut off from normal consumer power, are invading the space of those with consumer power. (p. 13)

Pressdee's shift from the religious metaphor to one of warfare signals his shift of focus from the powerful to the disempowered.

Thursday nights, which in Australia are the only ones on which stores stay open late, have become the high points of shopping, when the malls are at their most crowded and the cash registers ring up their profits most busily, and it is on Thursday nights that the youth "invasion" of consumer territory is most aggressive. Pressdee (1986) describes this invasion vividly:

> Thursday nights vibrate with youth, eager to show themselves:—it belongs to them, they have possessed it. This cultural response is neither spectacular nor based upon consumerism itself. Nor does it revolve around artifacts or dress, but rather around the possession of space, or to be more precise the possession of consumer space where their very presence challenges, offends and resists.

> Hundreds of young people pour into the centre every Thursday night, with three or four hundred being present at any one time. They parade for several hours, not buying, but presenting, visually, all the contradictions of employment and unemployment, taking up their natural public space that brings both life and yet confronts the market place. Security men patrol all night aided by several police patrols, hip guns visible and radios in use, bringing a new understanding to law and order.

> Groups of young people are continually evicted from this opulant and warm environment, fights appear, drugs seem plentiful, alcohol is brought in, in various guises and packages. The police close in on a group of young women, their drink is tested. Satisfied that it is only coca-cola they are moved on and out. Not wanted. Shopkeepers and shoppers complain. The security guards become agitated and begin to question all those seen drink-

ing out of cans or bottles who are under 20, in the belief that they *must* contain alcohol. They appear frightened, totally outnumbered by young people as they continue their job in keeping the tills ringing and the passage to the altar both free and safe. (p. 14).

Pressdee coins the term "proletarian shopping" (p. 16) to describe this window shopping with no intention to buy. The youths consumed images and space instead of commodities, a kind of sensuous consumption that did not create profits. The positive pleasure of parading up and down, of offending "real" consumers and the agents of law and order, of asserting their difference within, and different use of, the cathedral of consumerism became an oppositional cultural practice.

The youths were "tricksters" in de Certeau's terms—they pleasurably exploited their knowledge of the official "rules of the game" in order to identify where these rules could be mocked, inverted, and thus used to free those they were designed to discipline. De Certeau (1984) points to the central importance of the "trickster" and the "guileful ruse" throughout peasant and folk cultures. Tricks and ruses are the art of the weak that enables them to exploit their understanding of the rules of the system, and to turn it to their advantage. They are a refusal to be subjugated:

> The actual order of things is precisely what "popular" tactics turn to their own ends, without any illusion that it will change any time soon. Though elsewhere it is exploited by a dominant power . . . here order is *tricked* by an art. (de Certeau 1984: 26)

This trickery is evidence of "an ethics of *tenacity* (countless ways of refusing to accord the established order the status of a law, a meaning or a fatality)" (p. 26).

Shopping malls are open invitations to trickery and tenacity. The youths who turn them into their meeting places, or who trick the security guards by putting alcohol into some, but only some, soda cans, are not actually behaving any differently from lunch hour window shoppers who browse through the stores, trying on goods, consuming and playing with images, with no intention to buy. In extreme weather people exploit the controlled climate of the malls for their own pleasure—mothers take children to play in their air-conditioned comfort in hot summers, and in winter older people use their concourses for daily walks. Indeed, some malls now have notices welcoming "mall walkers," and a few have even provided exercise areas set up with equipment and instructions so that the walkers can exercise more than their legs.

Of course, the mall owners are not entirely disinterested or altruistic here—they hope that some of the "tricky" users of the mall will become real economic consumers, but they have no control over who will, how many will, how often, or how profitably. One boutique owner told me that she estimated that 1 in 30 browsers actually bought something. Shopping malls are where the strategy of the powerful is most vulnerable to the tactical raids of the weak.

References

De Certeau, M. (1984). *The Practice of Everyday Life.* Berkeley: University of California Press.

Pressdee, M. (1986). "Agony or Ecstasy: Broken Transitions and the New Social State of Working-Class Youth in Australia." Occasional Papers, S. Australian Centre for Youth Studies, S.A. College of A.E., Magill, S. Australia.

Schudson, M. (1984). *Advertising: The Uneasy Persuasion.* New York: Basic Books.

Sinclair, J. (1987). *Images Incorporated: Advertising as Industry and Ideology.* London: Croom Helm.

SUGGESTIONS FOR DISCUSSION

1. Why does Fiske challenge the cathedral metaphor as a useful one for analyzing the place of malls in our culture? How is the mall of today like the great cathedrals of the past? How does the metaphor of the mall as a place of warfare work in Fiske's analysis?

2. What do you think Fiske means when he says, "The equality of 'everyone' is, of course, an equality attainable only by those with purchasing power; those without are defined out of existence"?

3. Fiske has based most of what he says on his observations of malls in Australia. How would you describe mall culture in America?

SUGGESTIONS FOR WRITING

1. Write an essay on the "cathedral" and "warfare" metaphors that Fiske uses to describe malls. How does each metaphor change the way we might interpret the mall? Which metaphor would you choose?

2. Fiske tells us that, although malls are set up to control the public's response to and use of them, people end up using them for their own purposes anyway. Write an essay on another public space that you see as one that people use for their own purposes instead of—or in addition to—the purposes for which they are meant.

3. Go to a local mall with a group of your classmates. Spend time simply observing the people. Who buys? Who walks but ignores the stores? Who comes to the mall to socialize? You might wish to reread Guterson's article on the Mall of America since his conclusions are based on one week's worth of such observations. After you have gathered the kind of information that will help you answer those questions or questions like them, write a 3–5 page essay response to John Fiske in which you discuss his theory of mall behavior and the role of malls in this culture in relation to your observations of the mall and your discussions with your group who worked with you on this project.

Jean Baudrillard

NEW YORK

Jean Baudrillard is a French sociologist and cultural theorist who taught at the University of Nanterre from 1966 to 1987. Among his works translated into English are *In the Shadow of the Silent Majorities* and *Simulations and Simulacra*. When Baudrillard traveled to the United States in the late eighties on a cross-continental lecture tour, he spent part of his visit recording his impressions of America as a place of spectacle. The 1989 book *America*, from which the following selection has been excerpted, was written as a series of philosophical postcards about his experience of seeing this place as philosopher-tourist. Though these disjointed and highly personal descriptions are not meant to work out an extended philosophical argument, they do call up powerful images of modern America and the cultural values relayed through those images. We might locate this book of impressions within the very broad category of travel literature. As you read, think about your own impressions of new or foreign places and how your impressions might sound to the people who live in those places.

Suggestion for Reading

- As you read, annotate this selection with your own reactions to Baudrillard's description.

More sirens here, day and night. The cars are faster, the advertisements more aggressive. This is wall-to-wall prostitution. And total electric light too. And the game—all games—gets more intense. It's always like this when you're getting near the center of the world. But the people smile. Actually they smile more and more, though never to other people, always to themselves.

The terrifying diversity of faces, their strangeness, strained as they all are into unbelievable expressions. The masks old age or death conferred in archaic cultures are worn here by youngsters of twenty or twelve. But this reflects the city as a whole. The beauty other cities only acquired over centuries has been achieved by New York in fifty years.

Plumes of smoke, reminiscent of girls wringing out their hair after bathing. Afro or pre-Raphaelite hairstyles. Run-of-the-mill, multiracial. City of Pharoahs, all obelisks and needles. The blocks around Central Park are like flying buttresses, lending the huge park the appearance of a hanging garden. It isn't clouds that are fleecy here, but brains.

Clouds float over the city like cerebral hemispheres driven by the wind. The people have cirrus clouds in their heads or coming out of their eyes, like the spongy vapours that rise from earth cracked by hot rains. Sexual solitude of clouds in the sky; linguistic solitude of men on the earth.

The number of people here who think alone, sing alone, and eat and talk alone in the streets is mind-boggling. And yet they don't add up. Quite the reverse. They subtract from each other and their resemblance to one another is uncertain.

Yet there is a certain solitude like no other—that of the man preparing his meal in public on a wall, or on the hood of his car, or along a fence, alone. You see that all the time here. It is the saddest sight in the world. Sadder than destitution, sadder than the beggar is the man who eats alone in public. Nothing more contradicts the laws of man or beast, for animals always do each other the honour of sharing or disputing each other's food. He who eats alone is dead (but not he who drinks alone. Why is this?).

• • •

Why do people live in New York? There is no relationship between them. Except for an inner electricity which results from the simple fact of their being crowded together. A magical sensation of contiguity and attraction for an artificial centrality. This is what makes it a self-attracting universe, which there is no reason to leave. There is no human reason to be here, except for the sheer ecstasy of being crowded together.

SUGGESTIONS FOR DISCUSSION

1. This book of impressions of America has been called a collection of postcards. How does this passage seem to conform to or vary from postcard writing as you know it?
2. Baudrillard obviously wants to convey a particular attitude about New York (and America in general) through his descriptions. What attitude do you detect in this excerpt? What passages convey that attitude?
3. What kinds of places for you have been new, exciting, enigmatic, as New York was for Baudrillard?

SUGGESTIONS FOR WRITING

1. Baudrillard writes of New York, "This is wall-to-wall prostitution. And total electric light too. And the game—all games—gets more intense." Write an essay that explains what Baudrillard means in this passage. Compare his sense of the growing intensity of American life with your own sense of American life.
2. Think of five places that you can describe with postcard-like descriptions. You might choose places that are for you what New York was for Baudrillard: new, exciting, enigmatic. But you might also choose places that are familiar, comfortable, or predictable. Write a postcard-like description of each that briefly conveys your feelings or impressions of the place to a close friend or relative.
3. Use the postcard descriptions you have just written as a brainstorming device, a device that allows you to get down several ideas so that you can pick the best of them and develop them into an essay. Look back at the descriptions you have written.

Now, take the one you consider best and write a description of that place. Develop your description with sights, sounds, smells—any images that you think best evoke your impressions or memories of the place.

Mike Davis

FORTRESS LOS ANGELES: THE MILITARIZATION OF URBAN SPACE

Mike Davis teaches urban planning and political economy at the Southern California Institute of Architecture and at UCLA. He is the author of the 1992 book *City of Quartz,* nominated for the National Book Critics Circle Award, and *Prisoners of the American Dream.* The selection that follows, from *City of Quartz,* is an analysis of the way urban planning reflects cultural change and cultural biases. In it, Davis argues that downtown Los Angeles has become a kind of domestic militarized zone and a place where races and classes are visibly and aggressively separated.

Suggestion for Reading

• Before you begin reading, write a brief description of your personal image of the modern city. Think about what you base that image on and consider how Davis's description either corroborates or contradicts that image.

⧫

In Los Angeles—once a paradise of free beaches, luxurious parks, and "cruising strips"—genuinely democratic space is virtually extinct. The pleasure domes of the elite Westside rely upon the social imprisonment of a third-world service proletariat in increasingly repressive ghettos and barrios. In a city of several million aspiring immigrants (where Spanish-surname children are now almost two-thirds of the school-age population), public amenities are shrinking radically, libraries and playgrounds are closing, parks are falling derelict, and streets are growing ever more desolate and dangerous.

Here, as in other American cities, municipal policy has taken its lead from the security offensive and the middle-class demand for increased spatial and social insulation. Taxes previously targeted for traditional public spaces and recreational facilities have been redirected to support corporate redevelopment projects. A pliant city government—in the case of Los Angeles, one ironically professing to represent a liberal biracial coalition—has collaborated in privatizing public space and subsidizing new exclusive enclaves (benignly called "urban villages"). The celebratory language used to describe contemporary Los Angeles—"urban renaissance," "city of the future." and so on—is only a triumphal gloss laid over the brutalization of its inner-city neighborhoods and the stark divisions of class and race represented in its built environment. Urban form obediently follows repressive function. Los Angeles, as always in the vanguard, offers an especially disturbing guide to the emerging liaisons between urban architecture and the police state.

FORBIDDEN CITY

Los Angeles's first spatial militarist was the legendary General Harrison Gray Otis, proprietor of the *Times* and implacable foe of organized labor. In the 1890s, after locking out his union printers and announcing a crusade for "industrial freedom," Otis retreated into a new *Times* building designed as a fortress with grim turrets and battlements crowned by a bellicose bronze eagle. To emphasize his truculence, he later had a small, functional cannon installed on the hood of his Packard touring car. Not surprisingly, this display of aggression produced a response in kind. On October 1, 1910, the heavily fortified *Times* headquarters—the command-post of the open shop on the West Coast—was destroyed in a catastrophic explosion, blamed on union saboteurs.

Eighty years later, the martial spirit of General Otis pervades the design of Los Angeles's new Downtown, whose skyscrapers march from Bunker Hill down the Figueroa corridor. Two billion dollars of public tax subsidies have enticed big banks and corporate headquarters back to a central city they almost abandoned in the 1960s. Into a waiting grid, cleared of tenement housing by the city's powerful and largely unaccountable redevelopment agency, local developers and offshore investors (increasingly Japanese) have planted a series of block-square complexes: Crocker Center, the Bonaventure Hotel and Shopping Mall, the World Trade Center, California Plaza, Arco Center, and so on. With an increasingly dense and self-contained circulation system linking these superblocks, the new financial district is best conceived as a single, self-referential hyperstructure, a Miesian skyscape of fantastic proportions.

Like similar megalomaniacal complexes tethered to fragmented and desolate downtowns—such as the Renaissance Center in Detroit and the Peachtree and Omni centers in Atlanta—Bunker Hill and the Figueroa corridor have provoked a storm of objections to their abuse of scale and composition, their denigration of street life, and their confiscation of the vital energy of the center, now sequestered within their subterranean concourses or privatized plazas. Sam Hall Kaplan, the former design critic of the *Times,* has vociferously denounced the antistreet bias of redevelopment; in his view, the superimposition of "hermetically sealed fortresses" and random "pieces of suburbia" onto Downtown has "killed the street" and "dammed the rivers of life."[1]

Yet Kaplan's vigorous defense of pedestrian democracy remains grounded in liberal complaints about "bland design" and "elitist planning practices." Like most architectural critics, he rails against the oversights of urban design without conceding a dimension of foresight, and even of deliberate repressive intent. For when Downtown's new "Gold Coast" is seen in relation to other social landscapes in the central city, the "fortress effect" emerges, not as an inadvertent failure of design, but as an explicit—and, in its own terms, successful—socio-spatial strategy.

The goals of this strategy may be summarized as a double repression: to obliterate all connection with Downtown's past and to prevent any dynamic association with the non-Anglo urbanism of its future. Los Angeles is unusual among major urban centers in having preserved, however negligently, most of its Beaux Arts commercial core. Yet the city chose to transplant—at immense public cost—the entire corporate and financial district from around Broadway and Spring Street to Bunker Hill, a half-dozen blocks further west.

• • •

Photographs of the old Downtown in its 1940s prime show crowds of Anglo, black, and Mexican shoppers of all ages and classes. The contemporary Downtown "renaissance" renders such heterogeneity virtually impossible. It is intended not just to "kill the street" as Kaplan feared, but to "kill the crowd," to eliminate that democratic mixture that Olmsted believed was America's antidote to European class polarization. The new Downtown is designed to ensure a seamless continuum of middle-class work, consumption, and recreation, insulated from the city's "unsavory" streets. Ramparts and battlements, reflective glass and elevated pedways, are tropes in an architectural language warning off the underclass Other. Although architectural critics are usually blind to this militarized syntax, urban pariah groups—whether young black men, poor Latino immigrants, or elderly homeless white females—read the signs immediately.

• • •

MEAN STREETS

This strategic armoring of the city against the poor is especially obvious at street level. In his famous study of the "social life of small urban spaces," William Whyte points out that the quality of any urban environment can be measured, first of all, by whether there are convenient, comfortable places for pedestrians to sit. This maxim has been warmly taken to heart by designers of the high corporate precincts of Bunker Hill and its adjacent "urban villages." As part of the city's policy of subsidizing the white-collar residential colonization of Downtown, tens of millions of dollars of tax revenue have been invested in the creation of attractive, "soft" environments in favored areas. Planners envision a succession of opulent piazzas, fountains, public art, exotic shrubbery, and comfortable street furniture along a ten-block pedestrian corridor from Bunker Hill to South Park. Brochures sell Downtown's "livability" with idyllic representations of office workers and affluent tourists sipping cappuccino and listening to free jazz concerts in the terraced gardens of California Plaza and Grand Hope Park.

In stark contrast, a few blocks away, the city is engaged in a relentless struggle to make the streets as unlivable as possible for the homeless and the poor. The persistence of thousands of street people on the fringes of Bunker Hill and the Civic Center tarnishes the image of designer living Downtown and betrays the laboriously constructed illusion of an urban "renaissance." City Hall has retaliated with its own version of low-intensity warfare.

Although city leaders periodically propose schemes for removing indigents *en masse*—deporting them to a poor farm on the edge of the desert, confining them in camps in the mountains, or interning them on derelict ferries in the harbor—such "final solutions" have been blocked by council members' fears of the displacement of the homeless into their districts. Instead the city, self-consciously adopting the idiom of cold war, has promoted the "containment" (the official term) of the homeless in Skid Row, along Fifth Street, systematically transforming the neighborhood into an outdoor poorhouse. But this containment strategy breeds its own vicious cycle of contradiction. By condensing the mass of the desperate and helpless together in such a small space, and denying adequate housing, official policy has transformed Skid Row into probably the most dangerous ten square blocks in the world. Every night on Skid Row is Friday the 13th, and, unsurprisingly, many of the homeless seek to escape the area during the night at all costs, searching safer niches in other parts of Downtown. The city in turn tightens the noose with increased police harassment and ingenious design deterrents.

One of the simplest but most mean-spirited of these deterrents is the Rapid Transit District's new barrel-shaped bus bench, which offers a minimal surface for uncomfortable sitting while making sleeping impossible. Such "bumproof" benches are being widely introduced on the periphery of Skid Row. Another invention is the aggressive deployment of outdoor sprinklers. Several years ago the city opened a Skid Row Park; to ensure that the park could not be used for overnight camping, overhead sprinklers were programmed to drench unsuspecting sleepers at random times during the night. The system was immediately copied by local merchants to drive the homeless away from (public) storefront sidewalks. Meanwhile Downtown restaurants and markets have built baroque enclosures to protect their refuse from the homeless. Although no one in Los Angeles has yet proposed adding cyanide to the garbage, as was suggested in Phoenix a few years back, one popular seafood restaurant has spent $12,000 to build the ultimate bag-lady-proof trash cage: three-quarter-inch steel rod with alloy locks and vicious out-turned spikes to safeguard moldering fishheads and stale french fries.

Public toilets, however, have become the real frontline of the city's war on the homeless. Los Angeles, as a matter of deliberate policy, has fewer public lavatories than any other major North American city. On the advice of the Los Angeles police, who now sit on the "design board" of at least one major Downtown project, the redevelopment agency bulldozed the few remaining public toilets on Skid Row. Agency planners then considered whether to include a "free-standing public toilet" in their design for the upscale South Park residential development; agency chairman Jim Wood later admitted that the decision not to build the toilet was a "policy decision and not a design decision." The agency preferred the alternative of "quasi-public restrooms"—toilets in restaurants, art galleries, and office buildings—which can be made available selectively to tourists and white-collar workers while being denied to vagrants and other unsuitables. The same logic has inspired the city's transportation planners to exclude toilets from their designs for Los Angeles's new subway system.[2]

Bereft of toilets, the Downtown badlands east of Hill Street also lack outside water sources for drinking or washing. A common and troubling sight these days is the homeless men—many of them young refugees from El Salvador—washing, swimming, even drinking from the sewer effluent that flows down the concrete channel of the Los

Angeles River on the eastern edge of Downtown. The city's public health department has made no effort to post warning signs in Spanish or to mobilize alternative clean-water sources.

In those areas where Downtown professionals must cross paths with the homeless or the working poor—such as the zone of gentrification along Broadway just south of the Civic Center—extraordinary precautions have been taken to ensure the physical separation of the different classes. The redevelopment agency, for example, again brought in the police to help design "twenty-four-hour, state-of-the-art security" for the two new parking structures that serve the *Los Angeles Times* headquarters and the Ronald Reagan State Office Building. In contrast to the mean streets outside, both parking structures incorporate beautifully landscaped microparks, and one even boasts a food court, picnic area, and historical exhibit. Both structures are intended to function as "confidence-building" circulation systems that allow white-collar workers to walk from car to office, or from car to boutique, with minimum exposure to the public street. The Broadway-Spring Center, in particular, which links the two local hubs of gentrification (the Reagan Building and the proposed Grand Central Square) has been warmly praised by architectural critics for adding greenery and art to parking. It also adds a considerable dose of menace—armed guards, locked gates, and ubiquitous security cameras—to scare away the homeless and the poor.

The cold war on the streets of Downtown is ever escalating. The police, lobbied by Downtown merchants and developers, have broken up every attempt by the homeless and their allies to create safe havens or self-governed encampments. "Justiceville," founded by homeless activist Ted Hayes, was roughly dispersed; when its inhabitants attempted to find refuge at Venice Beach, they were arrested at the behest of the local council member (a renowned environmentalist) and sent back to Skid Row. The city's own brief experiment with legalized camping—a grudging response to a series of deaths from exposure during the cold winter of 1987—was abruptly terminated after only four months to make way for the construction of a transit maintenance yard. Current policy seems to involve perverse play upon the famous irony about the equal rights of the rich and poor to sleep in the rough. As the former head of the city planning commission explained, in the City of the Angels it is not against the law to sleep on the street per se— "only to erect any sort of protective shelter."[3] To enforce this proscription against "cardboard condos," the police periodically sweep the Nickel, tearing down shelters, confiscating possessions, and arresting resisters. Such cynical repression has turned the majority of the homeless into urban bedouins. They are visible all over Downtown, pushing their few pathetic possessions in stolen shopping carts, always fugitive, always in motion, pressed between the official policy of containment and the inhumanity of Downtown streets.

SEQUESTERING THE POOR

An insidious spatial logic also regulates the lives of Los Angeles's working poor. Just across the moat of the Harbor Freeway, west of Bunker Hill, lies the MacArthur Park district—once upon a time the city's wealthiest neighborhood. Although frequently characterized as a no-man's-land awaiting resurrection by developers, the district is, in fact, home to the largest Central American community in the United States. In the congested streets bordering the park, a hundred thousand Salvadorans and Guatemalans, including a large community of Mayan-speakers, crowd into tenements and boarding houses barely adequate for a fourth as many people. Every morning at 6 A.M. this Latino Bantustan dispatches armies of sewing *operadoras,* dishwashers, and janitors to turn the wheels of the Downtown economy. But because MacArthur Park is midway between Downtown and the famous Miracle Mile, it too will soon fall to redevelopment's bulldozers.

Hungry to exploit the lower land prices in the district, a powerful coterie of developers, represented by a famous ex-councilman and the former president of the planning commission, has won official approval for their vision of "Central City West": literally, a second Downtown comprising 25 million square feet of new office and retail space. Although local politicians have insisted upon a significant quota of low-income replacement housing, such a palliative will hardly compensate for the large-scale population displacement sure to follow the construction of the new skyscrapers and yuppified "urban villages." In the meantime, Korean capital, seeking *lebensraum* for Los Angeles's burgeoning Koreatown, is also pushing into the MacArthur Park area, uprooting tenements to construct heavily fortified condominiums and office complexes. Other Asian and European speculators are counting on the new Metrorail station, across from the park, to become a magnet for new investment in the district.

The recent intrusion of so many powerful interests into the area has put increasing pressure upon the police to "take back the streets" from what is usually represented as an occupying army of drug-dealers, illegal immigrants, and homicidal homeboys. Thus in the summer of 1990 the LAPD announced a massive operation to "retake crime-plagued MacArthur Park" and surrounding neighborhoods "street by street, alley by alley." While the area is undoubtedly a major drug market, principally for drive-in Anglo commuters, the police have focused not only on addict-dealers and gang members, but also on the industrious sidewalk vendors who have made the circumference of the park an exuberant swap meet. Thus Mayan women selling such local staples as tropical fruit, baby clothes, and roach spray have been rounded up in the same sweeps as alleged "narcoterrorists."[4] (Similar dragnets in other Southern California communities have focused on Latino day-laborers congregated at streetcorner "slave markets.")

By criminalizing every attempt by the poor—whether the Skid Row homeless or MacArthur Park venders—to use public space for survival purposes, law-enforcement agencies have abolished the last informal safety-net separating misery from catastrophe. (Few third-world cities are so pitiless.) At the same time, the police, encouraged by local businessmen and property owners, are taking the first, tentative steps toward criminalizing entire inner-city communities. The "war" on drugs and gangs again has been the pretext for the LAPD's novel, and disturbing, experiments with community blockades. A large section of the Pico-Union neighborhood, just south of MacArthur Park, has been quarantined since the summer of 1989; "Narcotics Enforcement Area" barriers restrict entry to residents "on legitimate business only." Inspired by the positive response of older residents and local politicians, the police have subsequently franchised "Operation Cul-de-Sac" to other low-income Latino and black neighborhoods.

Thus in November 1989 (as the Berlin Wall was being demolished), the Devonshire Division of the LAPD closed off a "drug-ridden" twelve-block section of the northern San Fernando Valley. To control circulation within this largely Latino neighborhood, the police convinced apartment owners to finance the construction of a permanent guard station. Twenty miles to the south, a square mile of the mixed black and Latino Central-Avalon community has also been converted into Narcotic Enforcement turf with concrete roadblocks. Given the popularity of these quarantines—save amongst the ghetto youth against whom they are directed—it is possible that a majority of the inner city may eventually be partitioned into police-regulated "no-go" areas.

The official rhetoric of the contemporary war against the urban underclasses resounds with comparisons to the War in Vietnam a generation ago. The LAPD's community blockades evoke the infamous policy of quarantining suspect populations in "strategic hamlets." But an even more ominous emulation is the reconstruction of Los Angeles's public housing projects as "defensible spaces." Deep in the Mekong Delta of the Watts-Willowbrook ghetto, for example, the Imperial Courts Housing Project has been fortified with chain-link fencing, RESTRICTED ENTRY signs, obligatory identity passes—and a substation of the LAPD. Visitors are stopped and frisked, the police routinely order residents back into their apartments at night, and domestic life is subjected to constant police scrutiny. For public-housing tenants and inhabitants of narcotic-enforcement zones, the loss of freedom is the price of "security."

References

1. *Los Angeles Times,* Nov. 4, 1978.
2. Tom Chorneau, "Quandary Over a Park Restroom," *Downtown News,* Aug. 25, 1986.
3. See "Cold Snap's Toll at 5 as Its Iciest Night Arrives," *Los Angeles Times,* Dec. 29, 1988.
4. Ibid., June 17, 1990.

SUGGESTIONS FOR DISCUSSION

1. Share the descriptions you wrote before reading Davis with a group of your classmates. Discuss how your impressions of cities compare with Davis's and with others' in your class. Where do most of the impressions come from?
2. Mike Davis makes it clear that one of the defining features of Los Angeles is the city planners' attempts to destroy public spaces, those places where people can congregate freely or just hang out. What problems do you see with the destruction of or the preservation of public space?
3. In his essay, Davis writes, "The American city is being systematically turned inward. The 'public' spaces of the new megastructures and supermalls have supplanted traditional streets and disciplined their spontaneity." This statement represents a judgment about what American cities once were and what they should be. With a group of your classmates, examine what that judgment is and respond with your own understanding of what American cities should be like as well as what they seem to be in your way of thinking.

SUGGESTIONS FOR WRITING

1. Each of the writers in this section is engaged in an interpretive act. Baudrillard, for example, interprets New York from the point of view of an outsider, a foreigner who will explain this great city to others. Keillor uses the State Fair as a backdrop for his story but also as a kind of microcosm, a picture of the world outside Lake Wobegon. FitzGerald uses the people, the social system, and the very appearance of the place to interpret the world of Sun City Center. And, of course, Edward

Abbey uses Arches National Monument as a place that represents one kind of life to him, another to developers in the National Park Service. Go back through the selections in this chapter and read over your notes. Reread passages that you think are important or interesting or difficult to remember or understand. In an effort to understand and sort out the positions that have been presented in this chapter thus far, write a three- to four-page essay in which you attempt to synthesize these positions. Synthesis suggests a bringing together, looking for similarities, recognizing differences, and suggesting ways of understanding the various attitudes or interpretations of several thinkers. When you synthesize, you do more than simply rehearse the arguments of several writers. You try to see the patterns of thinking of each, the ways in which the writers depart from one another, and you try to place your own thinking in relation to that of others.

2. Davis mentions several films that show the modern city as a dystopia, a place exactly the opposite of a utopia. Watch one of the films he mentions (*Bladerunner, Die Hard, Escape from New York*) and write an essay in which you compare the dystopian setting of that film with your own experience or impression of large American cities like Los Angeles or New York. Try to incorporate your reading of Mike Davis into your thinking as you write your comparison.

3. Mike Davis draws particular attention to the ways people in cities like Los Angeles must live. Davis's concerns are especially focused on the pushing out or segregation of the working poor and the homeless. In a three- to five-page essay, take a position on the American city planners' responsibility for living conditions within the city itself. You might consider such topics as urban planning, general assistance, low-cost housing, or private organizations such as church groups or Habitat for Humanity.

FOR FURTHER EXPLORATION

Public space raises several questions that make good topics for further research. You might be interested, for example, in reading the work of William Whyte, who has studied the ways in which architects build public spaces to attract some people and keep others moving. As well, you could look into issues of housing and development. Jonathan Kozol's *Rachel and Her Children* is a moving account of homelessness in New York and would make a useful addition to Mike Davis's analysis of Los Angeles. If you are interested in wilderness issues, try reading the work of Dave Foreman, Barry Lopez, or Terry Tempest Williams.

In addition, your explorations might include any of the following:

- Redwood Summer, the efforts of EarthFirst! to block Northwest logging operations
- The gentrification of urban areas
- Property rights versus public interest
- Landscape and architectural design

CHAPTER 8

STORYTELLING

Experience which is passed on from mouth to mouth is the source from which all storytellers have drawn. And among those who have written down the tales, it is the great ones whose written version differs least from the speech of the many nameless storytellers.

– Walter Benjamin,
"The Storyteller"

O ne of the pleasures of listening to stories is suspending disbelief and entering into the imaginary world that storytelling creates. It doesn't matter so much whether the story is true or could have happened. What matters is that listeners know that their feelings and their responses to a story are real. When people hear the words "Once upon a time. . . " at the beginning of a fairy tale (or Jason's footsteps in the *Friday the 13th* horror movies), they know they are entering a world that could never happen, but this knowledge does not stop them from trying on, at least temporarily, the version of reality (or unreality) the story offers.

Storytelling is a persistent form of popular entertainment, whether people tell ghost stories around a campfire or watch the electronic glow of a television set. Every culture has its own storytelling tradition of myths, legends, epics, fables, animal stories, fairy tales, and romances. Listeners take delight in the mythic powers of their heroes, laugh at the comic predicaments clowns and tricksters get themselves into, and feel awe—and sometimes terror—when they hear stories of unseen worlds and the supernatural. In every storytelling tradition, there is a repertoire of stock characters and plots that listeners recognize immediately—and know how to respond to through laughter, tears, excitement, fear and grief—as if the events in the story were actually taking place.

But the fact that people everywhere, in all known cultures, tell stories only raises a series of questions we will ask you to explore in this chapter. We will be asking you to recall stories from the past and present in order to think about the functions storytelling performs, the occasions on which stories are told, and the people who tell stories. The reading and writing assignments in this chapter will ask you to look at some of the stories circulating in contemporary America. We will be asking you to explore the familiar stories you hear from family and friends or watch on television and at the movies, to see what these stories can tell you about the culture you are living in and the kinds of knowledge the imaginary worlds of storytelling transmit.

One of the key functions of storytelling, aside from entertaining listeners, is a pedagogical one. Storytelling is one of the oldest forms of human communication, and stories are important ways young people learn about the world and what their culture values. In traditional societies, before the advent of the mass media and the entertainment industry, stories were passed along orally, from generation to generation by word of mouth. The elders were responsible for initiating young people into the lore of the tribe. In many respects, the same is true today, in the mass-mediated world of contemporary America. To be an adult and a full member of society means knowing the stories a particular culture tells about the world and about itself. The familiar stories everyone knows make up a charter of cultural belief about the world and why people do the things they do.

We have divided this chapter into two clusters of readings. The first concerns stories people tell and hear as part of everyday life—stories that are passed along by word of mouth. We will be asking you to recall the stories you tell in the course of casual conversation, when you explain what happened over the weekend or pass along the latest gossip, political controversy, or scandal. People love to tell and listen to stories about politicians, celebrities and professional athletes—who is dating whom, who is getting divorced, who is checking into a drug or alcohol abuse clinic, who is under investigation for what. These kinds of stories—personal anecdotes, gossip, bits and pieces of the evening news—may seem so trivial that they don't really merit the title of storytelling. But while telling and listening to these stories may appear to be no more than a way to pass the time with family, neighbors, co-workers, and friends, in fact storytelling performs a very useful social function within local communities. As people tell and listen to stories, perhaps without fully recognizing it, they are working out their own attitudes and evaluations of a wide range of social realities, from relations between the sexes to politics.

The second cluster of readings concerns the adventures of such legendary heroes as Robin Hood, Jesse James, and Pretty Boy Floyd. We will be asking you to explore popular legends of the outlaw-hero, the formulaic figure of ballad traditions, folk songs, dime novels, movies, and television shows. According to the formula, the outlaw-hero is an actual person who once lived, an honest man forced outside the law who stole from the rich and gave to the poor. The formula of the outlaw-hero, of course, is only one among many formulas in American storytelling. You can probably think of a number of others—hard-boiled private eyes, cowboys, interracial cop teams, urban vigilantes, gangsters, android terminators, martial arts masters, exorcists.

What makes these figures and their stories interesting is not just that they follow conventional formulas that rely on stock plots and characters—and thereby fit easily into television programming and movie marketing. The formulas enacted in these stories create imaginary worlds out of the tensions and ambiguities in contemporary American culture. The popularity of formulaic heroes depends in part on the self-identification of the average reader or viewer with the larger-than-life figures of popular entertainment. As the novelist and critic Umberto Eco suggests, the myth of Superman operates out of the secret hope of "any accountant in any American city . . . that one day, from the slough of his actual personality, there can spring forth a superman who is capable of redeeming years of mediocre existence." In comic books, television shows, and movies, the formulaic heroes of American popular culture are perpetually playing out the anxieties and aspirations of average people. These popular heroes inhabit imaginary worlds, often at the margins of society on the western frontier or in the criminal underworld of the city or the interstellar space of science fiction, where their stories explore the ambiguous boundaries in American culture between what is permitted and what is forbidden—when it is legitimate to use violence, when you can take the law into your own hands, when you must live outside of the law to be true to your self.

READING THE CULTURE OF STORYTELLING

Reading and writing about stories and storytelling will require you to listen again to the stories that surround you and to look for patterns in their familiar plots and characters. As Maxine Hong Kingston does in the opening selection, you might begin by recalling stories you heard when you were growing up. In "No Name Woman," Kingston retells a story from the Cantonese "talk story" tradition she heard from her mother in the Chinese-American community in Stockton, California. Her retelling offers a good example of how writers use familiar stories told within the family and the local community and what happens when they add their own voices to an ongoing tradition of storytelling.

In the next selection, "Oral Traditions," the anthropologist Shirley Brice Heath presents a different angle on storytelling, one that calls attention to cultural differences in storytelling style. Heath's study can be useful because it offers a comparative perspective on the storytelling traditions of two working-class communities in North Carolina—and by extension can help you to identify and compare the styles and traditions in the storytelling you are most familiar with. The next selection is the folklorist Jan Harold Brunvand's "'The Hook' and Other Teenage Horrors," a part of Brunvand's larger work of collecting what he calls "urban legends." These are stories people tell that are plausible and have realistic settings but are bizarre and sometimes horrifying—the baby-sitter on LSD who put an infant in the oven because she thought it was a chicken, the spiders who laid eggs in the scalp of a woman with a beehive hairdo, the mouse's head in the Dr. Pepper bottle. Our suspicion is that Brunvand is correct when he claims that such stories are widespread and adapted to local conditions. It will be interesting to see how many comparable tales you can recall from your own experience. In the final selection in the first cluster of readings, the well-known horror fiction writer Stephen King extends Brunvand's analysis of why people like a "good scare" by investigating "Why We Crave Horror Movies." For King, horror films owe their popularity to the way they offer viewers an experience of violating the normal boundaries of everyday life, while at the same time reestablishing a need for normality.

The second cluster of readings opens up ways to write about the legendary heroes of popular storytelling, the figures whose adventures we know through books, the media, and song rather than word of mouth. These readings ask you to think about the stories that make up such a large part of popular entertainment in American culture and the imaginary worlds they create.

We begin with "Thoughts on a Shirtless Cyclist, Robin Hood, and One or Two Other Things," in which Russell Hoban explores the role of Robin Hood and the "outlaw self" in his own imagination, suggesting that the heroes and heroines of popular culture compose an "inner society" in people's heads that offers a necessary refuge and alternative to the everyday world. Then we add the ballads of two American Robin Hood figures—Jesse James and Pretty Boy Floyd. The final selection, Robert Warshow's classic essay on the gangster film "The Gangster as Tragic Hero," brings the outlaw-hero up to date in the American metropolis.

As you read these selections on the popular legend of the outlaw-hero, you will no doubt recall more examples of such legendary figures from books and comics, songs, movies, and television shows, and you will be asked to think about why people from medieval England to the post-Civil War period in 19th century America to the Great Depression of the 1930s have made outlaws into popular heroes. As you will see, these outlaw-heroes—and their modern counterpart, the gangster—raise unsettling questions about a culture that is apparently devoted to law and order and the defense of private property and yet turns real historical figures into legends who live outside the law.

Throughout this chapter you will be asked to recall and retell stories you have heard or read in the past. One of the pleasures in such research is that of simply remembering, not just the story but the occasion on which you heard it and the people you were with at the time. Remembering the stories you learned growing up—bringing them back into view to think and write about—can help you to reconstruct the imaginary worlds they created and the versions of reality they transmitted. By the same token, looking for patterns in the familiar stories you hear in songs and see on television and at the movies can help you give shape to the larger popular culture and the fears and aspirations it represents.

Maxine Hong Kingston

NO NAME WOMAN

Maxine Hong Kingston is a Chinese-American writer who grew up in Stockton, California, and now lives in Hawaii. In two remarkable award-winning books, *The Woman Warrior* and *China Men,* Kingston combines autobiography, history, myth, folklore, and legend to tell and retell stories about her family and her girlhood in the Chinese-American community in Stockton. We have chosen the opening section of *The Woman Warrior* (1976), "No Name Woman," because it presents a striking example of how Kingston has recreated the mood of the "talk story," a Chinese tradition of storytelling she learned from her mother.

Suggestion for Reading

• Maxine Hong Kingston begins her story with her mother saying, "You must not tell anyone . . . what I am about to tell you." As you read, notice how this opening establishes a certain mood and announces certain purposes for her mother's "talk story."

◆

Y ou must not tell anyone," my mother said, "what I am about to tell you. In China your father had a sister who killed herself. She jumped into the family well. We say that your father had all brothers because it is as if she had never been born.

"In 1924 just a few days after our village celebrated seventeen hurry-up weddings—to make sure that every young man who went 'out on the road' would responsibly come home—your father and his brothers and your grandfather and his brothers and your aunt's new husband sailed for America, the Gold Mountain. It was your grandfather's last trip. Those lucky enough to get contracts waved good-bye from the decks. They fed and guarded the stowaways and helped them off in Cuba, New York, Bali, Hawaii. 'We'll meet in California next year,' they said. All of them sent money home.

"I remember looking at your aunt one day when she and I were dressing; I had not noticed before that she had such a protruding melon of a stomach. But I did not think, 'She's pregnant,' until she began to look like other pregnant women, her shirt pulling and the white tops of her black pants showing. She could not have been pregnant, you see, because her husband had been gone for years. No one said anything. We did not discuss it. In early summer she was ready to have the child, long after the time when it could have been possible.

"The village had also been counting. On the night the baby was to be born the villagers raided our house. Some were crying. Like a great saw, teeth strung with lights, files of people walked zigzag across our land, tearing the rice. Their lanterns doubled in the disturbed black water, which drained away through the broken bunds. As the villagers closed in, we could see that some of them, probably men and women we knew well, wore white masks. The people with long hair hung it over their faces. Women with short hair made it stand up on end. Some had tied white bands around their foreheads, arms, and legs.

"At first they threw mud and rocks at the house. Then they threw eggs and began slaughtering our stock. We could hear the animals scream their deaths—the roosters, the pigs, a last great roar from the ox. Familiar wild heads flared in our night windows; the villagers encircled us. Some of the faces stopped to peer at us, their eyes rushing like searchlights. The hands flattened against the panes, framed heads, and left red prints.

"The villagers broke in the front and the back doors at the same time, even though we had not locked the doors against them. Their knives dripped with the blood of our animals. They smeared blood on the doors and walls. One woman swung a chicken, whose throat she had slit, splattering blood in red arcs about her. We stood together in the middle of our house, in the family hall with the pictures and tables of the ancestors around us, and looked straight ahead.

"At that time the house had only two wings. When the men came back, we would build two more to enclose our courtyard and a third one to begin a second courtyard. The villagers pushed through both wings, even your grandparents' rooms, to find your aunt's, which was also mine until the men returned. From this room a new wing for one of the younger families would grow. They ripped up her clothes and shoes and broke her combs, grinding them underfoot. They tore her work from the loom. They scattered the cooking fire and rolled the new weaving in it. We could hear them in the kitchen breaking our bowls and banging the pots. They overturned the great waist-high earthenware jugs; duck eggs, pickled fruits, vegetables burst out and mixed in acrid torrents. The old woman from the next field swept a broom through the air and loosed the spirits-of-the-broom over our heads. 'Pig.' 'Ghost.' 'Pig.' they sobbed and scolded while they ruined our house.

"When they left, they took sugar and oranges to bless themselves. They cut pieces from the dead animals. Some of them took bowls that were not broken and clothes that were not torn. Afterward we swept up the rice and sewed it back up into sacks. But the smells from the spilled preserves lasted. Your aunt gave birth in the pigsty that night. The next morning when I went for the water, I found her and the baby plugging up the family well.

"Don't let your father know that I told you. He denies her. Now that you have started to menstruate, what happened to her could happen to you. Don't humiliate us.

You wouldn't like to be forgotten as if you had never been born. The villagers are watchful."

Whenever she had to warn us about life, my mother told stories that ran like this one, a story to grow up on. She tested our strength to establish realities. Those in the emigrant generations who could not reassert brute survival died young and far from home. Those of us in the first American generations have had to figure out how the invisible world the emigrants built around our childhoods fit in solid America.

The emigrants confused the gods by diverting their curses, misleading them with crooked streets and false names. They must try to confuse their offspring as well, who, I suppose, threaten them in similar ways—always trying to get things straight, always trying to name the unspeakable. The Chinese I know hide their names; sojourners take new names when their lives change and guard their real names with silence.

Chinese-Americans, when you try to understand what things in you are Chinese, how do you separate what is peculiar to childhood, to poverty, insanities, one family, your mother who marked your growing with stories, from what is Chinese? What is Chinese tradition and what is the movies?

If I want to learn what clothes my aunt wore, whether flashy or ordinary, I would have to begin, "Remember Father's drowned-in-the-well sister?" I cannot ask that. My mother has told me once and for all the useful parts. She will add nothing unless powered by Necessity, a riverbank that guides her life. She plants vegetable gardens rather than lawns; she carries the odd-shaped tomatoes home from the fields and eats food left for the gods.

Whenever we did frivolous things, we used up energy; we flew high kites. We children came up off the ground over the melting cones our parents brought home from work and the American movie on New Year's Day—*Oh, You Beautiful Doll* with Betty Grable one year, and *She Wore a Yellow Ribbon* with John Wayne another year. After the one carnival ride each, we paid in guilt; our tired father counted his change on the dark walk home.

Adultery is extravagance. Could people who hatch their own chicks and eat the embryos and the heads for delicacies and boil the feet in vinegar for party food, leaving only the gravel, eating even the gizzard lining—could such people engender a prodigal aunt? To be a woman, to have a daughter in starvation time was a waste enough. My aunt could not have been the lone romantic who gave up everything for sex. Women in the old China did not choose. Some man had commanded her to lie with him and be his secret evil. I wonder whether he masked himself when he joined the raid on her family.

Perhaps she encountered him in the fields or on the mountain where the daughters-in-law collected fuel. Or perhaps he first noticed her in the marketplace. He was not a stranger because the village housed no strangers. She had to have dealings with him other than sex. Perhaps he worked an adjoining field, or he sold her the cloth for the dress she sewed and wore. His demand must have surprised, then terrified her. She obeyed him; she always did as she was told.

When the family found a young man in the next village to be her husband, she stood tractably beside the best rooster, his proxy, and promised before they met that she would be his forever. She was lucky that he was her age and she would be the first wife, an advantage secure now. The night she first saw him, he had sex with her. Then he left for America. She had almost forgotten what he looked like. When she tried to envision him, she only saw the black and white face in the group photograph the men had had taken before leaving.

The other man was not, after all, much different from her husband. They both gave orders: she followed. "If you tell your family, I'll beat you. I'll kill you. Be here again next week." No one talked sex, ever. And she might have separated the rapes from the rest of living if only she did not have to buy her oil from him or gather wood in the same forest. I want her fear to have lasted just as long as rape lasted so that the fear could have been contained. No drawn-out fear. But women at sex hazarded birth and hence lifetimes. The fear did not stop but permeated everywhere. She told the man, "I think I'm pregnant." He organized the raid against her.

On nights when my mother and father talked about their life back home, sometimes they mentioned an "outcast table" whose business they still seemed to be settling, their voices tight. In a commensal tradition, where food is precious, the powerful older people made wrongdoers eat alone. Instead of letting them start separate new lives like the Japanese, who could become samurais and geishas, the Chinese family, faces averted but eyes glowering sideways, hung on to the offenders and fed them leftovers. My aunt must have lived in the same house as my parents and eaten at an outcast table. My mother spoke about the raid as if she had seen it, when she and my aunt, a daughter-in-law to a different household, should not have been living together at all. Daughters-in-law lived with their husbands' parents, not their own; a synonym for marriage in Chinese is "taking a daughter-in-law." Her husband's parents could have sold her, mortgaged her, stoned her. But they had sent her back to her own mother and father, a mysterious act hinting at disgraces not told me. Perhaps they had thrown her out to deflect the avengers.

She was the only daughter; her four brothers went with her father, husband, and uncles "out on the road" and for some years became western men. When the goods were divided among the family, three of the brothers took land, and the youngest, my father, chose an education. After my grandparents gave their daughter away to her husband's family, they had dispensed all the adventure and all the property. They expected her alone to keep the traditional ways, which her brothers, now among the barbarians, could fumble without detection. The heavy, deep-rooted women were to maintain the past against the flood, safe for returning. But the rare urge west had fixed upon our family, and so my aunt crossed boundaries not delineated in space.

The work of preservation demands that the feelings playing about in one's guts not be turned into action. Just watch their passing like cherry blossoms. But perhaps my aunt, my forerunner, caught in a slow life, let dreams grow and fade and after some months or years went toward what persisted. Fear at the enormities of the forbidden kept her desires delicate, wire and bone. She looked at a man because she liked the way the hair was tucked behind his ears, or she liked the question-mark line of a long torso curving at the shoulder and straight at the hip. For warm eyes or a soft voice or a slow walk—that's all—a few hairs, a line, a brightness, a sound, a pace, she gave up family. She offered us up for a charm that vanished with tiredness, a pigtail that didn't toss when the wind died. Why, the wrong lighting could erase the dearest thing about him.

It could very well have been, however, that my aunt did not take subtle enjoyment of her friend, but, a wild woman, kept rollicking company. Imagining her free with sex doesn't fit, though. I don't know any women like that, or men either. Unless I see her life branching into mine, she gives me no ancestral help.

To sustain her being in love, she often worked at herself in the mirror, guessing at the colors and shapes that would interest him, changing them frequently in order to hit on the right combination. She wanted him to look back.

On a farm near the sea, a woman who tended her appearance reaped a reputation for eccentricity. All the married women blunt-cut their hair in flaps about their ears or pulled it back in tight buns. No nonsense. Neither style blew easily into heart-catching tangles. And at their weddings they displayed themselves in their long hair for the last time. "It brushed the backs of my knees," my mother tells me. "It was braided, and even so, it brushed the backs of my knees."

At the mirror my aunt combed individuality into her bob. A bun could have been contrived to escape into black streamers blowing in the wind or in quiet wisps about her face, but only the older women in our picture album wear buns. She brushed her hair back from her forehead, tucking the flaps behind her ears. She looped a piece of thread, knotted into a circle between her index fingers and thumbs, and ran the double strand across her forehead. When she closed her fingers as if she were making a pair of shadow geese bite, the string twisted together catching the little hairs. Then she pulled the thread away from her skin, ripping the hairs out neatly, her eyes watering from the needles of pain. Opening her fingers, she cleaned the thread, then rolled it along her hairline and the tops of her eyebrows. My mother did the same to me and my sisters and herself. I used to believe that the expression "caught by the short hairs" meant a captive held with a depilatory string. It especially hurt at the temples, but my mother said we were lucky we didn't have to have our feet bound when we were seven. Sisters used to sit on their beds and cry together, she said, as their mothers or their slave removed the bandages for a few minutes each night and let the blood gush back into their veins. I hope that the man my aunt loved appreciated a smooth brow, that he wasn't just a tits-and-ass man.

Once my aunt found a freckle on her chin, at a spot that the almanac said predestined her for unhappiness. She dug it out with a hot needle and washed the wound with peroxide.

More attention to her looks than these pullings of hairs and pickings at spots would have caused gossip among the villagers. They owned work clothes and good clothes, and they wore good clothes for feasting the new seasons. But since a woman combing her hair hexes beginnings, my aunt rarely found an occasion to look her best. Women looked like great sea snails—the corded wood, babies, and laundry they carried were the whorls on their backs. The Chinese did not admire a bent back; goddesses and warriors stood straight. Still there must have been a marvelous freeing of beauty when a worker laid down her burden and stretched and arched.

Such commonplace loveliness, however, was not enough for my aunt. She dreamed of a lover for the fifteen days of New Year's, the time for families to exchange visits, money, and food. She plied her secret comb. And sure enough she cursed the year, the family, the village, and herself.

Even as her hair lured her imminent lover, many other men looked at her. Uncles, cousins, nephews, brothers would have looked, too, had they been home between journeys. Perhaps they had already been restraining their curiosity, and they left, fearful that their glances, like a field of nesting birds, might be startled and caught. Poverty hurt, and that was their first reason for leaving. But another, final reason for leaving the crowded house was the never-said.

She may have been unusually beloved, the precious only daughter, spoiled and mirror gazing because of the affection the family lavished on her. When her husband left, they welcomed the chance to take her back from the in-laws; she could live like the little daughter for just a while longer. There are stories that my grandfather was different from other people, "crazy ever since the little Jap bayoneted him in the head." He used to put his naked penis on the dinner table, laughing. And one day he brought home a baby girl, wrapped up inside his brown western-style greatcoat. He had traded one of his sons, probably my father, the youngest, for her. My grandmother made him trade back. When he finally got a daughter of his own, he doted on her. They must have all loved her, except perhaps my father, the only brother who never went back to China, having once been traded for a girl.

Brothers and sisters, newly men and women, had to efface their sexual color and present plain miens. Disturbing hair and eyes, a smile like no other, threatened the ideal of five generations living under one roof. To focus blurs, people shouted face to face and yelled from room to room. The immigrants I know have loud voices, unmodulated to American tones even after years away from the village where they called their friendships out across the fields. I have not been able to stop my mother's screams in public libraries or over telephones. Walking erect (knees straight, toes pointed forward, not pigeon-toed, which is Chinese-feminine) and speaking in an inaudible voice, I have tried to turn myself American-feminine. Chinese communication was loud, public. Only sick people had to whisper. But at the dinner table, where the family members came nearest one another, no one could talk, not the outcasts nor any eaters. Every word that falls from the mouth is a coin lost. Silently they gave and accepted food with both hands. A preoccupied child who took his bowl with one hand got a sideways glare. A complete moment of total attention is due everyone alike. Children and lovers have no singularity here, but my aunt used a secret voice, a separate attentiveness.

She kept the man's name to herself throughout her labor and dying; she did not accuse him that he be punished with her. To save her inseminator's name she gave silent birth.

He may have been somebody in her own household, but intercourse with a man outside the family would have been no less abhorrent. All the village were kinsmen, and the titles shouted in loud country voices never let kinship be forgotten. Any man within visiting distance would have been neutralized as a lover—"brother," "younger brother," "older brother"—one hundred and fifteen relationship titles. Parents researched birth charts probably not so much to assure good fortune as to circumvent incest in a population that has but one hundred surnames. Everybody has eight million relatives. How useless then sexual mannerisms, how dangerous.

As if it came from an atavism deeper than fear, I used to add "brother" silently to boys' names. It hexed the boys, who would or would not ask me to dance, and made them less scary and as familiar and deserving of benevolence as girls.

But, of course, I hexed myself also—no dates. I should have stood up, both arms waving, and shouted out across libraries, "Hey, you! Love me back." I had no idea, though, how to make attraction selective, how to control its direction and magnitude. If I made myself American-pretty so that the five or six Chinese boys in the class fell in love with me, everyone else—the Caucasian, Negro, and Japanese boys—would too. Sisterliness, dignified and honorable, made much more sense.

Attraction eludes control so stubbornly that whole societies designed to organize relationships among people cannot keep order, not even when they bind people to one another from childhood and raise them together. Among the very poor and the wealthy, brothers married their adopted sisters, like doves. Our family allowed some romance, paying adult brides' prices and providing dowries so that their sons and daughters could marry strangers. Marriage promises to turn strangers into friendly relatives—a nation of siblings.

In the village structure, spirits shimmered among the live creatures, balanced and held in equilibrium by time and land. But one human being flaring up into violence could open up a black hole, a maelstrom that pulled in the sky. The frightened villagers, who depended on one another to maintain the real, went to my aunt to show her a personal, physical representation of the break she had made in the "roundness." Misallying couples snapped off the future, which was to be embodied in true offspring. The villagers punished her for acting as if she could have a private life, secret and apart from them.

If my aunt had betrayed the family at a time of large grain yields and peace, when many boys were born, and wings were being built on many houses, perhaps she might have escaped such severe punishment. But the men—hungry, greedy, tired of planting in dry soil, cuckolded—had to leave the village in order to send food-money home. There were ghost plagues, bandit plagues, wars with the Japanese, floods. My Chinese brother and sister had died of an unknown sickness. Adultery, perhaps only a mistake during good times, became a crime when the village needed food.

The round moon cakes and round doorways, the round tables of graduated size that fit one roundness inside another, round windows and rice bowls—these talismans had lost their power to warn this family of the law: a family must be whole, faithfully keeping the descent line by having sons to feed the old and the dead, who in turn look after the family. The villagers came to show my aunt and her lover-in-hiding a broken house. The villagers were speeding up the circling of events because she was too short-sighted to see that her infidelity had already harmed the village, that waves of consequences would return unpredictably, sometimes in disguise, as now, to hurt her. This roundness had to be made coin-sized so that she would see its circumference: punish her at the birth of her baby. Awaken her to the inexorable. People who refused fatalism because they could invent small resources insisted on culpability. Deny accidents and wrest fault from the stars.

After the villagers left, their lanterns now scattering in various directions toward home, the family broke their silence and cursed her. "Aiaa, we're going to die. Death is coming. Death is coming. Look what you've done. You've killed us. Ghost! Dead ghost! Ghost! You've never been born." She ran out into the fields, far enough from the house so that she could no longer hear their voices, and pressed herself against the earth, her own land no more. When she felt the birth coming, she thought that she had been hurt. Her body seized together. "They've hurt me too much," she thought. "This is gall, and it will kill me." With forehead and knees against the earth, her body convulsed and then relaxed. She turned on her back, lay on the ground. The black well of sky and stars went out and out and out forever; her body and her complexity seemed to disappear. She was one of the stars, a bright dot in blackness, without home, without a companion, in eternal cold and silence. An agoraphobia rose in her, speeding higher and higher, bigger and bigger; she would not be able to contain it; there would be no end to fear.

Flayed, unprotected against space, she felt pain return, focusing her body. This pain chilled her—a cold, steady kind of surface pain. Inside, spasmodically, the other pain, the pain of the child, heated her. For hours she lay on the ground, alternately body and space. Sometimes a vision of normal comfort obliterated reality: she saw the family in the evening gambling at the dinner table, the young people massaging their elders' backs. She saw them congratulating one another, high joy on the mornings the rice shoots came up. When these pictures burst, the stars drew yet further apart. Black space opened.

She got to her feet to fight better and remembered that old-fashioned women gave birth in their pigsties to fool the jealous, pain-dealing gods, who do not snatch piglets. Before the next spasms could stop her, she ran to the pigsty, each step a rushing out into emptiness. She climbed over the fence and knelt in the dirt. It was good to have a fence enclosing her, a tribal person alone.

Laboring, this woman who had carried her child as a foreign growth that sickened her every day, expelled it at last. She reached down to touch the hot, wet, moving mass, surely smaller than anything human, and could feel that it was human after all—fingers, toes, nails, nose. She pulled it up on to her belly, and it lay curled there, butt in the air, feet precisely tucked one under the other. She opened her loose shirt and buttoned the child inside. After resting, it squirmed and thrashed and she pushed it up to her breast. It turned its head this way and that until it found her nipple. There, it made little snuffling noises. She clenched her teeth at its preciousness, lovely as a young calf, a piglet, a little dog.

She may have gone to the pigsty as a last act of responsibility: she would protect this child as she had protected its father. It would look after her soul, leaving supplies on her grave. But how would this tiny child without family find her grave when there would be no marker for her anywhere, neither in the earth nor the family hall? No one would give her a family hall name. She had taken the child with her into the wastes. At its birth the two of them had felt the same raw pain of separation, a wound that only the family pressing tight could close. A child with no descent line would not soften her life but only trail after her, ghost-like, begging her to give it purpose. At dawn the villagers on their way to the fields would stand around the fence and look.

Full of milk, the little ghost slept. When it awoke, she hardened her breasts against the milk that crying loosens. Toward morning she picked up the baby and walked to the well.

Carrying the baby to the well shows loving. Otherwise abandon it. Turn its face into the mud. Mothers who love their children take them along. It was probably a girl; there is some hope of forgiveness for boys.

• • •

"Don't tell anyone you had an aunt. Your father does not want to hear her name. She has never been born." I have believed that sex was unspeakable and words so strong and fathers so frail that "aunt" would do my father mysterious harm. I have thought that my family, having settled among immigrants who had also been their neighbors in the ancestral land, needed to clean their name, and a wrong word would incite the kinspeople even here. But there is more to this silence: they want me to participate in her punishment. And I have.

In the twenty years since I heard this story I have not asked for details nor said my aunt's name; I do not know it. People who can comfort the dead can also chase after them to hurt them further—a reverse ancestor worship. The real punishment was not the raid swiftly inflicted by the villagers, but the family's deliberately forgetting her. Her betrayal so maddened them, they saw to it that she would suffer forever, even after death. Always hungry, always needing, she would have to beg food from other ghosts, snatch and steal it from those whose living descendants give them gifts. She would have to fight the ghosts massed at crossroads for the buns a few thoughtful citizens leave to decoy her away from village and home so that the ancestral spirits could feast unharassed. At peace, they could act like gods, not ghosts, their descent lines providing them with paper suits and dresses, spirit money, paper houses, paper automobiles, chicken, meat, and rice into eternity—essences delivered up in smoke and flames, steam and incense rising from each rice bowl. In an attempt to make the Chinese care for people outside the family, Chairman Mao encourages us now to give our paper replicas to the spirits of outstanding soldiers and workers, no matter whose ancestors they may be. My aunt remains forever hungry. Goods are not distributed evenly among the dead.

My aunt haunts me—her ghost drawn to me because now, after fifty years of neglect, I alone devote pages of paper to her, though not origamied into houses and clothes. I do not think she always means me well. I am telling on her, and she was a spite suicide, drowning herself in the drinking water. The Chinese are always very frightened of the drowned one, whose weeping ghost, wet hair hanging and skin bloated, waits silently by the water to pull down a substitute.

SUGGESTIONS FOR DISCUSSION

1. Maxine Hong Kingston first gives her mother's version of her aunt's suicide and then she devotes the rest of this selection to her own reflections on it. Why do you think Kingston has organized "No Name Woman" this way? What effect does it have on you as a reader?
2. How would you describe the relationship between Kingston and her mother—as mother and daughter and as "story talkers"?
3. Kingston says of her aunt, "Unless I see her life branching into mine, she gives me no ancestral help." Explain the significance of this statement.

SUGGESTIONS FOR WRITING

1. Write an essay about the way Maxine Hong Kingston tells the story "No Name Woman." You might consider why Kingston makes the first voice that of her mother ("You must not tell anyone . . . what I am about to tell you") and why she breaks her mother's admonition to silence in order to retell the story of her aunt's suicide.
2. The story Maxine Hong Kingston's mother tells in "No Name Woman" might be considered a cautionary tale about the perils of growing up. Write an essay about a story you were told that transmitted some point about growing up or some lesson about life. You will want to take into account who told the story to you, the occasion on which the story was told, what gave the speaker the authority to tell you the story, and the point or lesson of the story. Recreate the setting and mood in order to retell the story through the voice of the person who told it to you. But also follow Kingston's example in "No Name Woman," and explore the effects on you of both the story and the person telling it.

3. In "No Name Woman" (and throughout much of her writing), Kingston makes family stories into tales of ancestral spirits and ghosts that haunt her imagination. Are
   there such figures in your family tradition? In your own imagination? Write an essay that tells a story about one of your ancestors and explains what he or she represents in your imagination.

Shirley Brice Heath

Oral Traditions

Shirley Brice Heath is a professor of English at Stanford University. The following selection is from *Ways With Words* (1983), Heath's study of how children learn to use spoken and written language in two working-class communities in North Carolina. As Heath describes them in the prologue to *Ways
With Words*, the "two communities—Roadville and Trackton—[are] only a
few miles apart in the Piedmont Carolinas. Roadville is a white working-class
community of families steeped for four generations in the life of the textile
mills. Trackton is a black working-class community whose older generations
grew up farming the land, but whose current members work in the mills." In
the selection we have chosen, Heath describes and compares how the two
communities have developed two quite distinct traditions of storytelling.

Suggestion for Reading

• As you read, notice how Shirley Brice Heath integrates the speaking voices
  of Roadville and Trackton residents into her account of the two storytelling
  traditions. Ethnographers like Heath are interested in recording stories, but
  they are also interested in how people make sense of the stories they tell.
  Underline and annotate passages where Heath draws upon the language
  Roadville and Trackton residents use to talk about storytelling and its function in the two communities.

———————————◆———————————

In Roadville

A Piece of Truth

Roadville residents worry about many things. Yet no Roadville home is a
somber place where folks spend all their time worrying about money, their
children's futures, and their fate at the hands of the mill. They create numerous occasions for celebration, most often with family members and
church friends. On these occasions, they regale each other with "stories." To an out-

sider, these stories seem as though they should be embarrassing, even insulting to people present. It is difficult for the outsider to learn when to laugh, for Roadville people seem to laugh at the story's central character, usually the story-teller or someone else who is present.

A "story" in Roadville is "something you tell on yourself, or on your buddy, you know, it's all in good fun, and a li'l something to laugh about." Though this definition was given by a male, women define their stories in similar ways, stressing they are "good fun," and "don't mean no harm." Stories recount an actual event either witnessed by others or previously told in the presence of others and declared by them "a good story."Roadville residents recognize the purpose of the stories is to make people laugh by making fun of either the story-teller or a close friend in sharing an event and the particular actions of individuals within that event. However, stories "told on" someone other than the story-teller are never told unless the central character or someone who is clearly designated his representative is present. The Dee children sometimes tell stories on their father who died shortly after the family moved to Roadville, but they do so only in Mrs. Dee's presence with numerous positive adjectives describing their father's gruff nature. Rob Macken, on occasion, is the dominant character in stories which make fun of his ever-present willingness to point out where other folks are wrong. But Rob is always present on these occasions, and he is clearly included in the telling ("Ain't that right, Rob?" "Now you know that's the truth, hain't it?"), as story-tellers cautiously move through their tale about him, gauging how far to go by his response to the story.

Outside close family groups, stories are told only in sex-segregated groups. Women invite stories of other women, men regale each other with tales of their escapades on hunting and fishing trips, or their run-ins (quarrels) with their wives and children. Topics for women's stories are exploits in cooking, shopping, adventures at the beauty shop, bingo games, the local amusement park, their gardens, and sometimes events in their children's lives. Topics for men are big-fishing expeditions, escapades of their hunting dogs, times they have made fools of themselves, and exploits in particular areas of their expertise (gardening and raising a 90-lb pumpkin, a 30-lb cabbage, etc.). If a story is told to an initial audience and declared a good story on that occasion, this audience (or others who hear about the story) can then invite the story-teller to retell the story to yet other audiences. Thus, an invitation to tell a story is usually necessary. Stories are often requested with a question: "Has Betty burned any biscuits lately?" "Brought any possums home lately?" Marked behavior—transgressions from the behavioral norm generally expected of a "good hunter," "good cook," "good handyman," or a "good Christian"—is the usual focus of the story. The foolishness in the tale is a piece of truth about everyone present, and all join in a mutual laugh at not only the story's central character, but at themselves as well. One story triggers another, as person after person reaffirms a familiarity with the kind of experience just recounted. Such stories test publicly the strength of relationships and openly declare bonds of kinship and friendship. When the social bond is currently strong, such stories can be told with no "hard feelings." Only rarely, and then generally under the influence of alcohol or the strain of a test in the relationship from another source (job competition, an unpaid loan), does a story-telling become the occasion for an open expression of hostility.

Common experience in events similar to those of the story becomes an expression of social unity, a commitment to maintenance of the norms of the church and of the roles within the mill community's life. In telling a story, an individual shows that he belongs to the group: he knows about either himself or the subject of the story, and he understands the norms which were broken by the story's central character. Oldtimers, especially those who came to Roadville in the 1930s, frequently assert their long familiarity with certain norms as they tell stories on the young folks and on those members of their own family who moved away. There is always an unspoken understanding that some experiences common to the oldtimers can never be known by the young folks, yet they have benefited from the lessons and values these experiences enabled their parents to pass on to them.

In any social gathering, either the story-teller who himself announces he has a story or the individual who invites another to tell a story is, for the moment, in control of the entire group. He manages the flow of talk, the staging of the story, and dictates the topic to which all will adhere in at least those portions of their discourse which immediately follow the story-telling. At a church circle meeting, many of the neighborhood women had gathered, and Mrs. Macken was responsible for refreshments on this occasion. The business and lesson of the circle had ended, and she was preparing the refreshments, while the women milled about waiting for her to signal she was ready for them. Mrs. Macken looked up from arranging cookies on a plate and announced Sue had a story to tell. This was something she could not normally have done, since as a relative newcomer, a schoolteacher, and a known malcontent in Roadville, her status was not high enough to allow her to announce a story for someone who was as much of an oldtimer as Sue. However, as the hostess of the circle, she had some temporary rank.

Roadville Text IV

Mrs. Macken: Sue, you oughta tell about those rolls you made the other day, make folks glad you didn't try to serve fancy rolls today.

Mrs. Dee: Sue, what'd you do, do you have a new recipe?

Mrs. Macken: You might call it that

Sue: [

                              I, hh wanna =

Martha: = Now Millie [Mrs. Macken], you hush and let Sue give us *her* story.

Sue: Well, as a matter of fact, I did have this new recipe, one I got out of *Better Homes and Gardens,* and I thought I'd try it, uh, you see, it called for scalded milk, and I had just started the milk when the telephone rang, and I went to get it. It was Leona/*casting her eyes at Mrs. Macken/*. I thought I turned the stove off, and when I came back, the burner was off, uh, so I didn't think anything about it, poured the milk in on the yeast, and went to kneading. Felt a little hot. Well, anyway, put the stuff out to rise, and came back, and it looked almost like Stone Mountain, thought that's a strange recipe, so I kneaded it again, and set it out in rolls. This time I had rocks, uh, sorta like 'em, the kind that roll up all smooth at the beach. Well, I wasn't gonna throw that stuff all out, so I cooked it. Turned out even harder than those rocks, if that's possible, and nobody would eat 'em, couldn't even soften 'em in buttermilk. I was trying to explain how the recipe was so funny, you know, see, how I didn't know what I did wrong, and Sally piped up and said 'Like yeah, when you was on the phone, I came in, saw this white stuff a-boiling, and I turned it off.' (pause). Then I knew, you know, that milk was too hot, killed the yeast/ *looking around at the women/*. Guess I'll learn to keep my mind on my own business and off other folks'.

The story was punctuated by gestures of kneading, turns of the head in puzzlement, and looks at the audience to see if they acknowledged understanding of the metaphors and similes. Stone Mountain is a campground in the region which everyone at the circle meeting had visited; it rises out of the ground like a giant smooth-backed whale. The beach is a favorite summer vacation spot for Roadville families, and the women often collect the smooth rocks from the beach to put on top of the dirt in their flower pots.

Several conventions of stories and story-telling in Roadville stand out in this incident. The highest status members present, Mrs. Dee and her granddaughter Martha, reannounce Sue's story and subtly convey that Mrs. Macken stepped out of line by asking Sue to tell a story on this occasion. Within her narrative, Sue follows a major requirement of a "good story": it must be factual, and any exaggeration or hyperbole must be so qualified as to let the audience know the story-teller does not accept such descriptions as literally true. Sue qualifies her Stone Mountain description with "almost," her equation of the rolls with rocks by "sorta like 'em," and her final comparison of the rolls to rocks with "if that's possible." She attempts to stick strictly to the truth and exaggerates only with hedges and qualifications.

Perhaps the most obligatory convention Sue follows is that which requires a Roadville story to have a moral or summary message which highlights the weakness admitted in the tale. "Stories" in these settings are similar to testimonials given at revival meetings and prayer sessions. On these occasions, individuals are invited to give a testimonial or to "tell your story." These narratives are characterized by a factual detailing of temporal and spatial descriptions and recounting of conversations by direct quotation ("Then the Lord said to me:"). Such testimonials frequently have to do with "bringing a young man to his senses" and having received answers to specific prayers. The detailing of the actual event is often finished off with Scriptural quotation, making it clear that the story bears out the promise of "the Word." Sue's story is confession-like, and its summing up carries a double meaning, both a literal one ("on my own business" = cooking) and a figurative one ("on my own business" = general affairs). Any woman in the group can quote Scripture describing the sins of which the tongue is capable (for example, James 3:6 which likens the tongue to a fire which spreads evil).

Unspoken here is the sin of Sue and Leona—gossip—the recounting and evaluating of the activities and personalities of others. Gossip is a frequent sermon topic and a behavior looked upon as a characteristic female weakness. Leona, who is not present at the circle meeting, is a known gossip, who occasionally telephones several of the women to fill them in on news in the neighborhood. All of the women know, but none says explicitly, that any phone call with Leona is likely to bring trouble, both to those who are the topics of her phone conversation and to those who are weak enough to listen to her. The story, told at the end of a church circle meeting, appears to be an innocent piece of female chatter, but it carries a message to all present which reminds them of their own weakness in listening to Leona. All the women have gossiped, and all have given in to listening to Leona at one time or another. Yet on this public occasion, all avoid direct negative talk about either Leona or anyone else, since engaging in this censured activity in such a public setting where more than two individuals are present would be foolish. Instead Sue's story is an occasion in which all recognize their common, but unspoken, Christian ideal of disciplined tongue. The major understandings and background knowledge on which a full interpretation of the story depends are unarticulated.

Sue's story carries subtle messages about the values and practices of the culture out of which the story comes. She reaffirms that the most frequent gossip in Roadville takes place between only two people, with an unstated and often unfulfilled agreement that neither will reveal her participation to others; breaches of such trust are frequent causes of female disagreement. Moreover, Sue asserts her maintenance of certain community norms for home-makers: she makes her bread "from scratch" instead of buying store goods; she is unwilling to throw out food; she has obviously trained Sally, her daughter, to be attentive to kitchen matters. Picking up, or recognizing all of this information depends on the familiarity with Roadville's norms and daily customs which the women of the church circle share.

In several ways, stories such as Sue's are similar to Biblical parables, a frequent source for sermons and Bible lessons, and a literary source familiar to all. Parables told by Jesus recount daily experiences common to the people of his day. Often parables end with a summary statement which is both a condemnation of one or more of the story's characters and a warning to those who would hear and understand the parable for its relevance to their own lives. In a parable, two items or events are placed side by side for comparison. The details of the story bring out its principal point or primary meaning, but there is little or no emotional expressiveness within the story evaluating the actions of the characters. The action is named and detailed, but its meaning to the characters is not set forth in exposition or through a report of the emotions of those involved. Biblical parables often open with formulas such as "The Kingdom of heaven is like unto this. . . " (Matthew 13:24, 13:31, 13:33, 13:44, 13:45, 20:1, 25:1), or admonitions to listen: "Listen then if you have ears" (Matthew 13:9) and "Listen and understand" (Matthew 15:10). Roadville's parable-like stories often open with announcement of the comparison of the events of the story to another situation: "That's like what happened to me. . . " Both men and women often open their stories with the simple comment "They say. . . " or a metaphor such as "We've got another bulldog on our hands" (referring to a fighting personality who is the central character in an upcoming story). In ways similar to Biblical parables, Roadville folks share with their listeners experiences which provide a lesson with a meaning for the life of all. The story is told using direct discourse whenever possible: "And he goes 'Now, you look out.'" or "Like yeah when you was on the phone. . . "

For the best of the parable-like stories, that is, those which are told repeatedly or are handed down in families over generations, the retelling of the entire story is often not necessary. Only its summary point need be repeated to remind listeners of the lesson behind the story. Proverbs or well-known sayings also carry lessons stating the general will of the community and ideals of Roadville families. Understanding of these depends, as do parable-like stories, on comparing one thing to another, for example, seeing similarities across nature.

A whistlin' girl and a crowin' hen will come to no good end.

A rollin' stone gather's no moss.

A stitch in time saves nine.

Rain before seven, clear by eleven.

For those activities which are traditionally part of the daily routine of mill families' lives—agriculture, weather, male-female relations, pregnancy and childbirth—proverbial guides to behavior abound. Proverbs help determine when certain crops are planted and harvested, predict rain, sunshine, good fishing or bad, link personality traits to physical features, and dictate behaviors of mothers-to-be. The anonymous and collective voices of those who have abided by these lessons in their experiences remind Roadville residents of behavioral norms and reinforce expectations of predictable actions and attitudes among community members.

The Bible's parables and proverbs are sometimes quite consciously used as a written model for Roadville's oral stories and proverbs. However, few written sources, other than the Bible, seem to influence either the content or the structure of oral stories in Roadville. Access to written stories, other than those in the Bible, is relatively rare. Women buy home and garden magazines and read their stories of successful remodeling or sewing projects—testimonials on the merits of budget shopping, thriftiness, and tenacity in do-it-yourself projects. Some women buy "True Story" magazines and publications which feature the personal stories of movie and television personalities, but they do not usually read these publicly. Some women occasionally buy paperback novels, and when asked about their hobbies, they often include reading, but then add comments such as "There's no time for it, for reading, you know, for pleasure or anything like that."

In church-related activities, they not only use stories from the Bible, but they occasionally hear certain other types of content-related stories. The circle meeting at which Sue was asked to tell her story is an example of one such activity. In such meetings, women share study of a designated Bible passage or a book of the Bible. The leader often reads from other short story-like materials to illustrate the need to follow the precepts covered in the Biblical passage. Throughout the discussion, however, there are numerous references to "our own stories [the experiences of those present]" which better relate to the Bible message than do the printed materials supplied for Bible study. Men's and women's Bible study groups prefer that a pastor or an elder lead them. The pastor sometimes suggests to lay leaders that they use a book of exposition of the Scriptures (especially when the Bible study focuses on a particular book of the Bible, such as Revelation). Some members of the Bible study group may be assigned portions of supplementary materials to read and discuss at the next Bible study. However, such efforts usually fail miserably. Roadville men and women do not like to read in public and do not wish to admit their lack of understanding of expository materials. They state strong preferences that, if any written materials are used to expand on Biblical passages, the pastor, and not they, should do it. As Mrs. Turner's mother explained. "I believe what the preacher speaks to be the truth, because I feel he is our leader, and I don't feel, well, I feel like *he* is tellin' us the right thing."

Thus, in interpreting the Bible, church members prefer either their own stories or Biblical accounts to written stories—whether factual expositions or tales of the lives of other modern-day Christians. Their own stories are often modeled on Biblical parables, but they are also personal accounts of what God's Word has meant to them. They reject depersonalized written accounts which come from unfamiliar sources. They use their own stories told on themselves and their friends to entertain and instruct, as they highlight personal and communal weaknesses and their struggles either to overcome them or to live with them. . . .

IN TRACKTON

Talkin' Junk

Trackton folks see the truth and the facts in stories in ways which differ greatly from those of Roadville. Good story-tellers in Trackton may base their stories on an actual event, but they creatively fictionalize the details surrounding the real event, and the outcome of the story may not even resemble what indeed happened. The best stories are "junk," and anyone who can "talk junk" is a good story-teller. Talkin' junk includes laying on highly exaggerated compliments and making wildly exaggerated comparisons as well as telling narratives. Straightforward factual accounts are relatively rare in Trackton and are usually told only on serious occasions: to give a specific piece of information to someone who has requested it, to provide an account of the troubles of a highly respected individual, or to exchange information about daily rounds of activities when neither party wishes to intensify the interaction or draw it out. Trackton's "stories," on the other hand, are intended to intensify social interactions and to give all parties an opportunity to share in not only the unity of the common experience on which the story may be based, but also in the humor of the wide-ranging language play and imagination which embellish the narrative.

From a very early age, Trackton children learn to appreciate the value of a good story for capturing an audience's attention or winning favors. Boys, especially on those occasions when they are teased or challenged in the plaza, hear their antics become the basis of exaggerated tales told by adults and older children to those not present at the time of the challenge. Children hear themselves made into characters in stories told again and again. They hear adults use stories from the Bible or from their youth to scold or warn against misbehavior. The mayor captures the boys' conflict in the story of King Solomon which features a chain of events and resolution of a conflict similar to that in which they are currently engaged. . . . Children's misdeeds provoke the punchline or summing up of a story which they are not told, but are left to imagine: "Dat póliceman'll come 'n git you, like he did Frog." The story behind this summary is never told, but is held out as something to be recreated anew in the imagination of every child who hears this threat.

Trackton children can create and tell stories about themselves, but they must be clever if they are to hold the audience's attention and to maintain any extended conversational space in an on-going discourse. Young children repeatedly try to break into adult discourse with a story, but if they do not succeed in relating the first few lines of their story to the on-going topic or otherwise exciting the listeners' interests, they are ignored. An adult's accusation, on the other hand, gives children an open stage for creating a story, but this one must also be "good," i.e. highly exaggerated, skillful in language play, and full of satisfactory comparisons to redirect the adult's attention from the infraction provoking the accusation.

Adults and older siblings do not make up sustained chronological narratives specially for young children, and adults do not read to young children. The flow of time in Trackton, which admits few scheduled blocks of time for routinized activities, does not lend itself to a bedtime schedule of reading a story. The homes provide barely enough space for the necessary activities of family living, and there is no separate room, book corner, or even outdoor seat where a child and parent can read together out of the constant flow of human interactions. The stage of the plaza almost always offers live action and is tough competition for book-reading. Stories exchanged among adults do not carry moral summaries or admonitions about behavior; instead they focus on detailing of events and personalities, and they stress conflict and resolution or attempts at resolution. Thus adults see no reason to direct these stories to children for teaching purposes. When stories are told among adults, young children are not excluded from the audience, even if the content refers to adult affairs, sexual exploits, crooked politicians, drunk ministers, or wayward choirleaders. If children respond to such stories with laughter or verbal comments, they are simply warned to "keep it to yo'self." Some adult stories are told only in sex-segregated situations. Men recount to their buddies stories they would not want their wives or the womenfolk to know about; women share with each other stories of quarrels with their menfolk or other women. Many men know about formulaic toasts (long epic-like accounts of either individual exploits or struggles of black people) from visitors from up-North or men returned from the armed services, but these are clearly external to the Trackton man's repertoire, and they do not come up in their social gatherings. Instead, Trackton men and their friends focus on stories which tell of their own current adventures or recount fairly recent adventures of particular personalities known to all present. All of these are highly self-assertive or extol the strength and cleverness of specific individuals.

Women choose similar topics for their stories: events which have happened to them, things they have seen, or events they have heard about. Considerable license is taken with these stories, however, and each individual is expected to tell the story, not as she has heard it, but with her own particular style. Women tell stories of their exploits at the employment office, adventures at work in the mill, or episodes in the lives of friends, husbands, or mutual acquaintances. Laced through with evaluative comments ("Didja ever hear of such a thing?" "You know how he ak [act] when he drunk." "You been like dat."), the stories invite participation from listeners. In fact, such participation is necessary reinforcement for the story-teller. Perhaps the most characteristic feature of story-telling by adults is the dramatic use of dialogue. Dovie Lou told the following story one afternoon to a group of six women sitting on the porch of Lillie Mae's house. The Henning family was transient and had been in Trackton only a few weeks.

Trackton Text V

Now you know me—I'm Dovie Lou, and you may think I'ma put up wid that stuff off Hennin's ol' lady, right? Who, who, after all, gives a hoot about her—or him, for dat matter? I been here quite a while—gonna be here a time yet too. She holler off her porch "Yo man, he over in Darby Sat'day nite." I say "Shit, what you know 'bout my man? My man." It was a rainy night, you know ain't no use gettin' fussied up to go out on a night like dat. Tessie 'n I go play bingo. But dat ol' woman, she ak like she some Channel Two reporter or sump'n:

> "P.B. Evans was seen today on the corner of Center and Main Street. He hadda bottle in each hip pocket, and one under his Lóndon Fóg hat. Sadie Lou [a well-known stripper in a local topless bar] was helpin' him across the street, holin' her white mink in front of him to keep his shíny shoes from gettin' wet. The weather tomorrow promises to be cloudy for some."

What she think she doin', tellin' *me/looks around to audience/*'bout my ol' man? Sayin' "He lookin' mighty fine, yes sireeeeee." (long pause) She betta keep/ *casting a sharp look in the direction of the Hennings' house/*her big mouf 'n stay shut up in dat house.

Throughout the story, the audience laughed, nodded, and provided "yeah," "you right," "you know it." Dovie Lou's shift to the exaggerated Standard English of the Channel Two reporter brought gales of laughter from the audience.

Numerous cultural assertions are made in the story. The evaluative introduction establishes Dovie Lou as an oldtimer, a fixture in the neighborhood, and Henning and his old lady as relative newcomers. Dovie Lou announces herself a victor before the story begins. Later, she makes it clear that she knew her man, P.B. Evans, was out that night, and that she had had a chance to go out with him, but had decided it was not worth getting "fussied up" to go out in the rain. Instead, she and a girlfriend had gone to play bingo. She uses the TV report to show exaggeration, to report her man out with a famous stripper, and also to brag about the fancy dress of her man who wears name-brand clothes and has a reputation for keeping himself "fine." The final point of the story asserts that her animosity to the Henning woman is not over. Dovie Lou warns that the newcomer should stay inside and not join the neighborhood women on their porches. Once Dovie Lou's anger wears off or she is reunited with her man publicly, she can fend off Henning's wife's stories. Dovie Lou's story is based on fact: Henning's wife had said something to Dovie Lou about her man being out with another woman. But beyond this basis in fact, Dovie Lou's story is highly creative, and she ranges far from the true facts to tell a story which extols her strengths and announces her faith in her ultimate victory over both her wayward man and her "big-mouth" neighbor. . . .

THE TRADITIONS OF STORY-TELLING

People in both Trackton and Roadville spend a lot of time telling stories. Yet the form, occasions, content, and functions of their stories differ greatly. They structure their stories differently; they hold different scales of features on which stories are recognized as *stories* and judged as good or bad. The patterns of interaction surrounding the actual telling of a story vary considerably from Roadville to Trackton. One community allows only stories which are factual and have little exaggeration; the other uses reality only as the germ of a highly creative fictionalized account. One uses stories to reaffirm group membership and behavioral norms, the other to assert individual strengths and powers. Children in the two communities hear different kinds of stories, they develop competence in telling stories in highly contrasting ways.

Roadville story-tellers use formulaic openings: a statement of a comparison or a question asked either by the story-teller or by the individual who has invited the telling of the story. Their stories maintain a strict chronicity, with direct discourse reported, and no explicit exposition of meaning or direct expression of evaluation of the behavior of the main character allowed. Stories end with a summary statement of a moral or a proverb, or a Biblical quotation. Trackton story-tellers use few formulaic openings, except the story-teller's own introduction of himself. Frequently, an abstract begins the story, asserting that the point of the story is to parade the strengths and victories of the story-teller. Stories maintain little chronicity; they move from event to event with numerous interspersions of evaluation of the behaviors of story characters and reiterations of the point of the story. Stories have no formulaic closing, but may have a reassertion of the strengths of the main character, which may be only the opening to yet another tale of adventure.

In Roadville, a story must be invited or announced by someone other than the story-teller. Only certain community members are designated good story-tellers. A story is recognized by the group as an assertion of community membership and agreement on behavioral norms. The marked behavior of the story-teller and audience alike is seen as exemplifying the weaknesses of all and the need for persistence in overcoming such weaknesses. Trackton story-tellers, from a young age, must be aggressive in inserting their stories into an on-going stream of discourse. Story-telling is highly competitive. Everyone in a conversation may want to tell a story, so only the most aggressive wins out. The stress is on the strengths of the individual who is the story's main character, and the story is not likely to unify listeners in any sort of agreement, but to provoke challenges and counterchallenges to the character's ways of overcoming an adversary. The "best stories" often call forth highly diverse additional stories, all designed not to unify the group, but to set out the individual merits of each member of the group.

Roadville members reaffirm their commitment to community and church values by giving factual accounts of their own weaknesses and the lessons learned in overcoming these. Trackton members announce boldly their individual strength in having been creative, persistent, and undaunted in the face of conflict. In Roadville, the sources of stories are personal experience and a familiarity with Biblical parables, church-related stories of Christian life, and testimonials given in church and home lesson-circles. Their stories are tales of transgressions which make the point of reiterating the expected norms of behavior of man, woman, hunter, fisherman, worker, and Christian. The stories of Roadville are true to the facts of an event; they qualify exaggeration and hedge if they might seem to be veering from an accurate reporting of events.

The content of Trackton's stories, on the other hand, ranges widely, and there is "truth" only in the universals of human strength and persistence praised and illustrated in the tale. Fact is often hard to find, though it is usually the seed of the story. Playsongs, ritual insults, cheers, and stories are assertions of the strong over the weak, of the power of the person featured in the story. Anyone other than the story-teller/main character may be subjected to mockery, ridicule, and challenges to show he is not weak, poor, or ugly.

In both communities, stories entertain; they provide fun, laughter, and frames for other speech events which provide a lesson or a witty display of verbal skill. In Roadville, a proverb, witty saying, or Scriptural quotation inserted into a story adds to both the entertainment value of the story and to its unifying role. Group knowledge of a proverb or saying, or approval of Scriptural quotation reinforces the communal experience which forms the basis of Roadville's stories. In Trackton, various types of language play, imitations of other community members or TV personalities, dramatic gestures and shifts of voice quality, and rhetorical questions and expressions of emotional evaluations add humor and draw out the interaction of story-teller and audience. Though both communities use their stories to entertain, Roadville adults see their stories as didactic: the purpose of a story is to make a point—a point about the conventions of behavior. Audience and story-teller are drawn together in a common bond through acceptance of the merits of the story's point for all. In Trackton, stories often have no point; they may go on as long as the audience enjoys the story-teller's entertainment. Thus a story-teller may intend on his first entry into a stream of discourse to tell only one story, but he may find the audience reception such that he can move from the first story into another, and yet another. Trackton audiences are unified by the story only in that they recognize the entertainment value of the story, and they approve stories which extol the virtues of an individual. Stories do not teach lessons about proper behavior; they tell of individuals who excel by outwitting the rules of conventional behavior.

SUGGESTIONS FOR DISCUSSION

1. Roadville residents distinguish between storytelling and gossip. What "rules" or criteria do they use to draw this distinction? Compare to your own experience. Do communities where you live or have lived make a distinction between storytelling and gossip? What criteria do people use? If you think they don't make a distinction, explain why.
2. Describe the identities storytellers in Roadville and Trackton take on when they tell stories. What kind of people do they want to be by telling stories?
3. Think about the stories people told in your family and local community when you were growing up. Who told stories? On what occasions were stories told? Did stories take a particular form? What counted as a good story? What role did storytelling play in the life of the group? Compare your recollections of storytelling with those of other members of the class.

SUGGESTIONS FOR WRITING

1. Write an essay that explains what Shirley Brice Heath sees as the significance of the differences and similarities between the two storytelling traditions.
2. "Talkin' junk" in Trackton, Heath explains, "includes laying on highly exaggerated compliments and making wildly exaggerated comparisons." Think of a story that you have told or heard that includes exaggeration. Write an essay that explains the effects of such exaggeration on the storyteller and listeners.
3. In a footnote to this section of her book *Ways With Words*, Heath notes that "[n]umerous studies of gossip in different cultures attest to the ways in which evaluative reporting confirms certain roles in the social group." Is this true of your experience? Write an essay that explains how gossip "confirms certain roles" in a social group you have been a member of.

Jan Harold Brunvand

"THE HOOK" AND OTHER TEENAGE HORRORS

Jan Harold Brunvand is a folklorist and professor of English at the University of Utah. The following selection "'The Hook' and Other Teenage Horrors" is a chapter from Brunvand's book *The Vanishing Hitchhiker: American Urban Legends and Their Meaning* (1981). In *The Vanishing Hitchhiker* and its two sequels, *The Choking Doberman* and *The Mexican Pet,* Brunvand has gathered examples of contemporary storytelling—strange, scary, funny, macabre, and embarrassing tales storytellers relate as true accounts of real-life experience. Brunvand calls these stories "urban legends" because they are, by and large, set in contemporary America and, like all legends, are alleged to be about real people and real events. These legends, often about someone the narrator knows or the "friend of a friend," are passed on by word of mouth, forming an oral tradition in the midst of America's print and media culture. As Brunvand says, urban legends "survive by being as lively and 'factual' as the television evening news, and, like the daily newscasts, they tend to concern deaths, injuries, kidnappings, tragedies, and scandals." Stories like "The Hook" are told and believed—or at least believable—as "human interest" stories that capture some of the fears and anxieties of contemporary America.

Suggestion for Reading

- As a folklorist, Brunvand is interested in interpreting urban legends as well as in gathering them. As you read through "'The Hook' and Other Teenage Horrors," underline and annotate the passages where Brunvand offers his own interpretations or those of other folklore scholars.

GROWING UP SCARED

P eople of all ages love a good scare. Early childlore is full of semiserious spooky stories and ghastly threats, while the more sophisticated black humor of Little Willies, Bloody Marys, Dead Babies, and other cycles of sick jokes enters a bit later. Among the favorite readings at school are Edgar Allan Poe's blood-soaked tales, and favorite stories at summer camp tell of maniacal ax-murderers and deformed giants lurking in the dark forest to ambush unwary Scouts. Halloween spook houses and Hollywood horror films cater to the same wish to push the level of tolerable fright as far as possible.

The ingredients of horror fiction change little through time, but the style of such stories does develop, even in oral tradition. In their early teens young Americans apparently reject the overdramatic and unbelievable juvenile "scaries" and adopt a new lore of more plausible tales with realistic settings. That is, they begin to enjoy urban legends, especially those dealing with "folks" like themselves—dating couples, students, and baby-sitters—who are subjected to grueling ordeals and horrible threats.

One consistent theme in these teenage horrors is that as the adolescent moves out from home into the larger world, the world's dangers may close in on him or her. Therefore, although the immediate purpose of many of these legends is to produce a good scare, they also serve to deliver a warning: Watch out! This could happen to you! Furthermore, the horror tales often contain thinly-disguised sexual themes which are, perhaps, implicit in the nature of such plot situations as parking in a lovers' lane or baby-sitting (playing house) in a strange home. These sexual elements furnish both a measure of further entertainment and definite cautionary notices about the world's actual dangers. Thus, from the teenagers' own major fears, concerns, and experiences, spring their favorite "true" oral stories.

The chief current example of this genre of urban legend—one that is even older, more popular, and more widespread than "The Boyfriend's Death"—is the one usually called "The Hook."

"THE HOOK"

On Tuesday, November 8, 1960, the day when Americans went to the polls to elect John F. Kennedy as their thirty-fifth president, thousands of people must have read the following letter from a teenager in the popular newspaper column written by Abigail Van Buren:

> DEAR ABBY: If you are interested in teenagers, you will print this story. I don't know whether it's true or not, but it doesn't matter because it served its purpose for me:
>
> A fellow and his date pulled into their favorite "lovers' lane" to listen to the radio and do a little necking. The music was interrupted by an announcer who said there was an escaped convict in the area who had served time for rape and robbery. He was described as having a hook instead of a right hand. The couple became frightened and drove away. When the boy took his girl home, he went around to open the car door for her. Then he saw—a hook on the door handle! I don't think I will ever park to make out as long as I live. I hope this does the same for other kids.
>
> JEANETTE

This juicy story seems to have emerged in the late 1950s, sharing some common themes with "The Death Car" and "The Vanishing Hitchhiker" and then . . . influencing "The Boyfriend's Death" as that legend developed in the early 1960s. The story of "The Hook" (or "The Hookman") really needed no national press report to give it life or credibility, because the teenage oral-tradition underground had done the job well enough long before the election day of 1960. Teenagers all over the country knew about "The Hook" by 1959, and like other modern legends the basic plot was elaborated with details and became highly localized.

One of my own students, originally from Kansas, provided this specific account of where the event supposedly occurred:

> Outside of "Mac" [McPherson, Kansas], about seven miles out towards Lindsborg, north on old highway 81 is an old road called "Hookman's Road." It's a curved road, a traditional parking spot for the kids. When I was growing up it [the legend] was popular, and that was back in the '60's, and it was old then.

Another student told a version of the story that she had heard from her baby-sitter in Albuquerque in 1960:

> . . . over the radio came an announcement that a crazed killer with a hook in place of a hand had escaped from the local insane asylum. The girl got scared and begged the boy to take her home. He got mad and stepped on the gas and roared off. When they got to her house, he got out and went around to the other side of the car to let her out. There on the door handle was a bloody hook.

But these two students were told, after arriving in Salt Lake City, that it had actually occurred *here* in Memory Grove, a well-wooded city park. "Oh, no," a local student in the class insisted, "This couple was parked outside of Salt Lake City *in a mountain canyon* one night, and. . . " It turned out that virtually every student in the class knew the story as adapted in some way to their hometowns.

Other folklorists have reported collecting "The Hook" in Maryland, Wisconsin, Indiana, Illinois, Kansas, Texas, Arkansas, Oregon, and Canada. Some of the informants' comments echo Dear Abby's correspondent in testifying to the story's effect (to discourage parking) even when its truth was suspect. The student said, "I believe that it *could* happen, and this makes it seem real," or "I don't really [believe it], but it's pretty scary; I sort of hope it didn't happen."

Part of the great appeal of "The Hook"—one of the most popular adolescent scare stories—must lie in the tidiness of the plot. Everything fits. On the other hand, the lack of loose ends would seem to be excellent testimony to the story's near impossibility. After all, what are the odds that a convicted criminal or crazed maniac would be fitted with a hook for a missing hand, that this same threatening figure would show up precisely when a radio warning had been broadcast of his escape, and that the couple would drive away rapidly just at the instant the hookman put his hook through the door handle? Besides, why wouldn't he try to open the door with his good hand, and how is it that the boy—furious at the interruption of their lovemaking—is still willing to go around politely to open the girl's door when they get home? Too much, too much—but it makes a great story.

In an adolescent novel titled *Dinky Hocker Shoots Smack!*, M. E. Kerr captured the way teenagers often react to such legends—with cool acceptance that it might have happened, and that's good enough:

> She told Tucker this long story about a one-armed man who was hanging around a lovers' lane in Prospect Park [Brooklyn]. There were rumors that he tried to get in the cars and carry off the girls. He banged on the windshields with his hooked

wooden arm and frothed at the mouth. He only said two words: *bloody murder;* and his voice was high and hoarse.

Dinky claimed this girl who went to St. Marie's was up in Prospect Park one night with a boyfriend. The girl and her boyfriend began discussing the one-armed man while they were parked. They both got frightened and decided to leave. The boy dropped the girl off at her house, and drove home. When he got out of his car, he found this hook attached to his door handle.

Dinky said, "They must have driven off just as he was about to open the door."

"I thought you weren't interested in the bizarre, anymore," Tucker said.

"It's a true story."

"It's still bizarre."

A key detail lacking in the *Dinky Hocker* version, however, is the boyfriend's frustrated anger resulting in their leaving the scene in a great hurry. Almost invariably the boy guns the motor and roars away: ". . . so he revs up the car and he goes torquing out of there." Or, "The boy floored the gas pedal and zoomed away," or "Her boyfriend was annoyed and the car screeched off. . . ." While this behavior is essential to explain the sudden sharp force that tears loose the maniac's hook, it is also a reminder of the original sexual purpose of the parking, at least on the boy's part. While Linda Dégh saw "the natural dread of the handicapped," and "the boy's disappointment and suddenly recognized fear as an adequate explanation for the jump start of the car," folklorist Alan Dundes disagreed, mainly because of the curtailed sex quest in the plot.

Dundes, taking a Freudian line, interpreted the hook itself as a phallic symbol which penetrates the girl's door handle (or bumps seductively against her window) but which is torn off (symbolic of castration) when the car starts abruptly. Girls who tell the story, Dundes suggests, "are not afraid of what a man lacks, but of what he has"; a date who is "all hands" may really want to "get his hooks into her." Only the girl's winding up the window or insisting upon going home at once saves her, and the date has to "pull out fast" before he begins to act like a sex maniac himself. The radio—turned on originally for soft, romantic background music—introduces instead "the consciencelike voice from society," a warning that the girl heeds and the boy usually scorns. Dundes concluded that this popular legend "reflects a very real dating practice, one which produces anxiety . . . particularly for girls."

"The Killer in the Backseat"

A similar urban legend also involves cars and an unseen potential assailant; this time a man threatens a woman who is driving alone at night. The following version of "The Killer in the Backseat" was contributed in 1967 by a University of Utah student who had heard other versions set in Denver and Aurora, Colorado:

A woman living in the city [i.e., Salt Lake City] was visiting some friends in Ogden. When she got into her car in front of this friend's house, she noticed that a car started up right behind her car. It was about 2:00 in the morning, and there weren't any other cars on the road. After she had driven to the highway, she began to think that this car was following her. Some of the time he would drive up real close to her car, but he wouldn't ever pass. She was really scared to death and kept speeding to try to get away from him.

When she got to Salt Lake, she started running stop lights to get away from him, but he would run right through them too. So when she got to her driveway she pulled in really fast, and this guy pulled in right behind her. She just laid on the horn, and her husband came running out. Just then, the guy jumped out of the car, and her husband ran over and said, "What the hell's goin' on here?" So he grabbed the guy, and his wife said, "This man's followed me all the way from Ogden." The man said, "I followed your wife because I was going to work, and as I got into my car, I noticed when I turned my lights on, a man's head bob down in her back seat." So the husband went over to her backseat, opened the door, and pulled this guy from out of the backseat.

This legend first appeared in print in 1968 in another version, also—coincidentally—set in Ogden, Utah, but collected at Indiana University, Bloomington. (This shows how the presence of folklorists in a locality will influence the apparent distribution patterns of folk material.) Twenty further texts have surfaced at Indiana University with, as usual, plenty of variations and localizations. In many instances the pursuing driver keeps flashing his headlights between the high and low beam in order to restrain the assailant who is popping up and threatening to attack the driver. Sometimes the pursuer is a burly truck driver or other tough-looking character, and in several of the stories the supposed would-be attacker (the pursuing rescuer) is specifically said to be a black man. (Both motifs clearly show white middle class fears of minorities or of groups believed to be socially inferior.)

In a more imaginative set of these legends the person who spots the dangerous man in back is a gas station attendant who pretends that a ten dollar bill offered by the woman driver in payment for gas is counterfeit. With this ruse he gets her safely away from her car before calling the police. In another version of the story, a passing motorist sharply warns the woman driver to roll up her window and follow him, driving in exactly the same manner he does. She obeys, speeding and weaving along the highway, until a suspected assailant—usually carrying an ax—is thrown from his perch on the roof of her car.

"The Baby-Sitter and the Man Upstairs"

Just as a lone woman may unwittingly be endangered by a hidden man while she is driving at night, a younger one may face the same hazard in a strange home. The horror legend of "The Baby-sitter and the Man Upstairs," similar in structure to "The Killer in the Backseat," is possibly a later variation of the same story relocated to fit teenagers' other direct experiences. This standard version is from a fourteen-year-old Canadian boy (1973):

There was this baby-sitter that was in Montreal baby-sitting for three children in a big house. She was watching TV when suddenly the phone rang. The children were all in bed. She picked up the phone and heard this guy on the other end laughing hysterically. She asked him what it was that he wanted, but he wouldn't answer and then hung up. She worried about it for a while, but then thought nothing more of it and went back to watching the movie.

Everything was fine until about fifteen minutes later when the phone rang again. She picked it up and heard the same voice laughing hysterically at her, and then hung up. At this point she became really worried and phoned the operator to tell her what had been happening. The operator told her to calm down and that if he called again to try and keep him on the line as long as possible and she would try to trace the call.

Again about fifteen minutes later the guy called back and laughed hysterically at her. She asked him why he was doing this, but he just kept laughing at her. He hung up and about five seconds later the operator called. She told the girl to get out of the house at once because the person who was calling was calling from the upstairs extension. She slammed down the phone and just as she was turning to leave she saw the man coming down the stairs laughing hysterically with a bloody butcher knife in his hand and meaning to kill her. She ran out onto the street but he didn't follow. She called the police and they came and caught the man, and discovered that he had murdered all the children.

The storyteller added that he had heard the story from a friend whose brother's girlfriend was the baby-sitter involved.

By now it should come as no surprise to learn that the same story had been collected two years earlier (1971) some 1500 miles southwest of Montreal, in Austin, Texas, and also in Bloomington, Indiana, in 1973 in a college dormitory. These three published versions are only samples from the wide distribution of the story in folk tradition. Their similarities and differences provide another classic case of folklore's variation within traditional boundaries. In all three legend texts the hour is late and the baby-sitter is watching television. Two of the callers make threatening statements, while one merely laughs. In all versions the man calls three times at regular intervals before the girl calls the operator, then once more afterwards. In both American texts the operator herself calls the police, and in the Indiana story she commands "Get out of the house immediately; don't go upstairs; don't do anything; just leave the house. When you get out there, there will be policemen outside and they'll take care of it." (One is reminded of the rescuers' orders not to look back at the car in "The Boyfriend's Death.") The Texas telephone operator in common with the Canadian one gives the situation away by adding, "The phone call traces to the upstairs." The murder of the child or children (one, two, or three of them—no pattern) is specified in the American versions: in Texas they are "chopped into little bitty pieces"; in Indiana, "torn to bits." All of the storytellers played up the spookiness of the situation—details that would be familiar to anyone who has every baby-sat—a strange house, a television show, an unexpected phone call, frightening sounds or threats, the abrupt orders from the operator, and finally the shocking realization at the end that (as in "The Killer in the Backseat") the caller had been there in the house (or behind her) all the time. The technical problems of calling another telephone from an extension of the same number, or the actual procedures of call-tracing, do not seem to worry the storytellers.

Folklorist Sue Samuelson, who examined hundreds of unpublished "Man Upstairs" stories filed in American folklore archives, concluded that the telephone is the most important and emotionally-loaded item in the plot: the assailant is harassing his victim through the device that is her own favorite means of communication. Baby-sitting, Samuelson points out, is an important socializing experience for young women, allowing them to practice their future roles, imposed on them in a male-dominated society, as homemakers and mothers. Significantly, the threatening male figure is *upstairs*—on top of and in control of the girl—as men have traditionally been in the sexual relationship. In killing the children who were in her care, the man brings on the most catastrophic failure any mother can suffer. Another contributing factor in the story is that the baby-sitter herself is too intent on watching television to realize that the children are being murdered upstairs. Thus, the tale is not just another scary story, but conveys a stern admonition to young women to adhere to society's traditional values.

Occasionally these firmly-believed horror legends are transformed from ghastly mysteries to almost comical adventures. The following Arizona version of "The Baby-sitter and the Man Upstairs," collected in 1976, is a good example:

It was August 8, 1969. She was going to baby-sit at the Smiths who had two children, ages five and seven. She had just put the children to bed and went back to the living room to watch TV.

The phone began to ring; she went to answer it; the man on the other end said, "I'm upstairs with the children; you'd better come up."

She hung the phone up immediately, scared to death. She decided that it must be a prank phone call; again she went to watch TV. The phone rang again; she went to answer it, this time more scared than last.

The man said, "I'm upstairs with the children," and described them in detail. So she hung up the phone, not knowing what to do. Should I call the police? Instead she decided, "I'll call the operator. They can trace these phone calls." She called the operator, and the operator said that she would try and do what she could. Approximately ten minutes later the phone rang again; this time she was shaking.

She answered the phone and the man again said, "I'm upstairs with the children; you'd better come quick!" She tried to stay on the phone as long as she could so that the operator could trace the call; this time the man hung up.

She called back, and the operator said, "Run out of the house; the man is on the extension."

She didn't quite know what to do; should she go and get the children? "No," she said, "he's up there; if I go and get the children, I'll be killed too!!"

She ran next door to the neighbor's house and called the police. The sirens came—there must have been at least ten police cars. They went inside the house, ran upstairs, and found not a man, but a seven-year-old child who was sitting next to the phone with a tape recorder. Later they found that a boy down the street had told this young boy to do this next time he had a baby-sitter. You see the boy didn't like his parents going out, and he didn't like having baby-sitters. So he felt this was the only way he could get rid of them. The boys [sic] don't have baby-sitters anymore; now they go to the nursery school.

"THE ROOMMATE'S DEATH"

Another especially popular example of the American adolescent shocker story is the widely-known legend of "The Roommate's Death." It shares several themes with other urban legends. As in "The Killer in the Backseat" and "The Baby-sitter and the Man Upstairs," it is usually a lone woman in the story who is threatened—or thinks she is—by a strange man. As in "The Hook" and "The Boyfriend's Death," the assailant is often said to be an escaped criminal or a maniac. Finally, as in the latter legend, the actual commission of the crime is never described; only the resulting mutilated corpse is. The scratching sounds outside the girl's place of refuge are an additional element of suspense. Here is a version told by a University of Kansas student in 1965 set in Corbin Hall, a freshman women's dormitory there:

> These two girls in Corbin had stayed late over Christmas vacation. One of them had to wait for a later train, and the other wanted to go to a fraternity party given that night of vacation. The dorm assistant was in her room—sacked out. They waited and waited for the intercom, and then they heard this knocking and knocking outside in front of the dorm. So the girl thought it was her date and she went down. But she didn't come back and she didn't come back. So real late that night this other girl heard a scratching and gasping down the hall. She couldn't lock the door, so she locked herself in the closet. In the morning she let herself out and her roommate had had her throat cut, and if the other girl had opened the door earlier, she [the dead roommate] would have been saved.

At all the campuses where the story is told the reasons for the girls' remaining alone in the dorm vary, but they are always realistic and plausible. The girls' homes may be too far away for them to visit during vacation, such as in Hawaii or a foreign country. In some cases they wanted to avoid a campus meeting or other obligation. What separates the two roommates may be either that one goes out for food, or to answer the door, or to use the rest room. The girl who is left behind may hear the scratching noise either at her room door or at the closet door, if she hides there. Sometimes her hair turns white or gray overnight from the shock of the experience (an old folk motif). The implication in the story is that some maniac is after her (as is suspected about the pursuer in "The Killer in the Backseat"); but the truth is that her own roommate needs help, and she might have supplied it had she only acted more decisively when the noises were first heard. Usually some special emphasis is put on the victim's fingernails, scratched to bloody stumps by her desperate efforts to signal for help.

A story told by a California teenager, remembered from about 1964, seems to combine motifs of "The Baby-sitter and the Man Upstairs" with "The Roommate's Death." The text is unusually detailed with names and the circumstances of the crime:

> Linda accepted a baby-sitting job for a wealthy family who lived in a two-storey home up in the hills for whom she had never baby-sat for before. Linda was rather hesitant as the house was rather isolated and so she asked a girlfriend, Sharon, to go along with her, promising Sharon half of the baby-sitting fee she would earn. Sharon accepted Linda's offer and the two girls went up to the big two-storey house.

The night was an especially dark and windy one and rain was threatening. All went well for the girls as they read stories aloud to the three little boys they were sitting for and they had no problem putting the boys to bed in the upstairs part of the house. When this was done, the girls settled down to watching television.

It was not long before the telephone rang. Linda answered the telephone, only to hear the heavy breathing of the caller on the other end. She attempted to elicit a response from the caller but he merely hung up. Thinking little of it and not wanting to panic Sharon, Linda went back to watching her television program, remarking that the caller had dialed a wrong number. Upon receiving the second call at which time the caller first engaged in a bit of heavy breathing and then instructed them to check on the children, the two girls became frightened and decided to call the operator for assistance. The operator instructed the girls to keep the caller on the line as long as possible should he call again so that she might be able to trace the call. The operator would check back with them.

The two girls then decided between themselves that one should stay downstairs to answer the phone. It was Sharon who volunteered to go upstairs. Shortly, the telephone rang again and Linda did as the operator had instructed her. Within a few minutes, the operator called back telling Linda to leave the house immediately with her friend because she had traced the calls to the upstairs phone.

Linda immediately hung up the telephone and proceeded to run to the stairway to call Sharon. She then heard a thumping sound coming from the stairway and when she approached the stairs she saw her friend dragging herself down the stairs by her chin, all of her limbs severed from her body. The three boys also lay dead upstairs in their beds.

Once again, the Indiana University Folklore Archive has provided the best published report on variants of "The Roommate's Death," Linda Dégh's summary of thirty-one texts and several subtypes and related plots collected since 1961. The most significant feature, according to her report, is the frequent appearance of a male rescuer at the end of the story. In one version, for example, two girls are left behind alone in the dorm by their roommate when she goes downstairs for food; they hear noises, and so stay in their room all night without opening the door. Finally the mailman comes around the next morning, and they call him from the window:

> The mailman came in the front door and went up the stairs, and told the girls to stay
> in their room, that everything was all right but that they were to stay in their rooms
> [sic]. But the girls didn't listen to him 'cause he had said it was all right, so they came
> out into the hall. When they opened the door, they saw they girlfriend on the floor
> with a hatchet in her head.

In other Indiana texts the helpful male is a handyman, a milkman, or the brother of one of the roommates.

According to folklorist Beverly Crane, the male-female characters are only one pair of a series of significant opposites, which also includes home and away, intellectual versus emotional behavior, life and death, and several others. A male is needed to resolve the female's uncertainty—motivated by her emotional fear—about how to act in a new situation. Another male has mutilated and killed her roommate with a blow to her head, "the one part of the body with which women are not supposed to compete." The girls, Crane suggested, are doubly out of place in the beginning, having left the haven of home to engage in intellectual pursuits, and having remained alone in the campus dormitory instead of rejoining the family on a holiday. Ironically, the injured girl must use her fingernails, intended to be long, lovely, feminine adornments, in order to scratch for help. But because her roommate fails to investigate the sound, the victim dies, her once pretty nails now bloody stumps. Crane concluded this ingenious interpretation with these generalizations:

> The points of value implicit in this narrative are then twofold. If women wish to depend on traditional attitudes and responses they had best stay in a place where these attitudes and responses are best able to protect them. If, however, women do choose to venture into the realm of equality with men, they must become less dependent, more self-sufficient, more confident in their own abilities, and, above all, more willing to assume responsibility for themselves and others.

One might not expect to find women's liberation messages embedded in the spooky stories told by teenagers, but Beverly Crane's case is plausible and well argued. Furthermore, it is not at all unusual to find up-to-date social commentary in other modern folklore—witness the many religious and sexual jokes and legends circulated by people who would not openly criticize a church or the traditional social mores. Folklore does not just purvey the old codes of morality and behavior; it can also absorb newer ideas. What needs to be done to analyze this is to collect what Alan Dundes calls "oral-literary criticism," the informants' own comments about their lore. How clearly would the girls who tell these stories perceive—or even accept—the messages extrapolated by scholars? And a related question: Have any stories with clear liberationist themes replaced older ones cautioning young women to stay home, be good, and—next best—be careful, and call a man if they need help?

SUGGESTIONS FOR DISCUSSION

1. Brunvand suggests that teenagers tell horror stories not only "to produce a good scare" but also "to deliver a warning" about the "world's actual dangers." To what extent do you think the stories in "The Hook" serve as cautionary tales? Do you think they would be heard and understood in different ways by male and female listeners?
2. Do you find Beverly Crane's interpretation of "The Roommate's Death" persuasive? How would you answer the question Brunvand poses at the end of this selection?
3. Work together with classmates to create your own collection of urban legends. Which of the stories in this selection or similar types of stories have you heard before? Where, when, and from whom did you hear a particular story? How were the details of the story adapted to local conditions? Did the narrator and the listeners seem to believe the story? What did the narrator and the listeners seem to feel were the most important meanings of the story? What fears, concerns, or experiences does the story seem to reflect?

SUGGESTIONS FOR WRITING

1. Jan Harold Brunvand begins this selection with the statement, "People of all ages love a good scare." Write an essay that explains why people enjoy being scared by ghost stories, horror films, and thrillers. To do this, you may want to compare the horror story with another kind of storytelling, such as fairy tales or adventure stories.

2. Reread "'The Hook' and Other Teenage Horrors," noticing the interpretations of the stories you have marked. Pick one of the interpretations you find particularly interesting or striking. Write an essay in which you summarize the interpretation and explain why it seems adequate or inadequate. Are there alternative interpretations you would offer?

3. Use the individual stories and commentaries in this selection ("The Hook," "The Killer in the Backseat," "The Baby-Sitter and the Man Upstairs," and "The Roommate's Death") as a model to recreate and comment on an urban legend you have heard. Be sure to set the scene of the storytelling—where, when, and who told it—and then give an account of the story. Follow this with a commentary of your own that interprets the dominant theme of the story.

Stephen King

WHY WE CRAVE HORROR MOVIES

Stephen King is a writer whose best-selling novels and short stories have taken the genre of horror fiction to new heights of popularity. A number of his fictions have been turned into successful Hollywood films, such as *Carrie* and *The Shining.* In the following essay, originally published in *Playboy* (December 1981), King seeks to identify the reasons why horror films have such a grip on the popular imagination. Before you read the essay, you might think about your own experience as a movie-goer and television-viewer. Are there particular forms of storytelling—thrillers, soap operas, romances, science fiction, action-adventure, cops and robbers, westerns, and so on—that you are particularly drawn to? The question he asks—Why do we crave horror movies?—could, of course, be applied as well to other forms of popular storytelling.

Suggestion for Reading

- Notice how Stephen King presents his assumptions about people in the opening paragraph. As you read, follow King's argument by underlining the reasons he gives. Consider how his initial assumptions have shaped the reasons he offers us answers to the question, Why do we crave horror movies?

---◆---

I think that we're all mentally ill; those of us outside the asylums only hide it a little better—and maybe not all that much better, after all. We've all known people who talk to themselves, people who sometimes squinch their faces into horrible grimaces when they believe no one is watching, people who have some hysterical fear—of snakes, the dark, the tight place, the long drop . . . and, of course, those final worms and grubs that are waiting so patiently underground.

When we pay our four or five bucks and seat ourselves at tenth-row center in a theater showing a horror movie, we are daring the nightmare.

Why? Some of the reasons are simple and obvious. To show that we can, that we are not afraid, that we can ride this roller coaster. Which is not to say that a really good horror movie may not surprise a scream out of us at some point, the way we may scream when the roller coaster twists through a complete 360 or plows through a lake at the bottom of the drop. And horror movies, like roller coasters, have always been the special province of the young; by the time one turns 40 or 50, one's appetite for double twists or 360-degree loops may be considerably depleted.

We also go to re-establish our feelings of essential normality; the horror movie is innately conservative, even reactionary. Freda Jackson as the horrible melting woman in *Die, Monster, Die!* confirms for us that no matter how far we may be removed from the beauty of a Robert Redford or a Diana Ross, we are still light-years from true ugliness.

And we go to have fun.

Ah, but this is where the ground starts to slope away, isn't it? Because this is a very peculiar sort of fun, indeed. The fun comes from seeing others menaced—sometimes killed. One critic has suggested that if pro football has become the voyeur's version of combat, then the horror film has become the modern version of the public lynching.

It is true that the mythic, "fairy-tale" horror film intends to take away the shades of gray. . . . It urges us to put away our more civilized and adult penchant for analysis and to become children again, seeing things in pure blacks and whites. It may be that horror movies provide psychic relief on this level because this invitation to lapse into simplicity, irrationality and even outright madness is extended so rarely. We are told we may allow our emotions a free rein . . . or no rein at all.

If we are all insane, then sanity becomes a matter of degree. If your insanity leads you to carve up women like Jack the Ripper or the Cleveland Torso Murderer, we clap you away in the funny farm (but neither of those two amateur-night surgeons was ever caught, heh-heh-heh); if, on the other hand, your insanity leads you only to talk to yourself when you're under stress or to pick your nose on your morning bus, then you are left alone to go about your business . . . though it is doubtful that you will ever be invited to the best parties.

The potential lyncher is in almost all of us (excluding saints, past and present; but then, most saints have been crazy in their own ways), and every now and then, he has to be let loose to scream and roll around in the grass. Our emotions and our fears form their own body, and we recognize that it demands its own exercise to maintain proper muscle tone. Certain of these emotional muscles are accepted—even exalted—in civilized society; they are, of course, the emotions that tend to maintain the status quo of civilization itself. Love, friendship, loyalty, kindness—these are all the emotions that we applaud, emotions that have been immortalized in the couplets of Hallmark cards and in the verses (I don't dare call it poetry) of Leonard Nimoy.

When we exhibit these emotions, society showers us with positive reinforcement; we learn this even before we get out of diapers. When, as children, we hug our rotten little puke of a sister and give her a kiss, all the aunts and uncles smile and twit and cry, "Isn't he the sweetest little thing?" Such coveted treats as chocolate-covered graham crackers often follow. But if we deliberately slam the rotten little puke of a sister's fingers in the door, sanctions follow—angry remonstrance from parents, aunts and uncles; instead of a chocolate-covered graham cracker, a spanking.

But anticivilization emotions don't go away, and they demand periodic exercise. We have such "sick" jokes as, "What's the difference between a truckload of bowling balls and a truckload of dead babies?" (You can't unload a truckload of bowling balls with a pitchfork . . . a joke, by the way, that I heard originally from a ten-year-old). Such a joke may surprise a laugh or a grin out of us even as we recoil, a possibility that confirms the thesis: If we share a brotherhood of man, then we also share an insanity of man. None of which is intended as a defense of either the sick joke or insanity but merely as an explanation of why the best horror films like the best fairy tales, manage to be reactionary, anarchistic, and revolutionary all at the same time.

The mythic horror movie, like the sick joke, has a dirty job to do. It deliberately appeals to all that is worst in us. It is morbidity unchained, our most base instincts let free, our nastiest fantasies realized . . . and it all happens, fittingly enough, in the dark. For those reasons, good liberals often shy away from horror films. For myself, I like to see the most aggressive of them—*Dawn of the Dead*, for instance—as lifting a trap door in the civilized forebrain and throwing a basket of raw meat to the hungry alligators swimming around in that subterranean river beneath.

Why bother? Because it keeps them from getting out, man. It keeps them down there and me up here. It was Lennon and McCartney who said that all you need is love, and I would agree with that.

As long as you keep the gators fed.

SUGGESTIONS FOR DISCUSSION

1. Look over the reasons you have underlined. Do you find some of the reasons King offers to explain why people "crave" horror movies more persuasive than others? Explain why his reasons are or are not persuasive to you. Are there reasons you can think of that King leaves out?
2. King begins his essay with a powerful assertion: "I think we're all mentally ill." How does this assumption guide the development of the rest of the essay? What other assumptions might you begin with to explain the appeal of horror movies?
3. King suggests that horror movies perform a social function that is "inherently conservative." To what extent do horror movies allow readers, in King's words, "to reestablish our feelings of essential normality"? Give specific examples of how particular horror movies do this. Can you make a similar argument about other kinds of movies, such as thrillers, romances, action-adventure, Westerns, and so on?

SUGGESTIONS FOR WRITING

1. Begin with King's suggestion that one of the social functions of the horror movie is first to violate and then to "re-establish our feelings of essential normality." Write an essay on a particular book, movie, or television show that uses this notion of violating and reestablishing social norms to analyze the story it tells and the appeal it has for readers or viewers.
2. Pick another genre of popular fiction, movies, or television shows with which you are familiar (such as soap operas, situation comedies, police shows, science fiction, fantasy, Westerns, and so on). Use King's essay as a model to write your own explanation of why we crave the form of storytelling you have chosen.

3. Choose a genre of storytelling with which you are not familiar or do not care for. Find someone—a friend, classmate, relative, or acquaintance—who really likes that particular form of storytelling, whether in the novels they read or in the movies and television shows they watch. Write an essay to explain the person's attraction to the genre and also to generalize about the larger popular appeal of the genre.

Russell Hoban

THOUGHTS ON A SHIRTLESS CYCLIST, ROBIN HOOD, AND ONE OR TWO OTHER THINGS

In "Thoughts on a Shirtless Cyclist, Robin Hood, and One or Two Other Things," taken from *Writers, Critics, and Children* (1976), Russell Hoban, the author of children's books and critically acclaimed novels, reflects on the place Robin Hood occupies in his imaginative life and, more generally, how "the fantasy of our legends, myths and stories" helps develop a sense of self in relation to the realities of the social world. Legends, as we saw in the earlier selection from Jan Harold Brunvand's *The Vanishing Hitchhiker and Other Urban Legends,* are stories narrators tell because they are entertaining and also because they are alleged to be true. Unlike other kinds of stories such as myths or fairy tales, legends retain a grip on their listeners because people believe they are about things that actually happened to real people. One of the longest-standing legendary figures is Robin Hood. Robin Hood is perhaps the earliest and best-known outlaw-hero in a tradition of storytelling that began in medieval England and entered the new world of America. Many of us know Robin Hood through the Walt Disney cartoon and the Hollywood feature films that revive the Robin Hood story periodically. But however you heard it, you are likely to think that Robin Hood was a real person in Sherwood Forest who robbed from the rich to give to the poor.

Suggestion for Reading

• Notice that Hoban opens his essay with an anecdote about a shirtless man, riding a bicycle and shouting. Then, at the very end of the essay, Hoban returns to this puzzling figure. As you read, keep the shirtless man in mind and consider how Hoban's essay on Robin Hood tries to account for his strange behavior.

◆

The other day when I was going to my office in the morning I saw a man without a shirt riding a bicycle in circles at a traffic light and shouting unintelligibly. It was a chilly morning, so he must have been uncomfortable without a shirt on, and he wasn't a hippy. He looked like a workman, and he didn't look drunk. So it seemed to me that he must be having a mental breakdown of some sort.

I thought about it for a while, and then it occurred to me that maybe the man's mind wasn't breaking down. Maybe what had broken down was the system of restraints and conventions inside him that ordinarily made him keep his shirt on and not shout. That system, I think, is part of what could be called an inner society. The inner society has its ballrooms and bedrooms and kitchens, its shops and offices, its narrow alleys and its open places, its figures of authority and rebellion, of usage and surprise, love and hate, should and should not, is and isn't. As in the outer society, some things are done and some are not.

When I had thought that far, my next thought was that on that particular day that particular man's inner society was rioting. The windows of the shops were being smashed, the offices were being deserted, and he was doing what he was doing.

My next thought was that the previous thought had been wrong: he was doing what he was doing because there were no rioters and no provision for riot in his inner society, and so there was no one for the job but him. His trouble, perhaps, was that his inner society was not sufficiently different from the outer one: too many of the same things were done and not done. And having no interior colleague to whom he could assign the task or delegate the responsibility, he himself had to take off his shirt and ride his bicycle in circles at a traffic light and shout. And it must have taken something out of him to do it.

Now my inner society, on the other hand, has always had that shirtless shouting cyclist in it. I know him of old as I know myself, even though I hadn't given him much thought until I actually saw him in the outer world. So it isn't likely that I shall ever have to go out into the street and do that myself; he's always there to take care of it for me. There may, of course, come a day when I shall riotously put on a bowler hat and a neat black suit, buy a tightly furled umbrella, and mingle in wild silence with the brokers in the City. One never knows what will come up.

Which brings me, by cobweb bridges perhaps invisible to the naked eye, to a book I once threw into an incinerator.

The book was *Robin Hood*. My edition, an American one, was bound in what I think was Lincoln Green. I don't remember who it was that wrote that particular version of the story, but it had large black type and was illustrated by an artist named Edwin John Prittie with line drawings and paintings in full colour. I used to read that book up in an old wild-cherry tree, and it was the coziest reading I can remember.

But there came a time when I got to be eighteen years old, and there was a war, and I was going off to be a soldier, and it seemed to me that I had better stop being a child and be a man altogether. So I took *Robin Hood* and pitched it into the incinerator. It's a crime that I am driven to confess from time to time, as I do now.

When I came home from the war and found myself, surprisingly, alive and having to go on with the business of growing up, I looked for that same edition that I had thrown away. Years later I found a copy. I haven't it with me now; it is gone again, lost in a removal. But I remember how it was when I held it in my hands again. There were all the pictures looking just as good as ever, and that whole dappled word-world of sun and shade with nothing lost whatever—Little John and Robin fighting on the plank bridge with their quarterstaves; the hateful Sheriff of Nottingham in his arrogance and his scarlet cloak; the beautiful Maid Marian and all the merry men in Lincoln Green: Robin in the *capul hide,* standing over the corpse of Guy of Gisborne. I've always liked the sound of the words *capul hide:* the skin of a horse, with the eyes of a man looking out through the eyeholes in the head—the skin of a dead beast hiding a live man, magical and murderous.

Obviously Robin Hood is a part of my inner society and has never stopped being in my thoughts, but it's only recently that I've become fully aware of how much he is to me, of how far the theme of that child's book has gone beyond childhood. Now as I think about him Robin Hood grows deeper and darker and stronger. Constantly he takes on new shadowy identities, and in his *capul hide* he sometimes evokes the dancing *shaman* in the drawing on the cave wall at Les Trois Frères, sometimes Fraser's *Rex Nemorensis,* doomed King of the Wood, the killer waiting for his killer who will be the next king.

In the absence of my found-and-lost again edition I bought Roger Lancelyn Green's Puffin *Robin Hood.* On the title page was a stanza from the Alfred Noyes poem, *Sherwood,* and it gave me gooseflesh when I read it:

> Robin Hood is here again: all his merry thieves
> Hear a ghostly bugle-note shivering through the leaves . . .
> The dead are coming back again, the years are rolled away
> In Sherwood, in Sherwood, about the break of day.

I wanted it to be Sherwood again, about the break of day. I turned the pages, reading with impatience. But it wasn't the same. This book started with Robin Hood's birth, and I didn't want that, I wanted the opening that had been in the cherry-tree book of childhood, and it wasn't there and I couldn't remember it.

Then, on page 19 I found it—the incident in which the Sheriff of Nottingham and his men capture a serf who had killed a royal deer. The beginning of my book came back to me then, just like Proust's Combray—all at once and clear and vivid. "Saxon hind" was what my book called the serf, and I could see the scene again as it first came to me through the words in the cherry tree. I could see that sunlight through the passing leaves, the prisoner trussed up on the sledge like meat, helpless, rolling his eyes in terror as the Sheriff's foresters drag him to his death. Robert Fitzooth, not yet Robin Hood the outlaw, encounters the group and questions the Sheriff's men. The Chief Forester taunts him about the power of the bow he carries, doubts that such a stripling can wield such a weapon. Fitzooth shows his strength and skill with a long shot that brings down one of the King's deer. And with that he has fallen into the forester's trap—like the prisoner, he has forfeited his life with that shot. The Sheriff's men attempt to take him, but he kills some of them and frees the "Saxon hind." They escape into the greenwood, and the outlaw life of Robin Hood begins.

The light and the air of that first encounter have never left my mind, and the sounds of the forest, the hissing of the sledge runners over the grass, the rattle of weapons, the shouts, the whizzing arrows. It is the metaphorical value of that action that has made it so memorable for me: the free and active wild self of the forest, armed and strong, freed the bound and helpless captive self and so became the outlaw self I recognized within me—the self indwelling always, sometimes kept faith with, sometimes betrayed.

Free and savage, the Robin Hood who has always walked the pathways of my inner society has been exemplary—a standard and a reminder to the unfree and unsavage boy that I was who lusted for that greenwood world: excellence was the price of Robin Hood's freedom, his untamedness, and his power. He was able to be what he was only because of his matchless skill; he was the archer who could shoot farther and truer than any other: he was a hero and a winner who had a thing that he could do better than anybody else.

Heroes who can do something well are still considered necessary for children. And if many of today's books for grown-ups offer us a selection of the infirm and the awkward, the losers who lap up defeat like chicken soup ladled out by a Jewish-mother kind of fate, we need those too: the composite hero of the collective, cumulative, juvenile-adult imagination has got to have some antiheroism about him in order to be complete. Certainly anything that closes the gap between the real and the ideal makes the hero more useful for everyday reference—and here I can't help thinking about the god Krishna, who disported himself with fifty or sixty cowgirls at a wonderful party out on the meadows that lasted many nights, during which he made all the cowgirls think he was making love with each of them. But despite his divine powers—or because of them—he did it all with his mind, which I think is charming. A hero no better than the reader, however, will scarcely last a lifetime. And I think that heroes who excel and win all kinds of good things are the best kind. Myself, I can't use a mythology in which there is nothing to win and consequently nothing to lose. I have to have something to try for, and the more excellence I can manage the better I feel. In that respect Robin Hood has been a great help to me all my life.

Reading the Roger Lancelyn Green version, I realize that there was a great deal more to the story and the archetypes than I had thought before. In my edition Marian was simply called Maid Marian, and nothing more was said about it. Once or twice as I grew older and more cynical I may have questioned the validity of her title. She was, after all, presumably sleeping rough like everyone else in the outlaw band, and Robin being her lover, what could have been more natural than for them to sleep together? But Green spells it out and no mistake: Marian *was* a maid; she kept her virginity the whole time that she and Robin lived together in the forest. Although she had pledged herself to him the marriage was not to be consummated until the return of Richard the Lion-Hearted, the true and lawful king.

Robin Hood has no other woman that I ever heard of in any of the stories. So I have to think of him as celibate, as putting off the assumption of a full male role, as being less than a complete, grown-up man. He is asexual and pure, mercurial, airy almost, Ariel-like—a natural innocent, murderous but sweet-natured, light and quick. And he shares with Marian that mystical virtue that chastity confers, so useful for catching unicorns. The male and the female elements, the *yang* and *yin* of this legend, are allied but not conjoined at the peak of their vigour, and when later a legitimate union is formed, they decline.

Robin Hood is more often with Little John than with Maid Marian. He and his giant companion are like a clean-cut, somewhat prim ego and id. They continually test and prove themselves, tempting fate, daring all comers, looking for trouble, never content with safety and boredom. They fight with quarterstaves at their first meeting; they quarrel from time to time; they rescue each other from capture; they compete with each other against the terrible strong beggar with the potent quarter-staff and the bag of meal that blinds the usually cunning Robin. And so they stay young and jolly until King Richard, the lawful ruler, the inevitable mature authority, returns.

And with that return Robin Hood is absorbed into grown-upness and legitimacy. He is pardoned, and no more an outlaw; he is married, and no more a child-man. His best men are called into the service of King Richard. Robin Hood's power is drained off into the power of lawful authority. The outlaw self is assimilated into the lawful self; the puissant youth becomes the waning man.

I'm no scholar, and I have no idea of the origin of the legend that is Robin Hood. What is inescapable is that the stone of legend is worn into shape by the sea of human perception and need that continually washes over it. Legends, myth and fantasy both ask and tell us how life is, and there seems to be a strong need in us to think about the theme that is in *Robin Hood:* the absorption into law and order of that mysterious, chthonic, demiurgic power that we vitally need but cannot socially tolerate. We regret the loss of it and we rationalize the necessity of that loss. We say to it, "Yes, be there. But lose yourself in us at the proper time. Grow up." But I wonder what the proper time is, and I wonder if the loss is necessary. And I wonder what growing up is. And I wonder whether young people now are not validly reconsidering and reshaping that theme, reclassifying it as well, so that the values assigned are no longer the same as those agreed upon until now. Maybe what we've always called growing up is sometimes growing down. It bears thinking about.

Robin Hood is only one development of that theme; there must be many others. In *Great Expectations,* for instance, Magwitch, the outlaw self, is content to subsidize anonymously Pip, the lawful self. And it is Magwitch the outlaw who refines what is base and shallow in the respectable youth. Pip thinks that Miss Havisham is financing him, but the money that makes it possible for him to cut a dash as a young gentleman does not come from her decaying beauty, wealth and gentility, but from the starveling and tenacious humanity of what in us is violent, inchoate, unshapen and fit only to be put in prison.

Again, in Conrad's *Secret Sharer,* a young captain, a young lawful authority in his first command, is appealed to by a young man who closely resembles him, a fugitive fleeing trial for killing a mate on another vessel. With characteristic genius Conrad opens his story with the unfledged captain taking the anchor watch alone at night on his ship that is still unfamiliar to him. He looks over the side and sees looking up at him from the water a face like his own, the face of a desperate swimmer. The captain shelters his criminal *doppelganger* aboard his ship during a period of self doubt before putting to sea. But when the barque leaves port the fugitive must be put ashore to take his chances alone. A wide-brimmed hat, given him by the captain as protection against the sun, falls into the water and becomes a sea mark by which the young master gauges the current while negotiating a difficult offing under sail in light and baffling airs.

The fugitive's hat gets the lawful master safely out to sea, but the fugitive cannot go with the ship. Magwitch gives Pip what he can and dies. Robin Hood is killed by the establishment that has no use for him. The predatory church that he has always fought will take him in, ailing and ageing, will bleed him to death at the end by the hand of the treacherous Prioress of Kirkleys Nunnery. Robin Hood, supported by Little John, will loose his last arrow from his deathbed and be buried where it falls. Marian, first magical maid and then magicless woman, will become a nun and Prioress in her turn. Robin in the earth and she in the nunnery will both regain their innocence and power.

After the first reading of the book, the death and the last arrow were always there waiting for Robin Hood and me; he carried that death with him, carried that last arrow in his quiver always. He seems such a year-king! He seems, in his green and lightsome strength, always to hasten toward his sacrificial death that will bring forth from the winter earth another spring. And like a year-king, he must be given up, cannot be kept.

But I cannot give him up entirely. I think that we need our outlaw strength alive and brother to our lawful vigour. The one is not healthy without the other. I keep calling the elements outlaw self and lawful self, but that is unfair, really, to the essence of the thing. Society defines the terms of lawful and unlawful, because society makes the laws. And society is a retarded child with a loaded gun in its hands; I don't completely accept society's terms. Something in us makes us retell that myth; some drive there is in us to find and name the demon in us that is more real than laws and conventions that tell us what is right and what is wrong. And that demon is, I think, the radical spirit of life: it is the dark and unseen root system of our human tree whose visible branches are so carefully labelled and scientifically pruned by us. Maybe we think we don't need to know more about that nameless creative chaos, but we do, because in it we must find all real order. Polite gentlemen wearing suits and ties and with neat haircuts sit around tables with the death of the world in their briefcases, and they do not hesitate to tell us what is order. But to me it seems disorder. Other polite gentlemen some years ago sent up human smoke signals from the chimneys of crematoria, and they too defined order with great clarity. I think that fewer definitive definitions and many more tentative ones are needed now.

The fantasy of our legends, myths and stories helps with those new definitions. It is as close as we can get to noumena through phenomena, as close as we can get to the thingness of things through the appearances of things. Fantasy isn't separate from reality; it is a vital approach to the essence of it. As to its importance, it is simply a matter of life and death. If we don't find out more about the truly essential thingness of things, then some future generation, if not this one, won't have anything left to find out about. So we must have fantasy constructed as scaffolding from which to work on actualities. And to work with fantasy is a risky business for the writer: it can change his whole world of actualities.

Which brings me back to the man on the bicycle, shirtless and shouting. I was sorry for that man. I know how he felt. I wish he had been able to do something better with the baffled demon in him. I think he might have found something better to do if he had had more workable material in his mind, more useful people in his inner society. Robin Hood would have helped him, perhaps Captain Ahab too, and Lord Jim and Raskolnikov and goodness knows who else, functioning as surrogate actors-out of extreme and exaggerated degrees of the human condition. They might have taken on for him certain time-consuming and self-defeating tasks. They might have shown him other ways to be, might have freed him to do something more effective than what he was doing, might have helped him to find an identity in that wild surge of random creation that vanished into silence on the indulgent and indifferent air.

Well, you may say, perhaps that man wasn't a reader, and whatever is in books won't help him. But books permeate both the outer and inner societies, moving through readers to non-readers with definitions and provision for societal roles, expectations and probabilities. Always more figures are needed to people our inner societies—personifications of all the subtly different modes of being, *avatars* of the sequential and often warring selves within us. Books in nameless categories are needed—books for children and adults together, books that can stand in an existential nowhere and find a centre that will hold.

SUGGESTIONS FOR DISCUSSION

1. Why does Russell Hoban open and close his essay with the image of the shirtless cyclist? What does this puzzling figure signify for Hoban?
2. What is the "inner society" Hoban speaks of? What functions does it perform? What is the "outlaw self" and what is its relationship, in Hoban's view, to the "lawful self"? Do you agree with him that we need both?
3. Who are the Robin Hoods in your "inner society"? Do they come from books or are they as likely to come from television, movies, and comics? Compile a list of the heroes and heroines who inhabit your "inner society." Then compare your list with those of your classmates. To what extent do they include the same figures? How do they differ? Do men and women in your class have the same heroes and heroines? How would you account for differences?

SUGGESTIONS FOR WRITING

1. Russell Hoban writes, "Heroes who can do something well are still considered necessary for children." Write an essay that explains why Hoban thinks heroes are "necessary for children" and what the heroes and heroines of your childhood represented for you. Are these figures still heroes and heroines for you? If so, explain why. If not, explain why this is so.
2. Write an essay that explains what Hoban means by an "inner society" and the role such an inner society plays in your life. Who are the figures who populate your inner society and what do they signify for you?
3. Write an essay that explains what Hoban sees as the role of the "outlaw self" in his imagination and what role such an outlaw self plays in your imagination.

John A. Lomax

HEROES AND HARD CASES

Anonymous

JESSE JAMES

Woody Guthrie

PRETTY BOY FLOYD

The following selections are well-known American ballads about the legendary outlaws. Jesse James and Pretty Boy Floyd. We have prefaced the ballad of Jesse James with introductory comments by John A. Lomax, one of the greatest American folklorists and song collectors, from his book *Folk Song USA* (1947). The second ballad, "Pretty Boy Floyd," was written by Woody Guthrie, the chronicler of the Dust Bowl migration from Oklahoma to California in the 1930s and the predecessor of such contemporary singer-songwriters as Bob Dylan. Both Jesse James and Pretty Boy Floyd were actual people (and robbers) who became legendary heroes during times of social crisis. Jesse James was a Confederate veteran in the chaotic times following the Civil War in Missouri. Pretty Boy Floyd's spree of bank robberies, like those of Bonnie and Clyde, Ma Barker, and John Dillinger, took place during the Depression of the 1930s. You might think about how such times of social crisis seem to call up the legendary outlaw-hero.

Suggestion for Reading

• As you read the lyrics to "Jesse James" and "Pretty Boy Floyd," keep in mind what Hoban said about the popularity of legendary outlaw-heroes.

HEROES AND HARD CASES

John A. Lomax

Bloody tragedy and violence have been the favored subjects for ballad-makers and their folk audience for centuries, just as they are today the bread and butter of the daily press. The longest-lived of the classical British ballads dealt with shocking tragedy. "Lord Thomas and Fair Eleanor":

> Lord Thomas he had a sword by his side,
> As he walked about the hall;
> He cut his bride's head from her shoulders
> And kicked it against the wall.

"Earl Brand" or "The Douglas Tragedy":

> She held his steed in her milk-white hand,
> And never shed one tear,
> Until she saw her seven brethren fall,
> And her father who loved her so dear.

American folk-singers treasured these medieval tales of passion and violence, but left them largely to the women to sing, calling them with unconscious scorn "old-time *love*-songs." The bear hunters, Indian fighters, six-gun artists, and eye-gougers who flourished on the frontier found these old tales rather tame in comparison with their own lives. They preferred a language that reeked with gore:

> I was raised on six-shooters till I got big enough to eat ground shotguns.

> The music of widders and orphans is music to me melancholy soul.

> I'll snatch you bald-headed and spit on the place where the hair come off.

> I'll take a leg off you and beat you over the head with the bloody end of it.

> I'll slap your head up to a peak and then knock the peak off.

> Take your eye out and eat it for a grape. . . .

The counterparts and opponents of these "ring-tailed roarers," these "half-man-half-horse-and-half-alligator" boys were the frontier peace officers, hard-eyed, quiet, and deadly. Of one of these it is told that he went after three bad men in a distant town with instructions to bring them back dead or alive. In a few days he wired home: "FOUND THEM. SEND TWO COFFINS AND A DOCTOR. JAKE." The American peace officer has always had a problem on his hands, since there seems to be a real ornery streak in the American character that inclines us to acts of "crime and disgrace." Some Kentucky mountaineer has left us a verse that describes and defines this American trait. "Hit comes natural to you," he indicates, "to be mean and lowdown when you are raised to hit."

> Rattlesnake, rattlesnake,
> What makes yore teeth so white?
> Why I've been in the bottom all of my life
> And I ain't done nothin' but bite, bite,
> I ain't done nothin' but bite.

Those of us who do not indulge in violence certainly enjoy hearing about such behavior and its consequences. At any rate, there is no question that stabbings, poisonings, floggings, beheadings, dismemberments, drownings, and gunplay have produced more American ballads than any other kind of subject. Little Frankie, Billy the Kid, Railroad Bill, Stagalee, John Dillinger, Pretty Boy Floyd, the Knoxville Boy, the Hatfields and the Coys, Jesse James, John Hardy—these outlaws and coldblooded killers make proper ballad heroes. Alongside these desperadoes stand the passion-murderer, whining his confession, and the prisoner, moaning out his agony and loneliness in the "hard-rock hotel,"—both everlasting folksong heroes and creators.

JESSE JAMES

The best-known and most singable of all our outlaw ballads is the story of Jesse James. Its creator, an anonymous people's poet said to have been a Negro convict, signed himself Billy Gashade in the final stanza—probably a pseudonym. Whatever the author's name, his song has carried the legend of Jesse James all over America and into a dozen ballad versions, Negro and white. Like outlaw heroes in the great tradition from Robin Hood to Pretty Boy Floyd, the Missouri train robber is portrayed as—

> . . . a man, friend to the poor,
> He never could see a man suffer pain,
> He robbed from the rich and he gave to the poor
> He'd a hand and a heart and a brain.

One of the classic stories in the James legend is the tale of the outlaw and the widow woman. They say that Jesse and his gang stopped at a widow woman's farm for dinner, and, as they ate their victuals, they noticed that she was crying.

Jesse kept asking questions. The woman said there was a mortgage due on her farm for $1400; it was overdue and this was her last day of grace. The man who held the mortgage was a hardhearted old miser and would be sure to turn her out. After they finished eating, Jesse produced a sack and counted out $1400 on the table. "Here, lady," said Jesse, "you take this money and pay off your mortgage."

The widow said she couldn't believe it was anything but a dream—things never happened that way—, but Jesse assured her it was good money and for her use.

They rode some distance from the house and hid in the bushes beside the rocky road along which the mortgage man was to come in his buggy. Presently they saw him driving toward the widow's house, and pretty soon, driving back, looking prosperous. He was humming "Ol Dan Tucker was a fine old feller" as he came opposite. The boys stepped out into the road, held him up, and recovered the $1400.

Just as this exploit of Jesse James fits the folklore pattern of the trickster hero, so the story of his death falls into the ancient tradition of hero-death, a tradition that embraces both Baldur and the carpenter of Nazareth. This story appeared in the St. Joseph, Missouri, *Evening News,* April 3, 1882, the day after Jesse "tumbled from the wall," showing that before the ballad-singers began their James saga, the newspaper stories had taken on the ballad flavor in their account of his death.

Between eight and nine o'clock yesterday morning Jesse James, the Missouri outlaw, before whom the deeds of Fra Diavolo, Dick Turpin and Schinderhannes dwindled into insignificance, was instantly killed by a boy twenty years old, named Robert Ford, at temporary residence on the corner of Thirteenth and Lafayette Streets, in this city.

In the light of all moral reasoning the shooting was unjustifiable; but the law was vindicated, and the $10,000 reward offered by the state for the body of the brigand will doubtless go to the man who had the courage to draw a revolver on the notorious outlaw even when his back was turned, as in this case.

There is little doubt that the killing was the result of a premeditated plan formed by Robert and Charles Ford several months ago. Charles had been an accomplice of Jesse James since the 3rd of last November and entirely possessed his confidence. Robert Ford, his brother, joined Jesse last Friday a week ago and accompanied Jesse and Charles to this city Sunday, March 23.

The opportunity they had long wished for came this morning. Breakfast was over. Charlie Ford and Jesse James been in the stable currying the horses preparatory to their night ride. On returning to the room where Robert Ford was, Jesse said:

"It's an awfully hot day. I guess I'll take off my pistols for fear somebody will see them if I walk in the yard."

He unbuckled the belt in which he carried two .45 calibre revolvers and laid them on the bed with his coat and vest. He then picked up a dusting brush with the intention of dusting some pictures which hung on the wall. To do this he got on a chair. His back was now turned to the brothers, who silently stepped between James and his revolvers.

At a motion from Charlie both drew their guns. Robert was the quicker of the two and in one motion he had the long weapon to a level of his eye, and with the muzzle not more than four feet from the back of the outlaw's head. . . . Even in that motion, quick as thought, there was something which did not escape the acute ears of the hunted man. He made a motion as if to turn his head to ascertain the cause of that suspicious sound, but too late. A nervous pressure on the trigger, a quick flash, a sharp report, and the well directed ball crashed through the outlaw's skull. . . . The shot had been fatal, and all the bullets in Charlie's revolver, still directed at Jesse's head could not more effectively have determined the fate of the greatest bandit and freebooter that ever figured in the pages of a country's history.

So, in the minds of folk-singers and, to some degree, for us all, Jesse James, train robber and gunman lives as a hero and his betrayer as another Judas Iscariot.

JESSE JAMES

Anonymous

[Jesse James was living under the alias Mr. Howard when he was killed.]
Jesse James was a lad,
    he killed many a man,
He robbed the Glendale train;
He took from the rich
    and he gave to the poor,
He'd a hand and a heart and a brain.
    Oh

(*Chorus*)
Jesse had a wife to mourn his life,
    Three children they were brave;
But that dirty little coward
    that shot Mister Howard,
He laid poor Jesse in his grave.
It was on a Saturday night and the
    moon was shining bright,
They robbed the Glendale train,
With the agent on his knees, he
    delivered up the keys
To these outlaws Frank and Jesse
    James. (*Chorus*)

The people held their breath when they
    heard of Jesse's death
They wondered how he ever came to
    fall;
Robert Ford, it was a fact, shot Jesse
    in the back
While Jesse hung a picture on the
    wall. (*Chorus*)

Oh, Jesse was a man, a friend of the
    poor
He'd never rob a mother or a child;
He took from the rich and he gave to
    the poor
So they shot Jesse James on the sly.
    (*Chorus*)

Well, this song was made by Billy
    Gashade,
As soon as the news did arrive;
He said there was no man with the law
    in his hand
Who could take Jesse James when
alive. (*Chorus*)

PRETTY BOY FLOYD

Woody Guthrie

If you'll gather round me children
A story I will tell,
About Pretty Boy Floyd, the outlaw
Oklahoma knew him well

It was in the town of Shawnee,
    It was Saturday afternoon.
    His wife beside him in the wagon
    As into town they rode.

There a deputy Sheriff approached him,
    In a manner rather rude,
    Using vulgar words of language,
    And his wife she overheard.

Pretty Boy grabbed a log chain,
    And the deputy grabbed a gun,
    And in the fight that followed
    He laid that deputy down.

He took to the trees and timbers,
    And he lived a life of shame,
    Every crime in Oklahoma
    Was added to his name.

Yes, he took to the trees and timbers,
    On that Canadian River's shore,
    And Pretty Boy found a welcome
    At many a farmer's door.

There's many a starvin farmer,
    The same old story told,
    How this outlaw paid their mortgage,
    And saved their little home.

Others tell you 'bout a stranger,
    That come to beg a meal,
    And underneath his napkin
    Left a thousand dollar bill.

It was in Oklahoma City
    It was on a Christmas Day,
    There came a whole car load of groceries,
    With a letter that did say.

"You say that I'm an outlaw,
    You say that I'm a thief,
    Here's a Christmas dinner
    For the families on relief."

Now as through this world I ramble,
    I see lots of funny men,
    Some will rob you with a six-gun,
    And some with a fountain pen.

But as through this life you travel,
    As through your life you roam,
    You won't never see an outlaw,
    Drive a family from their home.

SUGGESTIONS FOR DISCUSSION

1. John A. Lomax's introduction to the ballad of Jesse James suggests the role of the media in creating legendary outlaw-heroes. Reread the newspaper account Lomax presents of Jesse James's death. Can you think of other examples of the media creating a legendary hero?

2. Both Jesse James and Pretty Boy Floyd are portrayed in the ballad tradition as Robin Hood figures who robbed from the rich to give to the poor. For our purposes here, whether they did so or not is beside the point. Storytellers and traditions have insisted on it, and people have chosen to believe the legends. The question remains, though, why is this so? Why, in a culture ostensibly devoted to law and order and the preservation of private property, would such outlaws become popular heroes?

3. Generations of Americans grew up thinking of outlaws such as Jesse James, Billy the Kid, and Pretty Boy Floyd as folk heroes. Is this still the case, or are there other heroes who have taken their place in the popular imagination? If so, who are they and how would you explain the change?

SUGGESTIONS FOR WRITING

1. Write an essay that explains what Woody Guthrie means in the following verse from "Pretty Boy Floyd": "Now as through this world I ramble, / I see lots of funny men, / Some will rob you with a six-gun, / And some with a fountain pen." You will need to explain the distinction Guthrie is drawing between kinds of robbery and the version of justice Guthrie is advancing in the ballad.

2. Think of all the songs you know that tell the story of a hero—whether an outlaw-hero or not. Begin by listing as many songs as you can. Draw upon popular songs, folk songs, ballads, anything that comes to mind. Look over the list and pick one of the songs you find most memorable to write an essay about. In the essay, retell briefly but adequately the hero's story as the song presents it. The point of your essay, however, is not just to retell the tale. Your task here is to explain what makes the hero a hero. How would you define the formula that makes the character in the song recognizable to listeners as a hero?

3. "Jesse James" concerns how Jesse James was killed, in this case by treason. Pick a story in which the hero dies at the end and write an essay that explains the meaning of the hero's death.

Robert Warshow

THE GANGSTER AS TRAGIC HERO

Robert Warshaw was a film critic and one of the first American intellectuals to write seriously about popular culture. The following essay, "The Gangster as Tragic Hero," is taken from his book *The Immediate Experience,* published posthumously in 1962. (Warshow died in 1955.) The essay, though brief, is considered by many to be a classic example of film criticism and cultural analysis. The references Warshow makes to films such as *A Tree Grows in Brooklyn* and the original *Scarface* with Edward G. Robinson may seem dated, but the gangster film seems alive and well in contemporary America. *The Godfather, Goodfellas, Prizzi's Honor,* and a remake and update of *Scarface,* starring Al Pacino this time, have all been popular films, both with moviegoers and critics. We present "The Gangster as Tragic Hero" as the final reading in this sequence because it is the gangster who brings the legendary figure of the outlaw-hero into the city and contemporary American life.

Suggestion for Reading

- As you read, keep the title of the essay, "The Gangster as Tragic Hero," in mind. Underline and annotate passages in the essay where Warshow explains what makes gangsters tragic figures.

---◆---

A merica, as a social and political organization, is committed to a cheerful view of life. It could not be otherwise. The sense of tragedy is a luxury of aristocratic societies, where the fate of the individual is not conceived of as having a direct and legitimate political importance, being determined by a fixed and supra-political—that is, non-controversial—moral order or fate. Modern equalitarian societies, however, whether democratic or authoritarian in their political forms, always base themselves on the claim that they are making life happier; the avowed function of the modern state, at least in its ultimate terms, is not only to regulate social relations, but also to determine the quality and the possibilities of human life in general. Happiness thus becomes the chief political issue—in a sense, the only political issue—and for that reason it can never be treated as an issue at all. If an American or a Russian is unhappy, it implies a certain reprobation of his society, and therefore, by a logic of which we can all recognize the necessity, it becomes an obligation of citizenship to be cheerful; if the authorities find it necessary, the citizen may even be compelled to make a public display of his cheerfulness on important occasions, just as he may be conscripted into the army in time of war.

Naturally, this civic responsibility rests most strongly upon the organs of mass culture. The individual citizen may still be permitted his private unhappiness so long as it does not take on political significance, the extent of this tolerance being determined by how large an area of private life the society can accommodate. But every production of mass culture is a public act and must conform with accepted notions of the public good. Nobody seriously questions the principle that it is the function of mass culture to maintain public morale, and certainly nobody in the mass audience objects to having his morale maintained.[1] At a time when the normal condition of the citizen is a state of anxiety, euphoria spreads over our culture like the broad smile of an idiot. In terms of attitudes towards life, there is very little difference between a "happy" movie like *Good News,* which ignores death and suffering, and a "sad" movie like *A Tree Grows in Brooklyn,* which uses death and suffering as incidents in the service of a higher optimism.

But, whatever its effectiveness as a source of consolation and a means of pressure for maintaining "positive" social attitudes, this optimism is fundamentally satisfying to no one, not even to those who would be most disoriented without its support. Even within the area of mass culture, there always exists a current of opposition, seeking to express by whatever means are available to it that sense of desperation and inevitable failure which optimism itself helps to create. Most often, this opposition is confined to rudimentary or semiliterate forms: in mob politics and journalism, for example, or in certain kinds of religious enthusiasm. When it does enter the field of art, it is likely to be disguised or attenuated: in an unspecific form of expression like jazz, in the basically harmless nihilism of the Marx Brothers, in the continually reasserted strain of hopelessness that often seems to be the real meaning of the soap opera. The gangster film is remarkable in that it fills the need for disguise (though not sufficiently to avoid arousing uneasiness) without requiring any serious distortion. From its beginnings, it has been a consistent and astonishingly complete presentation of the modern sense of tragedy.[2]

In its initial character, the gangster film is simply one example of the movies' constant tendency to create fixed dramatic patterns that can be repeated indefinitely with a reasonable expectation of profit. One gangster film follows another as one musical or one Western follows another. But this rigidity is not necessarily opposed to the requirements of art. There have been very successful types of art in the past which developed such specific and detailed conventions as almost to make individual examples of the type interchangeable. This is true, for example, of Elizabethan revenge tragedy and Restoration comedy.

For such a type to be successful means that its conventions have imposed themselves upon the general consciousness and become the accepted vehicles of a particular set of attitudes and a particular aesthetic effect. One goes to any individual example of the type

---

[1] In her testimony before the House Committee on Un-American Activities, Mrs. Leila Rogers said that the movie *None But the Lonely Heart* was un-American because it was gloomy. Like so much else that was said during the unhappy investigation of Hollywood, this statement was at once stupid and illuminating. One knew immediately what Mrs. Rogers was talking about; she had simply been insensitive enough to carry her philistinism to its conclusion.

[2] Efforts have been made from time to time to bring the gangster film into line with the prevailing optimism and social constructiveness of our culture; *Kiss of Death* is a recent example. These efforts are usually unsuccessful; the reasons for their lack of success are interesting in themselves, but I shall not be able to discuss them here.

with very definite expectations, and originality is to be welcomed only in the degree that it intensifies the expected experience without fundamentally altering it. Moreover, the relationship between the conventions which go to make up such a type and the real experience of its audience or the real facts of whatever situation it pretends to describe is of only secondary importance and does not determine its aesthetic force. It is only in an ultimate sense that the type appeals to its audience's experience of reality; much more immediately, it appeals to previous experience of the type itself: it creates its own field of reference.

Thus the importance of the gangster film, and the nature and intensity of its emotional and aesthetic impact, cannot be measured in terms of the place of the gangster himself or the importance of the problem of crime in American life. Those European movie-goers who think there is a gangster on every corner in New York are certainly deceived, but defenders of the "positive" side of American culture are equally deceived if they think it relevant to point out that most Americans have never seen a gangster. What matters is that the experience of the gangster *as an experience of art* is universal to Americans. There is almost nothing we understand better or react to more readily or with quicker intelligence. The Western film, though it seems never to diminish in popularity, is for most of us no more than the folklore of the past, familiar and understandable only because it has been repeated so often. The gangster film comes much closer. In ways that we do not easily or willingly define, the gangster speaks for us, expressing that part of the American psyche which rejects the qualities and the demands of modern life, which rejects "Americanism" itself.

The gangster is the man of the city, with the city's language and knowledge, with its queer and dishonest skills and its terrible daring, carrying his life in his hands like a placard, like a club. For everyone else, there is at least the theoretical possibility of another world—in that happier American culture which the gangster denies, the city does not really exist; it is only a more crowded and more brightly lit country—but for the gangster there is only the city; he must inhabit it in order to personify it: not the real city, but that dangerous and sad city of the imagination which is so much more important, which is the modern world. And the gangster—though there are real gangsters—is also, and primarily, a creature of the imagination. The real city, one might say, produces only criminals; the imaginary city produces the gangster: he is what we want to be and what we are afraid we may become.

Thrown into the crowd without background or advantages, with only those ambiguous skills which the rest of us—the real people of the real city—can only pretend to have, the gangster is required to make his way, to make his life and impose it on others. Usually, when we come upon him, he has already made his choice or the choice has already been made for him, it doesn't matter which: we are not permitted to ask whether at some point he could have chosen to be something else than what he is.

The gangster's activity is actually a form of rational enterprise, involving fairly definite goals and various techniques for achieving them. But this rationality is usually no more than a vague background; we know, perhaps, that the gangster sells liquor or that he operates a numbers racket; often we are not given even that much information. So his activity becomes a kind of pure criminality: he hurts people. Certainly our response to the gangster film is most consistently and most universally a response to sadism; we gain the double satisfaction of participating vicariously in the gangster's sadism and then seeing it turned against the gangster himself.

But on another level the quality of irrational brutality and the quality of rational enterprise become one. Since we do not see the rational and routine aspects of the gangster's behavior, the practice of brutality—the quality of unmixed criminality—becomes the totality of his career. At the same time, we are always conscious that the whole meaning of this career is a drive for success: the typical gangster film presents a steady upward progress followed by a very precipitate fall. Thus brutality itself becomes at once the means to success and the content of success—a success that is defined in its most general terms, not as accomplishment or specific gain, but simply as the unlimited possibility of aggression. (In the same way, film presentations of businessmen tend to make it appear that they achieve their success by talking on the telephone and holding conferences and that success *is* talking on the telephone and holding conferences.)

From this point of view, the initial contact between the film and its audience is an agreed conception of human life: that man is a being with the possibilities of success or failure. This principle, too, belongs to the city; one must emerge from the crowd or else one is nothing. On that basis the necessity of the action is established, and it progresses by inalterable paths to the point where the gangster lies dead and the principle has been modified: there is really only one possibility—failure. The final meaning of the city is anonymity and death.

In the opening scene of *Scarface,* we are shown a successful man; we know he is successful because he has just given a party of opulent proportions and because he is called Big Louie. Through some monstrous lack of caution, he permits himself to be alone for a few moments. We understand from this immediately that he is about to be killed. No convention of the gangster film is more strongly established than this: it is dangerous to be alone. And yet the very conditions of success make it impossible not to be alone, for success is always the establishment of an *individual* preeminence that must be imposed on others, in whom it automatically arouses hatred; the successful man is an outlaw. The gangster's whole life is an effort to assert himself as an individual, to draw himself out of the crowd, and he always dies *because* he is an individual; the final bullet thrusts him back, makes him, after all, a failure. "Mother of God," says the dying Little Caesar, "is this the end of Rico?"—speaking of himself thus in the third person because what has been brought low is not the undifferentiated *man,* but the individual with a name, the gangster, the success; even to himself he is a creature of the imagination. (T. S. Eliot has pointed out that a number of Shakespeare's tragic heroes have this trick of looking at themselves dramatically; their true identity, the thing that is destroyed when they die, is something outside themselves—not a man, but a style of life, a kind of meaning.)

At bottom, the gangster is doomed because he is under the obligation to succeed, not because the means he employs are unlawful. In the deeper layers of the modern consciousness, *all* means are unlawful, every attempt to succeed is an act of aggression, leaving one alone and guilty and defenseless among enemies: one is *punished* for success. This is our intolerable dilemma: that failure is a kind of death and success is evil and dangerous, is—ultimately—impossible. The effect of the gangster film is to embody this dilemma in the person of the gangster and resolve it by his death. The dilemma is resolved because it is *his* death, not ours. We are safe; for the moment, we can acquiesce in our failure, we can choose to fail.

SUGGESTIONS FOR DISCUSSION

1. Warshow begins his essay by saying that "it is the function of mass culture to maintain public morale" and "to conform with accepted notions of the public good." Think about some of the movies you have seen recently. To what extent does Warshow's statement seem valid? What, in your view, are the benefits and limits of America's commitment "to a cheerful view of life"?
2. Warshow says that the gangster is "a consistent and astonishingly complete presentation of the modern sense of tragedy." What does Warshow mean by tragedy here? In what sense are gangster films tragic?
3. Warshow says that for the gangster "the whole meaning of his career is a drive for success." What does he mean by this statement? What do gangster films have to tell us about the American dream of success?

SUGGESTIONS FOR WRITING

1. According to Warshow, gangsters are more attractive figures than the "good" characters. Why is this so? Write an essay that explains why gangsters—or outlaw-heroes in general—have become such popular figures in song, television, and movies. Why would such figures become so popular in a society that is ostensibly devoted to law and order? Draw on points made by Warshow, Lomax, and Hoban, if they seem pertinent.
2. Use Warshow's treatment of the gangster as a tragic hero to analyze a movie, television show, or song you are familiar with. Write an essay that applies Warshow's view of the gangster as a tragic hero to a more recent character in popular culture. You might pick *Bonnie and Clyde*, *The Godfather*, or *Scarface*, but don't forget other recent gangsters in films such as *Colors*, *Boyz N the Hood*, and *New Jack City* or in rap songs by Ice-T and NWA.
3. Interview a number of people—friends, acquaintances, or relatives—who are a generation older than you. Ask them who their heroes were when they were growing up and why these figures held such an appeal for them. Write an essay that compares the heroes of an earlier generation with figures you believe to be heroes to your generation. Use the essay as an occasion to think about what changes and continuities are revealed by people's choices of heroes.

FOR FURTHER EXPLORATION

Much has been written about popular fiction—whether science fiction, "hard-boiled detective" novels, action-adventure, Westerns, romances, and thrillers. For example, Janice Radway's *Reading the Romance* is an illuminating study of why female readers read romances and what cultural purposes their reading serves. From a different perspective, John Cawelti's *Adventure, Mystery, and Romance* and *The Six-Gun Mystique* attempt to identify the formulas that characterize various types of popular fiction. To explore storytelling further, you might pick a genre of popular fiction that particularly appeals to you and research what writers have said about it. Or you might pick an archetypal figure, such as the trickster and "bad man" in African American oral and literary tradition, and read more about this folk hero in works such as John W. Roberts's *From Trickster to Badman: The Black Folk Hero in Slavery and Freedom* and Lawrence Levine's *Black Culture and Black Consciousness*.

CHAPTER 9

WORK

Never leave that to tomorrow, which you can do today.

> – Benjamin Franklin,
> *Poor Richard's Almanac*

McJob: A low-pay, low-prestige, low-benefit, no-future job in the service sector. Frequently considered a satisfying career choice by people who have never held one.

> – Douglas Coupland,
> *Generation X*

A mericans have historically had a love/hate relationship with their jobs. That may be due partially to the Protestant work ethic, a philosophy of living that has formed a part of the character of this nation from its beginnings. According to this ethic, "Idle hands are the devil's workshop." The contrast between fruitful labor and wasteful leisure is one that the Puritans brought with them as they traveled to the New World to explore and settle in this country. Its message is a simple one: Success is the reward for diligence. Failure is the consequence of idleness.

That this work ethic continues to fuel popular ideals is apparent in a recent phone company commercial that featured a worker telling viewers that she takes her job home, dreams about her work, and even gets up in the middle of the night to write notes to herself about the next day's tasks. For the phone company, this obsession with the job may seem like a good quality in a worker, but for the worker it can be a nightmare. In fact, that contrast between what we do for our jobs and what we do for ourselves is most often what is at issue when we talk about work.

Perhaps because many Americans suffer from stress-related illnesses and complain of having little time outside their jobs, the work ethic is now more frequently being called into question. Even with all our modern conveniences, many people have only energy enough when they get home from work to pop a frozen dinner into the microwave and sit down for an evening of television. Critics of this high-speed life-style point out that Americans need real leisure time, time to do those things that make a household run or time to pursue individual interests. Philosopher Bertrand Russell, for example, once argued that "there is far too much work done in the world, that immense harm is caused by the belief that work is virtuous, and that what needs to be preached in modern industrial countries is quite different from what always has been preached." For Russell, what needs to be preached is the necessity for time in which people do their own work, work that does not earn a wage but that makes for richer lives. According to Russell's philosophy, modern men and women ought to be able to work no more than four hours a day in order to earn enough for the basic necessities. The rest of the time should be free, with no one telling us that we are not career-minded and no one telling us what needs to be done next.

For others, the conflict is not between labor and leisure but instead between meaningless and meaningful work. Writer Tom Bender argues that work is a part of being human. It isn't work that is the problem, he says, it is the work that people do:

> Properly appreciated, work stands in the same relation to the higher faculties as food to the physical body. It nourishes and enlivens us and urges us to produce the best of which we are capable. To strive for leisure rather than work denies that work and leisure are complementary parts of the same living process and cannot be separated without destroying the joy of work and the bliss of leisure.

What, however, is meaningful work? That is one of the issues that the writers in this chapter will address, but you very likely already have some notions of what kind of work is meaningful to you.

From the time children start school, parents and teachers begin to ask them what they want to be when they grow up. And, though adults may smile when the small child says, "I want to drive a garbage truck," most aren't likely to be laughing when a

20-year-old says the same. In this culture, a 20-year-old is expected to be looking for a "career," a job that will support a family, provide opportunities for professional advancement, buy leisure time, perhaps contribute to community well-being, and be personally fulfilling all at once. Career-oriented people often don't consider jobs like trash collecting as meeting those demands, and yet trash collecting must be done, or our cities and towns will fall prey to disease, vermin, filth, and clutter. In other words, the social discrepancy between jobs that need to be done and jobs that are privileged as careers is a strong one in this culture.

In all cultures some jobs are privileged over others. America is no exception, perhaps because our life-style is such that most people have become farther and farther removed from the production of the things they consume. For example, migrant workers still pick the produce we eat, but most Americans know little about migrant labor. Office workers aren't subject to the whims of the weather, so their labor is often favored over the labor of workers in the field. In highly industrialized societies like our own, head work often seems to take precedence over hand work, and professions take precedence over clerical work. Certain kinds of work demand high levels of education, and every job seems to have its hierarchy of bosses, workers, and gofers.

READING THE CULTURE OF WORK

As you read, talk, and write about work, you will be asked to think about those jobs that must be done, who does those jobs, and what we mean when we talk about "meaningful" work. The selections in this chapter represent the experience of looking for work, working, and losing work. These writers help us explore our expectations and understand our disappointments in the work we do and with the situations we often find ourselves in because of age, sex, inexperience, class, race, or need.

We open with Philip Levine's "What Work Is," a poetic expression of how many of us feel about work, how it affects our lives and our ways of understanding each other. In the selection that follows, Sandra Cisneros writes of her first job, one she thought would be an easy summer wage. That job, though simple enough, carried with it an abrupt encounter between an inexperienced young girl and the adult world.

First jobs, however, are rarely the jobs we expect to keep, and yet many workers do find themselves working their entire lives in one place or doing one kind of job that never promises much beyond long hours and hard work. During the thirties, writer Betty Burke interviewed women who worked in meat packing plants, places that have had long histories of labor strife. Her interview with Estelle Zabritz, "I'll Tell You How I Got to Working in the Yards," might suggest to you how circumstance and economic situation can combine to hold any worker in a job that person might not choose in better times or under different conditions. The next selection, Alfred Benke's 1942 letter urging his son to find work, provides one example of how a work ethic can be expressed in real-life situations. The letter, as well, might suggest to you the ways history, age, and experience influence our attitudes about finding and holding a job.

Because ours is a wage labor culture (most people depend on earning some sort of wage to enable them to provide food, shelter, and clothing), it can be quite serious when a man or woman suddenly is without a job. Even if that job is as mind-numbing as the rivet-line job Ben Hamper describes in "I, Rivethead," the thought of being entirely without work is a frightening one. Being without work means standing in unemployment lines, moving away from home and family to where there might be work, and worrying over the possibility of not being able to bring home a living wage. Of course, our cultural heritage, drawing on that old Protestant work ethic, often characterizes the unemployed worker as lazy or incompetent. Hamper's article raises a more important issue than competence or incompetence, however. He asks us to think about what it might mean when the worker is capable and willing but the industry pulls out. What happens when the industrial marketplace makes it more profitable to leave a community in order to make more money? What happens to the worker whose job is gone?

As you read these selections, think about the reasons you have worked and the choices you, your friends, and your family have made as well as the options that seem closed. Think about the conditions that make for choices for all people, for though it is true that most people would like to choose their own work, it is also true that many women and men are severely limited in those choices. Choice, then, is a key component for many people when they talk about their work. Do they actually *choose* this work, or have they been forced by circumstance to take whatever they can get? In this culture, we have traditionally measured our freedom by how much choice we actually have to determine how we live. You will be asked to write about the ways you, your friends, and your family talk about work. How do those different people in your life make distinctions among work that must be done, work that could be done, and work that somehow enriches their lives? Do they even think of work as enriching, or is it simply the way we make our wage or the time we spend keeping our living spaces clean and in repair?

The next selections in this chapter ask you to reconsider what work means in a high-technology, work-oriented culture. Barbara Ehrenreich's "Good-bye to the Work Ethic" suggests that we throw our work obsessions out the window and start living a better life. She asks us to replace the slogan "Go for it!" with the much more heart-felt "Gimme a break!" Juliet B. Schor's introduction to her book-length study, *The Overworked American: The Unexpected Decline of Leisure,* raises questions about what the new efficiency actually accomplishes if it does not provide Americans with more but rather less leisure time—less time when the work we do is for us and more time when that work is for a corporation. Your own writing and thinking, as you read these selections, might lead you to consider what leisure time means to you, how you notice others using their leisure time, or how the technologized workplace changes the way Americans have traditionally described work.

A work-oriented culture can be hard on the worker who is suddenly retired after giving an entire life to the job. In his song "All Used Up," folksinger and activist Utah Phillips speaks of the man left to himself after he has given his whole life to work. Such a man or woman can feel empty, useless—all used up. Like Hamper and Zabritz, Phillips raises the issue of what our jobs mean to us when they are all we have.

We complete this chapter with a selection that questions entirely the role work plays in our personal lives and in our community as a whole. Wilfred Pelletier, an Odawan elder, writes of the role work plays in tribal or communal cultures as opposed to the role we have become familiar with in an industrial culture emerging from a Western European tradition. This selection from Pelletier's biography makes vivid the choices that many traditional American Indians, at least, must make when they decide to leave the reservation for work. These choices are not simply about succeeding or getting good jobs but about deciding on an entirely different tradition, a tradition in which work is not the work of the tribe or community but the work of the individual, work that provides a wage rather than a way of life.

Throughout this chapter, you will be asked to think and write not simply about jobs but about the role work plays in this culture. Think about how sex, class, race, age, and ethnic origin all come to mean something in the way we think of work and its place in our lives. Take time to talk to the people who work around you. Think and write about the work you have done in your life. Consider what it might mean to live in a culture in which wage labor is not the most valued labor but the least valued.

Philip Levine

WHAT WORK IS

Philip Levine was born in Detroit right before the Great Depression. The *Dictionary of Literary Biography* says of him, "Like other city children who came to individual consciousness before World War II, Levine met his enemies in the gray arenas of industrialism, where the grownups worked obsessively because *their* enemy was the Depression's spectre of idle poverty." In the poem reprinted below, from his 1992 collection *What Work Is*, Levine writes of waiting for work, standing in line and waiting with a crowd of others looking for work, any work, no matter how tedious or trivial.

Suggestion for Reading

• This poem might be said to have two parts. In the first, the speaker talks of standing in line waiting for work. In the second, he describes a worker's relationship with his brother. Underline the place in the poem in which Levine shifts from describing the waiting line to what seems to be the second topic. In an effort to identify what Levine is saying in those passages that describe the relationship with the brother, annotate that section of the poem.

We stand in the rain in a long line
waiting at Ford Highland Park. For work.
You know what work is—if you're
old enough to read this you know what
work is, although you may not do it.
Forget you. This is about waiting,
shifting from one foot to another.

Feeling the light rain falling like mist
into your hair, blurring your vision
until you think you see your own brother
ahead of you, maybe ten places.
You rub your glasses with your fingers,
and of course it's someone else's brother,
narrower across the shoulders than
yours but with the same sad slouch, the grin
that does not hide the stubbornness,
the sad refusal to give in to
rain, to the hours wasted waiting,
to the knowledge that somewhere ahead
a man is waiting who will say, "No,
we're not hiring today," for any
reason he wants. You love your brother,
now suddenly you can hardly stand
the love flooding you for your brother,
who's not beside you or behind or
ahead because he's home trying to
sleep off a miserable night shift
at Cadillac so he can get up
before noon to study his German.
Works eight hours a night so he can sing
Wagner, the opera you hate most,
the worst music ever invented.
How long has it been since you told him
you loved him, held his wide shoulders,
opened your eyes wide and said those words,
and maybe kissed his cheek? You've never
done something so simple, so obvious,
not because you're too young or too dumb,
not because you're jealous or even mean
or incapable of crying in
the presence of another man, no,
just because you don't know what work is.

SUGGESTIONS FOR DISCUSSION

1. Compare your annotations with annotations others in the class have written. Discuss what others noticed or wrote about that you did not.
2. What is the speaker trying to say by ending with the comment, "just because you don't know what work is"?
3. How would you compare Levine's attitude toward work, as it is revealed in this poem, to your own feeling about work or to the attitudes of your friends and classmates?

SUGGESTIONS FOR WRITING

1. Write a summary statement in which you paraphrase Levine's poem.
2. Write your own description of "what work is." You can make it in the form of a poem if you like, but that is not necessary. Be sure to use your own experience with work, and draw on the physical details of the work experience.

3. In "What Work Is," Levine writes that this poem isn't about "you"; it is about wait-ing. The narrator is waiting in line, watching people, watching "you," thinking about whether or not there will be work at the head of the line, thinking of you and your brother. The narrator ends the poem by reminding the waiting person of how much he loves his brother and how incapable he has been of expressing that love, "just because you don't know what work is." Write a response to Levine's poem in which you explore the connection he has made between being able to express emotion and knowing what work is. If you have experienced something that ex-plains that connection, you may wish to include that experience in your response. Your aim in this response is to work toward an understanding of the connections this poem makes among work, human relationships, and feeling. Your response may be in the form of a journal writing, an analysis of the poem, or a story you tell about yourself or about people you know.

Sandra Cisneros

THE FIRST JOB

Sanda Cisneros was born in Chicago, the daughter of a Mexican father and a Mexican-American mother. She has been a poet in the schools, a teacher for high school dropouts, and an arts administrator. Cisneros is the author of *My Wicked Ways* (1987), a volume of poetry, *The House on Mango Street* (1985), a collection of stories from which the following selection has been ex-cerpted, and *Woman Hollering Creek* (1991), her most recent collection of short stories.

Suggestion for Reading

• Write a brief description of a time you found yourself in a situation that was uncomfortable—something you did not expect. After you have read Cisneros's story, use your own memory piece to help you focus on what the event she writes of means to you.

♦

I t wasn't as if I didn't want to work. I did. I had even gone to the social security office the month before to get my social security number. I needed money. The Catholic high school cost a lot, and Papa said nobody went to public school unless you wanted to turn out bad. I thought I'd find an easy job, the kind other kids had, working in the dime store or maybe a hotdog stand. And though I hadn't started looking yet, I thought I might the week after next. But when I came home that afternoon, all wet because Tito had pushed me into the open water hydrant—only I had sort of let him—Mama called me in the kitchen before I could even go and change, and Aunt Lala was sitting there drinking her coffee with a spoon. Aunt Lala said she had found a job for me at the Peter Pan Photo Finishers on North Broadway where she worked and how old was I and to show up tomorrow saying I was one year older and that was that.

So the next morning I put on the navy blue dress that made me look older and borrowed money for lunch and bus fare because Aunt Lala said I wouldn't get paid 'til the next Friday and I went in and saw the boss of the Peter Pan Photo Finishers on North Broadway where Aunt Lala worked and lied about my age like she told me to and sure enough I started that same day.

In my job I had to wear white gloves. I was supposed to match negatives with their prints, just look at the picture and look for the same one on the negative strip, put it in the envelope, and do the next one. That's all. I didn't know where these envelopes were coming from or where they were going. I just did what I was told.

It was real easy and I guess I wouldn't have minded it except that you got tired after a while and I didn't know if I could sit down or not, and then I started sitting down only when the two ladies next to me did. After a while they started to laugh and came up to me and said I could sit when I wanted to and I said I knew.

When lunch time came I was scared to eat alone in the company lunchroom with all those men and ladies looking, so I ate real fast standing in one of the washroom stalls and had lots of time left over so I went back to work early. But then break time came and not knowing where else to go I went into the coatroom because there was a bench there.

I guess it was time for the night shift or middle shift to arrive because a few people came in and punched the time clock and an older Oriental man said hello and we talked for a while about my just starting and he said we could be friends and next time to go in the lunchroom and sit with him and I felt better. He had nice eyes and I didn't feel so nervous anymore. Then he asked if I knew what day it was and when I said I didn't he said it was his birthday and would I please give him a birthday kiss. I thought I would because he was so old and just as I was about to put my lips on his cheek, he grabs my face with both hands and kisses me hard on the mouth and doesn't let go.

SUGGESTIONS FOR DISCUSSION

1. Why does the narrator tell us "It wasn't as if I didn't want to work"? How would you describe her motivations for getting a job, and how would you explain the situation she finds herself in?
2. Compare the event you wrote about before you read this story with the events your classmates wrote about. Do any of them have anything in common with what Cisneros's narrator experienced? How common do you think an experience like hers is?
3. Why do you think the older man thought he could get away with his actions? Would anything comparable to this have happened to her had she been a young man?

SUGGESTIONS FOR WRITING

1. Reread Philip Levine's poem and Sandra Cisneros's story. Each one has a narrator who talks about what work means. Write a brief comparison of the narrator of each piece in which you explore the two characters for maturity, experience, and expectations. Would the young girl in "The First Job," for example, have expected

work to have anything at all to do with human relationships? Would the narrator in Levine's poem say that the young girl knows yet "what work is"?

2. Cisneros has written a story of a young girl's first day on a new job. Write a response to this story in which you explore the many topics this short piece of writing uncovers. These may include new responsibilities, parental pressure, the tedious and low-paying jobs many teenagers find themselves in, or even sexual harassment in the workplace.

3. Write a description of one of the first jobs you ever held (whether it was a paying job or just some new responsibility you were asked to take on in the family, in the community, in your peer group, or for church or school). In your description, try to recall those moments when you felt comfortable about the job and those moments when you were unsure of yourself. What did the job mean to you?

Estelle Zabritz

I'LL TELL YOU HOW I GOT TO WORKING IN THE YARDS

Between 1938 and 1942, as a part of the Federal Writers' Project, Betty Burke recorded the oral histories of women workers in the meat-packing industry, at a time when the Congress of Industrial Organizations (CIO) was attempting to organize the stockyards. The selection reprinted here is from one of those workers. Estelle Zabritz worked in meat packing from the time she was a teenager until she quit to stay home and raise her children in her early twenties.

Suggestion for Reading

• Unlike essays, short stories, and poems, oral histories may seem rambling and disconnected. As you read, remember the nature of the oral history and try to read almost as if you were listening to Estelle Zabritz tell a stranger a story of her life. Make notes or underlinings of places that are meaningful to you.

————————◆————————

I 'll tell you how I got to working in the yards. I wanted to finish high school but we had a lot of sickness and trouble in my family just then; my father got t.b. and they couldn't afford to send me anymore. Oh, I guess if I had begged and coaxed for money to go they would have managed, but I was too proud to do that. I thought I'd get a job downtown in an office or department store and then maybe make enough to go to school. Me and my girl friend used to look for work downtown every day. We lived right near the yards, but we wouldn't think of working in that smelly place for anything.

But we never got anything in office work and a year went by that way, so one time we took a walk and just for fun we walked into Armour's where they hire the girls. We were laughing and hoping they wouldn't give us applications—lots of times they send new girls away because there's so many laid-off girls waiting to get back, and we really thought working in the yards was awful. Lots of girls do even now, and some of them even have the nerve to tell people they don't work in the yards. They'll meet other girls who work there, at a dance or some wedding, and they'll say *they* don't. But you always know they're lying, because their fingernails are cracked and broken from always being in that pickle water; it has some kind of acid in it and it eats away the nails.

Well, in walks Miss McCann and she looks over everybody and what did she do but point at me and call me over to her desk. I guess she just liked my looks or something. She put me to work in Dry Casings. You might think it's dry there, but it isn't; they just call it that to distinguish it from Wet Casings, which is where they do the first cleaning out of pig guts. The workers call it the Gut Shanty and the smell of that place could knock you off your feet. Dry Casings isn't that bad, but they don't take visitors through unless it's some real important person who makes a point of it and wants to see. Lots of those ritzy ladies can't take it. They tighten up their faces at the entrance and think they're ready for anything, but before they're halfway through the place they're green as grass. The pickle water on the floors gets them all slopped up, just ruins their shoes and silk hose. And are they glad to get out! They bump into each other and fall all over themselves, just like cockroaches, they're so anxious to get away and get cleaned up. We feel sorry for them, they look so uncomfortable.

I operate a power machine in Dry Casings. It's better where I am because the casings are clean and almost dry by the time they come to the machine and I sew them at one end. Mine is a semi-skilled job and I get good pay, piecework, of course. On an average of from twenty-three to twenty-seven dollars a week. In my department there aren't so many layoffs like in the other places. I was lucky: I only got it three times in the five years I was there. I think they sort of like me, Miss McCann and some of them.

But the first week I was there, you should have seen my hands, all puffed and swollen. I wasn't on sewing then; I was on a stretching machine. That's to see the casing isn't damaged after the cleaning process it goes through. That pickle water causes salt ulcers and they're very hard to cure, nearly impossible if you have to keep working in the wet. The acids and salt just rot away a person's skin and bone if he gets the smallest scratch or cut at work. Most of the girls in Casings have to wear wooden shoes and rubber aprons. The company doesn't furnish them. They pay three dollars for the shoes and about a dollar and a half for the aprons.

My husband got the hog's itch from working there. He can't go near the yards now but what he gets it back again. He used to have his hands and arms wrapped up in bandages clear up to his elbows, it was so bad. The company paid his doctor bills for a while till it got a little better, but they broke up his seniority. They transferred him to another department after he had worked three and a half years in one place, and then after a couple of months they laid him off because they said he was new in that department. They just wanted to get rid of him now that he was sick and they had to keep paying doctors to cure him. Finally he got a job outside the yards so he said to hell with them.

SUGGESTIONS FOR DISCUSSION

1. How does the fact that this oral history was taken in 1939 affect the way you read it? Do you assume meat packing has changed significantly since then? What do you or your classmates know about the current state of the industry?
2. Estelle Zabritz describes herself as someone who could not stay in high school because finances were too tight and who wanted to work anywhere but where she ended up working. How common is that kind of situation today? Are jobs plentiful and well-paying enough that most people can choose when and where to work? Who would you say is in the best position to choose the kind of work they do? Who is in the worst?
3. As a class, make a list of jobs you would not want to do. Discuss why those jobs seem unappealing and how they rank in this culture. Who does those jobs?

SUGGESTIONS FOR WRITING

1. Reread Estelle Zabritz's story and write a brief description of her attitude toward the jobs she and her friends and family held in the meat-packing plant.
2. If someone were to interview you about a job you have held, what would you say? Write a notebook entry or brief diarylike piece in which you "talk" about work you have done. You may wish to reread Zabritz and Cisneros before you begin your writing.
3. In a written response to this oral history, write about how Zabritz's story makes you feel about her life, your own work experience, the work you have seen done by others, or the work you know you never want to have to do.

Alfred Benke

LETTER TO HIS SON

Alfred Benke worked as a machinist for the Tamarack Mining Company in the first part of this century. His home town of Laurium had, with much of Michigan's Upper Peninsula, gone through a copper mining boom and bust by the time this letter was written. World War II, as Alfred's letter suggests, did create a second boom, but that prosperity ended with the end of the war. A recommendation letter from his employer in 1907 describes Alfred as "a sober, industrious and faithful worker [who] has filled his position to my entire satisfaction." His son Fred was his only child, raised with the help of aunts after Alfred's wife Anna died in 1914 when Fred was approximately five years old. In the letter that follows, held in a private collection, Alfred tells his son why it is important to get work immediately. The letter is a vivid statement about work and responsibility in post-Depression America.

Suggestion for Reading

• You will notice that this letter is written in nonstandard English with many omissions and some strange syntax. (We have standardized the spelling so that the letter is more easily read by a broad audience.) The letter was also a difficult one for Alfred to write. In it he expresses his concern that Fred not get mad, and he asks Fred not to leave the letter lying around for others to read. Take your time as you read, and read for what the writer seems to be saying, remembering that much of what is written has both an emotional overtone and an argument for finding steady work.

◆

Laurium Mich 8. 20. 42
Saturday
11 .am

Son Fred

Your letter was received glad to hear from you. Sorry to hear you are not working. Well don't get mad when you read this letter.

We sure are dissapointed about you. I am any way. You spoiled my trip for this summer . . . and poor B. was crying last week about you because you are not working. And you know she don't work for 4 month. She has no income. She thought she would get a dollar now and then from you, for the summer.

Any way it's a shame. All last summer you were down there and didn't work. And this summer you are doing the same and when there [is] all kinds of work there. But, no, you would rather poke around. A lot of young kids go down from here and they rake in good money. Like that job you had at Packard. You could put away 2.00 dollars a month and would have 1.20 or 1.15 for spending money for a month. And in a year you would have saved a nice little bunch. But the old saying is can't stand prosperity.

You know if you wanted a dollar, B. would give it to you. And you know the girls are praying for you day and night. . . . And now you are going to school again. The same old story. You know son you had the best chance in the world. I told you time and again. When you went to M.C.M.[1] you would be through when you would be 21 or 22. No you could not see it. . . . And now its school school and get no where.

You must remember these times are not going to last. When the war is over there will be 10000s out of work and you will be one of them too. That's why you should make hay now so you would have something to show. Cause these times you [won't] see again for a long time.[2] And this jumping from one place to another is no go either. You never get any work.

The best thing to do is go back to your old job again. You are saying about good times, not having [any]. Well if you were working you could have good times too, but if

---

[1]Michigan Mining School, established in 1885, became Michigan College of Mines in 1897, Michigan College of Mining and Technology in 1927, and Michigan Technological University in 1964. Here, MCM clearly refers to the 1897 name.

[2]During the war years, the Keweenaw Peninsula in Upper Michigan experienced a temporary economic boom from the reopening of many of the previously closed copper mines.

you don't work you can't have them. Like the other boys. They work all year and then take 2 weeks off and have time. But this saying [you] can't have a good time. Well that's your hard luck. Just because some other boy gets 5 or 10 cents an hour more than you. Well maybe so. But you know he worked there longer. Now you tie yourself up with school again, and you don't get any where with it.

The same as last year. The summer will be over and the snow will be coming and you didn't make a dollar and the war will be over and you won't have nothing to show for. I was talking to one of Copper Range R.R. men Friday at Houghton. B. and I was down there to the store. There's where I saw him. He got back from Detroit last week. He said there is all kinds of work down [there] if a person wants to work. . . .

So Boy you want to make the money while you got a chance to make it. The rest make it, and no alibis eather. I told you last spring, think it over before you make a move. I told you when you were home here. I thought you made a mistake by leaving packard. Look [at] the nice little bunch of money you would have now and have a good time too. The little money you saved will be all gone and you have nothings. So the best is get a job and get to work. . . .

I thought I may not be down. If I did go and you not working, they would ask me about you if [you were] working. I would always to have alibis;. . . Well I guess I told you enough for today. So good bye son and good luck and good wishes and I hope you are working when we get the next letter.

As ever
Daddy xxx

PS When you read this tear it up after. not have lay around.

P.S. Geo. Gibb is Harry Gibb's father. Harry Gibb when to Detroit first of [the] month started work right away for G.M.

Cool today wind blowing

SUGGESTIONS FOR DISCUSSION

1. What would you say are Alfred Benke's underlying assumptions about work and his son's responsibility as an adult?
2. What importance does war time economy play in Alfred's plea to his son to get work now?
3. How does Alfred Benke's attitude toward school differ from or resemble the attitudes of your parents or guardians?

SUGGESTIONS FOR WRITING

1. Write a summary of Alfred Benke's letter in which you set forth his primary arguments to his son.
2. In an exploratory writing, respond to Alfred Benke's letter, his arguments on work and the economy, and his ways of pressing Fred to get work. You might want to include your own feelings about finding work and being a responsible worker.
3. Write a letter to your parents or family in which you explain the choices you are making in your work or your schooling.

Ben Hamper

I, Rivethead

Ben Hamper had worked at General Motors for six years when he wrote this column in 1986 for *Mother Jones*, now part of a recently published book with the same title. By the time he left his position on Rivet Line #1, Hamper had been laid off five times in five years as a part of the many GM shutdowns that hit Flint, Michigan, before the company left its birthplace entirely. His story is told in the movie *Roger and Me*, journalist Michael Moore's satiric film account of the GM pull-out in Flint, Michigan. At the time he wrote this essay, Ben Hamper did not know that the plant in which he was working, as well as many other plants in Flint, would eventually shut down and his job would leave with them. Hamper's essay tells of living in a factory town and trying to avoid the inevitable pull of the factory. It is also a story about what it means to spend an entire lifetime on the line.

Suggestion for Reading

- At points in his article, Hamper is angry, even sarcastic, about his job, the people he works with, and the company he works for. Underline those passages in which that anger and sarcasm seem strongest.

I knew in the tenth grade that I would become a shoprat. It was more an understanding of certain truisms found in my hometown than any form of game plan I might have been hatching. In Flint, Michigan, you either balled up your fists and got career motivated the moment the piano quit banging the commencement theme or, more likely, you'd still be left leanin' when the ancestors arrived to pass along your birthright. Here, kid, fetch.

At least up until recently, that's the way it worked. All roads led to General Motors in Flint. Father and son, sister and brother, each of 'em swingin' through the gates to play follow-the-earner.

The pattern began to dissolve with the cutbacks and technological gains of the early '80s. All of a sudden, trying to find an application for work at General Motors was like searching out buried treasure. It's now to a point where Flint youths can no longer entertain "shoprat" as a career option. The evolution of the critter appears at end, and unless I somehow manage to knock up a GMF spot-welding robot, I rather doubt I'll ever see any of my offspring inside the factory.

I almost didn't make it in myself. After high school, I wasted four prime earning years running around with my tongue stuck out at the smokestacks. I painted apartments. I swept floors. I got married and divorced. As long as I had my birthright stowed in my back pocket, I felt relatively safe in delaying destiny.

During this period, I would often-times get drunk and park by one of the factories just to watch the fools pile out at quit time. I hated the looks on their faces. I would sit there with a can of beer in my lap and try to focus in on one alternative career goal. There weren't any. All I ever came back to was the inevitable self-admission that I didn't want to do *anything*. And around these parts, that's just chicken-shit slang for "What time does the line start up on Monday?"

To be accurate, I hired in on a weekend. General Motors was in the midst of one of its boom-boom quota years, so reinforcements were being called in on Saturdays, Sundays, Salad Days—anytime was the right time. It was also the first time I could ever remember being asked out on a Saturday night by a Corporation.

Before we were to begin working, the group I was hiring in with was instructed to meet for physical examination in the plant hospital. We were a sluggish-looking crew. There were about 20 of us all together—each person chain-smoking and staring at the floor, waiting in silence to be pronounced fit for active drudgery. I had a hunch that there wasn't a marketable skill amongst us.

The urine test was up first. We were each handed a small vial and told to line up for the restroom. The guy in front of me kept looking over his shoulder at me. When it was his turn, he spun around and asked if it would be all right if I donated a little of my urine for his vial. He seemed to be undergoing a mild panic attack. Apparently, the fear was that the Company might look down upon any prospective serf who was incapable of bringing forth the pee when it mattered most. No piss, no job, ingrate!

"I just can't go right now," the guy moaned.

I didn't care much for the idea of passing my piss around with a total stranger. It didn't seem like a solid career move. Besides, for all either of us knew, I might be holding on to a bad batch. I had a background of hepatitis. My formative years were spent wolfing down a wide variety of menacing chemicals. I drank like a sieve. Heck, I never even wiped off the seat in public bathrooms. Who'd wanna take a crapshoot on the chance that any of that might come floating to the surface of their corporate dossier?

Evidently, this guy. He returned from the john and, true to his word, the vial he held before me was completely empty. "C'mon," he said, "just a squirt. I'll pay you for it."

Christ, that did it. "Gimme the thing," I groaned. It probably wasn't the most noble act of giving one had ever made in behalf of a needy Union brother, but somehow it sure seemed like it at the time.

We were almost through with our urine samples when a member of our group, a late arrival, walked in to the hospital and began to speak with our overseer. I could sense the guy was in deep trouble. He kept apologizing over and over—something to do with getting messed up in traffic and being detained. Judging by his performance, I doubted that he was lying.

It didn't matter. The man with the clipboard wasn't buying a single word. He stood there shaking his head from one side to the other—just another maggot in a short-sleeve shirt, deputized to protect the status quo. He did his job well.

"You were told to be prompt," he spouted. "There can be *no exceptions*."

The realization that he'd blown his big audition seemed to overwhelm the late guy. He looked down at the floor, his voice started breaking, and, right there in front of everyone, he began to cry. It all came spillin' out—what was he gonna tell his family and who would understand? For the sons and daughters of the assembly line, 1977 wasn't the best of years to go fumblin' the family baton.

We stood there clutching our little vials of piss as they escorted him out. We had been on time. We were going to build trucks for Chevrolet. The man with the bow tie and clipboard had written down all of our names. Our friend had been ten minutes late. He had proven himself undeserving of a hitch on the screw train. There could be no exceptions.

Now and again, I'll find myself still thinking about the late guy. It'll be one of those terribly humid shifts when the parts just aren't going together right and the clock begins to take two steps back for every step forward. Exhausted and desperate, I'll begin to see him over by the pool table in the tavern across the street. He'll have a cold beer in his hand and a grin a mile wide. I imagine myself walking up to him with my safety glasses, my locker key, and my plastic identification badge held out in my hand. "Here, it's all yours, buddy."

Immediately, the jukebox will stop playing. Everyone in the bar turns toward me and begins to laugh. The late guy slips his arm around the waitress and they both start shaking their heads. "We already started," he'll say. "There can be no exceptions."

I was assigned to the cab shop, an area more commonly known to its inhabitants as "the Jungle." Lifers will tell you that on a scale from one to ten—with one representing midtown Pompeii and ten being GM Chairman Roger Smith's summer digs—the Jungle rates about a minus-six.

It wasn't difficult to see how they had come up with the name for the place. Ropes, wires, and assorted black rubber cables drooped down and entangled everything. Sparks shot out in all directions—bouncing in the aisles, flying into the rafters and even ricocheting off the natives' heads. The noise level was deafening. It was like some hideous unrelenting tape-loop of trains having sex. I realized instantly that, as far as new homes go, the Jungle left a lot to be desired. Me Tarzan, you fucked.

I had been forewarned. As our group was being dispatched at various drop points throughout the factory, the guy walking beside me kept mumbling about our likely destination. "Cab Shop," the prophet would say. "We're headed for Cab Shop." I somehow wondered if this meant we would be building taxis.

The group would trudge on, leaving a few workers in each new area. We stopped by the Trim Line. The Axle Line. The Frame Line. The Fender Line. The Receding Hairline. When we arrived at the Motor Line, my friend with the bashful bladder hopped off. "Thanks," he said. It was kinda strange. All we had in common was a small, worthless vial of urine. "Have a nice career," I offered.

Soon, all but two rookies had been planted—the prophet and me. We took a freight elevator upstairs, and when the gate opened, my companion moaned loudly: "Goddamn, I knew it. The bastard's lettin' us off in Cab Shop." By this point, I couldn't have agreed with the guy more. Our overseer was the epitome of bastard. On top of that, he made for one lousy Johnny Appleseed. There could be no exceptions.

"Here you are, boys—the Cab Department. In this area you are advised to wear clothing made from a nonflammable fabric. Also, you will need to purchase a pair of steel-toed work boots, available at fair cost in the shoe store next to the workers cafeteria. Good luck, boys."

It turned out that the prophet would be working right across from me. His name was Roy and he'd come to Flint from Oklahoma to live with his brother and find work in the factory. Just your basic "Grapes-of-Wrath-run-aground-in-the-Pizza-Pizza Generation" story line, I suppose.

Our jobs were identical: install splash shields, pencil rods, and assorted nuts and bolts in the rear end of Chevy Blazers. To accomplish this, we worked on a portion of the line where the cabs would rise up on an elevated track. Once the cabs were about five feet off the ground, we'd have to duck inside the rear wheel wells and bust a little ass. Standing across from each other in those cramped wheel wells always reminded me of the two neighbors in the Right Guard commercial who met every morning in their communal medicine cabinet. "Hi, Guy! Care for a scoop of sealer on that pencil rod?"

We adjusted to the heat and grew accustomed to the noise. After a while, we even got used to the claustrophobia of the wheel wells. The idea that we were being paid handsome wages to mimic a bunch of overachieving simians suited us just dandy. In America there was nothing to accomplish as long as the numbers on your pay stub tumbled out in a sequence that served to justify your daily dread.

The one thing we couldn't escape was the monotony of our new jobs. Every minute, every hour, every truck, and every movement totaled nothing but a plodding replica of the one that had gone before. The monotony especially began to gnaw away at Roy. When the lunch horn sounded, we'd race out to his pickup and Roy would start pulling these enormous joints from a glove box. His stash was incredible. "Take one," he'd offer. Pot made me nervous, so I would stick to beer or slug a little whiskey.

The numbing process seemed to demand more every night. We'd go out to the truck and Roy would start burning two joints at once. Now and then, he'd slip down a hit of acid. "I don't know if I'm gonna make my 90 days," he'd tell me. Ninety days was the minimum amount of service required for a worker to apply for sick leave. It was all part of Roy's master plan: reach 90 days' seniority, round up a reliable quack, feign some mysterious injury and, with all the paperwork in order, semi-retire to an orbit of disco bars, women, and cocktails. The old Ozzie Nelson work ethic festering over and over in the hearts of the young.

Roy never did make his 90. To those who were on hand during his last days of service, it came as no real surprise. We all realized that Roy was cracking up.

First there was the incident involving the sacrificial rodent. Roy had managed to capture this tiny mouse that had been sneaking around under one of the stock bins. He built an elaborate little house for the creature and set it on his workbench. He fed it. He gave it water. He built windows in the house so that his pet could "watch me doin' my job." Any worker who passed through the area was summoned over and given a personal introduction to the mouse. For all the world, it seemed like a glorious love affair.

I could never figure out whether it was because of the dope or the drudgery or some unseen domestic quarrel, but things sure switched around in a hurry after each lunch break. Roy would rush through each job, run back to his workbench, and start screaming at the mouse through the tiny cardboard windows. He insisted that the mouse was mocking the way he performed the job. He ranted and raved. He began shaking the house. Keep in mind that, throughout all of this, we were still somehow managing to build 'em "*Chevy Tough!*"

Finally, it was over. Roy grabbed the mouse by the tail and stalked up the welder's platform. He took a brazing torch, gassed up a long blue flame, and right there in the middle of Jungleland, incinerated his little buddy at arm's length.

It didn't get any better. The day before he quit, Roy approached me with a box-cutter knife in his glove. His request was that I take the blade and give him a slice across the back of his hand. He felt flat sure that this ploy would land him a few days off the job.

I had to refuse. Once again, it didn't seem like a solid career move. Roy went on to the other workers where he received a couple of charitable offers to cut his throat, but no dice on the hand. He sulked back to his job.

After a half-dozen attempts on his own, Roy finally got himself a gash. He waited until the blood had a chance to spread out a bit and then went dashing off to see the boss. The damage was minimal. A hunk of gauze, an elastic bandage, and a slow, defeated shuffle back to the wheel wells.

After that day, I never saw Roy again. Personnel sent down a young Puerto Rican guy to help me do the Right Guard commercial and the two of us put in our 90 days without much of a squawk.

The money was right, even if we weren't.

• • •

The layoffs grabbed me in 1980. If you have a deep-rooted fear of standing in an unemployment line like I did, I advise that you do everything in your power to hang on to your job. Heap your employer with phony plaudits, offer to baby-sit his kids, gulp amphetamines and perform the work load of ten servants. If you have to, get down on all fours and smooch his dusty wing-tips anew with sheen. In your spare time go to church, pray to Allah, pray to Buddha, plead with Zeus, beg of Jah, implore the graces of whichever deity landed the '69 Mets a pennant to keep your little butt in the sling and outta the Michigan Employment Security Commission (MESC) logjam of human languish. No, this is not the place to be if you get clammy in a crowd.

First off, the MESC has no windows. Once you pop through the doors, it's like entering a holding tank for sodden sumo wrestlers. You're required to check in at the front desk where a nice little old lady (who appears to have been a teenager during the Spanish-American War) will put a red check next to your appointment time and ask you if you have any paperwork to turn in. Always answer no or you will be detained for a time approximately the same as was needed to build the Pyramids. Paperwork makes these people freeze, reducing them to slow-motion voyagers across the tar pits of eternity. If you have paperwork to hand in, wait until you are absolutely *commanded* to present it and then give weighty consideration to the benefits of suicide.

After your card has been checked at the front desk, you will be instructed to fall into line. Being a shoprat, the most popular of jobless hacks, I have my choice of line 10, 11, or 12, and without fail I always choose the wrong one. My method is to give a quick glance into the eyes of the prospective claims people and somehow determine just which one is herding them out the fastest. Sometimes I'll choose the stiff old man. Sometimes the pretty young woman. Sometimes the evil lady who looks like Agnes Moorehead ripped from the grave. The strategy never works. Either the pretty young woman gets bogged down with potential Romeos, the old guy has to go shuffling off to the can, or the huffy bat spends a half-hour gnawing on some piece of red tape gristle with some dunce who can't remember his age.

A friend of mine insists that the MESC has made a widespread effort to stock its ranks full of people with fetishes for dominance. Though I might hedge a bit on that assertion, it is true that many of its employees seem to delight in having you grovel, squirm, and plead total ignorance to their avalanche of legal brain boggle. They act as though you laid yourself off, that you have no intention of ever lifting another finger, that you're in a frantic rush to get back poolside to your bevy of naked stewardesses, that you hate this country and wanna take their money to buy explosives to lob at the governor's motorcade.

Reading through their standard probes, I'm always tempted to give them a jolt:

Q: "Have you received any income during the past two weeks?"

A: "Yes, I was paid $10,000 to carry out a hit on a U.S. senator."

Q: "Are you receiving any benefits from any other state?"

A: "Yes, I am on a retainer fee from the state of New York as a producer of male prostitutes."

Q: "Have you been able and available for work?"

A: "No, I haven't. I've been too busy selling cocaine and have been too wasted to hear the phone even if it rang."

One thing about being stranded in the unemployment line that I find preferable to a line at a grocery store or movie is that no one speaks to you. Of course, there is always the exception like the guy a few weeks ago who must have mistook me for a chaplain, a social worker, or the future biographer of his life's stupid deeds. As we edged closer and closer to the claims desk, at a pace not discernible to the naked eye, I was treated to every fact of this bumpkin's existence—the kids, his taxes, the deep green hue of his lawn, the hunting dog, his asthma, his perceptions of Blanchard, Reagan, Poland, and the *A-Team*. What is it that makes people think that I have the slightest interest in what's going on in their lives? I hardly have any interest in mine.

Occasionally you'll see people get really irked over a development in their claim. The last time I was in for my check, the desk people dropped this big ugly bomb stating that because of blah-blah-blah (read: unlimited technical bullshit), the extended benefits program was being cut and that the majority of these jobless folks had run the old money meter bone dry. Believe me, this message was not received with cheers and beers—as proven by the fact that one enraged castoff, being of sound strength, if not entirely sound mind, saw fit to retreat to the MESC personnel parking lot, pull out a knife and proceed to play Zorro on the office worker's radials. He was apprehended and stashed in the pokey, where I guess he's pretty much accomplished his objective—the State is still gonna be footing his meal money.

The thing you want to avoid at all costs when visiting the unemployment office is to be detained in the section of seats over by the side wall. That is where they send you if you develop complications in your claim, if you need to file a new claim, if you act unappreciative, or if you go to the bathroom in your pants. If you are instructed to have a seat over in this dreadful limbo, it is advisable that you pack a hefty lunch, bring the complete works of your favorite authors, have your mail delivery halted, and prepare to wait, wait, wait. So far, I've been lucky to avoid taking up a perch in the Land That Time Forgot. What they do with these people is not apparent. Every now and then you see some wire-rimmed weasel in a suit coat poke his head out from beyond the partition and summon one of the waiting few to follow him.

Never, but never, have I ever seen people reappear once ushered in to the boundless back chambers of the MESC. At first I thought that they were merely ducking out a side exit, but casual research into this possible explanation has shown me that *there is no side exit.*

I take it now that this is how it ends. A silent trudge down a narrow hallway, led by a cranky claims executioner with cold eyes and blue lips. Finally having your benefits exhausted, you are a total non-entity. No one misses you. No one can see you. You disappear from the unemployment statistics. You no longer exist.

A miniature Auschwitz has been assembled far behind the clicking of the cashier's keys, far removed from the lazy shuffle of the fresh claimant's feet, off in back where you now only wait for the pellets to drop and the air to get red.

Oh, it could have been worse. You could have been burnt in a house fire. You could have been snagged in a plane prop. You could have been trampled at a Paul Anka concert. You could have had to go find a job.

I was fortunate to be called back to work just one week before my claim was to expire. In a roundabout way, I have only one man to thank for this swell turn of fate—Caspar Weinberger. It was this man's dogged lust for a few billion dollars' worth of military trucks that reopened the doors and pumped new life into my sagging career as a shoprat.

Who could argue? When the call came in askin' if I'd like to come back and help assemble Ronnie's new Death Wagon, I was quick to respond. "Hell yes, I will go!" Conscientious objection might be a noble path on draft day, but I had to admit to having developed a strong desire to eat food every day, and I didn't think it would be an easy habit to break.

SUGGESTIONS FOR DISCUSSION

1. At one point in his article, Hamper tells us that his family has logged about 126 years working for General Motors in Flint, Michigan. Why do you think he wants his readers to know this?
2. Why do you think that Hamper tells the story of the crazy worker with his pet mouse? What is he getting at with that story?
3. Though Ben Hamper's narrative is about his working life at General Motors, his story might extend to many other jobs. What is there in Hamper's story that applies to careers in general?

SUGGESTIONS FOR WRITING

1. Ben Hamper begins his article by telling us that he never intended to be a shoprat. He avoided the factory as long as he could. With that information, he is suggesting there is something he wanted for himself that he did not see in the factory shop. Write a letter to your family in which you explain what kind of work you never want to do. Explain why you want to avoid that work. What is it about that work that doesn't seem fulfilling to you? Can you understand why others might take or even want the same work you would go out of your way to avoid?
2. At the center of his article, Hamper provides a long description of life in the unemployment line. As he describes it, the unemployed don't like being there and the so-

cial workers aren't very sympathetic. All cities and towns in this country have some unemployment. Write an essay that explains what you believe is the attitude of most of your friends or family toward the unemployed. Do you think that attitude is justified? On what basis do you come to your opinion?

3. Write an essay in which you explain what it is that you believe gives a job meaning and what kind of work is meaningful for you. In your essay, take into account the discussions of work you have read thus far in this chapter as well as your own goals for the work you do or hope to do someday. If you wrote the letter suggested in #1 above, you can even draw upon some of the thinking you laid out in that letter.

Barbara Ehrenreich

GOOD-BYE TO THE WORK ETHIC

Essayist Barbara Ehrenreich's articles have become popular social criticisms, appearing in such newspapers and magazines as *The New York Times, The Nation, Atlantic, New Republic, Mother Jones,* and *Ms.* Possibly her most talked about book-length work is *Fear of Falling,* a study of the life-styles and insecurities of middle-class Americans. Her 1990 collection of essays, *The Worst Years of Our Lives: Irreverent Notes from a Decade of Greed,* from which the following selection has been taken, is a satiric look at life in the 1980s. In this essay, written originally in 1988 for *Mother Jones,* Ehrenreich calls for a ban on the work ethic, which, she tells us, yuppies took too far.

Suggestion for Reading

- In order to understand the satiric tone and the target audience for this article, you might wish to look at an issue of *Mother Jones,* the publication in which "Good-bye to the Work Ethic" originally appeared.

T he media have just buried the last yuppie, a pathetic creature who had not heard the news that the great pendulum of public consciousness has just swung from Greed to Compassion and from Tex-Mex to meatballs. Folks are already lining up outside the mausoleum bearing the many items he had hoped to take with him, including a quart bottle of raspberry vinegar and the Cliff Notes for *The Wealth of Nations.* I, too, have brought something to throw onto the funeral pyre—the very essence of yupdom, its creed and its meaning. Not the passion for money, not even the lust for tiny vegetables, but the *work ethic.*

Yes, I realize how important the work ethic is. I understand that it occupies the position, in the American constellation of values, once held by motherhood and Girl Scout cookies. But yuppies took it too far; they *abused* it.

In fact, one of the reasons they only lived for three years (1984–87) was that they *never* rested, never took the time to chew between bites or gaze soulfully past their computer screens. What's worse, the mere rumor that someone—anyone—was not holding up his or her end of the work ethic was enough to send them into tantrums. They blamed lazy workers for the Decline of Productivity. They blamed lazy welfare mothers for the Budget Deficit. Their idea of utopia (as once laid out in that journal of higher yup thought, the *New Republic*) was the "Work Ethic State": no free lunches, no handouts, and too bad for all the miscreants and losers who refuse to fight their way up to the poverty level by working eighty hours a week at Wendy's.

Personally, I have nothing against work, particularly when performed, quietly and unobtrusively, by someone else. I just don't happen to think it's an appropriate subject for an "ethic." As a general rule, when something gets elevated to apple-pie status in the hierarchy of American values, you have to suspect that its actual *monetary* value is skidding toward zero.

Take motherhood: nobody ever thought of putting it on a moral pedestal until some brash feminists pointed out, about a century ago, that the pay is lousy and the career ladder nonexistent. Same thing with work: would we be so reverent about the "work ethic" if it wasn't for the fact that the average working stiff's hourly pay is shrinking, year by year, toward the price of a local phone call?

In fact, let us set the record straight: the work ethic is not a "traditional value." It is a johnny-come-lately value, along with thin thighs and nonsmoking hotel rooms. In ancient times, work was considered a disgrace inflicted on those who had failed to amass a nest egg through imperial conquest or other forms of organized looting. Only serfs, slaves, and women worked. The yuppies of ancient Athens—which we all know was a perfect cornucopia of "traditional values"—passed their time rubbing their bodies with olive oil and discussing the Good, the True, and the Beautiful.

The work ethic came along a couple of millennia later, in the form of Puritanism—the idea that the amount of self-denial you endured in this life was a good measure of the amount of fun awaiting you in the next. But the work ethic only got off the ground with the Industrial Revolution and the arrival of the factory system. This was—let us be honest about it—simply a scheme for extending the benefits of the slave system into the age of emancipation.

Under the new system (aka capitalism in this part of the world), huge numbers of people had to be convinced to work extra hard, at pitifully low wages, so that the employing class would not have to work at all. Overnight, with the help of a great number of preachers and other well-rested propagandists, work was upgraded from an indignity to an "ethic."

But there was a catch: the aptly named *working class* came to resent the resting class. There followed riots, revolutions, graffiti. Quickly, the word went out from the robber barons to the swelling middle class of lawyers, financial consultants, plant managers, and other forerunners of the yuppie: Look busy! Don't go home until the proles have punched out! Make 'em think *we're* doing the work and that they're lucky to be able to hang around and help out!

The lawyers, managers, etc., were only too happy to comply, for as the perennially clever John Kenneth Galbraith once pointed out, they themselves comprised a "new leisure class" within industrial society. Of course, they "work," but only under the most pleasant air-conditioned, centrally heated, and fully carpeted conditions, and then only in a sitting position. It was in their own interest to convince the working class that what looks like lounging requires intense but invisible effort.

The yuppies, when they came along, had to look more righteously busy than anyone, for the simple reason that they did nothing at all. Workwise, that is. They did not sow, neither did they reap, but rather sat around pushing money through their modems in games known as "corporate takeover" and "international currency speculation." Hence their rage at anyone who actually works—the "unproductive" American worker, or the woman attempting to raise a family on welfare benefits set below the average yuppie's monthly health spa fee.

So let us replace their cruel and empty slogan—"Go for it!"—with the cry that lies deep in every true worker's heart: "Gimme a break!" What this nation needs is not the work ethic, but a *job* ethic: If it needs doing—highways repaired, babies changed, fields plowed—let's get it done. Otherwise, take five. Listen to some New Wave music, have a serious conversation with a three-year-old, write a poem, look at the sky. Let the yuppies Rest in Peace; the rest of us deserve a break.

SUGGESTIONS FOR DISCUSSION

1. How would you describe Ehrenreich's tone in this essay? Identify places in the essay where the tone seems informal and funny and places where the tone seems slightly more serious.
2. Explain what Ehrenreich means when she says, "I understand that [the work ethic] occupies the position, in the American constellation of values, once held by motherhood and Girl Scout cookies." After reading the selections in this chapter, do you agree?
3. What do you suppose Alfred Benke would say to Barbara Erhenreich about her attitudes toward the work ethic?

SUGGESTIONS FOR WRITING

1. Write a summary of Ehrenreich's history of the work ethic.
2. Review the writers you have read thus far in this chapter and write a response to Ehrenreich's essay that draws on your own feelings about work and the work ethic but also takes into account the experiences with work you have been reading about.
3. After reviewing the writers in this chapter, write a work ethic for the 1990s. In your discussion, explain how your updated work ethic emerges from but is different than that handed down to us by our ancestors and, more recently, the Boomers Ehrenreich writes of.

Juliet B. Schor

THE OVERWORKED AMERICAN

Economist Juliet Schor argues in the following excerpt from *The Overworked American: The Unexpected Decline of Leisure* that, despite the fact that we can now produce as much in four hours as it once took eight hours to produce, Americans work longer, less productive hours than ever before. Her analysis of contemporary working conditions raises questions about how our work and leisure time are spent and what it is that we call leisure. At the time of this book's publication, Juliet Schor was Associate Professor of Economics at Harvard University.

Suggestion for Reading

- Although Schor's analysis is about work, it is more specifically about the loss of leisure time. As you read, pay particular attention to and annotate those passages in which Schor makes her argument about how the decline of leisure in America today affects our lives.

---◆---

In the last twenty years the amount of time Americans have spent at their jobs has risen steadily. Each year the change is small, amounting to about nine hours, or slightly more than one additional day of work. In any given year, such a small increment has probably been imperceptible. But the accumulated increase over two decades is substantial. When surveyed, Americans report that they have only sixteen and a half hours of leisure a week, after the obligations of job and household are taken care of. Working hours are already longer than they were forty years ago. If present trends continue, by the end of the century Americans will be spending as much time at their jobs as they did back in the nineteen twenties.

The rise of worktime was unexpected. For nearly a hundred years, hours had been declining. When this decline abruptly ended in the late 1940s, it marked the beginning of a new era in worktime. But the change was barely noticed. Equally surprising, but also hardly recognized, has been the deviation from Western Europe. After progressing in tandem for nearly a century, the United States veered off into a trajectory of declining leisure, while in Europe work has been disappearing. Forty years later, the differences are large. U.S. manufacturing employees currently work 320 more hours—the equivalent of over two months—than their counterparts in West Germany or France.

The decline in Americans' leisure time is in sharp contrast to the potential provided by the growth of productivity. Productivity measures the goods and services that result from each hour worked. When productivity rises, a worker can either produce the current output in less time, or remain at work the same number of hours and produce more. Every time productivity increases, we are presented with the possibility of either more free time or more money. That's the productivity dividend.

Since 1948, productivity has failed to rise in only five years. The level of productivity of the U.S. worker has more than doubled. In other words, we could now produce our 1948 standard of living (measured in terms of marketed goods and services) in less than half the time it took in that year. We actually could have chosen the four-hour day. Or a working year of six months. Or, *every worker in the United States could now be taking every other year off from work—with pay.* Incredible as it may sound, this is just the simple arithmetic of productivity growth in operation.

But between 1948 and the present we did not use any of the productivity dividend to reduce hours. In the first two decades after 1948, productivity grew rapidly, at about 3 percent a year. During that period, worktime did not fall appreciably. Annual hours per labor force participant fell only slightly. And on a per-capita (rather than a labor force) basis, they even rose a bit. Since then, productivity growth has been lower, but still positive, averaging just over 1 percent a year. Yet hours have risen steadily for two decades. In 1990, the average American owns and consumes more than twice as much as he or she did in 1948, but also has less free time.

How did this happen? Why has leisure been such a conspicuous casualty of prosperity? In part, the answer lies in the difference between the markets for consumer products and free time. Consider the former, the legendary American market. It is a veritable consumer's paradise, offering a dazzling array of products varying in style, design, quality, price, and country of origin. The consumer is treated to GM versus Toyota, Kenmore versus GE, Sony, or Magnavox, the Apple versus the IBM. We've got Calvin Klein, Anne Klein, Liz Claiborne, and Levi-Strauss; McDonald's, Burger King, and Colonel Sanders. Marketing experts and advertisers spend vast sums of money to make these choices appealing—even irresistible. And they have been successful. In cross-country comparisons, Americans have been found to spend more time shopping than anyone else. They also spend a higher fraction of the money they earn. And with the explosion of consumer debt, many are now spending what they haven't earned.

After four decades of this shopping spree, the American standard of living embodies a level of material comfort unprecedented in human history. The American home is more spacious and luxurious than the dwellings of any other nation. Food is cheap and abundant. The typical family owns a fantastic array of household and consumer appliances: we have machines to wash our clothes and dishes, mow our lawns, and blow away our snow. On a per-person basis, yearly income is nearly $22,000 a year—or sixty-five times the average income of half the world's population.

On the other hand, the "market" for free time hardly even exists in America. With few exceptions, employers (the sellers) don't offer the chance to trade off income gains for a shorter work day or the occasional sabbatical. They just pass on income, in the form of annual pay raises or bonuses, or, if granting increased vacation or personal days, usually do so unilaterally. Employees rarely have the chance to exercise an actual choice about how they will spend their productivity dividend. The closest substitute for a "market in leisure" is the travel and other leisure industries that advertise products to occupy our free time. But this indirect effect has been weak, as consumers crowd increasingly expensive leisure spending into smaller periods of time.

Nor has society provided a forum for deliberate choice. The growth of worktime did not occur as a result of public debate. There has been little attention from government, academia, or civic organizations. For the most part, the issue has been off the agenda, a nonchoice, a hidden trade off. It was not always so. As early as 1791, when Philadelphia carpenters went on strike for the ten-hour day, there was public awareness about hours of work. Throughout the nineteenth century, and well into the twentieth, the reduction of worktime was one of the nation's most pressing social issues. Employers and workers fought about the length of the working day, social activists delivered lectures, academics wrote treatises, courts handed down decisions, and government legislated hours of work. Through the Depression, hours remained a major social preoccupation. Today these debates and conflicts are long forgotten. Since the 1930s, the choice between work and leisure has hardly been a choice at all, at least in any conscious sense.

• • •

In its starkest terms, my argument is this: Key incentive structures of capitalist economies contain biases toward long working hours. As a result of these incentives, the development of capitalism led to the growth of what I call "long hour jobs." The eventual recovery of leisure came about because trade unions and social reformers waged a protracted struggle for shorter hours. Some time between the Depression and the end of the Second World War, that struggle collapsed. As the inevitable pressures toward long hours reasserted themselves, U.S. workers experienced a new decline that now, at the century's end, has created a crisis of leisure time. I am aware that these are strong claims which overturn most of what we have been taught to believe about the way our economy works. . . .

Ironically, the tendency of capitalism to expand work is often associated with a growth in joblessness. In recent years, as a majority have taken on the extra month of work, nearly one-fifth of all participants in the labor force are unable to secure as many hours as they want or need to make ends meet. While many employees are subjected to mandatory overtime and are suffering from overwork, their co-workers are put on involuntary part-time. In the context of my story, these irrationalities seem to make sense. The rational, and humane, solution—reducing hours to spread the work—has practically been ruled out of court.

In speaking of "long hour jobs" exclusively in terms of the capitalist marketplace, I do not mean to overlook those women who perform their labor in the privacy of their own homes. Until the late nineteenth century, large numbers of single and married women did participate in the market economy, either in farm labor or through various entrepreneurial activities (taking in boarders, sewing at home, and so on). By the twentieth century, however, a significant percentage of married women, particularly white women, spent all their time outside the market nexus, as full-time "domestic laborers," providing goods and, increasingly, services for their families. And they, too, have worked at "long hour jobs."

Studies of household labor beginning in the 1910s and continuing through to the 1970s show that the amount of time a full-time housewife devoted to her work remained virtually unchanged for over fifty years—despite dramatic changes in household technology. As homes, like factories, were "industrialized," refrigerators, laundry machines, vacuum cleaners, and microwaves took up residence in the American domicile. Ready-made clothes and processed food supplanted the home-produced variety. Yet with all these labor-saving innovations, no labor has been saved. Instead, housework expanded to fill the available time. Norms of cleanliness rose. Standards of mothering grew more rigorous. Cooking and baking became more complicated. At the same time, a variety of cheaper and more efficient ways of providing household services failed in the market, and housewives continued to do their own.

The stability of housewives' hours was due to a particular bias in the incentives of what we may term the "labor market for housewives." Just as the capitalist labor market contains structural biases toward long hours, so too has the housewife's situation. . . . And in neither case has technology automatically saved labor. It has taken women's exodus from the home itself to reduce their household labor. As women entered paid employment, they cut back their hours of domestic work signifi- . cantly—but not by enough to keep their total working time unchanged. According to my estimates, when a woman takes a paying job, her schedule expands by at least twenty hours a week. The overwork that plagues many Americans, especially married women, springs from a combination of full-time male jobs, the expansion of housework to fill the available hours, and the growth of employment among married women.

● ● ●

However scarce academic research on the rising workload may be, what we do know suggests it has contributed to a variety of social problems. For example, work is implicated in the dramatic rise of "stress." Thirty percent of adults say that they experience high stress nearly every day; even higher numbers report high stress once or twice a week. A third of the population says that they are rushed to do the things they have to do—up from a quarter in 1965. Stress-related diseases have exploded, especially among women, and jobs are a major factor. Workers' compensation claims related to stress tripled during just the first half of the 1980s. Other evidence also suggests a rise in the demands placed on employees on the job. According to a recent review of existing findings, Americans are literally working themselves to death—as jobs contribute to heart disease, hypertension, gastric problems, depression, exhaustion, and a variety of other ailments. Surprisingly, the high-powered jobs are not the most dangerous. The most stressful workplaces are the "electronic sweatshops" and assembly lines where a demanding pace is coupled with virtually no individual discretion.

Sleep has become another casualty of modern life. According to sleep researchers, studies point to a "sleep deficit" among Americans, a majority of whom are currently getting between 60 and 90 minutes less a night than they should for optimum health and performance. The number of people showing up at sleep disorder clinics with serious problems has skyrocketed in the last decade. Shiftwork, long working hours, the growth of a global economy (with its attendant continent-hopping and twenty-four-hour business culture), and the accelerating pace of life have all contributed to sleep deprivation. If you need an alarm clock, the experts warn, you're probably sleeping too little.

The juggling act between job and family is another problem area. Half the population now says they have too little time for their families. The problem is particularly acute for women: in one study, half of all employed mothers reported it caused either "a lot" or an "extreme" level of stress. The same proportion feel that "when I'm at home I try to make up to my family for being away at work, and as a result I rarely have any time for myself." This stress has placed tremendous burdens on marriages. Two-earner couples have less time together, which researchers have found reduces the happiness and satisfaction of a marriage. These couples often just don't have enough time to talk to each other. And growing numbers of husbands and wives are like ships passing in the night, working sequential schedules to manage their child care. Among young parents, the prevalence of at least one partner working outside regular daytime hours is now close to one half. But this "solution" is hardly a happy one. According to one parent: "I work 11–7 to accommodate my family—to eliminate the need for babysitters. However, the stress on myself is tremendous."

A decade of research by Berkeley sociologist Arlie Hochschild suggests that many marriages where women are doing the "second shift" are close to the breaking point. When job, children, and marriage have to be attended to, it's often the marriage that is neglected. The failure of many men to do their share at home creates further problems. A twenty-six-year-old legal secretary in California reports that her husband "does no cooking, no washing, no anything else. How do I feel? Furious. If our marriage ends, it will be on this issue. And it just might."

Serious as these problems are, the most alarming development may be the effect of the work explosion on the care of children. According to economist Sylvia Hewlett, "child neglect has become endemic to our society." A major problem is that children are increasingly left alone, to fend for themselves while their parents are at work. Nationwide, estimates of children in "self"—or, more accurately, "no"—care range up to seven million. Local studies have found figures of up to one-third of children caring for themselves. At least half a million preschoolers are thought to be left at home part of each day. One 911 operator reports large numbers of frightened callers: "It's not uncommon to hear from a child of six or seven who has been left in charge of even younger siblings."

Even when parents are at home, overwork may leave them with limited time, attention, or energy for their children. One working parent noted, "My child has severe emotional problems because I am too tired to listen to him. It is not quality time; it's bad quantity time that's destroying my family." Economist Victor Fuchs has found that between 1960 and 1986, the time parents actually had available to be with children fell ten hours a week for whites and twelve for blacks. Hewlett links the "parenting deficit" to a variety of problems plaguing the country's youth: poor performance in school, mental problems, drug and alcohol use, and teen suicide. According to another expert, kids are being "cheated out of childhood. . . . There is a sense that adults don't care about them."

Of course, there's more going on here than lack of time. Child neglect, marital distress, sleep deprivation and stress-related illnesses all have other causes. But the growth of work has exacerbated each of these social ailments. Only by understanding why we work as much as we do, and how the demands of work affect family life, can we hope to solve these problems.

• • •

The past forty years should provide a warning. They have brought us nothing in the way of leisure time and a saner pace of life. The bias of the system is strongly toward the status quo. But time poverty is straining the social fabric. Continued growth threatens environmental balance, and gender equality requires new work patterns. Despite these obstacles, I am hopeful. By understanding how we came to be caught up in the cycle of work-and-spend, perhaps we can regain a reasonable balance between work and leisure.

SUGGESTIONS FOR DISCUSSION

1. Make a list of some of the people you know well who hold jobs outside the home. How much leisure time would you estimate most of them have? Do you think any of them would identify a lack of leisure time as a particular problem for them?
2. Explain the connection Schor makes between the loss of leisure time and the rise of conspicuous consumption.
3. With a group of classmates, discuss why or why not the loss of leisure time should be a serious concern for anyone about to enter the job market or for others who have been working for many years.

SUGGESTIONS FOR WRITING

1. Summarize Shor's arguments for the reevaluation of work loads. Make sure you include her historical argument as well as her discussion of the problems connected with diminished leisure time.
2. As others have, Schor argues that labor-saving technology may end up increasing rather than decreasing our work load. Write an essay in which you identify specific labor-saving technology that has actually increased your own work. (Some would argue, for example, that word processors make us work more rather than less on our writing.)
3. Write an essay in which you spell out your own position on the value of, loss of, or usefulness of leisure time. Write from your reading, from your experience, and from your observations of others.

Utah Phillips

ALL USED UP

Folksinger and storyteller Utah Phillips has been a tramp, an IWW (Industrial Workers of the World) organizer, and a labor activist. He often speaks out for the underprivileged and the outcasts in our culture. In the following song, Phillips tells a story of a man who gave his entire life to his job so that, when the job was over, he had nothing left. In the album notes, Phillips introduces this song by saying, "There is an old man who sits in the window of the Clem Hotel here in Spokane and looks out on the parking lot day after day. I don't know if this song is his story. It's not going to be mine if I can help it, and I hope it's not going to be any of yours." "All Used Up" is a folk song. That means it tells a simple story about ordinary people. It is written, not just as a melody but as a message. If you would like to hear the song, it appears on Utah Phillips's album *All Used Up: A Scrapbook,* on the Philo label.

Suggestion for Reading

- Even if you are not able to listen to Utah Phillips sing, you might wish to know that Phillips believes strongly in people helping each other as a community. And, he believes that much knowledge comes from hardship. In the album's liner notes, he writes of a friend who used to say: "When you're theorisin' on a full stomach, you hain't the least idea what you'd do if you was practicing on an empty one." His songs, like "All Used Up," ask us to understand those who are practicing on empty. As you read these lyrics, annotate the song with your own reactions to this old man's dilemma.

———————◆———————

I spent my whole life makin' somebody rich;
I busted my ass for that son-of-a-bitch:
And he left me to die like a dog in a ditch
And told me I'm all used up.
He used up my labor, he used up my time,
He plundered my body and squandered my mind
And gave me a pension of handouts and wine
And told me I'm all used up.

My kids are in hock to a God you call work,
Slaving their lives out for some other jerk;
My youngest in Frisco just made shipping clerk
And he don't know I'm all used up.
Young people reaching for power and gold
Don't have respect for anything old
For pennies they're bought and for promises sold,
Someday they'll all be used up.

They use up the oil, they use up the trees
They use up the air and they use up the sea;
Well how about you, friend, and how about me?
What's left when we're all used up?
I'll finish my life in this crummy hotel,
It's lousy with bugs and my God what a smell,
But my plumbing still works and I'm clear as a bell,
Don't tell me I'm all used up.

Outside my window the world passes by,
It gives me a handout and spits in my eye,
And no one can tell me 'cause no one knows why
I'm livin' but I'm all used up.
Sometimes in my dreams I sit by a tree;
My life is a book of how things used to be,
And kids gather 'round and they listen to me,
And they don't think I'm all used up.

And there's songs and there's laughter and things I can do,
And all that I've learned I can give back to you;
I'd give my last breath just to make it come true—
No, I'm not all used up.
They use up the oil and they use up the trees
They use up the air and they use up the sea;
Well, how about you, friend, and how about me?
What's left when we're all used up?

SUGGESTIONS FOR DISCUSSION

1. What is Utah Phillips saying about the old man in this song?
2. Although it might be tempting to say, as Phillips does, that none of us intends to end up like this old man, discuss why a person might feel "all used up" after retirement or a lifetime of hard work.
3. In his introduction to this song, Utah Phillips says that this won't be his fate and he hopes it won't be ours. How you might go about avoiding the fate of being "all used up" once your job ends?

SUGGESTIONS FOR WRITING

1. Write an essay that summarizes Utah Phillips's message in this song and explains the assumptions he is making about the world of work.
2. Write an essay that compares the message in "All Used Up" to Ben Hamper's description of factory life, Estelle Zabritz's description of the meat-packing plant, or Philip Levine's description of waiting for work.
3. Interview someone you know who is retired or near retirement. If you are able to, take a tape recorder with you. Ask that person about his or her work, what in the work is satisfying and what is not, how important the work is to this person's concept self-worth, and what the person thinks retirement will be like. Reread Alfred Benke's letter to his son, Philip Levine's poem, Estelle Zabritz's oral history, and Ben Hamper's story in order to refresh your memory of how others talk about work, and then write up your interview, editing it so that the those points you consider the most important come out in your retelling of it. In the written presentation of your interview, choose comments that convey your subject's attitude toward work, especially as that attitude seems to reflect a particular point of view about work, retirement, or unemployment that you believe is common in this culture.

Wilfred Pelletier and Ted Poole

HOME IS HERE

Wilfred Pelletier is an Odawan elder from Manitoulin Island on Lake Huron. He has worked as co-director of the Nishnawbe Institute, an Indian educational and cultural project in Toronto. The following selection is taken from

Pelletier's 1973 biography, *No Foreign Land: The Biography of a North American Indian.* In this excerpt, Pelletier explains the difference between Western European assumptions and American Indian tribal assumptions about work and its place in the community. Pelletier's biography touches on much more than the story of one person's life. It is a story about how people live together, about how different cultures understand their world, and about how these cultures might try to understand each other. What a culture thinks of as "work," he argues, has very much to do with community and cultural assumptions about how work functions in that community. Like Studs Terkel's interviews of workers, this biography is oral history. Wilfred Pelletier told his story to Ted Poole, who wrote it down as Pelletier told it. In writing the biography, Poole has retained as much of the oral nature of Pelletier's story as possible, in keeping with the oral tradition in American Indian history and storytelling.

Suggestion for Reading

- As you read, underline passages in which Pelletier talks about the difference between his job off the reservation that provides him with a wage and the jobs he and others do for their community to keep that community going.

◆

I had no money, no credit. There was no work on the reserve I could make money at. Once again, I was just another damn Indian. I had fallen back into survival, Indian style. What that means is that you work—sometimes you work like hell—but you're not an employee and you don't get paid money. You get paid in a different way—satisfactions, I suppose you'd call them—the good feeling of your body coming together with hard work, the good feeling of your life coming together because all the non-essentials have fallen away and the whole thing is just simple, very simple and primary. There's a direct line between your head and your hands and your belly. Money, the middleman of survival, has been eliminated. Everything you do is directly related to survival: the wood you cut, the water you draw, the garden you plant, the berries you pick, the fish you catch—and that's your life. And that was our life, but not all of it. There was another element in our survival: the people.

Every day somebody would drop in—some woman would drop in and say, "Well, we had this soup last night. If you want it, it's left over. There's enough there for three or four people, but I can't heat it up now because there's eight of us." And there were three of us, so we'd have soup. Or somebody'd drop in with potatoes, or after they'd made bread: "I want you to try my bread." And every day they came. It had nothing to do with then wanting us to try their bread. They were feeding us. And it wasn't just kindness or thoughtfulness, not charity. It was a way of life, or survival. They sustained us because, with Indians, if the community doesn't survive, no one survives.

● ● ●

I've come home dozens of times, hundreds of times, and no one has ever asked me where I came from or what I'm doing now or where I'm living now or how much money I make or what sort of job I have or any of these questions which are so common in white society. What that means is that the people in that community don't place any importance on these things. They like me and love me as I like and love them, and when I come home they are happy to see me and they don't see anyone except Wilf, who was once a little boy and who's now older and bigger and a man, but who is still Wilf, really unchanged. I haven't become anything, I'm not somebody; I'm just who I always was—Wilf. I don't have to account for myself, I don't have to impress anyone, I don't have to explain myself, I don't have to do anything. I'm allowed just to be, and that is the greatest freedom I know. That is what I mean when I say I've come home. And that is life, total life. And that is the world. There isn't anything outside of that.

Yeah, that's all there is except that one other thing, and that one other thing—I don't know what it is. It can be called "the job," or I guess it could be given lots of names. Anyway, there are hundreds of Indian people like me who go home, but only for a few days, a weekend or whatever, and then they go back to that job. They're a tool-maker or a student or a factory worker or something; they leave and go back to that job. Even though the reserve is all there is. And I don't know . . . oh, I can talk about economic necessity, the need to survive and so on, and there aren't any jobs on the reserve so you have to go outside to find a job. All that. But I know that doesn't explain it. You're damned if you do and damned if you don't. Everyone has to decide for himself what poverty is, what survival is—to be rich in relationships and poor in possessions, or the other way around. For Indians, it seems to be a choice between staying home and having very little (which is really everything) and going away in order to achieve relative affluence (which is nothing). I do know that the whole thing I'm talking about of going home, that's what religion is all about. Those people want to go home, all the people in the world. And I wonder . . . I don't think there are very many who get home any more through organized religion because the people who are trying to lead the way don't know where they're going. What I mean by going home is finding your own people—not just your blood relations, your *whole* family, wherever they may be anywhere in the world. And I guess that means recognition: knowing the members of your family at a glance and having them know you. People who accept you without question. Because if your medium of exchange is not love, you can't survive.

• • •

Then I took a look around. I saw city halls, courthouses, houses of parliament, churches, schools, and universities by the hundreds and thousands. I saw systems—systems for managing the land, the air, and the water; systems for managing human behavior; systems for managing religion; systems for managing learning; systems for managing food, shelter, clothing; systems for managing love and procreation: a vast complex of carefully engineered systems. I saw millions of people working, not for themselves, but for someone else. I saw millions of people doing, not what they themselves want to do, but what someone else wants them to do. I saw the depressing evidence of a people who have externalized and institutionalized—in fact, have tried to standardize—the very nature of humanity. I saw a whole people who've lost the way of life and in its place have built a mechanical monster which does most of their hard work, carries their water, delivers their food, raises their kids, makes their decisions, says their prayers, transports them, "informs" them, entertains them, and controls the people it serves, absolutely. I also saw that the monster, unable to manage itself, was running wild, totally out of control, ripping the land to pieces, spreading poisons, filling the air with filth, dumping garbage and shit in the rivers and lakes and oceans. I saw all that, and I saw the people, millions of them, crowded together in cities, living side by side in towns, villages, rural areas. But I didn't see a single community.

Still, I knew of some. There were a few *bona fide* communities left in America, all of them Indian or Eskimo. A community is invisible from the outside—just a collection of people. But from the inside it is a living organism that manages itself. Not engineered, not planned; just growing there—a sort of happening that flourishes or shrivels depending on the climate around it. A community has no institutions, no agencies, no forms of extraneous government, because *there are no departments of activity.* There's only a way of life, and all the activities are just naturally in that flow, all the things that people find it necessary to do in order to survive. In the communities I was thinking of, the people know nothing of Justice or Religion or Education or Equality or Culture or any of those big institutional concepts. Their language has no words of that sort in it. But the people themselves are just and learned and religious and equal. Those people don't even know they are a community. The word itself has no meaning for them.

Another thing they have no awareness of and certainly no word for, but which I have observed lots of times, is something I have come to call community consciousness. I'm not sure I can describe it except to say it's common ground, a kind of corporate consciousness that is shared by everybody in that community and used by everyone. Maybe the best word for it is "trust"—a kind of trust that people outside that community can hardly imagine and which the people inside that community cannot name. I think it must be closely related to the kind of consciousness you see in a flock of sandpipers. Fifty or sixty individual birds are all packed together into one dense flock and they're going to beat hell, turning this way and that, diving and climbing, cutting around in tight circles, and that flock stays right together, stays the same shape all the time. And not one bird runs into another. Each bird acts, flies, moves like every other bird. The flock behaves as one, one single organism. You can see the same thing in a school of fish and in some swarms of insects, too.

Now, I don't know how they do that, those creatures, except that *they* don't do it; *it* does it. And I think this same thing, this same sensitivity or alertness or whatever, is present in tribal communities. For one thing, work is shared and produce is shared. People survive together as a group, not as individuals. They aren't into competition. But they aren't into cooperation either—never heard of either of those words. What they do just happens, just flows along. And they're not into organization either; no need for it, because that community is *organic.* Wherever people feel the need to organize it's because the normal condition of their society is disorganized (not together). But I don't think the Western European way of organizing brings things together anyway, in the sense of human relations. From what I've seen, it usually does just the opposite. It gets things done, but it alienates people.

Let's say the council hall in an Indian community needs a new roof—maybe that would be a good example. Well, everybody knows that. It's been leaking here and there for quite a while and it's getting worse. And people have been talking about it, saying, "I guess the old hall needs a new roof." So all of a sudden one morning here's a guy up on the roof, tearing off the old shingles, and down on the ground there's several bundles of new, handsplit shakes—probably not enough to do the whole job, but enough to make a good start. Then after a while another guy comes along and sees the first guy on the roof. So he comes over and he doesn't say, "What are you doing up here?" because that's obvious, but he may say, "How's she look? Pretty rotten, I guess." Something like that. Then he takes off, and pretty soon he's back with a hammer or shingle hatchet and maybe some shingle nails or a couple of rolls of tarpaper. By afternoon there's a whole crew working on that roof, a pile of materials building up down there on the ground, kids taking the old shingles away—taking them home for kindling—dogs barking, women bringing cold lemonade and sandwiches. The whole community is involved and there's a lot of fun and laughter. Maybe next day another guy arrives with more bundles of shakes. In two or three days that whole job is finished, and they all end up having a big party in the "new" council hall.

All that because one guy decided to put a new roof on the hall. Now who was that guy? Was he a single isolated individual? Or was he the whole community? How can you tell? No meeting was called, no committees formed, no funds raised. There were no arguments about whether the roof should be covered with aluminum or duroid or tin or shakes and which was the cheapest and which would last the longest and all that. There was no foreman and no-one was hired and nobody questioned that guy's right to rip off the old roof. But there must have been some kind of "organization" going on in all that, because the job got done. It got done a lot quicker than if you hired professionals. And it wasn't work; it was fun.

SUGGESTIONS FOR DISCUSSION

1. What distinction does Pelletier make between working for a wage and working for the survival of a community?
2. Why do you think Pelletier wants to stay on the reservation even though there is no "job" for him there? What assumptions is he making about the role of work in his life?
3. Explain what you think Pelletier means by the organic nature of tribal communities. How does he connect that organicism to the ways in which tribal communities seem to characterize work?

SUGGESTIONS FOR WRITING

1. Write an essay in which you compare the idea of work in Western European traditions as Ehrenreich and Schor write of them and as Pelletier describes them to its role in tribal cultures.
2. Pelletier explains that work in his culture is valued in terms of its worth to the entire community. Write an essay in which you explain how work is depicted in mainstream American culture. You may wish to draw on images of work or workers as they appear in the popular stories, film, television, or advertising you know. Such popular sources often depict the most generalized attitudes about a given cultural convention and might help you sort out at least the broad image of work in American culture today.
3. Most of the writers you have read in this chapter write of individuals' experiences with work. Pelletier's biography, on the contrary, writes of work as a way of understanding an entire culture. In doing that, he actually questions basic assumptions many Americans hold about why we work in this culture and what kind of work we should do. Write an essay in which you explain what cultural influences have acted on you to help you decide what is meaningful work in your life and what is not. In other words, what values of this culture that relate to work are you adhering to in your own hopes and aspirations for future work and in your own ideas about

work? In preparation for your essay, reread those selections in this chapter that seemed to you to most closely resemble attitudes toward work you hold or that you have encountered before. You might consider, for example, how closely your ideas about work resemble those of Ben Hamper or Sandra Cisneros or Juliet B. Schor or Barbara Ehrenreich or Utah Phillips.

FOR FURTHER EXPLORATION

The reading in this chapter can lead you in several different directions if you decide to do library research. You may, for example, wish to know more about the history of the Protestant work ethic so that you understand some of the ways work has been talked about in American culture. Daniel Rodgers's *The Work Ethic in Industrial America: 1850–1920* is a full-length history of that concept that may be useful in your research. Estelle Zabritz's story of her work in the meat-packing industry might lead you to Sinclair Lewis's fictional account of that industry, *The Jungle,* or you can find out information on the more recent Hormel strike that occurred in Wisconsin in the 1980s. Consider, as well, the many labor issues that are of interest to workers today:

- Sexual harrassment in the workplace
- The North American Free Trade Agreement
- Right-to-work laws.
- The AARP's (American Association of Retired Persons) position on social security, pension, and retirement funds

CHAPTER 10

HISTORY

One of the marks of a good professional historian is the consistency with which he reminds his readers of the purely provisional nature of his characterization of events, agents, and agencies found in the always incomplete historical record.

— Hayden White,
Tropics of Discourse

I f you asked what history is, most people would probably say that it is the story of what happened in the past, and they might think of the dates they memorized and the events they learned in school. Most Americans encounter history in school as a set of facts about the Louisiana Purchase, the Mexican-American War, or the Homestead Act. Accounts of these events can be verified by records and evidence from the past, and so we take them to be true—to be based on the facts.

But it is precisely because history claims an authority based on fact that we need to ask a further question, namely, where do the facts come from in the writing of history? It is true, of course, that in one sense the facts are simply there—in historical records, newspapers, government documents, archives, and so forth. The facts, however, cannot come forward on their own to speak for themselves. So, while it seems incontestable that Columbus did indeed sail from Spain to the West Indies in 1492, the meanings of the event people have brought forward can vary considerably. Among our concerns in this chapter are the perspectives from which historians and other writers look at the past and how these ways of looking bring certain facts into view while ignoring or suppressing others.

The purpose of this chapter, in other words, is to investigate the writing of history—and why individuals and groups might tell different versions of the past. In this chapter you will be asked to read, think, and write about the version of American history you learned in school. You will be asked to recall not only what you learned but also what lessons you were led to draw from the study of the past. You will be asked to think about whose version of the American past you learned, and whose perspectives are included and whose are excluded in the story. And you will be asked to consider whether American history needs to be rewritten in order to embody those perspectives that are absent, the voices from the past that have been silent in the history Americans learn in school.

There are some things in school that students have to learn by heart. The alphabet. The multiplication tables. The names of the continents and oceans. But students also learn history by heart—and it's worth examining for a moment just what that phrase "to learn by heart" might mean. On the one hand, of course, it means memorizing dates, names, and events—and probably getting tested on them. On the other hand, however, learning something by heart also suggests an emotional investment. To learn the history of the American revolution or the Civil War by heart is not just to acquire the facts. It also means acquiring judgments and attitudes and forming social allegiances and loyalties. History, most students understand, despite the ostensibly objective tone of their textbooks, is a moral drama that contains lessons to teach them about which side they belong to in the unfolding story of the American nation.

The story Americans learn through school and history textbooks is a tale of national destiny—of how hard-working Americans developed a democratic society in the New World and how America prospered and grew bigger and stronger to become an industrial and geopolitical power in the twentieth century. According to this story, the expansion of America's borders and productivity is simply the natural growth and development of the nation, the inevitable unfolding of the country's role in history. This sense of destiny and national purpose is closely linked to Americans' image of themselves and their mission as a people. For many Americans, history is a form of collective memory that joins the country together in a national identity and explains how America became what it is today. American history, in this regard, is not just a matter of the facts. It takes on a mythic dimension by telling of the founding events, heroic acts, and tragic sacrifices that have made this country a powerful nation.

Until fairly recently there existed a broad consensus about the meaning of American history and its principles of development. Nowadays, however, the version of American history that has prevailed in schools and textbooks has been called into question. Historians have started to reread the historical record, to see what voices have been silenced or ignored in the story of America's national development. New perspectives—from women, African Americans, Hispanics, American Indians, Asian Americans, and working-class people—are being added to America's collective history, presenting alternative accounts that complicate the picture of the American past considerably. The westward expansion, for example, from the perspective of Native Americans, looks less like the progressive development of the land and its agricultural and mineral resources and more like the military conquest and occupation of traditional tribal holdings.

One of the things you will be asked to do in this chapter is to read for the plot in historians' and other writers' accounts of the past—to describe what their perspectives bring into view about the past and how they have selected and arranged the events to tell a story. By looking at how historians and writers construct versions of the past (always from their particular perspective in the present), you can identify not only the techniques they use to tell a story but also the different versions of the past they make available to us today. In contemporary America, to think about history is to think about competing versions of the past, and you will want to consider how the plots differ—and what is thereby at stake—in the various accounts of the past you read in the following selections. We have chosen the readings in this chapter to include contrasting examples of historical writing—official versions of American history taken from textbooks, as well as efforts of revisionist historians and writers to retell the story of the American past. What you will see is that the differences in plots and perspectives raise profound questions about who is entitled to write American history and whose voices are heard.

The answers you get to these and to other questions you will discover in the following readings are concerned finally not just with the study of the past but also with how you as a reader and writer align yourself in the present—how you know what the sides are in American history and where your sympathies reside. The purpose of this chapter in the most general sense is to ask you to think about the role history plays in your own and other people's lives and how it defines (or challenges) our sense of identity as a people and as a nation.

READING THE CULTURE OF HISTORY

One way to think about the role history plays in people's lives is to think about how you have learned about the past. The opening two selections offer perspectives on how learning about history is not simply a matter of learning what happened in the past. As Mary Gordon suggests in "More Than Just a Shrine: Paying Homage to the Ghosts of Ellis Island," visiting historical sites can be more than a history lesson. It can also offer an occasion to honor ancestors, in this case the Irish, Italians, and Lithuanian Jews in

Gordon's family who immigrated to the United States around the turn of the century and whose lives show up only as statistics in the official historical record. By the same token, in "Columbus in Chains," a chapter selected from the novel *Annie John*, Jamaica Kincaid reveals how a young West Indian schoolgirl learns which "side" she is on by studying the history of Columbus's voyages to the New World. Taken together, these two readings selections indicate how writers have constructed their own histories, against the grain of the familiar stories of immigration or Christopher Columbus, by retelling these stories for their own purposes. What these readings suggest is that the meaning of the past can never be complete. We can never fully exhaust the meaning of the past because reasons and urgencies in the present seem to compel new versions of history, new plots, and new interpretations.

The next selection, "Unsettling the Old West," by Richard Bernstein, is a feature story on revisionist historians that raises questions about how professional historians do history. As Bernstein notes, a generation of Western historians are at work revising the dominant view of westward expansion and settlement, offering new perspectives on what Frederick Jackson Turner called "the significance of the frontier in American history" in his seminal essay by that name, originally published in 1890. Turner's hypothesis that the frontier decisively influenced the development of individualism, democracy, and nationalism has shaped generations of American historians and is still echoed in American history textbooks. But the frontier hypothesis has also entered into the national mythology, portraying the pioneering experience of the nineteenth century as the source of a hardy, independent, freedom-loving people. According to Bernstein, to challenge Turner's view of American history, therefore, is to challenge the national mythology with which it has become intertwined. To retell the story of the frontier, as revisionist historians are making clear, is also to rethink the matter of what purposes are being enacted—the taming and settlement of the wilderness or the military conquest of the original inhabitants? The mastery of nature through logging, mining, and irrigation systems in the West or the courting of ecological disaster?

The next cluster of readings all concern the Vietnam War and make up a short case study of how the history of this traumatic time gets told and interpreted, not only by professional historians but also by participants and by Hollywood. The first selection pairs two readings, "The Tragedy of Vietnam," from George B. Tindall and David E. Shi's textbook *America: A Narrative History*, and a number of passages, grouped under the title "God's Country and American Know-How," from Loren Baritz's book-length study of the cultural causes of the Vietnam War, *Backfire: A History of How American Culture Led Us Into the Vietnam War*. Each selection, as you will see, offers an explanation of American military involvement in Vietnam but differs considerably in scope and emphasis.

The next three readings offer personal accounts of the Vietnam War, giving us voices from the war of ordinary people who are not always heard in the official record. In the first, "When Heaven and Earth Changed Places," Le Ly Hayslip explains the war from the perspective of Vietnamese peasants in the countryside, while "Private First Class Reginald 'Malik' Edwards," an oral history from Wallace Terry's book *Bloods*, offers the recollections of an American soldier. The third selection, Molly Ivin's "A Short Story About the Vietnam War Memorial" recreates the visit of a young woman to the

Vietnam War Memorial in Washington, D.C., and reveals how events from the past live on in the memories of ordinary people.

In the final selection, "Historical Memory, Film, and the Vietnam Era," Michael Klein analyzes how Hollywood movies have represented the Vietnam War. Klein suggests that the cultural meanings of historical events are determined not only by textbooks and official accounts but also by movies, novels, songs, and television shows that shape the living historical memory of a people in selective ways.

As you read, think, talk, and write about how American history has been constructed, you will be asked to consider where the meanings Americans ascribe to their history come from and how the meanings we give to the past position people in relation to the social, cultural, and political realities of the present. What do Americans as a people choose to remember and commemorate about their past? How does historical memory influence life in contemporary America?

Mary Gordon

MORE THAN JUST A SHRINE: PAYING HOMAGE TO THE GHOSTS OF ELLIS ISLAND

Mary Gordon is an acclaimed novelist and short-story writer who teaches at Barnard College. Her novels *Final Payments, The Company of Women,* and *The Other Side* explore the history and culture of Irish Catholics in America. In the following selection, an essay originally published in the *New York Times* (1987), Gordon offers her personal reflections on the history of immigration that brought her ancestors—Irish, Italian, and Lithuanian Jews—to the United States by way of Ellis Island, the point of entry in New York Harbor for over 16 million immigrants between 1892 and 1924. In her essay, Gordon suggests that history is a living relationship to the past, in this case to the "ghosts of Ellis Island" she wants to honor.

Suggestion for Reading

- As you read, notice that Mary Gordon provides a good deal of historical information about Ellis Island and yet her main point is to establish her own personal connection to this American landmark. Mark passages where Gordon locates herself in relation to what took place in the past.

◆

I once sat in a hotel in Bloomsbury trying to have breakfast alone. A Russian with a habit of compulsively licking his lips asked if he could join me. I was afraid to say no; I thought it might be bad for détente. He explained to me that he was a linguist and that he always liked to talk to Americans to see if he could make any connection between their speech and their ethnic background. When I told him about my mixed ancestry—my mother is Irish and Italian, my father was a Lithuanian Jew—he began jumping up and down in his seat, rubbing his hands together and licking his lips even more frantically.

"Ah," he said, "so you are really somebody who comes from what is called the boiling pot of America." Yes, I told him; yes, I was; but I quickly rose to leave. I thought it would be too hard to explain to him the relation of the boiling potters to the main course, and I wanted to get to the British Museum. I told him that the only thing I could think of that united people whose backgrounds, histories, and points of view were utterly diverse was that their people had landed at a place called Ellis Island.

I didn't tell him that Ellis Island was the only American landmark I'd ever visited. How could I describe to him the estrangement I'd always felt from the kind of traveler who visits shrines to America's past greatness, those rebuilt forts with muskets behind glass and sabers mounted on the walls and gift shops selling maple sugar candy in the shape of Indian headdresses, those reconstructed villages with tables set for fifty and the Paul Revere silver gleaming? All that Americana—Plymouth Rock, Gettysburg, Mount Vernon, Valley Forge—it all inhabits for me a zone of blurred abstraction with far less hold on my imagination than the Bastille or Hampton Court. I suppose I've always known that my uninterest in it contains a large component of the willed: I am American, and those places purport to be my history. But they are not mine.

Ellis Island is, though; it's the one place I can be sure my people are connected to. And so I made a journey there to find my history, like any Rotarian traveling in his Winnebago to Antietam to find his. I had become part of that humbling democracy of people looking in some site for a past that has grown unreal. The monument I traveled to was not, however, a tribute to some old glory. The minute I set foot upon the island I could feel all that it stood for: insecurity, obedience, anxiety, dehumanization, the terrified and careful deference of the displaced. I hadn't traveled to the Battery and boarded a ferry across from the Statue of Liberty to raise flags or breathe a richer, more triumphant air. I wanted to do homage to the ghosts.

I felt them everywhere, from the moment I disembarked and saw the building with its high-minded brick, its hopeful little lawn, its ornamental cornices. The place was derelict when I arrived; it had not functioned for more than thirty years—almost as long as the time it had operated at full capacity as a major immigration center. I was surprised to learn what a small part of history Ellis Island had occupied. The main building was constructed in 1892, then rebuilt between 1898 and 1900 after a fire. Most of the immigrants who arrived during the latter half of the nineteenth century, mainly northern and western Europeans, landed not at Ellis Island but on the western tip of the Battery, at Castle Garden, which had opened as a receiving center for immigrants in 1855.

By the 1880s, the facilities at Castle Garden had grown scandalously inadequate. Officials looked for an island on which to build a new immigration center, because they thought that on an island immigrants could be more easily protected from swindlers and quickly transported to railroad terminals in New Jersey. Bedloe's Island was considered, but New Yorkers were aghast at the idea of a "Babel" ruining their beautiful new treasure, "Liberty Enlightening the World." The statue's sculptor, Frédéric-Auguste Bartholdi, reacted to the prospect of immigrants landing near his masterpiece in horror; he called it a "monstrous plan." So much for Emma Lazarus.

Ellis Island was finally chosen because the citizens of New Jersey petitioned the federal government to remove from the island an old naval powder magazine that they thought dangerously close to the Jersey shore. The explosives were removed; no one wanted the island for anything. It was the perfect place to build an immigration center.

I thought about the island's history as I walked into the building and made my way to the room that was the center in my imagination of the Ellis Island experience: the Great Hall. It had been made real for me in the stark, accusing photographs of Louis Hine and others, who took those pictures to make a point. It was in the Great Hall that everyone had waited—waiting, always, the great vocation of the dispossessed. The room was empty, except for me and a handful of other visitors and the park ranger who showed us around. I felt myself grow insignificant in that room, with its huge semicircular windows, its air, even in dereliction, of solid and official probity.

I walked in the deathlike expansiveness of the room's disuse and tried to think of what it might have been like, filled and swarming. More than sixteen million immigrants came through that room; approximately 250,000 were rejected. Not really a large proportion, but the implications for the rejected were dreadful. For some, there was nothing to go back to, or there was certain death; for others, who left as adventurers, to return would be to adopt in local memory the fool's role, and the failure's. No wonder that the island's history includes reports of three thousand suicides.

Sometimes immigrants could pass through Ellis Island in mere hours, though for some the process took days. The particulars of the experience in the Great Hall were often influenced by the political events and attitudes on the mainland. In the 1890s and the first years of the new century, when cheap labor was needed, the newly built receiving center took in its immigrants with comparatively little question. But as the century progressed, the economy worsened, eugenics became both scientifically respectable and popular, and World War I made American xenophobia seem rooted in fact.

Immigration acts were passed; newcomers had to prove, besides moral correctness and financial solvency, their ability to read. Quota laws came into effect, limiting the number of immigrants from southern and eastern Europe to less than 14 percent of the total quota. Intelligence tests were biased against all non-English-speaking persons, and medical examinations became increasingly strict, until the machinery of immigration nearly collapsed under its own weight. The Second Quota Law of 1924 provided that all immigrants be inspected and issued visas at American consular offices in Europe, rendering the center almost obsolete.

On the day of my visit, my mind fastened upon the medical inspections, which had always seemed to me most emblematic of the ignominy and terror the immigrants ensured. The medical inspectors, sometimes dressed in uniforms like soldiers, were particularly obsessed with a disease of the eyes called trachoma, which they checked for by flipping back the immigrants' top eyelids with a hook used for buttoning gloves—a method that sometimes resulted in the transmission of the disease to healthy people.

Mothers feared that if their children cried too much, their red eyes would be mistaken for a symptom of the disease and the whole family would be sent home. Those immigrants suspected of some physical disability had initials chalked on their coats. I remembered the photographs I'd seen of people standing, dumbstruck and innocent as cattle, with their manifest numbers hung around their necks and initials marked in chalk upon their coats: "E" for eye trouble, "K" for hernia, "L" for lameness, "X" for mental defects, "H" for heart disease.

I thought of my grandparents as I stood in the room: my seventeen-year-old grandmother, coming alone from Ireland in 1896, vouched for by a stranger who had found her a place as a domestic servant to some Irish who had done well. I tried to imagine the assault it all must have been for her; I've been to her hometown, a collection of farms with a main street—smaller than the athletic field of my local public school. She must have watched the New York skyline as the first- and second-class passengers were whisked off the gangplank with the most cursory of inspections while she was made to board a ferry to the new immigration center.

What could she have made of it—this buff-painted wooden structure with its towers and its blue slate roof, a place *Harper's Weekly* described as "a latter-day watering place hotel"? It would have been the first time she had heard people speaking something other than English. She would have mingled with people carrying baskets on their heads and eating foods unlike any she had ever seen—dark-eyed people, like the Sicilian she would marry ten years later, who came over with his family at thirteen, the man of the family, responsible even then for his mother and sister. I don't know what they thought, my grandparents, for they were not expansive people, nor romantic; they didn't like to think of what they called "the hard times," and their trip across the ocean was the single adventurous act of lives devoted after landing to security, respectability, and fitting in.

What is the potency of Ellis Island for someone like me—an American, obviously, but one who has always felt that the country really belonged to the early settlers, that, as J. F. Powers wrote in *Morte D'Urban,* it had been "handed down to them by the Pilgrims, George Washington and others, and that they were taking a risk in letting you live in it." I have never been the victim of overt discrimination; nothing I have wanted has been denied me because of the accidents of blood. But I suppose it is part of being an American to be engaged in a somewhat tiresome but always self-absorbing process of national definition. And in this process, I have found in traveling to Ellis Island an important piece of evidence that could remind me I was right to feel my differentness. Something had happened to my people on that island, a result of the eternal wrongheadedness of American protectionism and the predictabilities of simple greed. I came to the island, too, so I could tell the ghosts that I was one of them, and that I honored them—their stoicism, and their innocence, the fear that turned them inward, and their pride. I wanted to tell them that I liked them better than I did the Americans who made them pass through the Great Hall and stole their names and chalked their weaknesses in public on their clothing. And to tell the ghosts what I have always thought: that American history was a very classy party that was not much fun until they arrived, brought the good food, turned up the music, and taught everyone to dance.

SUGGESTIONS FOR DISCUSSION

1. Mary Gordon describes the "estrangement I'd always felt from the kind of traveler who visits shrines to America's past greatness" and goes on to say that "those places purport to be my history. But they are not mine." Why does Gordon feel this way? What is she suggesting about the way we experience the history of America? Do some parts belong to you but not others?

2. What historical landmarks have you visited, with your family or on class trips in elementary or high school? What were your feelings about these trips? Compare your experience to Gordon's. Did you experience these historical sites as part of your history? Explain.

3. Gordon says that Ellis Island is "the one place I can be sure my people are connected to." Name a place your people are connected to, where you could, as Gordon puts it, "do homage to the ghosts." To what extent is the place you've named alike or different from the places your classmates have named?

SUGGESTIONS FOR WRITING

1. Mary Gordon says the one thing that unifies her ancestors—Irish, Italian, and Lithuanian Jews "whose backgrounds, histories, and points of view were utterly diverse"—is that they all landed at Ellis Island. Write an essay that explores the diversity among your ancestors and considers whether there is something—a place such as Ellis Island or a historical event such as immigration—that unites them.

2. Use Gordon's account of her visit to Ellis Island as a model to write an essay that explains your response to visiting a historical site. Make sure you explain the historical importance of the place you visited, but also follow Gordon's example to explain your own personal relation to that history. Did you experience the place as part of a history you felt connected to or did you, for some reason, feel estranged?

3. Gordon's essay suggests that history is as much a matter of paying "homage to the ghosts" as it is learning a chronology of events. Pick a historical figure, place, or event in American history with which you feel an especially strong personal identification. Describe the person, place, or event and then explain the reasons for your identification. Use the essay as an occasion to pay homage, to explain your personal allegiances and why the person, place, or event seems important to you.

Jamaica Kincaid

COLUMBUS IN CHAINS

Jamaica Kincaid is an award-winning novelist, short-story writer, and essayist who grew up on the West Indian island of Antigua and now lives in Vermont. Her fiction, *At the Bottom of the River, Annie John,* and *Lucy,* concerns the coming of age of a young West Indian woman, the intense emotional bonds between mothers and daughters, and the struggles of Kincaid's main character to assert her independence and individuality. The following selection,

"Columbus in Chains," was originally published as a short story in the *New Yorker* and then became a chapter in *Annie John* (1985). Here, Annie John, Kincaid's precious heroine, offers readers an alternative perspective on Columbus's voyages to the New World.

Suggestion for Reading

- The following reading explores, among other things, the interaction of two cultures in the West Indies—the British culture of the schools and the local Antiguan culture. As you read, annotate passages where the narrator Annie John gives us clues to the two cultures and to their relationship.

———————————◆———————————

Outside, as usual, the sun shone, the trade winds blew; on her way to put some starched clothes on the line, my mother shooed some hens out of her garden; Miss Dewberry baked the buns, some of which my mother would buy for my father and me to eat with our afternoon tea; Miss Henry brought the milk, a glass of which I would drink with my lunch, and another glass of which I would drink with the bun from Miss Dewberry; my mother prepared our lunch; my father noted some perfectly idiotic thing his partner in housebuilding, Mr. Oatie, had done, so that over lunch he and my mother could have a good laugh.

The Anglican church bell struck eleven o'clock—one hour to go before lunch. I was then sitting at my desk in my classroom. We were having a history lesson—the last lesson of the morning. For taking first place over all the other girls, I had been given a prize, a copy of a book called *Roman Britain,* and I was made prefect of my class. What a mistake the prefect part had been, for I was among the worst-behaved in my class and did not at all believe in setting myself up as a good example, the way a prefect was supposed to do. Now I had to sit in the prefect's seat—the first seat in the front row, the seat from which I could stand up and survey quite easily my classmates. From where I sat I could see out the window. Sometimes when I looked out, I could see the sexton going over to the minister's house. The sexton's daughter, Hilarene, a disgusting model of good behavior and keen attention to scholarship, sat next to me, since she took second place. The minister's daughter, Ruth, sat in the last row, the row reserved for all the dunce girls. Hilarene, of course, I could not stand. A girl that good would never do for me. I would probably not have cared so much for first place if I could be sure it would not go to her. Ruth I liked, because she was such a dunce and came from England and had yellow hair. When I first met her, I used to walk her home and sing bad songs to her just to see her turn pink, as if I had spilled hot water all over her.

Our books, *A History of the West Indies,* were open in front of us. Our day had begun with morning prayers, then a geometry lesson, then it was over to the science building for a lesson in "Introductory Physics" (not a subject we cared much for), taught by the most dingy-toothed Mr. Slacks, a teacher from Canada, then precious recess, and now this, our history lesson. Recess had the usual drama: this time, I coaxed Gwen out of her disappointment at not being allowed to join the junior choir. Her father—how many times had I wished he would become a leper and so be banished to a leper colony for the rest of my long and happy life with Gwen—had forbidden it, giving as his reason that she lived too far away from church, where choir rehearsals were conducted, and that it would be dangerous for her, a young girl, to walk home alone at night in the dark. Of course, all the streets had lamplight, but it was useless to point that out to him. Oh, how it would have pleased us to press and rub our knees together as we sat in our pew while pretending to pay close attention to Mr. Simmons, our choirmaster, as he waved his baton up and down and across, and how it would have pleased us even more to walk home together, alone in the "early dusk" (the way Gwen had phrased it, a ready phrase always on her tongue), stopping, if there was a full moon, to lie down in a pasture and expose our bosoms in the moonlight. We had heard that full moonlight would make our breasts grow to a size we would like. Poor Gwen! When I first heard from her that she was one of ten children, right on the spot I told her that I would love only her, since her mother already had so many other people to love.

Our teacher, Miss Edward, paced up and down in front of the class in her usual way. In front of her desk stood a small table, and on it stood the dunce cap. The dunce cap was in the shape of a coronet, with an adjustable opening in the back, so that it could fit any head. It was made of cardboard with a shiny gold paper covering and the word "DUNCE" in shiny red paper on the front. When the sun shone on it, the dunce cap was all aglitter, almost as if you were being tricked into thinking it a desirable thing to wear. As Miss Edward paced up and down, she would pass between us and the dunce cap like an eclipse. Each Friday morning, we were given a small test to see how well we had learned the things taught to us all week. The girl who scored lowest was made to wear the dunce cap all day the following Monday. On many Mondays, Ruth wore it—only, with her short yellow hair, when the dunce cap was sitting on her head she looked like a girl attending a birthday party in *The Schoolgirl's Own Annual.*

It was Miss Edward's way to ask one of us a question the answer to which she was sure the girl would not know and then put the same question to another girl who she was sure would know the answer. The girl who did not answer correctly would then have to repeat the correct answer in the exact words of the other girl. Many times, I had heard my exact words repeated over and over again, and I liked it especially when the girl doing the repeating was one I didn't care about very much. Pointing a finger at Ruth, Miss Edward asked a question the answer to which was "On the third of November 1493, a Sunday morning, Christopher Columbus discovered Dominica." Ruth, of course, did not know the answer, as she did not know the answer to many questions about the West Indies. I could hardly blame her. Ruth had come all the way from England. Perhaps she did not want to be in the West Indies at all. Perhaps she wanted to be in England, where no one would remind her constantly of the terrible things her ancestors had done; perhaps she had felt even worse when her father was a missionary in Africa. I could see how Ruth felt from looking at her face. Her ancestors had been the masters, while ours had been the slaves. She had such a lot to be ashamed of, and by being with us every day she was always being reminded. We could look everybody in the eye, for our ancestors had done nothing wrong except just sit somewhere, defenseless. Of course, sometimes, what with our teachers and our books, it was hard for us to tell on which side we really now belonged—with the masters or the slaves—for it was all history, it was all in the past, and everybody behaved differently now; all of us celebrated Queen Victoria's birthday, even though she had been dead a long time. But we, the descendants of the slaves, knew quite well what had really happened, and I was sure that if the tables had been turned we would have acted differently;

I was sure that if our ancestors had gone from Africa to Europe and come upon the people living there, they would have taken a proper interest in the Europeans on first seeing them, and said, "How nice," and then gone home to tell their friends about it.

I was sitting at my desk, having these thoughts to myself. I don't know how long it had been since I lost track of what was going on around me. I had not noticed that the girl who was asked the question after Ruth failed—a girl named Hyacinth— had only got a part of the answer correct. I had not noticed that after these two attempts Miss Edward had launched into a harangue about what a worthless bunch we were compared to girls of the past. In fact, I was no longer on the same chapter we were studying. I was way ahead, at the end of the chapter about Columbus's third voyage. In this chapter, there was a picture of Columbus that took up a whole page, and it was in color—one of only five color pictures in the book. In this picture, Columbus was seated in the bottom of a ship. He was wearing the usual three-quarter trousers and a shirt with enormous sleeves, both the trousers and shirt made of maroon-colored velvet. His hat, which was cocked up on one side of his head, had a gold feather in it, and his black shoes had huge gold buckles. His hands and feet were bound up in chains, and he was sitting there staring off into space, looking quite dejected and miserable. The picture had as a title "Columbus in Chains," printed at the bottom of the page. What had happened was that the usually quarrelsome Columbus had got into a disagreement with people who were even more quarrelsome, and a man named Bobadilla, representing King Ferdinand and Queen Isabella, had sent him back to Spain fettered in chains attached to the bottom of a ship. What just desserts, I thought, for I did not like Columbus. How I loved this picture—to see the usually triumphant Columbus, brought so low, seated at the bottom of a boat just watching things go by. Shortly after I first discovered it in my history book, I heard my mother read out loud to my father a letter she had received from her sister, who still lived with her mother and father in the very same Dominica, which is where my mother came from. Ma Chess was fine, wrote my aunt, but Pa Chess was not well. Pa Chess was having a bit of trouble with his limbs; he was not able to go about as he pleased; often he had to depend on someone else to do one thing or another for him. My mother read the letter in quite a state, her voice rising to a higher pitch with each sentence. After she read the part about Pa Chess's stiff limbs, she turned to my father and laughed as she said, "So the great man can no longer just get up and go. How I would love to see his face now!" When I next saw the picture of Columbus sitting there all locked up in his chains, I wrote under it the words "The Great Man Can No Longer Just Get Up and Go." I had written this out with my fountain pen, and in Old English lettering—a script I had recently mastered. As I sat there looking at the picture, I traced the words with my pen over and over, so that the letters grew big and you could read what I had written from not very far away. I don't know how long it was before I heard that my name, Annie John, was being said by this bellowing dragon in the form of Miss Edward bearing down on me.

I had never been a favorite of hers. Her favorite was Hilarene. It must have pained Miss Edward that I so often beat out Hilarene. Not that I liked Miss Edward and wanted her to like me back, but as the other teachers regarded me with much affection, would always tell my mother that I was the most charming student they had ever had, beamed at me when they saw me coming, and were very sorry when they had to write some version of this on my report card: "Annie is an unusually bright girl. She is well behaved in class, at least in the presence of her masters and mistresses, but behind their backs and outside the classroom quite the opposite is true." When my mother read this or something like it, she would burst into tears. She had hoped to display, with a great flourish, my report card to her friends, along with whatever prize I had won. Instead, the report card would have to take a place at the bottom of the old trunk in which she kept any important thing that had to do with me. I became not a favorite of Miss Edward's in the following way: Each Friday afternoon, the girls in the lower forms were given, instead of a last lesson period, an extra-long recess. We were to use this in lady-like recreation—walks, chats about the novels and poems we were reading, showing each other the new embroidery stitches we had learned to master in home class, or something just as seemly. Instead, some of the girls would play a game of cricket or rounders or stones, but most of us would go to the far end of the school grounds and play band. In this game, of which teachers and parents disapproved and which was sometimes absolutely forbidden, we would place our arms around each other's waist or shoulders, forming lines of ten or so girls, and then we would dance from one end of the school grounds to the other. As we danced, we would sometimes chat these words: "Tee la la la, come go. Tee la la la, come go." At other times we would sing a popular calypso song which usually had lots of unladylike words to it. Up and down the school-yard, away from our teachers, we would dance and sing. At the end of recess—forty-five minutes—we were missing ribbons and other ornaments from our hair, the pleats of our linen tunics became unset, the collars of our blouses were pulled out, and we were soaking wet all the way down to our bloomers. When the school bell rang, we would make a whooping sound, as if in a great panic, and then we would throw ourselves on top of each other as we laughed and shrieked. We would then run back to our classes, where we prepared to file into the auditorium for evening prayers. After that, it was home for the weekend. But how could we go straight home after all that excitement? No sooner were we on the street than we would form little groups, depending on the direction we were headed in. I was never keen on joining them on the way home, because I was sure I would run into my mother. Instead, my friends and I would go to our usual place near the back of the churchyard and sit on the tombstones of people who had been buried there way before slavery was abolished, in 1833. We would sit and sing bad songs, use forbidden words, and, of course, show each other various parts of our bodies. While some of us watched, the others would walk up and down on the large tombstones showing off their legs. It was immediately a popular idea; everybody soon wanted to do it. It wasn't long before many girls—the ones whose mothers didn't pay strict attention to what they were doing—started to come to school on Fridays wearing not bloomers under their uniforms but underpants trimmed with lace and satin frills. It also wasn't long before an end came to all that. One Friday afternoon, Miss Edward, on her way home from school, took a shortcut through the churchyard. She must have heard the commotion we were making, because there she suddenly was, saying, "What is the meaning of this?"—just the very thing someone like her would say if she came unexpectedly on something like us. It was obvious that I was the ringleader. Oh, how I wished the ground would open up and take her in, but it did not. We all, shamefacedly, slunk home, I with Miss Edward at my side. Tears came to my mother's eyes when she heard what I had done. It was apparently such a bad thing that my mother couldn't bring herself to repeat my misdeed to my father in my presence. I got the usual punishment of dinner alone, outside under the breadfruit tree, but added on to that, I was not

allowed to go to the library on Saturday, and on Sunday, after Sunday school and dinner, I was not allowed to take a stroll in the botanical gardens, where Gwen was waiting
for me in the bamboo grove.

• • •

That happened when I was in the first form. Now here Miss Edward stood. Her
whole face was on fire. Her eyes were bulging out of her head. I was sure that at any
minute they would land at my feet and roll away. The small pimples on her face, already looking as if they were constantly irritated, now ballooned into huge, on-the-
verge-of-exploding boils. Her head shook from side to side. Her strange bottom,
which she carried high in the air, seemed to rise up so high that it almost touched the
ceiling. Why did I not pay attention, she said. My impertinence was beyond endurance. She then found a hundred words for the different forms my impertinence
took. On she went. I was just getting used to this amazing bellowing when suddenly
she was speechless. In fact, everything stopped. Her eyes stopped, her bottom
stopped, her pimples stopped. Yes she had got close enough so that her eyes caught a
glimpse of what I had done to my textbook. The glimpse soon led to closer inspec-
tion. It was bad enough that I had defaced my schoolbook by writing in it. That I
should write under the picture of Columbus "The Great Man. . ." etc. was just too
much. I had gone too far this time, defaming one of the great men in history,
Christopher Columbus, discoverer of the island that was my home. And now look at
me. I was not even hanging my head in remorse. Had my peers ever seen anyone so
arrogant, so blasphemous?

I was sent to the headmistress, Miss Moore. As punishment, I was removed
from my position as prefect, and my place was taken by the odious Hilarene. As an
added punishment, I was ordered to copy Books I and II of *Paradise Lost,* by John
Milton, and to have it done a week from that day. I then couldn't wait to get home to
lunch and the comfort of my mother's kisses and arms. I had nothing to worry about
there yet; it would be a while before my mother and father heard of my bad deeds.
What a terrible morning! Seeing my mother would be such a tonic—something to
pick me up.

When I got home, my mother kissed me absentmindedly. My father had got
home ahead of me, and they were already deep in conversation, my father regaling
her with some unusually outlandish thing the oaf Mr. Oatie had done. I washed my
hands and took my place at table. My mother brought me my lunch. I took one
smell of it, and I could tell that it was the much hated breadfruit. My mother said
not at all, it was a new kind of rice imported from Belgium, and not breadfruit,
mashed and forced through a ricer, as I thought. She went back to talking to my father. My father could hardly get a few words out of his mouth before she was a jelly-
fish of laughter. I sat there, putting my food in my mouth. I could not believe that
she couldn't see how miserable I was and so reach out a hand to comfort me and ca-
ress my cheek, the way she usually did when she sensed that something was amiss
with me. I could not believe how she laughed at everything he said, and how bitter it
made me feel to see how much she liked him. I ate my meal. The more I ate of it,
the more I was sure that it was breadfruit. When I finished, my mother got up to re-

move my plate. As she started out the door, I said, "Tell me, really, the name of the thing I just ate."

My mother said, "You just ate some breadfruit. I made it look like rice so that you would eat it. It's very good for you, filled with lots of vitamins." As she said this, she laughed. She was standing half inside the door, half outside. Her body was in the shade of our house, but her head was in the sun. When she laughed, her mouth opened to show off big, shiny, sharp white teeth. It was as if my mother had suddenly turned into a crocodile.

SUGGESTIONS FOR DISCUSSION

1. Describe the perspective of the narrator in *Annie John*. Identify passages where Annie John locates herself in relation to the history of her people. In what sense is Annie's "defacing" her textbook a rewriting of history? What is Annie's version of the story of Columbus and what is its relation to the official version in the schools and textbooks?

2. The key event in the chapter "Columbus in Chains" involves an act of writing—when Annie John letters "The Great Man Can No Longer Just Get Up and Go" under the picture of Columbus in chains—but there are also a number of other references to reading and writing and to written materials throughout the chapter. Identify passages where reading and writing take place or Annie John mentions written material of one kind or another. What role, literally and symbolically, do reading and writing play in this chapter?

3. Describe your own experience learning history in school. How does it compare to Annie's? Take into account how teachers and textbooks represented the history of your people.

SUGGESTIONS FOR WRITING

1. In the following passage, Annie John records Miss Edwards' reaction to writing in her textbook:

> It was bad enough that I had defaced my textbook by writing in it. That I should write under the picture of Columbus "The Great Man. . . " etc. was just too much. I had gone too far this time, defaming one of the great men in history, Christopher Columbus, discoverer of the island that was my home.

Write an essay that explains why Annie John has "gone too far" and what makes her act of writing (in Miss Edwards's words) "arrogant" and "blasphemous." Begin by analyzing Miss Edwards' reaction, but use this analysis to explore the versions of history presented in this chapter. Provide your own evaluation of what makes Annie's act appear to be a such a transgression.

2. Speaking of the history of her ancestors, Annie John says, "Of course, sometimes what with our teachers and our books, it was hard for us to tell on which side we really now belonged—with the masters or the slaves—for it was all history, it was all in the past, everybody behaved differently then." A line or two later, however, Annie John says that "we, the descendants of the slaves, knew quite well what had really happened." Write an essay that explains how learning history in school has taught you to which side you belong. How does the history you learned in school present "sides"? You might want to consider whether the history of your ancestors and their side of things is presented in history textbooks or whether you, like Annie John, have learned the history of your people elsewhere.

3. Part of the attraction of this reading is the delight readers feel, perhaps in secret, when Annie John writes in her textbook to debunk the myth of Columbus and to set the record straight. Can you think of a historical figure or a historical event you've always wanted to debunk and set the record straight about? Write an essay in which you represent a historical figure or event, as Annie does with Columbus, for what in your judgment it really is. You'll want to pick something in history that has acquired mythic proportions but that you can show another and perhaps more revealing side to. Begin your essay with the conventional view of the event or person but then replace this view with your own and draw out the significance of your rewriting of history.

Richard Bernstein

UNSETTLING THE OLD WEST

Richard Bernstein is the author of *Fragile Glory,* a portrait of France and French culture, and a correspondent for *The New York Times* who writes frequently about cultural and intellectual affairs. His feature article "Unsettling the Old West" appeared originally in *The New York Times* (March 18, 1990). Bernstein explains how professional historians are revising the standard textbook version of the American frontier—presented around the turn of the century by Frederick Jackson Turner—that the pioneer experience and westward expansion were instrumental in shaping the American national character and the country's commitments to individualism, democracy, and nationalism. Bernstein's article suggests that the way we look at the past is shaped to a large extent by the cultural mood of the present.

Suggestion for Reading

• As you read, you will notice that Richard Bernstein has written brief profiles of four new historians of the American West—Patricia Nelson Limerick, Donald Worster, Peggy Pascoe, and Richard White. Underline and annotate passages in the article where Bernstein introduces each of the historians and explains the focus of their research.

---◆---

Ghost towns are among her first exhibits. Patricia Nelson Limerick, who teaches Western history at the University of Colorado, takes out a bundle of glossy black-and-white prints that she keeps at her home in Boulder and shows me scenes of dilapidated cabins, saloons, sagging mining shacks amid empty landscapes.

"If you live in Western America, you know that there are relics all over the place of things that didn't work out," she says, using her exhibits to make a broader point. Limerick, along with a growing number of scholars, is busily promoting an entirely unromantic vision of the history of the American West, a vision where failure thrusts itself rudely into former, more comforting notions of success. "The West is the place where everybody was supposed to escape failure," she continues, "but it didn't happen that way."

Limerick, who is 38 years old, and other—generally young—historians of the American West are saying that traditional Western history, the stuff we were taught in elementary schools and universities alike, the narrative that Limerick sometimes calls "the old hat frontier history" in which "heroic pioneers brought civilization to a savage wilderness," is distorted, misleading, exclusive, chauvinistic and, in the words of some more rhetorically radical historians, even "racist" and "sexist." As an example of this objectionable approach, she offers a key sentence in the standard textbook in the field, the fifth edition of "Westward Expansion: A History of the American Frontier," by Ray Allen Billington and Martin Ridge: "The history of the American West is, almost by definition, a triumphal narrative for it traces a virtually unbroken chain of successes in national expansion." The myth, say the rebellious, dissenting historians, assumes an untamed land subdued by ruggedly independent white male settlers who created democracy, prosperity and the glories of American life. The myth, they vigorously contend, is wrong.

Indeed, as Limerick shows her pictures and slides, she seems to take a certain sardonic pleasure in pointing out evidence of how shaky the West really was—the busts that followed booms in the frontier economy, the sudden abandonment of newly settled places after brief periods of habitation. There is, for example, a sagging mineshaft house in Caribou, Colo. And there is a row of wind-battered wood buildings lining an empty street in a town surrounded by treeless mountains; Limerick calls the town "the ironically named Apex." One of her favorites is Ashcroft, Colo., an abandoned mining town just a few miles from Aspen, where the beautiful people congregate. Ashcroft, whose buildings are laid out "as if a sculptor had placed them," is a town of such great natural beauty that it might inspire the sort of romantic sighs that once emanated from British romantics as they gazed upon the ruins of Greece and Rome. Limerick entertains no illusions of past glories. She told an audience in Casper, Wyo., last January: "Towns with Ashcroft's natural beauty do not stand a good chance of making us backslide from the new Western history, back to the vision of pioneers putting up quaint buildings in lovely open spaces, evidently for the pure pleasure of having rooms they could sit in and look out at the mountains."

For Limerick, the ghost towns provide undeniable proof that the West has a complicated, ambiguous history, a history as much of suffering as of fulfillment. Such skeptical notions no longer seem iconoclastic. Every other week there seems to be another academic conference in some Western locale. The pile of journal articles furthering the new historians' ideas grows higher and the shelf space taken up by their books ever longer—books like "Many Tender Ties: Women in Fur-Trade Society," by Sylvia Van Kirk; "Far From Home: Families of the Westward Journey," by Lillian Schlissel, Byrd Gibbens, and Elizabeth Hampsten; "Cannery Women, Cannery Wives: Mexican Women, Unionization, and the California Food Processing Industry," by Vicki L. Ruiz; "Forgotten Frontier: A History of Wyoming Coal Mining," by A. Dudley Gardner and Verla R. Flores. The regional political establishment has become increasingly receptive to a vision of the West as a place of pitiless struggle involving not only Gary Cooper white guys, but just about every human type—Indian chiefs and black newspaper men, society dames and prostitutes, missionaries and Chinese real estate investors, fur trappers and squaws. The Western Governors Association is publishing a collection of essays on new ways of looking at the West; the one by Limerick—"The Rendezvous Model of Western American History"—stresses the view of the West, dear to the new historians, as the most ethnically diverse part of the country.

But wait. What is new here? Did Limerick, Van Kirk, Schlissel, and their colleagues discover ghost towns? Are they the first to penetrate the myth of the heroic West? One need only think of such famous American historians as Charles Beard or C. Vann Woodward to get a flavor of a revisionist, iconoclastic history of America, or of such historians of the West as Gerald Nash, Earl Pomeroy and Howard Lamar, whose works laid the foundation for today's frontal assault on the Hollywood version of Western expansion. These historians also described its costs, its violence, the destruction of both men and nature that the march across the continent entailed.

One of the main targets of the new historians is the very granddaddy, the great progenitor of modern Western American history, Frederick Jackson Turner, the Wisconsin-born scholar against whose turn-of-the-century frontier thesis all other interpretations of Western history have long been measured. For Turner, the existence of the frontier, that steadily receding zone of wilderness being invaded by the forces of civilization, gave America its special character, its rough-and-ready democracy, its stress on adaptability and innovation. The new historians charge Turner with being ethnocentric—of excluding everybody but white males from his account of the West. But earlier schools of thought had already subjected Turner to merciless, unfavorable scrutiny. He and his followers, some critics say, exaggerated the role of the frontier, making it not just an element in the Western story but the story itself.

What then, if anything, is truly different in the new history? Some scholars, perhaps a bit miffed at the attention Patricia Limerick is getting, whisper discontentedly that the whole thing is a media event, that there isn't much new in the new historians' work. But even these skeptics allow that the new scholarship represents a point of view, an attitude about the country, that in at least one key and potentially controversial respect marks it off from much of the revisionist scholarship on America that has appeared in the past. It is this: Many historians, skeptical of both Turner and Hollywood, took it as axiomatic that the Westward expansion was violent and often tragic for many—especially the Indians. Yet they saw it as an inevitable process, a historic good whose end, a free and powerful country stretching from sea to shining sea, justified the price. The new historians are not so sure. They are blazing a pioneer's trail toward an altered view of the moral status of America itself. The new historians question the very idea of a Western—and thus an American—success story. They represent a tipping of the moral scales to that unhappy point where national faults and imperfections seem to balance national virtues.

"My argument in Casper was that this region has had an advanced curriculum in failure," Limerick said during my visit to her home, a bungalow in the shadows of the Rocky Mountain foothills. Limerick is erudite and witty. She punctuates her scholarly points with anecdotes about everybody from Silverheels, a legendary Colorado prostitute, to Coronado, the ill-fated Spanish explorer. She has a pleasant self-deprecating sense of humor. At the same time, she sees it as her mission to impart lessons about environmental destruction and the costs of a boom-and-bust economy before, in her view, it's too late. "Failure has its tragic, injurious side," she told me. "It also has its educational side. Failure is one of the great opportunities to learn."

But read the works of these scholars and a certain gloom sets in. Things were not as great as we thought they were. More than half of the people who came out to strike it rich in gold and silver lost everything and went back, if they went back at all, nearly destitute. There was suffering and oppression, of women and of those who were black, Asian or Hispanic—and, of course, most conspicuously of all, Indians, who were cheated and massacred wholesale.

In his latest book, "Rivers of Empire," Donald Worster, a leading exponent of the new history who teaches at the University of Kansas, describes the great Western irrigation projects, the same projects that made deserts blossom, as an ecological and political misfortune. Western development brought about a "hydraulic society," he writes, one in which Federal and state bureaucracies combined with agribusiness to impose what was "increasingly a coercive, monolithic and hierarchical system, ruled by a power elite based on the ownership of capital and expertise." The result is "sharply alienating." It represents the brutality of the thirst for "total power" and "total possession." The original dream of a land of small, independent farmers was ruined.

Limerick, talking last fall to a group of Government space policy planners, poked fun at the "new frontier" metaphor, particularly as it applied to the exploration of space. Ronald Reagan, she reminded her audience, once compared the landing of the space shuttle Columbia—that emblem of "true grit"—to "the driving of the golden spike which completed the first transcontinental railroad." Limerick jumped all over the metaphor. "To anyone who is serious about history," she told the space planners, the golden spike "is also a reference to enterprises done with too much haste and grandstanding, and with too little care for detail." She listed, among the faults in the great transcontinental railroad venture, "executive misbehavior, large-scale corruption, shoddy construction, brutal labor exploitation, financial inefficiency." (It might be noted in this connection that Limerick's next book is tentatively entitled "Troubled Land: Failure and Defeat in Western Expansion." It's about "the working men and women whose dreams evaporated" and "the moral failure involved in building profitable enterprises on the basis of unrestrained, inhumane exploitation of labor.")

So persistently have the new historians debunked the Western myth that a number of other historians (including those who agree that some myths need smashing) feel uneasy, sensing that the pendulum is swinging too far in the other direction. A gentle critic, but also a mentor, is Howard R. Lamar, Sterling Professor of History at Yale, who taught Limerick and several other members of the new Western historians' group. They did their doctoral degrees under his direction. Professor Lamar distances himself from some of his pupils' ideas, even while praising them for their enthusiasm and energy. "I think that what we have here is an image of an ideal West, and the real West doesn't come up to it," he says. "So they tend to look at the dark side of things. There, I have to part company, but in a friendly way. I'm an optimist."

Less gentle is William H. Goetzmann, a Pulitzer Prize winner who teaches history and American studies at the University of Texas—and is also a former student of Lamar's at Yale. His harsher view of Limerick and company mingles skepticism over the supposed newness of some of the new historians' discoveries with a strong sense that the scales of judgment have tipped too far toward the negative. "They've discovered that there were Indian atrocities, that there were fights over water, that Mexicans were discriminated against, that mining stripped some of the land, that life was hard, and so on," Goetzmann objects, contending that these "discoveries" had already been made by other scholars, including himself, scholars who put the new elements of the picture into a more balanced perspective. "But that doesn't mean that the American Western experience wasn't important or that it doesn't have its positive side in American history."

● ● ●

To find all the practitioners of the new Western history you would have to travel a great deal, most of it in the West itself, to the great state and private universities and to tiny community colleges alike. For the most part, the new historians are Westerners themselves, and, as Professor Lamar remarked, they have a "ferocious" regional pride.

Limerick, born and raised in Banning, Calif.—a place that seemed dull to her as a child but whose cattle ranchers, Indian reservation, large black and Hispanic populations make it seem to her now a prototypical Western place—is clearly the most prominent and most visible of the new historians. This seems in part due to tremendous energy, to her wry sense of humor and skills as a public speaker, in part to her book "The Legacy of Conquest: the Unbroken Past of the American West," which is widely regarded as the most complete and intellectually compelling summary of the new historians' views. But she herself, a little uncomfortable with the attention she's gotten, is quick to name others in the new historians' school whose work she admires.

One of them is Peggy Pascoe, 35 years old, a soft-spoken woman who teaches at the University of Utah in Salt Lake City and is about to publish an expanded version of her doctoral thesis as a book. Pascoe was born in Butte, Mont. She went East to Sarah Lawrence College for a master's degree and then to Stanford University for her doctorate. She remembers Butte as a "town in decline. People lived in the past as much as in the present. Everybody had stories of the miners' strikes of 70 years before." Butte, she recalls, was once dominated by the Anaconda Copper Mining Company: "it was a town with a very large immigrant base."

There is nothing to suggest a revolutionary about Pascoe. She is trim and sedate, pensive and deliberate. Yet her chief concern, the history of women in the West, represents some of the bolder and more intensely revisionist themes of the new historians. Her forthcoming book, "Relations of Rescue: The Search for Female Moral Authority in the American West, 1874–1939," is a study of efforts by four middle-class white women of generally Victorian values to set up "rescue homes" for the female victims of "male abuse"—Chinese prostitutes in San Francisco, Mormon wives of polygamous husbands in Salt Lake City, Indian women on the Omaha Reservation in Nebraska and unmarried mothers in Denver. One of her underlying themes is that the inclusion of women does not merely enrich the overall picture; it changes it dramatically. She notes in this regard that some historians, aware of feminist scholarship, have added paragraphs here and there on women in an effort to redress the imbalance in favor of men—but in her view, this is inadequate compensation.

"It's 'add women and stir,'" says Pascoe. "It's adding the word 'women' without changing much of anything else." Or, as Limerick put it in her "Legacy of Conquest": "Exclude women from Western history, and unreality sets in. Restore them, and the Western drama gains a fully human cast of characters—males and females whose urges, needs, failings, and conflicts we can recognize and even share."

For Pascoe, the study of women also provides a point of departure to yet another central theme of the new historians: that American life has been unfair, even tragic to many. "I'd be inclined to say that the interesting questions about American history are questions about inequality," she says. Does that make her a radical? An academic revolutionary who would discount the very notion of American opportunity? "I'm not saying that inequality is the central factor of history, but that those are the questions that are most important for us as Americans to have answers to." It is this concern that prompts her to invoke what has become a common trinity in scholarly research these days: "Class, race and gender are the axes of inequality," she says, "and so for a historian interested in one sort of inequality—that is, gender inequality—theoretically it makes a great deal of sense to pay attention to other sorts of inequality, such as class and race."

Across the hall from Pascoe at the University of Utah is Richard White, whose specialty is the history of the environment and Indian history. White, 42, whose shoulder-length hair, mustache and casual dress suggest the 60's culture of protest, has just completed a textbook on Western history that he hopes will supplant Billington and Ridge, authors of the standard textbook in the field. He describes his entry into the historians' ranks as a kind of happy accident arising out of his 60's political activism.

"In 1968," he said, talking in his office at the university, where the windows frame the stunning Wasatch Mountains on the outskirts of Salt Lake City, "an Indian friend and I were going to the Democratic National Convention in Chicago." They were on their way to the anti-war demonstrations there. "The bus broke down," White recalled. "Many things happened. After a long interlude, we ended up in the Pacific Northwest at demonstrations for Indian fishing rights on the Nisqually River." White became interested in the Indians and then in the environment. He went to graduate school at the University of Washington where he wrote a doctoral dissertation on the environmental history of Island County, near Seattle.

That kind of history, studying the landscape the way other historians might read a document—determining how the land was shaped by human habitation and how it in turn shaped its habitants—represents a major concern of the new historians, one that White has developed in his book, "It's Your Misfortune and None of Mine: A History of the American West," soon to be published by the University of Oklahoma Press.

"My text doesn't mention the frontier," White observes, marking himself off from Turner and such Turnerians as Billington and Ridge. His point is that the very notion of a frontier is an ethnocentric one, deriving entirely from the point of view of the European settlers in the East. For the Indians and even for the early Spanish settlers of the Southwest, the "frontier" was, quite simply, home. The settlers coming from the East saw this vast territory as a "wilderness," but White argues that it was actually a landscape already deeply shaped and profoundly altered by centuries of Indian habitation. Competition among different peoples over the land—not its settlement by European pioneers—is, for White, the crux of Western history.

"I treat the West as a region," he says. "The whites moving in to the West represent one of a series of migrations but not the only one. For Western historians, the great challenge has been that Turner gave such a gratifying meaning, while the meaning that we get from Western history is not nearly as clear and not nearly as gratifying." What "we" are saying, he continued, "is that there are people left out, that the continent wasn't empty, that bad things happened that have to be mentioned. And so it does seem more pessimistic."

But what of criticisms like those of Professor Goetzmann, who believes that this stress on the "bad things" obscures a larger, happier reality—that many millions of people, not all of them white, have achieved a free and prosperous life in the American West? Do the new Western historians really intend to portray our collective past as a disaster?

"I wouldn't say it's a history of disaster," White said. "What we emphasize is costs. In the old Western history, the only costs were the obstacles that had to be overcome. One of the things we emphasize is that it matters where you're looking. If Indians are looking at American history, it's hard to see a triumph. Hispanics looking at American history, it's hard to see a triumph. That's not the whole story, but it's part of the story."

• • •

As I read and talked with the new historians, I began to realize that this eagerness to tell a different part of the story reflected a broader transformation in American intellectual life, encompassing more than just our conception of the territory west of the Mississippi. The work of White, Pascoe, Worster, Limerick and their colleagues bears a resemblance to efforts taking place elsewhere. Recently, the Board of Regents of the New York public school system, eager to compensate for centuries of European ethnocentrism, mandated a new curriculum that would give recognition to the contributions of non-whites. Two years ago, Stanford University provoked a national debate on the scholarly "canon" when its faculty voted to revise required courses based on a list of Western classics, substituting for some traditional works on the syllabus works whose emphasis is "women, minorities, and persons of color." In the same spirit, a recent book entitled "Colorado Profiles" carefully included an ethnic cross-section: White tycoons and gunslingers stood cheek by jowl between its covers with the Cheyenne chief Black Kettle; the New York Jewish Indian fighter Sigmund Schlesinger; with Chin Lin Sou, a Canton-born railroad foreman and gold miner; and Lewis Price, a black former slave who won and lost a fortune as a Denver real estate baron.

The curriculum fights at Stanford and the effort to write a history of the West that stresses darker themes are symptomatic of a basic change in American universities that has occurred over the last 20 years. It represents the migration into tenured positions of men and women with ideas that seemed radical during the protests of the 1960's. Richard White, sitting in his office in Utah, recalls that "many of the people who are grouped together in the new Western history were in college in the 1960's and for many of them the formative experience was the anti-war movement." Peggy Pascoe concurs. "At the time I got to college in Montana," she recalls of the 70's, "the 60's were still alive and well. I felt like I was growing up in the 60's."

The new history of the American West incorporates the post-Vietnam mood. It reflects the willingness of the 60's generation to find the invisible worm eating away at the once blushing rose of the American self-image. And who is to say that is a bad thing? Nobody who has read the works of Worster, Limerick, White and others would disparage the seriousness of their scholarship. And it *is* hard to look at those photographs of ghost towns without sharing some of Patricia Limerick's Gibbonesque gloom. Sentimental illusions are not a good basis for national creeds, and certainly the creed of the West has been among the most sentimental of all. But it is useful to bear in mind that, just as Turner and the Turnerians were products of their time, the most optimistic period in American history, so too are the new historians. They are products of a more complicated, more ambivalent epoch, one that has led many of their generation to look at their country and find it wanting. It's hardly surprising that the new historians, in searching the West for our national origins, for clues to our national character, have found it wanting as well.

SUGGESTIONS FOR DISCUSSION

1. The dominant view of westward expansion is, as Bernstein quotes the historian Patricia Nelson Limerick saying, that "heroic pioneers brought civilization to a savage wilderness." How have the new generations of historians challenged this view? What are the results?
2. Bernstein connects the new history of the American West to what he calls the "post-Vietnam mood." What does he mean by this mood? How and why would this mood lead to reinterpretation of the past?
3. In the final section of the article, Bernstein says the work of the new historians "bears a resemblance to efforts taking place elsewhere" to change the curriculum in history courses. What are the grounds of change? Does American history need to be rewritten? If so, why and in what respects? To answer these questions, recall the version of American history you learned in school.

SUGGESTIONS FOR WRITING

1. Write an essay that explains how you learned American history in school. Try to recall specific lessons. The point of his assignment, however, is not just to describe the details of your education in American history. You will want also to explain what values were transmitted to you through the study of the past.
2. Bernstein writes that the new historians "are blazing a pioneer's trail toward an altered view of the moral status of America itself." In what sense does the writing of history inevitably involve moral judgments? Pick an event or episode in American history that you think raises questions about America's "moral status." Write an essay that explains what you see as the moral issues involved. You might begin by describing how the event or episode is traditionally treated in school and textbooks. Then you will want to identify what you see as the moral issues raised and what they reveal about the American past.
3. One of the points of studying the past—besides accounting for how the present turned out the way it did—is to understand how people lived in another time and place, to see the past not just as a preparation for the present and the future but as a human possibility and state of affairs in its own right. Write an essay that identifies a period in the past when you would like to have been alive and explain why.

George B. Tindall and David E. Shi

THE TRAGEDY OF VIETNAM

Loren Baritz

GOD'S COUNTRY AND AMERICAN KNOW-HOW

The following two selections offer very different perspectives on the Vietnam War, raising questions about how professional historians seek to explain the causes and meanings of particular historical events. The first selection, "The Tragedy of Vietnam," appeared originally in George B. Tindall and David E. Shi's textbook *America: A Narrative History* (1989). The second selection, "God's Country and American Know-How," is taken from Loren Baritz's book *Backfire: A History of How American Culture Led Us Into Vietnam* (1985). The first selection may appear at first reading to be simply a historical narrative of U.S. involvement in Vietnam, while the second is clearly tied to Baritz's thesis that long-standing patterns in American culture led to military intervention in Vietnam. Your task as a reader is to make sense of these two treatments of the Vietnam War and to decide whether Tindall and Shi offer an interpretation as much as Baritz does.

Suggestion for Reading

• As you read, consider whether Tindall and Shi's "The Tragedy of Vietnam" simply describes events that led the United States into a deepening involvement in Vietnam or offers an interpretation to explain this involvement. You might think about why they have titled this section of their textbook, "The Tragedy of Vietnam."

THE TRAGEDY OF VIETNAM

George B. Tindall and David E. Shi

As violence was escalating in America's inner cities, the war in Vietnam also reached new levels of intensity and destruction. At the time of President Kennedy's death there were 16,000 American military advisors in Vietnam. Lyndon Johnson inherited a commitment to prevent a Communist takeover in South Vietnam along with a reluctance to assume the military burden for fighting the war. One president after another had done just enough to avoid being charged with having "lost" Vietnam. Johnson did the same, fearing that any other course would undermine his influence and endanger his Great Society programs in Congress. But this path took him and the United States inexorably deeper into intervention in Asia.

ESCALATION

The official sanction for America's "escalation"—a Defense Department term coined in the Vietnam era—was the Tonkin Gulf Resolution, voted by Congress on August 7, 1964. Johnson reported in a national television address that two American destroyers had been attacked by North Vietnamese vessels on August 2 and 4 in the Gulf of Tonkin off the coast of North Vietnam. Although he described the attacks as unprovoked, in truth the destroyers had been monitoring South Vietnamese raids against two North Vietnamese islands—raids planned by American advisors. The Tonkin Gulf Resolution authorized the president to "take all necessary measures to repel any armed attack against the forces of the United States and to prevent further aggression."

Three months after Johnson's landslide victory over Goldwater, he and his advisors made the crucial decisions that shaped American policy in Vietnam for the next four years. On February 5, 1965, Vietcong guerrillas killed 8 and wounded 126 Americans at Pleiku. Further attacks on Americans later that week led Johnson to order operation "Rolling Thunder," the first sustained American bombings of North Vietnam, which were intended to stop the flow of soldiers and supplies into the south. Six months later a task force concluded that the bombing had little effect on the supplies pouring down the "Ho Chi Minh Trail" from North Vietnam through Laos. Still, the bombing continued.

In March 1965 the new American army commander in Vietnam, Gen. William C. Westmoreland, requested and got the first installment of combat troops, ostensibly to defend American airfields. By the end of 1965 there were 184,000 American troops in Vietnam; in 1966 the troop level reached 385,000. And as combat operations increased, so did the list of American casualties, announced each week on the nightly news along with the "body count" of alleged enemy dead. "Westy's War," although fought with helicopter gunships, chemical defoliants, and napalm, became like the trench warfare of World War I—a grinding war of attrition.

THE CONTEXT FOR POLICY

Johnson's decision to "Americanize" the war, so ill-starred in retrospect, was entirely consistent with the foreign policy principles pursued by all American presidents after World War II. The version of the containment theory articulated in the Truman Doctrine, endorsed by Eisenhower and Dulles throughout the 1950s, and reaffirmed by Kennedy, pledged United States opposition to the advance of communism anywhere in the world. "Why are we in Vietnam?" Johnson asked rhetorically at Johns Hopkins University in 1965. "We are there because we have a promise to keep. . . . To leave Vietnam to its fate would shake the confidence of all these people in the value of American commitment." Secretary of State Dean Rusk repeated this rationale before countless congressional committees, warning that Thailand, Burma, and the rest of Southeast Asia would fall to communism if American forces withdrew. American military intervention in Vietnam was thus no aberration, but a logical culmination of the assumptions widely shared by the foreign policy establishment and leaders of both political parties since the early days of the Cold War.

Nor did the United States blindly "stumble into a quagmire" in Vietnam, as some commentators maintained. Johnson insisted from the start that American military involvement must not reach levels that would provoke the Chinese or Soviets into direct intervention. He therefore exercised a tight rein over the bombing campaign, once boasting that "they can't even bomb an outhouse without my approval." Such a restrictive policy meant, in effect, that military victory in any traditional sense of the term was never possible. "It was startling to me to find out," the new secretary of defense, Clark Clifford, recalled in 1968, "that we had no military plan to end the war." America's goal was not to win the war in a conventional sense by capturing enemy territory, but to prevent the North Vietnamese and Vietcong from winning. This meant that America would have to maintain a military presence as long as the enemy retained the will to fight.

As it turned out, American public support for the war eroded faster than the will of the North Vietnamese leaders to tolerate casualties. Opposition to the war broke out on college campuses with the escalation of 1965. And in January 1966 Sen. J. William Fulbright of Arkansas, chairman of the Senate Foreign Relations Committee, began congressional investigations into American policy. George Kennan, the founding father of the containment doctrine, told Fulbright's committee that the doctrine was appropriate for Europe, but not Southeast Asia. By 1967 opposition to the war had become so pronounced that antiwar demonstrations in New York and at the Pentagon attracted massive support. Nightly television accounts of the fighting—Vietnam was the first war to receive extended television coverage, and hence has been dubbed the "living room war"—brought the horrors of guerrilla warfare into American dens. As Secretary of Defense McNamara admitted, "The picture of the world's greatest superpower killing or injuring 1,000 noncombatants a week, while trying to pound a tiny backward nation into submission on an issue whose merits are hotly disputed, is not a pretty one."

In a war of political will, North Vietnam had the advantage. Johnson and his advisors never came to appreciate the tenacity of North Vietnam's commitment to unify Vietnam and expel the United States. Ho Chi Minh had warned the French in the 1940s that "You can kill ten of my men for every one I kill of yours, but even at those odds, you will lose and I will win." He knew that in a battle of attrition, the

Vietnamese Communists had the advantage, for they were willing to sacrifice all for their cause. Indeed, just as General Westmoreland was assuring Johnson and the American public that his forces in early 1968 were on the verge of gaining the upper hand, the Communists again displayed their resilience.

THE TURNING POINT

On January 31, 1968, the first day of the Vietnamese New Year (Tet), the Vietcong and North Vietnamese defied a holiday truce to launch a wave of surprise assaults on American and South Vietnamese forces throughout South Vietnam. The old capital city of Hué fell to the Communists, and Vietcong units temporarily occupied the grounds of the American embassy in Saigon. But within a few days American and South Vietnamese forces organized a devastating counterattack. General Westmoreland justifiably proclaimed the Tet offensive a major defeat for the Vietcong. But while Vietcong casualties were enormous, the psychological impact of the offensive on the American public was more telling. *Time* and *Newsweek* soon ran antiwar editorials urging American withdrawal. Walter Cronkite, the dean of American television journalists, confided to his viewers that he no longer believed the war was winnable. "If I've lost Walter," Johnson was reported to say, "then it's over. I've lost Mr. Average Citizen." Polls showed that Johnson's popularity declined to 35 percent, lower than any president since Truman's darkest days. In 1968 the United States was spending $322,000 on every enemy killed in Vietnam; the poverty programs at home received only $53 per person.

During 1968 Johnson grew increasingly isolated. The secretary of defense reported that a task force of prominent soldiers and civilians saw no prospect for a military victory. Robert Kennedy was considering a run for the presidency in order to challenge Johnson's Vietnam policy. And Sen. Eugene McCarthy of Minnesota had already decided to oppose Johnson in the Democratic primaries. With antiwar students rallying to his candidacy, McCarthy polled 42 percent of the vote to Johnson's 48 percent in New Hampshire's March primary. Though voters had to write in Johnson's name to vote for the president, it was still a remarkable showing for a little-known senator, and each presidential primary now promised to become a referendum on Johnson's Vietnam policy.

Despite Johnson's troubles in the conduct of foreign policy, he remained a master at reading the political omens. On March 31 he announced a limited halt to the bombing of North Vietnam and fresh initiatives for a negotiated cease-fire. Then he added a dramatic postscript: "I have concluded that I should not permit the Presidency to become involved in the partisan divisions that are developing in this political year. Accordingly, I shall not seek, and I will not accept, the nomination of my party for another term as your President." Although American troops would remain in Vietnam for five more years and the casualties would mount, the quest for military victory had ended. Now the question was how the most powerful nation in the world could extricate itself from Vietnam with a minimum of damage to its prestige. It would not be easy. When direct negotiations with the North Vietnamese finally began in Paris in May 1968 they immediately bogged down over North Vietnam's demand for an American bombing halt as a precondition for further discussion.

Suggestion for Reading

- As you read, notice how Loren Baritz develops his idea that America's quest for moral leadership led policymakers to involve the United States in Vietnam. Compare this perspective on American military intervention in Vietnam to the perspective Tindall and Shi offer in "The Tragedy of Vietnam." When you finish reading, you will want to think about what these perspectives have in common and how they differ.

◆

GOD'S COUNTRY AND AMERICAN KNOW-HOW

Loren Baritz

Americans were ignorant about the Vietnamese not because we were stupid, but because we believe certain things about ourselves. Those things necessarily distorted our vision and confused our minds in ways that made learning extraordinarily difficult. To understand our failure we must think about what it means to be an American.

The necessary text for understanding the condition of being an American is a single sentence written by Herman Melville in his novel *White Jacket:* "And we Americans are the peculiar, chosen people—the Israel of our time; we bear the ark of the liberties of the world." This was not the last time this idea was expressed by Americans. It was at the center of thought of the men who brought us the Vietnam War. It was at the center of the most characteristic American myth.

This oldest and most important myth about America has an unusually specific origin. More than 350 years ago, while in mid-passage between England and the American wilderness, John Winthrop told the band of Puritans he was leading to a new and dangerous life that they were engaged in a voyage that God Himself not only approved, but in which He participated. The precise way that Brother Winthrop expressed himself echoes throughout the history of American life. He explained to his fellow travelers, "We shall find that the God of Israel is among us, when ten of us shall be able to resist a thousand of our enemies, when he shall make us a praise and glory, that men shall say of succeeding plantations [settlements]: the Lord make it like that of New England: for we must Consider that we shall be as a City upon a Hill, the eyes of all people are upon us." The myth of America as a city on a hill implies that America is a moral example to the rest of the world, a world that will presumably keep its attention riveted on us. It means that we are a Chosen People, each of whom, because of God's favor and presence, can smite one hundred of our heathen enemies hip and thigh.

The society Winthrop meant to establish in New England would do God's work, insofar as sinners could. America would become God's country. The Puritans would have understood this to mean that they were creating a nation of, by, and for the Lord. About two centuries later, the pioneers and the farmers who followed the Puritans translated God's country from civilization to the grandeur and nobility of nature, to virgin land, to the purple mountains' majesty. Relocating the country of God from civilization to nature was significant in many ways, but the conclusion that this New World is specially favored by the Lord not only endured but spread.

In countless ways Americans know in their gut—the only place myths can live—that we have been Chosen to lead the world in public morality and to instruct it in political virtue. We believe that our own domestic goodness results in strength adequate to destroy our opponents who, by definition, are enemies of virtue, freedom, and God. Over and over, the founding Puritans described their new settlement as a beacon in the darkness, a light whose radiance could keep Christian voyagers from crashing on the rocks, a light that could brighten the world. In his inaugural address John Kennedy said, "The energy, the faith, the devotion which we bring to this endeavor [defending freedom] will light our country and all who serve it—and the glow from that fire can truly light the world." The city on a hill grew from its first tiny society to encompass the entire nation. As we will see, that is one of the reasons why we compelled ourselves to intervene in Vietnam.

An important part of the myth of America as the city on a hill has been lost as American power increased. John Winthrop intended that his tiny settlement should be only an example of rectitude to the cosmos. It could not have occurred to him that his small and weak band of saints should charge about the world to impose the One Right Way on others who were either too wicked, too stupid, or even too oppressed to follow his example. Because they also had domestic distractions, the early American Puritans could not even consider foreign adventures. In almost no time they had their hands full with a variety of local malefactors: Indians, witches, and, worst of all, shrewd Yankees who were more interested in catching fish than in catching the spirit of the Lord. Nathaniel Hawthorne, brooding about these Puritans, wrote that civilization begins by building a jail and a graveyard, but he was only two-thirds right. Within only two generations, the New England saints discovered that there was a brothel in Boston, the hub of the new and correct Christian order.

The New World settlement was puny, but the great ocean was a defensive moat that virtually prohibited an onslaught by foreign predators. The new Americans could therefore go about perfecting their society without distracting anxiety about alien and corrupting intrusions from Europe. This relative powerlessness coupled with defensive security meant that the city on a hill enjoyed a favorable "peculiar situation." It was peculiarly blessed because the decadent world could not come here, and we did not have to go there. The rest of the world, but especially Europe, with its frippery, pomp, and Catholicism, was thought to be morally leprous. This is what George Washington had in mind when he asked a series of rhetorical questions in his farewell address in 1796:

> Why forego the advantages of so peculiar a situation? Why quit our own to stand upon foreign ground? Why, by interweaving our destiny with that of any part of Europe, entangle our peace and prosperity in the toils of European ambition, rivalship, interest, humor, of caprice?

This is also what Thomas Jefferson told his countrymen when he was inaugurated five years later. This enlightened and skeptical philosopher-President announced that this was a "chosen country" which had been "kindly separated by nature and a wide ocean from the exterminating havoc of one quarter of the globe." He said that the young nation could exult in its many blessings if it would only keep clear of foreign evil. His prescription was that America should have "entangling alliances with none."

One final example of the unaggressive, unimperial interpretation of the myth is essential. The entire Adams family had a special affinity for old Winthrop. Perhaps it was that they grew up on the soil in which he was buried. On the Fourth of July, in 1821, John Quincy Adams gave a speech that captured every nuance of the already ancient myth. His speech could have been the text for the Vietnam War critics. He said that America's heart and prayers would always be extended to any free and independent part of the world. "But she goes not abroad in search of monsters to destroy." America, he said, hoped that freedom and independence would spread across the face of the earth. "She will recommend the general cause by the countenance of her voice, and by the benignant sympathy of her example." He said that the new nation understood that it should not actively intervene abroad even if such an adventure would be on the side of freedom because "she would involve herself beyond the power of extrication." It just might be possible for America to try to impose freedom elsewhere, to assist in the liberation of others. "She might," he said, "become the dictatress of the world. She would no longer be the ruler of her own spirit."

In 1966, this speech was quoted by George F. Kennan, the thoughtful analyst of Soviet foreign affairs, to the Senate Foreign Relations Committee which was conducting hearings on the Vietnam War. Perhaps not knowing the myth, Mr. Kennan said that he was not sure what Mr. Adams had in mind when he spoke almost a century and a half earlier. But whatever it was, Mr. Kennan told the senators who were then worrying about Vietnam, "He spoke very directly and very pertinently to us here today."

The myth of the city on a hill became the foundation for the ritualistic thinking of later generations of Americans. This myth helped to establish nationalistic orthodoxy in America. It began to set an American dogma, to fix the limits of thought for Americans about themselves and about the rest of the world, and offered a choice about the appropriate relationship between us and them.

The benevolence of our national motives, the absence of material gain in what we seek, the dedication to principle, and our impenetrable ignorance were all related to the original myth of America. It is temptingly easy to dismiss this as some quaint idea that perhaps once had some significance, but lost it in this more sophisticated, toughminded, modern America. Arthur Schlesinger, Jr., a close aide to President Kennedy, thought otherwise. He was concerned about President Johnson's vastly ambitious plans to create a "Great Society for Asia." Whatever the President meant, according to Professor Schlesinger, such an idea

> . . . demands the confrontation of an issue deep in the historical consciousness of the United States: whether this country is a chosen people, uniquely righteous and wise, with a moral mission to all mankind . . . The ultimate choice is between messianism and maturity.

The city myth should have collapsed during the war. The war should have taught us that we could not continue to play the role of moral adviser and moral enforcer to the world. After the shock of the assassinations, after the shock of Tet, after President Johnson gave up the presidency, after the riots, demonstrations, burned neighborhoods, and the rebellion of the young, it should have been difficult to sustain John

Winthrop's optimism. It was not difficult for Robert Kennedy who, after Senator Eugene McCarthy had demonstrated LBJ's vulnerability in New Hampshire, finally announced that he would run for the presidency himself. The language he used in his announcement speech proved that the myth was as alive and as virulent as it had ever been: "At stake," Senator Kennedy said, "is not simply the leadership of our party, and even our own country, it is our right to the moral leadership of this planet." Members of his staff were horrified that he could use such language because they correctly believed that it reflected just the mind-set that had propelled us into Vietnam in the first place. He ignored their protests. This myth could survive in even the toughest of the contemporary, sophisticated, hard-driving politicians. Of course, he may have used this language only to persuade his listeners, to convince the gullible. But, even so, it showed that he believed that the myth was what they wanted to hear. In either case, the city on a hill continued to work its way.

• • •

The myth of the city on a hill combined with solipsism in the assumptions about Vietnam made by the American war planners. In other words, we assumed that we had a superior moral claim to be in Vietnam, and because, despite their quite queer ways of doing things, the Vietnamese shared our values, they would applaud our intentions and embrace our physical presence. Thus, Vice-President Humphrey later acknowledged that all along we had been ignorant of Vietnam. He said that "to LBJ, the Mekong and the Pedernales were not that far apart." Our claim to virtue was based on the often announced purity of our intentions. It was said, perhaps thousands of times, that all we wanted was freedom for other people, not land, not resources, and not domination.

Because we believed that our intentions were virtuous, we could learn nothing from the French experience in Vietnam. After all, they had fought only to maintain their Southeast Asian colonies and as imperialists deserved to lose. We assumed that this was why so mighty a European power lost the important battle of Dien Bien Phu to General Giap's ragged army. America's moral authority was so clear to us that we assumed that it also had to be clear to the Vietnamese. This self-righteousness was the clincher in the debate to intensify the conflict in Vietnam, according to George W. Ball, an undersecretary of state for Presidents Kennedy and Johnson. Washington's war planners, Mr. Ball said in 1973, had been captives of their own myths. Another State Department official also hoped, after the fact, that Americans "will be knocked out of our grandiosity . . . [and] will see the self-righteous, illusory quality of that vision of ourselves offered by the high Washington official who said that while other nations have 'interests' the United States has 'a sense of responsibility.'" Our power, according to this mentality, gives us responsibility, even though we may be reluctant to bear the burden. Other peoples' greed or selfishness gives them interests, even though they may not be strong enough to grab all they want.

Our grandiosity will, however, not be diminished so easily. At least since World War II, America's foreign affairs have been the affairs of Pygmalion. We fall in love with what we create. We create a vision of the world made in what we think is our own image. We are proud of what we create because we are certain that our intentions are pure, our motives good, and our behavior virtuous. We know these things to be true because we believe that we are unique among the nations of the world in our collective idealism.

• • •

Although the nationalists of the world all share a peoples' pride in who they are, a loyalty to place and language and culture, there are delicate but important differences. Because of its Puritan roots, it is not surprising that America's nationalism is more Protestant than that of other countries. It is more missionary in its impulses, more evangelical. It typically seeks to correct the way other people think rather than to establish its own physical dominion over them. It is, as it were, more committed to the Word, as befits serious Protestants, than other nationalisms.

One of the peculiarities of American Protestant nationalism, especially in its most aggressive mood, is its passion about ideas. What we want is to convert others to the truth as we understand it. We went to war in Vietnam in the name of ideas, of principles, of abstractions. Thus, President Johnson said in his inaugural, "We aspire to nothing that belongs to others." And added in his important address at Johns Hopkins in April 1965: "Because we fight for values and we fight for principles, rather than territory or colonies, our patience and our determination are unending." This is what we mean when we think of ourselves as idealists, magnanimous and moral. It is what cold warriors mean when they say over and over that we are engaged with the Soviet Union "in a competition of ideas."

• • •

Tangled up in old myths, fearful of speaking plain English on the subject, the political conscience of many Americans must be troubled. There is bad faith in accepting the city myth of American uniqueness as if the myth can be freed from its integral Protestantism, almost always of a fundamentalist flavor. Conservatives have less need to launder the myth of its religion. Because liberals require a secular version of nationalism, and if they need or want to retain some sense of the unique republic, they are required to rest their case on a secular basis. Wilsonian idealism was the answer in the 1960s, as liberals argued that America was the only society capable of creating social justice and genuine democracy at home and abroad. These ideals merged with the cold war and persuaded the best of American liberals to bring us Vietnam.

In America, as elsewhere, elected officials are especially susceptible to the fundamental myths of nationalism because they must embody them to get elected and act on them to govern. The vision of the world that suffused Mr. Wilson's Fourteen Points and League of Nations was also the vision of John Kennedy and his circle. They were pained by the knowledge that a people anywhere in the world struggled toward freedom but was frustrated by the imposition of force. So it was that John F. Kennedy's inspired inaugural address carried the burden of Woodrow Wilson's idealism, and also carried the deadly implication that America was again ready for war in the name of goodness.

President Kennedy's language must be understood in the light of what was just around the corner in Vietnam. He announced to the world, "We shall pay any price, bear any burden, meet any hardship, support any friend, oppose any foe to assure the survival and the success of liberty." He said that it was the rare destiny of his generation to defend freedom when it was at its greatest risk. "I do not shrink from this responsibility—I welcome it."

The difference between the two sons of the Commonwealth of Massachusetts, John Quincy Adams and John Fitzgerald Kennedy, was the difference between good wishes and war, but also the difference between a tiny and isolated America and the world's most powerful nation. Presidents Wilson and Kennedy both fairly represented American liberalism at its most restless and energetic. This was a liberalism that wanted, as President Wilson put it, to make the world safe for democracy, or as President Kennedy said, to defend "those human rights to which this nation has always been committed, and to which we are committed today at home and around the world." JFK described this as "God's work."

An important part of the reason we marched into Vietnam with our eyes fixed was liberalism's irrepressible need to be helpful to those less fortunate. But the decency of the impulse, as was the case with President Wilson, cannot hide the bloody eagerness to kill in the name of virtue. In 1981, James C. Thomson, an aide in the State Department and a member of the National Security Council under President Johnson, finally concluded that our Vietnamese intervention had been motivated by a national missionary impulse, a "need to do good to others." In a phrase that cannot be improved, he and others called this "sentimental imperialism." The purity of intention and the horror of result is unfortunately the liberal's continuing burden.

American conservatives had it easier, largely because they believed in the actuality of evil. In his first public statement, President Eisenhower informed the American public, "The forces of good and evil are massed and armed and opposed as rarely before in history." For him the world struggle was not merely between conflicting ideologies. "Freedom is pitted against slavery; lightness against the dark."

Conservatives in America are closer than liberals to the myth of the city on a hill because they are not embarrassed by public professions of religion. They are therefore somewhat less likely to ascribe American values and behavior to other cultures. This is so because of the conservatives' conviction that America is so much better—more moral, godly, wise, and especially rich—than other nations that they could not possibly resemble us. Thus, President Eisenhower announced that one of America's fixed principles was the refusal to "use our strength to try to impress upon another people our own cherished political and economic institutions." The idea of uniqueness means, after all, that we are alone in the world.

Conservatives shared with liberals the conviction that America could act, and in Vietnam did act, with absolute altruism, as they believed only America could. Thinking of this war, President Nixon, another restless descendent of Mr. Wilson, declared that "never in history have men fought for less selfish motives—not for conquest, not for glory, but only for the right of a people far away to choose the kind of government they want." This was especially attractive because in this case the kind of government presumably sought by this faraway people was opposed to Communism, our own enemy. It was therefore an integral part of the universal struggle between freedom and slavery, lightness and dark. As a result it was relatively easy for conservatives to think of Vietnam as a laboratory to test ways to block the spreading stain of political atheism.

Power is sometimes a problem for liberals and a solution for conservatives. When Senator Goldwater rattled America's many sabers in his presidential campaign of 1964, and when General Curtis LeMay wanted to bomb North Vietnam "back to the stone age," they both made liberals cringe, partly from embarrassment, and partly because the liberals were appalled at the apparent cruelty. In the 1950s, Dr. Kissinger cleverly argued that the liberal embarrassment over power made its use, when necessary, even worse than it had to be. "Our feeling of guilt with respect to power," he wrote, "has caused us to transform all wars into crusades, and then to apply our power in the most absolute ways." Later, when he ran America's foreign policy, his own unambivalent endorsement of the use in Vietnam of enormous power inevitably raised the question of whether bloody crusades are caused only by the squeamishness of liberals or also by the callousness of conservatives.

• • •

Implicit in John Winthrop's formulation of the city myth was the idea that the new Americans could, because of their godliness, vanquish their numerically superior enemies. The idea that warriors, because of their virtue, could beat stronger opponents, is very ancient. Pericles spoke of it in his funeral oration to the Athenians. The Christian crusaders counted on it. *Jibad,* Islam's conception of a holy war, is based on it. The Samurai believed it. So did the Nazis.

In time, the history of America proved to Americans that we were militarily invincible. The Vietnam War Presidents naturally cringed at the thought that they could be the first to lose a war. After all, we had already beaten Indians, French, British (twice), Mexicans, Spaniards, Germans (twice), Italians, Japanese, Koreans, and Chinese. Until World War II, the nation necessarily had to rely on the presumed virtue, not the power, of American soldiers to carry the day, and the war. This was also the case in the South during our Civil War.

Starting in the eighteenth century, the nation of farmers began to industrialize. As the outcome of war increasingly came to depend on the ability to inject various forms of flying hardware into the enemy's body, victory increasingly depended on technology. The acceleration of industrialization in the late nineteenth century inevitably quickened the pace of technological evolution. By then no other power could match the Americans' ability to get organized, to commit resources to development, and to invent the gadgets that efficiently produced money in the marketplace, and, when necessary, death on the battlefield. The idea of Yankee ingenuity, American know-how, stretches back beyond the nineteenth century. Our admiration for the tinkerer whose new widget forms the basis of new industry is nowhere better shown than in our national reverence of Thomas Edison.

Joining the American sense of its moral superiority with its technological superiority was a marriage made in heaven, at least for American nationalists. We told ourselves that each advantage explained the other, that the success of our standard of living was a result of our virtue, and our virtue was a result of our wealth. Our riches, our technology, provided the strength that had earlier been missing, that once had forced us to rely only on our virtue. Now, as Hiroshima demonstrated conclusively, we could think of ourselves not only as morally superior, but as the most powerful nation in history. The inevitable offspring of this marriage of an idea with a weapon was the conviction that the United States could not be beaten in war—not by any nation, and not by any combination of nations. For that moment we thought that we could fight where, when, and how we wished, without risking failure. For that moment we thought that we could impose our will on the recalcitrant of the earth.

A great many Americans, in the period just before the war in Vietnam got hot, shared a circular belief that for most was probably not very well formed: America's technological supremacy was a symptom of its uniqueness, and technology made the nation militarily invincible. In 1983, the playwright Arthur Miller said, "I'm an American. I believe in technology. Until the mid-60s I never believed we could lose because we had technology."

The memory of World War II concluding in a mushroom cloud was relatively fresh throughout the 1950s. It was unthinkable that America's military could ever fail to establish its supremacy on the battlefield, that the industrial, scientific, and technological strength of the nation would ever be insufficient for the purposes of war. It was almost as if Americans were technology. The American love affair with the automobile was at its most passionate in the 1950s, our well-equipped armies stopped the Chinese in Korea, for a moment our nuclear supremacy was taken for granted, and affluence for many white Americans seemed to be settling in as a way of life.

It is, of course, unfortunate that the forces of evil may be as strong as the forces of virtue. The Soviet Union exploded its first atomic bomb way ahead of what Americans thought was a likely schedule. This technology is not like others because even a weak bomb is devastating. Even if our bombs are better than theirs, they can still do us in. America's freedom of action after 1949 was not complete. President Eisenhower and John Foster Dulles, the Secretary of State, threatened "massive retaliation" against the Soviet Union if it stepped over the line. They knew, and we knew, that this threat was not entirely real, and that it freed the Soviets to engage in peripheral adventures because they correctly believed that we would not destroy the world over Korea, Berlin, Hungary, or Czechoslovakia.

Our policy had to become more flexible. We had to invent a theory that would allow us to fight on the edges without nuclear technology. This theory is called "limited war." Its premise is that we and the Soviets can wage little wars, and that each side will refrain from provoking the other to unlock the nuclear armory.

Ike threatened the Chinese, who at the time did not have the bomb, with nuclear war in Korea. JFK similarly threatened the Soviets, who had nuclear capability, over Cuba. But, although some military men thought about using nuclear weapons in Vietnam, the fundamental assumption of that war was to keep it limited, not to force either the Soviets or the Chinese, who now had their own sloppy bombs, to enter the war. Thus, we could impose our will on the recalcitrant of the earth if they did not have their own nuclear weapons, and if they could not compel the Soviets or the Chinese to force us to quit.

In Vietnam we had to find a technology to win without broadening the war. The nuclear stalemate reemphasized our need to find a more limited ground, to find, so to speak, a way to fight a domesticated war. We had to find a technology that would prevail locally, but not explode internationally. No assignment is too tough for the technological mentality. In fact, it was made to order for the technicians who were coming into their own throughout all of American life. This war gave them the opportunity to show what they could do. This was to be history's most technologically sophisticated war, most carefully analyzed and managed, using all of the latest wonders of managerial procedures and systems. It was made to order for bureaucracy.

James C. Thomson, who served both JFK and LBJ as an East Asia specialist, understood how the myths converged. He wrote of "*the rise of a new breed of American ideologues who see Vietnam as the ultimate test of their doctrine.*" These new men were the new missionaries and had a trinitarian faith: in military power, technological superiority, and our altruistic idealism. They believed that the reality of American culture "provides us with the opportunity and obligation to ease the nations of the earth toward modernization and stability: toward a full-fledged *Pax Americana Technocratica.*" For these parishioners in the church of the machine, Vietnam was the ideal laboratory.

SUGGESTIONS FOR DISCUSSION

1. How are these two accounts alike and different in the way they explain U.S. involvement in Vietnam? What do the titles these historians have given to the selections "The Tragedy of Vietnam" and "God's Country and American Know-How" indicate about their respective points of view? What advantages and disadvantages do you see in each selection's attempt to explain the origins of the Vietnam War?
2. Recall how and what you have learned about the Vietnam War. What has shaped your understanding—school, friends, relatives, movies, books, television shows? How does your own sense of the Vietnam War compare to the perspectives presented by the two reading selections?
3. Baritz describes the "trinitarian faith" of American policymakers in "military power, technological superiority, and altruistic idealism" that he believes led the country into the Vietnam War. Is this "faith" still strongly held today? What, if any, relation do you see between this faith and post-Vietnam military interventions in Grenada, Panama, Iraq, Somalia, and Haiti? What problems or issues does such "faith" ignore or suppress?

SUGGESTIONS FOR WRITING

1. Write an essay that compares Tindall's and Shi's and Baritz's accounts of the origins of the Vietnam War. Take into account both differences and similarities in their explanations of causes. End the essay with your own sense of the relative strengths and weaknesses of each way of doing and explaining history.
2. Write an essay on what Baritz calls America's "missionary impulse." What do you see as the problems, if any, with this "altruistic idealism"? Does it invariably lead, as Baritz suggests, to "purity of intention," on one hand, and "the horror of result," on the other? It will help your essay to look at a particular instance with which you are familiar, where the desire to act "in that name of goodness" backfired on the benefactors. You needn't limit yourself here to matters of international or military policy. There may well be instances much closer to home in which someone or some group seeking to do good actually produces the opposite effect. Your task here is to analyze why and how this is the case.
3. Write an essay that locates your own understanding of the Vietnam War in relation to the accounts of these professional historians. Agree and disagree with them as you see fit, but the main point is to use their versions of the Vietnam War to develop your own. Make sure you explain how you learned about the Vietnam War, through which sources—school, friends, relatives, popular media—and how these sources shaped your understanding.

Le Ly Hayslip

WHEN HEAVEN AND EARTH CHANGED PLACES

Le Ly Hayslip was born into a peasant family in central Vietnam and, when she was a teenager, fought for the Viet Cong. The following selection is taken from the Prologue to her book, *When Heaven and Earth Changed Places* (1989), which recounts her experiences with the Viet Cong and, after she fled from the fighting in the countryside, in the bars, brothels, and black markets of war-torn Saigon (now Ho Chi Minh City). Hayslip married an American civilian working in Vietnam and, in 1970, followed him to the United States, where she founded the East Meets West Foundation, a charitable relief organization dedicated to healing the wounds of the Vietnam War.

Suggestion for Reading

- As you read, notice that Hayslip, like the authors of the two previous selections, is attempting to explain the causes of the Vietnam War and why people took sides to fight. Consider how the perspective of Vietnamese peasants differs from those of professional historians.

◆

E verything I knew about the war I learned as a teenaged girl from the North Vietnamese cadre leaders in the swamps outside Ky La. During these midnight meetings, we peasants assumed everything we heard was true because what the Viet Cong said matched, in one way or another, the beliefs we already had.

The first lesson we learned about the new "American" war was why the Viet Cong was formed and why we should support it. Because this lesson came on the heels of our war with the French (which began in 1946 and lasted, on and off, for eight years), what the cadre leaders told us seemed to be self-evident.

First, we were taught that Vietnam was *con rong chau tien*—a sovereign nation which had been held in thrall by Western imperialists for over a century. That all nations had a right to determine their own destiny also seemed beyond dispute, since we farmers subsisted by our own hands and felt we owed nothing to anyone but god and our ancestors for the right to live as we saw fit. Even the Chinese, who had made their own disastrous attempt to rule Vietnam in centuries past, had learned a painful lesson about our country's zeal for independence. "Vietnam," went the saying that summarized their experience, "is nobody's lapdog."

Second, the cadres told us that the division of Vietnam into North and South in 1954 was nothing more than a ploy by the defeated French and their Western allies, mainly the United States, to preserve what influence they could in our country.

"Chia doi dat nuoc?" the Viet Cong asked, "Why should outsiders divide the land and tell some people to go north and others south? If Vietnam were truly for the Vietnamese, wouldn't we choose for ourselves what kind of government our people wanted? A nation cannot have *two* governments," they said, "any more than a family can have two fathers."

Because those who favored America quickly occupied the seats of power formerly held by the French, and because the North remained pretty much on its own, the choice of which side best represented independence was, for us, a foregone conclusion. In fact, the Viet Cong usually ended our indoctrination sessions with a song that played on our worst fears:

> Americans come to kill our people,
> Follow America, and kill your relatives!
> The smart bird flies before it's caught.
> The smart person comes home before Tet.
> Follow us, and you'll always have a family.
> Follow America, and you'll always be alone!

After these initial "lessons," the cadre leaders introduced us to the two Vietnamese leaders who personified each view—the opposite poles of our tiny world. On the South pole was President Ngo Dinh Diem, America's staunch ally, who was Catholic like the French. Although he was idolized by many who said he was a great humanitarian and patriot, his religion alone was enough to make him suspicious to Buddhists on the Central Coast. The loyalty we showed him, consequently, was more duty to a landlord than love for a founding father. Here is a song the Republican schoolteachers made us learn to praise the Southern president:

> In stormy seas, Vietnam's boat rolls and pitches.
> Still we must row; our President's hand upon the helm.
> The ship of state plows through heavy seas,
> Holding fast its course to democracy.
> Our President is celebrated from Europe to Asia,
> He is the image of philanthropy and love.
> He has sacrificed himself for our happiness.
> He fights for liberty in the land of the Viet.
> Everyone loves him earnestly, and behind him we will march
> Down the street of freedom, lined with fresh flowers,
> The flag of liberty crackling above our heads!

In the North, on the other pole, was Ho Chi Minh, whom we were encouraged to call *Bac Ho*—Uncle Ho—the way we would refer to a trusted family friend. We knew nothing of his past beyond stories of his compassion and his love for our troubled country—the independence of which, we were told, he had made the mission of his life.

Given the gulf between these leaders, the choice of whom we should support again seemed obvious. The cadre leaders encouraged our natural prejudices (fear of outsiders and love of our ancestors) with stirring songs and tender stories about Uncle Ho in which the Communist leader and our ancient heroes seemed to inhabit one congenial world. Like an unbroken thread, the path from our ancestors and legends seemed to lead inevitably to the Northern leader—then past him to a future of harmony and peace.

But to achieve that independence, Ho said, we must wage total war. His cadremen cried out "We must hold together and oppose the American empire. There is nothing better than freedom, independence, and happiness!"

To us, these ideas seemed as obvious as everything else we had heard. *Freedom* meant a Vietnam free of colonial domination. *Independence* meant one Vietnamese people—not two countries, North and South—determining its own destiny. *Happiness* meant plenty of food and an end to war—the ability, we assumed, to live our lives in accordance with our ancient ways. We wondered: how can the Southerners oppose these wonderful things? The answer the Viet Cong gave us was that the Republicans prized Yankee dollars more than the blood of their brothers and sisters. We did not think to question with our hearts what our minds told us must be true.

Although most of us thought we knew what the Viet Cong meant by freedom, independence, and happiness, a few of us dared to ask what life the Northerners promised when the war was over. The answer was always the same: "Uncle Ho promises that after our victory, the Communist state will look after your rights and interests. Your highest interest, of course, is the independence of our fatherland and the freedom of our people. Our greatest right is the right to determine our own future as a state." This always brought storms of applause from the villagers because most people remembered what life was like under the French.

Nonetheless, despite our vocal support, the Viet Cong never took our loyalty for granted. They rallied and rewarded and lectured us sternly, as the situation demanded, while the Republicans assumed we would be loyal because we lived south of a line some diplomats had drawn on a map. Even when things were at their worst—when the allied forces devastated the countryside and the Viet Cong themselves resorted to terror to make us act the way they wanted—the villagers clung to the vision the Communists had drummed into us. When the Republicans put us in jail, we had the image of "Communist freedom"—freedom from war—to see us through. When the Viet Cong executed a relative, we convinced ourselves that it was necessary to bring "Communist happiness"—peace in the village—a little closer. Because the Viet Cong encouraged us to voice our basic human feelings through patriotic songs, the tortured, self-imposed silence we endured around Republicans only made us hate the government more. Even on those occasions when the Republicans tried to help us, we saw their favors as a trick or sign of weakness. Thus, even as we accepted their kindness, we despised the Republicans for it.

As the war gathered steam in the 1960s, every villager found his or her little world expanded—usually for the worse. The steady parade of troops through Ky La meant new opportunities for us to fall victim to outsiders. Catholic Republicans spurned and mistreated Buddhists for worshiping their ancestors. City boys taunted and cheated the "country bumpkins" while Vietnamese servicemen from other provinces made fun of our funny accents and strange ways. When the tactics on both sides got so rough that people were in danger no matter which side they favored, our sisters fled to the cities where they learned about liquor, drugs, adultery, materialism, and disrespect for their ancestors. More than one village father died inside when a "stranger from Saigon" returned in place of the daughter he had raised.

In contrast to this, the Viet Cong were, for the most part, our neighbors. Even though our cadre leaders had been trained in Hanoi, they had all been born on the Central Coast. They did not insult us for our manners and speech because they had been raised exactly like us. Where the Republicans came into the village overburdened with American equipment designed for a different war, the Viet Cong made do with what they had and seldom wasted their best ammunition—the goodwill of the people. The cadremen pointed out to us that where the Republicans wore medals, the Viet Cong wore rags and never gave up the fight. "Where the Republicans pillage, rape, and plunder," they said, "we preserve your houses, crops, and family"; for they knew that it was only by these resources—our food for rations, our homes for hiding, our sons and brothers for recruits—that they were able to keep the field.

Of course, the Viet Cong cadremen, like the Republicans, had no desire (or ability, most of them) to paint a fairer picture. For them, there could be no larger reason for Americans fighting the war than imperialist aggression. Because we peasants knew nothing about the United States, we could not stop to think how absurd it would be for so large and wealthy a nation to covet our poor little country for its rice fields, swamps, and pagodas. Because our only exposure to politics had been through the French colonial government (and before that, the rule of Vietnamese kings), we had no concept of democracy. For us, "Western culture" meant bars, brothels, black markets, and *xa hoi van minh*—bewildering machines—most of them destructive. We couldn't imagine that life in the capitalist world was anything other than a frantic, alien terror. Because, as peasants, we defined "politics" as something other people did someplace else, it had no relevance to our daily lives—except as a source of endless trouble. As a consequence, we overlooked the power that lay in our hands: our power to achieve virtually anything we wanted if only we acted together. The Viet Cong and the North, on the other hand, always recognized and respected this strength.

We children also knew that our ancestral spirits demanded we resist the outsiders. Our parents told us of the misery they had suffered from the invading Japanese ("small death," our neighbors called them) in World War II, and from the French, who returned in 1946. These soldiers destroyed our crops, killed our livestock, burned our houses, raped our women, and tortured or put to death anyone who opposed them—as well as many who did not. Now, the souls of all those people who had been mercilessly killed had come back to haunt Ky La—demanding revenge against the invaders. This we children believed with all our hearts. After all, we had been taught from birth that ghosts were simply people we could not see.

There was only one way to remove this curse. Uncle Ho had urged the poor to take up arms so that everyone might be guaranteed a little land on which to cultivate some rice. Because nearly everyone in Central Vietnam was a farmer, and because farmers must have land, almost everyone went to war: with a rifle or a hoe; with vigilance to give the alarm; with food and shelter for our fighters; or, if one was too little for anything else, with flowers and songs to cheer them up. Everything we knew commanded us to fight. Our ancestors called us to war. Our myths and legends called us to war. Our parents' teachings called us to war. Uncle Ho's cadre called us to war. Even President Diem had called us to fight for the very thing we now believe he was betraying—an independent Vietnam. Should an obedient child be less than an ox and refuse to do her duty?

And so the war began and became an insatiable dragon that roared around Ky La. By the time I turned thirteen, that dragon had swallowed me up.

SUGGESTIONS FOR DISCUSSION

1. This selection closes with the lines, "And so the war began and became an insatiable dragon that roared around Ky La. By the time I turned thirteen, that dragon had swallowed me up." How does Hayslip explain the origins of the Vietnam War in the countryside and why Vietnamese peasants fought for the Viet Cong? How does Hayslip's account differ from the accounts offered by Tindall and Shi in "The Tragedy of Vietnam" and by Baritz in "God's Country and American Know-How"? What implications about the nature of the war do you draw from your answer?

2. The Vietnam War was not only an encounter between the American military and the Viet Cong and North Vietnamese forces. It was also a cross-cultural encounter between Americans and Vietnamese. Hayslip offers the perspective of Vietnamese villagers on the arrival of "Western culture" in their country. What can you learn about the nature and meaning of the war by taking this perspective into account?

3. History is often presented in school and in popular opinion as the story of how the leaders of great nations shaped historical events. People, therefore, often think of history in terms of prominent figures such as George Washington, Napoleon, Abraham Lincoln, V. I. Lenin, Adolf Hitler, Mao Zedong, and Mohandas Gandhi. Hayslip, on the other hand, offers a view of history as it is lived at the local level, through the experience of ordinary people. What can you learn about the meaning of history from this local perspective? What does it bring to light that gets overlooked in other historical accounts?

SUGGESTIONS FOR WRITING

1. Write an essay that compares Hayslip's account of the origins of the Vietnam War to the accounts offered by Tindall and Shi in "The Tragedy of Vietnam" and by Baritz in "God's Country and American Know-How." The point here is not to decide which account is more accurate (they could all be accurate, from the perspectives they take) but to consider how the three quite different perspectives on the Vietnam War offer quite different representations of the nature and meaning of the war.

2. Hayslip says, "Our ancestors called us to war. Our myths and legends called us to war." She seems to suggest here that a people's willingness to wage a war of national liberation is not simply a matter of geopolitical conflicts but is deeply ingrained in their culture. Write an essay that considers whether Hayslip's statement, "Everything we knew commanded us to fight," can be applied to your "ancestors," to the "myths and legends" passed down to you. How you define ancestors, myths, and legends for this essay is up to you. Don't feel restricted to the perspective of American culture, its ancestors, myths, and legends. Depending on your own background, you might write, for example, about African American, Armenian, Irish, or Puerto Rican ancestors, myths, and legends. In any case, consider whether and how the desire for independence is expressed through your people's culture and what the consequences have been.

3. By representing the lived experience of Vietnamese villagers, Hayslip offers an account of the Vietnam War that differs dramatically from the two previous accounts, in which the Vietnamese are largely invisible. The Vietnam War, of course, is not the only encounter of Americans with another culture. Pick another instance where Americans have encountered another people and write an essay that develops the perspective of ordinary people in that culture to the arrival of Americans. Don't feel you have to write only about military encounters. You might want to consider other cross-cultural encounters such as those between New England missionaries and American Indians or between slave traders and West Africans.

Wallace Terry

PRIVATE FIRST CLASS REGINALD "MALIK" EDWARDS

The following selection is a chapter from *Bloods: An Oral History of the Vietnam War by Black Veterans* (1984) by the journalist and documentary film producer Wallace Terry. *Bloods* consists of twenty oral histories Terry gathered from African Americans who served in Vietnam, enlisted men and officers, from the U.S. Army, Navy, Marines, and Air Force—what Terry calls "a representative cross-section of the black combat force." As Terry says, these men's "stories are not to be found in the expanding body of Vietnam literature" but "deservedly belong in the forefront because of the unique experience of the black Vietnam veteran." We have chosen the story told by Malik Edwards, but all of the stories are equally eloquent, telling of life in combat, racism in the military, relations between Americans and Vietnamese, and the difficulties of returning to civilian life in a racially divided society.

Suggestion for Reading

- As you read, notice how Malik Edwards offers both anecdotal accounts of particular incidents in the war and his own commentary on the meaning of the war. Mark those passages where Edwards explains his feelings about the war.

◆

Rifleman
9th Regiment
U.S. Marine Corps
Danang
June 1965–March 1966

I'm in the Amtrac with Morley Safer, right? The whole thing is getting ready to go down. At Cam Ne. The whole bit that all America will see on the *CBS Evening News,* right? Marines burning down some huts. Brought to you by Morley Safer. Your man on the scene. August 5, 1965.

When we were getting ready for Cam Ne, the helicopters flew in first and told them to get out of the village 'cause the Marines are looking for VC. If you're left there, you're considered VC.

They told us if you receive one round from the village, you level it. So we was coming into the village, crossing over the hedges. It's like a little ditch, then you go through these bushes and jump across, and start kickin' ass, right?

Not only did we receive one round, three Marines got wounded right off. Not only that, but one of the Marines was our favorite Marine, Sergeant Bradford. This brother that everybody loved got shot in the groin. So you know how we felt.

The first thing happened to me, I looked out and here's a bamboo snake. That little short snake, the one that bites you and you're through bookin'. What do you do when a bamboo snake comin' at you? You drop your rifle with one hand, and shoot his head off. You don't think you can do this, but you do it. So I'm so rough with this snake, everybody thinks, well, Edwards is shootin' his ass off today.

So then this old man runs by. This other sergeant says, "Get him, Edwards." But I missed the old man. Now I just shot the head off a snake. You dig what I'm sayin'? Damn near with one hand. M-14. But all of a sudden, I missed this old man. 'Cause I really couldn't shoot him.

So Brooks—he's got the grenade launcher—fired. Caught my man as he was comin' through the door. But what happened was it was a room full of children. Like a schoolroom. And he was runnin' back to warn the kids that the Marines were coming. And that's who got hurt. All those little kids and people.

Everybody wanted to see what had happened, 'cause it was so fucked up. But the officers wouldn't let us go up there and look at what shit they were in. I never got the count, but a lot of people got screwed up. I was telling Morley Safer and his crew what was happening, but they thought I was trippin', this Marine acting crazy, just talking shit. 'Cause they didn't want to know what was going on.

So I'm going on through the village. Like the way you go in, you sweep, right? You fire at the top of the hut in case somebody's hangin' in the rafters. And if they hit the ground, you immediately fire along the ground, waist high, to catch them on the run. That's the way I had it worked out, or the way the Marines taught me. That's the process.

All of a sudden, this Vietnamese came runnin' after me, telling me not to shoot: "Don't shoot. Don't shoot." See, we didn't go in the village and look. We would just shoot first. Like you didn't go into a room to see who was in there first. You fired and go in. So in case there was somebody there, you want to kill them first. And we was just gonna run in, shoot through the walls. 'Cause it was nothin' to shoot through the walls of a bamboo hut. You could actually set them on fire if you had tracers. That used to be a fun thing to do. Set hootches on fire with tracers.

So he ran out in front of me. I mean he's runnin' into my line of fire. I almost killed him. But I'm thinking, what the hell is wrong? So then we went into the hut, and it was all these women and children huddled together. I was gettin' ready to wipe them off the planet. In this one hut. I tell you, man, my knees got weak. I dropped down, and that's when I cried. First time I cried in the 'Nam. I realized what I would have done. I almost killed all them people. That was the first time I had actually had the experience of weak knees.

Safer didn't tell them to burn the huts down with they lighters. He just photographed it. He could have got a picture of me burning a hut, too. It was just the way they did it. When you say level a village, you don't use torches. It's not like in the 1800s. You use a Zippo. Now you would use a Bic. That's just the way we did it. You went in there with your Zippos. Everybody. That's why people bought Zippos. Everybody had a Zippo. It was for burnin' shit down.

I was a Hollywood Marine. I went to San Diego, but it was worse in Parris Island. Like you've heard the horror stories of Parris Island—people be marchin' into the swamps. So you were happy to be in San Diego. Of course, you're in a lot of sand, but it was always warm.

At San Diego, they had this way of driving you into this base. It's all dark. Back roads. All of a sudden you come to this little adobe-looking place. All of a sudden, the lights are on, and all you see are these guys with these Smokey the Bear hats and big hands on their hips. The light is behind them, shining through at you. You all happy to be with the Marines. And they say, "Better knock that shit off, boy. I don't want to hear a goddamn word out of your mouth." And everybody starts cursing and yelling and screaming at you.

My initial instinct was to laugh. But then they get right up in your face. That's when I started getting scared. When you're 117 pounds, 150 look like a monster. He would just come screaming down your back, "What the hell are you looking at, shit turd?" I remembered the time where you cursed, but you didn't let anybody adult hear it. You were usually doing it just to be funny or trying to be bold. But these people were actually serious about cursing your ass out.

Then here it is. Six o'clock in the morning. People come in bangin' on trash cans, hittin' my bed with night sticks. That's when you get really scared, 'cause you realize I'm not at home anymore. It doesn't look like you're in the Marine Corps either. It looks like you're in jail. It's like you woke up in a prison camp somewhere in the South. And the whole process was not to allow you to be yourself.

I grew up in a family that was fair. I was brought up on the Robin Hood ethic, and John Wayne came to save people. So I could not understand that if these guys were supposed to be the good guys, why were they treating each other like this?

I grew up in Plaquemines Parish. My folks were poor, but I was never hungry. My stepfather worked with steel on buildings. My mother worked wherever she could. In the fields, pickin' beans. In the factories, the shrimp factories, oyster factories. And she was a housekeeper.

I was the first person in my family to finish high school. This was 1963. I knew I couldn't go to college because my folks couldn't afford it. I only weighed 117 pounds, and nobody's gonna hire me to work for them. So the only thing left to do was go into the service. I didn't want to go into the Army, 'cause everybody went into the Army. Plus the Army didn't seem like it did anything. The Navy I did not like 'cause of the uniforms. The Air Force, too. But the Marines was bad. The Marine Corps built men. Plus just before I went in, they had all these John Wayne movies on every night. Plus the Marines went to the Orient.

Everybody laughed at me. Little, skinny boy can't work in the field going in the Marine Corps. So I passed the test. My mother, she signed for me 'cause I was seventeen.

There was only two black guys in my platoon in boot camp. So I hung with the Mexicans, too, because in them days we never hang with white people. You didn't have white friends. White people was the aliens to me. This is '63. You don't have integration really in the South. You expected them to treat you bad. But somehow in the Marine Corps you hoping all that's gonna change. Of course, I found out this was not true, because the Marine Corps was the last service to integrate. And I had an Indian for a platoon commander who hated Indians. He used to call Indians blanket ass. And then we had a Southerner from Arkansas that liked to call you chocolate bunny and Brillo head. That kind of shit.

I went to jail in boot camp. What happened was I was afraid to jump this ditch on the obstacle course. Every time I would hit my shin. So a white lieutenant called me a nigger. And, of course, I jumped the ditch farther than I'd ever jumped before. Now I can't run. My leg is really messed up. I'm hoppin'. So it's pretty clear I can't do this. So

I tell the drill instructor, "Man, I can't fucking go on." He said, "You said what?" I said it again. He said, "Get out." I said, "Fuck you." This to a drill instructor in 1963. I mean you just don't say that. I did seven days for disrespect. When I got out of the brig, they put me in a recon. The toughest unit.

We trained in guerrilla warfare for two years at Camp Pendleton. When I first got there, they was doing Cuban stuff. Cuba was the aggressor. It was easy to do Cuba because you had a lot of Mexicans. You could always let them be Castro. We even had Cuban targets. Targets you shoot at. So then they changed the silhouettes to Vietnamese. Everything to Vietnam. Getting people ready for the little gooks. And, of course, if there were any Hawaiians and Asian-Americans in the unit, they played the roles of aggressors in the war games.

Then we are going over to Okinawa, thinking we're going on a regular cruise. But the rumors are that we're probably going to the 'Nam. In Okinawa we was trained as raiders. Serious, intense jungle-warfare training. I'm gonna tell you, it was some good training. The best thing about the Marine Corps, I can say for me, is that they teach you personal endurance, how much of it you can stand.

The only thing they told us about the Viet Cong was they were gooks. They were to be killed. Nobody sits around and gives you their historical and cultural background. They're the enemy. Kill, kill, kill. That's what we got in practice. Kill, kill, kill. I remember a survey they did in the mess hall where we had to say how we felt about the war. The thing was, get out of Vietnam or fight. What we were hearing was Vietnamese was killing Americans. I felt that if people were killing Americans, we should fight them. As a black person, there wasn't no problem fightin' the enemy. I knew Americans were prejudiced, were racist and all that, but basically, I believed in America 'cause I was an American.

I went over with the original 1st Battalion 9th Marines. When we got there, it was nothing like you expect a war to be. We had seen a little footage of the war on TV. But we was on the ship dreaming about landing on this beach like they did in World War II. Then we pulled into this area like a harbor almost and just walked off the ship.

And the first Vietnamese that spoke to me was a little kid up to my knee. He said, "You give me cigarette. You give me cigarette." That really freaked me out. This little bitty kid smokin' cigarettes. That is my first memory of Vietnam. I thought little kids smokin' was the most horrible thing that you could do. So the first Vietnamese words I learned was *Toi khong hut thuoc lo.* "I don't smoke cigarettes." And *Thuoc la co hai cho suc khoe.* "Cigarettes are bad for your health."

Remember, we were in the beginning of the war. We wasn't dealing with the regular army from the North. We was still fightin' the Viet Cong. The NVA was moving in, but they really hadn't made their super move yet. So we were basically runnin' patrols out of Danang. We were basically with the same orders that the Marines went into Lebanon with. I mean we couldn't even put rounds in the chambers at first.

It was weird. The first person that died in each battalion of the 9th Marines that landed was black. And they were killed by our own people. Comin' back into them lines was the most dangerous thing then. It was more fun sneakin' into Ho Chi Minh's house than comin' back into the lines of Danang. Suppose the idiot is sleeping on watch and he wake up. All of a sudden he sees people. That's all he sees. There was a runnin' joke around Vietnam that we was killing more of our people than the Vietnamese were. Like we were told to kill any Vietnamese in black. We didn't know

that the ARVN had some black uniforms, too. And you could have a platoon commander calling the air strikes, and he's actually calling on your position. It was easy to get
killed by an American.

They called me a shitbird, because I would stay in trouble. Minor shit, really. But
they put me on point anyway. I spent most of my time in Vietnam runnin'. I ran
through Vietnam 'cause I was always on point, and points got to run. They can't walk
like everybody else. Specially when you hit them open areas. Nobody walked through
an open area. After a while, you develop a way to handle it. You learned that the point
usually survived. It was the people behind you who got killed.

And another thing. It's none of that shit, well, if they start shootin' at you, now all
of a sudden we gonna run in there and outshoot them. The motherfuckers hit, you call
in some air. Bring in some heavy artillery, whatever you need to cool them down. You
wipe that area up. You soften it up. Then you lay to see if you receive any fire. And *then*
you go on in.

I remember the first night we had went out on patrol. About 50 people shot this
old guy. Everybody claimed they shot him. He got shot 'cause he started running. It
was an old man running to tell his family. See, it wasn't s'posed to be nobody out at
night but the Marines. Any Vietnamese out at night was the enemy. And we had guys
who were frustrated from Korea with us. Guys who were real gung ho, wanted a name
for themselves. So a lot of times they ain't tell us shit about who is who. People get out
of line, you could basically kill them. So this old man was running like back towards his
crib to warn his family. I think people said "Halt," but we didn't know no Vietnamese
words.

It was like shootin' water buffaloes. Somebody didn't tell us to do this. We did it
anyway. But they had to stop us from doing that. Well, the water buffaloes would actually attack Americans. I guess maybe we smelled different. You would see these little
Vietnamese kids carrying around this huge water buffalo. That buffalo would see some
Marines and start wantin' to run 'em down. You see the poor little kids tryin' to hold
back the water buffalo, because these Marines will kill him. And Marines, man, was
like, like we was always lookin' for shit to go wrong. Shit went wrong. That gave us the
opportunity.

I remember we had went into this village and got pinned down with a Australian
officer. When we finally went on through, we caught these two women. They smelled
like they had weapons. These were all the people we found. So the Australian dude told
us to take the women in. So me and my partner, we sittin' up in this Amtrac with these
women. Then these guys who was driving the Amtrac come in there and start unzippin'
their pants as if they gonna screw the women. So we say, "Man, get outta here. You
can't do it to our prisoners." So they get mad with us. Like they gonna fight us. And we
had to actually lock and load to protect the women. They said, "We do this all the
time."

One time we had went into this place we had hit. We was takin' prisoners. So this
one guy broke and ran. So I chased him. I ran behind him. Everybody say, "Shoot him.
Shoot him." 'Cause they was pissed that I was chasin' him. So I hit him. You know I
had to do something to him. I knew I couldn't just grab him and bring him back. And
his face just crumbled. Then I brought him back, and they said, "You could have got a
kill, Edwards."

The first time we thought we saw the enemy in big numbers was one of these operations by Marble Mountain. We had received fire. All of a sudden we could see people in front of us. Instead of waiting for air, we returned the fire, and you could see people fall. I went over to this dude and said, "Hey, man, I saw one fall." Then everyone started yelling, "We can see 'em fall. We can see 'em fall." And they were fallin'. Come to find out it was Bravo Company. What the VC had done was suck Bravo Company in front of us. 'Cause they attacked us and Bravo Company at the same time. They would move back as Bravo Company was in front of us. It was our own people. That's the bodies we saw falling. They figured out what was happening, and then they ceased fire. But the damage is done real fast. I think we shot up maybe 40 guys in Bravo Company. Like I said, it was easy to get killed by an American.

The first time I killed somebody up close was when we was tailing Charlie on a patrol somewhere around Danang. It was night. I was real tired. At that time you had worked so hard during the day, been on so many different details, you were just bombed out.

I thought I saw this dog running. Because that white pajama top they wore at night just blend into that funny-colored night they had over there. All of a sudden, I realized that somebody's runnin'. And before I could say anything to him, he's almost ran up on me. There's nothing I can do but shoot. Somebody get that close, you can't wait to check their ID. He's gonna run into you or stop to shoot you. It's got to be one or the other. I shot him a bunch of times. I had 20-round clip, and when he hit the ground, I had nothing. I had to reload. That's how many times he was shot.

Then the sergeant came over and took out the flashlight and said, "Goddamn. This is fucking beautiful. This is fucking beautiful."

This guy was really out of it. He was like moanin'. I said, "Let me kill him." I couldn't stand the sound he was makin'. So I said, "Back off, man. Let me put this guy out of his misery." So I shot him again. In the head.

He had a grenade in his hand. I guess he was committing suicide. He was just runnin' up to us, pullin' a grenade kind of thing. I caught him just in time.

Everybody was comin' congratulatin' me, saying what a great thing it was. I'm tryin' to be cool, but I'm really freakin' out. So then I start walking away, and they told me I had to carry the body back to base camp. We had a real kill. We had one we could prove. We didn't have to make this one up.

So then I start draggin' this body by the feet. And his arm fell off. So I had to go back and get his arm. I had to stick it down his pants. It was a long haul.

And I started thinkin'. You think about how it feels, the weight. It was rainin'. You think about the mist and the smells the rain brings out. All of a sudden I realize this guy is a person, has got a family. All of a sudden it wasn't like I was carrying a gook. I was actually carrying a human being. I started feeling guilty. I just started feeling really badly.

I don't feel like we got beat in Vietnam. We never really fought the war. People saying that America couldn't have won that war is crazy.

The only way we could actually win the war was to fight every day. You couldn't fight only when you felt like it. Or change officers every month. Troops would learn the language, learn the people, learn the areas. If you're gonna be fighting in an area, you get to know everybody in the area and you stay there. You can't go rotate your troops every 12 months. You always got new people coming in. Plus they may not get to learn anything. They may die the first day. If you take a guy on patrol and he gets killed the first day, what good is he? See, if you have seasoned troops, you can move in and out of the bush at will. You get the smell of the country on you. You start to eat the food. You start to smell like it. You don't have that fresh smell so they can smell you when you're comin'. Then you can fight a war. Then you can just start from one tip of South Vietnam and work your way to the top. To China. Of course, if we had used the full might of the military, we'd be there now. We could never give the country back up. Plus we'd have to kill millions of Vietnamese. Do we want to do that? What had they done to us to deserve all that? So to do it would have been wrong. All we did was give our officers the first combat training they had since Korea. It was more like a big training ground. If it was a real war, you either would have come out in a body bag or you would have come out when the war was over.

Sometimes I think we would have done a lot better by getting them hooked on our life-style than by trying to do it with guns. Give them credit cards. Make them dependent on television and sugar. Blue jeans works better than bombs. You can take blue jeans and rock 'n' roll records and win over more countries than you can with soldiers.

When I went home, they put me in supply, probably the lowest job you can have in the Marines. But they saw me drawing one day and they said, "Edwards can draw." They sent me over to the training-aids library, and I became an illustrator. I reenlisted and made sergeant.

When I went to Quantico, my being black, they gave me the black squad, the squad with most of the blacks, especially the militant blacks. And they started hippin' me. I mean I was against racism. I didn't even call it racism. I called it prejudice. They hipped me to terms like "exploitation" and "oppression." And by becoming an illustrator, it gave you more time to think. And I was around people who thought. People who read books. I would read black history where the white guys were going off on novels or playing rock music. So then one day, I just told them I was black. I didn't call them *blanco,* they didn't have to call me Negro. That's what started to get me in trouble. I became a target. Somebody to watch.

Well, there was this riot on base, and I got busted. It started over some white guys using a bunch of profanity in front of some sisters. I was found guilty of attack on an unidentified Marine. Five months in jail, five months without pay. And a suspended BCD. In jail they didn't want us to read our books, draw any pictures, or do anything intellectually stimulating or what they thought is black. They would come in my cell and harass me. So one day I was just tired of them, and I hit the duty warden. I ended up with a BCD in 1970. After six years, eight months, and eight days, I was kicked out of the Corps. I don't feel it was fair. If I had been white, I would never have went to jail for fighting. That would have been impossible.

With a BCD, nothing was happenin'. I took to dressin' like the Black Panthers, so even blacks wouldn't hire me. So I went to the Panther office in D.C. and joined. I felt the party was the only organization that was fighting the system.

I liked their independence. The fact that they had no fear of the police. Talking about self-determination. Trying to make Malcolm's message reality. This was the first time black people had stood up to the state since Nat Turner. I mean armed. It was obvious they wasn't gonna give us anything unless we stood up and were willing to die. They obviously didn't care anything about us, 'cause they had killed King.

For me the thought of being killed in the Black Panther Party by the police and the thought of being killed by Vietnamese was just a qualitative difference. I had left one war and came back and got into another one. Most of the Panthers then were veterans. We figured if we had been over in Vietnam fighting for our country, which at that point wasn't serving us properly, it was only proper that we had to go out and fight for our own cause. We had already fought for the white man in Vietnam. It was clearly his war. If it wasn't, you wouldn't have seen as many Confederate flags as you saw. And the Confederate flags was an insult to any person that's of color on this planet.

I rose up into the ranks. I was an artist immediately for the newspaper. Because of my background in the military, obviously I was able to deal with a lot of things of a security nature. And eventually I took over the D.C. chapter.

At this time, Huey Newton and Bobby Seale were in jail and people sort of idealized them. The party didn't actually fall apart until those two were released, and then the real leader, David Hilliard, was locked up. Spiro Agnew had a lot to do with the deterioration when he said take the Panthers out of the newspapers and then they will go away. And the FBI was harassing us, and we started turning on each other because of what they were spreading. And the power structure started to build up the poverty programs. Nobody was going to follow the Panthers if they could go down to the poverty program and get a check and say they are going to school.

We just didn't understand the times. All we wanted to do was kick whitey's ass. We didn't think about buying property or gaining economic independence. We were, in the end, just showing off.

I think the big trip America put us on was to convince us that having money was somehow harmful. That building businesses and securing our economic future, and buying and controlling areas for our group, our family, our friends like everybody else does, was wrong. Doing that doesn't make you antiwhite. I think white people would even like us better if we had more money. They like Richard Pryor. And Sammy Davis. And Jabbar.

Economically, black folks in America have more money than Canada or Mexico. It's obvious that we are doing something wrong. When people say we're illiterate, that doesn't bother me as much. Literacy means I can't read these books. Well neither does a Korean or a Vietnamese. But where they're not illiterate is in the area of economics. Sure, we're great artists, great singers, play great basketball. But we're not great managers yet. It's pretty obvious that you don't have to have guns to get power. People get things out of this country and they don't stick up America to do it. Look at the Vietnamese refugees running stores now in the black community where I live.

Right now, I'm an unemployed artist, drawing unemployment. I spent time at a community center helping kids, encouraging kids to draw.

I work for the nuclear-freeze movement, trying to convince people nuclear war is insane. Even when I was in the Marine Corps, I was against nuclear war. When I was a child, I was against nuclear weapons, because I thought what they did to Hiroshima and Nagasaki was totally cold. There's nothing any human being is doing on the planet that I could want to destroy the planet for future generations. I think we should confine war to our century and our times. Not to leave the residue around for future generations. The residue of hate is a horrible thing to leave behind. The residue of nuclear holocaust is far worse.

I went to see *Apocalypse Now,* because a friend paid my way. I don't like movies about Vietnam 'cause I don't think that they are prepared to tell the truth. *Apocalypse Now,* didn't tell the truth. It wasn't real. I guess it was a great thing for the country to get off on, but it didn't remind me of anything I saw. I can't understand how you would have a bridge lit up like a Christmas tree. A USO show at night? Guys attacking the women on stage. That made no sense. I never saw us reach the point where nobody is in charge in a unit. That's out of the question. If you don't know anything, you know the chain of command. And the helicopter attack on the village? Fuckin' ridiculous. You couldn't hear music comin' out of a helicopter. And attacking a beach in helicopters was just out of the question. The planes and the napalm would go in first. Then, the helicopters would have eased in after the fact. That was wild.

By making us look insane, the people who made that movie was somehow relieving themselves of what they asked us to do over there. But we were not insane. We were not insane. We were not ignorant. We knew what we were doing.

I mean we were crazy, but it's built into the culture. It's like institutionalized insanity. When you're in combat, you can do basically what you want as long as you don't get caught. You can get away with murder. And the beautiful thing about the military is there's always somebody that can serve up as a scapegoat. Like Calley. I wondered why they didn't get Delta Company 1-9 because of Cam Ne. We were real scared. But President Johnson came out and defended us. But like that was before My Lai. When they did My Lai, I got nervous again. I said my God, and they have us on film.

I was in Washington during the National Vietnam Veterans Memorial in 1982. But I didn't participate. I saw all these veterans runnin' around there with all these jungle boots on, all these uniforms. I didn't want to do that. It just gave me a bad feeling. Plus some of them were braggin' about the war. Like it was hip. See, I don't think the war was a good thing. And there's no memorial to Cam Ne, to My Lai. To all those children that was napalmed and villages that were burned unnecessarily.

I used to think that I wasn't affected by Vietnam, but I been livin' with Vietnam ever since I left. You just can't get rid of it. It's like that painting of what Dali did of melting clocks. It's a persistent memory.

I remember most how hard it was to just shoot people.

I remember one time when three of our people got killed by a sniper from this village. We went over to burn the village down. I was afraid that there was going to be shootin' people that day, so I just kind of dealt with the animals. You know, shoot the chickens. I mean I just couldn't shoot no people.

I don't know how many chickens I shot. But it was a little pig that freaked me out more than the chickens. You think you gonna be shootin' a little pig, it's just gonna fall over and die. Well, no. His little guts be hangin' out. He just be squiggling around and freakin' you out.

See, you got to shoot animals in the head. If we shoot you in your stomach, you may just fall over and die. But an animal, you got to shoot them in the head. They don't understand that they supposed to fall over and die.

SUGGESTIONS FOR DISCUSSION

1. Compare the passages you marked with the passages marked by your classmates. See if you can decide what Edwards's feelings are about the Vietnam War. How would you characterize his understanding of why the war was fought and what it means? If you think his feelings are contradictory or inconsistent, how would you explain this?

2. Edwards says that the "only thing they told us about the Viet Cong was they were gooks. They were to be killed. Nobody sits around and gives you their historical and cultural background. They're the enemy. Kill, kill, kill." Explain the meaning of this passage. How, in wartime, is the "enemy" created? What might have happened if American soldiers knew the historical and cultural background of the Vietnamese people?

3. Edwards says that when he returned to the United States, he "had left one war and got into another one." What does he mean? How are these two "wars" alike and different?

SUGGESTIONS FOR WRITING

1. Write an essay that develops your own personal response to reading the selection by Malik Edwards. How did it make you feel about the Vietnam War? What changes, if any, occurred in your understanding of the war? Why do you think you reacted as you did?

2. Edwards says, "You can take blue jeans and rock 'n' roll records and win over more countries than you can with soldiers." Write an essay that explains what Edwards means by this statement. Use the essay to develop your own position on what it means for the United States to "hook" other countries "on our life-style." How does this (or does it not) differ from "trying to do it with guns"? What are the wider issues—ethical, cultural, and political—that you see involved here?

3. Write an essay that compares Edwards's experience of the Vietnam War to that of Le Ly Hayslip. What do you see as the significance of these two descriptions of the war?

Molly Ivins

A SHORT STORY ABOUT THE VIETNAM WAR MEMORIAL

Molly Ivins is an award-winning journalist who has written for the *Texas Observer* and *The New York Times* and contributes regularly to magazines such as *Ms., The Progressive,* and *The Nation.* The following selection was written as a column for the *Dallas Times-Herald* (November 30, 1982) shortly after the Vietnam War Memorial was dedicated. Ivins's writing is often witty and irreverent, but in this column her tone is restrained, even solemn, as she recreates a woman's visit to the Vietnam War Memorial in Washington, D.C. Ivins tells the woman's story in a simple, unadorned way that reveals the impact of the war, years after it ended, on the lives of ordinary people.

Suggestion for Reading

- As you read, notice how Ivins uses fictional techniques to represent the thoughts and memories of her character. Ivins offers little commentary but, by the end, the story has taken on considerable significance. Annotate those passages where Ivins unfolds the meaning of the story.

———————◆———————

S he had known, ever since she first read about the Vietnam War Memorial, that she would go there someday. Sometime she would be in Washington and would go and see his name and leave again.

So silly, all that fuss about the memorial. Whatever else Vietnam was, it was not the kind of war that calls for some *Raising the Flag at Iwo Jima* kind of statue. She was not prepared, though, for the impact of the memorial. To walk down into it in the pale winter sunshine was like the war itself, like going into a dark valley and damned if there was ever any light at the end of the tunnel. Just death. When you get closer to the two walls, the number of names start to stun you. It is terrible, there in the peace and the pale sunshine.

The names are listed by date of death. There has never been a time, day or night, drunk or sober, for thirteen years that she could not have told you the date. He was killed on August 13, 1969. It is near the middle of the left wall. She went toward it as though she had known beforehand where it would be. His name is near the bottom. She had to kneel to find it. Stupid clichés. His name leaped out at her. It was like being hit.

She stared at it and then reached out and gently ran her fingers over the letters in the cold black marble. The memory of him came back so strong, almost as if he were there on the other side of the stone, she could see his hand reaching out to touch her fingers. It had not hurt for years and suddenly, just for a moment, it hurt again so horribly that it twisted her face and made her gasp and left her with tears running down her face. Then it stopped hurting but she could not stop the tears. Could not stop them running and running down her face.

There had been a time, although she had been an otherwise sensible young woman, when she had believed she would never recover from the pain. She did, of course. But she is still determined never to sentimentalize him. He would have hated that. She had thought it was like an amputation, the severing of his life from hers, that you could live on afterward but it would be like having only one leg and one arm. But it was only a wound. It healed. If there is a scar, it is only faintly visible now at odd intervals.

He was a biologist, a t.a. at the university getting his Ph.D. They lived together for two years. He left the university to finish his thesis but before he lined up a public school job—teachers were safe in those years—the draft board got him. They had friends who had left the country, they had friends who had gone to prison, they had friends who had gone to Nam. There were no good choices in those years. She thinks now he unconsciously wanted to go even though he often said, said in one of his last letters, that it was a stupid, f---in' war. He felt some form of guilt about a friend of theirs who was killed during the Tet offensive. Hubert Humphrey called Tet a great victory. His compromise was to refuse officer's training school and go as an enlisted man. She had thought then it was a dumb gesture and they had a half-hearted quarrel about it.

He had been in Nam less than two months when he was killed, without heroics, during a firefight at night by a single bullet in the brain. No one saw it happen. There are some amazing statistics about money and tonnage from that war. Did you know that there were more tons of bombs dropped on Hanoi during the Christmas bombing of 1972 than in all of World War II? Did you know that the war in Vietnam cost the United States $123.3 billion? She has always wanted to know how much that one bullet cost. Sixty-three cents? $1.20? Someone must know.

The other bad part was the brain. Even at this late date, it seems to her that was quite a remarkable mind. Long before she read C. P. Snow, the ferociously honest young man who wanted to be a great biologist taught her a great deal about the difference between the way scientists think and the way scientists think and the way humanists think. Only once has she been glad he was not with her. It was at one of those bizarre hearings about teaching "creation science." He would have gotten furious and been horribly rude. He had no patience with people who did not understand and respect the process of science.

She used to attribute his fierce honesty to the fact that he was a Yankee. She is still prone to tell "white" lies to make people feel better, to smooth things over, to prevent hard feelings. Surely there have been dumber things for lovers to quarrel over than the social utility of hypocrisy. But not many.

She stood up again, still staring at his name, stood for a long time. She said, "There it is," and turned to go. A man to her left was staring at her. She glared at him. The man had done nothing but make the mistake of seeing her weeping. She said, as though daring him to disagree, "It was a stupid, f---in' war," and stalked past him.

She turned again at the top of the slope to make sure where his name is, so whenever she sees a picture of the memorial she can put her finger where his name is. He never said goodbye, literally. Whenever he left he would say, "Take care, love." He could say it many different ways. He said it when he left for Vietnam. She stood at the top of the slope and found her hand half-raised in some silly gesture of farewell. She brought it down again. She considered thinking to him, "Hey, take care, love" but it seemed remarkably inappropriate. She walked away and was quite entertaining for the rest of the day, because it was expected of her.

She thinks he would have liked the memorial. He would have hated the editorials. He did not sacrifice his life for his country or for a just or noble cause. There just were no good choices in those years and he got killed.

SUGGESTIONS FOR DISCUSSION

1. Compare your annotations with those written by other members of the class. Work together to construct the meaning of Ivins's column. See if you can state its theme and purpose in one or two sentences.
2. Ivins says, "Whatever else Vietnam was, it was not the kind of war that calls for some *Raising the Flag at Iwo Jima* kind of statue." Find photographs of the Vietnam War Memorial and Raising the Flag at Iwo Jima to bring to class. Explain Ivins's statement by referring to the two photographs.
3. At the end of the column, Ivins writes, "She thinks he would have liked the memorial." What do you make of this judgment?

SUGGESTIONS FOR WRITING

1. Ivins says, "there were just no good choices in those days and he died." What does she mean by this statement? Write an essay that begins by explaining why Ivins makes the statement and then give your own assessment of the choices available—leaving the country, going to prison, fighting in Vietnam, finding a job with a draft deferment.
2. Both Malik Edwards and the woman in Ivins's story visit the Vietnam War Memorial. If they had met there and talked, what do you think they would have said to each other? Write a dialogue between the two that expresses their feelings about the Vietnam War Memorial and about their memories of the war.
3. This selection and the previous reading, "Malik Edwards," suggest that history lives in ordinary people's memories, that they carry the past with them into the present. Interview someone who lived through the Vietnam years—someone who went to Vietnam, who was active in the antiwar movement, whose son or daughter was in the military. How does your subject remember those years? What lasting effects did the war have on the person? What memories does the person carry with him or her? Use the interview to write a character sketch of the Vietnam War as a living memory.

Michael Klein

HISTORICAL MEMORY, FILM, AND THE VIETNAM ERA

Michael Klein teaches media and American studies at the University of Ulster in Northern Ireland. The following selection is taken from a longer article, published in *From Hanoi to Hollywood: The Vietnam War in American Film* (1990), that analyzes how the Vietnam War has been represented in Hollywood films, from *The Green Berets* (1968) to *Platoon* (1987). Klein suggests that Americans learn history not only through school textbooks and official accounts but also through the popular media, whether movies, television shows, or popular songs. According to Klein, such popular versions of historical events often reinterpret the past "in an attempt to heal national and class divisions that were rooted in still-unresolved social and political contradictions." In this sense, the version of the past provided by Hollywood movies and television shows is always a selective one, constructed to serve particular cultural and political purposes in the present.

Suggestion for Reading

- Michael Klein ends the opening paragraph by describing reinterpretations of wars and significant social crises as a "process of organized forgetting" that "takes a people's complex past away." As you read, notice how Klein develops this argument. Mark key passages and examples.

———————◆———————

HOLLYWOOD AND HISTORICAL MEMORY: THE ROAD TO *PLATOON*

> We need to question discourse in order to identify not its deeper meaning, its concealed residue, but what is at stake in this or that interpretation.
>
> Catherine Belsey, *The Politics of Meaning*

fter a war or significant social crisis that has been divisive, and especially during a period of conservatism following an era of radical social or cultural action, the history of the recent past is often reinterpreted. Those with access to the means of cultural production, in accordance with the new dominant political attitudes, are likeliest to be behind such major shifts in interpretation. Radical or oppositional moments in the history of a nation are effectively excised from the cultural memory. A process of organized forgetting takes people's complex past away, substituting comfortable myths that reinforce rather than challenge the status quo.

Thus, in the years after the American Civil War and the failure of radical Reconstruction, cultural production about the preceding period was dominated by revisionist myths, myths still apparent many years later in D. W. Griffith's *The Birth of a Nation* (1915), in *Gone With the Wind* (1939), and in the recent television series *North and South*. Griffith's film is part of a thematic trend in popular narrative about the Civil War and Reconstruction, a trend governed by an ideology of reconciliation and national unity. Historians, novelists, and later filmmakers revised the history of the recent past in an attempt to heal national and class divisions that were rooted in still-unresolved social and political contradictions. After the radical forces that had achieved a certain degree of hegemony in the late 1860s were marginalized, compromised, or suppressed, the war that in a formal sense had ended slavery was reinterpreted from a conservative white Southern point of view by Southern Bourbons and the Ku Klux Klan with the tacit support of Northern business interests. They developed a reactionary Southern myth of a harmonious slave society and divisive war into a key aspect of the new national consensus. In time, the radicalism and achievements of the Civil War and Black Reconstruction eras were exorcised from historical memory.

A series of historical narratives produced in the following decades shifted sympathy from abolitionists, reformers, and Negro slaves to patriarchal former slave owners, Southern belles, and Confederate soldiers as victims of the war and Reconstruction. For example, *The Birth of a Nation,* endorsed and promoted by the U.S. president and the chief justice of the Supreme Court, stereotypes Blacks and radicals as threats to law and order, sexual morality, and the social fabric; it celebrates the reestablishment of the nation on the basis of the conservative prewar national consensus. The popularity of Griffith's film, and later *Gone With the Wind,* are indexes of complacent acceptance of Jim Crow in the South and segregation elsewhere in insecure economic times. Later, scholarship and narratives that began to challenge the revisionist interpretation of the Civil War and Reconstruction signalled a thaw in American society and the start of the Civil Rights era.

An analogous process has taken place in our own period, through the reinterpretation of the American war in Vietnam. During the period of the war, *and* of the movement against the war—which was part of a broad movement whose concerns included equal rights and equal opportunities for Blacks, other minorities, and women—the independent media produced a number of works opposed to American military involvement, and in some cases were sympathetic to the cause of the Vietnamese National Liberation Front. More covert statements critical of U.S. intervention in Vietnam were also made through Hollywood genre films. Subsequently, as America entered the Reagan era and began engaging in interventions in Central America, Grenada, and the Middle East, Hollywood produced a series of films that glorified the war in Vietnam. They have on the whole been permeated with macho-warrior and racist ideology, reaffirming a neo–Cold War perspective of the world and depicting radical and liberal-minded people as weak or deviant. Some recent films have countered the excesses of this revisionism, but generally they have failed to do justice to antiwar attitudes at home, within the army, or among Vietnam veterans, and to the effect that this opposition had on people's consciousness of themselves and their society. They are therefore a distorted representation of the national past.

During the years of the Vietnam War and the protests against it, only one Hollywood fiction film was set in Vietnam—John Wayne's *The Green Berets* (1968). Drawing heavily upon established conventions of the World War II and Korean War film and exploiting the image of its star, *The Green Berets* was an unqualified defense of American military involvement in Vietnam. At the same time, however, horrific images of the consequences of American military presence and reports of worldwide antiwar protests were seen by the American public on television news and in independently produced 16mm documentary films such as *Inside North Vietnam* (1968), *In the Year of the Pig* (1968), and *Hearts and Minds* (1974). Images and counterimages of the war were an important aspect of the midsixties debate between doves and hawks about the war and conscription.

Indirect criticism of the war also appeared in one established Hollywood film genre, the Western, and expanded its conventions in new directions. Both Ralph Nelson's *Soldier Blue* (1970) and Arthur Penn's *Little Big Man* (1970) suggest in their condemnation of cavalry massacres and genocidal policy towards American Indians allegories of the war in Vietnam, perhaps with particular reference to the massacre of Vietnamese civilians in the village of My Lai and the U.S. Air Force's indiscriminate use of napalm in free-fire zones. Both films also offer a critique of white U.S. civilization as essentially colonialist, barbarous, hypocritical, and life-denying. Significantly, both films present Indian life, and by extension non-Anglo life, as more holistic and life-enhancing than competitive materialistic American society. In doing so they not only express a certain solidarity with the struggle of Third World people against cultural, military, and economic penetration but also affirm the social values of the Civil Rights movement and the counterculture, which were an integral aspect of the antiwar movement both within and outside the army.

Vietnam as a subject initially returned to the Hollywood screen after the conclusion of the war, in the form of a series of coming-home films that focused on the situation of the returning veteran. Again Hollywood only seemed able to confront the Vietnam experience by situating it within an established genre. For example, *I Am a Fugitive from a Chain Gang* (1932) and *The Best Years of Our Lives* (1946) were post–World War I and post–World War II coming-home films that focused on a wounded, alienated, or rejected veteran's return to American society; such films have often been vehicles for social criticism and thus were a recognizable popular cultural form. Liberal and radical Vietnam-era coming-home films range from sympathetic portraits of the problem of rehabilitation that challenge mainstream American constructions of masculinity (*Coming Home* in 1978) to portraits of the vet as crazed protofascist victim (*Tracks* in 1976) to parables like *Cutter's Way* (1981), in which a mutilated veteran becomes an avenger, arrayed against semi-criminal capitalist establishment figures. One film in this genre, *Heroes* (1977), flashes back to the war, which is superimposed, in a horrifying hallucinatory scene, upon the landscape of Middle America. *Friendly Fire* (1979), which is set in the wheat belt, is concerned with developing political activism against the draft by the parents of a young soldier who has been killed by artillery fire from his own company, and with government surveillance and intimidation of their antiwar activity. The film incorporates several themes within its narrative about parents coming to terms with their son's death: campus teach-ins about the war; testimony by Vietnam Veterans Against the War before a congressional committee; peace demonstrations; criticisms of racism within the army, economic injustice in America, and unquestioning pro-establishment conformity. In the final sense these are films of closure: the war is exorcised and placed in the confines of the recent American past. These films' narratives generally advance from the war experience to criticize American society of the 1970s from alternative cultural perspectives. Their subject is not so much the war or combat experience—very few war scenes are presented—but the effect of the war on American veterans and the implications of the failure of the post-Vietnam United States to fully implement the countervision of the sixties at home or abroad.

The Deer Hunter (1978) initiates a different interpretation of the Vietnam era in Hollywood fiction film. Unlike, for example, *Go Tell the Spartans* (1978), which is set in Vietnam in 1964 at the start of the escalation of significant U.S. military presence, *The Deer Hunter* neither attempts a realistic recreation in fictional terms of the complexities of the war nor repudiates U.S. military involvement in Vietnam. Its subject is not the war, or the effect of the war and the antiwar movement upon American culture from 1964 to 1973, but American culture and society after the war as the 1970s drew to a close. Thus scenes set in Vietnam during the war are no more historically specific then depictions of Tombstone or the OK Corral in Westerns or of plantations and cotton fields in films about the Civil War and Reconstruction. They are nonetheless quite significant.

The Deer Hunter marks the beginning of a series of post-Vietnam films that negate the contradiction between doves and hawks and use the era as a period and a setting in order to construct parables that reinterpret the Vietnam experience in the context of the concerns and developing climate of opinion of the late 1970s and the 1980s. What is occurring in Hollywood narrative fiction film in the years after the war is that Vietnam, like the West in the days of Indians and cowboys or the South in the time of plantations, has become a setting within which ideological constructs are explored and contested. Given the illusionist power of the cinema and the technical skill of special effects teams, these fiction films may indeed seem to be detailed reenactments of history. They are, however, highly encoded generic melodramas and thus should be evaluated with an eye to their ideology and the ways they interpret a recent period of American history that is part of our national experience.

For example, the Vietnam sections of *The Deer Hunter* are pervaded by racist and Cold War stereotypes: images of "the yellow peril," of "Russian roulette" as a routine form of Communist torture and an expression of Oriental decadence. At the conclusion of *The Deer Hunter* the characters, whose lives have been damaged by the Vietnam War, gather around a table and sing "God Bless America." Cimino's fable is fraught with contradiction and reveals more than it intends about the developing conservative climate of opinion in the United States in the late seventies. It is, perhaps, significant that it was screened on television by New York City's WOR-TV on the eve of Reagan's election. The film is permeated with a bewildered sense of nativist pride, bruised innocence and loss, a structure of feeling that is resolved in a vision of a beleaguered but unified America—standing together, standing tall—in a hostile, evil, and incomprehensible world of Asian and Communist demons.

In the 1980s, as U.S. economic and political hegemony declined throughout most of the world, the decline was manifested, in excess, in a series of films that not only refight the Vietnam War and justify it on the basis of an anti-Asian racism and anti-Communist demonology, but create the illusion that the U.S. won the battle and in a sense the war (or that it won the battle but was betrayed, hence denied total victory in the war). Notable among these films were *Uncommon Valor* (1983); *Missing in Action* (1984); *Missing in Action 2: The Beginning* (1985); *Rambo: First Blood Part II* (1985); and *The Hanoi Hilton* (1987). In these films Vietnam has become the setting for fables that ideologically reproduce their time with clear implications for the direction of American foreign policy. This was recognized by President Reagan, who prepared the nation for the possibility of military intervention in the Middle East by commenting: "Boy, I saw *Rambo* last night; now I know what to do next time." Fifty years earlier, President Wilson had also conflated revisionist fable and history when he praised *The Birth of a Nation* as "history written like lightning." What is at stake in the interpretation is not only the memory of the past but the consciousness that will affect future policy.

Rambo and *The Birth of a Nation* revise history and justify vigilante-style military intervention (U.S. military/Ku Klux Klan) against alien peoples to sustain the construction of national consensus and the related discourse of them and us. Frantz Fanon, in writing about the literature and art of neocolonialism in *The Wretched of the Earth* (1961), has illustrated that the culture of the dominant forces in society tends to stereotype colonized peoples as "others"—as slaves (inferiors) or monsters (threats)—or simply to marginalize them beyond the fringes of society or historical memory. Excluded, they become invisible men and women. In recent Hollywood fiction film narratives about the Vietnam era there is a tendency for both the Vietnamese, who fought in what they call the American war, and the majority of Americans, who ultimately came to oppose that war (in and out of the army), to be dematerialized or demonized. They are not the tellers of the tale any more than the slaves or abolitionists are in the conventional Civil War/Reconstruction film or the Indians in the traditional Western. These two separate but related dematerializations of the colonized or oppressed and their political allies work together to forward the interests of the dominant classes and their allies. The situation is thus fraught with contradiction. It is as if the recent past is being recounted by a victim of historical amnesia or by a narrator whose tunnel vision compels him/her to censor or repress certain material.

The narratives of films as diverse in quality as *Rambo: First Blood Part II* (1985), *Missing in Action* (1984), *American Commandos* (1985), *The Deer Hunter* (1978), and, as we will see, *Platoon* (1987), as well as those of popular novels such as J. C. Pollock's *Mission M.I.A.* (1982) and John Del Vecchio's *The Thirteenth Valley* (1982), reduce the complexities of the Vietnam era to the morality of soldiering. This is an effort to reconcile the ambiguities and silence the contradictions of a period that was a watershed in American politics—a period of opposition to the war and to the worldview that sustained it, as well as of challenge to racial and economic inequalities at home. In these works Vietnamese and other Third World people are dematerialized or stereotyped as dehumanized others, as shadowy aliens. The war is mystified as a tragic mistake or an existentialist adventure through which the White American hero discovers or realizes his identity. There is no sense of the existence of the significant antiwar movement at home—a broad movement for the transformation of American society—that ultimately gained a degree of hegemony, if only for a few years. The perspective of those soldiers who opposed the war, and in some cases fragged their officers, is silently erased from historical memory. There is no recognition that the war was hardly an accident but rather a historical development from long-standing and ultimately counterproductive French and American colonialist and imperialist policies.

SUGGESTIONS FOR DISCUSSION

1. Michael Klein sees Vietnam War films as offering different and changing interpretations over a twenty-year period, 1968 to 1987. How does he see these changes taking place? Use Klein's article to create a chronology of Vietnam War films, noting when and why he believes representations of the war change.
2. Klein compares reinterpretations of the Vietnam War to reinterpretations of slavery, the Civil War, and Reconstruction that took place after Reconstruction ended in 1877. Consider the way slavery, the Civil War, and Reconstruction are represented in history textbooks you studied in school and in popular accounts you're familiar with from movies, novels, and television shows. The point here is not so much to recall details as to think about the dominant images in American culture of the old slave South and plantation culture, the Civil War, and Reconstruction. To what extent do you think these images and historical accounts are, as Klein argues, the result of "a conservative white Southern point of view"?
3. What is the dominant image of the Vietnam War in your experience, taking into account what you've learned in school, heard from friends and relatives, or seen in movies or television shows? What differences and similarities can you identify among your classmates? How do your representations of the Vietnam War compare to those Klein sees in Hollywood movies?

SUGGESTIONS FOR WRITING

1. Pick one of the movies Klein discusses in the reading selection or one that has appeared more recently, such as *Full Metal Jacket, Born on the Fourth of July,* or *Good Morning, Vietnam.* Write an essay that explains how the movie interprets the Vietnam War. The point of the essay is not to decide whether the interpretation is an accurate portrayal but rather to analyze the political and cultural meanings the movie ascribes to the war.
2. Take Klein's idea that representations of the past are often the result of a "process of organized forgetting" to write an essay about a significant historical event with which you are familiar. You can write about the Vietnam War if you wish but don't feel limited to it. In your essay, consider how the event you're writing about is represented in popular consciousness and whether the dominant image of the event, as Klein puts it, "takes people's complex past away, substituting comfortable myths that reinforce rather than challenge the status quo." What, in your view, has been excised or suppressed in popular representations of the event you're analyzing?
3. Klein suggest that Hollywood movies have represented the Vietnam War by silently erasing the Vietnamese people, the antiwar movement, and the colonialist and imperialist policies he believes caused the war in the first place. Compare Klein's account to one or more of the other interpretations of the Vietnam War in this chapter. Your task here is not to come up with a definitive account of the war but rather to consider how each of the interpretations you discuss bring some things to light and ignore others. How do you position your own thinking about the war in relation to the accounts and interpretations you discuss?

FOR FURTHER EXPLORATION

The readings in this chapter suggest numerous opportunities for further exploration. For example, in "Unsettling the Old West," Richard Bernstein lists some of the books written by revisionist Western historians Patricia Limerick Nelson, Donald Worster, Peggy Pascoe, and Richard White. You might read one or more of these works in order to develop your own view of how these historians are revising the history of the American West. Or you may want to explore issues related to the Vietnam War. The following topics are by no means exhaustive but are meant to give you some leads:

- The Tet offensive (1968)
- The antiwar movement
- The history of Vietnamese nationalism
- Media coverage of the war
- The effects of Agent Orange
- Literature of the Vietnam War: reporting such as Gloria Emerson's *Winners and Losers* and Michael Herr's *Dispatches,* or novels such as Tim O'Brien's *Going After Cacciato,* Charles Mason's *Chickenhawk,* and Stephen Wright's *Meditation in Green*

CHAPTER 11

MULTICULTURAL AMERICA

How does it happen that in the United States, where the inhabitants have only recently immigrated to the land which they now occupy, and brought neither customs nor traditions with them there; where they met one another for the first time with no previous acquaintances; where, in short, the instinctive love of country can scarcely exist; how does it happen that everyone takes as zealous an interest in the affairs of his township, his county, and the whole state as if they were his own?
—Alexis de Tocqueville

"No, I'm not an American. I'm one of the 22 million black people who are the victims of Americanism."
—Malcolm X

America has always been a multicultural society. From Columbus's first contact with the Taino tribe in the West Indies, the exploration and settlement of America by Europeans has involved a series of encounters with peoples outside the dominant white, Protestant, middle-class culture— not only with American Indians but also with the West Africans forcibly brought to America through the slave trade; with Mexicans when the United States appropriated California, Texas, and the Southwest in the Mexican War; with Irish and Chinese laborers recruited to build the transcontinental railroad; and with the Italian Catholics and Eastern European Jews who immigrated to the United States between 1880 and 1920 to work in the mines, steel mills, garment trades, and other industries of an expanding capitalist economy.

The founding premise of the early American republic was that Americans would become one people, with a common culture, by forging a new national identity. When the French writer Hector St. John de Crevecoeur visited America in the eighteenth century, he marveled at the diversity of the settlers—"[a] mixture of English, Scotch, Irish, Dutch, Germans, and Swedes . . . a promiscuous breed" intermarrying and giving birth to a new people rather than preserving the old ethnic cultures and traditions. "Here," de Crevecoeur said, "individuals of all nations are melted into a new race of men."

This vision of the assimiliation of many diverse peoples into one common culture, of course, has become a fixture in American consciousness, expressed in the image of the melting pot and the national slogan *E pluribus unum.* But it has also remained just that—a vision of an imaginary unified America without cultural differences. The fact of the matter is that a lot of people did not melt in, as de Crevecoeur thought they would, but instead have been marginalized and subordinated, rendered politically powerless and culturally invisible. The American experiment to form a new people has in actuality produced not a common culture and national identity but a multicultural society, divided along racial and ethnic lines.

The issue Americans have always faced, then, is not whether they can establish a unified culture but whether they can learn to live and work together with their differences. The historical record is an uneven one, and for every instance of cooperation across cultural differences or racial lines, such as the Underground Railroad to assist runaway slaves before the Civil War or the unity of black and white workers during the union organizing drives in the 1930s, there have been far too many cases where the dominant culture has sanctioned the oppression of Americans who are different. The Jim Crow laws and lynchings of southern blacks that followed the end of Reconstruction, the genocidal military campaigns to dispossess American Indians, and the internment of Japanese Americans during World War II are only the most obvious examples of a nation turning to force instead of negotiating its cultural differences.

The point, though, is that Americans now live, as they always have, whether they have recognized it or not, in a multicultural society—and the skills of negotiating differences have become a matter of urgency, not to undo differences but to discover new ways to arrange our collective life. Despite what is often presented in the media and popular press, multiculturalism is neither a new phenomenon nor a plot by leftwing college professors to dismantle the Western tradition. Debates about multicultural education have been raging for a number of years now and are likely to continue throughout the 1990s. These are important debates, and they are touched on in some of the selections in this chapter. But in another sense, debates about whether or not the curriculum students study and teachers teach should be multicultural make it sound as if there were a choice to be made—for or against multiculturalism. The purpose of this chapter, on the other hand, is not to offer a choice but to explore the consequences of a fact: multiculturalism is, and always has been, deeply embedded in the lived experience of Americans.

Americans are living, as Mary Louise Pratt puts it, in a "contact zone," where encounters with cultural differences, whether they are based on race, class, gender, ethnicity, religion, or sexual orientation, are simply not optional. The United States is changing, and current demographic trends indicate the country is becoming less white and less middle class. The recent wave of immigration from Southeast Asia and Latin America has been the largest since the turn of the century. If anything, the future of America is going to be more multicultural than ever. For some, this is a troubling prospect, and there have been disturbing outbreaks of violence against recent immigrants, attempts to close the border, and initiatives to make English the official language. Old myths die hard, and the belief that America was once a unified nation with a common culture continues to hang on in the face of evidence to the contrary.

The decade of the 1990s will be a difficult one for many Americans. As the readings we have gathered here reveal, the contact zones of multicultural America are problematic places in which individuals and groups work out their identities and aspirations in relation both to the identities and aspirations of other groups of Americans and to the structures of power that organize and maintain the dominant culture. The purpose of this closing chapter, then, is to invite you to read America as a multicultural society, to locate yourself and your own heritage in relation to the various cultures and ethnic groups that now populate the country, and to consider the cultural meanings of multiculturalism for life in contemporary America.

READING MULTICULTURAL AMERICA

The readings we have assembled here look at the realities of multicultural America from a variety of perspectives and propose a variety of terms to describe contemporary American experience. The first two reading selections each see America as a multicultural society, but the first emphasizes the diversity and mix of cultures while the second emphasizes conflict. The first selection, Ishmael Reed's "America: The Multinational Society," refers to American culture as a "bouillabaise," a rich mixture of disparate cultural elements that blurs the lines between cultures without melting them together into a common stock. Adrienne Rich's "Split at the Root: An Essay on Jewish Identity," on the other hand, offers Rich's self-analysis of the multiple conflicting selves—"split at the root"—she inhabits as the result of growing up in an anti-Semitic, racially divided, heterosexual culture.

In the next selection, "Arts of the Contact Zone," Mary Louise Pratt proposes another term—"contact zone"—to characterize the interactions of various cultures in the Americas and how these cultures represent themselves to each other. In "How to Tame a Wild Tongue," Gloria Anzaldua offers still another term—"borderlands"—to describe the experience of Chicanos in the Southwest, located between Anglo and Mexican cultures. Elaine H. Kim, in "Home Is Where the *Han* Is: A Korean-American Perspective on the Los Angeles Upheavals," sees Korean Americans caught in the middle—in her word, "squeezed"—between the dominant white culture, on one hand, and African American and Latino communities, on the other.

In the final selection, "The Multicultural Wars," Hazel V. Carby develops an analysis of both the opposition to multiculturalism and the limits and contradictions of a curriculum that emphasizes cultural diversity and cultural differences in a society that remains divided along racial, class, ethnic, and gender lines.

As you read the selections in this chapter, you will be asked to think and write about the way each writer characterizes the multicultural realities of contemporary America. Taken together, these writers challenge conventional views that American culture is a coherent unified one and that there is a single national identity that binds all Americans together. Instead, these writers repeatedly emphasize the mix of cultures, the splits and conflicts of life in the "contact zone," at the "border," or "squeezed" between cultures. In this sense, the writers we have gathered not only raise important issues about multicultural America. They also complicate what it might mean to read culture, to picture American culture as a place where people negotiate their differences.

Ishmael Reed

AMERICA: THE MULTINATIONAL SOCIETY

Ishmael Reed is one of the foremost novelists in America today. In *Flight to Canada, Mumbo Jumbo, The Last Days of Louisiana Red,* and other novels, Reed uses the experimentalism of postmodernist fiction to create a body of African American fictions. Reed is also a critic and essayist, as you will see in the following selection. The essay "America: The Multinational Society" appeared in Reed's collection of essays and reviews, *Writin' Is Fightin'* (1988). Here Reed raises the perspective that despite textbook accounts of American history, America has always been a multinational culture—not exactly a melting pot so much as a stew of disparate peoples.

Suggestion For Reading

- As you read, you will notice that Ishmael Reed opens the essay with a series of examples, including the lead quote from the *New York Times*. Notice how this sets Reed up to step back and generalize. Underline and annotate the passage where Reed first announces the theme of the essay.

> At the annual Lower East Side Jewish Festival yesterday, a
> Chinese woman ate a pizza slice in front of Ty Thuan Duc's
> Vietnamese grocery store. Beside her a Spanish-speaking
> family patronized a cart with two signs: "Italian Ices" and
> "Kosher by Rabbi Alper." And after the pastrami ran out,
> everybody ate knishes.
> —*New York Times,* 23 June 1983

◆

On the day before Memorial Day, 1983, a poet called me to describe a city he had just visited. He said that one section included mosques, built by the Islamic people who dwelled there. Attending his reading, he said, were large numbers of Hispanic people, forty thousand of whom lived in the same city. He was not talking about a fabled city located in some mysterious region of the world. The city he'd visited was Detroit.

A few months before, as I was leaving Houston, Texas, I heard it announced on the radio that Texas's largest minority was Mexican-American, and though a foundation recently issued a report critical of bilingual education, the taped voice used to guide the passengers on the air trams connecting terminals in Dallas Airport is in both Spanish and English. If the trend continues, a day will come when it will be difficult to travel through some sections of the country without hearing commands in both English and Spanish; after all, for some western states, Spanish was the first written language and the Spanish style lives on in the western way of life.

Shortly after my Texas trip, I sat in an auditorium located on the campus of the University of Wisconsin at Milwaukee as a Yale professor—whose original work on the influence of African cultures upon those of the Americas has led to his ostracism from some monocultural intellectual circles—walked up and down the aisle, like an old-time southern evangelist, dancing and drumming the top of the lectern, illustrating his points before some serious Afro-American intellectuals and artists who cheered and applauded his performance and his mastery of information. The professor was "white." After his lecture, he joined a group of Milwaukeeans in a conversation. All of the participants spoke Yoruban, though only the professor had ever traveled to Africa.

One of the artists told me that his paintings, which included African and Afro-American mythological symbols and imagery, were hanging in the local McDonald's restaurant. The next day I went to McDonald's and snapped pictures of smiling youngsters eating hamburgers below paintings that could grace the walls of any of the country's leading museums. The manager of the local McDonald's said, "I don't know what you boys are doing, but I like it," as he commissioned the local painters to exhibit in his restaurant.

Such blurring of cultural styles occurs in everyday life in the United States to a greater extent than anyone can imagine and is probably more prevalent than the sensational conflict between people of different backgrounds that is played up and often encouraged by the media. The result is what the Yale professor, Robert Thompson, referred to as a cultural bouillabaisse, yet members of the nation's present educational and cultural Elect still cling to the notion that the United States belongs to some vaguely defined entity they refer to as "Western civilization," by which they mean, presumably, a civilization created by the people of Europe, as if Europe can be viewed in monolithic terms. Is Beethoven's Ninth Symphony, which includes Turkish marches, a part of Western civilization, or the late nineteenth- and twentieth-century French paintings, whose creators were influenced by Japanese art? And what of the cubists, through whom the influence of African art changed modern painting, or the surrealists, who were so impressed with the art of the Pacific Northwest Indians that, in their map of North America, Alaska dwarfs the lower forty-eight in size?

Are the Russians, who are often criticized for their adoption of "Western" ways by Tsarist dissidents in exile, members of Western civilization? And what of the millions of Europeans who have black African and Asian ancestry, black Africans having occupied several countries for hundreds of years? Are these "Europeans" members of Western civilization, or the Hungarians, who originated across the Urals in a place called Greater Hungary, or the Irish, who came from the Iberian Peninsula?

Even the notion that North America is part of Western civilization because our "system of government" is derived from Europe is being challenged by Native American historians who say that the founding fathers, Benjamin Franklin especially, were actually influenced by the system of government that had been adopted by the Iroquois hundreds of years prior to the arrival of large numbers of Europeans.

Western civilization, then, becomes another confusing category like Third World, or Judeo-Christian culture, as man attempts to impose his small-screen view of political and cultural reality upon a complex world. Our most publicized novelist recently said that Western civilization was the greatest achievement of mankind, an attitude that flourishes on the street level as scribbles in public restrooms: "White Power," "Niggers and Spics Suck," or "Hitler was a prophet," the latter being the most telling, for wasn't Adolph Hitler the archetypal monoculturalist who, in his pigheaded arrogance, believed that one way and one blood was so pure that it had to be protected from alien strains at all costs? Where did such an attitude, which has caused so much misery and depression in our national life, which has tainted even our noblest achievements, begin? An attitude that caused the incarceration of Japanese-American citizens during World War II, the persecution of Chicanos and Chinese-Americans, the near-extermination of the Indians, and the murder and lynchings of thousands of Afro-Americans.

Virtuous, hardworking, pious, even though they occasionally would wander off after some fancy clothes, or rendezvous in the woods with the town prostitute, the Puritans are idealized in our schoolbooks as "a hardy band" of no-nonsense patriarchs whose discipline razed the forest and brought order to the New World (a term that annoys Native American historians). Industrious, responsible, it was their "Yankee ingenuity" and practicality that created the work ethic. They were simple folk who produced a number of good poets, and they set the tone for the American writing style, of lean and spare lines, long before Hemingway. They worshiped in churches whose colors blended in with the New England snow, churches with simple structures and ornate lecterns.

The Puritans were a daring lot, but they had a mean streak. They hated the theater and banned Christmas. They punished people in a cruel and inhuman manner. They killed children who disobeyed their parents. When they came in contact with those whom they considered heathens or aliens, they behaved in such a bizarre and irrational manner that this chapter in the American history comes down to us as a late-movie horror film. They exterminated the Indians, who taught them how to survive in a world unknown to them, and their encounter with the calypso culture of Barbados resulted in what the tourist guide in Salem's Witches' House refers to as the Witchcraft Hysteria.

The Puritan legacy of hard work and meticulous accounting led to the establishment of a great industrial society; it is no wonder that the American industrial revolution began in Lowell, Massachusetts, but there was the other side, the strange and paranoid attitudes toward those different from the Elect.

The cultural attitudes of that early Elect continue to be voiced in everyday life in the United States: the president of a distinguished university, writing a letter to the *Times,* belittling the study of African civilizations; the television network that promoted its show on the Vatican art with the boast that this art represented "the finest achievements of the human spirit." A modern up-tempo state of complex rhythms that depends upon contacts with an international community can no longer behave as if it dwelled in a "Zion Wilderness" surrounded by beasts and pagans.

When I heard a schoolteacher warn the other night about the invasion of the American educational system by foreign curriculums, I wanted to yell at the television set, "Lady, they're already here." It has already begun because the world is here. The world has been arriving at these shores for at least ten thousand years from Europe, Africa, and Asia. In the late nineteenth and early twentieth centuries, large numbers of Europeans arrived, adding their cultures to those of the European, African, and Asian settlers who were already here, and recently millions have been entering the country from South America and the Caribbean, making Yale Professor Bob Thompson's bouillabaisse richer and thicker.

One of our most visionary politicians said that he envisioned a time when the United States could become the brain of the world, by which he meant the repository of all of the latest advanced information systems. I thought of that remark when an enterprising poet friend of mine called to say that he had just sold a poem to a computer magazine and that the editors were delighted to get it because they didn't carry fiction or poetry. Is that the kind of world we desire? A humdrum homogeneous world of all brains and no heart, no fiction, no poetry; a world of robots with human attendants bereft of imagination, of culture? Or does North America deserve a more exciting destiny? To become a place where the cultures of the world crisscross. This is possible because the United States is unique in the world: The world is here.

SUGGESTIONS FOR DISCUSSION

1. Western civilization, in Reed's view, has become a "confusing category." What do you understand the term "Western civilization" to mean? Where did you learn the meaning of the term? Compare your sense of the term to those of classmates. How would you account for differences and similarities? Do you agree with Reed that it is a "confusing category"? If so, what exactly makes it "confusing"?
2. Describe Reed's perspective on the Puritans. What about the Puritans is he trying to bring into view? How does his portrait differ from ones you have read in history textbooks? What does Reed see as the result of the "Puritan legacy"? Do you find his characterization of the Puritans and their legacy to be a useful one? What would you add or leave out?
3. The metaphor of the melting pot has been used widely by American historians and other writers to describe the intermingling of immigrants to form one people. Reed,

on the other hand, draws on a different metaphor—that of a "cultural bouil-labaisse." What do you see as the main differences between the two metaphors? What does each reveal and conceal? What, in your view, are the advantages and disadvantages of each?

SUGGESTIONS FOR WRITING

1. Use the opening section of Ishmael Reed's essay as a model to create your own scenes and examples of America as a "cultural bouillabaisse." Write three or four sketches of things you have seen and experienced. Then, following Reed's example, step back and generalize about the significance of your sketches.
2. One of Reed's central points is that American culture has always been a "blurring of cultural styles." Pick an example of cultural expression you are familiar with—whether in music, art, literature, everyday speech, fashion, or whatever—and write an essay that explains and analyzes the components from different cultures that are combined and "blurred" together.
3. Reed points to the "cultural attitudes of the early Elect," the Puritans, in explaining the sources of resistance to recognizing America as a "multinational" instead of a "monocultural" society. Write an essay that extends Reed's analysis of the sources of resistance to portraying America as a multicultural society.

Adrienne Rich

SPLIT AT THE ROOT: AN ESSAY ON JEWISH IDENTITY

Adrienne Rich is one of America's leading poets, an essayist, and a committed feminist. She teaches English and feminist studies at Stanford University, and her poetry has won numerous awards, including the National Book Award in 1974 for *Diving into the Wreck*. In the following selection, from *Blood, Bread, and Poetry: Selected Prose 1979–85*, Rich performs a kind of self-analysis by looking at the sources of her own divided identities in her experiences growing up and seeing the world from "too many disconnected angles: white, Jewish, anti-Semite, racist, anti-racist, once-married, lesbian, middle-class, exmatriate southerner, *split at the root*."

Suggestion for Reading

• As you read, notice how Adrienne Rich analyzes her identity as "split at the root," composed of multiple and sometimes conflicting selves. Annotate those passages where Rich identifies these various selves and their relations to each other.

———————————◆———————————

For about fifteen minutes I have been sitting chin in hand in front of the typewriter, staring out at the snow. Trying to be honest with myself, trying to figure out why writing this seems to be so dangerous an act, filled with fear and shame, and why it seems so necessary. It comes to me that in order to write this I have to be willing to do two things: I have to claim my father, for I have my Jewishness from him and not from my gentile mother; and I have to break his silence, his taboos; in order to claim him I have in a sense to expose him.

And there is, of course, the third thing: I have to face the sources and the flickering presence of my own ambivalence as a Jew; the daily, mundane anti-Semitisms of my entire life.

These are stories I have never tried to tell before. Why now? Why, I asked myself sometime last year, does this question of Jewish identity float so impalpably, so ungraspably around me, a cloud I can't quite see the outlines of, which feels to me to be without definition?

And yet I've been on the track of this longer than I think.

• • •

In a long poem written in 1960, when I was thirty-one years old, I described myself as "Split at the root, neither Gentile nor Jew,/Yankee nor Rebel."[1] I was still trying to have it both ways: to be neither/nor, trying to live (with my Jewish husband and three children more Jewish in ancestry than I) in the predominantly gentile Yankee academic world of Cambridge, Massachusetts.

But this begins, for me, in Baltimore, where I was born in my father's workplace, a hospital in the Black ghetto, whose lobby contained an immense white marble statue of Christ.

• • •

My father was then a young teacher and researcher in the department of pathology at the Johns Hopkins Medical School, one of the very few Jews to attend or teach at that institution. He was from Birmingham, Alabama; his father, Samuel, was Ashkenazic, an immigrant from Austria-Hungary, and his mother, Hattie Rice, a Sephardic Jew from Vicksburg, Mississippi. My grandfather had had a shoe store in Birmingham, which did well enough to allow him to retire comfortably and to leave my grandmother income on his death. The only souvenirs of my grandfather, Samuel Rich, were his ivory flute, which lay on our living-room mantel and was not to be played with; his thin gold pocket watch, which my father wore; and his Hebrew prayer book, which I discovered among my father's books in the course of reading my way through his library. In this prayer book there was a newspaper clipping about my grandparents' wedding, which took place in a synagogue.

My father, Arnold, was sent in adolescence to a military school in the North Carolina mountains, a place for training white southern Christian gentlemen. I suspect

---

[1] Adrienne Rich, "Readings of History," in *Snapshots of a Daughter-in-Law* (New York: W. W. Norton, 1967), pp. 35–40.

that there were few, if any, other Jewish boys at Colonel Bingham's, or at "Mr. Jefferson's university" in Charlottesville, where he studied as an undergraduate. With whatever conscious forethought, Samuel and Hattie sent their son into the dominant southern WASP culture to become an "exception," to enter the professional class. Never, in describing these experiences, did he speak of having suffered—from loneliness, cultural alienation, or outsiderhood. Never did I hear him use the word *anti-Semitism.*

• • •

It was only in college, when I read a poem by Karl Shapiro beginning "To hate the Negro and avoid the Jew / is the curriculum," that it flashed on me that there was an untold side to my father's story of his student years. He looked recognizably Jewish, was short and slender in build with dark wiry hair and deep-set eyes, high forehead and curved nose.

My mother is a gentile. In Jewish law I cannot count myself a Jew. If it is true that "we think back through our mothers if we are women" (Virginia Woolf)—and I myself have affirmed this—then even according to lesbian theory, I cannot (or need not?) count myself a Jew.

The white southern Protestant woman, the gentile, has always been there for me to peel back into. That's a whole piece of history in itself, for my gentile grandmother and my mother were also frustrated artists and intellectuals, a lost writer and a lost composer between them. Readers and annotators of books, note takers, my mother a good pianist still, in her eighties. But there was also the obsession with ancestry, with "background," the southern talk of family, not as people you would necessarily know and depend on, but as heritage, the guarantee of "good breeding." There was the inveterate romantic heterosexual fantasy, the mother telling the daughter how to attract men (my mother often used the word "fascinate"); the assumption that relations between the sexes could only be romantic, that it was in the woman's interest to cultivate "mystery," conceal her actual feelings. Survival tactics of a kind, I think today, knowing what I know about the white woman's sexual role in the southern racist scenario. Heterosexuality as protection, but also drawing white women deeper into collusion with white men.

It would be easy to push away and deny the gentile in me—that white southern woman, that social christian. At different times in my life I have wanted to push away one or the other burden of inheritance, to say merely *I am a woman; I am a lesbian.* If I call myself a Jewish lesbian, do I thereby try to shed some of my southern gentile white woman's culpability? If I call myself only through my mother, is it because I pass more easily through a world where being a lesbian often seems like outsiderhood enough?

• • •

According to Nazi logic, my two Jewish grandparents would have made me a *Mischling, first-degree*—nonexempt from the Final Solution.

• • •

The social world in which I grew up was christian virtually without needing to say so—christian imagery, music, language, symbols, assumptions everywhere. It was also a genteel, white, middle-class world in which "common" was a term of deep opprobrium. "Common" white people might speak of "niggers"; *we* were taught never to use that word—*we* said "Negroes" (even as we accepted segregation, the eating taboo, the assumption that Black people were simply of a separate species). Our language was more polite, distinguishing us from the "rednecks" or the lynch-mob mentality. But so charged with negative meaning was even the word "Negro" that as children we were taught never to use it in front of Black people. We were taught that any mention of skin color in the presence of colored people was treacherous, forbidden ground. In a parallel way, the word "Jew" was not used by polite gentiles. I sometimes heard my best friend's father, a Presbyterian minister, allude to "the Hebrew people" or "people of the Jewish faith." The world of acceptable folk was white, gentile (christian, really), and had "ideals" (which colored people, white "common" people, were not supposed to have). "Ideals" and "manners" included not hurting someone's feelings by calling her or him a Negro or a Jew—naming the hated identity. This is the mental framework of the 1930s and 1940s in which I was raised.

(Writing this, I feel dimly like the betrayer; of my father, who did not speak the word; of my mother, who must have trained me in the messages; of my caste and class; of my whiteness itself.)

Two memories: I am in a play reading at school of *The Merchant of Venice*. Whatever Jewish law says, I am quite sure I was *seen* as Jewish (with a reassuringly gentile mother) in that double vision that bigotry allows. I am the only Jewish girl in the class, and I am playing Portia. As always, I read my part aloud for my father the night before, and he tells me to convey, with my voice, more scorn and contempt with the word "Jew": "Therefore, Jew . . . " I have to say the word out, and say it loudly. I was encouraged to pretend to be a non-Jewish child acting a non-Jewish character who has to speak the word "Jew" emphatically. Such a child would not have had trouble with the part. But *I* must have had trouble with the part, if only because the word itself was really taboo. I can see that there was a kind of terrible, bitter bravado about my father's way of handling this. And who would not dissociate from Shylock in order to identify with Portia? As a Jewish child who was also a female, I loved Portia—and, like every other Shakespearean heroine, she proved a treacherous role model.

A year or so later I am in another play, *The School for Scandal,* in which a notorious spendthrift is described as having "many excellent friends . . . among the Jews." In neither case was anything explained, either to me or to the class at large, about this scorn for Jews and the disgust surrounding Jews and money. Money, when Jews wanted it, had it, or lent it to others, seemed to take on a peculiar nastiness; Jews and money had some peculiar and unspeakable relation.

At this same school—in which we had Episcopalian hymns and prayers, and read aloud through the Bible morning after morning—I gained the impression that Jews were in the Bible and mentioned in English literature, that they had been persecuted centuries ago by the wicked Inquisition, but that they seemed not to exist in everyday life. These were the 1940s, and we were told a great deal about the Battle of Britain, the noble French Resistance fighters, the brave, starving Dutch—but I did not learn of the resistance of the Warsaw ghetto until I left home.

I was sent to the Episcopal church, baptized and confirmed, and attended it for about five years, though without belief. That religion seemed to have little to do with belief or commitment; it was liturgy that mattered, not spiritual passion. Neither of my parents ever entered that church, and my father would not enter *any* church for any reason—wedding or funeral. Nor did I enter a synagogue until I left Baltimore. When I came home from church, for a while, my father insisted on reading aloud to me from Thomas Paine's *The Age of Reason*—a diatribe against institutional religion. Thus, he explained, I would have a balanced view of these things, a choice. He—they—did not give me the choice to be a Jew. My mother explained to me when I was filling out forms for college that if any question was asked about "religion," I should put down "Episcopalian" rather than "none"—to seem to have no religion was, she implied, dangerous.

But it was white social christianity, rather than any particular christian sect, that the world was founded on. The very word *Christian* was used as a synonym for virtuous, just, peace-loving, generous, etc., etc.[2] The norm was christian: "religion: none" was indeed not acceptable. Anti-Semitism was so intrinsic as not to have a name. I don't recall exactly being taught that the Jews killed Jesus—"Christ killer" seems too strong a term for the bland Episcopal vocabulary—but certainly we got the impression that the Jews had been caught out in a terrible mistake, failing to recognize the true Messiah, and were thereby less advanced in moral and spiritual sensibility. The Jews had actually allowed *moneylenders in the Temple* (again, the unexplained obsession with Jews and money). They were of the past, archaic, primitive, as older (and darker) cultures are supposed to be primitive; christianity was lightness, fairness, peace on earth, and combined the feminine appeal of "The meek shall inherit the earth" with the masculine stride of "Onward, Christian Soldiers."

● ● ●

Sometime in 1946, while still in high school, I read in the newspaper that a theater in Baltimore was showing films of the Allied liberation of the Nazi concentration camps. Alone, I went downtown after school one afternoon and watched the stark, blurry, but unmistakable newsreels. When I try to go back and touch the pulse of that girl of sixteen, growing up in many ways so precocious and so ignorant, I am overwhelmed by a memory of despair, a sense of inevitability more enveloping than any I had ever known. Anne Frank's diary and many other personal narratives of the Holocaust were still unknown or unwritten. But it came to me that every one of those piles of corpses, mountains of shoes and clothing had contained, simply, individuals, who had believed, as I now believed of myself, that they were intended to live out a life of some kind of meaning, that the world possessed some kind of sense and order; yet *this* had happened to them. And I, who believed my life was intended to be so interesting and meaningful, was connected to those dead by something—not just mortality but a taboo name, a hated identity. Or was I—did I really have to be? Writing this now, I feel belated rage that I was so impoverished by the family and social worlds I lived in, that I had to try to figure out by myself what this did indeed mean for me. That I had never been taught about resistance, only about passing. That I had no language for anti-Semitism itself.

---

[2] In a similar way the phrase "That's white of you" implied that you were behaving with the superior decency and morality expected of white but not of Black people

When I went home and told my parents where I had been, they were not pleased. I felt accused of being morbidly curious, not healthy, sniffing around death for the thrill of it. And since, at sixteen, I was often not sure of the sources of my feelings or of my motives for doing what I did, I probably accused myself as well. One thing was clear: there was nobody in my world with whom I could discuss those films. Probably at the same time, I was reading accounts of the camps in magazines and newspapers; what I remember were the films and having questions that I could not even phrase, such as *Are those men and women "them" or "us"?*

To be able to ask even the child's astonished question *Why do they hate us so?* means knowing how to say "we." The guilt of not knowing, the guilt of perhaps having betrayed my parents or even those victims, those survivors, through mere curiosity—these also froze in me for years the impulse to find out more about the Holocaust.

• • •

1947: I left Baltimore to go to college in Cambridge, Massachusetts, left (I thought) the backward, enervating South for the intellectual, vital North. New England also had for me some vibration of higher moral rectitude, of moral passion even, with its seventeenth-century Puritan self-scrutiny, its nineteenth-century literary "flowering," its abolitionist righteousness, Colonel Shaw and his Black Civil War regiment depicted in granite on Boston Common. At the same time, I found myself, at Radcliffe, among Jewish women. I used to sit for hours over coffee with what I thought of as the "real" Jewish students, who told me about middle-class Jewish culture in America. I described my background—for the first time to strangers—and they took me on, some with amusement at my illiteracy, some arguing that I could never marry into a strict Jewish family, some convinced I didn't "look Jewish," others that I did. I learned the names of holidays and foods, which surnames are Jewish and which are "changed names"; about girls who had had their noses "fixed," their hair straightened. For these young Jewish women, students in the late 1940s, it was acceptable, perhaps even necessary, to strive to look as gentile as possible; but they stuck proudly to being Jewish, expected to marry a Jew, have children, keep the holidays, carry on the culture.

I felt I was testing a forbidden current, that there was danger in these revelations. I bought a reproduction of a Chagall portrait of a rabbi in striped prayer shawl and hung it on the wall of my room. I was admittedly young and trying to educate myself, but I was also doing something that *is* dangerous: I was flirting with identity.

• • •

One day that year I was in a small shop where I had bought a dress with a too-long skirt. The shop employed a seamstress who did alterations, and she came in to pin up the skirt on me. I am sure that she was a recent immigrant, a survivor. I remember a short, dark woman wearing heavy glasses, with an accent so foreign I could not understand her words. Something about her presence was very powerful and disturbing to me. After marking and pinning up the skirt, she sat back on her knees, looked up at me, and asked in a hurried whisper: "You Jewish?" Eighteen years of training in assimilation sprang into the reflex by which I shook my head, rejecting her, and muttered, "No."

What was I actually saying "no" to? She was poor, older, struggling with a foreign tongue, anxious; she had escaped the death that had been intended for her, but I had no imagination of her possible courage and foresight, her resistance—I did not see in her a heroine who had perhaps saved many lives, including her own. I saw the frightened immigrant, the seamstress hemming the skirts of college girls, the wandering Jew. But I was an American college girl having her skirt hemmed. And I was frightened myself, I think, because she had recognized me ("It takes one to know one," my friend Edie at Radcliffe had said) even if I refused to recognize myself or her, even if her recognition was sharpened by loneliness or the need to feel safe with me.

But why should she have felt safe with me? I myself was living with a false sense of safety.

There are betrayals in my life that I have known at the very moment were betrayals: this was one of them. There are other betrayals committed so repeatedly, so mundanely, that they leave no memory trace behind, only a growing residue of misery, of dull, accreted self-hatred. Often these take the form not of words but of silence. Silence before the joke at which everyone is laughing; the anti-woman joke, the racist joke, the anti-Semitic joke. Silence and then amnesia. Blocking it out when the oppressor's language starts coming from the lips of one we admire, whose courage and eloquence have touched us: *She didn't really mean that; he didn't really say that.* But the accretions build up out of sight, like scale inside a kettle.

● ● ●

1948: I come home from my freshman year at college, flaming with new insights, new information. I am the daughter who has gone out into the world, to the pinnacle of intellectual prestige, Harvard, fulfilling my father's hopes for me, but also exposed to dangerous influences. I have already been reproved for attending a rally for Henry Wallace and the Progressive party. I challenge my father: "Why haven't you told me that I am Jewish? Why do you never talk about being a Jew?" He answers measuredly, "You know that I have never denied that I am a Jew. But it's not important to me. I am a scientist, a deist. I have no use for organized religion. I choose to live in a world of many kinds of people. There are Jews I admire and others who I despise. I am a person, not simply a Jew." The words are as I remember them, not perhaps exactly as spoken. But that was the message. And it contained enough truth—as all denial drugs itself on partial truth—so that it remained for the time being unanswerable, leaving me high and dry, split at the root, gasping for clarity, for air.

At that time Arnold Rich was living in suspension, waiting to be appointed to the professorship of pathology at Johns Hopkins. The appointment was delayed for years, no Jew ever having held a professional chair in that medical school. And he wanted it badly. It must have been a very bitter time for him, since he had believed so greatly in the redeeming power of excellence, of being the most brilliant, inspired man for the job. With enough excellence, you could presumably make it stop mattering that you were Jewish; you could become the *only* Jew in the gentile world, a Jew so "civilized," so far from "common," so attractively combining southern gentility with European cultural values that no one would ever confuse you with the raw, "pushy" Jew of New York, the "loud, hysterical" refugees from eastern Europe, the "overdressed" Jews of the urban South.

We—my sister, mother, and I—were constantly urged to speak quietly in public, to dress without ostentation, to repress all vividness or spontaneity, to assimilate with a world which might see us as too flamboyant. I supposes that my mother, pure gentile though she was, could be seen as acting "common" or "Jewish" if she laughed too loudly or spoke aggressively. My father's mother, who lived with us half the year, was a model of circumspect behavior, dressed in dark blue or lavender, retiring in company, ladylike to an extreme, wearing no jewelry except a good gold chain, a narrow brooch, or a string of pearls. A few times, within the family, I saw her anger flare, felt the passion she was repressing. But when Arnold took us out to a restaurant or on a trip, the Rich women were always tuned down to some WASP level my father believed, surely, would protect us all—maybe also make us unrecognizable to the "real Jews" who wanted to seize us, drag us back to the *shtetl*, the ghetto, in its many manifestations.

For, yes, that *was* a message—that some Jews would be after you, once they "knew," to rejoin them, to re-enter a world that was messy, noisy, unpredictable, maybe poor—"even though," as my mother once wrote me, criticizing my largely Jewish choice of friends in college, "some of them will be the most brilliant, fascinating people you'll ever meet." I wonder if that isn't one message of assimilation—of America—that the unlucky or the unachieving want to pull you backward, that to identify with them is to court downward mobility, lose the precious chance of passing, of token existence. There was always within this sense of Jewish identity a strong class discrimination. Jews might be "fascinating" as individuals but came with huge unruly families who "poured chicken soup over everyone's head" (in the phrase of a white southern male poet). Anti-Semitism could thus be justified by the bad behavior of certain Jews; and if you did not effectively deny family and community, there would always be a remote cousin claiming kinship with you who was the "wrong kind" of Jew.

I have always believed his attitude toward other Jews depended on who they were. . . . It was my impression that Jews of this background looked down on Eastern European Jews, including Polish Jews and Russian Jews, who generally were not as well educated. This from a letter written to me recently by a gentile who had worked in my father's department, whom I had asked about anti-Semitism there and in particular regarding my father. This informant also wrote me that it was hard to perceive anti-Semitism in Baltimore because the racism made so much more intense an impression: *I would almost have to think that blacks went to a different heaven than the whites, because the bodies were kept in a separate morgue, and some white persons did not even want blood transfusions from black donors.* My father's mind was predictably racist and misogynist; yet as a medical student he noted in his journal that southern male chivalry stopped at the point of any white man in a streetcar giving his seat to an old, weary Black woman standing in the aisle. Was this a Jewish insight—an outsider's insight, even though the outsider was striving to be on the inside?

Because what isn't named is often more permeating than what is, I believe that my father's Jewishness profoundly shaped my own identity and our family existence. They were shaped both by external anti-Semitism and my father's self-hatred, and by his Jewish pride. What Arnold did, I think, was call his Jewish pride something else: achievement, aspiration, genius, idealism. Whatever was unacceptable got left back under the rubric of Jewishness or the "wrong kind" of Jews—uneducated, aggressive, loud. The message I got was that we were really superior: nobody else's father had collected so many books, had traveled so far, knew so many languages. Baltimore was a musical city, but for the most part, in the families of my school friends, culture was for women. My father was an amateur musician, read poetry, adored encyclopedic knowledge. He prowled and pounced over my school papers, insisting I use "grownup" sources; he criticized my poems for faulty technique and gave me books on rhyme and meter and form. His investment in my intellect and talent was egotistical, tyrannical, opinionated, and terribly wearing. He taught me, nevertheless, to believe in hard work, to mistrust easy inspiration, to write and rewrite; to feel that I *was* a person of the book, even though a woman; to take ideas seriously. He made me feel, at a very young age, the power of language and that I could share in it.

The Riches were proud, but we also had to be very careful. Our behavior had to be more impeccable than other people's. Strangers were not to be trusted, nor even friends; family issues must never go beyond the family; the world was full of potential slanderers, betrayers, *people who could not understand.* Even within the family, I realize that I never in my whole life knew what my father was really feeling. Yet he spoke— monologued—with driving intensity. You could grow up in such a house mesmerized by the local electricity, the crucial meanings assumed by the merest things. This used to seem to me a sign that we were all living on some high emotional plane. It was a diffi- cult force field for a favored daughter to disengage from.

Easy to call that intensity Jewish; and I have no doubt that passion is one of the qual- ities required for survival over generations of persecution. But what happens when passion is rent from its original base, when the white gentile world is softly saying "Be more like us and you can be almost one of us"? What happens when survival seems to mean closing off one emotional artery after another? His forebears in Europe had been forbidden to travel or expelled from one country after another, had special taxes levied on them if they left the city walls, had been forced to wear special clothes and badges, restricted to the poorest neighborhoods. He had wanted to be a "free spirit," to travel widely, among "all kinds of people." Yet in his prime of life he lived in an increasingly withdrawn world, in his house up on a hill in a neighborhood where Jews were not supposed to be able to buy property, depending almost exclusively on interactions with his wife and daughters to provide emo- tional connectedness. In his home, he created a private defense system so elaborate that even as he was dying, my mother felt unable to talk freely with his colleagues or others who might have helped her. Of course, she acquiesced in this.

The loneliness of the "only," the token, often doesn't feel like loneliness but like a kind of dead echo chamber. Certain things that ought to don't resonate. Somewhere Beverly Smith writes of women of color "inspiring the behavior" in each other. When there's nobody to "inspire the behavior," act out of the culture, there is an atrophy, a dwindling, which is partly invisible.

● ● ●

Sometimes I feel I have seen too long from too many disconnected angles: white, Jewish, anti-Semite, racist, anti-racist, once-married, lesbian, middle-class, feminist, ex- matriate southerner, *split at the root*—that I will never bring them whole. I would have liked, in this essay, to bring together the meanings of anti-Semitism and racism as I have experienced them and as I believe they intersect in the world beyond my life. But I'm not able to do this yet. I feel the tension as I think, make notes: *If you really look at the one reality, the other will waver and disperse.* Trying in one week to read Angela Davis and Lucy Davidowicz;[3] trying to hold throughout to a feminist, a lesbian, perspective—

---

[3] Angela Y. Davis, *Woman, Race and Class* (New York: Random House, 1981); Lucy S. Davidowicz, *The War against the Jews 1933–1945* (1975; New York: Bantam, 1979).

what does this mean? Nothing has trained me for this. And sometimes I feel inadequate to make any statement as a Jew; I feel the history of denial within me like an injury, a scar. For assimilation has affected *my* perceptions; those early lapses in meaning, those blanks, are with me still. My ignorance can be dangerous to me and to others.

Yet we can't wait for the undamaged to make our connections for us; we can't wait to speak until we are perfectly clear and righteous. There is no purity and, in our lifetimes, no end to this process.

This essay, then, has no conclusions: it is another beginning for me. Not just a way of saying, in 1982 Right Wing America, *I too, will wear the yellow star.* It's a moving into accountability, enlarging the range of accountability. I know that in the rest of my life, the next half century or so, every aspect of my identity will have to be engaged. The middle-class white girl taught to trade obedience for privilege. The Jewish lesbian raised to be a heterosexual gentile. The woman who first heard oppression named and analyzed in the Black Civil Rights struggle. The woman with three sons, the feminist who hates male violence. The woman limping with a cane, the woman who has stopped bleeding are also accountable. The poet who knows that beautiful language can lie, that the oppressor's language sometimes sounds beautiful. The woman trying, as part of her resistance, to clean up her act.

SUGGESTIONS FOR DISCUSSION

1. Adrienne Rich suggests that what we experience as our "self" is never a whole, formed independently, but rather is always multiple and divided, formed in relation to other people in a society divided by prejudice. Explain how Rich analyzes her divided identities as relations to others. What conflicts arise from these relations?
2. Rich's father plays a prominent part in her personal reminiscence. Explain his role in her divided consciousness. What might have led him to deny his Jewish heritage? What do you see as the personal costs?
3. Rich notes "the white woman's role in the southern racist scenario" but doesn't really develop the idea at any length. What, do you think, is she pointing to here? What does Rich mean by the "inveterate romantic heterosexual fantasy"? How might this draw "white women deeper into collusion with white men" in maintaining racial hierarchies?

SUGGESTIONS FOR WRITING

1. Write an essay that analyzes Rich's self-analysis. Identify Rich's multiple, conflicting selves and explain the various and sometimes contradictory demands they make of her. Notice at the end of the essay Rich says she "will never bring them whole," but nonetheless she does call on herself to "mov[e] into accountability." Explain in your essay what "accountability" might mean when personal identity is "split at the root."
2. In her discussion of her father, Rich notes that despite his racism and misogyny, nonetheless as a medical student he had observed in his journal "that southern male chivalry stopped at the point of any white man in a streetcar giving his seat to an old, weary Black woman standing in the aisle." Rich goes on to wonder, "Was this a Jewish insight—an outsider's insight. . . ?" Write an essay that uses Rich's notion of an "outsider's insight." What is it that outsiders might see about the dominant American culture that those in the mainstream may be altogether blind to?

Focus your essay around a particular moment of such insight. The outsider in the essay could be you, someone you know, or someone you have read or heard about. The task here is first to locate the person as an outsider, to explain what exactly puts the person outside of the mainstream, and then to explain what insight that person might have about the workings, customs, attitudes, beliefs, or practices of the insiders.

3. Write an essay that uses the reading selection from Rich as a model to perform your own self-analysis. What you will need to do is to identify the multiple yet overlapping selves that you contain and to explain the demands they make of you and how and why they conflict. In doing this essay, it will help to recall how Rich locates her own divided identities as relationships to other people and to the conflicting cultural meanings of a divided society. Don't expect to integrate all your various selves into one whole person but do indicate what "accountability" toward these various selves might mean to you.

Mary Louise Pratt

ARTS OF THE CONTACT ZONE

Mary Louise Pratt teaches in the departments of Comparative Literature and Spanish and Portuguese at Stanford University, where she was involved in designing a freshman culture program to replace the Western civilization course that Stanford had traditionally required of its incoming students. As Pratt notes toward the end of her essay, the course she teaches in the new program, "Europe and the Americas," focuses on the "multiple cultural histories (including European ones) that have intersected" in the Americas. The title of Pratt's essay, "Arts of the Contact Zone," originally published in *Profession 91,* captures her notion of America as a multicultural place where "peoples geographically and historically separated come into contact with each other and establish ongoing relations, usually involving conditions of coercion, radical inequality, and intractable conflict." The "arts" of the contact zone refer, then, to what Pratt sees as the "interactive, improvisational dimensions of colonial encounters," whereby both colonizers and colonized come to an understanding of themselves through their mutual if unequal relations.

Suggestion for Reading

• As you read, you will notice that Mary Louise Pratt's essay is a wide-ranging one that makes considerable demands on readers to put its parts together. She ranges from talking about her children to discussing the letter *New Chronicle and Good Government* written in 1613 by the Incan Guaman Poma to King Philip III of Spain to recounting a brief history of

European literacy to describing the curriculum reform at Stanford. To help you follow the main line of thought, notice where the essay divides into sections. Annotate passages where Pratt develops her general argument across the various sections.

◆

W henever the subject of literacy comes up, what often pops first into my mind is a conversation I overheard eight years ago between my son Sam and his best friend, Willie, aged six and seven, respectively: "Why don't you trade me Many Trails for Carl Yats . . . Yesits . . . Yastrum-scrum." "That's not how you say it, dummy, it's Carl Yes . . . Yes . . . oh, I don't know." Sam and Willie had just discovered baseball cards. Many Trails was their decoding, with the help of first-grade English phonics, of the name Manny Trillo. The name they were quite rightly stumped on was Carl Yastrzemski. That was the first time I remembered seeing them put their incipient literacy to their own use, and I was of course thrilled.

Sam and Willie learned a lot about phonics that year by trying to decipher surnames on baseball cards, and a lot about cities, states, heights, weights, places of birth, stages of life. In the years that followed, I watched Sam apply his arithmetic skills to working out batting averages and subtracting retirement years from rookie years; I watched him develop senses of patterning and order by arranging and rearranging his cards for hours on end, and aesthetic judgment by comparing different photos, different series, layouts, and color schemes. American geography and history took shape in his mind through baseball cards. Much of his social life revolved around trading them, and he learned about exchange, fairness, trust, the importance of processes as opposed to results, what it means to get cheated, taken advantage of, even robbed. Baseball cards were the medium of his economic life too. Nowhere better to learn the power and arbitrariness of money, the absolute divorce between use value and exchange value, notions of long- and short-term investment, the possibility of personal values that are independent of market values.

Baseball cards meant baseball card shows, where there was much to be learned about worlds as well. And baseball cards opened the door to baseball books, shelves and shelves of encyclopedias, magazines, histories, biographies, novels, books of jokes, anecdotes, cartoons, even poems. Sam learned the history of American racism and the struggle against it through baseball; he saw the depression and two world wars from behind home plate. He learned the meaning of commodified labor, what it means for one's body and talents to be owned and dispensed by another. He knows something about Japan, Taiwan, Cuba, and Central America and how men and boys do things there. Through the history and experience of baseball stadiums he thought about architecture, light, wind, topography, meteorology, the dynamics of public space. He learned the meaning of expertise, of knowing about something well enough that you can start a conversation with a stranger and feel sure of holding your own. Even with an adult— especially with an adult. Throughout his preadolescent years, baseball history was Sam's luminous point of contact with grown-ups, his lifeline to caring. And, of course, all this time he was also playing baseball, struggling his way through the stages of the local Little League system, lucky enough to be a pretty good player, loving the game and coming to know deeply his strengths and weaknesses.

Literacy began for Sam with the newly pronounceable names on the picture cards and brought him what has been easily the broadest, most varied, most enduring, and most integrated experience of his thirteen-year life. Like many parents, I was delighted to see schooling give Sam the tools with which to find and open all these doors. At the same time I found it unforgivable that schooling itself gave him nothing remotely as meaningful to do, let alone anything that would actually take him beyond the referential, masculinist ethos of baseball and its lore.

However, I was not invited here to speak as a parent, nor as an expert on literacy. I was asked to speak as an MLA member working in the elite academy. In that capacity my contribution is undoubtedly supposed to be abstract, irrelevant, and anchored outside the real world. I wouldn't dream of disappointing anyone. I propose immediately to head back several centuries to a text that has a few points in common with baseball cards and raises thoughts about what Tony Sarmienro, in his comments to the conference, called new visions of literacy. In 1908 a Peruvianist named Richard Pietschmann was exploring in the Danish Royal Archive in Copenhagen and came across a manuscript. It was dated in the city of Cuzco in Peru, in the year 1613, some forty years after the final fall of the Inca empire to the Spanish and signed with an unmistakably Andean indigenous name: Felipe Guaman Poma de Ayala. Written in a mixture of Quechua and ungrammatical, expressive Spanish, the manuscript was a letter addressed by an unknown but apparently literate Andean to King Philip III of Spain. What stunned Pietschmann was that the letter was twelve hundred pages long. There were almost eight hundred pages of written text and four hundred of captioned line drawings. It was titled *The First New Chronicle and Good Government*. No one knew (or knows) how the manuscript got to the library in Copenhagen or how long it had been there. No one, it appeared, had ever bothered to read it or figured out how. Quechua was not thought of as a written language in 1908, nor Andean culture as a literate culture.

Pietschmann prepared a paper on his find, which he presented in London in 1912, a year after the rediscovery of Machu Picchu by Hiram Bingham. Reception, by an international congress of Americanists, was apparently confused. It took twenty-five years for a facsimile edition of the work to appear, in Paris. It was not till the late 1970s, as positivist reading habits gave way to interpretive studies and colonial elitisms to postcolonial pluralisms, that Western scholars found ways of reading Guaman Poma's *New Chronicle and Good Government* as the extraordinary intercultural tour de force that it was. The letter got there, only 350 years too late, a miracle and a terrible tragedy.

I propose to say a few more words about this erstwhile unreadable text, in order to lay out some thoughts about writing and literacy in what I like to call the *contact zones*. I use this term to refer to social spaces where cultures meet, clash, and grapple with each other, often in contexts of highly asymmetrical relations of power, such as colonialism, slavery, or their aftermaths as they are lived out in many parts of the world today. Eventually I will use the term to reconsider the models of community that many of us rely on in teaching and theorizing and that are under challenge today. But first a little more about Guaman Poma's giant letter to Philip III.

Insofar as anything is known about him at all, Guaman Poma exemplified the sociocultural complexities produced by conquest and empire. He was an indigenous Andean who claimed noble Inca descent and who had adopted (at least in some sense)

Christianity. He may have worked in the Spanish colonial administration as an interpreter, scribe, or assistant to a Spanish tax collector—as a mediator, in short. He says he learned to write from his half brother, a mestizo whose Spanish father had given him access to religious education.

Guaman Poma's letter to the king is written in two languages (Spanish and Quechua) and two parts. The first is called the *Nueva corónica* 'New Chronicle.' The title is important. The chronicle of course was the main writing apparatus through which the Spanish represented their American conquests to themselves. It constituted one of the main official discourses. In writing a "new chronicle," Guaman Poma took over the official Spanish genre for his own ends. Those ends were, roughly, to construct a new picture of the world, a picture of a Christian world with Andean rather than European peoples at the center of it—Cuzco, not Jerusalem. In the *New Chronicle* Guaman Poma begins by rewriting the Christian history of the world from Adam and Eve (fig. 1), incorporating the Amerindians into it as offspring of one of the sons of Noah. He identifies five ages of Christian history that he links in parallel with the five ages of canonical Andean history—separate but equal trajectories that diverge with Noah and reintersect not with Columbus but with Saint Bartholomew, claimed to have preceded Columbus in the Americas. In a couple of hundred pages, Guaman Poma constructs a veritable encyclopedia of Inca and pre-Inca history, customs, laws, social forms, public offices, and dynastic leaders. The depictions resemble European manners and customs description, but also reproduce the meticulous detail with which knowledge in Inca society was stored on *quipus* and in the oral memories of elders.

Guaman Poma's *New Chronicle* is an instance of what I have proposed to call an *autoethnographic* text, by which I mean a text in which people undertake to describe themselves in ways that engage with representations others have made of them. Thus if ethnographic texts are those in which European metropolitan subjects represent to themselves their others (usually their conquered others), autoethnographic texts are representations that the so-defined others construct *in response to* or in dialogue with those texts. Autoethnographic texts are not, then, what are usually thought of as autochthonous forms of expression or self-representation (as the Andean *quipus* were). Rather they involve a selective collaboration with and appropriation of idioms of the metropolis or the conqueror. These are merged or infiltrated to varying degrees with indigenous idioms to create self-representations intended to intervene in metropolitan modes of understanding. Autoethnographic works are often addressed to both metropolitan audiences and the speaker's own community. Their reception is thus highly indeterminate. Such texts often constitute a marginalized group's point of entry into the dominant circuits of print culture. It is interesting to think, for example, of American slave autobiography in its autoethnographic dimensions, which in some respects distinguish it from Euramerican autobiographical tradition. The concept might help explain why some of the earliest published writing by Chicanas took the form of folkloric manners and customs sketches written in English and published in English-language newspapers or folklore magazines (see Treviño). Autoethnographic representation often involves concrete collaborations between people, as between literate ex-slaves and abolitionist intellectuals, or between Guaman Poma and the Inca elders who were his informants. Often, as in Guaman Poma, it involves more than one language. In recent decades autoethnography, critique, and resistance have reconnected with writing in a contemporary creation of the contact zone, the *testimonio*.

Figure 1 Adam and Eve.

Guaman Poma's *New Chronicle* ends with a revisionist account of the Spanish conquest, which, he argues, should have been a peaceful encounter of equals with the potential for benefiting both, but for the mindless greed of the Spanish. He parodies Spanish history. Following contact with the Incas, he writes, "In all Castille, there was a great commotion. All day and at night in their dreams the Spaniards were saying 'Yndias, yndias, oro, plata, oro, plata del Piru'" ("Indies, Indies, gold, silver, gold, silver from Peru") (fig. 2). The Spanish, he writes, brought nothing of value to share with the Andeans, nothing "but armor and guns con la codicia de oro, plata, oro y plata, yndias, a las Yndias, Piru" ("with the lust for gold, silver, gold and silver, Indies, the Indies, Peru") (372). I quote these words as an example of a conquered subject using the conqueror's language to construct a parodic, oppositional representation of the conqueror's own

Figure 2 Conquista Meeting of Spaniard and Inca. The Inca says in Quechua. "You
eat this gold?" Spaniard replies in Spanish. "We eat this gold."

speech. Guaman Poma mirrors back to the Spanish (in their language, which is alien to
him) an image of themselves that they often suppress and will therefore surely recognize.
Such are the dynamics of language, writing, and representation in contact zones.

The second half of the epistle continues the critique. It is titled *Buen gobierno y
justicia* 'Good Government and Justice' and combines a description of colonial society
in the Andean region with a passionate denunciation of Spanish exploitation and abuse.
(These, at the time he was writing, were decimating the population of the Andes at a
genocidal rate. In fact, the potential loss of the labor force became a main cause for reform of the system.) Guaman Poma's most implacable hostility is invoked by the
clergy, followed by the dreaded *corregidores,* or colonial overseers (fig. 3). He also praises
good works, Christian habits, and just men where he finds them, and offers at length
his views as to what constitutes "good government and justice." The Indies, he argues,
should be administered through a collaboration of Inca and Spanish elites. The epistle
ends with an imaginary question-and-answer session in which, in a reversal of hierar-

Figure 3 Corregidor de minas. Catalog of Spanish abuses of indigenous labor force.

chy, the king is depicted asking Guaman Poma questions about how to reform the empire—a dialogue imagined across the many lines that divide the Andean scribe from the imperial monarch, and in which the subordinated subject single-handedly gives himself authority in the colonizer's language and verbal repertoire. In a way, it worked—this extraordinary text did get written—but in a way it did not, for the letter never reached its addressee.

To grasp the import of Guaman Poma's project, one needs to keep in mind that the Incas had no system of writing. Their huge empire is said to be the only known instance of a full-blown bureaucratic state society built and administered without writing. Guaman Poma constructs his text by appropriating and adapting pieces of the representational repertoire of the invaders. He does not simply imitate or reproduce it; he selects and adapts it along Andean lines to express (bilingually, mind you) Andean interests and aspirations. Ethnographers have used the term *transculturation* to describe processes whereby members of subordinated or marginal groups select and invent from materials transmitted by a dominant or metropolitan culture. The term, originally coined by Cuban sociologist Fernando Ortiz in the 1940s, aimed to replace overly reductive concepts of acculturation and assimilation used to characterize culture under conquest. While subordinate peoples do not usually control what emanates from the dominant culture, they do determine to varying extents what gets absorbed into their own and what it gets used for. Transculturation, like autoethnography, is a phenomenon of the contact zone.

As scholars have realized only relatively recently, the transcultural character of Guaman Poma's text is intricately apparent in its visual as well as its written component. The genre of the four hundred line drawings is European—there seems to have been no tradition of representational drawing among the Incas—but in their execution they deploy specifically Andean systems of spatial symbolism that express Andean values and aspirations.[1]

In figure 1, for instance, Adam is depicted on the left-hand side below the sun, while Eve is on the right-hand side below the moon, and slightly lower than Adam. The two are divided by the diagonal of Adam's digging stick. In Andean spatial symbolism, the diagonal descending from the sun marks the basic line of power and authority dividing upper from lower, male from female, dominant from subordinate. In figure 2, the Inca appears in the same position as Adam, with the Spaniard opposite, and the two at the same height. In figure 3, depicting Spanish abuses of power, the symbolic pattern is reversed. The Spaniard is in a high position indicating dominance, but on the "wrong" (right-hand) side. The diagonals of his lance and that of the servant doing the flogging mark out a line of illegitimate, though real, power. The Andean figures continue to occupy the left-hand side of the picture, but clearly as victims. Guaman Poma wrote that the Spanish conquest had produced "un mundo al reves" 'a world in reverse.'

In sum, Guaman Poma's text is truly a product of the contact zone. If one thinks of cultures, or literatures, as discrete, coherently structured, monolingual edifices, Guaman Poma's text, and indeed any autoethnographic work, appears anomalous or chaotic—as it apparently did to the European scholars Pietschmann spoke to in 1912. If one does not think of cultures this way, then Guaman Poma's text is simply heterogeneous, as the Andean region was itself and remains today. Such a text is heterogeneous on the reception end as well as the production end: it will read very differently to people in different positions in the contact zone. Because it deploys European and Andean systems of meaning making, the letter necessarily means differently to bilingual Spanish-Quechua speakers and to monolingual speakers in either language; the drawings mean differently to monocultural readers, Spanish or Andean, and to bicultural readers responding to the Andean symbolic structures embodied in European genres.

In the Andes in the early 1600s there existed a literate public with considerable intercultural competence and degrees of bilingualism. Unfortunately, such a community did not exist in the Spanish court with which Guaman Poma was trying to make contact. It is interesting to note that in the same year Guaman Poma sent off his letter, a text by another Peruvian was adopted in official circles in Spain as the canonical Christian mediation between the Spanish conquest and Inca history. It was another huge encyclopedic work, titled the *Royal Commentaries of the Incas,* written, tellingly, by a mestizo, Inca Garcilaso de la Vega. Like the mestizo half brother who taught Guaman Poma to read and write, Inca Garcilaso was the son of an Inca princess and a Spanish official, and had lived in Spain since he was seventeen. Though he too spoke Quechua, his book is written in eloquent, standard Spanish, without illustrations. While Guaman Poma's life's work sat somewhere unread, the *Royal Commentaries* was edited and reedited in Spain and the New World, a mediation that coded the Andean past and present in ways thought unthreatening to colonial hierarchy.[2] The textual hierarchy persists: the *Royal Commentaries* today remains a staple item on PhD reading lists in Spanish, while the *New Chronicle and Good Government,* despite the ready availability of several fine editions, is not. However, though Guaman Poma's text did not reach its destination, the transcultural currents of expression it exemplifies continued to evolve in the Andes, as they still do, less in writing than in storytelling, ritual, song, dance-drama, painting and sculpture, dress, textile art, forms of governance, religious belief, and many other vernacular art forms. All express the effects of long-term contact and intractable, unequal conflict.

Autoethnography, transculturation, critique, collaboration, bilingualism, mediation, parody, denunciation, imaginary dialogue, vernacular expression—these are some of the literate arts of the contact zone. Miscomprehension, incomprehension, dead letters, unread masterpieces, absolute heterogeneity of meaning—these are some of the perils of writing in the contact zone. They all live among us today in the transnationalized metropolis of the United States and are becoming more widely visible, more pressing, and, like Guaman Poma's text, more decipherable to those who once would have ignored them in defense of a stable, centered sense of knowledge and reality.

CONTACT AND COMMUNITY

The idea of the contact zone is intended in part to contrast with ideas of community that underlie much of the thinking about language, communication, and culture that gets done in the academy. A couple of years ago, thinking about the linguistic theories I knew, I tried to make sense of a utopian quality that often seemed to characterize social analyses of language by the academy. Languages were seen as living in "speech communities," and these tended to be theorized as discrete, self-defined, coherent entities, held together by a homogeneous competence or grammar shared identically and equally among all the members. This abstract idea of the speech community seemed to reflect, among other things, the utopian way modern nations conceive of themselves as what Benedict Anderson calls "imagined communities."[3] In a book of that title, Anderson observes that with the possible exception of what he calls "primordial villages," human communities exist as *imagined* entities in which people "will never know most of their fellow-members, meet them or even hear of them, yet in the minds of each lives the image of their communion." "Communities are distinguished," he goes on to say, "not by their falsity/genuineness, but by *the style in which they are imagined*" (15; emphasis mine). Anderson proposes three features that characterize the style in which the modern nation is imagined. First, it is imagined as *limited,* by "finite, if elastic, boundaries"; second, it is imagined as *sovereign,* and, third, it is imagined as *fraternal,* "a deep, horizontal comradeship" for which millions of people are prepared "not so much to kill as willingly to die" (15). As the image suggests, the nation-community is embodied metonymically in the finite, sovereign, fraternal figure of the citizen-soldier.

Anderson argues that European bourgeoisies were distinguished by their ability to "achieve solidarity on an essentially imagined basis" (74) on a scale far greater than that of elites of other times and places. Writing and literacy play a central role in this argument. Anderson maintains, as have others, that the main instrument that made bourgeois nation-building projects possible was print capitalism. The commercial circulation of books in the various European vernaculars, he argues, was what first created the invisible networks that would eventually constitute the literate elites and those they ruled as nations. (Estimates are that 180 million books were put into circulation in Europe between the years 1500 and 1600 alone.)

Now obviously this style of imagining of modern nations, as Anderson describes it, is strongly utopian, embodying values like equality, fraternity, liberty, which the societies often profess but systematically fail to realize. The prototype of the modern nation as imagined community was, it seemed to me, mirrored in ways people thought about language and the speech community. Many commentators have pointed out how modern views of language as code and competence assume a unified and homogeneous social world in which language exists as a shared patrimony—as a device, precisely, for imagining community. An image of a universally shared literacy is also part of the picture. The prototypical manifestation of language is generally taken to be the speech of individual adult native speakers face-to-face (as in Saussure's famous diagram) in monolingual, even monodialectal situations—in short, the most homogeneous case linguistically and socially. The same goes for written communication. Now one could certainly imagine a theory that assumed different things—that argued, for instance, that the most revealing speech situation for understanding language was one involving a gathering of people each of whom spoke two languages and understood a third and held only one language in common with any of the others. It depends on what workings of language you want to see or want to see first, on what you choose to define as normative.

In keeping with autonomous, fraternal models of community, analyses of language use commonly assume that principles of cooperation and shared understanding are normally in effect. Descriptions of interactions between people in conversation, classrooms, medical and bureaucratic settings, readily take it for granted that the situation is governed by a single set of rules or norms shared by all participants. The analysis focuses then on how those rules produce or fail to produce an orderly, coherent exchange. Models involving games and moves are often used to describe interactions. Despite whatever conflicts or systematic social differences might be in play, it is assumed that all participants are engaged in the same game and that the game is the same for all players. Often it is. But of course it often is not, as, for example, when speakers are from different classes or cultures, or one party is exercising authority and another is submitting to it or questioning it. Last year one of my children moved to a new elementary school that had more open classrooms and more flexible curricula than the conventional school he started out in. A few days into the term, we asked him what it was like at the new school. "Well," he said, "they're a lot nicer, and they have a lot less rules. But know *why* they're nicer?" "Why?" I asked. "So you'll obey all the rules they don't have," he replied. This is a very coherent analysis with considerable elegance and explanatory power, but probably not the one his teacher would have given.

When linguistic (or literate) interaction is described in terms of orderliness, games, moves, or scripts, usually only legitimate moves are actually named as part of the system, where legitimacy is defined from the point of view of the party in authority—regardless of what other parties might see themselves as doing. Teacher-pupil language, for example, tends to be described almost entirely from the point of view of the teacher and teaching, not from the point of view of pupils and pupiling (the word doesn't even exist, though the thing certainly does). If a classroom is analyzed as a social world unified and homogenized with respect to the teacher, whatever students do other than what the teacher specifies is invisible or anomalous to the analysis. This can be true in practice as well. On several occasions my fourth grader, the one busy obeying all the rules they didn't have, was given writing assignments that took the form of answering a series of questions to build up a paragraph. These questions often asked him to identify with the interests of those in power over him—parents, teachers, doctors, public authorities. He invariably sought ways to resist or subvert these assignments. One assignment, for instance, called for imagining "a helpful invention." The students were asked to write single-sentence responses to the following questions:

> What kind of invention would help you?
> How would it help you?
> Why would you need it?
> What would it look like?
> Would other people be able to use it also?
> What would be an invention to help your teacher?
> What would be an invention to help your parents?

Manuel's reply read as follows:

> A grate adventchin
>
> Some inventchins are GRATE!!!!!!!!!!! My inventchin would be a shot that would put every thing you learn at school in your brain. It would help me by letting me graduate right now!! I would need it because it would let me play with my friends, go on vacachin and, do fun a lot more. It would look like a regular shot. Ather peaple would use to. This inventchin would help my teacher parents get away from a lot of work. I think a shot like this would be GRATE!

Despite the spelling, the assignment received the usual star to indicate the task had been fulfilled in an acceptable way. No recognition was available, however, of the humor, the attempt to be critical or contestatory, to parody the structures of authority. On that score, Manuel's luck was only slightly better than Guaman Poma's. What is the place of unsolicited oppositional discourse, parody, resistance, critique in the imagined classroom community? Are teachers supposed to feel that their teaching has been most successful when they have eliminated such things and unified the social world, probably in their own image? Who wins when we do that? Who loses?

Such questions may be hypothetical, because in the United States in the 1990s, many teachers find themselves less and less able to do that even if they want to. The composition of the national collectivity is changing and so are the styles, as Anderson put it, in which it is being imagined. In the 1980s in many nation-states, imagined national syntheses that had retained hegemonic force began to dissolve. Internal social groups with histories and lifeways different from the official ones began insisting on those histories and lifeways *as part of their citizenship,* as the very mode of their membership in the national collectivity. In their dialogues with dominant institutions, many groups began asserting a rhetoric of belonging that made demands beyond those of representation and basic rights granted from above. In universities we started to hear, "I don't just want you to let me be here, I want to belong here; this institution should belong to me as much as it does to anyone else." Institutions have responded with, among other things, rhetorics of diversity and multiculturalism whose import at this moment is up for grabs across the ideological spectrum.

These shifts are being lived out by everyone working in education today, and everyone is challenged by them in one way or another. Those of us committed to educational democracy are particularly challenged as that notion finds itself besieged on the public agenda. Many of those who govern us display, openly, their interest in a quiescent, ignorant, manipulable electorate. Even as an ideal, the concept of an enlightened citizenry seems to have disappeared from the national imagination. A couple of years ago the university where I work went through an intense and wrenching debate over a narrowly defined Western-culture requirement that had been instituted there in 1980. It kept boiling down to a debate over the ideas of national patrimony, cultural citizenship, and imagined community. In the end, the requirement was transformed into a much more broadly defined course called Cultures, Ideas, Values.[4] In the context of the change, a new course was designed that centered on the Americas and the multiple cultural histories (including European ones) that have intersected here. As you can imagine, the course attracted a very diverse student body. The classroom functioned not like a homogeneous community or a horizontal alliance but like a contact zone. Every single text we read stood in specific historical relationships to the students in the class, but the range and variety of historical relationships in play were enormous. Everybody had a stake in nearly everything we read, but the range and kind of stakes varied widely.

It was the most exciting teaching we had ever done, and also the hardest. We were struck, for example, at how anomalous the formal lecture became in a contact zone (who can forget Atahuallpa throwing down the Bible because it would not speak to him?). The lecturer's traditional (imagined) task—unifying the world in the class's eyes by means of a monologue that rings equally coherent, revealing, and true for all, forging an ad hoc community, homogeneous with respect to one's own words—this task became not only impossible but anomalous and unimaginable. Instead, one had to work in the knowledge that whatever one said was going to be systematically received in radically heterogeneous ways that we were neither able nor entitled to prescribe.

The very nature of the course put ideas and identities on the line. All the students in the class had the experience, for example, of hearing their culture discussed and objectified in ways that horrified them; all the students saw their roots traced back to legacies of both glory and shame; all the students experienced face-to-face the ignorance and incomprehension, and occasionally the hostility, of others. In the absence of community values and the hope of synthesis, it was easy to forget the positives; the fact, for instance, that kinds of marginalization once taken for granted were gone. Virtually every student was having the experience of seeing the world described with him or her in it. Along with rage, incomprehension, and pain, there were exhilarating moments of wonder and revelation, mutual understanding, and new wisdom—the joys of the contact zone. The sufferings and revelations were, at different moments to be sure, experienced by every student. No one was excluded, and no one was safe.

The fact that no one was safe made all of us involved in the course appreciate the importance of what we came to call "safe houses." We used the term to refer to social and intellectual spaces where groups can constitute themselves as horizontal, homogeneous, sovereign communities with high degrees of trust, shared understandings, temporary protection from legacies of oppression. This is why, as we realized, multicultural curricula should not seek to replace ethnic or women's studies, for example. Where there are legacies of subordination, groups need places for healing and mutual recognition, safe houses in which to construct shared understandings, knowledges, claims on the world that they can then bring into the contact zone.

Meanwhile, our job in the Americas course remains to figure out how to make that crossroads the best site for learning that it can be. We are looking for the pedagogical arts of the contact zone. These will include, we are sure, exercises in storytelling and in identifying with the ideas, interests, histories, and attitudes of others; experiments in transculturation and collaborative work and in the arts of critique, parody, and comparison (including unseemly comparisons between elite and vernacular cultural forms); the redemption of the oral; ways for people to engage with suppressed aspects of history (including their own histories), ways to move *into and out of* rhetorics of authenticity; ground rules for communication across lines of difference and hierarchy that go beyond politeness but maintain mutual respect; a systematic approach to the all-important concept of *cultural mediation*. These arts were in play in every room at the extraordinary Pittsburgh conference on literacy. I learned a lot about them there, and I am thankful.

Notes

1. For an introduction in English to these and other aspects of Guaman Poma's work, see Rolena Adorno. Adorno and Mercedes Lopez-Baralt pioneered the study of Andean symbolic systems in Guaman Poma.

2. It is far from clear that the *Royal Commentaries* was as benign as the Spanish seemed to assume. The book certainly played a role in maintaining the identity and aspirations of indigenous elites in the Andes. In the mid-eighteenth century, a new edition of the *Royal Commentaries* was suppressed by Spanish authorities because its preface included a prophecy by Sir Walter Raleigh that the English would invade Peru and restore the Inca monarchy.

3. The discussion of community here is summarized from my essay "Linguistic Utopias."

4. For information about this program and the contents of courses taught in it, write Program in Cultures, Ideas, Values (CIV), Stanford Univ., Stanford, CA 94305.

Works Cited

Adorno, Rolena. *Guaman Poma de Ayala: Writing and Resistance in Colonial Peru.* Austin: U of Texas P, 1986.

Anderson, Benedict. *Imagined Communities: Reflections on the Origins and Spread of Nationalism.* London: Verso, 1984.

Garcilaso de la Vega, El Inca. *Royal Commentaries of the Incas.* 1613. Austin: U of Texas P, 1966.

Guaman Poma de Ayala, Felipe. *El primer nueva corónica y buen gobierno.* Manuscript. Ed. John Murra and Rolena Adorno. Mexico: Siglo XXI, 1980.

Pratt, Mary Louise. "Linguistic Utopias." *The Linguistics of Writing.* Ed. Nigel Fabb et al. Manchester: Manchester UP, 1987. 48–46.

Treviño, Gloria. "Cultural Ambivalence in Early Chicano Prose Fiction." Diss. Stanford U, 1985.

SUGGESTIONS FOR DISCUSSION

1. Compare with other students how you have divided Mary Louise Pratt's essay into sections and how you have annotated it. The point here is not to decide whether one set of divisions and annotations is better than another but to use all those available to put together a reading of the essay by reconstructing its development and its general line of argument. Your task here is to explain how (or whether) the essay establishes a central perspective from its various parts.

2. Pratt's notion of the "arts of the contact zone" is not without its difficulties. At the end of her discussion of Guaman Poma's letter, she offers the following summary:

> Autoethnography, transculturation, critique, collaboration, bilingualism, mediation, parody, denunciation, imaginary dialogue, vernacular expression—these are some of the literate arts of the contact zone. Miscomprehension, incomprehension, dead letters, unread masterpieces, absolute heterogeneity of meaning—these are some of the perils of writing in the contact zone. They all live among us today in the transnationalized metropolis of the United States and are becoming more widely visible, more decipherable to those who once would have ignored them in defense of a stable, centered sense of knowledge and reality.

Take your time deciphering this passage, for it is a complicated one. At the same time, it is a crucial passage in the essay where Pratt is summing up what she sees as the significance of Guaman Poma's letter and where she is preparing readers for the final sections of the essay. Work together with other students to clarify the meaning of this passage and how it represents Pratt's overall line of thought.

3. Each of the first three selections in this chapter relies on a central metaphor to describe the lived realities of multicultural America. Ishmael Reed uses "bouillabaise," in contrast to the conventional image of America as a melting pot. Adrienne Rich describes her personal identity as "split at the root," in contrast to a readily available and singular American identity. By the same token, Pratt offers the metaphor of the "contact zone" to describe culture as a complicated intersection and interaction of various languages, cultural practices, knowledges, beliefs, and perspectives, in contrast to the representation of culture as "discrete, coherently structured, monolingual edifices." Compare these metaphors of cultural experience. What do

they have in common? How do they differ? What changes do they ask readers to make in their understandings of American culture? What do you see as the benefits or liabilities of these changes?

SUGGESTIONS FOR WRITING

1. Write a letter to a friend at another college who has not read Mary Louise Pratt's "Arts of the Contact Zone." Assume that your friend is interested in thinking about new ways to describe and analyze American culture. In the letter, explain what Pratt's main line of thought is and what she is arguing about the nature of American culture. You will need to explain the meanings Pratt derives from Guaman Poma's letter, but it may help your friend, who has not read the essay, to use other examples of the "contact zone" as well. Since this is a letter to a friend, you will also want to describe your own experience working through Pratt's essay and to explain your own sense of the value of thinking about American culture as a "contact zone."

2. In many respects, Pratt's analysis of Guaman Poma's letter is the centerpiece of her essay, the occasion she uses to develop her notion of the "literate arts of the contact zone." If her term is useful, then you should be able to apply it to other, more contemporary forms of cultural expression. Write an essay that works with the notion of the "contact zone," that uses it as a practical tool of analysis to discuss what you see as a form of cultural expression written, produced, or performed in the contact zone. The choice of materials is up to you, but keep in mind how Guaman Poma's letter represents the experience of outsiders to the dominant culture. You might think, for example, of how African Americans, Hispanics, Asians, Jews, Irish, Italians, or gays and lesbians represent themselves to mainstream American culture, or how children and young people represent themselves to adult society.

3. Pratt is offering a view of American culture and the communities Americans live in that contrasts dramatically with conventional ideas about a common, unified national culture and communities that share a common way of life. Think of the various communities in which you have lived—the particular neighborhood, town, or region of the country you have grown up in, the community you participate in at school or at work, in the military, in church, and so forth. Write an essay that uses Pratt's notion of the "contact zone" to contrast the view that particular community holds of itself as a unified body with Pratt's sense that communities are invariably based on the interactions of cultural differences as much as on the similarities of its members. Begin your essay by describing how the community you are writing about represents itself in terms of common values and beliefs. Then use Pratt's notion of "contact zones" to redescribe that community as insiders and outsiders representing themselves and their differences to each other.

Gloria Anzaldua

HOW TO TAME A WILD TONGUE

Gloria Anzaldua writes in a language that grows out of the multiple cultures in the American Southwest—a mosaic of English (both standard and slang), Spanish (both Castilian and Mexican), northern Mexican and Chicano Spanish dialects, Tex-Mex, *Pachuco* (the vernacular of urban zoot suiters), and the Aztec language Nahuatl. The following selection is a chapter from her book, *Borderlands/La Frontera,* originally published in 1987. As the title of her book indicates, Anzaldua sees herself as a "border woman." "I grew up between two cultures," she says, "the Mexican (with a heavy Indian influence) and the Anglo (as a member of a colonized people in our own territory). I have been straddling that *tejas*-Mexican border, and others, all my life." Like Mary Louise Pratt's notion of the "contact zone," Anzaldua's "borderland" refers to those places "where two or more cultures edge each other, where people of different races occupy the same territory, where under, lower, middle, and upper classes touch, where the space between two individuals shrinks with intimacy."

Suggestion for Reading

• As you read, you will notice how Gloria Anzaldua combines English and Spanish in a sentence or a paragraph. Consider the effects of Anzaldua's prose and how it locates you as a reader on the border where two cultures and languages touch.

"We're going to have to control your tongue," the dentist says, pulling out all the metal from my mouth. Silver bits plop and tinkle into the basin. My mouth is a motherlode.

The dentist is cleaning out my roots. I get a whiff of the stench when I gasp. "I can't cap that tooth yet, you're still draining," he says.

"We're going to have to do something about your tongue," I hear the anger rising in his voice. My tongue keeps pushing out the wads of cotton, pushing back the drills, the long thin needles. "I've never seen anything as strong or as stubborn," he says. And I think, how do you tame a wild tongue, train it to be quiet, how do you bridle and saddle it? How do you make it lie down?

Who is to say that robbing a people of

its language is less violent than war?

—Ray Gwyn Smith[1]

I remember being caught speaking Spanish at recess—that was good for three licks on the knuckles with a sharp ruler. I remember being sent to the corner of the classroom for "talking back" to the Anglo teacher when all I was trying to do was tell her how to pronounce my name. "If you want to be American, speak 'American.' If you don't like it, go back to Mexico where you belong."

"I want you to speak English. *Pa' hallar buen trabajo tienes que saber hablar el inglés bien. Qué vale toda tu educación si todavía hablas inglés con un* 'accent,'" my mother would say, mortified that I spoke English like a Mexican. At Pan American University, I and all Chicano students were required to take two speech classes. Their purpose: to get rid of our accents.

Attacks on one's form of expression with the intent to censor are a violation of the First Amendment. *El Anglo con cara de inocente nos arrancó la lengua.* Wild tongues can't be tamed, they can only be cut out.

Overcoming the Tradition of Silence

> *Ahogadas, escupimos el oscuro.*
> *Peleando con nuestra propia sombra*
> *el silencio nos sepulta.*

En boca cerrada no entran moscas. "Flies don't enter a closed mouth" is a saying I kept hearing when I was a child. *Ser habladora* was to be a gossip and a liar, to talk too much. *Muchachitas bien criadas,* well-bred girls don't answer back. *Es una falta de respeto* to talk back to one's mother or father. I remember one of the sins I'd recite to the priest in the confession box the few times I went to confession: talking back to my mother, *hablar pa' 'tras, repelar. Hocicona, repelona, chismosa,* having a big mouth, questioning, carrying tales are all signs of being *mal criada.* In my culture they are all words that are derogatory if applied to women—I've never heard them applied to men.

• • •

The first time I heard two women, a Puerto Rican and a Cuban, say the word "*nosotras,*" I was shocked. I had not known the word existed. Chicanas use *nosotros* whether we're male or female. We are robbed of our female being by the masculine plural. Language is a male discourse.

> And our tongues have become dry the wilderness has dried out our tongues
> and we have forgotten speech.
>
> —Irena Klepfisz[2]

Even our own people, other Spanish speakers *nos quieren poner candados en la boca.* They would hold us back with their bag of *reglas de academia.*

Oyé como ladra: el lenguaje de la frontera

> *Quien tiene boca se equivoca.*
> —Mexican saying

"*Pocho,* cultural traitor, you're speaking the oppressor's language by speaking English, you're ruining the Spanish language," I have been accused by various Latinos and Latinas. Chicano Spanish is considered by the purist and by most Latinos deficient, a mutilation of Spanish.

But Chicano Spanish is a border tongue which developed naturally. Change, *evolución, enriquecimiento de palabras nuevas por invención o adopción* have created variants of Chicano Spanish, *un nuevo lenguaje. Un lenguaje que corresponde a un modo de vivir.* Chicano Spanish is not incorrect, it is a living language.

For a people who are neither Spanish nor live in a country in which Spanish is the first language; for a people who live in a country in which English is the reigning tongue but who are not Anglo; for a people who cannot entirely identify with either standard (formal, Castilian) Spanish nor standard English, what recourse is left to them but to create their own language? A language which they can connect their identity to, one capable of communicating the realities and values true to themselves—a language with terms that are neither *español ni inglés,* but both. We speak a patois, a forked tongue, a variation of two languages.

Chicano Spanish sprang out of the Chicanos' need to identify ourselves as a distinct people. We need a language with which we could communicate with ourselves, a secret language. For some of us, language is a homeland closer than the Southwest—for many Chicanos today live in the Midwest and the East. And because we are a complex, heterogeneous people, we speak many languages. Some of the languages we speak are

1. Standard English

2. Working class and slang English

3. Standard Spanish

4. Standard Mexican Spanish

5. North Mexican Spanish dialect

6. Chicano Spanish (Texas, New Mexico, Arizona, and California have regional variations)

7. Tex-Mex

8. *Pachuco* (called *caló*)

My "home" tongues are the languages I speak with my sister and brothers, with my friends. They are the last five listed, with 6 and 7 being closest to my heart. From school, the media, and job situations, I've picked up standard and working class English. From Mamagrande Locha and from reading Spanish and Mexican literature, I've picked up Standard Spanish and Standard Mexican Spanish. From *los recién llegados,* Mexican immigrants, and *braceros,* I learned the North Mexican dialect. With Mexicans I'll try to speak either Standard Mexican Spanish or the North Mexican dialect. From my parents and Chicanos living in the Valley, I picked up Chicano Texas Spanish, and I speak it with my mom, younger brother (who married a Mexican and who rarely mixes Spanish with English), aunts, and older relatives.

With Chicanas from *Nuevo México* or *Arizona* I will speak Chicano Spanish a little, but often they don't understand what I'm saying. With most California Chicanas I
speak entirely in English (unless I forget). When I first moved to San Francisco, I'd rattle off something in Spanish, unintentionally embarrassing them. Often it is only with
another Chicana *tejano* that I can talk freely.

• • •

Words distorted by English are known as anglicisms or *pochismos*. The *pocho* is an angli-
cized Mexican or American of Mexican origin who speaks Spanish with an accent characteristic of North Americans and who distorts and reconstructs the language according
to the influence of English.[3] Tex-Mex, or Spanglish, comes most naturally to me. I may
switch back and forth from English to Spanish in the same sentence or in the same
word. With my sister and my brother Nune and with Chicano *tejano* contemporaries I
speak in Tex-Mex.

From kids and people my own age I picked up *Pachuco*. *Pachuco* (the language
of the zoot suiters) is a language of rebellion, both against Standard Spanish and
Standard English. It is a secret language. Adults of the culture and outsiders cannot
understand it. It is made up of slang words from both English and Spanish. *Ruca*
means girl or woman, *vato* means guy or dude, *chale* means no, *simón* means yes,
churro is sure, talk is *periquiar*, *pigionear* means petting, *que gacho* means how
nerdy, *ponte águila* means watch out, death is called *la pelona*. Through lack of
practice and not having others who can speak it, I've lost most of the *Pachuco*
tongue.

CHICANO SPANISH

Chicanos, after 250 years of Spanish/Anglo colonization, have developed significant
differences in the Spanish we speak. We collapse two adjacent vowels into a single syllable and sometimes shift the stress in certain words such as *maíz/maiz, cohete/cuete*. We
leave out certain consonants when they appear between vowels: *lado/lao, mojado/mojao*.
Chicanos from South Texas pronounce *f* as *j* as in *jue (fue)*. Chicanos use "archaisms,"
words that are no longer in the Spanish language, words that have been evolved out.
We say *semos, truje, haiga, ansina*, and *naiden*. We retain the "archaic" *j*, as in *jalar*, that
derives from an earlier *h* (the French *halar* or the Germanic *halon* which was lost to
standard Spanish in the sixteenth century), but which is still found in several regional
dialects such as the one spoken in South Texas. (Due to geography, Chicanos from the
Valley of South Texas were cut off linguistically from other Spanish speakers. We tend
to use words that the Spaniards brought over from Medieval Spain. The majority of the
Spanish colonizers in Mexico and the Southwest came from Extremadura—Hernán
Cortés was one of them—and Andalucía. Andalucians pronounce *ll* like a *y*, and their
d's tend to be absorbed by adjacent vowels: *tirado* becomes *tirao*. They brought *el
lenguaje popular, dialectos y regionalismos*.)[4]

Chicanos and other Spanish speakers also shift *ll* to *y* and *z* to *s*.[5] We leave out initial syllables, saying *tar* for *estar*, *toy* for *estoy*, *hora* for *ahora* (*cubanos* and *puertor-
riqueños* also leave out initial letters of some words). We also leave out the final syllable
such as *pa* for *para*. The intervocalic *y*, the *ll* as in *tortilla, ella, botella*, gets replaced by

tortia or *tortiya, ea, botea.* We add an additional syllable at the beginning of certain words: *atocar* for *tocar, agastar* for *gastar.* Sometimes we'll say *lavaste las vacijas,* other times *lavates* (substituting the *ates* verb endings for the *aste*).

We used anglicisms, words borrowed from English: *bola* from ball, *carpeta* from carpet, *máchina de lavar* (instead of *lavadora*) from washing machine. Tex-Mex argot, created by adding a Spanish sound at the beginning or end of an English word such as *cookiar* for cook, *watchar* for watch, *parkiar* for park, and *rapiar* for rape, is the result of the pressures on Spanish speakers to adapt to English.

We don't use the word *vosotros/as* or its accompanying verb form. We don't say *claro* (to mean yes), *imagínate,* or *me emociona,* unless we picked up Spanish from Latinas, out of a book, or in a classroom. Other Spanish-speaking groups are going through the same, or similar, development in their Spanish.

LINGUISTIC TERRORISM

> *Deslenguadas. Somos los del español deficiente.* We are your linguistic nightmare, your linguistic aberration, your linguistic *mestisaje,* the subject of your *burla.* Because we speak with tongues of fire we are culturally crucified. Racially, culturally, and linguistically *somos huérfanos*—we speak an orphan tongue.

Chicanas who grew up speaking Chicano Spanish have internalized the belief that we speak poor Spanish. It is illegitimate, a bastard language. And because we internalize how our language has been used against us by the dominant culture, we use our language differences against each other.

Chicana feminists often skirt around each other with suspicion and hesitation. For the longest time I couldn't figure it out. Then it dawned on me. To be close to another Chicana is like looking into the mirror. We are afraid of what we'll see there. *Pena.* Shame. Low estimation of self. In childhood we are told that our language is wrong. Repeated attacks on our native tongue diminish our sense of self. The attacks continue throughout our lives.

Chicanas feel uncomfortable talking in Spanish to Latinas, afraid of their censure. Their language was not outlawed in their countries. They had a whole lifetime of being immersed in their native tongue; generations, centuries in which Spanish was a first language, taught in school, heard on radio and TV, and read in the newspaper.

If a person, Chicana or Latina, has a low estimation of my native tongue, she also has a low estimation of me. Often with *mexicanas y latinas* we'll speak English as a neutral language. Even among Chicanas we tend to speak English at parties or conferences. Yet, at the same time, we're afraid the other will think we're *agringadas* because we don't speak Chicano Spanish. We oppress each other trying to out-Chicano each other, vying to be the "real" Chicanas, to speak like Chicanos. There is no one Chicano language just as there is no one Chicano experience. A monolingual Chicana whose first language is English or Spanish is just as much a Chicana as one who speaks several variants of Spanish. A Chicana from Michigan or Chicago or Detroit is just as much a Chicana as one from the Southwest. Chicano Spanish is as diverse linguistically as it is regionally.

By the end of this century, Spanish speakers will comprise the biggest minority group in the United States, a country where students in high schools and colleges are encouraged to take French classes because French is considered more "cultured." But for a language to remain alive it must be used.[6] By the end of this century English, and not Spanish, will be the mother tongue of most Chicanos and Latinos.

• • •

So, if you want to really hurt me, talk badly about my language. Ethnic identity is twin skin to linguistic identity—I am my language. Until I can take pride in my language, I cannot take pride in myself. Until I can accept as legitimate Chicano Texas Spanish, Tex-Mex, and all the other languages I speak, I cannot accept the legitimacy of myself. Until I am free to write bilingually and to switch codes without having always to translate, while I still have to speak English or Spanish when I would rather speak Spanglish, and as long as I have to accommodate the English speakers rather than having them accommodate me, my tongue will be illegitimate.

I will no longer be made to feel ashamed of existing. I will have my voice: Indian, Spanish, white. I will have my serpent's tongue—my woman's voice, my sexual voice, my poet's voice. I will overcome the tradition of silence.

> My fingers
> move sly against your palm
> Like women everywhere, we speak in code. . . .

—Melanie Kaye/Kantrowitz[7]

"*VISTAS,*" *CORRIDOS, Y COMIDA:* MY NATIVE TONGUE

In the 1960s, I read my first Chicano novel. It was *City of Night* by John Rechy, a gay Texan, son of a Scottish father and a Mexican mother. For days I walked around in stunned amazement that a Chicano could write and could get published. When I read *I Am Joaquín*[8] I was surprised to see a bilingual book by a Chicano in print. When I saw poetry written in Tex-Mex for the first time, a feeling of pure joy flashed through me. I felt like we really existed as a people. In 1971, when I started teaching High School English to Chicano students, I tried to supplement the required texts with works by Chicanos, only to be reprimanded and forbidden to do so by the principal. He claimed that I was supposed to teach "American" and English literature. At the risk of being fired, I swore my students to secrecy and slipped in Chicano short stories, poems, a play. In graduate school, while working toward a Ph.D., I had to "argue" with one adviser after the other, semester after semester, before I was allowed to make Chicano literature an area of focus.

Even before I read books by Chicanos or Mexicans, it was the Mexican movies I saw at the drive-in—the Thursday night special of $1.00 a carload—that gave me a sense of belonging. "*Vámonos a las vistas,*" my mother would call out and we'd all—grandmother, brothers, sister, and cousins—squeeze into the car. We'd wolf down cheese and bologna white bread sandwiches while watching Pedro Infante in melodramatic tearjerkers like *Nosotros los pobres,* the first "real" Mexican movie (that was not an imitation of European movies). I remember seeing *Cuando los hijos se van* and surmising that all Mexican movies played up the love a mother has for her children and what ungrateful sons and daughters suffer when they are not devoted to their mothers. I remember the singing-type "westerns" of Jorge Negrete and Miquel Aceves Mejía. When watching Mexican movies, I felt a sense of homecoming as well as alienation. People who were to amount to something didn't go to Mexican movies, or *bailes,* or tune their radios to *bolero, rancherita,* and *corrido* music.

• • •

The whole time I was growing up, there was *norteño* music sometimes called North Mexican border music, or Tex-Mex music, or Chicano music, or *cantina* (bar) music. I grew up listening to *conjuntos,* three- or four-piece bands made up of folk musicians playing guitar, *bajo sexto,* drums, and button accordion, which Chicanos had borrowed from the German immigrants who had come to Central Texas and Mexico to farm and build breweries. In the Rio Grande Valley, Steve Jordan and Little Joe Hernández were popular, and Flaco Jiménez was the accordion king. The rhythms of Tex-Mex music are those of the polka, also adapted from the Germans, who in turn had borrowed the polka from the Czechs and Bohemians.

I remember the hot, sultry evenings when *corridos*—songs of love and death on the Texas-Mexican borderlands—reverberated out of cheap amplifiers from the local *cantinas* and wafted in through my bedroom window.

Corridos first became widely used along the South Texas/Mexican border during the early conflict between Chicanos and Anglos. The *corridos* are usually about Mexican heroes who do valiant deeds against the Anglo oppressors. Pancho Villa's song, *"La cucaracha,"* is the most famous one. *Corridos* of John F. Kennedy and his death are still very popular in the Valley. Older Chicanos remember Lydia Mendoza, one of the great border *corrido* singers who was called *la Gloria de Tejas.* Her *"El tango negro,"* sung during the Great Depression, made her a singer of the people. The ever-present *corridos* narrated one hundred years of border history, bringing news of events as well as entertaining. These folk musicians and folk songs are our chief cultural mythmakers, and they made our hard lives seem bearable.

I grew up feeling ambivalent about our music. Country-western and rock-and-roll had more status. In the fifties and sixties, for the slightly educated and *agringado* Chicanos, there existed a sense of shame at being caught listening to our music. Yet I couldn't stop my feet from thumping to the music, could not stop humming the words, nor hide from myself the exhilaration I felt when I heard it.

• • •

There are more subtle ways that we internalize identification, especially in the forms of images and emotions. For me food and certain smells are tied to my identity, to my homeland. Woodsmoke curling up to an immense blue sky; woodsmoke perfuming my grandmother's clothes, her skin. The stench of cow manure and the yellow patches on the ground; the crack of a .22 rifle and the reek of cordite. Homemade white cheese sizzling in a pan, melting inside a folded *tortilla.* My sister Hilda's hot, spicy *menudo, chile colorado* making it deep red, pieces of *panza* and hominy floating on top. My brother Carito barbequing *fajitas* in the backyard. Even now and 3,000 miles away, I can see my mother spicing the ground beef, pork, and venison with *chile*. My mouth salivates at the thought of the hot steaming *tamales* I would be eating if I were home.

SI LE PREGUNTAS A MI MAMÁ, "¿QUÉ ERES?"

> Identity is the essential core of who we are as individuals, the conscious experience of the self inside.
>
> —Gershen Kaufman[9]

Nosotros los Chicanos straddle the borderlands. On one side of us, we are constantly exposed to the Spanish of the Mexicans, on the other side we hear the Anglos' incessant clamoring so that we forget our language. Among ourselves we don't say *nosotros los americanos, o nosotros los españoles, o nosotros los hispanos.* We say *nosotros los mexicanos* (by *mexicanos* we do not mean citizens of Mexico; we do not mean a national identity, but a racial one). We distinguish between *mexicanos del otro lado* and *mexicanos de este lado.* Deep in our hearts we believe that being Mexican has nothing to do with which country one lives in. Being Mexican is a state of soul—not one of mind, not one of citizenship. Neither eagle nor serpent, but both. And like the ocean, neither animal respects borders.

> *Dime con quien andas y te diré quien eres.*
>
> (Tell me who your friends are and I'll tell you who you are.)
>
> —Mexican saying

Si le preguntas a mi mamá, "¿Qué eres?" te dirá, "Soy mexicana." My brothers and sister say the same. I sometimes will answer *"soy mexicana"* and at others will say *"soy Chicana" o "soy tejana."* But I identified as *"Raza"* before I ever identified as *"mexicana"* or "Chicana."

As a culture, we call ourselves Spanish when referring to ourselves as a linguistic group and when copping out. It is then that we forget our predominant Indian genes. We are 70–80 percent Indian.[10] We call ourselves Hispanic or Spanish-American or Latin American or Latin when linking ourselves to other Spanish-speaking peoples of the Western hemisphere and when copping out. We call ourselves Mexican-American[12] to signify we are neither Mexican nor American, but more the noun "American" than the adjective "Mexican" (and when copping out).

Chicanos and other people of color suffer economically for not acculturating. This voluntary (yet forced) alienation makes for psychological conflict, a kind of dual identity—we don't identify with the Anglo-American cultural values and we don't totally identify with the Mexican cultural values. We are a synergy of two cultures with various degrees of Mexicanness or Angloness. I have so internalized the borderland conflict that sometimes I feel like one cancels out the other and we are zero, nothing, no one. *A veces no soy nada ni nadie. Pero hasta cuando no lo soy, lo soy.*

When not copping out, when we know we are more than nothing, we call our-selves Mexican, referring to race and ancestry; *mestizo* when affirming both our Indian and Spanish (but we hardly ever own our Black) ancestry; Chicano when referring to a politically aware people born and/or raised in the United States; *Raza* when referring to Chicanos; *tejanos* when we are Chicanos from Texas.

Chicanos did not know we were a people until 1965 when Cesar Chavez and the farmworkers united and *I Am Joaquín* was published and *la Raza Unida* party was formed in Texas. With that recognition, we became a distinct people. Something momentous happened to the Chicano soul—we became aware of our reality and ac-quired a name and a language (Chicano Spanish) that reflected that reality. Now that we had a name, some of the fragmented pieces began to fall together—who we were, what we were, how we had evolved. We began to get glimpses of what we might eventually become.

Yet the struggle of identities continues, the struggle of borders is our reality still. One day the inner struggle will cease and a true integration take place. In the mean-time, *tenémos que hacer la lucha. ¿Quién está protegiendo los ranchos de mi gente? ¿Quién está tratando de cerrar la fisura entre la india y el blanco en nuestra sangre? El Chicano, si, el Chicano que anda como un ladrón en su propia casa.*

● ● ●

Los Chicanos, how patient we seem, how very patient. There is the quiet of the Indian about us.[13] We know how to survive. When other races have given up their tongue we've kept ours. We know what it is to live under the hammer blow of the dominant *norteamericano* culture. But more than we count the blows, we count the days the weeks the years the centuries the aeons until the white laws and commerce and customs will rot in the deserts they've created, lie bleached. *Humildes* yet proud, *quietos* yet wild, *nosotros los mexicanos-Chicanos* will walk by the crumbling ashes as we go about our business. Stubborn, persevering, impenetrable as stone, yet possessing a malleability that renders us unbreakable, we, the *mestizas* and *mestizos,* will remain.

Notes

1. Ray Gwyn Smith, *Moorland Is Cold Country,* unpublished book.
2. Irena Klepfisz, "*Di rayze aheym*/The Journey Home," in *The Tribe of Dina: A Jewish Women's Anthology,* Melanie Kaye/Kantrowitz and Irena Klepfisz, eds. (Montpelier, VT: Sinister Wisdom Books, 1986), 49.
3. R. C. Ortega, *Dialectología Del Barrio,* trans. Hortencia S. Alwan (Los Angeles, CA: R. C. Ortega Publisher & Bookseller, 1977), 132.
4. Eduardo Hernandéz-Chávez, Andrew D. Cohen, and Anthony F. Beltramo, *El Lenguaje de los Chicanos: Regional and Social Characteristics of Language Used by Mexican Americans* (Arlington, VA: Center for Applied Linguistics, 1975), 39.
5. Hernandéz-Chávez, xvii.
6. Irena Klepfisz, "Secular Jewish Identity: Yidishkayt in America," in *The Tribe of Dina,* Kaye/Kantrowitz and Klepfisz, eds., 43.
7. Melanie Kaye/Kantrowitz, "Sign," in *We Speak in Code: Poems and Other Writings* (Pittsburgh, PA: Motheroot Publications, Inc., 1980), 85.

8. Rodolfo Gonzales, *I Am Joaquín/Yo Soy Joaquín* (New York, NY: Bantam Books, 1972). It was first published in 1967.

9. Gershen Kaufman, *Shame: The Power of Caring* (Cambridge, MA: Schenkman Books, Inc., 1980), 68.

10. John R. Chávez, *The Lost Land: The Chicano Images of the Southwest* (Albuquerque, NM: University of New Mexico Press, 1984), 88–90.

11. "Hispanic" is derived from *Hispanis* (*España,* a name given to the Iberian Peninsula in ancient times when it was a part of the Roman Empire) and is a term designated by the U.S. government to make it easier to handle us on paper.

12. The Treaty of Guadalupe Hidalgo created the Mexican-American in 1848.

13. Anglos, in order to alleviate their guilt for dispossessing the Chicano, stressed the Spanish part of us and perpetrated the myth of the Spanish Southwest. We have accepted the fiction that we are Hispanic, that is Spanish, in order to accommodate ourselves to the dominant culture and its abhorrence of Indians. Chávez, 88–91.

SUGGESTIONS FOR DISCUSSION

1. Compare your experience reading Gloria Anzaldua's polyglot prose with the experiences of others in your class. As we have suggested the purpose of Anzaldua's mix of language is to recreate the conditions of the borderland, where the use of one language leaves out or excludes those who know only the other language. But what are readers to do with such prose? If you don't know Spanish, how did you try to make sense of the Spanish words and phrases Anzaldua uses? Even if you do know Spanish, are you familiar with the terms she draws from regional dialects? What does your experience reading "How to Tame a Wild Tongue" reveal to you about the nature of cultural encounters at the borderlands?

2. Anzaldua has composed the chapter "How to Tame a Wild Tongue" like a mosaic, in which she juxtaposes seven separate sections without offering an overarching statement of purpose or meaning to unify the sections. At the same time, the sections do seem to go together in an associative, nonlinear way. Look back over the sections of the chapter to identify how (or whether) the separate parts work together to form a whole. What in your view is the principle of combination that links them together?

3. Anzaldua says that the "voluntary (yet forced) alienation [of Chicanos and other people of color] makes for psychological conflict, a kind of dual identity—we don't identify with the Anglo-American cultural values and we don't totally identify with the Mexican cultural values. We are a synergy of two cultures with various degrees of Mexicanness or Angloness. I have so internalized the borderland conflict that sometimes I feel like one cancels out the other and we are zero, nothing, no one." Yet she also says, a few lines later, "Stubborn, perserving, impenetrable as stone, yet possessing a malleability that renders us unbreakable, we, the *mestizas* and *mestizos,* will remain." What is the struggle of identities Anzaldua articulates here? How do you account for the abrupt shift from the pessimism of the first statement to the optimism of the second? How does Anzaldua's sense of dual identity compare to Adrienne Rich's notion of herself as "split at the root"?

SUGGESTIONS FOR WRITING

1. Write an essay describing and analyzing your experience reading "How to Tame a Wild Tongue." How do the mix of languages and the fragmentary character of the text put special demands on you as a reader? How and in what sense is this

reading experience equivalent to what Anzaldua calls the "borderland"? What does your position as a reader on the border reveal to you about the nature of encounters across cultures in multicultural America?

2. Write an essay that compares Anzaldua's position as a *mestiza* of the borderlands to Adrienne Rich's portrayal of herself as a middle-class Jewish southerner "split at the root." To what extent are their experiences similar? In what respects do they differ? Don't settle in your essay for just describing differences and similarities. The issue is how you explain what they have in common and what makes them different. What in your view is the significance of these differences and similarities?

3. Use Anzaldua's chapter as a model to write your own essay about the contradictory and conflicting meanings of language use and cultural expression in your life. This assignment is meant to be an experiment in writing that asks you to emulate Anzaldua in incorporating multiple voices, dialects, slangs, and languages and in composing by way of a collage that juxtaposes fragments of thought and experience instead of developing a linear piece of writing with a main point and supporting evidence. To develop ideas for this essay, you might begin by thinking of the different voices, musics, foods, and other cultural forms that are part of your experience, the conflicting ways of life you have lived, and the multiple identities you inhabit.

Elaine H. Kim

HOME IS WHERE THE *HAN* IS: A KOREAN-AMERICAN PERSPECTIVE ON THE LOS ANGELES UPHEAVALS

Elaine H. Kim teaches Asian American Studies at the University of California—Berkeley. She has written and edited a number of books on Asian American writers and artists, and she has been involved in the production of television documentaries on Asian women. The following selection originally appeared as a chapter in a collection of essays, *Reading Rodney King/Reading Urban Uprising* (1993). In her chapter, Kim suggests that the uprising that followed the acquittal of four police officers in the Rodney King beating case was a "baptism into what it really means for a Korean to 'become American' in the 1990s." The failure of the Los Angeles police to respond to the looting and burning of stores and homes in Koreatown revealed to the Korean community, Kim says, the contradiction between the American dream and American reality and what she calls the "interstitial position" of Korean Americans, caught in a racially divided society between "predominantly Anglo and mostly African American and Latino communities."

Suggestion for Reading

- As you read, notice how Elaine H. Kim combines commentary on the Los Angeles uprising with the history of the Korean people and an analysis of readers' responses to the "My Turn" column she wrote for *Newsweek* magazine. To help you follow Kim's line of thought, underline and annotate key passages that develop her central ideas. How do the various sections locate Korean Americans as caught in the middle—on the one hand, between the dominant Anglo and the minority African American and Latino communities, and on the other, between the United States and Korea?

◆

A bout half of the estimated $850 million in estimated material losses incurred during the Los Angeles upheavals was sustained by a community no one seems to want to talk much about. Korean Americans in Los Angeles, suddenly at the front lines when violence came to the buffer zone they had been so precariously occupying, suffered profound damage to their means of livelihood.[1] But my concern here is the psychic damage which, unlike material damage, is impossible to quantify.

I want to explore the questions of whether or not recovery is possible for Korean Americans, and what will become of our attempts to "become American" without dying of *han*. *Han* is a Korean word that means, loosely translated, the sorrow and anger that grow from the accumulated experiences of oppression. Although the word is frequently and commonly used by Koreans, the condition it describes is taken quite seriously. When people die of *han*, it is called dying of *hwabyong*, a disease of frustration and rage following misfortune.

Situated as we are on the border between those who have and those who have not, between predominantly Anglo and mostly African American and Latino communities, from our current interstitial position in the American discourse of race, many Korean Americans have trouble calling what happened in Los Angeles an "uprising." At the same time, we cannot quite say it was a "riot." So some of us have taken to calling it *sa-i-ku*, April 29, after the manner of naming other events in Korean history—3.1 (*sam-il*) for March 1, 1919, when massive protests against Japanese colonial rule began in Korea; 6.25 (*yook-i-o*), or June 25, 1950, when the Korean War began; and 4.19 (*sa-il-ku*), or April 19, 1960, when the first student movement in the world to overthrow a

[1] I am deeply indebted to the activists in the Los Angeles Korean American community, especially Bong Hwan Kim and Eui-Young Yu, whose courage and commitment to the empowerment of the disenfranchised, whether African American, Latino, or Korean American, during this crisis in Los Angeles has been a continuous source of inspiration for me. I would also like to thank Barry Maxwell for critically reading this manuscript and offering many insightful suggestions; my niece Sujin Kim, David Lloyd, and Caridad Souza for their encouragement; and Mia Chung for her general assistance.

government began in South Korea. The ironic similarity between 4.19 and 4.29 does not escape most Korean Americans.

Los Angeles Koreatown has been important to me, even though I visit only a dozen times a year. Before Koreatown sprang up during the last decade and a half, I used to hang around the fringes of Chinatown, although I knew that this habit was pure pretense. For me, knowing that Los Angeles Koreatown existed made a difference; one of my closest friends worked with the Black-Korean Alliance there, and I liked to think of it as a kind of "home"—however idealized and hypostatized—for the soul, an anchor, a potential refuge, a place in America where I could belong without ever being asked, "Who are you and what are you doing here? Where did you come from and when are you going back?"

Many of us watched in horror the destruction of Koreatown and the systematic targeting of Korean shops in South Central Los Angeles after the Rodney King verdict. Seeing those buildings in flames and those anguished Korean faces, I had the terrible thought that there would be no belonging and that we were, just as I had always suspected, a people destined to carry our *han* around with us wherever we went in the world. The destiny (*p'aljja*) that had spelled centuries of extreme suffering from invasion, colonization, war, and national division had smuggled itself into the U.S. with our baggage.

AFRICAN AMERICAN AND KOREAN AMERICAN CONFLICT

As someone whose social consciousness was shaped by the African American–led civil rights movement of the 1960s, I felt that I was watching our collective dreams for a just society disintegrating, cast aside as naive and irrelevant in the bitter and embattled 1990s. It was the courageous African American women and men of the 1960s who had redefined the meaning of "American," who had first suggested that a person like me could reject the false choice between being treated as a perpetual foreigner in my own birthplace, on the one hand, and relinquishing my identity for someone else's ill-fitting and impossible Anglo American one on the other. Thanks to them, I began to discern how institutional racism works and why Korea was never mentioned in my world-history textbooks. I was able to see how others besides Koreans had been swept aside by the dominant culture. My American education offered nothing about Chicanos or Latinos, and most of what I was taught about African and Native Americans was distorted to justify their oppression and vindicate their oppressors.

I could hardly believe my ears when, during the weeks immediately following *sa-i-ku,* I heard African American community leaders suggesting that Korean American merchants were foreign intruders deliberately trying to stifle African American economic development, when I knew that they had bought those liquor stores at five times gross receipts from African American owners, who had previously bought them at two times gross receipts from Jewish owners after Watts. I saw anti-Korean flyers that were being circulated by African American political candidates and read about South Central residents petitioning against the reestablishment of swap meets, groups of typically Korean immigrant-operated market stalls. I was disheartened with Latinos who related the pleasure they felt while looting Korean stores that they believed "had it coming" and who claimed that it was because of racism that more Latinos were arrested during *sa-i-ku* than Asian Americans. And I was filled with despair when I read about Chinese Americans wanting to dissociate themselves from us. According to one Chinese American reporter assigned to cover Asian American issues for a San Francisco daily, Chinese and Japanese American shopkeepers, unlike Koreans, always got along fine with African Americans in the past. "Suddenly," admitted another Chinese American, "I am scared to be Asian. More specifically, I am afraid to be mistaken for Korean." I was enraged when I overheard European Americans discussing the conflicts as if they were watching a dogfight or a boxing match. The situation reminded me of the Chinese film "Raise the Red Lantern," in which we never see the husband's face. We only hear his mellifluous voice as he benignly admonishes his four wives not to fight among themselves. He can afford to be kind and pleasant because the structure that pits his wives against each other is so firmly in place that he need never sully his hands or even raise his voice.

BATTLEGROUND LEGACY

Korean Americans are squeezed between black and white and also between U.S. and South Korean political agendas. Opportunistic American and South Korean presidential candidates toured the burnt ruins, posing for the television cameras but delivering nothing of substance to the victims. Like their U.S. counterparts, South Korean news media seized upon *sa-i-ku,* featuring sensational stories that depicted the problem as that of savage African Americans attacking innocent Koreans for no reason. To give the appearance of authenticity, Seoul newspapers even published articles using the names of Korean Americans who did not in fact write them.

Those of us who chafe at being asked whether we are Chinese or Japanese as if there were no other possibilities or who were angered when the news media sought Chinese and Japanese but not Korean American views during *sa-i-ku* are sensitive to an invisibility that seems particular to us. To many Americans, Korea is but the gateway to or the bridge between China and Japan, or a crossroads of major Asian conflicts.

It can certainly be said that, although little known or cared about in the Western world, Korea has been a perennial battleground. Besides the Mongols and the Manchus, there were the *Yŏjin* (Jurched), the *Koran* (Khitan), and the *Waega* (Wäkö) invaders. In relatively recent years, there was the war between China and Japan that ended in 1895 and the war between Japan and Russia in 1905; both of which were fought on Korean soil and resulted in extreme suffering for the Korean people. Japan's 36 years of brutal colonial rule ended with the U.S. and what was then the Soviet Union dividing the country in half at the 38th parallel. Thus, Korea was turned into a Cold War territory that ultimately became a battleground for world superpowers during the conflict of 1950–53.

BECOMING AMERICAN

One of the consequences of war, colonization, national division, and superpower economic and cultural domination has been the migration of Koreans to places like Los

Angeles, where they believed their human rights would be protected by law. After all, they had received U.S.-influenced political educations. They started learning English in the seventh grade. They all knew the story of the poor boy from Illinois who became president. They all learned that the U.S. Constitution and Bill of Rights protected the common people from violence and injustice. But they who grew up in Korea watching "Gunsmoke," "Night Rider," and "McGyver" dubbed in Korean were not prepared for the black, brown, red, and yellow America they encountered when they disembarked at the Los Angeles International Airport. They hadn't heard that there is no equal justice in the U.S. They had to learn about American racial hierarchies. They did not realize that, as immigrants of color, they would never attain political voice or visibility but would instead be used to uphold the inequality and the racial hierarchy they had no part in creating.

Most of the newcomers had underestimated the communication barriers they would face. Like the Turkish workers in Germany described in John Berger and Jean Mohr's *A Seventh Man,* their toil amounted to only a pile of gestures and the English they tried to speak changed and turned against them as they spoke it. Working 14 hours a day, six or seven days a week, they rarely came into sustained contact with English-speaking Americans and almost never had time to study English. Not feeling at ease with English, they did not engage in informal conversations easily with non-Koreans and were hated for being curt and rude. They did not attend churches or do business in banks or other enterprises where English was required. Typically, the immigrant, small-business owners utilized unpaid family labor instead of hiring people from local communities. Thanks to Eurocentric American cultural practices, they knew little or nothing good about African Americans or Latinos, who in turn and for similar reasons knew little or nothing good about them. At the same time, Korean shopowners in South Central and Koreatown were affluent compared with the impoverished residents, whom they often exploited as laborers or looked down upon as fools with an aversion to hard work. Most Korean immigrants did not even know that they were among the many direct beneficiaries of the African American–led civil rights movement, which helped pave the way for the 1965 immigration reforms that made their immigration possible.

Korean-immigrant views, shaped as they were by U.S. cultural influences and official, anticommunist, South Korean education, differed radically from those of many poor people in the communities Korean immigrants served: unaware of the shameful history of oppression of nonwhite immigrants and other people of color in the U.S., they regarded themselves as having arrived in a meritocratic "land of opportunity" where a person's chances for success are limited only by individual lack of ability or diligence. Having left a homeland where they foresaw their talents and hard work going unrecognized and unrewarded, they were desperate to believe that the "American dream" of social and economic mobility through hard work was within their reach.

SA-I-KU

What they experienced on 29 and 30 April was a baptism into what it really means for a Korean to "become American" in the 1990s. In South Korea, there is no 911, and no one really expects a fire engine or police car if there is trouble. Instead, people make arrangements with friends and family for emergencies. At the same time, guns are not part of Korean daily life. No civilian in South Korea can own a gun. Guns are the exclusive accoutrement of the military and police who enforce order for those who rule the society. When the Korean Americans in South Central and Koreatown dialed 911, nothing happened. When their stores and homes were being looted and burned to the ground, they were left completely alone for three horrifying days. How betrayed they must have felt by what they had believed was a democratic system that protects its people from violence. Those who trusted the government to protect them lost everything; those who took up arms after waiting for help for two days were able to defend themselves. It was as simple as that. What they had to learn was that, as in South Korea, protection in the U.S. is by and large for the rich and powerful. If there were a choice between Westwood and Koreatown, it is clear that Koreatown would have to be sacrificed. The familiar concept of privilege for the rich and powerful would have been easy for the Korean immigrant to grasp if only those exhortations about democracy and equality had not obfuscated the picture. Perhaps they should have relied even more on whatever they brought with them from Korea instead of fretting over trying to understand what was going on around them here. That Koreatown became a battleground does seem like the further playing out of a tragic legacy that has followed them across oceans and continents. The difference is that this was a battle between the poor and disenfranchised and the invisible rich, who were being protected by a layer of clearly visible Korean American human shields in a battle on the buffer zone.

This difference is crucial. Perhaps the legacy is not one carried across oceans and continents but one assumed immediately upon arrival, not the curse of being Korean but the initiation into becoming American, which requires that Korean Americans take on this country's legacy of five centuries of racial violence and inequality, of divide and rule, of privilege for the rich and oppression of the poor. Within this legacy, they have been assigned a place on the front lines. Silenced by those who possess the power to characterize and represent, they are permitted to speak only to reiterate their acceptance of this role.

SILENCING THE KOREAN AMERICAN VOICE

Twelve years ago, in Kwangju, South Korea, hundreds of civilians demonstrating for constitutional reform and free elections were murdered by U.S.-supported and -equipped South Korean elite paratroopers. Because I recorded it and played it over and over again, searching for a sign or a clue, I remember clearly how what were to me heartrendingly tragic events were represented in the U.S. news media. For a few fleeting moments, images of unruly crowds of alien-looking Asians shouting unintelligible words and phrases and wearing white headbands inscribed with unintelligible characters flickered across the screen. The Koreans were made to seem like insane people from another planet. The voice in the background stated simply that there were massive demonstrations but did not explain what the protests were about. Nor was a single Korean ever given an opportunity to speak to the camera.

The next news story was about demonstrations for democracy in Poland. The camera settled on individuals' faces which one by one filled the screen as each man or woman was asked to explain how he or she felt. Each Polish person's words were translated in a voice-over or subtitle. Solidarity leader Lech Walesa, who was allowed to speak often, was characterized as a heroic human being with whom all Americans could surely identify personally. Polish Americans from New York and Chicago to San Francisco, asked in man-on-the-street interviews about their reactions, described the canned hams and blankets they were sending to Warsaw.

This was for me a lesson in media representation, race, and power politics. It is a given that Americans are encouraged by our ideological apparatuses to side with our allies (here, the Polish resisters and the anti-communist South Korean government) against our enemies (here, the communist Soviet Union and protesters against the South Korean government). But visual-media racism helps craft and reinforce our identification with Europeans and whites while distancing us from fearsome and alien Asiatic hordes.

In March of last year, when two delegates from North Korea visited the Bay Area to participate in community-sponsored talks on Korean reunification, about 800 people from the Korean American community attended. The meeting was consummately newsworthy, since it was the first time in history that anyone from North Korea had ever been in California for more than 24 hours just passing through. The event was discussed for months in the Korean-language media—television, radio, and newspapers. Almost every Korean-speaking person in California knew about it. Although we sent press releases to all the commercial and public radio and television stations and to all the Bay Area newspapers, not a single mainstream media outfit covered the event. However, whenever there was an African American boycott of a Korean store or whenever conflict surfaced between Korean and African Americans, community leaders found a dozen microphones from all the main news media shoved into their faces, as if they were the president's press secretary making an official public pronouncement. Fascination with interethnic conflicts is rooted in the desire to excuse or minimize white racism by buttressing the mistaken notion that all human beings are "naturally" racist, and when Korean and African Americans allow themselves to be distracted by these interests, their attention is deflected from the social hierarchies that give racism its destructive power.

Without a doubt, the U.S. news media played a major role in exacerbating the damage and ill will toward Korean Americans, first by spotlighting tensions between African Americans and Koreans above all efforts to work together and as opposed to many other newsworthy events in these two communities, and second by exploiting racist stereotypes of Koreans as unfathomable aliens, this time wielding guns on rooftops and allegedly firing wildly into crowds. In news programs and on talk shows, African and Korean American tensions were discussed by blacks and whites, who pointed to these tensions as the main cause of the uprising. I heard some European Americans railing against rude and exploitative Korean merchants for ruining peaceful race relations for everyone else. Thus, Korean Americans were used to deflect attention from the racism they inherited and the economic injustice and poverty that had been already well woven into the fabric of American life, as evidenced by a judicial system that could allow not only the Korean store owner who killed Latasha Harlins but also the white men who killed Vincent Chin and the white police who beat Rodney King to go free, while Leonard Peltier still languishes in prison.

As far as I know, neither the commercial nor the public news media has mentioned the many Korean and African American attempts to improve relations, such as joint church services, joint musical performances and poetry readings, Korean merchant donations to African American community and youth programs, African American volunteer teachers in classes for Korean immigrants studying for citizenship examinations, or Korean translations of African American history materials.

While Korean immigrants were preoccupied with the mantra of day-to-day survival, Korean Americans had no voice, no political presence whatsoever in American life. When they became the targets of violence in Los Angeles, their opinions and views were hardly solicited except as they could be used in the already-constructed mainstream discourse on race relations, which is a sorry combination of blaming the African American and Latino victims for their poverty and scapegoating the Korean Americans as robotic aliens who have no "real" right to be here in the first place and therefore deserve whatever happens to them.

THE *NEWSWEEK* EXPERIENCE

In this situation, I felt compelled to respond when an editor from the "My Turn" section of *Newsweek* magazine asked for a 1000-word personal essay. Hesitant because I was given only a day and a half to write the piece, not enough time in light of the vastness of American ignorance about Koreans and Korean Americans, I decided to do it because I thought I could not be made into a sound bite or a quote contextualized for someone else's agenda.

I wrote an essay accusing the news media of using Korean Americans and tensions between African and Korean Americans to divert attention from the roots of racial violence in the U.S. I asserted that these lie not in the Korean-immigrant-owned corner store situated in a community ravaged by poverty and police violence, but reach far back into the corridors of corporate and government offices in Los Angeles, Sacramento, and Washington, D.C. I suggested that Koreans and African Americans were kept ignorant about each other by educational and media institutions that erase or distort their experiences and perspectives. I tried to explain how racism had kept my parents from ever really becoming Americans, but that having been born here, I considered myself American and wanted to believe in the possibility of an American dream.

The editor of "My Turn" did everything he could to frame my words with his own viewpoint. He faxed his own introductory and concluding paragraphs that equated Korean merchants with cowboys in the Wild West and alluded to Korean/African American hatred. When I objected, he told me that my writing style was not crisp enough and that as an experienced journalist, he could help me out. My confidence wavered, but ultimately I rejected his editing. Then he accused me of being overly sensitive, confiding that I had no need to be defensive—because his wife was a Chinese American. Only after I had decided to withdraw the piece did he agree to accept it as I wrote it.

Before I could finish congratulating myself on being able to resist silencing and the kind of decontextualization I was trying to describe in the piece, I started receiving hate mail. Some of it was addressed directly to me, since I had been identified as a University of California faculty member, but most of it arrived in bundles, forwarded by *Newsweek*. Hundreds of letters came from all over the country, from Florida to Washington state and from Massachusetts to Arizona. I was unprepared for the hostility expressed in most of the letters. Some people sent the article, torn from the magazine and covered with angry, red-inked obscenities scratched across my picture. "You should see a good doctor," wrote someone from Southern California, "you have severe problems in thinking, reasoning, and adjusting to your environment."

A significant proportion of the writers, especially those who identified themselves as descendants of immigrants from Eastern Europe, wrote *Newsweek* that they were outraged, sickened, disgusted, appalled, annoyed, and angry at the magazine for providing an arena for the paranoid, absurd, hypocritical, racist, and childish views of a spoiled, ungrateful, whining, bitching, un-American bogus faculty member who should be fired or die when the next California earthquake dumps all of the "so-called people of color" into the Pacific Ocean.

I was shocked by the profound ignorance of many writers' assumptions about the experiences and perspectives of American people of color in general and Korean and other Asian Americans in particular. Even though my essay revealed that I was born in the U.S. and that my parents had lived in the U.S. for more than six decades, I was viewed as a foreigner without the right to say anything except words of gratitude and praise about America. The letters also provided some evidence of the dilemma Korean Americans are placed in by those who assume that we are aliens who should "go back" and at the same time berate us for not rejecting "Korean-American identity" for "American identity."

How many Americans migrate to Korea? If you are so disenchanted, Korea is still there. Why did you ever leave it? Sayonara.

Ms. Kim appears to have a personal axe to grind with this country that has given her so much freedom and opportunity. . . . I should suggest that she move to Korea, where her children will learn all they ever wanted about that country's history.

[Her] whining about the supposedly racist U.S. society is just a mask for her own acute inferiority complex. If she is so dissatisfied with the United States why doesn't she vote with her feet and leave? She can get the hell out and return to her beloved Korea—her tribal afinity [*sic*] where her true loyalty and consciousness lies [*sic*].

You refer to yourself as a Korean American and yet you have lived all your life in the United States . . . you write about racism in this country and yet you are the biggest racist by your own written words. If you cannot accept the fact that you are an American, maybe you should be living your life in Korea.

My stepfather and cousin risked their lives in the country where your father is buried to ensure the ideals of our country would remain. So don't expect to find a sympathetic ear for your pathetic whining.

Many of the letter writers assumed that my family had been the "scum" of Asia and that I was a college teacher only because of American justice and largesse. They were furious that I did not express gratitude for being saved from starvation in Asia and given the opportunity to flourish, no doubt beyond my wildest dreams, in America.

Where would she be if her parents had not migrated to the United States? For a professor at Berkeley University [*sic*] to say the American dream is only an empty promise is ludicrous. Shame, shame, shame on Elaine!

[Her father and his family] made enough money in the USA to ship his corpse home to Korea for burial. Ms. Kim herself no doubt has a guaranteed life income as a professor paid by California taxpayers. Wouldn't you think that she might say kind things about the USA instead of whining about racism?

At the same time some letters blamed me for expecting "freedom and opportunity":

It is wondrous that folks such as you find truth in your paranoia. No one ever promised anything to you or your parents.

Besides providing indications of how Korean Americans are regarded, the letters revealed a great deal about how American identity is thought of. One California woman explained that although her grandparents were Irish immigrants, she was not an Irish American, because "if you are not with us, you are against us." A Missouri woman did not seem to realize that she was conflating race and nationality and confusing "nonethnic" and "nonracial," by which she seems to have meant "white," with "American." And, although she insists that it is impossible to be both "black" and "American," she identifies herself at the outset as a "white American."

I am a white American. I am proud to be an American. You cannot be black, white, Korean, Chinese, Mexican, German, French, or English or any other and still be an American. Of course the culture taught in schools is strictly American. That's where we are and if you choose to learn another [culture] you have the freedom to settle there. You cannot be a Korean American which assumes you are not ready to be an AMERICAN. Do you get my gist?

The suggestion that more should be taught in U.S. schools about America's many immigrant groups and people of color prompted many letters in defense of Western civilization against non-Western barbarism:

You are dissatisfied with current school curricula that excludes Korea. Could it possibly be because Korea and Asia for that matter has [*sic*] not had . . . a noticeable impact on the shaping of Western culture, and Korea has had unfortunately little culture of its own?

Who cares about Korea, Ms. Kim? . . . And what enduring contributions has the Black culture, both here in the US and on the continent contributed to the world, and mankind? I'm from a culture, Ms. Kim, who put a man on the moon 23 years ago, who established medical schools to train doctors to perform open heart surgery, and . . . who created a language of music so that musicians, from Beethoven to the Beatles, could easily touch the world with their brilliance forever and ever and ever. Perhaps the dominant culture, whites obviously, "swept aside Chicanos . . . Latinos . . . African-Americans . . . Koreans," because they haven't contributed anything that made—be mindful of the cliche—a world of difference?

Koreans' favorite means of execution is decapitation . . . Ms. Kim, and others like her, came here to escape such injustice. Then they whine at riots to which they have contributed by their own fanning of flames of discontent. . . . Yes! Let us all study more about Oriental culture! Let us put matters into proper perspective.

Fanatical multiculturalists like you expect a country whose dominant culture has been formed and influenced by Europe. . . , nearly 80% of her population consisting of persons whose ancestry is European, to include the history of every ethnic group who has ever lived here. I truly feel sorry for you. You and your bunch need to realize that white Americans are not racists. . . . We would love to get along, but not at the expense of our own culture and heritage.

Kim's axe-to-grind confirms the utter futility of race-relations—the races were never meant to live together. We don't get along and never will. . . . Whats [sic] needed is to divide the United States up along racial lines so that life here can finally become livable.

What seemed to anger some people the most was their idea that, although they worked hard, people of color were seeking handouts and privileges because of their race, and the thought of an ungrateful Asian American siding with African Americans, presumably against whites, was infuriating. How dare I "bite the hand that feeds" me by siding with the champion "whiners who cry 'racism'" because to do so is the last refuge of the "terminally incompetent"?

The racial health in this country won't improve until minorities stop erecting "me first" barriers and strive to be Americans, not African-Americans or Asian-Americans expecting privileges.

Ms. Kim wants preferential treatment that immigrants from Greece-to-Sweden have not enjoyed. . . . Even the Chinese . . . have not created any special problems for themselves or other Americans. Soon those folk are going to express their own resentments to the insatiable demands of the Blacks and other colored peoples, including the wetbacks from Mexico who sneak into this country then pilfer it for all they can.

The Afroderived citizens of Los Angeles and the Asiatic derivatives were not suffering a common imposition. . . . The Asiatics are trying to build their success. The Africans are sucking at the teats of entitlement.

As is usual with racists, most of the writers of these hate letters saw only themselves in their notions about Korea, America, Korean Americans, African Americans. They felt that their own sense of American identity was being threatened and that they were being blamed as individuals for U.S. racism. One man, adept at manipulating various fonts on his word processor, imposed his preconceptions on my words:

Let me read between the lines of your little hate message:

... "The roots ... stretch far back into the corridors of corporate and government offices in Los Angeles, Sacramento, and Washington, D.C."

All white America and all American institutions are to blame for racism.

... "I still want to believe the promise is real."

I have the savvy to know that the American ideals of freedom and justice are a joke but if you want to give me what I want I'm willing to make concessions.

Ms. Kim, ... if you want to embody the ignorant, the insecure, and the emotionally immature, that's your right! Just stop preaching hate and please, please, quit whining.

Sincerely, A proud White-American teaching
my children not to be prejudicial

Especially since my essay had been subdued and intensely personal, I had not anticipated the fury it would provoke. I never thought that readers would write over my words with their own. The very fact that I used words, and English words at that, particularly incensed some: one letter writer complained about my use of words and phrases like "manifestation" and "zero-sum game," and "suzerain relationship," which is the only way to describe Korea's relationship with China during the T'ang Dynasty. "Not more than ten people in the USA know what [these words] mean," he wrote. "You are on an ego trip." I wondered if it made him particularly angry that an Asian American had used those English words, or if he would make such a comment to George Will or Jane Bryant Quinn.

Clearly I had encountered part of America's legacy, the legacy that insists on silencing certain voices and erasing certain presences, even if it means deportation, internment, and outright murder. I should not have been surprised by what happened in Koreatown or by the ignorance and hatred expressed in the letters to *Newsweek,* any more than African Americans should have been surprised by the Rodney King verdict. Perhaps the news media, which constituted *sa-i-ku* as news, as an extraordinary event in no way continuous with our everyday lives, made us forget for a moment that as people of color many of us simultaneously inhabit two Americas: the America of our dreams and the America of our experience.

Who among us does not cling stubbornly to the America of our dreams, the promise of a multicultural democracy where our cultures and our differences might be affirmed instead of distorted in an effort to destroy us?

After *sa-i-ku,* I was able to catch glimpses of this America of my dreams because I received other letters that expressed another American legacy. Some people identified themselves as Norwegian or Irish Americans interested in combating racism. Significantly, while most of the angry mail had been sent not to me but to *Newsweek,* almost all of the sympathetic mail, particularly the letters from African Americans, came directly to me. Many came from Korean Americans who were glad that one of their number had found a vehicle for self-expression. Others were from Chinese and Japanese Americans who wrote that they had had similar experiences and feelings. Several were written in shaky longhand by women fervently wishing for peace and understanding among people of all races. A Native American from Nashville wrote a long description of cases of racism against African, Asian, and Native Americans in the U.S. criminal-justice system. A large number of letters came from African Americans, all of them supportive and sympathetic—from judges and professors who wanted better understanding between Africans and Koreans to poets and laborers who scribbled their notes in pencil while on breaks at work. One man identified himself as a Los Angeles African American whose uncle had married a Korean woman. He stated that as a black man in America, he knew what other people feel when they face injustice. He ended his letter apologizing for his spelling and grammar mistakes and asking for materials to read on Asian Americans. The most touching letter I received was written by a prison inmate who had served twelve years of a 35-to-70-year sentence for armed robbery during which no physical injuries occurred. He wrote:

> I've been locked in these prisons going on 12 years now . . . and since being here I have studied fully the struggles of not just blacks, but all people of color. I am a true believer of helping "your" people "first," but also the helping of all people no matter where there at or the color of there skin. But I must be truthful, my struggle and assistance is truly on the side of people of color like ourselves. But just a few years ago I didn't think like this.
>
> I thought that if you wasn't black, then you was the enemy, but . . . many years of this prison madness and much study and research changed all of this. . . . [I]t's not with each other, blacks against Koreans or Koreans against blacks. No, this is not what it's about. Our struggle(s) are truly one in the same. What happened in L.A. during the riot really hurt me, because it was no way that blacks was suppose to do the things to your people, my people (Koreans) that they did. You're my sister, our people are my people. Even though our culture may be somewhat different, and even though we may worship our God(s) different . . . white-Amerikkka [doesn't] separate us. They look at us all the same. Either you're white, or you're wrong. . . . I'm just writing you to let you know that, you're my sister, your people's struggle are my people's struggle.

This is the ground I need to claim now for Korean American resistance and recovery, so that we can become American without dying of *han*.

Although the sentiments expressed in these letters seemed to break down roughly along racial lines—that is, all writers who were identifiably people of color wrote in support—and one might become alarmed at the depth of the divisions they imply, I like to think that I have experienced the desire of many Americans, especially Americans of color, to do as Rodney King pleaded on the second day of *sa-i-ku:* "We're all stuck here for awhile. . . . Let's try to work it out."

In my view, it's important for us to think about *all* of what Rodney King said and not just the words "we all can get along," which have been depoliticized and transformed into a Disneyesque catchphrase for Pat Boone songs and roadside billboards in Los Angeles. It seems to me the emphasis is on the being "stuck here for awhile" together as we await "our day in court."

Like the African American man who wrote from prison, the African American man who had been brutally beaten by white police might have felt the desire to "love everybody," but he had to amend—or rectify—that wish. He had to speak last about loving "people of color." The impulse to "love everybody" was there, but the conditions were not right. For now, the most practical and progressive agenda may be people of color trying to "work it out."

FINDING COMMUNITY THROUGH NATIONAL CONSCIOUSNESS

The place where Korean and American legacies converge for Korean Americans is the exhortation to "go home to where you belong."

One of the letters I received was from a Korean American living in Chicago. He had read a translation of my essay in a Korean language newspaper. "Although you were born in the U.S.A.," he wrote, noticing what none of the white men who ordered me to go back to "my" country had, "your ethnical background and your complexion belong to Korea. It is time to give up your U.S. citizenship and go to Korea."

Some ruined merchants are claiming that they will pull up stakes and return to Korea, but I know that this is not possible for most of them. Even if their stores had not been destroyed, even if they were able to sell their businesses and take the proceeds to Korea, most of them would not have enough to buy a home or business there, since both require total cash up front. Neither would they be able to find work in the society they left behind because it is plagued by recession, repression, and fierce economic competition.

Going back to Korea. The dream of going back to Korea fed the spirit of my father, who came to Chicago in 1926 and lived in the United States for 63 years, during which time he never became a U.S. citizen, at first because the law did not allow it and later because he did not want to. He kept himself going by believing that he would return to Korea in triumph one day. Instead, he died in Oakland at 88. Only his remains returned to Korea, where we buried him in accordance with his wishes.

Hasn't the dream of going back home to where you belong sustained most of America's unwanted at one time or another, giving meaning to lives of toil and making it possible to endure other people's hatred and rejection? Isn't the attempt to find community through national consciousness natural for people refused an American identity because racism does not give them that choice?

Korean national consciousness, the resolve to resist and fight back when threatened with extermination, was all that could be called upon when the Korean Americans in Los Angeles found themselves abandoned. They joined together to guard each other's means of livelihood with guns, relying on Korean-language radio and newspapers to communicate with and help each other. On the third day after the outbreak of violence, more than 30,000 Korean Americans gathered for a peace march in downtown L.A. in what was perhaps the largest and most quickly organized mass mobilization in Asian American history. Musicians in white, the color of mourning, beat traditional Korean drums in sorrow, anger, and celebration of community, a call to arms like a collective heartbeat. I believe that the mother of Edward Song Lee, the Los Angeles–born college student mistaken for a looter and shot to death in the streets, has been able to persevere in great part because of the massive outpouring of sympathy expressed by the Korean-American community that shared and understood her *han*.

I have been critical lately of cultural nationalism as detrimental to Korean Americans, especially Korean American women, because it operates on exclusions and fosters intolerance and uniformity of thought while stifling self-criticism and encouraging sacrifice, even to the point of suicide. But *sa-i-ku* makes me think again: what remains for those who are left to stand alone? If Korean Americans refuse to be victims or political pawns in the U.S. while rejecting the exhortation that we go back to Korea where we belong, what will be our weapons of choice?

In the darkest days of Japanese colonial rule, even after being stripped of land and of all economic means of survival, Koreans were threatened with total erasure when the colonizers rewrote Korean history, outlawed the Korean language, forced the subjugated people to worship the Japanese emperor, and demanded that they adopt Japanese names. One of the results of these cultural-annihilation policies was Koreans' fierce insistence on the sanctity of Korean national identity that persists to this day. In this context, it is not difficult to understand why nationalism has been the main refuge of Koreans and Korean Americans.

While recognizing the potential dangers of nationalism as a weapon, I for one am not ready to respond to the antiessentialists' call to relinquish my Korean American identity. It is easy enough for the French and Germans to call for a common European identity and an end to nationalisms, but what of the peoples suppressed and submerged while France and Germany exercised their national prerogatives? I am mindful of the argument that the resurgence of nationalism in Europe is rooted in historical and contemporary political and economic inequality among the nations of Europe. Likewise, I have noticed that many white Americans do not like to think of themselves as belonging to a race, even while thinking of people of color almost exclusively in terms of race. In the same way, many men think of themselves as "human beings" and of women as the ones having a gender. Thus crime, small businesses, and all Korean-African American interactions are seen and interpreted through the lens of race in the same dominant culture that angrily rejects the use of the racial lens for viewing yellow/white or black/white interactions and insists suddenly that we are all "American" whenever we attempt to assert our identity as people of color. It is far easier for Anglo Americans to call for an end to cultural nationalisms than for Korean Americans to give up national consciousness, which makes it possible to survive the vicious racism that would deny our existence as either Korean Americans or Americans.

Is there anything of use to us in Korean nationalism? During one thousand years of Chinese suzerainty, the Korean ruling elite developed a philosophy called *sadaejui,* or reliance of the weak on the strong. In direct opposition to this way of thought is what is called *jaju* or *juche sasang,* or self-determination. Both *sadaejui* and *juche sasang* are ways of dealing with unequal power relationships and resisting the transformation of one's homeland into a battlefield for others, but *sadaejui* has never worked any better for Koreans than it has for any minority group in America. *Juche sasang,* on the other hand, has the kind of oppositional potential needed in the struggle against silence and invisibility. From Korean national consciousness, we can recover this fierce refusal to accept subjugation, which is the first step in the effort to build community, so that we can work with others to challenge the forces that would have us annihilate each other instead of our mutual oppression.

What is clear is that we cannot "become American" without dying of *han* unless we think about community in new ways. Self-determination does not mean living alone. At least for now, that may mean mining the rich and haunted lode of Korean national consciousness while we struggle to understand how our fate is entwined with the fate of others lying prostrate before the triumphal procession of the winners of History. During the past fifteen years or so, many young Korean nationalists have been studying the legacies of colonialism and imperialism that they share with peoples in many Asian, African, and Latin American nations. At the same time that we take note of this work, we can also try to understand how nationalism and feminism can be worked together to demystify the limitations and reductiveness of each as a weapon of empowerment. If Korean national consciousness is ever to be such a weapon for us, we must use it to create a new kind of nationalism-in-internationalism to help us call forth a culture of survival and recovery, so that our *han* might be released and we might be freed to dream fiercely of different possibilities.

SUGGESTIONS FOR DISCUSSION

1. Elaine H. Kim describes *han* as a Korean term for "the sorrow and anger that grow from the accumulated experiences of oppression." Why, do you think, has she titled her chapter "Home Is Where the *Han* Is"? How does the notion of *han* inform Kim's line of thought throughout the chapter?
2. Kim presents the Korean American community as one that is "squeezed between black and white and also between U.S. and South Korean political agendas." Explain what Kim means by this "squeeze." What are the effects of this "interstitial position [of Korean Americans] in the American discourse of race"? In what sense have African American and Korean American conflicts been used to justify the racial divisions in contemporary America? How and by whom?
3. Kim compares the television coverage of South Korean demonstrations for constitutional reform and free elections to the coverage of the prodemocratic Solidarity movement in Poland. How does she explain the differences in coverage? How in a more general sense does the media represent minority communities of Asian Americans, African Americans, Latinos, and so on? What are the effects of these representations on social, cultural, and political life in contemporary America?

SUGGESTIONS FOR WRITING

1. Kim suggests that minority groups such as Korean Americans are silenced or incorporated into a drama of interethnic conflict (thereby showing how all humans are "naturally" racist) by the media. Write an essay that analyzes how a particular minority or ethnic group is represented by the media—on the news, in films, or in television shows. What are the social, cultural, and political effects of such representations?
2. Use the letters from *Newsweek* readers that Kim quotes to write an essay that analyzes the responses she received to her "My Turn" column, which appeared in *Newsweek* on May 18, 1992. First of all, go to the library and read the column.

Then reread the responses she quotes in the essay, both positive and negative. The point of your essay is not simply to dismiss (or denounce) the responses that are racist or ethnocentric, though some of them certainly are. The point rather is to identify what the letters indicate about deeply entrenched beliefs and attitudes about the nature of American culture, the position of immigrants, the multicultural debates, and so on. Consider how readers are making sense of the multicultural realities of contemporary America and what they reveal about life today in the "contact zone."

3. The central metaphor Kim uses in this essay differs from those in earlier selections, whether Reed's "bouillabaise," Rich's "split roots," or Anzaldua's "borderland." For Kim, the lives of Korean Americans are "squeezed between black and white and also between U.S. and South Korean political agendas." Notice how Kim develops her own position of being "squeezed," caught between the lessons she learned from the African American–led civil rights movement and her feelings of dismay and sorrow at anti-Korean sentiments expressed by African Americans in Los Angeles. Along the same lines, she is also caught between her desire to affirm her Korean identity and her anger that the South Korean media depicted the Los Angeles uprising as "savage African Americans attacking innocent Koreans for no reason." Kim's position in the "contact zone" is a complicated one, but in certain respects there are no doubt ways in which many other Americans also feel "squeezed," caught in the middle of contending cultural and political forces. Use Kim's essay as a model to write an essay in which you describe and analyze how you are, or have been, in some sense "squeezed," caught in the middle. In this essay, you will need to explain carefully how you were caught in the middle, between which communities and contending forces. You will need too to explain what conflicting loyalties you experienced and what you did (or did not do) to deal with the "squeeze" you felt.

Hazel V. Carby

THE MULTICULTURAL WARS

Hazel V. Carby teaches English and Afro-American Studies at Yale University and is the author of the prize-winning study of African American women writers, *Reconstructing Womanhood: The Emergence of the Afro-American Woman Novelist.* The following selection was originally presented at a conference on Black Popular Culture, organized by Michele Wallace, and later appeared in a collection of essays (1992) by the same title, taken from the conference. Carby raises some troubling questions about the multicultural debates and how the interest in "diversity" and "difference" in the curriculum is too often expressed in terms of identity and otherness rather than power and domination. Carby asks, at what point does the emphasis on cultural differences "become totally compatible with, rather than a threat to, the rigid frameworks of segregation and ghettoization at work throughout our society?"

Suggestion for Reading

- As you read, notice the complexity of Hazel V. Carby's thinking about multiculturalism. On the one hand, she wants to defend multicultural education against its critics. On the other hand, however, she also wants to point out limits and contradictions in a movement for educational change that calls for diversity in the curriculum but fails to address the deeper structural patterns of segregation and ghettoization in a racially divided society. To follow the turns in Carby's line of thought, it will help to underline and annotate key passages, noticing where (and why) she is defending multiculturalism against its opponents and where (and why) she is pointing out its limits and contradictions.

A s a black intellectual, I am both intrigued and horrified by the contradictory nature of the black presence in North American universities. We are, as students, as teachers, and as cultural producers, simultaneously visibly present in, and starkly absent from, university life. Although it costs approximately $20,000 a year to attend Yale and approximately $50,000 a year to reside in a New York jail, black males are being incarcerated at unprecedented rates. The press and the culture industry, having "discovered" the black woman writer for the first time in the seventies, are now finding it increasingly profitable to market narratives of the lives of successful black men. Articles about black males who have "made it" are no longer found only in the entertainment or sports sections of national newspapers: musicians and basketball stars have been joined by film directors and academics in the pages of our Sunday magazines.

In particular, the very existence of black male professors seems to fascinate the *New York Times.* On April 1, 1990, the *Times* ran a cover story entitled "Henry Louis Gates, Jr.: Black Studies' New Star." Stanley Fish, chair of the English Department at Duke University, patronizingly described Professor Gates's professional success as "entrepreneurial P.T. Barnumism." Adam Begley, the author of the story, concludes that with "a phone in his Mercedes-Benz, a literary agent in New York and an impressive network of contacts in the academy, publishing and the arts, [Professor Gates] seems more like a mogul than a scholar."[1] The *Times* article is, at best, ambivalent toward its black subject and frequently adopts such an incisive tone of ridicule that one wonders if the newspaper's editorial staff consciously decided to create an April 1 cartoon of black studies as a ship of fools. A much more serious, considered, and sober article about Cornel West appeared in the same magazine, describing him as "Princeton's Public Intellectual."[2]

In stark contrast to the attention paid to individual black professors is the glaring absence of any equivalent publicity about the paltry presence of nonwhite ladder faculty in universities: 4.1 percent are Black, 3.8 percent are Asian, 1.3 percent are Latino, and 0.4 percent are Native American.[3] Derrick Bell, a professor at the Harvard Law School, has argued that

A widespread assumption exists that there is an irreconcilable conflict between achieving diversity in law school faculties and maintaining academic excellence. . . . It serves as the primary reason why most college and university faculties across the nation remain all-white and mostly-male almost four decades after the law barred them from continuing their long-practiced policies of excluding minorities and women because of their race and sex without regard to their academic qualifications.[4]

These "contentions" Bell maintains "are simultaneously racially insulting and arrogantly wrong": They are insulting because they insinuate that the old rules of racial segregation rightly correlated color with intellectual inferiority. They are arrogant in that they assume that all of those with upper-class–based qualifications are by definition exemplary scholars and teachers.[5]

Bell continues by stressing that "minorities who achieve are deemed exceptions," whereas those "who fail are deemed painful proof that we must adhere to hiring standards that subsidize the well-placed members of our society while penalizing those, white as well as black, from disadvantaged backgrounds."[6] That more than ninety percent of all faculty members across the nation are white is a scandal but is not, apparently, a cause for journalistic outrage or newspaper headlines.

The percentage of black students in college populations has steadily decreased throughout the last decade, as has the number of B.A.s awarded to black students, even though the absolute number of bachelor's degrees awarded has been increasing nationally. In graduate schools, the proportion of American graduate students who are black is decreasing and the proportion of doctorates awarded to black people is also in significant decline. The number of tenured black professors has increased slightly, but the number of untenured black appointees is decreasing.[7] Clearly, if the black student population continues to decline at the undergraduate and graduate levels, the current black intellectual presence in academia, small as it is, will not be reproduced.

During the past two years, debate about the inclusion of people from a variety of ethnic, national, and class backgrounds as appropriate subjects for educational study and research has become focused on what is now commonly referred to as the multicultural curriculum. Multiculturalism appears as a controversial issue at all levels of the national educational system; the debate is not confined to universities. Despite apparent uniformity of the issues being fought over in these multicultural wars of position, there are, in fact, significantly different interests in play and at stake as these battles take place regionally and in the public and private spheres of education. However, it is important to recognize that even though this debate is differently inflected at different levels, all aspects constitute a debate about contemporary meanings of race in North America. Indeed, I would argue that multiculturalism is one of the current code words for race— a code just as effective as the word "drugs" or the phrase "inner-city violence" at creating a common-sense awareness that race is, indeed, the subject being evoked.

Since the fall of 1990, we have witnessed a barrage of journalistic attacks on the concept of multiculturalism and attempts to institute multicultural curricula. These reports have either implicitly or explicitly acknowledged multiculturalism as a discourse about race, and many have frequently asserted that there are close and disturbing links between multiculturalism, affirmative action, and threats to freedom of speech guaranteed by the first amendment.

In common-sense terms, affirmative action is no longer referenced by the media as a necessary corrective social policy but as a social problem that itself needs correction. The press's perceptions of the threats to freedom of speech and expression have shaped a moral panic about allegedly terroristic attempts to institute "politically correct" thought and behavior. Indeed, this danger is thought to be so real that it has elicited condemnation from President Bush himself. It is as if the historical contradictions between the original Constitution, which sanctioned slavery, and the fourteenth and fifteenth amendments, have returned to haunt us yet again—only to be dispelled by a form of executive exorcism.

The fundamental contradictions of a society structured by racial inequality from its founding moment have been shaped in the 1990s by an administration in Washington that is not only unsympathetic toward any demands for civil rights but also blatantly antagonistic to such demands. If we also consider the moral panics about affirmative action, antisexist and antiracist codes of behavior, and multiculturalism in the pages of numerous journals like *Time, Newsweek,* the *Atlantic Quarterly,* the *New Republic,* the *Chronicle of Higher Education,* the *Boston Globe,* and the *New York Times,* it would appear as if liberal, as well as conservative, opposition to increasing cultural and ethnic diversity in higher education is becoming entrenched.[8]

For those of us who recognize the need for transformations in our educational systems and in the ways in which we organize fields of knowledge, it is frequently dismaying to consider what is sometimes thought to constitute change in educational policy and practice. Departments and programs in many private universities, for example, will proudly point to an "integrated" curriculum while being unable to point to an integrated student body—except in the photographs in their student handbooks, photographs that contrive to demonstrate "diversity" by self-consciously including the pitiful handful of black/Latino/Asian/Chicano/ and perhaps even fewer American Indian students on campus. As Nicolaus Mills has argued in his survey of 1990 college publications, the contemporary college view book presents an idealized world in which the dominant code word is "diversity."[9]

> "Diversity is the hallmark of the Harvard/Radcliffe experience," the first sentence in the Harvard University register declares. "Diversity is the virtual core of University life," the University of Michigan bulletin announces. "Diversity is rooted deeply in the liberal arts tradition and is key to our educational philosophy," Connecticut College insists. "Duke's 5,800 undergraduates come from regions which are truly diverse," the Duke University bulletin declares. "Stanford values a class that is both ethnically and economically diverse," the Stanford University bulletin notes. Brown University says, "When asked to describe the undergraduate life at The College—and particularly their first strongest impression of Brown as freshmen—students consistently bring up the same topic: the diversity of the student body."[10]

In this context, Mills concludes, diversity means that "a college is doing its best to abolish the idea that it caters to middle-class whites."[11]

The various cultural and political presences of black women in universities provide particularly good examples of the contradictions embedded in the various curricular practices that occur under the aegis of "diversity." On many campuses, coalitions of marginalized and nonmarginalized women, students, and professors have formed alliances to ensure the inclusion of the histories of black women, and other previously excluded categories of women, in the university curriculum. But the result has been a patchwork of success and spectacular failure. Clearly, the syllabi of some courses, particularly within women's studies and African-American studies programs, have been transformed, and the demand for the establishment of programs in ethnic studies is both vocal and assertive. However, changes too frequently amount only to the inclusion of one or two new books in an already established syllabus rather than a reconsideration of the basic conceptual structure of a course.

Within women's studies programs, and within some literature departments, black women writers have been used and, I would argue, abused as cultural and political icons. In spite of the fact that the writing of black women is extraordinarily diverse, complex, and multifaceted, feminist theory has frequently used and abused this material to produce an essential black female subject for its own consumption, a black female subject that represents a single dimension—either the long-suffering or the triumphantly noble aspect of a black community throughout history. Because this black female subject has to carry the burden of representing what is otherwise significantly absent in the curriculum, issues of complexity disappear under the pressure of the demand to give meaning to blackness.

Certainly, we can see how the black female subject has become very profitable for the culture industry. The Harper Collins reprinting of all the previously published books of Zora Neale Hurston, for example, has been an extraordinarily profitable publishing enterprise based primarily on sales within an academic market.[12] We need to ask why black women, or other women who are non-white, are needed as cultural and political icons by the white middle class at this particular moment? What cultural and political need is being expressed, and what role is the black female subject being reduced to play? I would argue that it is necessary to recognize the contradictions between elevating the black female subject to the status of major text within multiculturalism and failing to lead students toward an integrated society, between making the black female a subject in the classroom and failing to integrate university student and faculty bodies on a national scale. Instead of recognizing these contradictions, the black female subject is frequently the means by which many middle-class white students and faculty cleanse their souls and rid themselves of the guilt of living in a society that is still rigidly segregated. Black cultural texts have become fictional substitutes for the lack of any sustained social or political relationships with black people in a society that has retained many of its historical practices of apartheid in housing and schooling.

The cultural, political, and social complexity of black people is consistently denied in those strands of feminist and multicultural theory that emphasize "difference" and use it to mark social, cultural, and political differences as if they were unbridgeable human divisions.[13] This theoretical emphasis on the recognition of difference, of otherness, requires us to ask, different from and for whom? In practice, in the classroom, black texts have been used to focus on the complexity of response in the (white) reader/student's construction of self in relation to a (black) perceived "other." In the motivation of that response, the text has been reduced to a tool. The theoretical paradigm of difference is obsessed with the construction of identities rather than relations of power and domination[14] and, in practice, concentrates on the effect of this difference on a (white) norm. Proponents of multiculturalism and feminist theorists have to interrogate some of their basic and unspoken assumptions: to what extent are fantasized black female and male subjects invented, primarily, to make the white middle class feel better about itself? And at what point do theories of "difference," as they inform academic practices, become totally compatible with, rather than a threat to, the rigid frameworks of segregation and ghettoization at work throughout our society?

We need to recognize that we live in a society in which systems of dominance and subordination are structured through processes of racialization that continuously interact with all other forces of socialization. Theoretically, we should be arguing that everyone in this social order has been constructed in our political imagination as a racialized subject. In this sense, it is important to think about the invention of the category of whiteness as well as that of blackness and, consequently, to make visible what is rendered invisible when viewed as the normative state of existence: the (white) point in space from which we tend to identify difference.

If, instead, we situated all North American peoples as racialized subjects of our political imagination, we would see that processes of racialization are determining to all our work. But processes of racialization, when they are mentioned at all in multicultural debate, are discussed as if they were the sole concern of those particular groups perceived to be racialized subjects. Because the politics of difference work with concepts of individual identity, rather than structures of inequality and exploitation, processes of racialization are marginalized and given symbolic and political meaning only when the subjects are black.

My argument for the centrality of the concept of race is not the same as the assertion, from within the politics of difference, that everyone has an ethnicity. I am not arguing for pluralistic research paradigms or for a politics of pluralism, the result of much work on ethnicity. But, I am arguing for an educational politics that would reveal the structures of power relations at work in the racialization of our social order.

As a final exercise in thinking about the ways the black female subject has been addressed and, to a great extent, invented within the curricular practices designed to increase "diversity," I would like to question the marginalization of the concept of race in the phrase "women of color." This phrase carries a series of complex meanings. Historically, it has its origin in the need of subordinated, marginalized, and exploited groups of women to find common ground with each other, and in the assertion of their desire to establish a system of alliances as "women of color." But what happens when this phrase is then taken up and inserted into the language of difference and diversity? Does "women of color" have other meanings inflected by theories of difference and diversity? I know we are all supposed to be familiar with who is being evoked by this term, but do we honestly think that some people lack color? Do white women and men have no color? What does it mean socially, politically, and culturally not to have color? Are those without color not implicated in a society structured in dominance by race? Are those without color outside of the hierarchy of social relations and not racialized? Are only the so-called colored to be the subjects of a specialized discourse of difference? And, most important, do existing power relations remain intact and unchallenged by this discourse?

We need to ask ourselves some serious questions about our culture and our politics. Is the emphasis on cultural diversity making invisible the politics of race in this increasingly segregated nation, and is the language of cultural diversity a convenient substitute for the political action needed to desegregate? In considering a response, we would be wise to remember Malcolm X's words: "There is nothing that the white man will do to bring about true, sincere citizenship or civil rights recognition for black people in this country . . . They will always talk it but they won't practice it."[15]

While the attention of faculty and administrators has been directed toward increasing the representation of different social groups in the curriculum or the college handbook, few alliances have been forged with forces across this society that will significantly halt and reverse the declining numbers of black, working-class, and poor people among university student bodies and faculty.

From one perspective, academic language in the decade of the eighties appeared to be at odds with the growing conservatism of the Reagan years. It seemed, at times, as if life in the academy was dominated by questions about the monolithic (and mono-ethnic) nature of courses in Western civilization; about texts that constituted all white and male literary and historical "canons"; and about issues of "diversity" and "difference." Students on campuses all over the country formed movements that condemned apartheid in South Africa and vigorously worked to persuade university administrations to divest their economic holdings in that country. However, we have to confront the fact that the white middle and upper classes in this country, from which these students predominantly come, have, simultaneously, sustained and supported apartheid-like structures that maintain segregation in housing and education in the United States. Comparisons with South African apartheid are a part of the language of black American daily life: the Bronx becomes "New York's Johannesburg"; Chicago is called "Joberg by the Lake"; and the *Minneapolis Star Tribune* is known by black politicians as the "Johannesburg Times."[16]

In Connecticut, the state where I live and work, the state constitution provides for free public elementary and secondary schools and specifically states that "No person shall be subjected to Segregation or Discrimination because of Religion, Race, Color, Ancestry or National Origin."[17] According to a recent report, there are 450,000 children at school in Connecticut, and one out of every four is non-white. But eight out of ten so-called minority students "are concentrated in ten percent of the school districts. By the year 2000, minority enrollments in Hartford, Bridgeport, and New Haven public schools will be approaching one hundred percent."[18]

Such systems of segregation ensure that the black working class and the urban poor will not encroach on the privileged territory of the white middle and upper classes or into the institutions that are the gatekeepers and providers of legitimated access to power, universities included. The integration that has occurred has been primarily on the grounds of class assimilation, and affirmative action has become an important mechanism for advancing a very limited number of black people into the middle class. The admissions practices at Harvard University, discussed in a recent report on affirmative action, are a good example: Harvard has sought to avoid the problem [of attrition] by ensuring that most of its black students come from middle-class families and predominantly white schools. As an admissions officer explained, "It is right for Harvard and better for the students, because there is better adjustment and less desperate alienation."[19]

Because entry into the professions is a major port of entry into the middle class, universities have been important and contested sites within which to accomplish the transformation of the previously outcast into an acceptable body for integration. The social and political consciousness of the undergraduate population currently enrolled in universities has been formed entirely during the Reagan and Bush years, and the disparity between the groups which have benefited from, and those that have been radically disadvantaged by, the social policies of conservatism is stark. Public systems of education in particular regions have had to respond rather differently from overwhelmingly white private or public universities to questions of diversity and difference.

The New York City educational system, for example, has a population of students, in some schools and colleges, where the so-called minority groups are overwhelmingly in the majority and where issues of difference and diversity are not theoretical playthings at odds with the context in which teaching occurs. New York public schools, which seem to have the most radically diverse and transformed curriculum in the country, find that this curriculum is now under vigorous attack by the New York regents. At the same time, it is precisely the state and city educational systems that have a majority population of black and Hispanic students that are disastrously underfunded. The withdrawal of federal financing and, now, the drastic decline in state and city financing will soon decimate what is left of the promise of the city's schools and colleges.

Meanwhile, in the universities with money, the National Association of Scholars, its friends and allies, and the media campaign against curricular reform have had significant effects in shifting the general climate against educational reform and against affirmative action. Not the least of these effects is the example of the $20 million donation to Yale University for the promotion of scholarship in Western civilization, a donation that was only one of four equivalent donations from the same family within one year. No equivalent donation has ever been made to institute courses in non-Western civilizations that I have been able to find, but I can imagine the difference to the New Haven public school system an injection of $80 million might make.[20] In the public sphere, the most recent presidential educational initiative seeks to replace federal funding of the public schools with corporate funding. One has to ask, will this mean corporate control of the curriculum as well?

In the post–civil rights era, then, one has to wonder at the massive resources being mobilized in opposition to programs or courses that focus on non-white or ethnically diverse topics and issues. One wonders, too, about the strength of the opposition to affirmative action, when social mobility has been gained by so few black people, and black entry into the so-called mainstream has been on the grounds of middle-class acceptability and not the end of segregation. Perhaps it is not too cynical to speculate that the South African government has learned a significant lesson by watching the example of the United States in the last two decades: some of the most important aspects of an apartheid system can be retained without having to maintain rigid apartheid legislation. It is in this social, political, and economic context that I feel it is appropriate and important to question the disparity between the vigor of debates about the inclusion of black subjects on a syllabus and the almost total silence about, and utter disregard for, the material conditions of most black people.

From the vantage point of the academy, it is obvious that the publishing explosion of the fiction of black women has been a major influence in the development of the multicultural curriculum, and I have tried to point to the ways in which the texts of black women and men sit uneasily in a discourse that seems to act as a substitute for the political activity of desegregation. But it is also evident that in white suburban libraries, bookstores, and supermarkets an ever-increasing number of narratives of black lives are easily available. The retention of segregated neighborhoods and public schools and the apartheid-like structures of black inner-city versus white suburban life mean that those who read these texts lack the opportunity to grow up in any equitable way with each other.

Indeed, those same readers are part of the white suburban constituency that refuses to support the building of affordable housing in its affluent suburbs, aggressively opposes the busing of children from the inner city into its neighborhood schools, and would fight to the death to prevent its children from being bused into the urban blight that is the norm for black children. For white suburbia, as well as for white middle-class students in universities, these texts are becoming a way of gaining knowledge of the "other," a knowledge that appears to satisfy and replace the desire to challenge existing frameworks of segregation. Have we, as a society, successfully eliminated the need for achieving integration through political agitation for civil rights and opted instead for knowing each other through cultural texts?

References

1. Adam Begley, "Henry Louis Gates, Jr.: Black Studies' New Star," *New York Times Magazine,* April 1, 1990, 24–27.
2. Robert S. Boynton, "Princeton's Public Intellectual," *New York Times Magazine,* September 15, 1991, 39, 43, 45, 49.
3. These figures are from the American Council on Education, Office of Minority Concerns, "Seventh Annual Status Report on Minorities in Higher Education," Table 13, as quoted in "Recruitment and Retention of Minority Group Members on the Faculty at Yale," the report of a committee chaired by Judith Rodin, Yale University, 1.
   In the National Research Council's report *A Common Destiny,* the outlook for black faculty is gloomy: "Figures for 1977–1983 show a drop of 6.2 percent in the number of full-time black faculty at public four-year institutions and of 11.3 percent at private institutions. Black under-representation is greatest at elite universities and at two-year colleges. There is little prospect for growth in black representation in light of the declines in both the percentage of blacks going on to college and the percentage pursuing graduate and professional degrees." Gerald David Jaynes and Robin M. Williams, eds., *A Common Destiny: Blacks and American Society,* National Research Council, (Washington, D.C.: National Academy Press, 1989), 375.
4. Derrick Bell, "Why We Need More Black Professors in Law School," *Boston Sunday Globe,* April 29, 1991, A1.
5. Ibid.
6. Ibid.
7. "Recruitment and Retention of Minority Group Members on the Faculty at Yale," 1.
8. A number of articles in the national and local press have been extremely critical of what is called the "hegemony of the politically correct" and described attempts to transform the canon as "liberal fascism" or terrorism. See, for example, *New York Times,* October 28, 1990, 1, 4; *New York Times,* December 9, 1990, 5; *Chronicle of Higher Education,* November 28, 1990, A5. An issue of *Newsweek* even went so far as to inscribe the words "Thought Police" on stone on its cover: December 24, 1990, 48–55. In contrast, the *Boston Globe Magazine* ran a much more

sympathetic account of multiculturalism as a phenomenon of the "melting pot," entitled "The New World." However, it concluded with a negative article on multicultural education, "Too Many Have Let Enthusiasm Outrun Reason," by Kenneth Jackson: October 13, 1991, 27–32.

9. Nicolaus Mills, "The Endless Autumn," *The Nation*, April 16, 1990, 529–531.

10. Ibid.

11. Ibid.

12. Presumably influenced by the possibility of sharing some of the massive profits realized by the publishing industry through marketing the black female subject, film distribution companies have recently begun to vigorously market films about black women to university professors for course use. See Hazel V. Carby, "In Body and Spirit: Representing Black Women Musicians," *Black Music Research Journal* 11 (Fall 1991), 177–192.

13. I would like to thank Paul Gilroy for the many conversations we have had on this issue. His influence upon my thinking has been profound.

14. See Elizabeth Weed, "Introduction: Terms of Reference" in *Coming to Terms: Feminism, Theory, Politics*, ed. Elizabeth Weed (London: Routledge, 1989), xvii.

15. Video interview with Malcolm X, from an installation by David Hammons at the New Museum (1989), as quoted in Maurice Berger, "Are Art Museums Racist?" *Art in America* (September 1990), 69–77.

16. John Matisonn, reporting for National Public Radio's "All Things Considered, Weekend Edition," February 2, 1991, Transcript, 21.

17. Constitution of the State of Connecticut, 1965, as quoted on the PBS special "Schools in Black and White," produced and written by Vivian Eison and Andrea Haas Hubbell, broadcast September 4, 1991.

18. Ibid.

19. Andrew Hacker, "Affirmative Action: The New Look," *The New York Review*, October 12, 1989, 64.

20. Giving this extraordinary amount of money, $80 million, to an already well-endowed institution needs to be measured against initiatives to support inner-city schools by using black churches as sites for supplemental educational classes and activities. The Association for the Advancement of Science has spent $800,000 over a period of four years for educational programs in eight hundred churches in seventeen cities. The largest donation by a private foundation for church-based educational programs seems to be $2.3 million spread among nine cities from the Carnegie Foundation. See the *New York Times*, August 7, 1991, A1.

SUGGESTIONS FOR DISCUSSION

1. Compare your underlinings and annotations with your classmates' in order to put together a reading of the selection from Carby. What is her overall assessment of multiculturalism and what she calls "the multicultural wars"? To what extent and why does she defend multiculturalism against its opponents? How is this defense connected to her sense of the "contradictions" in multicultural education? Your task here is to identify Carby's position in all of its complexity and to uncover the assumptions that have led her to it.

2. Carby says that "everyone in this social order has been constructed in our political imagination as a racialized subject. In this sense, it is important to think about the invention of the category of whiteness as well as blackness and, consequently, to make visible what is rendered invisible when viewed as the normative state of existence: the (white) point in space from which we tend to identify difference." What would thinking about the "invention of the category of whiteness" entail? What would it make visible that is currently invisible?

3. The question that Carby raises repeatedly throughout her essay is whether the language of cultural diversity and difference has in fact become a substitute for political action to desegregate this society. She notes the widespread popularity of black female writers (presumably writers such as Toni Morrison, Alice Walker, Gloria Naylor, and Zora Neale Hurston), but she closes her essay with this question: "Have we, as a society, successfully eliminated the need for achieving integration through political agitation for civil rights and opted instead for knowing each other through cultural texts?" How would you answer Carby's question? You might begin by explaining what Carby is referring to as the "post–civil rights era." What is she suggesting about the nature of race relations in contemporary America?

SUGGESTIONS FOR WRITING

1. Write an essay that compares Carby's thinking about multiculturalism to one or more of the other selections in this chapter. You will first need to summarize Carby's general line of argument and then to indicate what it has in common with and how you would distinguish it from the other perspectives offered in this chapter. The point of the essay is not simply an exercise in comparing and contrasting. To make your essay a meaningful one, you will need to point out what you see as the significance of the differences and similarities for the social, cultural, and political meanings of life in contemporary America.
2. Both Carby and Elaine H. Kim point out ways in which the dominant white middle-class American culture represents itself as simply "human beings" without racial, ethnic, class, or gender identities, as an unspoken and universal norm according to which all the "others"—African Americans, Asians, Latinos, working-class people, women, gays, and lesbians—are marked as "different." At the same time, however, neither Carby nor Kim gives many examples to make all that goes unspoken about the dominant culture more visible, more available for analysis. Write an essay that extends and fills in their thinking about the mainstream culture in contemporary America. What you want to do in this essay is to make more concrete and more visible some of the unspoken norms. Your task is to put into words what usually goes without saying: what the dominant mainstream culture takes for granted and how such unspoken norms operate to construct cultural differences.
3. One of the most troubling arguments Carby makes is that the emphasis on cultural diversity and cultural differences in the multicultural curriculum may in fact serve to "make the white middle class feel better about itself" by distracting attention from "the rigid frameworks of segregation and ghettoization at work throughout our society." Notice here that Carby is not arguing against a fuller, more representative curriculum but rather is raising questions about the limits and contradictory effects of multicultural education in a society that remains divided along racial, ethnic, class, and gender lines. Write an essay that develops your own position on the relation between the "multicultural wars" and the persistent patterns of social, cultural, and political inequality in a multicultural society. One way to think about this essay is as one that offers your own answer to Carby's question, "Have we, as a society, successfully eliminated the need for achieving integration through political agitation for civil rights and opted instead for knowing each other through cultural texts?"

FOR FURTHER EXPLORATION

A good deal has been written about what Hazel V. Carby calls the "multicultural wars" in the American university. One line of investigation you might pursue is to read your way into this debate, to identify the various positions writers have taken and to locate your own thinking in relation to theirs. Take into account discussions on your own campus. If there have been proposals to make the curriculum more representative and multicultural, you might interview key spokespersons from the faculty, student body, and administration. Another possibility is to look at American attitudes toward immigration. Popular magazines such as *Time* and *Newsweek* have run feature stories recently on the "new immigration" and on changing views of what it means to be an American. One way to focus this research is to investigate the English Only movement's efforts to make English the official language in a number of states. Or you might want to develop a historical perspective by researching American attitudes toward immigration in the period 1880–1920.

ACKNOWLEDGMENTS

"The New Lost Generation" by David Leavitt. Reprinted by permission of Wylie, Aitken & Stone, Inc.

"When Black Feminism Faces the Music, and the Music Is Rap" by Michele Wallace. Copyright © 1989/90 by The New York Times Company. Reprinted by permission.

"Kiswana Browne", from THE WOMEN OF BREWSTER PLACE by Gloria Naylor. Copyright © 1980, 1982 by Gloria Naylor. Used by permission of Viking Penguin, a division of Penguin Books USA Inc.

"Profiles of Today's Youth: They Couldn't Care Less" by Michael Oreskes. Copyright © 1989/90 by The New York Times Company. Reprinted by permission.

"What High School Is" from HORACE'S COMPROMISE by Theodore Sizer. Copyright © 1984 by Theodore R. Sizer. Reprinted by permission of Houghton Mifflin Co. All rights reserved.

"The Classroom World" from *Reading, Writing, and Resistance: Adolescence and Labor in Junior High School* by Robert B. Everhart. Copyright © 1983 by Robert B. Everhart. Reprinted by permission of Routledge, a division of Routledge, Chapman & Hall Ltd.

Reprinted with the permission of The Free Press, an imprint of Simon & Schuster from LIVES ON THE BOUNDARY by Mike Rose. Copyright © 1989 by Mike Rose.

"Nobody Mean More to Me Than You and the Future Life of Willie Jordan" by June Jordan. First appeared in *Harvard Educational Review* (August 1988). Copyright © 1988 by June Jordan. All rights reserved. Reprinted by permission.

"Cultural Literacy and the Schools" by E. D. Hirsch, Jr. from *American Educator* (Summer 1985), the quarterly journal of the American Federation of Teachers. Copyright © 1985 by American Federation of Teachers. Reprinted by permission.

"In the Shadow of the Image" from CHANNELS OF DESIRE by Stuart and Elizabeth Ewen.

"Beauty . . . And the Beast of Advertising" by Jean Kilbourne, from *Media & Values* (Winter 1989). Reprinted by permission of the Center for Media and Values.

"Sex as Symbol in Advertising" from MEDIA ANALYSIS TECHNIQUES by Arthur Asa Berger. Reprinted by permission of Sage Publications, Inc.

"A Growing Awareness: Environmental Groups and the Media" by Joel Connelly, from *Aperture* No. 120 (Late Summer 1990). Reprinted by permission of Aperture Foundation.

"Straightening Our Hair" by bell hooks, from *Z Magazine* (September 1988). Copyright © 1988 by the Institute for Social and Cultural Communications. Reprinted by permission of *Z Magazine*, 150 West Canton Street, Boston, MA 02118.

"I, Riverhead" by Ben Hamper. Reprinted with permission from MOTHER JONES Magazine, Copyright © 1986, Foundation for National Progress.

"All Used Up" by Bruce [Utah] Phillips. Reprinted by permission of Thomas R. Levy and Music Management.

From NO FOREIGN LAND by Wilfred Pelletier and Ted Poole. Copyright © 1973 by Wilfred Pelletier and Ted Poole. Reprinted by permission of Pantheon Books, a division of Random House, Inc.

Reprinted by permission of Farrar, Straus & Giroux, Inc. "Columbus in Chains" from ANNIE JOHN by Jamaica Kincaid. Copyright © 1985 by Jamaica Kincaid.

"Unsettling the Old West" by Richard Bernstein. Copyright © 1990 by The New York Times Company. Reprinted by permission.

Reprinted with the permission of Atheneum Publishers, an imprint of Macmillan Publishing Company from WRITIN' IS FIGHTIN': Thirty-Seven Years of Boxing on Paper by Ishmael Reed. Copyright © 1988 by Ishmael Reed.

"Youth and American Identity" [editor's title], from *It's A Sin: Essays on Postmodernism, Politics, and Culture* by Lawrence Grossberg. Copyright © 1988 by Lawrence Grossberg. Reprinted by permission of Power Publications.

"Hard-Core Rap Lyrics Stir Backlash" by Michel Marriott. Copyright © 1993 by The New York Times Company. Reprinted by permission.

"Ice T: Is the Issue Social Responsibility. . . " Copyright © 1992 by Time Inc. Reprinted by permission.

". . . Or Is It Creative Freedom?" by Barbara Ehrenreich. Copyright © 1992 by Time Inc. Reprinted by permission.

"The Rap Attitude" from NEWSWEEK, 3/19/90, Copyright © 1990 by Newsweek, Inc. All rights reserved. Reprinted by permission.

"Niggas With Attitude" from BUPPIES, B-BOYS, BAPS, AND BOHOS by Nelson George. Copyright © 1993 by Nelson George. Reprinted by permission of HarperCollins Publishers, Inc.

"Move Over, Boomers" by Laura Zinn. Reprinted from December 14, 1992 issue of Business Week by special permission, copyright © 1992 by McGraw-Hill, Inc.

"The New Generation Gap" by Neil Howe and William Strauss. Reprinted by permission of Raphael Sagalyn, Inc.

"Sexism in the Schoolroom of the 80's" by Myra and David Sadker. Reprinted With Permission From Psychology Today Magazine, Copyright © 1985 by Sussex Publishers, Inc.

"To Our Readers" by Susan Lyne, Premiere Magazine. Reprinted by permission.

"Buy Any Means Necessary" by Danny Duncan Collum. Reprinted with permission from Sojourners, 2401 15th St. NW, Washington, DC 20009.

"Malcolm X: Consumed By Images" by bell hooks. Reprinted by permission of the author.

"The Female Body" © O. W. Toad Ltd., 1992. Reprinted from GOOD Bones with the permission of Coach House Press. Reprinted with the permission of the author. To be part of a collection published by Doubleday Books titled GOOD BONES AND SIMPLE MURDERS.

by permission of Doubleday, a division of Bantam Doubleday Dell Publishing Group, Inc.

From BLOODS by Wallace Terry, Copyright © 1984 by Wallace Terry. Reprinted by permission of Random House, Inc.

From MOLLY IVINS CAN'T SAY THAT, CAN SHE? by Molly Ivins. Copyright © 1991 by Molly Ivins. Reprinted by permission of Random House, Inc.

"Historical Memory, Film, the Vietnam Era" by Michael Klein from *From Hanoi to Hollywood.* Copyright © 1990 by Rutgers University Press. Used by permission of Rutgers University Press.

"Home is Where the Han Is: A Korean American Perspective on the Los Angeles Upheavals" by Elaine H. Kim. Reprinted from READING RODNEY KING, READING URBAN UPRISING 1993 by permission of the publisher, Routledge, New York.

"The Multicultural Wars" by Hazel V. Carby from BLACK POPULAR CULTURE reprinted by permission of Bay Press

Reprinted from AMERICA: A Narrative History, Brief Second Edition by George B. Tindall and David E. Shi, with the permission of W. W. Norton & Company, Inc. Copyright © 1989, 1988, 1984 by W. W. Norton & Company, Inc.

"Letter to My Son" by Alfred Benke. Reprinted by permission of Ruth McGinnis and Evelyn Nofs.

From Borderlands/LaFrontera: The New Mestiza © 1987 by Gloria Anzaldua. Reprinted with permission from Aunt Lute Books (415) 826-1300.

Reprinted by permission of the Modern Language Association of America from *Profession '91,* "Art of the Contact Zone" by Mary Louise Pratt.

"Split at the Root: An Essay on Jewish Identity" is reprinted from BLOOD, BREAD, AND POETRY, Selected Prose, 1979–1985, by Adrienne Rich, by permission of W. W. Norton & Company, Inc. Copyright © 1986 by Adrienne Rich.